# Adventure Tourism

# Adventure Tourism

**Ralf Buckley**

*International Centre for Ecotourism Research*
*Griffith University*
*Gold Coast, Australia*

*With contributions by:*
Carl Cater
Ian Godwin
Rob Hales
Jerry Johnson
Claudia Ollenburg
Julie Schaefers

www.cabi.org

**CABI is a trading name of CAB International**

| | |
|---|---|
| CABI Head Office | CABI North American Office |
| Nosworthy Way | 875 Massachusetts Avenue |
| Wallingford | 7th Floor |
| Oxfordshire OX10 8DE | Cambridge, MA 02139 |
| UK | USA |
| | |
| Tel: +44 (0)1491 832111 | Tel: +1 617 395 4056 |
| Fax: +44 (0)1491 833508 | Fax: +1 617 354 6875 |
| E-mail: cabi@cabi.org | E-mail: cabi-nao@cabi.org |
| Website: www.cabi.org | |

A catalogue record for this book is available from the British Library, London, UK.

**Library of Congress Cataloging-in-Publication Data**

Buckley, Ralf
 Adventure tourism / Ralf Buckley.
   p. cm.
 Includes bibliographical refences and index.
 ISBN 1-84593-122-X
 1. Adventure travel. 2. Tourism. I. Title.

 G516.B83 2006
 338.4'791--dc22

                        2005037063

ISBN-10: 1 84593 122 X
ISBN-13: 978 1 84593 122 3


Typeset by MRM Graphics Ltd, Winslow, Bucks.
Printed and bound in the UK by Biddles Ltd, King's Lynn.

# Contents

# Contributors

## Principal author

**Ralf Buckley** is Professor and Director of the International Centre for Ecotourism Research, established in 1993 at Griffith University, Australia. He has published over 200 journal articles and ten books, including five on ecotourism and related topics. He has several decades' experience in various forms of adventure recreation, and used to work as a tour guide for a US-based international natural history tour company. His current research focuses on ways in which new trends in tourism affect conservation of the natural environment.

Mailing address: International Centre for Ecotourism Research, Griffith University, Gold Coast, Qld 9726, Australia. E-mail: r.buckley@ griffith.edu.au

## Contributing authors

**Carl Cater** is a member of the International Centre for Ecotourism Research at Griffith University, specializing in marine ecotourism, the psychology of adventure tourism, and adventure destinations. He co-leads the University's field courses in adventure and ecotourism and is an experienced mountaineer and rock climber.

Mailing address: International Centre for Ecotourism Research, Griffith University, Gold Coast, Qld 9726, Australia. E-mail: c.cater@ griffith.edu.au

**Ian Godwin** is a programme manager in the Department of Education at Montana State University. His postgraduate qualifications are in geography and earth sciences, and his current research focuses on the content, administration and distance delivery of higher education. He has been climbing for 25 years and an Outward Bound mountaineering instructor and course director for 13. His current outdoor pursuits include kayaking, squirt boating and climbing ice.

Mailing address: Department of Education, Montana State University, Bozeman, MT 59717, USA. E-mail: igodwin@montana.edu

**Rob Hales** is a member of the International Centre for Ecotourism Research at Griffith University, specializing in outdoor environmental education, eco-adventure tourism impacts, and the sociology of leisure and the environment. He is a skilled whitewater kayaker, rock climber and mountaineer with experience in Australia, North America, Europe, Asia and Antarctica, and used to operate his own mountain guiding company.
Mailing address: International Centre for Ecotourism Research, Griffith University, Gold Coast, Qld 9726, Australia. E-mail: r.hales@ griffith.edu.au

**Jerry Johnson** is Professor and Head of the Department of Political Science at Montana State University in Bozeman. His research focuses on rural land use change and tourism impacts. His work has been supported by most of the federal land management agencies including NSF, NASA, US National Park Service and several foundations. Johnson has made ascents of many of the ice classics in the Canadian Rockies and in Montana. He has climbed and kayaked in Europe, Alaska, Turkey and Russia.
Mailing address: Department of Political Science, Montana State University, Bozeman, MT 59717, USA. E-mail: jdj@montana.edu

**Claudia Ollenburg** is a member of the International Centre for Ecotourism Research at Griffith University, specializing in equestrian tourism and farm tourism. Originally trained in agricultural science and economics at the University of Kiel, Germany, she has worked with horses since the age of six and has extensive practical experience in working farm tourism businesses. She recently wrote a successful US$150,000 grant application for a new farm tourism hub in northern NSW, Australia.
Mailing address: International Centre for Ecotourism Research, Griffith University, Gold Coast, Qld 9726, Australia. E-mail: c.ollenburg@ griffith.edu.au

**Julie Schaefers** is a fanatic mountain biker who has ridden the trails of North America from Alaskan mud to Utah slickrock. Her contribution in this volume is written in a private capacity, but in her day job she is a social scientist for the US Forestry Service, seeing the adventure tourists from a land manager's perspective.
Mailing address: USDA Forest Service, Golden, CO 80401, USA. E-mail: jschaefers@fs.fed.us

# Lists of Tables and Figures

## List of Tables

## List of Figures

# Preface

Jane on Ranger, New Zealand. Photo Ralf Buckley.

## DEDICATION

For my mother Jane, who can run up mountains, ski down them, swim across lakes, gallop horses, sail yachts, pilot gliders, and race cars on and off-road; and expected her children to do likewise regardless of age or sex.

Adventure means different things to different people. For the past 5 or 10 years the term 'adventure', and images of adventure activities, have been used worldwide to advertise holidays, equipment, clothing, lifestyles, property and more.

Adventure may also mean different things to different tourists. What fills one person with fear fills another with boredom, and vice versa.

Adventure tourism products, however, form a relatively well-defined and recognizable sector of the tourism industry. Adventure tours are retail-level commercial tour products which clients purchase specifically to take part in an outdoor activity which is more exciting than contemplative, and where the outdoor environment is enjoyed more as a setting for the activity than for its scenery, plants or animals.

These definitions are not clear-cut, and in practice many tour products focus on nature and/or culture at the same time as adventure. This has been recognized through terms such as ACE, adventure-culture-ecotourism (Fennell, 1999, 2001) and NEAT, nature-eco-adventure-tourism (Buckley, 2000).

The adventure component of such tour products is recognizable by the activity and sometimes also by the location. Diving and snorkelling, whitewater rafting and kayaking, skiing and snowboarding, hiking and biking, climbing and mountaineering, sailing and seakayaking: all of these form the basis for adventure tours. Visiting polar regions, deserts, jungles or mountaintops, or looking for large, dangerous or unusual wildlife, also contains a strong element of adventure.

There are tens or hundreds of thousands of individual adventure tourism products worldwide, and many millions of tourists buying them each year. And adventure tours are rarely cheap, not least because they commonly require expensive specialist equipment: from hiking boots to diving regulators, surfboards to yachts and ice-strengthened expedition vessels.

So adventure tourism is big business. It is a major part of the tourism industry. It is one of the main reasons people travel. To date, however, it has been little studied. Tourism researchers have turned their attention quite extensively to people who: visit friends and relatives; go to meetings and conventions; go to sporting events, art galleries and even rave parties; lie on the beach in the sun; eat and drink or visit shopping malls – but not much, apparently, to people who travel specifically to have fun.

Adventure tourism is not, of course, entirely unstudied. There is quite an extensive literature on the psychological aspects of various adventure activities, but these studies are largely from an outdoor education or parks and recreation perspective, not from a commercial tourism perspective. There is barely any published work, apparently, which describes and analyses the structure of adventure tourism products. This is analogous, for example, to studying the psychology of drivers and passengers before knowing what a car looks like, let alone how it works.

Ideally a book on adventure tourism would be able to synthesize an extensive published literature on all aspects of adventure tourism products, before proceeding to the finer social details of the people who purchase them. But this basic literature simply does not seem to exist.

This book, therefore, makes a small start to remedy that defect, by providing analyses of over 100 real, retail-level, individual adventure tour products featuring a range of activities in various parts of the world. There are tens of thousand of such products, changing daily. A book such as this can only hope to present a small sample. It is a start. I shall count the work a success if it gives tourism students some of the basic data they need to understand adventure tourism products and compare them with other types of tourism, and if it provokes other tourism researchers to expand it to more places, more products and more parameters.

One caveat is in order. This is a book about commercial adventure tourism products: retail products available for sale to anyone with the requisite skills, interests and funds. It is not a book about individual adventures, intentional or otherwise: either the author's or anyone else's. There are many such books, and some of them are classics; but they are not texts on tourism.

# Disclaimer

Adventure tour operations change continually, and certainly faster than any one author can keep checking them. Information in the case studies and elsewhere in this volume has been compiled from a variety of written and electronic documents, and personal observations and experiences, which themselves date from different years or even decades. Where possible, publicly available statistical information has been updated during 2005 from tour operator websites and similar sources. These sources, however, may be outdated or inaccurate and no guarantees are expressed or implied regarding any such data.

Similarly, experiences reported are generally for a single occasion, which may or may not be representative of the tour product studied, and which may potentially reflect the personal interests of the author and other contributors as well as the characteristics of the commercial package.

Inclusion of a tour operator, company or product in this volume does not necessarily represent endorsement by the author(s), their employers and professional institutions, or the publishers. We have endeavoured to present a range of individual products from a variety of adventure tourism sectors, but this selection necessarily reflects historical coincidences as well as deliberate choices. Some of the tours described here, for example, were taken before the author first commenced academic research in adventure tourism. They are relevant, but not necessarily representative.

This book is intended for researchers, lecturers and students engaged in the academic analysis of adventure tourism. It is not intended as a tourist guidebook. As we checked and re-checked information during 2005, we found that relevant websites often changed several times within months; and different websites apparently referring to the same tours often contained conflicting information. If, after reading any of the case studies in this volume, you consider taking that tour yourself, please obtain up-to-date information directly from the operator.

# 1 Introduction

## Aims and Scope

Adventure tourism has grown rapidly in recent years as outdoor recreation has become increasingly commercialized (Buckley, 2000, 2004a; Travel Industry Association of America, 2005). To date, however, the actual commercial products offered by adventure tourism operators do not seem to have been subject to any coherent and comprehensive review and analysis. This book is a first attempt at such an approach.

Other sectors of the tourism industry have been analysed extensively. Many volumes, for example, have been written about conventions and coastal resorts, events and ecotourism. Many aspects of outdoor recreation have also received detailed scrutiny, and much of that literature is relevant to the modern adventure tourism industry.

The ways in which tour operators have packaged outdoor recreation activities as commercial products, however, do not seem to have experienced equivalent attention. The defining features of most adventure tourism products include the geographic setting as well as the adventure activity.

Customer experience also depends on guides and service, so people are also critical to the commercial success of adventure tourism. The role of adventure guides has indeed received some attention in the academic literature, as outlined below, and the experiences and attitudes of participants have been examined quite extensively. These more psychological components of tour products, however, are largely beyond the scope of the current contribution.

## Defining Adventure Tourism

The distinctions between nature tourism, ecotourism, adventure tourism, adventure travel, commercial expeditions, outdoor recreation and outdoor education are blurred (Weaver, 1998; Fennell, 1999; Manning, 1999; Buckley, 2000; Newsome *et al.*, 2001). Here I shall use the term adventure tourism to mean guided commercial tours where the principal attraction is an outdoor activity that relies on features of the natural terrain, generally requires specialized sporting or similar equipment, and is exciting for the tour clients. This definition does not require that the clients themselves operate the equipment: they may simply be passengers, whether in a dogsled, a whitewater raft or a tandem parachute harness.

As with most aspects of tourism, this is an artificial definition in the sense that it identifies one particular set of human behaviours from a broad multi-dimensional continuum, with no prior evidence that it corresponds to any empirically identified clumping within that continuum. Individual people have many different expectations and experiences from outdoor activities, and excitement is only one of these. The same tour can mean different things to different people. The distances people travel and the times they spend in outdoor activities are continuously variable. Levels of individual skill, self-sufficiency and equipment ownership, as compared to commercial support, also vary continuously. There is no definitive distinction between adventure and non-adventure, between commercial tourism and individual recreation, between remote and local sites, and so on. Such distinctions may or may not be significant from the various perspectives of, for example, an economic statistician, an outdoor equipment manufacturer, a tour operator and equipment rental agency, a protected area management agency, a public liability insurer or an individual person planning a holiday trip (Buckley, 2004a).

Whilst the boundaries of adventure tourism are not well defined, its core activities are. An archetypal example, perhaps, would be a multi-day whitewater rafting tour, where the tour operator provides all the equipment, the clients need no prior skills and the principal attraction is running rapids rather than riverside scenery. Climbing, abseiling, seakayaking and whitewater kayaking, skiing and snowboarding, caving, ballooning, skydiving and parapenting, mountain biking, diving and snorkelling, surfing and sailboarding, snowmobiling and off-road driving, heliskiing and many similar activities may also form the basis for adventure tourism.

## Difficult Distinctions

### Travel threshold

There are three commonly drawn distinctions that are particularly difficult to apply in the case of adventure tourism. The first is that for the purposes of economic statistics, a leisure activity only qualifies as tourism if it includes an overnight stay and/or travel away from the participant's place of residence. In Australia, the minimum threshold travel distance is set at 40 km, but this does not necessarily apply worldwide. Many commercial adventure activities are single-day tours. Most of their clients, however, are holidaymakers who are already far from home and so qualify as tourists. In addition, many single-day adventure tours travel more than 40 km from the pick-up point in the nearest gateway town to the location of the day's activity itself. Hence it is reasonable to consider these one-day activities as tours, which is indeed how they are marketed.

### Recreation and tourism

The second difficult distinction is between adventure *tourism*, where a client pays a tour operator to provide an adventure experience, and adventure *recreation*, where individual participants carry out the same activity on their own. From a legal perspective, e.g. in regard to liability insurance or access and operating permits for a particular site, this distinction is clear and very significant.

As noted earlier, however, in terms of practical logistics there is considerable overlap. Private recreational groups, particularly non-profit groups such as schools, may be much larger than small commercial tours. A commercial tour may provide all the equipment and specialized clothing that participants need, so they can show up in street clothes with no prior skills. At the other extreme, the tour company may provide only a guide, with participants expected to arrive with all their own equipment and the skills to use it. So-called tagalong 4WD tours operate this way, for example, and so also do some hiking tours and mountaineering expeditions.

The distinction between a group of skilled and well-equipped people led by a paid guide, by a volunteer guide whose expenses are paid, by one of their own number who is particularly experienced, or by a process of consensus, is a rather fine one. And to complicate matters even further, a private group with a private leader may contract an outfitter to provide equipment, guides and catering for a private trip. Again, the distinction between a private group that charters a tour company to guide and outfit them, and a similar group that makes a group booking on a scheduled but otherwise identical tour, is also a fine one, especially where the tour operator is the same in each case, and their tours are irregular and depart only if a large enough group signs up by a specified pre-departure date. A dive tour company that runs a large high-speed wave-piercing catamaran to the Great Barrier Reef every day is a very different operation from one that takes a single small group of highly experienced divers under the ice in the Arctic or Antarctic.

## Fixed and mobile activities

A third significant distinction is between fixed-site and mobile activities. Again, the dividing line is not clear. A ski resort, for example, has a fixed site, whereas a backcountry ski tour is mobile. But heliskiing, for example, is a mobile activity with a fixed base. Similarly, a dive boat on the Great Barrier Reef is mobile, but it relies on a fixed wharf or marina to load passengers and supplies, and some boats journey routinely to elaborate pontoon facilities moored permanently on the outer reef. Some surf tours operate entirely from live-aboard boats; others operate from lodges or resorts near particular surf breaks.

Skiing and snowboarding are certainly excitement-based outdoor leisure activities that require specialist skills and equipment and rely on features of the natural terrain: i.e. an adventure activity. Tourist expenditure at ski resorts makes up a large component of Mallett's (1998) estimate of the economic scale of adventure tourism in North America, and the figure increases enormously if associated real estate development is also included (Johnson *et al.*, 2003). Corresponding attractions for resort-residential development in subtropical areas, however, such as marinas and golf courses (Warnken and Buckley, 1997), would not be considered as adventure tourism, even if some of the boats based at the marinas do operate adventure tours.

## Social Contexts and Changes

As societies in developed Western nations become increasingly urbanized, greater numbers of people have lifestyles that lack any outdoor component except during leisure activities. Many of these people are relatively well-off but have little leisure time: they are cash-rich, time-poor. They see wilderness environments and wildlife through television programmes and travel magazines, perhaps without appreciating just how much time, equipment and expertise is required to make a wildlife documentary film. They also see athletes engaging in a variety of outdoor sports and recreational activities, perhaps without appreciating that these are a select and sponsored few who have made a career in the outdoor sport concerned.

These factors have created a cohort of people who have the desire, money and basic fitness for outdoor recreation in remote areas, but not necessarily the time, skills, equipment or experience. In addition, there are people who have prior experience and skills, but do not have the time to organize their own expeditions, no longer have their full former strength and skills, or simply prefer to pay for support services rather than organizing their own trips. It is these groups that provide the increasing market for commercial adventure tourism.

In the past, people interested in outdoor recreation would commonly buy their own equipment and learn relevant skills gradually, either from friends or through clubs. Both for social and financial reasons, therefore, this led them to focus on one particular activity. As equipment has become more sophisticated and expensive, the option of renting it as part of a commercial adventure tour product has become more attractive financially. If people no longer need to buy their own equipment, however, and if they can rely on guides for trip planning, leadership, safety and basic skills training, then they no longer need to focus on a single outdoor recreation activity.

It therefore appears that outdoor recreation is now treated much more as a purchasable short-time holiday experience than as a gradually acquired lifetime skill with its own set of social rewards and responsibilities (Johnson and Edwards, 1994; Buckley, 1998, 2000, 2004a; Kane and Zink, 2004).

Although commercial adventure recreation has absorbed a proportion of the outdoor recreation market, individual outdoor recreation has continued to grow at the same time. For most such activities, individual adventure recreation is probably still many times larger than commercial adventure tourism, though there do not yet seem to be any published quantitative analyses either of the number of people involved, or patterns of expenditure. Of course, the same individual may take part in the same activity sometimes as an individual, sometimes as part of a private group and sometimes as part of a commercial tour.

## Equipment, Clothing and Entertainment

Over the past few years, quite strong and mutually reinforcing business links have arisen between adventure tour operators, equipment and clothing manufacturers, and the entertainment industry (Buckley, 2003b). These business ties are essentially mediated by fashion rather than any fundamental logistic links, so in the longer term they may well prove ephemeral. Currently, however, they are strong enough to have quite significant financial implications for the adventure tourism sector.

The way it works is similar for many different activities, but can be illustrated well by the surfing subsector (Buckley, 2003b). There are similar patterns for other types of adventure tourism. Snowboarding, for example, is used to sell winter street clothing. Rock climbing provides adventure images used to advertise a wide range of lifestyle consumer goods, from mobile phones to chewing tobacco. Manufacturers of expensive recreational equipment, especially motorized equipment such as snowmobiles, personal watercraft (jetskis), off-road and all-terrain vehicles (ATVs), and sport utility vehicles rely heavily on adventure imagery to maintain sales.

Historically, the hunting and fishing industries have also promoted their own clothing styles, and these are still used as status symbols amongst particular social groups. Hunting, for example, enjoys particular status amongst well-off Germans, and fly-fishing amongst residents of the UK or the western USA. These styles, however, have not penetrated mass urban streetwear markets to the same degree as modern adventure-style clothing. Fashionable clothing based on riding gear may also have enjoyed prominence in upper-class European societies at one time, and the Australian Drizabone® coat, now used as a city raincoat, was developed for mountain horsemen. Again, however, these did not become general streetwear. The closest historical analogue to the modern link between streetwear and outdoor sport clothing is, perhaps, the highly successful use of sports athletes such as professional basketballers to market specialized sports shoes as mainstream urban streetwear. This, however, lacks the commercial adventure tourism component that applies for surfing and snowboarding, for example (Buckley, 2003b).

## Overlaps with Other Subsectors

The commercial adventure tourism sector has grown rapidly but recently, and has received rather little academic attention to date. There is a long history of literature, from researchers and practitioners alike, in related areas such as outdoor recreation, outdoor education, leisure studies and protected area visitor management. There are a number of cross-links from these fields of study into the tourism literature. Individual recreational visitors to national parks, for example, make significant contributions to regional economies through their use of off-park tourist accommodation and services. Similarly, the psychological experiences of participants in outdoor education and recreation programmes may be very similar to those in commercial adventure tours.

The development, marketing, management, economics and general business practices in the commercial adventure tourism sector itself, however, have received very little attention in comparison to similar aspects of other tourism sectors. This lack of attention is all the more remarkable since the adventure tourism sector seems to be significantly larger and more widespread than specialist sectors such as ecotourism (Weaver, 2001; Buckley, 2003a), farm tourism (Ollenburg, 2006) or even volunteer tourism (Wearing, 2001).

The relation between adventure travel and ecotourism, in particular, has been taken into account by organizations such as the Adventure Travel Trade Association (2005), which for many years has run an annual World Congress on Adventure Travel and Ecotourism. Organizations focusing on ecotourism, however, such as The International Ecotourism Society (2005), have focused more on links with mainstream urban, rural and nature tourism through environmental management and education practices than on the links with outdoor and adventure tourism through product packaging.

## Information on Adventure Tours

There is one previous text specifically on adventure tourism (Swarbrooke *et al.*, 2003), but it focuses more on the psychological experiences of young backpackers than on the commercial adventure tourism sector more broadly. There is also one text nominally on sport and adventure tourism (Hudson, 2002), but which in fact focuses heavily on fixed-site sports. A new book due out contemporaneously with the current volume (Easson, 2006) examines adventure and extreme sports, but only from a philosophical and psychological perspective.

There are a number of journal articles addressing issues such as participant expectations and experiences, risks and injuries, but relatively few that describe what products are available worldwide and how they work. Of course, individual adventure tour companies describe their products in their own brochures and websites, but such marketing materials cannot necessarily be relied upon as an accurate description for academic analysis of actual practices. The same applies to descriptions of adventure destinations and tour operators in specialist recreational magazines for individual outdoor recreation sectors.

For the individual tourist searching for information on adventure tourism products, there are currently several different options, depending on specialization, prior skill and price range. The first option, generally common amongst time-rich, cash-poor tourists, is to visit a well-known adventure tourism destination such as Queenstown in New Zealand, Cairns in Australia or Victoria Falls in Zimbabwe, and then select one or more adventure activities from those on offer at that destination. This is a common practice, for example, in the backpacker market and applies particularly for short-duration, low-skill products such as half-day whitewater rafting trips, tandem skydiving or hang gliding, softboard surfing or introductory diving. Many travel agents sell package tours to such destinations that include one or more short-duration adventure activities. For less heavily visited destinations, guides such as the *Lonely Planet*® series provide information on activities as well as accommodation, often including contact details for individual commercial operators.

At a more specialist level and commonly a higher price range, there are commercial tour operators that retail a range of adventure tourism products. These are generally marketed through brochures, presentations and websites in the same way as specialist natural history tour products. Indeed, some firms offer both nature and adventure tourism products in the same brochures. Some of these companies focus on a single country or a single activity, whereas others include several activities and operate worldwide. Commonly, such operators also advertise in specialist recreational magazines for the activity concerned, such as surfing, diving, kayaking or skiing. That is, these products are aimed more at clients with strong interests and skills in one particular activity than at those who simply want a dose of excitement as part of a holiday package. Tour companies that advertise routinely in such specialist magazines are also likely to seek editorial coverage, e.g. by sponsoring places for travel writers or other journalists.

## Base and Apex of the Adventure Sector

The bread-and-butter business base of the adventure sector is in so-called soft adventure, where unskilled clients show up in street clothes and a tour operator provides transport, equipment, specialized clothing, skilled guides and sufficient on-the-spot training for participants to enjoy a safe and usually short set of thrills (Buckley, 2004a). The broad-scale trend in adventure tourism is thus towards reducing risk, remoteness and skill requirements so as to broaden market demand.

At the same time that one end of the adventure tourism sector is expanding its appeal to mainstream mass tourism, however, the other end is expanding into smaller volume, higher cost products that require higher prior skills and involve greater individual risk for clients, and operate in more remote and inhospitable areas. If you have the necessary skills as well as money, commercial adventure tour operators can now take you climbing on 8000 m peaks, kayaking Himalayan rivers in flood, diving under Antarctic ice, parachuting on to the North Pole or skiing across Greenland. Experiences such as these, which were at the frontiers of human endeavour only a few decades ago, now form a recognizable subsector of the tourism industry. This might be abbreviated as SCARRA, Skilled Commercial Adventure Recreation in Remote Areas (Buckley, 2004a) and represents the apex of the commercial adventure tourism industry.

Note that even the most remote and risky adventure tour products are still over-shadowed by adventure recreation exploits and one-off expeditions. The apex of commercial adventure tourism is not the apex of adventure (Fig. 1.1).

Adventure tourism seems to be at the edge of the tourism industry structurally as well as geographically (Buckley, 2004a). In particular, some commercial adventure activities and destinations have evolved quite rapidly from extreme to soft adventure, whereas others have not. This depends on the balance between the driving pressures of market demand and the resistance of costs and technologies. Worldwide, social and technological changes make it easier and cheaper to visit remote parts of the globe, and reduce at least some of the risks.

Such expansion, of course, is not necessarily to the advantage of the individual tourism businesses that pioneered the particular products concerned. It moves them from a niche market where they have a strong competitive advantage or even a monopoly, to a larger and broader market where there may be a substantial competition on price. This price competition may exert downward pressures on safety, guiding skills, equipment quality, etc. At the same time, shifting towards a larger but softer adventure tourism market is likely to require changes in accommodation and transport logistics, so as to support more people in greater comfort. Typically, this needs considerably greater capital investment, which may take it beyond the financial reach of pioneer operators.

## Skill, Risk, Reward, Remoteness

The critical factors differentiating the low-volume apex from the high-volume base of the adventure tourism sector are skill and remoteness. The requirement for prior skills in the relevant activity distinguishes specialist adventure tours from the broader nature, eco and adventure tourism (NEAT) sector, where tour operators strive to make their products accessible to unskilled clients so as to maximize their potential market size. The remoteness factor distinguishes such tours from skilled outdoor adventure recreation in more developed areas, such as heavily used rock climbing and scuba diving sites, or so-called park-and-play whitewater kayaking rivers.

Associated with the skill requirements and remoteness is an increased level of risk. This, however, is a consequence rather than a defining factor, and tour operators take steps to minimize risks, to maintain their future reputation as well as to minimize immediate liability. For skilled clients, adventure tours to remote areas offer rewards that they cannot obtain at their own local recreational areas, but with greater convenience and efficiency and lower risk than organizing a private recreational trip. Risk is reduced through the tour operator's local knowledge, guide skills, logistic support and, commonly, arrangements for emergency medical assistance and/or evacuation if needed.

As commercial tourism, small-scale skilled adventure tours to remote areas can be distinguished from private adventure recreation, competitive adventure sports, etc., but the distinction can be rather fine. As noted earlier, for example, if a private group uses a local commercial outfitter to provide equipment for a particular trip, but provides its own leader, this would be considered as private recreation. If the same group uses the same outfitter to make the same trip, but with a leader provided by the outfitter, it would be considered as commercial tourism.

## Evolution of Skilled Adventure Tours in Remote Areas

Historically, travel in the most remote areas and difficult terrain has nearly always been pioneered by scientific or sponsored expeditions, with commercial tourism lagging far behind. It is only recently that the opportunity to make a first ascent or descent, a first traverse or crossing, or to be the first to carry out a particular recreational activity at a new site, has been marketed as a component of commercial tours. Organizations such as the Explorers Club (2005) in the USA and the World Expeditionary Association (WEXAS, 2005) in the UK, focus on private rather than commercial expeditions. It is only in the last decade or so that organizations such as the Adventure Travel Trade Association (2005) have begun to cater equally for adventure tour operators as well as individuals. Even now, in areas of the world with local populations, transport and accommodation, tourism is commonly pioneered by individual travellers, with commercial tours establishing much later once the destination is well known (Fig. 1.1).

The way in which adventure tourism has developed thus differs between regions. Broadly, four categories of remoteness can be distinguished:

- Rural areas and parks in developed countries, typically within a few days from a roadhead and within range of rescue services; human habitation may be restricted by land tenure or economic factors but not by terrain or climate.
- Inhabited areas in developing nations, with purchasable access to local transport, shelter and food supplies.
- Sparsely inhabited areas with no regular mechanized access or local transport, no communications infrastructure and traditional subsistence lifestyles only.
- Areas that are uninhabited because of extreme environments: oceans, poles, some deserts, highest mountain peaks.

In developed nations, new high-skilled adventure tour products typically focus on more and more challenging recreational activities, such as: whitewater kayaking down previously unrun rivers; skiing or snowboarding down previously unrun slopes; ascents of previously unclimbed routes on cliffs and mountains; explorations of previously unvisited caves; or traverses of previously uncrossed terrain. The risk level may be high or extreme, but rescue services are at least potentially available.

Activities such as these are nearly always attempted first by private individuals, sometimes sponsored either for a one-off attempt or as part of professional teams. These are followed typically by other private groups, often from recreational clubs and associations. Once the volume of visitors provides a sufficient market, local outfitters may establish to provide on-site equipment rental and/or guiding services. Adventure tour operations can then use these outfitters, or their own gear and guides, to offer commercial trips. Commonly these are sporadic at first, with departure dates customized to individual groups of clients, and trips running only if fully pre-booked. At this stage, prices typically remain somewhat negotiable,

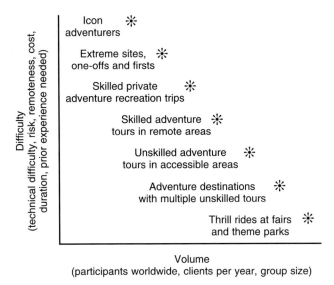

Difficulty (technical difficulty, risk, remoteness, cost, duration, prior experience needed)

Icon adventurers ☀

Extreme sites, ☀ one-offs and firsts

Skilled private ☀ adventure recreation trips

Skilled adventure ☀ tours in remote areas

Unskilled adventure ☀ tours in accessible areas

Adventure destinations ☀ with multiple unskilled tours

Thrill rides at fairs ☀ and theme parks

Volume (participants worldwide, clients per year, group size)

**Fig. 1.1.** The adventure activity pyramid: volume cf. difficulty.

calculated trip-by-trip depending on numbers. Only once such charters are well-established will operators begin to schedule routine departures with fixed per-client prices.

Inhabited areas in developing nations are visited routinely by local merchants and other domestic travellers, and their first international tourists are often backpackers relying entirely on local facilities: what might be described as the *Lonely Planet*® market. These, however, are – almost by definition – not engaged in high-risk high-skill recreational activities, first because such activities need logistic support, and secondly because they often need access to locally little-used areas, just as in developed nations. As in the latter, therefore, high-skill adventure activities are most often pioneered by private recreational groups, with or without sponsorship.

The first commercial adventure tours in these areas usually are self-supported expeditions, bringing all their own equipment. If these are successful, they may lead to the establishment of local operational bases and hiring of local guides, who then pioneer additional new trips. Sometimes, areas with an established industry in one adventure tourism sector may simply expand to add new activities from existing bases. Trekking and mountaineering outfitters and tour operators in Nepal, for example, branched into whitewater rafting once early descents showed that this activity was both feasible and commercially viable.

In areas occupied by indigenous societies with little link to the rest of the world, almost any travel has a significant adventure element. Worldwide, there are few such societies remaining. There are, however, all possible gradations between complete tribalism and complete urbanization, and there are still many societies where adventure recreation and its associated high-tech equipment are completely unfamiliar. The development of an adventure tourism industry in such areas may be inseparable from other aspects of so-called Westernization.

Most remote in perception and practical effect, if not in geographic distance, are the extreme environments where human life cannot be sustained for long without technological means to supply oxygen, warmth or water. These include the so-called forbidden landscapes of the Arctic and Antarctic (Splettstoesser *et al.*, 2004) and high montane environments above 6000 m, including the so-called dead zone. They also include sections of the world's hyper-arid deserts such as the Rub'al Khali or the Taklamakan, away from oases that form traditional camel-crossing routes. Any human venture into such areas is as a self-supported expedition, and any permanent human base is completely dependent upon continuing resupplies from outside the region. Independent travel is generally not possible since all visitors need expedition support, whether through an official, scientific, sponsored, private or commercial expedition.

Within these areas, the degree of skill and risk depend on the activity involved. To visit the Arctic or Antarctic as a passenger on a cruise liner requires neither skill nor fitness (Splettstoesser *et al.*, 2004). To take part in a so-called expedition cruise, with frequent landings by inflatable boats, requires only basic balance and mobility. Multi-day seakayaking tours along the shores of Baffin or Ellesmere Island in the Canadian Arctic are available to any reasonably fit person with some experience in backcountry camping, though prior cold-weather seakayaking experience would certainly be an advantage.

Diving at the edge of polar ice, climbing 8000 m peaks, cross-country skiing in Greenland or the Arctic icecap (North Pole Expeditions, 2005a) or skydiving on to the North Pole (North Pole Expeditions, 2005b) require considerable prior skill and experience so as not to endanger either oneself or other members of the group. Beyond this, trips such as unsupported seakayak journeys in the Antarctic, or ski-mountaineering traverses of the sub-Antarctic South Georgia Island, are too difficult even for experienced commercial clients, and have been achieved only by highly skilled and experienced private groups.

## Structure of Adventure Subsectors

Commercial tour products for different adventure activities feature different levels of risks, remoteness and prior skill requirements. For each activity, there are some products aimed at beginners, others at experts. Some adventure activities lend themselves to the design of tour products where clients are essentially passengers, whereas others require active participation. For activities that require active participation, such as kayaking, diving, surfing, ice climbing, horse riding or mountain biking, there are commercial tour products that offer training at basic or advanced level, and there are commercial tour products that take skilled participants to remote areas or icon sites and guide them once they get there.

There are other activities where prior skill is essential, such as heliskiing or boarding, or mountaineering expeditions. Skills must be learned elsewhere before joining a commercial tour. For expedition cruises, tandem parachuting, and many rafting and wildlife watching tours, in contrast, the clients would have no opportunity to exercise any relevant skills in any event, and take part purely as passengers.

For most of the adventure activities covered in this volume, a range of tour products are presented, with a corresponding range of prior skill requirements, risk and remoteness.

# 2 Adventure Recreation Research

## Adventure in Tourism and Recreation Texts

Adventure tourism has received relatively little attention in the academic literature, and most of the focus has been on accidents or injuries. Adventure tourism is mentioned in some texts on ecotourism, outdoor recreation and park management, but not explored in much detail. Page and Dowling (2002, pp. 75–77) summarize various definitions and subdivisions, citing Christiansen (1990), Fennell and Eagles (1990), Dyers (1997), Beeh (1999), Fennell (1999), Bentley and Page (2001), Bentley *et al.* (2001a, b, c), and the Canadian Tourism Commission (1995). They also include typologies (pp. 13–14) of adventure tourism activities, drawn from Bentley and Page (2001), and operators drawn from Bentley *et al.* (2000, 2001a, b, c). In addition, many of the activities they list as ecotourism (Page and Dowling, 2002, pp. 99–102) might equally be considered as adventure tourism.

Other texts on ecotourism such as Fennell (1999), Weaver (2001), Fennell and Dowling (2003), Garrod and Wilson (2004) and Diamantis (2004) say little or nothing about adventure tourism, and the same applies for texts on recreational tourism such as Ryan (2003). The now classic text by Hammitt and Cole (1998) on wildland recreation includes past surveys and future projections of the use of US Forest Service lands for activities such as off-road driving, rock climbing, horse riding, boating and diving (pp. 131–137), but with no distinction between private recreation and commercial outfitters. The more recent text by Eagles and McCool (2002) on tourism in protected areas does mention kayaking and diving briefly (pp. 218, 228), but the index does not list climbing, rafting or horse riding.

Another recent North American text, the voluminous compendium by Hendee and Dawson (2002) on wilderness management, makes rather brief mention of commercial outfitting, guiding and stock and equipment rental (pp. 375–376). It notes, for example, that there were 57 licensed outfitters in the Bob Marshall Wilderness in 1986 and 78 in the Selway-Bitterroot Wilderness (p. 376), and that up to 50% of visitors in some areas are on horseback (p. 376). This is important for wilderness management for several reasons. Most complaints to land managers are about horses and packstock (p. 454); horse riders pay much less attention to minimal-impact messages than other users do (p. 451); and horses generate substantial ecological impacts (pp. 423–453).

There seem to be only two texts to date whose titles refer specifically to adventure tourism: Hudson (2002) and Swarbrooke *et al.* (2003). The former, however, is principally on sports tourism rather than on adventure. The latter focuses far more on human psychology than on tourism products, with material covering characteristics of casino gamblers, urban adventure playgrounds, UK clubbers and party tours, and postcards to home, for example. There is one further forthcoming text (Easson, 2006) focusing on philosophy and psychology of extreme sports.

Some of the most detailed and relevant information available to date is in an edited volume by Wilks and Page (2003) on tourist health and safety, notably a chapter by Page *et al.* (2003a) on adventure tourism. In addition, the chapter by Page *et al.* (2003b) summarizes New Zealand accident statistics in whitewater rafting, canoeing, caving and diving. Ewert and Jamieson (2003) examine characteristics of adventure tours and tourists, covering issues such as skills at specific outdoor activities, risk management and safety, remote areas and self-reliance, weather and seasonality, cost and preparation and the critical role of skilled guides. They reviewed participation rates in adventure tourism activities such as hiking, biking, climbing, rafting and diving as recorded by surveys in 1993, 1995 and 1997; they also note, for example, that of the 1114 people who had summited Mt Everest up to and including 2001, 183 of these (16.5%) made the ascent in 2001.

In the same volume Bentley *et al.* (2003) indicate that 11% of visitors to New Zealand in 1999 took part in an adventure tourism activity, with a total of 400 operators providing such products. They also tabulate injuries per million participant hours (p. 94) for different activities. The highest rate is 7401 for cycle tours, followed by 6636 for caving, 3164 for fishing and 3096 for riding quad bikes or ATVs. Adventure activities more commonly thought of as risky, in contrast, actually had far lower rates of injury per million participant hours: 718 for horse riding, 537 for whitewater rafting, 483 for blackwater (cave) rafting, 125 for diving and only 14 for kayaking.

## Products

A few authors, certainly, have indeed described individual adventure tourism products as a core component of their analyses. The now classic contribution by Ewert (1989) reviewed 'outdoor adventure pursuits'. Tabata (1992) described the structure of diving tours. Shackley (1996a, b, 1998) described wildlife tours, camel tours and stingray snorkelling tours, respectively. Johnson and Edwards (1994) referred to the 'commodification' of mountaineering, and Livet (1997) gave a similar analysis for diving. Analyses of whaleshark tours by Davis *et al.* (1997), or crocodile tours by Ryan (1998) and Ryan and Harvey (2000) describe the structure of the tours as well as tourist behaviour, demographics or expenditure. Wilson and Tisdell (2001) report on product aspects such as access, seasonality and price in their analyses of sea turtle tourism. Scott and Laws (2004) examine Australian whalewatching tours from a small-business perspective. More broadly, Cater and Cater (2000), and later Jennings (2003), reviewed the marine tourism sector; Beedie and Hudson (2003) described the emergence of adventure tourism in mountaineering; Sung *et al.* (2000) classified American adventure tourists into six subgroups; and Cloutier (2003) summarized the business aspects of adventure tourism more generally.

Even these authors, however, have rarely focused on the structure and composition of adventure tours as saleable products. As noted by More and Averill (2003) in a somewhat broader context: 'The most neglected part of recreation research may be the actual composition of an activity'.

Somewhat more attention has, in fact, been paid to the structure of outdoor recreation activities at particular sites and places. This is a broader perspective than individual products, and includes individual private recreation as well as commercial tours, but it provides a useful context none the less.

Descriptions of mountain tourism are available for France (Giard, 1997; Bourdeau *et al.*, 2002); Switzerland (Wyder, 1987); India (Bisht, 1994; Kayastha, 1997); Nepal (Zurick, 1992); Japan (Suzuki and Kawamura, 1994); New Zealand (Booth and Cullen, 2001; Davidson, 2002); and sub-Antarctic islands (Hall, 1993). Skiing in Sweden is described by Fredman and Heberlein (2003). Diving and dive sites have been described in Hawaii (Tabata, 1989); the Caribbean (Hawkins and Roberts, 1992, 1993, 1994; Hawkins *et al.*, 1999; Williams and Polunin, 2000); in Egypt (Prior *et al.*, 1995); in Spain (Mundet and Ribera, 2001); in Australia (Davis and Tisdell, 1995, 1996, 1998; Davis *et al.*, 1997) and elsewhere.

Whalewatching has been examined in western Canada (Duffus and Dearden, 1993; Duffus, 1996); in the St Lawrence River in eastern Canada (Blane and Jaakson, 1994); in New Zealand (Constantine, 1999; Curtin, 2003); in Ireland (Berrow, 2003); and in Scotland (MacLellan, 1999; Parsons *et al.*, 2003; Woods-Ballard *et al.*, 2003). Descriptions of wildlife tourism include, for example, Sournia (1996) in West and Central Africa; Sekhar (2003) for tigers in India; and a very thorough analysis by Lamprey and Reid (2004) for the Maasai Mara region in East Africa. Geographically oriented descriptions also include Goeft and Alder (2000) for mountain biking in south-western Western Australia, and Berno *et al.* (1996) for a range of adventure tourism activities in Queenstown, New Zealand.

The overall size, scale and trends in adventure tourism have attracted attention both for economic reasons and for land management. Hof and Kaiser (1983), Cordell and Bergstrom (1991), Watson *et al.* (1995) and Cole (1996), for example, were all interested in analysing and/or forecasting trends in outdoor recreation with particular reference to public lands in the USA. Chavez (1996a, b) and Schuett (1997) focused specifically on mountain biking, and Bowker (2001) on off-road driving, again in the USA. More recently, Cape (2003) examined the global market for recreational diving, and Chen *et al.* (2003) reviewed forecasting methods with specific reference to seasonality. There are many more publications that also quote the broad scale of different activities in different regions, either in demographic or economic terms, but principally as a precursor or context to other types of analysis. These are reviewed later in this chapter.

## Impacts

### Ecological impacts

The impacts of adventure tourism on the natural and human environment have been analysed much more extensively for some areas and activities than for others. There are recent reviews of environmental impacts caused by hiking and backcountry camping (Cole, 2004; Marion and Leung, 2004), by horse riding (Newsome *et al.*, 2004a), by off-road driving (Buckley, 2004d) and by recreational boating (Mosisch and Arthington, 2004; Warnken and Byrnes, 2004). Likewise, there are reviews of impacts on vegetation and soils (Cole, 2004), on birds (Buckley, 2004b) and on other wildlife (Beale and Monaghan, 2004; Buckley, 2004c). As one example, the impacts of tourists on various species of penguin have been examined by Giese (1996) and Fowler (1999).

The impacts of skiing, particularly alpine skiing and ski resorts, have also been examined in some detail. General reviews are provided by Buckley *et al.* (2000) and Hadley and Wilson (2004). In particular, the impacts of ski resorts have been examined for soil fauna and Orthoptera (the grasshopper family) in Austria (Meyer, 1993; Illich and Haslett, 1994); for ptarmigan in Scotland (Watson and Moss, 2004); for mountain pygmy possums in Australia (Mansergh and Scotts, 1989; Broome, 2001); and for various environmental impacts in New Zealand (Fahey *et al.*, 1999). Snowmobile impacts have been considered by Neumann and Merriam (1972), Pesant (1987) and Vail and Heldt (2004). The impacts of mountain biking have been examined by Weaver and Dale (1978), Goeft and Alder (2000), Symmonds *et al.* (2000), Thurston and Reader (2001) and Cessford (2002); those of horse riding by Weaver and Dale (1978), Summer (1980, 1986), Whinam *et al.* (1994), Newsome *et al.* (2002, 2004a); and those of rock climbing by Camp and Knight (1998) and Farris (1998).

Impacts of diving, snorkelling, and watching whales and other marine vertebrates have been examined in some detail: indeed, a complete review is beyond the scope of this contribution. Impacts of diving on coral reefs in Florida and the Caribbean have been described by Hawkins and Roberts (1992, 1993, 1999), Dixon *et al.* (1993), Talge (1993), Marion and Rogers (1994), Hawkins *et al.* (1999), Williams and Polunin (2000), Tratalos and Austin (2001) and Townsend (2003). In Europe, Petreas (2003) reported the environmental impacts of diving in Greece. In the Red Sea there are reports from Riegl and Velimirov (1991), Hawkins and Roberts (1994), Jameson *et al.* (1999) and Zakai and Chadwick-Furman (2002). Further south, Schleyer and Tomalin (2000) and Walters and Samways (2001) have studied the impacts of diving in South Africa. Salm (1986) reviewed impacts in the Indian Ocean, and Allison (1996) in the Maldives. Examples from Australia include Davis and Tisdell (1995), Harriott *et al.* (1997), Rouphael and Inglis (2001) and Newsome *et al.* (2004b). Musa (2003) studied impacts at Sipadan in Indonesia, and Howard (1999) in Vanuatu.

Most of these authors report breakage of branching corals, principally by inexperienced divers. Contacts with coral are also commonly made by skilled photographers steadying themselves for close-up shots. Fewer contacts are made by experienced divers, and also by divers who have received briefing on minimal-impact behaviours (Medio *et al.*, 1997). Impacts can also occur from divers resuspending sediment (Rogers, 1983, 1990; Neil, 1990), or by direct trampling on reef flats (Liddle and Kay, 1987; Kay and Liddle, 1989; Hawkins and Roberts, 1992, 1993; Woodland and Hooper, 1977). By far the majority of diving impact studies are in warm-water coral reef ecosystems, but Garrabou (1998) also studied impacts on bryozoans, and Schaeffer *et al.* (1999) on kelp forest.

Impacts of tourism on marine mammals have also been studied quite extensively (Higham and Lusseau, 2004). Species studied include: harp seals in Canada (Kovacs and Innes, 1990); manatees in Florida (Nowacek *et al.*, 2004); bottlenose dolphins (Janik and Thompson, 1996; Constantine, 2000; Scarpaci *et al.*, 2000; Nowacek *et al.*, 2001); Hector's dolphins (Bejder *et al.*, 1999; Nichols *et al.*, 2001); beluga (Blane and Jaakson, 1994); grey whales at Cape Cod (Watkins, 1986); humpback whales in Hervey Bay, Australia (Corkeron, 1995); and sperm whales in New Zealand (Gordon *et al.*, 1992). Behavioural changes include: avoiding swimmers and/or boats; changes to surfacing patterns; and different vocalization patterns. Impacts on other marine vertebrates such as whalesharks, rays and turtles have also been examined, though less extensively.

## Social impacts and conflicts

The human impacts of adventure tourism can usefully be considered in three categories: impacts on non-tourist residents and communities; impacts on other tourists, commonly phrased as conflicts of various types; and impacts on the tour participants themselves, and their guides. Impacts on resident host communities are usefully divided into social and economic categories.

There are a number of reported instances where tourism was expected to contribute to local residents, especially in developing nations, but has either failed to do so or has done so inequitably. Examples include wildlife tourism in the Maasai Mara (Thompson and Homewood, 2002); Zambia (Mvula, 2001); Uganda (Archabald and Naughton-Treves, 2001; Adams and Infield, 2003); and India (Sekhar, 2003). There are also examples where tourism has successfully contributed to local communities (Buckley, 2003a).

Conflicts associated with adventure tourism have been the subject of quite detailed study in some instances. Some general reviews and introductions include: Jacob and Schreyer (1980), Devall and Harry (1981), Gramann and Burdge (1981), Ruddell and Gramann (1994), Gibbons and Ruddell (1995), Hendricks (1995), Watson (1995), Mace *et al.* (1999), Schneider (2000) and Vaske *et al.* (2004).

Conflicts have also been examined between devotees of different types of adventure tourism recreation. Many of these are between motorized and non-motorized users in the same area, or between those with and without livestock. There are also finer-scale conflicts associated with fashion, age, gender and experience, for example between skiers and snowboarders, or different styles of climbing. In some cases, especially where sites are crowded, there is antagonism between those present for private recreation, and those there for commercial tours or instruction. Jakus and Shaw (1997), for example, found that 13% of climbers at one site wanted professional climbing instruction banned at that site. There have also been conflicts between recreational surfers and surf schools, and between independent surfers and commercial surf resorts and charters claiming exclusive access to particular areas.

Conflicts between skiers and snowmobiles in the backcountry have been identified, and in some cases analysed, by Knopp and Tyger (1973), Jackson and Wong (1982), Hultkrantz and Mortazavi (1999), Vaske *et al.* (2000), Vail and Heldt (2004) and Vitterso *et al.* (2004). Conflicts between skiers and snowboarders are reported by Williams *et al.* (1994), Vaske *et al.* (2000, 2004), Thapa and Graefe (2003) and Needham and Rollins (2005). My own observations suggest that this particular antipathy has now largely disappeared, perhaps thanks to the 'new school' skiers who ski more like snowboarders than traditional skiers.

Many national parks and wilderness areas, especially in North America, have reported conflicts between hikers and riders or livestock packers (e.g. Watson *et al.*, 1994; Blahna *et al.*, 1995) and especially between hikers and mountain bikers (Jacoby, 1990; Watson *et al.*, 1991; Chavez *et al.*, 1993; Hopkin and Moore, 1995; Ramthun, 1995; Chavez, 1996a, b, 1999; Schuett, 1997; Carothers *et al.*, 2001; Mosedale, 2002).

User conflicts are not restricted to terrestrial activities. They are also reported between marine divers and anglers (Lynch *et al.*, 2004), anglers and river boaters (Driver and Bassett, 1975), and between paddlers and motorboaters (Shelby, 1980; Adelman *et al.*, 1982; Donnelly *et al.*, 1986). Conflicts between different types of users are so commonplace in North America that large sections of a national recreation management conference in 1999 were devoted to this issue. Commonly, such conflicts are asymmetrical: the motorized users declare themselves quite prepared to 'share', apparently unaware of the impacts they have on non-motorized users seeking silence, solitude and safety.

## Economic impacts

The economic impacts of various forms of adventure tourism have been examined at different scales, from single sites to worldwide, using various approaches. The overall economic scale of adventure tourism in the USA, for example, was estimated at more than US$200 billion per annum over a decade ago (Mallett, 1998). This estimate included ski resorts and motorized recreational equipment.

More recently Page *et al.* (2005) reported that the domestic adventure industry in Scotland has an annual turnover of UKP1.6 billion (US$2.9 billion), with the outbound sector an additional UKP1.9 billion (US$3.4 billion) per annum. In Australia the scale of the nature, eco and adventure tourism sector was estimated at around 25–33% of the entire tourism industry, AUD15 billion, a decade ago (Buckley, 1998). This included purely contemplative nature tourism, however, with no adventure component.

The annual turnover of the Caribbean diving industry has been estimated at US$1.2 billion (Green and Donnelly, 2003), with the suggestion that this represents 57% of the industry worldwide. If so, the global scale of recreational diving revenue would be around US$2.3 billion per annum. International markets for recreational diving have also been examined by Cope (2003). The global scale of the whale-watching industry has been estimated at around US$1 billion per annum (Hoyt, 2000; Rodger and Moore, 2004).

Data, assumptions and calculations underlying these figures are often poorly defined, so they are approximations at best. They do, however, suggest that adventure tourism is indeed a significant component of the tourism industry. Since nearly all adventure tourism takes place well outside urban areas, it has considerable potential to contribute to rural and regional economies.

At a more localized level, there are estimates of the economic scale of: climbing in Scotland (Hanley *et al.*, 2001, 2003; Hanley, 2002) and the USA (Grijalva *et al.*, 2002); mountain biking at Moab, Utah (Fix and Loomis, 1997); snorkelling in Florida (Park *et al.*, 2002); and whitewater rafting on certain southern US rivers (Bowker *et al.*, 1996; English and Bowker, 1996) and eastern Australian rivers (Buultjens and Davis, 2001). The economic scale of the whalewatching industry (including other marine vertebrates) has been estimated for various sites and species in Canada (Duffus and Dearden, 1993), Australia (Davis and Tisdell, 1996, 1998), Scotland (Parsons *et al.*, 2003; Woods-Ballard *et al.*, 2003) and elsewhere (Hoyt, 2000; Rodger and Moore, 2004).

The economic scale of tourism based on wildlife and parks has been estimated for particular species and areas in, for example, Zambia (Mvula, 2001), Namibia (Barnes *et al.*, 1999), the Congo (Wilkie and Carpenter, 1999a, b) and Indonesia (Walpole and Goodwin, 2001). The distribution of this tourist revenue, particularly to local residents, has been examined for: mountain travel in Nepal (Hoffman, 2001); gorilla watching in Uganda (Archabald and Naughton-Treves, 2001; Adams and Infield, 2003); and various southern African parks and game reserves, for example.

Economic estimates can be highly sensitive to the details of the methods used

(Shaw and Jakus, 1996; English and Bowker, 1996b; Barnes *et al.*, 1999; Wielgus *et al.*, 2003). Economic approaches have also been used to examine how either landholders or participants in various adventure activities at crowded sites might respond to different potential management measures (Barnes and Jager, 1996; Davis and Tisdell, 1996; Hanley *et al.*, 2001, 2003; Hanley, 2002; Siderelis and Attarian, 2004).

## Risks and Accidents

Risks and accidents have been investigated more rigorously than most aspects of adventure tourism and recreation: perhaps partly because of insurance and lawsuits, and partly because medical science may be more meticulous than its social counterparts. As noted by Page *et al.* (2005), 'much of the influential research on adventure highlights risk as the key element, but interestingly, the conceptual bases have been developed not by tourism researchers but by those working in outdoor recreation'. General considerations of tourist health and safety are available in books such as Clift *et al.* (1997) and Wilks and Page (2003). Page *et al.* (2005), though writing specifically about Scotland, also provide a review of adventure activities and accident statistics, drawing on previous work in New Zealand by Bentley *et al.* (2001a, b, c). The most risky activities, judging from such statistics, are horse riding, quad bikes and snow sports. The most detailed investigations, however, seem to be in mountaineering, skiing and snowboarding, and diving.

Williamson (1999), for example, reviewed accidents for mountaineering in North America, and Malcolm (2001) reported fatalities for mountaineering in Mt Cook National Park in New Zealand. Hackett and Rennie (1976) examined the incidence of altitude sickness and Musa *et al.* (2004) found that 89% of visitors to Sagarmartha National Park (Mt Everest) get either altitude sickness, respiratory ailments or intestinal infections. Snow sports injuries have attracted attention for over three decades, with early work by Garrick and Kurland (1971) and Requa *et al.* (1977). More recently there have been analyses by Aitkens (1990), Prall *et al.* (1995), Johnson *et al.* (1997), Deibert *et al.* (1998), Goulet *et al.* (1999), Tarazi *et al.* (1999), Machold *et al.* (2000, 2002), Macnab *et al.* (2002), Ronning *et al.* (2000, 2001), Yamakawa *et al.* (2001), Federiuk *et al.* (2002), Levy *et al.* (2002), Matsumoto *et al.* (2002) and Hagel *et al.* (2004), for example. These report not only basic statistics, but details such as differences between skiers and snowboarders in the frequencies of injuries to different parts of the body; the effect of helmets and wrist guards; and the effects of skill and experience.

Diving injuries have also been examined closely, perhaps partly because of the requirements for specialist medical examinations as one component of diving certification systems. According to Trevett *et al.* (2001), for example, in 1999 one in every 178 divers at Scapa Flow in the Orkney Islands, north of Scotland, experienced a 'significant' accident, and in 2001 the proportion was 1 in 102. These are high rates. Wilks and Davis (2000) reported diving mortality rates as 1 per 430,000 dives in Queensland, 1 per 120,000 dives in Australia as a whole, 1 per 100,000 dives in the USA and 6.5 per 100,000 dives in Japan. Earlier data on diving safety and accidents in Australia were provided by Edmonds and Walker (1989) and Wilks (1992, 1993, 1999). Byrd and Hamilton (1997) reported statistics for cave diving deaths in Florida, and Gorman (1994) and Taylor *et al.* (2003) reviewed diving injuries more generally. There is much more limited information for other adventure sports, such as surfing (Nathanson *et al.*, 2002), whitewater rafting and kayaking (Schoen and Stano, 2002).

# Participant Perceptions and Psychology

## Thrills, fear and risk

As noted by Cater (2005), participants in commercial adventure tours commonly want to experience thrills and even fear, but do not want to be subject to actual risk. As also noted by Page *et al.* (2005) for research on actual physical and medical risk, much of the research on participant perception of risk has been carried out in relation to outdoor recreation rather than tourism. Clearly, there are strong parallels, particularly for the more skilled and experienced commercial clients, though perhaps less so for unskilled tourists taking part in a one-day adventure activity as part of a more general tour.

The outdoor recreation literature is replete with terms such as risk recreation and sensation seeking (McIntyre, 1992). There are general discussions of psychology and participation, such as Cheron and Ritchie (1982), Ewert and Hollenhurst (1989, 1997), Crawford *et al.* (1991), Slanger and Rudestam (1997), Jack and Ronan (1998), McIntyre and Roggenbuck (1998), Holyfield (1999), Schrader and Wann (1999) and Fluker and Turner (2000). Climbing and mountaineering seem to have received particular attention, including Bratton *et al.* (1979), Ewert (1985, 1994), Breivik (1996), Jakus and Shaw (1996), Feher *et al.* (1998), Delle Fave *et al.* (2003) and Pomfret (2005), for example.

## Attitudes and experiences

The psychology of individual participants in adventure activities seems to have been studied in more detail than any other aspect of adventure recreation. This general field includes motivations and attitudes, experience and emotions, learning and satisfaction (e.g. Driver and Knopf, 1976; Geva and Goldman, 1991), and a wide range of factors that may influence any of these. There are particular subsets of research on behavioural norms and compliance. Much of the research has been associated with mountain environments and North American wilderness areas, from Lucas (1964) and Mitchell (1983) to Hendee and Dawson (2002).

The attitudes of climbers to fixed bolts have been studied by Schuster *et al.* (2001) and Borrie and Harding (2002) and the perceptions of hikers by Martin and Priest (1986), Borrie and Roggenbuck (2001), Chhetri *et al.* (2004), Manning (2004), Manning and Freimund (2004) and Manning *et al.* (2004), for example. Skiers and snowboarders have received attention from, e.g. Gilbert and Hudson (2000), Heino (2000) and Anderson (2000), though from rather different perspectives. Farmer (1992) examined surfing subcultures; Hollenhorst *et al.* (1995) analysed the attitudes of mountain bikers; Knopf *et al.* (1983), Hall and McArthur (1991) and Brookes (2001) studied whitewater rafters; Lipscombe (1999) studied skydivers; and Schänzel and McIntosh (2000) investigated the emotions experienced by visitors to a New Zealand penguin colony.

Gyimothy and Mykletun (2004) described the behaviour of a bunch of Norwegian schoolteachers on two snowmobiling holidays in Svalbard, though just why this should merit attention is not well explained. Equally unusual is recent research reported by Loeffler (2004) on 'photo-elicitation' – i.e. show me your holiday photos and tell me about them. Some of these social science analyses do indeed contain interesting insights: for example, that of Anderson (1999) on gender in snowboarding. Others report what would, perhaps, already be well-known to adventure tour guides and participants, if not to tourism academics: examples include Beedie and Hudson (2003) and Pomfret (2005).

## Behavioural norms

Behavioural norms for various aspects of outdoor recreation and adventure tourism have received particular attention: what they are, how they develop, how to measure them and how to change them. Recent reviews include Manning *et al.* (2002, 2004) and Manning and Freimund (2004). The main focus has been on crowding, often expressed as number of encounters with other people. Examples include Vaske *et al.* (1986) for backcountry hikers; Shelby (1981) and Wellman *et al.* (1982) for river runners and canoeists; Manning *et al.* (1996) for tour boats in Alaska's Glacier Bay; Jakus and Shaw (1997) for rock climbing; Inglis *et al.* (1999) for snorkellers on Australia's Great Barrier Reef; and Needham *et al.* (2004) and Needham and Rollins (2005) for summer use of ski areas. Additional discussions are available in Roggenbuck *et al.* (1991), Basman *et al.* (1996), Shelby *et al.* (1996), Donnelly *et al.* (2000), Heywood and Murdock (2002), Vaske and Donnelly (2002), Manning *et al.* (2002, 2004) and More and Averill (2003), for example.

One behavioural norm of particular interest to both land managers and tour guides is compliance with codes of conduct. This issue has been examined in most detail for the whalewatching industry. Some countries have legally enforceable regulations to govern commercial whalewatching, and others rely on codes of conduct, which are generally similar in substance but not enforceable. Whalewatching codes have been reviewed, compared and analysed by Gjerdalen and Williams (2000), Carlson (2001) and Garrod and Fennell (2004). Carlson (2001) compiled 58 different codes, and Garrod and Fennell (2004) analysed their content. They found that many codes do not refer at all to the more substantive and controversial issues.

Scarpaci and Dayanthi (2003) examined actual compliance with a legislated code of conduct by operators of swim-with-dolphin tours in Port Philip Bay, Victoria, Australia. This code formed part of the permit conditions for these operators, but even so, many failed to comply. One-third of the approaches to dolphin pods breached the conditions; one-third of the swims were illegal because they were longer than the maximum allowable time and two-thirds because they were closer than the minimum allowable distance. These breaches occurred even though the operator knew the observers were on board. This certainly suggests that without enforcement, even legislated codes have little effect.

## Guides

Most of the research literature on the psychology of adventure tourism and recreation has focused on the participants. A few researchers, however, have examined the perspective of the guides. The service aspects of adventure tours have been recognized and examined for many years, e.g. by Lopez (1980) and more recently by Arnould and Price (1993) for river trips, and O'Neill *et al.* (2002) for diving tours. Only recently, however, has the psychology of the guides been considered. Parker and Avant (2000) found that whilst mountain climbing guides saw their role as educational, backcountry horse packers saw themselves simply as providing a service. Beedie (2003) described mountain guiding in terms of choreography; and most recently Sharpe (2005) has applied the term 'emotional labour' to river guiding.

# 3  Case Study Approach

## On-site Audits and Activity Sector

There are too few published descriptions of adventure tourism products to carry out an analysis from secondary data. The bulk of this book, therefore, contains a set of case studies from over 100 individual adventure tourism products that I have experienced in person. Some of these are similar products from the same company in different places, and some are similar products from different companies in the same places. In such cases I have presented several individual tour products in a single case study to avoid repetition.

It is one of the characteristic features of adventure tourism, as with individual outdoor recreation, that a certain degree of individual skill and experience in the activity concerned is a prerequisite for purchasing and participating in many products – particularly those that might be labelled as more 'extreme'. You generally don't need prior skills to go bungee jumping, tandem parachuting, seakayaking or whitewater rafting, but you certainly do in order to go diving, mountaineering, surfing or whitewater kayaking.

As a result, my own case study observations only cover adventure activities in which I myself have sufficient skill and experience to take part in commercial tours. For other activities, chapters have been contributed by colleagues with greater expertise in the activities concerned: horse riding by Claudia Ollenburg, mountain biking by Julie Schaefers, mountaineering by Rob Hales and ice climbing by Jerry Johnson and Ian Godwin. All are highly expert in their respective fields. In addition, the chapter on the self-styled adventure capital of the world was contributed by Carl Cater, who has made this a particular subject of study.

There are other activities that are offered as adventure tourism products but that are not featured in this book, either because they have been examined in more detail elsewhere, or because neither I nor my colleagues have relevant experience. The former category includes, for example, resort skiing and snowboarding, described by Hudson *et al.* (2002), or whalewatching and other forms of marine tourism described by Cater and Cater (forthcoming). The latter includes caving, blackwater rafting and zorbing, for example. There are also adventure recreation activities that are relatively recent in origin and do not yet feature significantly as commercial tourism products. Kiteboarding is a good example.

In addition to the case studies as above, I have included one or two where we have no first-hand observations, but that are of sufficient interest to merit inclusion none the less, as examples of what the adventure tourism industry is offering. Cross-country skiing to the North Pole is one such instance. For some of the case studies presented, I have only indirect experience, by taking part in the same activity at the same place independently, and later learning of commercial tour providers offering packaged products that are not dissimilar. Such cases are identified in the text.

## Advantages and Limitations of Case Studies

The focus of this volume is on the actual practice of adventure tourism at the ground level, the operational detail of individual adventure tourism products in different sectors. These case studies are then used as a basis for cross-case analysis so as to comment on broad issues facing the sector as a whole, and comparative differences between different adventure activities. A number of broad trends in the adventure tourism sector have been identified previously (e.g. Buckley, 2002a, b, 2003b, 2004a; Swarbrooke *et al.*, 2003). The case-study approach used here can shed additional light on some of these issues, but rather less for others.

As noted earlier, for example, it has been suggested that growth in commercial adventure tourism is due at least in part to large-scale social factors such as: increased urbanization; links to the clothing and entertainment industries; and a broad trend for many people to treat outdoor recreation more as a purchasable holiday experience than a lifetime skill and vocation (Buckley, 1998, 2003b, 2004a). In addition, this last trend has led to growth in low-skill adventure tourism products aimed at mass markets, at the same time as the expansion of so-called extreme or expeditionary tours marketed to those who do have skill and expertise in a particular recreational activity (Buckley, 2004a).

Many of the case studies presented in this book do indeed appear to exemplify these patterns. The inclusion of particular case studies, however, has necessarily been rather opportunistic, so the information presented here cannot be interpreted as a representative, random or stratified sample of the global adventure tourism sector. More methodical sampling has indeed been used on occasion in individual nations, such as that carried out in Australia by Buckley (2000) or in the USA by the Outdoor Industry Association (2005).

Similarly, because the focus is on the practical management of individual tour products, the case studies described in this book cannot answer broader questions such as the contribution of adventure tourism to regional economies, the demographics of adventure tour participants, or the personal experiences of individual tour participants and associated lifestyle implications. Such issues are indeed significant and have been addressed elsewhere, as summarized in the previous chapter. Generally, however, they need either far more case studies than are currently available, or a different analytical approach from that adopted here.

Despite these deficiencies, which in many ways parallel those identified for a previous compilation of 170 case studies in ecotourism (Buckley, 2003a), the present volume does appear to be the most extensive academic analysis of the adventure tourism sector yet conducted. Twenty-five of the tourism products reviewed here have been examined previously from an environmental perspective (Buckley, 2003a). These cases are presented here from an adventure-oriented product perspective. The other 90 products outlined here do not appear to have been analysed previously. We trust that the information in this volume will prove valuable for tourism studies more generally, and will catalyse further research in the adventure tourism sector specifically.

## Parameters and Products

The aim of this book is to analyse the commercial adventure tourism industry. The emphasis is on actual adventure tourism products sold to commercial clients by reputable operators. The case studies present a range of such products in a standardized manner, with a range of routine statistics and descriptive information, and a commentary on various aspects of the client experience. These case studies then provide the basis for cross-case analysis both within and between different activities or subsectors.

To obtain descriptive data on individual adventure tour products that can be used with confidence in subsequent cross-case analysis requires on-the-spot audits by observers with relevant comparative experience. For most adventure tourism products, this means that the observer must take part in the tour or activity concerned and examine aspects such as access, logistics, equipment, safety procedures, management practices and the behaviour of staff and clients.

Auditors thus require not only the time and funding to take part, but also relevant skills for the adventure activity concerned. The same constraints apply, of course, to analyses of outdoor recreation and education, which may explain why those literatures are somewhat self-contained. In practical terms, it is relatively straightforward to study single-day, low-cost, low-skill 'soft' adventure tours, but much more difficult to study multi-day, high-cost, high-skill 'hard' adventure tours. This applies particularly to those that take place in remote areas (Buckley, 2004a).

## Access and Sponsorship

There are tens of thousands of adventure tourism products worldwide, and it is impossible for any one researcher to investigate any more than a tiny sample. Indeed, since many adventure tourism products are only available to individuals skilled in particular outdoor recreational activities, it is difficult for any one researcher to examine the full breadth of activities offered, let alone a representative worldwide selection from each.

In compiling this volume I have drawn on personal experience of over 100 commercial adventure tourism products over a period of several decades. For many of these I took part completely incognito as a paying client. For others I took part as an unpaid member of staff, e.g. as an extra safety kayaker on whitewater raft trips; or in some supernumerary capacity as an independent researcher; or occasionally, as a sponsored participant, as for a journalist or industry familiarization tour. There are also one or two instances where I did not take part in a commercial trip, but examined the area and activities independently. Case studies in this last category contain only general information on commercial tour operations in these areas, rather than personal experience with a particular tour.

Limitations on funding can be overcome to a degree through sponsorship, but this is not always available, usually only partial, and rarely covers air travel to the tour's starting point. Most importantly, tour operators who provide sponsored places may expect a favourable report, in the same way as they would do from a journalist or magazine writer. To overcome this difficulty, the parameters of any sponsorship must be agreed clearly at the outset. For the more expensive and upmarket adventure tourism products, sponsorship is probably the only realistic option for any individual academic to make comparative studies. A number of the case study audits reported in this volume were carried out with at least partial sponsorship.

The procedure adopted in these cases was the same as for audits reported by Buckley (2003a) in the ecotourism sector, as follows:

**1.** The first approach was always made by the researcher, requesting sponsorship, rather than by the company offering it.

**2.** Approaches were made only to established and reputable operators.

**3.** Before any approach was made, opinions were sought from competing operators in the same sector, from commercial clients who had experience both with the operator concerned and with competing operators, and/or from professionals and researchers in related areas who could comment on the company concerned.

**4.** Requests for sponsorship specified at the outset:

**a.** that the information was for academic research, not the popular press;

**b.** that the case study report would be brief and phrased in technical rather than marketing language;

**c.** that inclusion of any particular case study in the research text was not guaranteed;

**d.** that description and analysis of any individual case study would be the same irrespective of whether sponsorship was provided; and

**e.** that the amount of sponsorship that could be offered was left to the discretion of the company concerned;

**f.** at the same time, this initial approach also made clear that the ability to include the more expensive tour products in the book at all was constrained by cost and hence sponsorship; and

**g.** that the researcher requesting sponsorship had an established record of reliable publication in related fields.

In practice, only a few operators were approached for sponsorship and all of them did in fact offer it, except for one very small specialist company with high prices and very small client numbers, where the effective cost of sponsoring a place might well have had a significant impact on total annual revenue.

In addition to the time and cost involved in on-the-spot audits of individual adventure tour products, and the complexities of sponsorship, case study audits suffer from two further deficiencies. The first is that any one researcher can only audit a limited number of products, particularly for multi-day tours in remote areas. If different people audit different products, however, there is no guarantee of comparative consistency. Ideally, perhaps, one would use a team of adventure tourism researchers worldwide, with a certain subset of products being audited by more than one researcher to ensure consistent treatment. Adventure tourism research, however, has not progressed to this degree. For this volume, therefore, almost all the case studies reported have been audited in person by the principal author, or by individual chapter authors for the climbing, horse riding and mountain biking chapters. Other tour products are mentioned as appropriate, but distinguished clearly from those that have been audited.

A second deficiency is that each audit is effectively a single snapshot of the particular tour product concerned, whereas that tour is probably offered repeatedly and may not always run in quite the same way. External factors such as wind and weather, snow or surf conditions, the behaviour of wildlife or local communities, or political changes in the country concerned, as well as internal factors such as the personalities of guides and clients, can make a major difference to the tour experience. The greater a researcher's comparative experience, perhaps, the greater the ability to allow for such factors, but such compensation mechanisms are still very imperfect.

## Limitations on Scope

### Commercial tour products

This appears to be the first book to attempt the analysis of the adventure tourism sector from this product perspective. It may therefore be useful to summarize some of the things that this book does not do. It is not a description of individual adventure and achievement. The heroic exploits of great explorers such as Scott, Speke or Shackleton, or modern mountaineers such as Boukhreev, Lowe or Simpson are in another realm of difficulty and danger relative to the more pedestrian pursuits described here.

It is not a book about independent outdoor recreation. There are many guide books, such as the *Lonely Planet*® series, that list adventure activities available in various geographic areas. Such guides frequently feature outdoor recreation suppliers at the sites they describe, including local tours and guides as well as equipment rentals. This information is intended, however, principally for people who are visiting these areas as free and independent travellers, not those who arrive as part of an international package tour to carry out a particular outdoor activity.

There are many specialist magazines that describe sites and opportunities worldwide, some mundane and others extreme, for individual outdoor sports and recreational activities. Such magazines often feature commercial adventure tours as well as independent private trips. There are also detailed guidebooks for particular activities in particular places, such as 4WD tours in Australia or hiking routes in a particular national park. This book does not attempt to substitute for any of these.

Nor is it a text on outdoor recreation planning, outdoor recreation management, outdoor education, outdoor programme planning or wilderness visitor management. There is an extensive body of literature in each of these fields, including a number of recent textbooks. None of this literature, however, focuses specifically on the structure of commercial adventure tourism products.

Finally, this is not a text on individual psychology, experience or emotion, whether of guides or clients, instructors or students. Again, there seems to be quite an extensive literature on these aspects.

### Selected subsectors

There are a number of commercial outdoor sports that could clearly qualify as adventure tourism and are commonly included in adventure tourism statistics, but that are not covered in this volume simply because they are already well known. The prime example is the downhill ski industry, which has been subject to extensive economic analysis and is arguably driven more by real estate sales than actual skiing, as the value of residential housing and commercial retail precincts at ski areas now greatly exceeds ski lift ticket sales. In this book, therefore, only backcountry skiing and snowboarding are considered, whether heliskiing and boarding, or cross-country touring.

There are other adventure tourism activities that are not included simply because we have not yet compiled a sufficient number of case studies. There are some activities, such as caving, where I have taken part in a limited number of commercial tours, but do not have the skills or experience for a comparative analysis.

There are some, such as sailboarding and hang-gliding, where I have low-key private recreational or competitive experience over several decades, but little or no experience in commercial tours. For example, I took part in some of the events in the first world sailboarding championship in the late 1970s, and the Australian national hang-gliding championship a couple of years later; but I have not taken part in any commercial sailboarding or hang-gliding tours.

There are outdoor sports such as kiteboarding that have grown greatly in popularity over recent years, that have an international following and their own specialist magazines, and where I have learned a little myself, but that do not yet seem to have developed a commercial tour industry.

Naturally, no insult is intended to the devotees of any adventure activity that has been omitted, and I should be very pleased to hear from researchers with relevant skills to write new chapters for the next edition. I can be contacted at the International Centre for Ecotourism Research, r.buckley@ griffith.edu.au. I look forward to a second volume or a second edition of this book, with a significantly expanded set of authors who can cover a more comprehensive set of adventure tourism activities and case studies.

## Anglophone operators

In particular, all the case studies presented here are from companies that communicate with their clients in English, even if they operate in countries where English is not the first language. Yet many of the world's adventure tourists are from countries such as Italy, Germany, France and Japan. They have their own adventure tour companies and their own guides and whilst some may subcontract the same local operators as their Anglophone counterparts, others may not. Whether they structure their adventure tourism products in the same way or face the same issues, we do not know. This applies even more strongly for countries such as China, where adventure tourism is a relatively new but rapidly growing concept.

## Academic Disciplines, Methods and Data

Academics argue with each other a lot. Sometimes it's fruitful, sometimes not. When the subject matter crosses the boundaries of academic disciplines, the debate can often be at cross purposes. It may therefore be useful to address the issue of academic context, at least briefly.

The purpose of this volume is to contribute to reliable data and understanding of commercial adventure tourism products. This falls under the general rubric of tourism studies. To the extent that the differences between regions are examined, it may also be of interest to tourism geographers.

For each product examined, issues such as price, land tenure, environmental management, safety and marketing are considered briefly, but only as components of the product. Some cross-case comparisons are considered, but this volume does not purport to contribute to theoretical advancement in tourism economics, management, marketing or law.

The case studies presented were chosen to cover a reasonably broad range of activities and countries, but they are not necessarily a random or representative sample, and the number of cases from each adventure activity sector is small. Whilst the data presented for each individual product can provide some general indications of variation between subsectors, they are not intended to provide a basis for statistical analysis of differences between activities or regions.

Thus we can conclude, for example, that certain types of tours are usually more expensive than others, measured per person per day; but we cannot calculate meaningful significance probabilities. Indeed, for many types of tours, all we can say is that their price ranges overlap.

Prices and costs, incidentally, are shown throughout in three-letter currency codes for all local currencies, with $ symbols used only for conversions to US$ (at 2005 rates).

Similar considerations apply, e.g. for group size, client-to-guide ratios and trip lengths. For parameters that are described only in qualitative terms, such comparisons are even less rigorous.

As noted earlier, observations of a particular tour product may well depend on the specific departure date, weather, guide and client group. No two tours are identical. This does not make those particular observations inaccurate or unreliable: it means merely that they may not be representative.

There seems to be some kind of controversy within the social sciences as to the different roles and values of qualitative vs quantitative data, external observations vs social immersion, hypothesis testing vs narrative accounts, and no doubt many more besides. To a natural scientist, these debates seem to miss the point. All observations of any type differ in reliability and representativeness, and different types of data can be used to answer different questions.

A single observation of a viable seed in mud on a tourist's boot or tent peg, for example, may be 100% accurate and reliable as far as it goes, but it only shows that the plant species could potentially be dispersed by tourists. To determine how likely it is that a particular plant species in a particular place is actually dispersed there by tourists takes vastly more information. A single observation of poor safety procedures or environmental management by an adventure tour operator shows only that such problems sometimes occur, not that they are routine. That specific observation, however, is no less accurate or reliable because it may not be representative.

There also appears to be some debate, perhaps more semantic than substantive, over what constitutes a 'case study', and how case studies should be used in research. A very clear review was provided recently by Beeton (2005). In this volume the phrase is used in its lay or non-technical sense to mean simply an example, an instance of the topic under discussion, which can be described in order to contribute data to the debate.

To compare case studies, each one needs to present similar information, and I have therefore used the same headings for each (Table 3.1). This, however, could easily become repetitive and boring. In an attempt to minimize this risk, I have used some of the case studies, generally the earlier ones in each chapter, to present some general issues related to the adventure activities concerned. In addition, I have inserted occasional anecdotal comments here and there as a small reminder that adventure tour guides, adventure tour clients and adventure tourism researchers all have their accidents and foibles. After all, a dust-dry text is of little use if people don't read it.

**Table 3.1.** Format of case study descriptions.

| Subheading | Issues examined |
| --- | --- |
| Place | Where does the tour itself take place? |
| Company | Who operates the tour? |
| Activity | What is the major adventure activity involved? |
| Equipment | What does the operator provide and what must clients bring? |
| Accommodation | Where do clients stay overnight during the tour, for multi-day trips? |
| Statistics | Group size, client/guide ratio, duration, price range and structure |
| Access | Land and sea access, permits and fees |
| Community | Local involvement and conflicts |
| Experience | Client comfort, excitement and satisfaction |
| Environment | Environmental management and education |
| Safety | Risk level and safety procedures |
| Marketing | Accuracy of claims in marketing materials |

## Experience, Audits and Case Studies

Information about adventure tourism, as presented in this volume, is derived from several different sources. Published literature is reviewed in the previous chapter. Marketing materials from companies, destinations and associations have been examined where relevant. Most importantly, however, the bulk of this book is derived from personal experience by the principal and contributing authors.

This experience is summarized in Table 3.2, which lists: the main activity subsectors in the adventure tourism industry; the degree to which the author(s) are familiar with each; the number of commercial tour products audited in person; and the number of case studies presented.

**Table 3.2.** Adventure activities and case studies.

| Activity | Author's recreational experience[1] | Commercial product audits[3] | Case studies presented here[3] |
| --- | --- | --- | --- |
| Abseiling | * | * | — |
| Aircraft (aerobatic) | * | — | — |
| Ballooning | * | * | 1 |
| Blackwater rafting | — | — | — |
| Bungee jumping | ** | ** | — |
| Caving | * | * | — |
| Cross-country skiing | ** | * | 3[5] |
| Diving | *** | ** | 9 |
| Downhill ski/snowboard | *** | ** | — |
| Expedition cruises | * | * | 3 |
| Gliding | * | — | — |
| Hang-gliding | ** | — | — |
| Heliski/boarding | ** | ** | 6 |
| Hiking | *** | * | 6 |

**Table 3.2.** *Continued.*

| Activity | Author's recreational experience[1] | Commercial product audits[3] | Case studies presented here[3] |
|---|---|---|---|
| Horse riding | **, ***[1] | **[2] | 3 |
| Ice climbing | –, ***[1] | **[2] | 3 |
| Jetboating | * | * | – |
| Kiteboarding | * | – | – |
| Mountain biking | *, ***[1] | *[2] | 3 |
| Mountaineering | *, ***[1] | *[2] | 2 |
| Off-road 4WD | *** | ** | 5 |
| Parapente/paragliding | – | – | – |
| Quad biking/ATV | * | * | – |
| River expeditions | ** | ** | 6 |
| Rock climbing | *, ***[1] | – | – |
| Sailboarding | *** | – | – |
| Sailing | ** | * | – |
| Seakayaking | ** | ** | 7 |
| Skydiving/parachuting[6] | * | * | 1 |
| Snowshoeing | – | – | – |
| Surfing | *** | ** | 5 |
| Whalewatching | ** | ** | – |
| Whitewater kayaking | *** | *** | 6 |
| Whitewater rafting | * | *** | 8 |
| Wildlife watching[4] | ** | ** | 6 |
| Zorbing | – | – | – |

Notes: * = limited, e.g. 1–5 trips or days; ** = moderate, e.g. 5–50; *** = extensive, e.g. 50–1000. [1]For rock climbing, horse riding, ice climbing, mountain biking and mountaineering, the symbols after the commas are for the individual chapter authors, and those before the commas are for the principal author. [2]For horse riding, mountain biking, mountaineering and ice climbing, these symbols refer to the individual chapter authors. [3]Some case studies include more than one individual product. [4]Large animals in remote locations only. [5]Including one case study not audited by any of the authors. [6]Tandem only.

There are some activities where the authors do have relevant experience but that have not been covered by product audits. The case studies do not match the audits directly: first, because some products audited have not been presented; and secondly because some case studies include several commercial products (Table 3.3).

**Table 3.3.** Adventure tourism case studies audited.

| Country | Place | Tour operator[1] | Case study presented | No. of audits[2] |
|---|---|---|---|---|
| *River journeys* | | | | |
| China | Lancang Jiang | Shangri-La River Expeditions | – | 1 |
| China | Yangbi River | Earth Science Expeditions | * | 1 |
| Tibet | Qamdo Gorge, Mekong | SSEA and ESE (jointly) | * | 1 |
| Nepal | Karnali, Sun Khosi, Trisuli, Marsyangdi River | David Allardice's Ultimate Descents | * | 4 |
| Brazil | Jatapu River | Fabio Bueno Neto and Carlos Colares (jointly) | * | 1 |
| Australia | Drysdale River | Raleigh International, USNOLS | * | 2 |
| USA | Grand Canyon | Expeditions Inc., OARS | * | 2 |
| *Whitewater kayaking* | | | | |
| Chile | Rios Futaleufu, Fuy | Expediciones Chile | * | 2 |
| Argentina | Rio Manso | Expediciones Chile | * | 1 |
| Costa Rica | Reventazon, Pacuare, Pejibaye, Sarapiqui | Endless River Adventures | * | 1 |
| Zimbabwe | Upper Zambezi | Shearwater, others | * | 1 |
| New Zealand | Karamea River | Ultimate Descents NZ | * | 1 |
| Australia | Franklin River | World Expeditions | * | 1 |
| USA | Cataract Canyon | Various | – | 1 |
| USA | Lochsa River | Various | – | 2 |
| USA | Payette North Fork | Various | – | 1 |
| USA | White Salmon River | Various | – | 1 |
| USA | Westwater Canyon | Various | – | 3 |
| *Whitewater rafting* | | | | |
| Ecuador | Rios Toachi, Blanco | Yacu Amu Rafting | * | 1 |
| Uganda | White Nile | Adrift | * | 1 |
| Zimbabwe | Zambezi River | Shearwater Adventures | * | 1 |
| New Zealand | Kawarau River | Queenstown Rafting, others | * | 2 |
| New Zealand | Rangitata River | Rangitata Rafts | * | 1 |
| New Zealand | Shotover River | Queenstown Rafting, others | * | 2 |
| New Zealand | Buller River | Ultimate Descents NZ, Buller River Rafting | – | 2 |
| Australia | Nymboida River | World Expeditions, others | * | 3 |
| Australia | Gwydir River | Wildwater Adventures, others | – | 1 |
| Australia | Tully River | R'n'R, Raging Thunder | * | 2 |
| USA | Green River | Various | – | 1 |
| USA | San Juan River | Wild Rivers Expeditions | – | 1 |
| USA | Flathead River | Glacier Raft Co., others | – | 1 |
| *Seakayaking* | | | | |
| Australia | Hinchinbrook Island | Southern Sea Ventures (SSV) | * | 1 |
| New Zealand | Abel Tasman | Ocean River, Natural High | * | 2 |
| Alaska | Admiralty Island | Kayak Express | – | 1 |
| Alaska | Prince William Sound | USNOLS | * | 1 |
| Canada | Baffin Island | Blackfeather Inc | * | 1 |
| USA | San Juan Islands | Sea Quest Kayaks | – | 1 |
| Norway | Svalbard | SSV and Aurora Expeditions | * | 1 |
| Samoa | Upolu Coastline | Ecotour Samoa | – | 1 |
| Thailand | Phang Nga Bay | John Gray's Sea Canoe | * | 1 |
| *Diving* | | | | |
| Australia | Lizard Island | Lizard Island Lodge | – | 1 |
| Australia | Osprey Reef | Taka Dive | * | 1 |
| Australia | Port Douglas Reefs | Quicksilver Cruises | * | 1 |
| Australia | Ningaloo Reef | Ningaloo Blue, King Dive | * | 2 |
| Maldives | Paradise Island | Delphis | * | 1 |

**Table 3.3.** *Continued.*

| Country | Place | Tour operator[1] | Case study presented | No. of audits[2] |
|---|---|---|---|---|
| Zanzibar | Mnemba Island | CCAfrica | * | 1 |
| South Africa | Rocktail Bay | Wilderness Safaris | * | 1 |
| Papua New Guinea | Walindi Bay | Walindi Plantation Resort | * | 1 |
| *Expedition cruises* | | | | |
| Antarctic | Antarctic Peninsula | Explorer Shipping | * | 1 |
| Norway | Spitzbergen | Aurora Expeditions | * | 1 |
| Papua New Guinea | Sepik River | MTS *Discoverer*, MV *Sepik Spirit* | * | 2 |
| *Surfing* | | | | |
| Australia | East and South Coast | Various | – | 1 |
| South Africa | Jeffreys Bay | Various | – | 1 |
| Western Samoa | Savaii | Savaii Surfaris | * | 1 |
| Western Samoa | Upolu | Salani Surf Resort | * | 1 |
| Maldives | Dhonveli | Atoll Adventures | * | 1 |
| Indonesia | Mentawai Islands | Mentawai Sanctuary | * | 1 |
| *Heliski and snowboard* | | | | |
| New Zealand | Harris Mts | The Helicopter Line | * | 1 |
| New Zealand | Arrowsmith Mts | Methven Heliski | * | 1 |
| Canada | Whistler | Tyax Heliski | – | 1 |
| Canada | Monashees | Canadian Mountain Holidays | * | 1 |
| Canada | Galena | Canadian Mountain Holidays | * | 1 |
| Canada | Blue River | Mike Wiegele Helicopter Skiing | * | 1 |
| India | Manali | Himachal Helicopter Skiing | * | 1 |
| *Cross-country skiing* | | | | |
| Australia | Mt Kosciuszko | Paddy Pallins Ltd | * | 1 |
| USA | Yellowstone National Park | Various | * | 1 |
| USA | Banff National Park | Various | * | – |
| *Off-road safaris* | | | | |
| Australia | Simpson Desert | Various | * | 1 |
| Australia | Gibson, Great Victoria | Various | – | 2 |
| Kenya | Chalbi Desert | Various | * | 1 |
| China | Gobi Desert | China Academy of Sciences | – | 1 |
| China | Taklamakan Desert | Various | * | 1 |
| Namibia | Namib Desert | Various | * | 1 |
| Namibia | Skeleton Coast | Various | – | 1 |
| Chile | Atacama Desert | Various | – | 1 |
| *Hiking and bushwalking* | | | | |
| Australia | Purnululu National Park | Willis's Walkabouts | * | 1 |
| Ecuador | Podocarpus National Park | Surtrek | * | 1 |
| Kenya | Mt Kenya | Various | * | 1 |
| Nepal | Jomson/Annapurna | World Expeditions | * | 1 |
| Alaska, USA | Denali National Park | Various | – | 1 |
| USA | Salmon-Huckleberry | Various | – | 1 |
| USA | Mt Adams | Various | – | 1 |
| Canada | Yoho National Park | Various | – | 1 |
| New Zealand | Routeburn Track | Ultimate Hikes | * | 1 |
| *Wildlife* | | | | |
| Tanzania | Northern Circuit | Conservation Corporation Africa | * | 5 |
| Tanzania | Southern Circuit | Conservation Corporation Africa | – | 3 |
| South Africa | Sabi Sands Lodges | CCA, Sabi Sabi, Chitwa Chitwa | – | 5 |
| South Africa | Phinda, Greater St Lucia | Conservation Corporation Africa | – | 1 |
| South Africa | Ndumu | Wilderness Safaris | – | 1 |

**Table 3.3.** *Continued.*

| Country | Place | Tour operator[1] | Case study presented | No. of audits[2] |
|---------|-------|------------------|---------------------|-------------------|
| Botswana | Jack's Camp | Uncharted Africa/Wilderness Safaris | * | 1 |
| Russia | Kamchatka, Grizzly Bears | Explore Kamchatka | * | 1 |
| USA | Alaska, Grizzly Bears | Various | – | 1 |
| Canada | Churchill, Polar Bears | Natural Habitat Adventures | * | 1 |
| Nepal | Bardia, Tigers | Tiger Tops Karnali | * | 1 |
| Uganda | Bwindi, Gorillas | African Wildlife Safaris | * | 1 |
| China | Chengdu, Panda | Various | – | 1 |

Notes: [1]Operators joined by 'and' run the same trip jointly; operators separated by a comma run similar trips separately. [2]The case studies presented have been selected to illustrate the range of adventure tourism products. Others have also been audited but not presented, as indicated in this table. The fact that a particular audited product is not presented as a case study does not imply any criticism of that product or its operator. Some of the cases have been presented elsewhere. In other cases my visit did not audit specific tour products. And some of the products audited are very similar to those that are presented as case studies.

# 4 River Journeys

Earth Science Expeditions, Mekong, China. Photo Ralf Buckley.

Ralf Buckley, Fitzroy River, Australia. Photo Scott Sumner.

## Sector Structure

Whitewater raft and kayak tour companies range in size from a single person with a single raft, to worldwide operations such as Mountain Travel Sobek (2005), owned by the Microsoft Corporation. The majority of these operators, however, are small and medium-sized enterprises (SMEs) that own their own rafts and kayaks, operate on a restricted and localized set of rivers that they know well, hire whitewater guides trip-by-trip as required, and get most of their clients either through multi-activity outdoor tourism retailers such as World Expeditions (2005b), or by basing themselves in well-known adventure tourism destinations where they can rely on walk-ins.

Whitewater rapids and rivers are classified on an international scale of I–V in degree of difficulty, with Class V subdivided in recent years into V.i, V.ii and V.iii as equipment and techniques continue to improve, and rapids previously considered unrunnable are now being run. Most commercial whitewater rafting tours operate on rivers rated at Class II–III for family trips including children, or Class III–IV for thrill-seeking clients who expect to be flipped into the river at some point. Some commercial rafting trips do run rivers with Class V rapids, but there is a degree of latitude in what is interpreted as Class V. Swimming in serious Class V whitewater involves a considerable and immediate risk to life.

A small number of companies specialize in Class V whitewater. An example is provided by Expediciones Chile, operating on the Futaleufu and neighbouring rivers in Patagonian Chile. Whilst the company has now expanded to include fly-fishing and rafting, it started as an experts-only kayak camp, where internationally renowned professional kayak guides would lead skilled kayaking clients down sections of the river ranging from Class IV+ to Class V.iii, depending on ability (Buckley, 2003a; Expediciones Chile, 2005). A similar company, Endless River Adventures (Buckley, 2003a; Endless River Adventures, 2005) operates in Costa Rica and Ecuador, but using local accommodation instead of a purpose-built camp. Whilst both these companies offer challenging whitewater, neither offers first descents. The same applies for companies such as Adrift Adventure (2005) in Uganda and Ultimate Descents in Nepal (2005) and New Zealand (2005). The latter, however, now also operates in Bhutan, and their first Bhutan trip a few years ago was offered commercially as a first descent.

Many companies add to their repertoire of rivers at intervals by exploring new options, and one or two companies also offer first descents of significant rivers in remote areas. For whitewater rafters and kayakers, the first descent of a major river is a significant international event, in the same way that the first ascent of a previously unclimbed peak is significant in mountaineering circles. Tradition-ally, the first person to run each individual rapid gets the right to name it, in the same way that rock climbers name individual routes (though usually less imaginatively).

Since most first descents are made by experienced private recreational groups, or by professional teams sponsored by major kayak manufacturers, the cachet of a first descent adds significantly to the appeal and value of a whitewater trip for many commercial clients. From an operational perspective, however, a first descent is very different from a routine river-running tour. The river is unknown, the logistics are untested, and the tour is a one-off. Hence the participants, even though they are paying customers, need to have sufficient whitewater and backcountry skills to take part safely and make a net contribution to the expedition, rather than behaving as paying passengers. They also need to be sufficiently good-humoured and flexible to blend well into a group and to adjust to whatever unexpected circumstances may arise.

A few companies specialize almost entirely in first descents. A prime example is Earth Science Expeditions (ESE) (2005) and its subsidiary Shangri-La River Expeditions (2005), run from the USA but specializing in first descents on the big rivers of the Himalayas, in northwest China and southeast Tibet (Buckley, 2003a; Earth Science Expeditions, 2005). Broadly, ESE's owners identify, plan and obtain permission for new first descents, and provide equipment and full logistic support, and then sell a limited number of expedition places to skilled kayakers and rafters. The rivers run by Earth Science Expeditions are selected for their size, geographic location and global significance rather than degree of difficulty, but some of them are in fact extremely challenging.

There are world-famous gorges (such as Tiger Leap Gorge on the Yangtze and the Great Bend of the Tsangpo – or indeed the Grand Canyon of the Stikine or Devil's Canyon on the Susitna in Canada) that have been run or attempted by expert private expeditions, in some cases involving loss of life, but that would currently be considered far too dangerous for a commercial trip. On the other hand, to be marketable to experienced whitewater aficionados, even a first descent needs a degree of challenge, and besides, first descents are only available on rivers too difficult for local watercraft.

In 2003, for example, Earth Science Expeditions offered a first descent by raft of a section of the Salween, one of the major rivers of the Himalayas, and first descents by kayak only of a series of smaller but more difficult Class V rivers in China's Gonga Shan area. In 2004, the company attempted a first descent of the Class V+ Qamdo Gorge of the Mekong River in Tibet, reported in this volume.

Do first descents such as these lead to expansions in commercial adventure tourism? In many cases, yes; but not automatically. Successful operations such as Expediciones Chile and Endless River Adventures show that there are skilled recreational kayakers who are prepared to pay for guides and for logistics in unfamiliar areas: the cash-rich, time-poor section of the adventure tourism market (Buckley, 2002a). Similarly, the commercial success of companies such as Adrift Adventure and Ultimate Descents shows that there is a significant market of unskilled adventure tourists prepared to pay for fully guided Class IV–V whitewater trips in relatively remote areas.

The difference between these operations, and the first descents offered by Earth Science Expeditions, is principally one of cost, timing and reliability. First descents command a price premium that generally cannot be maintained in a routine adventure tourism product. In addition, first-descent clients will commonly accept greater uncertainty and less efficient logistics than clients on a routine whitewater trip. For most whitewater rivers, therefore, even challenging rivers in remote areas, it is a combination of political and market factors that determine whether a new first descent will lead to a routine tour offering.

Whitewater adventure tours differ so much in duration, difficulty and watercraft that the case studies presented here are divided into three separate chapters. The first whitewater chapter examines case studies where the emphasis is on a multi-day journey down a remote river, typically using both rafts and kayaks. Some of these case studies describe first descents, others routine trips. Some are Class V or harder, others mere riffles, but all involve barriers that must be negotiated actively. That is, they are not float trips where the focus is on scenery and wildlife.

The second chapter covers case studies where the focus is on kayaking, and the tour operators aim to provide equipment, logistic support, local knowledge and expert guiding for experienced whitewater kayakers. Some of these companies cater for kayakers only; some offer separate raft or kayak trips; and some offer suitably skilled kayakers the opportunity to paddle their own boats alongside guided rafts, as commercial clients, with their equipment carried on the rafts and all off-river activities carried out jointly with the rafting clients.

The third focuses on short-duration, high-adrenalin raft trips aimed at unskilled clients. Many of the clients are backpackers, and such trips often form an iconic component of the product mix at adventure tourism destinations. The day's activities are highly scheduled and standardized. Clients receive only minimal instruction, focusing on paddling commands and safety. These companies generally do not offer a kayak option, and the only way to kayak with a rafting group is as an informal safety boater.

## Yangbi River, China: Earth Science Expeditions

### Place

The Yangbi River is a major tributary of the Mekong River, known in China as the Lancang Jiang. The Yangbi flows from the mountains north of Dali in Yunnan Province, southwestern China, through a relatively inaccessible area inhabited principally by the people of Bai and Yi ethnic origin rather than the majority Han Chinese. It enters the Mekong from its eastern side, in a section of the Mekong currently subject to massive dam construction for hydroelectric power development. The upper catchment near Dali has been subject to large-scale industrial logging. Except for one medium-scale mine, the lower gorges are apparently occupied only by villagers who practice a local subsistence farming lifestyle. At least, this was the situation when we visited in the mid-1990s.

### Operator

Earth Science Expeditions (ESE) is a small US-based company that specializes in river-based exploratory trips and expeditions in remote areas of China and Tibet. Its directors combine expertise in exploration geology and prospecting with expertise in remote-area travel, river running and commercial tourism. Their primary focus is on first descents of large remote rivers draining the major catchments of the Himalayas. Many of these rivers run through areas occupied by minority peoples, and in some cases disputed territories. In these areas, maps and aerial photographs are still treated as military intelligence, and there is little or no up-to-date scientific information on the geology or ecology, at least in the international English-language scientific literature.

These expeditions have been run effectively as commercial tours, advertised in whitewater circles and open to anyone with relevant interests. The first descent of the Yangbi River was ESE's first such adventure tour, and entailed very considerable organizational effort and expense by the company's directors, not least because the period whilst the trip was being planned was interrupted by the Tiananmen Square massacre in China, which severed diplomatic relations between China and the USA for several years. Following the successful first descent of the Yangbi, ESE and its subsidiary Shangri-La River Expeditions have carried out a number of similar trips and explorations.

I have taken part in three of these: the 1994 Yangbi trip described here (Buckley, 1995); a 1997 trip on a section of the Lancang Jiang (Mekong) in Yunnan, China (Earth Science Expeditions, 2005); and a 2004 trip in the Qamdo Gorge in the Tibetan section of the Mekong, described in the next case study.

## Activity

ESE's trips are expeditions in the senses that each is a one-off exercise involving complex logistics; they operate in remote and relatively inaccessible parts of the globe; they involve first descents of rivers that have not been run previously; all expedition members contribute to the costs as participants, rather than being separated into paying clients and paid staff; and the organization is set up as a non-profit corporation. The trips are tours in the senses that they take people who have paid for the privilege to parts of the world they would not otherwise visit; and whilst some of the expedition members may be engaged in scientific research, others are there simply to experience nature, culture and adventure.

The Yangbi River Expedition had three main purposes. It was a geological exploration, carried out as a scientific project in conjunction with the Chinese Academy of Sciences. It was a commercial tour, an opportunity for participants to make a first descent of a major and previously unrun river in a remote part of the world. And it was an attempt to demonstrate to Chinese provincial government officials that adventure tourism could be a commercially valuable activity, with better long-term economic prospects than logging and pulp mills.

The trip required considerable investment by ESE in establishing a working relationship with the Chinese Academy of Sciences, and the group was accompanied by an interpreter from the Academy. There was no road access to the river between the put-in and take-out points, and for most of the stretch the Yangbi flows through a deep steep-sided gorge. The only maps of the area available outside China were over 50 years old and showed very little detail. The Chinese Government refused to allow access to its own maps, which were treated as military intelligence.

Hence ESE knew very little about the river, except for its overall drop in elevation between put-in and take-out. The descent was therefore made in early spring, when river levels are lowest, so that the group could camp on exposed gravel bars. The days are short at this time of year, and we had to use all available daylight to travel down river. We therefore started breaking camp in the dark every morning so as to be on the river shortly after dawn.

## Equipment

As with ESE's other first descents in China, the group used a combination of kayaks and catarafts. The catarafts carry the food, camping and cooking equipment so that the kayakers can paddle their boats empty for maximum manoeuvrability. The kayakers paddle ahead and check whether each rapid is runnable or needs to be scouted and perhaps portaged, and signal back to the rafts. Catarafts, which are essentially twin inflatable pontoons held together with a rowing and equipment frame, cannot carry as many passengers as a conventional floored oval raft of similar dimensions, but are much more manoeuvrable.

Participants brought their own camping equipment, and the kayakers brought their own kayaks and all associated gear. ESE does keep some whitewater kayaks in China, available for use by its kayakers, but most expedition members bring their own boats specifically for the trip, taking them home again afterwards. The dismantled rafts, rigging, oars and accessories are stored in China between trips, along with tents, cooking gear and other camping equipment. For the Yangbi trip, the participants brought their own camping equipment, but ESE now has tents and sleeping bags available for loan if required. ESE provides river gear for rafters, but kayakers bring their own personal gear such as helmets, lifejackets, sprayskirts and paddles.

## Accommodation

All accommodation on the river itself was in tents, camped on gravel bars, riverbanks or wherever else was possible. On the road trips between the river and the gateway city of Kunming, accommodation was in local hotels or guesthouses, as available. Each cataraft had two large plastic cooler boxes that were continually splashed or partially immersed in the river, and at that time of the year the air was also cool, so it was possible to bring fresh vegetables as well as dry and packaged foods.

## Statistics

The Yangbi descent is not run as a routine tour, and indeed, since the ESE descent, the river has been largely dammed and heavily polluted and has, apparently, never been run again. There are therefore no up-to-date statistics on price, duration and group size. For the 1994 descent we had three kayakers, including the expedition leader; two catarafts; and eight participants in total. Including travel, the entire trip took about 3 weeks, of which 10 days were spent on the river itself. The total cost was several thousand US dollars per participant, plus international airfares. A significant proportion of this represented a permit and in-country logistics fee paid to the Chinese Academy of Science, as outlined below.

## Access

Access was by air to Kunming and by road to the river via Dali. Much of this road is now a large modern highway, but at the time it was a narrow dirt road used by livestock, horse-drawn and motorized carts and other contrivances, and aging trucks and buses, all driven furiously with little regard to life or limb. The road was heavily potholed and its verges were littered with the remains of road accidents. Our put-in and take-out points were at road bridges and there was no other road access to the river.

There is apparently no routine process to obtain river-running permits in China. Currently, it requires negotiation with local and provincial authorities. Various individuals and organizations, with differing degrees of influence and credibility, have set themselves up as permit brokers. At the time of the Yangbi Expedition, however, ESE was able to deal directly with the Yunnan provincial branch of the

Chinese Academy of Science, which is a national government organization. They charged a significant fee, amounting to about US$1000 per participant, but this was still far less expensive than other permit options, and significantly less than fees charged by provincial government authorities for later ESE expeditions.

Nominally, these fees are not permit fees as such, but payments for in-country logistic costs such as local transport and accommodation. It is not difficult to ascertain these individual cost components, however, and it certainly appears that they add up to considerably less than the total fees paid. The remainder effectively constitutes a payment for permission to run the river, levied by persons who have the power to deny or enforce such permission. Whether or not this should be described as a permit fee is perhaps a question of semantics or political perception.

## Community

Local residents along the Yangbi River were largely Bai and Yi peoples, rather than Han Chinese. Each has its own traditional building styles, recognizable in villages beside the river. The houses are well-made, from hand-hewn rock and timber. Livelihood is largely by subsistence farming, with houses built from locally quarried stone and locally logged timber. In calm sections of the river, locals cross using bamboo rafts. There are mines near the riverbank and locals have the habit, disconcerting to passing river runners, of fishing with dynamite.

We were visited by villagers at a number of our riverbank campsites and were able to communicate since several of the rafters spoke Chinese. At one village there was one young girl who was learning English at her school 30 km away, walking there and back each week to study.

At two sites the villagers were hunting birds and small mammals with shotguns, and at least one of these guns was a muzzle-loader using the hard spherical fruit of a local plant as shot. When they saw we had empty glass jars and bottles that we were carrying out for disposal they were very keen to take them from us, and gave us local pickles in return. In the calmer stretches of the river, they crossed using long bamboo rafts propelled by a kind of wooden hoe, where the blade is mounted perpendicular to the shaft rather than parallel to it as for a conventional oar or paddle.

Since the ESE group was continually proceeding downstream, our encounters with local communities were necessarily brief, but cordial within the limits of communication. We had a limited opportunity for conversation when one group visited our evening campfire, and on our one lay-over day at the junction of the Yangbi and Mekong, we climbed up to a small village set high on the steep valley slopes.

## Experience

This was ESE's first river trip in China and, for essentially political reasons, took many years of planning and preparation. It was therefore somewhat disconcerting, not to say disappointing, to discover that during this period of planning a pulp mill had been constructed on the Yangbi, immediately upstream of our proposed put-in point, and the river was severely polluted with its effluents. Indeed, when we first saw the river we debated seriously whether we would have to abort the entire river trip. Fortunately, we went ahead and were indeed able to make the first descent of the Yangbi.

Most of the group had already travelled previously in China, but there were new experiences none the less. Some of these were positive, such as finding probable tracks of a red panda on an isolated beach. Others were negative, such as finding a red panda skin hanging on a post. From a whitewater perspective, a first descent of an effectively unmapped river is always a memorable experience, particularly for the lead kayaker or 'probe'.

## Environment

The directors of Earth Science Expeditions are experienced river runners, and one is a long-term former ranger from Grand Canyon National Park in the USA, so they are very familiar with minimal-impact environmental practices whilst on the river and in camp.

The environmental impacts of a raft trip, however, are insignificant in comparison with those of a pulp mill, or even those of local villagers and agriculture. On all of ESE's first descents in China, glass containers, which elsewhere would be considered recyclable garbage, were in demand for immediate reuse by local residents. All the villages in the areas concerned use fuel wood for cooking, and there is abundant dead driftwood on the riverine gravel bars which are reworked and flooded during the wet season every year, so campfires provide the best minimal-impact option for expedition cooking. Self-contained pump-out toilets, such as used on the Grand Canyon, would be pointless in China where human waste is collected for agricultural fertilizer. Accordingly, the group used pit toilets. All litter, however, including cigarette butts and similar small items, was collected and carried out.

The Yangbi area receives so few visitors that there are no artefacts or other items manufactured for sale to tourists, and hence no concern over possible secondary impacts on endangered species which might be used in such artefacts.

One of the major aims of the trip was to demonstrate the commercial viability of river tourism as an economical alternative to industrial logging, paper production and large-scale dams. Whilst tourism has indeed played an economic and political role in conservation in some parts of the world, and this effort is now continuing in China through initiatives such as The Nature Conservancy's Great Rivers Project, it was not successful in the case of the Yangbi. When we returned to the river in mid-2004 it was so severely dammed and polluted that no runnable whitewater remained.

## Safety

For a first descent of an unknown river in a remote area, safety issues are considerably broader than for a routine tour on a well-known river. At its broadest level, safety depends on overall trip planning, including the best available knowledge of terrain, gradient, geology and seasonal rainfall patterns. Taken together these provide some prediction of the likely shape and severity of the rapids, the frequency of potential campsites, and the probable distance travelled per day. Information on air and water temperature is also needed to determine what clothing and camping equipment may be required.

Opportunities for access to the river and for emergency evacuation, if any, also need to be planned in advance. For this part of China, reliable maps are unobtainable and in any event are at such a small scale that they give only a broad indication of topography. Aerial photographs are treated as military intelligence, and likewise unavailable. International satellite imagery is very expensive and does not show individual rapids in enough detail to be much use. Local villages may be sparse and residents may speak only local dialects. They may or may not be friendly to river runners arriving unexpectedly. They may or may not be able to describe downstream river conditions in terms meaningful to rafters and kayakers.

In such circumstances a river expedition must proceed with caution. Rapids that elsewhere would tempt kayakers to hours of play can only be run once. Rapids that elsewhere might be run by the most difficult route are instead run using easier lines. Rapids where all routes are difficult but not impossible may instead be portaged. All this is necessary to conserve equipment and energy for those rapids that are difficult but must be run none the less.

For first descents such as these, Earth Science Expeditions uses catarafts to carry gear and hardshell kayaks to scout ahead. The kayaking participants must be skilled paddlers. Their task is to run the river ahead of the rafts, signalling routes on easily runnable sections, and signalling a stop above more difficult rapids. With this advance warning, the rafts can pull safely to the riverbank when necessary, and wait for the much more manoeuvrable kayaks to scout a route through the next rapid.

For rapids that are long or have blind sections, kayakers can descend section by section and relay signals back to the rafters. If rapids cannot safely be 'boat-scouted' in this way, kayakers and rafters may have to scout the rapids from the shore. Once a rapid is scouted and the rafts start their run, the kayakers provide safety support in case any of the rafts capsize or anyone is thrown out. If this does happen, a kayaker will try to paddle to the swimmer as quickly as possible, and ferry them to safety. In a large, wide or violent rapid this is not always possible, but often kayaks can drag swimmers away from the more dangerous features of the rapid.

Safety kayakers are used routinely by many commercial whitewater rafting tour companies. The difference for a first descent is that neither the kayakers nor the rafters know what is coming downstream, so the kayakers must treat every new rapid as potentially unrunnable until proven otherwise, and the rafts must be alert and always ready to stop at a kayaker's signal.

Access points to the river are limited for most first descents in remote areas, and expeditions can carry only limited food. The ability to cover distance each day can hence become critical. If the kayakers halt the rafts unnecessarily, too much time is lost. The skill, judgement and teamwork of the rafters and kayakers are vital for overall safety.

Safety practices on the river itself included measures such as maintaining visual contact from boat to boat; scouting rapids in advance in the case of any uncertainty; taking safe and conservative lines through rapids where possible, rather than the lines one might take if it were a well-known river; wearing lifejackets at all times except in camp; keeping throw-ropes ready on rafts as well as kayaks; setting up back-ups and rescue plans for major rapids; and positioning the kayaks so they could rescue rafters or each other if need be. All these measures were followed during the ESE Yangbi trip. The most risky parts of the expedition, almost certainly, were the road journeys to and from the river, where accidents were clearly frequent and safety was beyond our control.

## Marketing

Marketing for a specialist one-off but relatively expensive trip such as this, especially by a newly formed company as ESE was then, presents particular difficulties. A company that already has a large repertoire of well-known routine tours and a heavily visited website can advertise a specialist one-off trip quite easily, relying on their existing customer base. Indeed, they may send direct mail or e-mail invitations to past clients who they think might be interested.

For a newly formed enterprise, however, there is no existing corporate customer base, and the trip leaders have to rely principally on personal contacts. If they can obtain sponsorship from any organization which publishes its own magazine or newsletter, that organization may also be prepared to provide publicity. Commercial advertising is generally not feasible, because the cost has to be spread across too few participants.

For a trip such as this, where costs have to be shared between all participants and most participants need to be skilled, there is a further difficulty: those with the necessary skills rarely have the necessary funds and vice versa. Many such proposed trips, in fact, do not succeed in attracting a sufficient number of skilled and paying participants to cover costs, and do not take place. It is a tribute to ESE's skills in marketing, as well as politics, planning and logistics that this trip took place at all, especially after a 7-year lead time.

## Qamdo Gorge of the Mekong, Tibet: Shangri-La River Expeditions

### Place

The Mekong River, thirteenth longest in the world, rises in Tibet and flows through Yunnan Province in Western China, into southeast Asia. As it leaves the Tibetan plateau, the river cuts down through a giant gorge several kilometres deep and over 100 km in length. Other great Asian rivers such as the Brahmaputra, the Salween and the Yangtze cut similar and parallel gorges.

Although still over 2000 km from the ocean, the Mekong is a large-volume river as it flows south from Qamdo in southern Tibet. Indeed, even at its lowest seasonal flow at the end of winter, it is still similar in size to the Grand Canyon of the Colorado at normal dam-release water levels. At high flow, the Qamdo Gorge probably carries as much water as monsoon flows in western Himalayan rivers such as the Sun Khosi in Nepal.

The section of the Mekong River immediately below Qamdo is relatively open, and there is a dirt road alongside and several local bridges. Once the river enters the main gorge, however, there is only an extremely narrow, precarious and intermittent track along cliffs and screes high above the river, and tiny isolated villages making a subsistence living at the junctions of side streams. The tracks are built up with stones from far below, so that in some places it is like walking along the top of a 10 m wall. In other places the tracks are carved out of vertical or overhanging cliffs. At one cliff there are some very large and solid ancient wooden pillars set beside the track, bored through with hand-cut rectangular holes. Presumably these are the remains of an ancient gate.

The villages, especially the smallest ones furthest into the gorges, appear to subsist almost entirely on the traditional Tibetan tsampa, barley meal ground between hand-hewn granite grindstones in mills driven by wooden paddle wheels. The barley is grown on small terraced fields irrigated by ramshackle but effective aqueducts from the side streams. Rainfall is very low, and houses are built with earth and stone walls, and earth and timber roofs. All structural timber, whether hollowed trunks for aqueducts or beams for houses, must be brought down from mountain forests thousands of metres higher in elevation. Despite this isolation, which must be extreme in winter, in 2004 at least one of the larger villages had a solar-powered video player! The river is cold and silty and the air is extremely dry.

## Operator

Shangri-La River Expeditions is a subsidiary of Earth Science Expeditions, a US-based company that has run a number of first descents on Chinese rivers, combining adventure tourism with scientific exploration. The Shangri-La subsidiary had previously run a first descent of the upper reaches of the Mekong on the Tibet plateau (Shangri-La River Expeditions, 2005). In April 2004, the company combined forces with a Japanese rafting group from the Exploration Club of the Tokyo University of Agriculture, and a Chinese group from Szechuan Scientific Explorations, to attempt a first descent of the Qamdo Gorge. Pete Winn, owner of Shangri-La River Expeditions, was the overall leader of this attempt. Szechuan Scientific Explorations is a commercial organization that arranged permits and logistics in China.

## Activity

The aim of the expedition was to make a first descent of the Mekong River from Qamdo through the gorge to the border between Tibet and Yunnan, a distance of 240 km. To cover this distance in the time available, most of the day was necessarily spent either on the water, scouting rapids or making and breaking camp. Since this section contains numerous Class IV and V rapids, all equipment had to be packed carefully and tied very thoroughly to the rafts, which took additional time. There were no detailed maps or large-scale aerial photographs, so navigation was a constant concern. There was no opportunity to replenish supplies whilst on the river and the rafts carried only enough food for the planned duration of the descent. Managing food consumption and checking the rate of progress downstream were therefore also important activities.

## Equipment

The group had three 5–6 m catarafts and four hardshell whitewater kayaks. Camping equipment and food were carried on the rafts so that the kayaks could paddle unladen. The catarafts were equipped with rowing frames and oar rigs for power and manoeuvrability in big water. Each carried one rower and up to three other expedition members. Two of the rafts were provided by Shangri-La River Expeditions, and one by the Japanese team.

My own kayak was sponsored by Current Craft Perception® in New Zealand. Some expedition participants brought their own camping equipment, others used gear supplied by Shangri-La. Chinese, Japanese and American participants brought separate food and cooking equipment, but soon combined them. Three expedition members brought handheld global positioning system (GPS) equipment. Three also brought commercial broadcast-quality video recorders, one from each national group. A separate Chinese TV video team also followed the expedition's progress from the banks where possible. However, they had no access into the main gorge. One member of the expedition brought a satellite telephone. This worked only intermittently, but proved very valuable later in the trip.

## Accommodation

The trip commenced in Chengdu in Yunnan Province and ended in Kunming. Travel to Qamdo was by truck and minibus. Accommodation during this section was in local hotels. On the river, accommodation was in tents on the riverbanks. In the upper sections of the river there were large sandbars, which provided good campsites, but as we came into the gorge, campsites were extremely few, small and cramped. At two sites we put our tents inside small room-sized rectangular stone walls built on the only available ledges of flat ground. At one site these were apparently disused and unroofed. At the other they had rudimentary brush roofs and were likely used to overwinter livestock.

## Statistics

The trip took a month in total, including travel within China. According to the plan, the group would have spent 18 days on the river. In practice, after 9 days on the river it was forced to abandon the descent and haul all its equipment out over a 5000 m snowbound pass, taking 6 days. This was an expeditionary first descent, and there was no clear distinction between guides and clients as in more routine commercial tours. Expedition members differed in their whitewater experience, expeditionary and outdoor experience, and experience in China. Similarly, different members of the expedition took part under different financial arrangements. Essentially, the international participants paid for the journeys, and probably also for a significant Chinese profit. It was an expensive trip.

## Access

Access to the Qamdo Gorge is complicated and difficult, both physically and legally. There is an airport about 80 km away from Qamdo, but it is often closed at short notice because of poor weather and is not considered reliable. Accordingly, expedition members flew to Chengdu and drove for several days to reach Qamdo. Downstream from Qamdo there is a riverside road for the first 60 km or so, then an increasingly narrow, precarious and intermittent track, and then nothing. About two-thirds of the way through the gorge there is a road bridge high above the river, but no road access to the river itself. Within the gorge section the only access is on foot, up side streams and over mountain ranges and passes at 5000 m elevation and higher.

To carry out this expedition, and indeed to enter this area of Tibet at all, we had to obtain permits from various government agencies including the Provincial Government of Tibet and the local government of the Qamdo area. Permit arrangements were handled by Szechuan Scientific Explorations on behalf of Shangri-La River Expeditions. Even so, some conflict between permitting authorities, never fully explained, detained us for 3 days at Qamdo before we were permitted to launch. Whitewater rafting and kayaking in China, especially first descents, always seem to involve endless difficulties with permits.

## Community

Our dealings with local communities in this expedition can be considered at several levels. We had dealings with Chinese government officials for permits. These were formal and ceremonial. For example, we were required to take part in a televised launch ceremony involving commoditized Tibetan customs, somewhat ironic as Qamdo is an old Tibetan monastery town that is now overrun by frontier-style Chinese economic development.

We had various interactions with the Chinese members of the expedition itself and those who had associated themselves with it. Clearly, we presented a promotional and moneymaking opportunity that some of our associates were keen to capitalize on. The dynamics between different Chinese members of our expedition were sometimes quite confusing for the Westerners.

The clash of traditional Tibetan and modern Han Chinese customs and cultures was also very apparent. Once we left the last road and came to isolated villages accessible only on foot or perhaps donkey, we encountered small traditional Tibetan communities with very little outside contact. Since our intended Tibetan guide had been unable to join us, however, our communications with these villagers were only through our Chinese expedition members, who by that time were substantially stressed. Communication was therefore not as relaxed as one might have wished for an effective cultural interaction.

## Experience

The expedition did not succeed in running the full 360 km length of the Qamdo Gorge. About 135 km below Qamdo the rapids became too difficult for the rafts to run safely and the gorge became too steep and sheer-walled for portages to be possible. The kayakers considered continuing unsupported, but had neither equipment nor permission to do so. To have carried on regardless would have endangered not only their own safety, but the opportunities for future whitewater descents in China. The expedition therefore dismantled all of its equipment, and with the assistance of local villagers and a number of small donkeys, carried it out over the nearest pass, 5000 m in elevation and snowbound, taking 6 days. This walk was very interesting, but not why we were there.

## Environment

Environmental management whilst on the river was similar to that by Earth Science Expeditions elsewhere, as described for the Yangbi River case study. The riverbanks in the city of Qamdo are heavily polluted with human excrement and the impacts of a small raft trip are entirely negligible in comparison. Several of the Japanese and Chinese members of the group were smokers. Each of the Japanese carried an empty film canister to store used cigarette butts. The Chinese initially threw their butts to the ground or the river, but later noted the Japanese practices and indeed mentioned them in written reports on the expedition in the Chinese press.

As with the Yangbi River Expedition a decade earlier, one of the aims of this trip was to demonstrate the potential economic significance of river tourism, in the hope that it could prove valuable as part of a conservation initiative. The Nature

Conservancy (2005), a large US-based international NGO, currently has a major conservation initiative in this region, known as the Great Rivers Project. Its objectives are similar but larger scale, better resourced and better connected than ours. Hopefully it will be successful.

## Safety

Safety procedures on the river were generally similar to those of ESE elsewhere. The kayaks paddle ahead of the rafts, scouting the river. Where they encounter easily run rapids, they proceed downstream and then signal the safest route to the rafts. For more difficult rapids, the kayaks first signal the rafts to halt at the riverbank, and investigate the rapids more carefully before deciding how to proceed. For the most difficult rapids, both kayakers and rowers halt upstream and scout the rapids from the bank before attempting to run them. Whilst rafts are running a rapid, the kayaks position themselves so as to rescue anyone who falls overboard.

One difference from earlier ESE trips was the lack of a common language. All but the most basic communications between the Chinese-, Japanese- and English-speaking members had to be relayed and interpreted. The Chinese members were inexperienced and it took several days before they learnt to pack their raft properly. Neither the Chinese nor the Japanese group had oarsmen with the same skills and experience as the American raft. The expedition leader overcame these difficulties to some degree by mixing group members between rafts to improve communications and by training oarsmen on the river, but such measures could only go so far.

Overall, the politics of assembling such a multinational expedition in order to obtain permission to attempt the descent led to shortcomings in the skills and experience of the expedition members. This meant that we had to portage rapids which a more experienced group might have run; that we fell behind schedule because of portages and because we were slow to break camp; and that the more experienced members, including the kayakers, had to devote considerable effort to assisting the group in tasks such as packing and portaging rafts, rather than being free to scout rapids.

A more detailed discussion is available on the expedition website (Shangri-La River Expedition, 2005). Congratulations are due especially to the expedition leader for maintaining coherence and making difficult decisions, and to the Japanese contingent for unflagging energy and efficiency. Nobody was injured despite some potentially dangerous situations.

## Marketing

As noted for the Yangbi River Expedition case study, assembling a trip such as this is not easy. For this trip it was further complicated by several factors. First, the Japanese crew wanted to run the same section, and the groups had to be combined. And secondly, the Chinese organization that brokered the permit not only wanted to be included, but also charged a very high price that restricted the number of potential participants.

# Chuya and Katun Rivers, Russia: Team Gorky

## Place

The Katun River flows north from the Altai Mountains in southern Siberia, joining the River Ob near the town of Barnaul. The headwaters of the Katun, and its tributaries such as the Chuya and Argut, are close to the international borders between Russia, China and Mongolia, in the Altai region at the western end of Central Asia's Sayan mountain range. Parts of the Altai are listed as a World Heritage Area.

The Katun is one of Russia's better-known and more popular rafting rivers. The Jenisei River, which flows north from the Sayan Mountains further east, is also used for rafting. These rivers are also popular for fishing. There are numerous sandy beaches along the central and lower stretches of the Katun River, and these are popular summer holiday destinations for Russian self-drive domestic tourists and school groups, who camp in grassy areas along raised river terraces.

Peak runoff is in June, but varies considerably from year to year. The rivers have a high silt load that colours the waters accordingly: the Chuya to a milky grey-brown and the Katun to a translucent green. The river valleys are high and steep-sided, with sparsely vegetated eroding slopes and sharp and heavily dissected ridge lines. The principal vegetation types include open conifer woodlands, birch groves, juniper heaths on the slopes, mixed herbaceous meadows on the river terraces, and dense but narrow stands of shrubs along side streams. There are wild strawberries, raspberries, gooseberries and other fruit and mushrooms. The area is famous for its honey.

There are rock art sites with ancient petroglyphs, which appear to depict ibex with their very characteristic large curled horns. Hunters still visit the region in winter. Unlike most of Siberia, the Katun is known for being largely free of mosquitoes. Presumably this is because the landscape is generally dry, steep and free-draining with no marshes, and the rivers are cold and fast-flowing. This feature certainly adds greatly to its attractiveness as a holiday destination. At the time of my visit there were immense clouds of small black flies over the river itself. These did not bite, but they did fly into one's eyes in large numbers, causing some difficulties whilst running rapids. There were also ticks, which can carry a Siberian encephalitis that is particularly virulent.

## Operator

Team Gorky is a well-respected and long-established outdoor tour operator that offers a range of land- and river-based trips throughout Siberia and elsewhere in Russia and overseas. The majority of its clients are Russian, but it also acts as the local provider for international tour companies such as Mountain Travel – Sobek. It has been operating for several decades, with permanent headquarters in Nizhny Novgorod and a summer base in Barnaul.

A number of other Russian firms offer rafting trips on the Katun River, but most of these seem to be low-key 1-day float trips on the lower Katun, below the whitewater sections described here. There are one or two other Russian operators who offer trips on the upper Katun and its tributaries, including the Class V+ Argut, but to judge from their respective websites, Team Gorky appears to be the most professional and well-established operator in the area. There is also at least one Russian operator based in the USA that offers rafting trips on the Chuya and Katun with the same itineraries as team Gorky, but at three times the price. International tour retailers that offer Team Gorky's trip under their own name also charge several times Team Gorky's own prices.

Team Gorky's name, incidentally, comes from the town of Nizhny Novgorod, which was at one time known as Gorky. The company is led and co-owned by Andrey Kapitanov, a very skilled and experienced rafter and kayaker who is still the chief guide and leads trips continuously during the summer season. Of course, since trips run simultaneously on different rivers, the company also employs additional lead guides. The rafting season in this area is from May to September, so most of Team Gorky's river guides and staff have other employment during winter.

## Activity

Both the Chuya and the Katun are relatively fast shallow rivers with many small rapids and riffles interspersed between the major rapids, and numerous pourovers and other hazards. Except in a few slower stretches towards the end of the trip, the rafters and kayakers must be alert and active throughout the entire trip. At this time of year, the days are long, with light from around 5 am until 9 pm. Whilst one or two of the clients were up early, the majority waited until the guides, who got up at 7 am, had breakfast ready at about 8:30 am. Dismantling the camp and packing the boats was a leisurely procedure, and often we were not on the water until 11 am.

On the Chuya there is a road alongside the river and all gear was transported from camp to camp in a truck so that the boats could be paddled empty. This is a significant consideration since the more difficult rapids are on the Chuya rather than the Katun. On the Katun, there is no road near the river until close to the take-out point, but the river is wide enough, and the rapids sufficiently straightforward, for the group to be accompanied by an oar-rigged baggage raft which carried communal camp equipment.

On most days the group stopped around 2 pm for an extended lunch break and then continued in the afternoon for another couple of hours on the river. Dinners were generally quite late, typically 9 or 9:30 pm, and on several nights many of the clients carried on the party until the early hours of the morning.

At two of the campsites the guides constructed a banya, a sauna-style steam tent. A couple of dozen football-sized rounded river rocks are piled into a hollow heap. A large fire is built beneath and around them and is kept stoked for several hours until the rocks are extremely hot. The embers are raked away, the ashes blown out from between the rocks, and the remains of the charred area covered with damp sand. A double-skinned tent is erected over the rock pile and its edges sealed to the ground with more sand. Guides and clients then take it turns to get into the tent in groups of six or eight, pour water on to the rocks and whip themselves with leaf-covered bunches of birch twigs. When the steam becomes too scalding one can squeeze out of the tent and leap into the river. On each occasion, the men went first, taking a couple of hours in all for everyone to have several turns in the tent, and then the women took over and followed suit. Apparently this is traditional.

On one occasion, we camped for two consecutive nights at the same site on the Katun River, and spent the day hiking up a small peak nearby which provided a panoramic view up and downstream. Overall, there was a good balance between active paddling and leisurely camping and riverside activities.

## Equipment

Team Gorky provided all the rafting and camping equipment, including sleeping bags. Clients provided only their own clothing, both for on- and off-river use. Whilst the Team Gorky (2005) website says only that one needs two sets of clothing, in practice many of the clients brought their own wetsuits or waterproof river jackets. Many of the clients were repeat customers and knew what to expect. In my own case, I used a kayak borrowed from Team Gorky, but brought all my own kayaking equipment and clothing. The water temperature was about 15°C.

All the equipment provided by Team Gorky was of good quality and in good condition. The camping gear was of Russian manufacture, the kayaks imported. Except for the oar-rigged baggage raft on the Katun section, the rafts were rigged as paddle rafts with six clients and one guide each. There were four such rafts, plus three kayaks and one privately owned two-person cataraft.

These small two-person catarafts, which seem to be quite common in Russia, are very different from the large oar-rigged catarafts used by Earth Science Expeditions in China and Tibet. They are small and narrow, with each of the inflatable pontoons little larger than an old-style whitewater kayak. One paddler kneels astride each pontoon, with their knees held in padded loops and their feet wedged against one of the aluminium cross-bars. They paddle using long-shafted single-bladed paddles, one paddling right-handed and one left-handed. These catarafts are fast and manoeuvrable, and can surf waves in the same way as a hardshell kayak. If they flip, they can be righted by standing on one pontoon, hooking the paddle tee-piece into a baggage strap on the other, and leaning outward. On the Katun, we saw a number of private trips using these craft.

## Accommodation

Accommodation on the rivers is in two-person tents. There were enough tents that clients travelling on their own could take a tent for themselves if they wished. On the first night, after a 12-h bus journey from Barnaul, the clients arrive at the Chuya River to find their tents already set up by the guides. On subsequent days, they are responsible for pitching and striking their own tents. The tents are of a straightforward design, but proved capable of handling high winds and heavy rains on several occasions.

At each camp the guides also set up several large tarpaulins for shelter in the centre of the camp, including one set up over a row of collapsible tables where food was laid out. All cooking was done by the guides, who also did all the washing up and all the work associated with the main camp and with loading and unloading boats, unless clients volunteered to help. Every morning, for example, two of the guides, using two frying pans each, would cook over 100 pancakes for breakfast. There were fresh fruit, fresh vegetables and fresh meat every day, including a sheep purchased from a farmer at one point. A number of clients had brought beer, wine and spirits, which added to the general conviviality. On the final night of the trip, after the group had driven back to Barnaul, accommodation was provided in a basic but adequate Soviet-era hotel.

## Statistics

The Chuya–Katun river trip takes a total of 10 days, including a day at each end spent travelling from Barnaul to the river and back. Of this, 3 days are spent on the

Chuya and five on the Katun, including the one rest day. The rafts take six clients and one guide each, and there were also two safety kayakers in addition to myself. The overall client-to-guide ratio was about 3:1. The trip costs €700 ex Barnaul, including all food and local transport and the final night's hotel accommodation. This corresponds to a little under US$90 per person per day, which is comparable to costs for corresponding high-volume trips in Nepal and well below the rates for specialist low-volume or one-off trips in Chile or China.

## Access

Access to the put-in point on the Chuya River is by an all-day road journey in a Team Gorky bus from Barnaul. The bus stops for lunch at a village market famous for various local foods such as honey, various pickled vegetables and other delicacies. The rafts, kayaks and camping equipment are driven to the river a day earlier by truck. Barnaul is accessible by air from Moscow. For international travellers arriving from the east, it is somewhat inconvenient to fly across the whole of Russia to Moscow and then back to Barnaul, but it appears that there are no long-haul flights into Barnaul, or even nearby Novosibirsk, from eastern gateways such as Vladivostok. Moscow has two major airport complexes, and ground transfers between them apparently take several hours. For flights to Barnaul that leave from Domodedovo airport, Team Gorky apparently provides a local courier to assist with connections (Team Gorky, 2005). This does not apply for those transiting through Sheremetyevo, who must make their own way between the international and domestic airports.

In the Chuya River valley there is a road running parallel to the river, and various points at which a carefully manoeuvred truck can get down to riverbank campsites, as outlined earlier. On the section of the Katun River below the confluence of the Chuya, there is no road access for three river days downstream. Below that, there are numerous access points, used by riverbank campers as well as rafters. It seems that some sections, and perhaps all of the section rafted by Team Gorky on this trip, flow through land managed by a forestry agency, which charges an access and/or camping fee for rafters. These fees were paid directly by Team Gorky and were included in the package price.

## Community

The Chuya and upper Katun catchments support low-density agriculture, with free-range cattle grazing predominant. In the villages, every house has a large yard, and every square metre is planted with potatoes and other vegetables. There are dilapidated remains of large farm buildings from the Soviet collective-farm era, but these are no longer operational. The riverbank terraces produce a rich meadow, and at the Katun take-out point this was being mowed by a tractor, presumably for winter hay. It appears that with the disintegration of the collective farms, the area has reverted to a small-scale mixed farming economy.

It seems that tourism is also making a growing contribution. There are a number of recently constructed tourist bungalows along the river banks, for example, and organized tented camps as well as individual people camping with their own tents and cars. Tourist minibuses, often with rafts on the roofs, are a common sight on the main access road. There is a roadside spring, which has become a tourist attraction, and a large line of permanent kiosks selling a range of craft items and other souvenirs. Few if any of the items for sale, incidentally, seem to be manufactured locally: they are bought in purely for sale to tourists, principally domestic tourists. Even the food market referred to earlier attracts tourists as well as locals.

As one of the pioneers of rafting on the Katun River and its tributaries, Team Gorky and its clients have presumably made a significant strategic contribution to the growth of this tourist economy, even though its quantitative significance is currently small relative to the flow of self-drive domestic tourists. In day-to-day terms, the group had little interaction with local residents, except when we stopped to buy a sheep. Most of the Team Gorky guides are from Nizhny Novgorod rather than the local area, and Barnaul is a large city where adventure tourism is not a significant component of the economy.

## Experience

The river gorges through the Altai Mountains are extremely scenic, particularly when the sun is shining. At the time of this trip, in late July, a large number of herbaceous meadow plants were in flower, adding to the effect. The area is still agricultural, and some of the riverbank campsites are rather heavily contaminated with cow by-products, but this is a minor consideration. Of particular significance, this area seems to be relatively free of mosquitoes, which makes camping a far more relaxing experience than would otherwise be the case. There were swarms of black flies, but these did not bite. Ticks were present but infrequent. They are of particular concern in this area since they can transmit the particularly virulent Siberian form of Russian spring–summer encephalitis virus, which has a high fatality rate and no known treatment.

Team Gorky proved to be a highly professional organization with well-organized logistics and very confident, hard-working and friendly guides. There was only one raft flip and everyone was quickly rescued. The day spent hiking gave us a chance to see a little of the surrounding terrain, and the banyas were certainly a bonus.

## Environment

Campsites along the Chuya and Katun Rivers are used by private rafting groups and other tour operators as well as Team Gorky, and those accessible by road are also used by private self-drive domestic tourists. From an aesthetic perspective, some of these campsites are quite heavily impacted by large amounts of litter, broken bottles and numerous unburied human waste deposits. At an ecosystem level these factors are probably negligible relative to roads, mines, logging and livestock, but they do detract from the experience. Of course, since Team Gorky does not control these sites and is generally not in communication with other users, there is little it can do to improve the situation overall. In addition, most of the river beaches are presumably washed through by annual floods, though of course these only redeposit litter further downstream.

Team Gorky's own environmental management practices are better than local norms, but would not be considered as best practice at a world scale. All group litter, principally food packaging, is collected at each campsite and burnt on the morning of departure. Combustion, however, is not always complete. Burnt cans are thrown into the river rather than being carried out. No attempt was made to collect and burn rubbish left by previous campsite users. There did not seem to be any environmental or minimal-impact briefing for clients. Many of the clients and guides were heavy smokers and threw their cigarette butts to the ground rather than putting them in the garbage bags. In addition, where clients were drinking in their own tents they sometimes left empty bottles at the tent sites. At each campsite the staff dug a hole to bury food scraps, and inorganic waste was sometimes also thrown into this hole.

## Safety

All rafting equipment was in good condition, the raft guides were skilled, and all clients were issued with lifejackets and helmets. There were two safety kayakers in addition to myself. Before taking to the river on the first morning's rafting, the trip leader gave a safety briefing. Since this was in Russian, I cannot comment on detailed content. There were demonstrations on how to get back into a raft, but not of how to orient oneself if swimming, or how to act in a rope-assisted or kayak-assisted rescue. In practice, there was one major raft flip, and everyone was quickly rescued with kayaks standing by.

Attitudes to safety off-river were not entirely consistent. On the day we spent hiking up a nearby peak, the guides were concerned to keep us together, even though the route was clearly marked and visible, and the weather good, so risks were small. Perhaps the greatest risk, combining high probability and high severity, was of falling into the extremely hot stones in the centre of the banya tent whilst moving in and out. Nothing, however, was said or done to minimize this risk, presumably because all Russians are expected to be familiar with such issues.

One risk that was not mentioned at all on the trip, but that potentially could be quite significant, is that of encephalitis transmitted by tick bites. The area concerned lies within the range of RSSEV, Russian spring–summer encephalitis virus, which can be transmitted by ticks and also by unpasteurized dairy products. The Siberian form of RSSEV is apparently more serious than the Far Eastern form. Indeed, this particular part of Siberia appears to be one of the world's highest-risk areas for severe tick-born encephalitis. Greatest risks are experienced by people walking away from the river, especially in relatively dense moist vegetation alongside streams. I was, in fact, bitten by such a tick whilst collecting raspberries, and later blood tests specific to RSSEV proved positive. Fortunately, I proved to be somewhat resistant, probably because of innumerable previous tick bites. None of this, however, is mentioned in Team Gorky's (2005) website, perhaps because risks from RSSEV are already well-known to Russian clients.

Despite this unexpected issue, Team Gorky's Chuya–Katun trip ranks world-class in scenery, rapids, guiding and value.

## Marketing

Most of Team Gorky's clients fall into one of two categories: domestic Russian clients booking individually; and international clients, principally from the USA, booking in groups through overseas tour operators. Team Gorky seemed to be relatively well known within Russia, particularly in the Nizhny Novgorod area where it is based. Most international clients probably do not know anything at all about Team Gorky itself until they arrive. Rather, they book a Katun rafting trip through a tour operator in their own country.

From Team Gorky's perspective, therefore, the critical marketing issue is to maintain active links with such companies and continue to provide satisfaction for client groups. It would seem it does so successfully since US-based companies such as Mountain Travel – Sobek and Steve Currey Expeditions apparently both use Team Gorky routinely. The company does have its own English-language website, which is easily found by searching for raft tours on the Katun, but it seems that relatively few international clients contact the company without some form of intermediate link.

## Sun Khosi, Karnali, Trisuli, Marsyangdi, Nepal: David Allardice's Ultimate Descents

### Place

Though politically unstable of late (2005), Nepal has a long history as a relatively low-cost destination for backpacker tourism and mountain trekking. During the last two decades it has also become well known for whitewater rafting. Commercial raft tour operators have offered multi-day raft trips on rivers such as the Sun Khosi, Karnali, Kali Gandaki and Trisuli, and less frequently on rivers such as the Marsyangdi and the Bhote Khosi (Knowles and Allardice, 1992). The volume of water in these rivers varies greatly from season to season. Immediately after the monsoon rains, flows in the larger rivers such as the Sun Khosi and Karnali are typically around 3000 cubic metres per second, which is about five times the normal dam-controlled flow in the Colorado Grand Canyon.

### Operator

At least 30 different companies in Kathmandu offer whitewater rafting tours. Only some of these, however, actually own and operate their own rafts; the others simply sell seats on commission. The best-known whitewater raft and kayak company in Nepal was established in the 1980s by a New Zealander, David Allardice, co-author of the definitive guide to Nepal's whitewater (Knowles and Allardice, 1992). I took part in several of their high-water commercial raft descents some years ago, as an additional kayaker. I also paddled the Marsyangdi with one of their safety kayakers, but not with a raft group.

In 2002, however, one of their Nepalese associates apparently carried out a hostile takeover of the company, causing a significant interruption until Allardice was able to establish a new operation. The original company's website now contains a mixture of descriptive material from prior to the takeover and new material describing the company as if it had been established by the takeover owner. It also contains materials attempting to denigrate Allardice's new company, in a way that would not be considered acceptable in a developed country. I am not familiar with any of the details of the takeover and cannot comment on the operations of the Nepal-owned company.

My experience with the company was whilst it was under Allardice's management, and my observations may or may not apply currently. Under Allardice's management this was a world-class operation, and no doubt this still applies for Allardice's current company. It seems unlikely that the local takeover company can match these standards, but I have not audited their operations to check this directly.

Allardice's company is now trading internationally under its original name of Ultimate Descents, and runs river trips in a variety of Himalayan nations. In Nepal the takeover company is called Ultimate Descents Nepal, and Allardice trades as The Last Resort (2005) to distinguish his company from the current operation using the original name. The Last Resort is the name of a lodge he has built on the Bhote Khosi, as a base for whitewater and other adventure activities.

## Activity

Descents of the Karnali and Sun Khosi are multi-day trips that start in the foothills of the Himalayas and end in the flatlands of the Terai, Nepal's low-altitude southern fringe. The majority of the trip is spent either on the river in the rafts, or making and breaking camp on riverbank sandbars. Each of the trips in which I took part was the first descent of the season after the end of the monsoon rains, when the water level was first beginning to fall and expose the sandbars. As a result, campsites were comparatively infrequent, and each day's rafting was designed accordingly. The remainder of the riverbank, especially in the Karnali, is relatively steep, rocky and heavily forested.

Each trip included 1 lay-over day, an insurance against any unforeseen difficulties. On these days we camped 2 nights at the same site, and had the opportunity to hike up side creeks and explore the forest. The upper sections of the Karnali, traversed in the early days of the trip, are relatively steep, narrow and fast-flowing with major rapids where the rafters and safety kayakers must remain alert. In the lower stretches, however, the river is wider, less steep and slower-flowing, and rapids are small and infrequent. In these sections, some of the rafting clients took the opportunity to borrow kayaks and practice paddling, whilst the safety boaters took their places on the rafts. On the Sun Khosi, however, even the lower sections of the river have major rapids.

The Karnali trip, in far western Nepal, started with a 3-day hike from the nearest roadhead to the put-in point on the Karnali River. The rafting clients carried their own personal gear, and porters carried the rafts, kayaks and communal cooking and camping equipment. This provides a very interesting opportunity to visit some of the hill villages in a relatively remote part of the country, not visited by trekkers. This area is currently (December, 2005) off-limits to tourists because of civil unrest.

The take-out point on the lower Karnali is close to Bardia National Park, which provides opportunities to search for tiger and rhinoceros on elephant-back. A number of clients took the opportunity to visit Bardia before returning to Kathmandu.

The Sun Khosi, Marsyangdi and Trisuli are much closer to Kathmandu. The Trisuli is a much shorter trip with fewer and smaller rapids. Much of the river, including the one overnight campsite, is accessible by road, so there is no need to carry camping equipment in the rafts unless the trip leader decides to camp on the side of the river away from the road. This is apparently advisable during the peak rafting season, for safety and serenity. When I took part in this trip, however, there were only a few groups on the river, and we camped undisturbed on the roadside riverbank.

## Equipment

Even though these rivers are wide enough for oar rafts, in practice paddle rafts are used, because most of the clients prefer active participation. In addition, for the Karnali descent there is less equipment to carry in for paddle rafts than for oar rafts, which would also require rowing frames. One of the main features distinguishing different raft tour operators in Nepal is the age and condition of their rafts. Allardice's rafts were all relatively new and in good condition, but some of the other rafts on the rivers were extremely old and patched. It is commonplace in many developing countries for smaller local operators to buy their equipment second-hand when larger operators, sometimes owned by expatriates, replace their own equipment.

Allardice's trips are fully equipped and catered, and accessible to backpackers and other tourists who turn up in Kathmandu with no whitewater equipment or experience. This includes tents, cooking and camping equipment, as well as rafting safety gear. Nepal is, of course, known for the high peaks of the Himalayas, but the major rivers used for rafting are in deep valleys at much lower altitude, and both water and weather are quite warm. In addition to rafting equipment, the operator provides dry bags for personal gear and waterproof plastic barrels for cameras. Clients bring their own sleeping mats and bags or can hire them cheaply in Kathmandu.

## Accommodation

All accommodation during the river trips was in tents on riverbank campsites. Tents were also used during the 3-day walk-in for the Karnali descent. Clients were collected from their accommodation in Kathmandu before the trip, but this accommodation was not included in the tour. A wide range of accommodation is available in Kathmandu. For clients who elected to stay on at Bardia National Park after the Karnali descent, there were several accommodation options, including the Tiger Tops Jungle Lodge. Rafting operators can make these arrangements, but they are not included in the river trip itself. Allardice now also offers accommodation in his river lodge, The Last Resort, but only for trips on the Bhote Khosi.

## Statistics

The Trisuli tour was a 2-day trip with a single overnight. Sun Khosi trips took 8–9 days. Karnali tours took a total of 10 days, excluding any additional time spent at Bardia National Park, but including the days spent driving to the roadhead and hiking to the river. The rafts used carried six or seven clients and one guide, and each trip would generally have several rafts, with the exact number depending on the season. Each trip also included one or more safety kayakers. Prices are currently around US$85 for the Trisuli, US$400 for the Sun Khosi and US$650 for the Karnali when last listed. This corresponds to around US$50 per person per day.

## Access

Access to and from the Trisuli and Sun Khosi is by road from Kathmandu, in the tour operator's buses. For the Karnali, access is by road to the nearest roadhead and on foot to the river as outlined above. The return to Kathmandu is either by road with the rafts and equipment, or by air from a nearby town. For the last few years, access to western Nepal, including the Karnali, has been problematic for internal political reasons. This may currently apply to Nepal as a whole, despite official assurances that tourists are not at risk.

## Experience

High-water rafting on high-volume rivers such as these is always an exciting experience, particularly in more sparsely inhabited valleys such as Karnali. There are some giant, though technically straightforward, rapids. At high water, few of these have stable waves which a kayak can surf, but those which do are memorable indeed. There was one such wave on the Karnali where one of our safety kayakers, an internationally famous whitewater boater, was flung from the peak to the trough of the wave with such force that his paddle snapped and he had to get back to the bank using only one blade and the stump of the shaft, Canadian-style. Evenings on the riverbank campsites, in contrast, were very mellow, with guides and clients sprawled around the campfire until late.

## Community

Tourism is – or was – a major component of the Nepal economy, and most components of Nepal's tourism industry are run and staffed largely or entirely by Nepalese. As in most countries, the people concerned do not necessarily work in the same area as they were born. Allardice's staff included both Nepalese and international raft guides and office personnel. Suppliers and support staff were all local. On the Karnali descent, the group camped near local villages. The tour groups were self-sufficient, but clients had opportunities to meet local children and other residents. The company contributed to a local school on the Karnali River.

## Environment

In comparison to subsistence agriculture, rafting has relatively low impacts. Allardice's company contributed to the Nepal River Conservation Trust, and generally adopted environmental management standards in line with best practice in the commercial rafting industry (Buckley, 1999), but there were one or two deficiencies. Pit toilets were dug at each campsite by the clients in rotation. These were generally too shallow and tended to collapse. In addition, both clients and guides left numerous cigarette butts and other small items of litter around campsites, and guides made no attempt or request to clean them up. Indeed, even though I did so myself each morning, only one or two of the other clients assisted, and these were generally the non-smokers. When I mentioned this to expatriate staff in Kathmandu headquarters after the trip, however, they summoned the guides and gave them firm instructions to remedy this situation in future.

## Safety

Allardice's company has a good safety record. It uses well-maintained equipment, supplies adequate safety gear for its clients and sends safety kayakers with all its major multi-day raft trips. Allardice's raft guides are internationally experienced and trained in first aid, CPR and swiftwater rescue. Lifejackets and safety gear are replaced regularly. Clients are also advised to bring hats, sunscreen and lip balm because of the extended period of exposure to high-altitude sun.

Even so, some safety issues did arise. On our lay-over day on the Karnali, when most clients were hiking up a side creek, the clients remaining at camp decided to try their skills at kayaking. They borrowed all the kayaks at once, and paddled out into a large eddy near camp. One of them capsized and bailed out. He was able to swim safely to shore, but the boat drifted downstream. Since all the kayaks were in use there was a significant delay before safety kayakers could pursue the empty boat downstream. The guides then had to drag the boat several kilometres back upstream along the riverbank through dense forest.

## Marketing

Allardice's new company is still marketed internationally as Ultimate Descents. Within Nepal it seems to be marketed through The Last Resort (2005). As noted earlier, the former company name is now in use by a local operation, but since Allardice evidently owns the US web address, the local operation uses an abbreviation. At one time, Allardice operated in Nepal under the name Ultimate Rivers, but this name no longer seems to be in use.

I am not familiar with the circumstances under which Allardice's Nepali associates carried out the hostile takeover. It is clear from the historical record, however, that David Allardice was one of the major whitewater pioneers in Nepal, and has devoted much of his life to this rafting business. Irrespective of politics, personalities and legalities, it must be extremely galling to find his efforts and success effectively hijacked, and it is impressive that he has managed to build a new business so quickly and tenaciously. The attacks featured on the company's website are likely to backfire, as is commonplace with most negative marketing of this type, and as long as Nepal's political situation allows Allardice to continue operating and to attract sufficient clients, I trust that his new company will prosper.

# Drysdale River, Australia: Raleigh International and NOLS

## Place

The Drysdale River is one of several substantial but little-known rivers that flow across the Kimberley region of north-western Australia. One of these, the Ord, is dammed to provide water for agricultural irrigation. The others are free-flowing and highly seasonal: barely flowing in the dry season, and torrential during the wet season.

The headwaters of the Drysdale are in a low plateau at the southern margin of the Kimberley region, and the upper stretches wind through swamps of pandanus trees. Further downstream the river drops over a giant horseshoe-shaped waterfall, Solea Falls. Below the Falls the topography is varied. In some sections the river crosses broad plains where it can spread to many hundreds of metres in width during flood flows; elsewhere it is confined in narrow, vertically walled rock gorges, so flood flows rise many tens of metres. The river reaches the ocean on the northern coastline, near the small Aboriginal township of Kalumburu. Part of the surrounding landscape is protected in a national park, and the remainder lies within large, privately owned grazing properties.

## Operator

The first known descent of the Drysdale River was made in 1988 by an international team from an organization then known as Operation Raleigh, and later renamed as Raleigh International (2005). This group ran the entire length through to the ocean. Raleigh International (2005) describes itself as a 'youth development charity'. It was set up essentially to provide adventure opportunities for people of school-leaving and university age (17–25), through a wide range of expeditions in different countries across the globe. Like its predecessor, Operation Drake, it had strong ties to the British Army and its counterparts in other nations, including Australia. Raleigh International now incorporates two subsidiaries, known respectively as Raleigh Adventures and Raleigh Explorers.

The second and subsequent descents of the Drysdale River have been made by the US-based National Outdoor Leadership School (NOLS, 2005), which has run semester courses in Australia since 1996. NOLS is described in more detail in Chapter 7. It is an outdoor education provider with a strong focus on backcountry travel skills, including the practicalities of navigation, camping, climbing, kayaking, etc.; leadership and group management; and minimal-impact techniques. The semester courses in Australia include 5 weeks canoeing on the Drysdale River, 3 weeks hiking in the adjacent Carson escarpment and 1 week visiting the Bardi Aboriginal community. I took part in the Drysdale River section of the first NOLS course in the Kimberley.

Neither NOLS nor Raleigh International would consider themselves as adventure tourism providers, but both offer the opportunity to take part in adventurous activities in remote settings, for a price. They may indeed teach backcountry travel and leadership skills, but so also do some avowed adventure tour operators.

## Activity

The NOLS and Raleigh descents were different in detail but similar in the overall activities: paddling downriver, navigating through multiple channels in some areas, portaging around rapids and camping on the riverbanks. In each case there was little opportunity to explore off river until near the end of the trip. The Raleigh trip camped for several days by the estuarine stretch of the river, and was able to explore caves and rock art in that area. The NOLS group camped for several days on Drysdale River Station below Solea Falls and explored a nearby scarp, also with rock art. The NOLS group had two food resupplies. The Raleigh group had one food drop and also caught fish and shot feral animals for food. The NOLS trip involved extensive practical instruction for students. On the Raleigh trip, the leader did consult participants on critical issues, but then made military-style decisions.

## Equipment

The two groups used different equipment. The Raleigh descent was made using two-person Metzeler® inflatable canoes, carrying food in plastic barrels and personal gear in backpacks. Each canoe was equipped with a specially constructed lightweight folding stretcher to help in carrying the barrels during portages. The inflatable canoes are of tough construction and could be paddled safely through shallow rocky stretches, of which there were many, and most rapids, of which there were few.

The NOLS courses use two-person collapsible canoes with aluminium frames and a rubberized fabric skin. These are far less resistant to wear and impact than the inflatables. The frameworks are easily bent even by minor collisions, and the skins constantly became worn through where they were in contact with the longitudinal stringers, as the boats were often run over rocks and gravel. This may indeed have helped to teach the NOLS students to paddle carefully so as to protect their boats, but it also slowed down progress considerably, as the canoes had to be manhandled or passed hand-to-hand rather than paddled through even the smallest rapids. Indeed, at many points the group had to move rocks to create a deep enough channel for the canoes to pass through without grounding, or cut pandanus trees to clear an easy route. Each evening the boats were turned over, dried and repaired as well as possible using duct tape and glue.

In the Raleigh trip, each participant brought their own camping gear, but all cooking was done in a group using campfires and camp ovens. The NOLS instructional system is highly standardized and relies on four-person 'tent groups' who share a tent and cook together using fuel stoves. NOLS also issue its students with standardized lists of equipment, which can be bought or in some cases rented from NOLS if students do not have their own gear.

## Accommodation

Once on the river, both groups camped by the riverbanks each night. NOLS used tents as above. The Raleigh group left it to individual choice whether or not to bring or use a tent. Most used only a mosquito net. The Raleigh group was given quarters in a large canvas tent at the Darwin army barracks before and after the trip. Operation Raleigh logistics for northern Australia were run in cooperation with the army. The NOLS group proceeded directly from the canoeing phase to a backpacking phase, using the same tents.

## Statistics

The Raleigh expedition took 9 weeks to traverse the Drysdale River from source to sea. The NOLS courses spend 5 weeks on the river, but do not run its entire length. The Raleigh group consisted of about 20 people in all, of whom six were considered as staff in the terminology of Raleigh International (2005), and the remainder as 'Venturers' – i.e. participants aged 17–25 and paying to join the expedition. All of these, however, were personally selected by Operation Raleigh Australia for this particular expedition, which was treated as more difficult than the other Australian projects. Several of them had considerable relevant experience. Whilst the nominal client-to-guide or student-to-staff ratio was about 2:1, none of the participants was entirely inexperienced. The NOLS course included three leaders on the river section, plus myself. There were about 20 students.

The logistics and finances of Operation Raleigh were designed so that all 'Venturers' paid the same amount regardless of the specific expedition or project in which they finally took part. According to Operation Raleigh this contribution covered only part of the pro rata costs of the overall programme, with the reminder being met by corporate sponsorships and in-kind assistance from the army. Participants were also permitted, and widely encouraged, to raise their own contributions from local sponsors. This was intended to provide equitable access irrespective of their parents' financial means. There is thus no figure for a market-comparable price for the Raleigh trip.

The current cost of the NOLS Semester in Australia is US$9660 for a 70-day course in 2006, or US$11,235 for a 75-day course, plus a US$600 equipment deposit in each case (NOLS, 2005). This is not partitioned between the different components, but calculated pro rata per day spent on each activity; the Drysdale River canoeing section would represent a little over half of this, about US$140 per person per day.

## Access

The Drysdale River is accessible by vehicle at relatively few points. Cattle station roads provide access near the headwaters and again below Solea Falls. The estuary is accessible from the ocean, but the nearest port is a long distance away. Operation Raleigh used a military transport plane to take the participants to their put-in point, and to deliver a food drop 2 weeks downstream. I joined the group by taking the mail plane to the Drysdale River Station airstrip. At the estuary we were airlifted out in a large helicopter, sponsored by an oil exploration company, to its local operations base on an offshore island. From there we flew to Darwin in a charter flight.

NOLS courses also start from a road access point in the upper reaches of the river. They use the Drysdale River Station access as their take-out point. I joined the NOLS group by helicopter at the junction of a tributary part way downstream. Access through Drysdale River National Park requires a permit from the state government parks agency, and access through cattle stations requires prior arrangements with the station owners or managers. These arrangements were made by the trip leaders in each case, with no direct involvement by paying participants.

## Community

There are two main communities along the Drysdale River: the cattle stations, and Aboriginal residents at Kalumburu and surrounding areas. The former are straightforward for these trips to deal with, as long as leaders and participants are polite, leave any gates as they find them, leave no litter and bring an occasional thank you, such as a case or two of beer. Dealings with the latter are potentially more complex, because there are multiple levels of interactions.

The Drysdale River area is particularly rich in Aboriginal rock art, in three different major styles. Some of these date back many thousands of years. These sites have current cultural importance for present-day inhabitants, as well as their artistic, archaeological and historic significance. Besides rock art sites there are other culturally important sites that may not be immediately apparent except to traditional owners. Indeed, arguably the entire landscape is a mosaic or tapestry of cultural significance, well known to its traditional owners even if they now live largely in the township of Kalumburu. Finally, there was a Christian mission station at Kalumburu that introduced an additional layer of complexity in interaction with local people.

The Raleigh expedition passed through this country with little interaction with cattle stations and even less with Aboriginal residents, though it did note a number of rich rock art sites. The first NOLS course on the Drysdale experienced a major internal controversy because its leaders had intended to teach rock climbing techniques after the canoeing section, and had sent two additional leaders ahead to identify an appropriate site; but the only site suitable from a climbing perspective was also heavily endowed with rock art. The American NOLS staff were unconcerned about this, as they are apparently used to climbing at Anasazi sites in the southwestern USA. It took some time for two Australian members of the group to convey the message that some of the Aboriginal rock art on the Drysdale was roughly ten times older, comparable in age to Neolithic cave paintings in Europe.

In addition, whilst the Anasazi are gone, represented now only by descendent races such as the Hopi, the Australian Aboriginal custodians of the Drysdale rock art are very much alive and indeed were living a short distance away at Kalumburu. Ultimately it was the students themselves who agreed, after extended debate, that if any members of the group were uncomfortable with climbing at the sites concerned, then other members should respect their views even if they themselves did not share these concerns personally.

There was one further component of the Australian community with whom the first NOLS group experienced an indirect interaction. Even though they had a permit from the land management agency, one day when they were away from their camp, the area was firebombed by that agency as part of its fire management strategy, and a considerably quantity of equipment was lost.

## Experience

The Operation Raleigh descent of the Drysdale River was the culmination of many months of planning. It included a scientific research component that was my own responsibility. We collected aquatic plants, and we searched – successfully – for an endangered bird species, the purple-backed wren. One of the other expedition members also searched, very successfully, for aboriginal rock art, particularly of the 'Wandjina' design. There were a number of communication problems with last-minute additions to the group, but these did not interfere with a successful descent. We made the descent after the end of the wet season, when the river flow was low enough for safety, but high enough to float the canoes. The actual boating was very easy, with no significant rapids, but the terrain was remote and unknown.

The NOLS descent was also the culmination of a long planning process, but one carried out largely from the USA. The choice of collapsible canoes rather than inflatable kayaks created some difficulties, and there were also some problems with map-reading and some tensions between the leaders. The trip proceeded successfully none the less, and the students certainly had a memorable experience.

## Environment

The main anthropogenic impacts in the Kimberley region are from farming and mining, and the main impacts in the national park are from feral animals, including livestock. The main impacts of tourism are probably from people visiting Aboriginal rock art sites in their own 4WD vehicles. The NOLS group employed minimal-impact camping practices throughout the trip, but did use a helicopter at one point.

The Operation Raleigh trip managed some impacts well, e.g. making sure not to leave litter. On the other hand, some participants shot duck without knowing what actual species they were. This could potentially have created significant impacts if the species concerned were in fact endangered. The Raleigh group used a transport plane and a helicopter.

## Safety

There were no serious injuries on either trip, but a number of potential hazards. The Operation Raleigh trip carried a large army radio and was generally able to stay in touch with Darwin most days. The greatest safety concern was in the lowermost parts of the river, the saltwater estuarine section. In this stretch we saw a very large estuarine crocodile, swimming on the surface. The expedition leader therefore sent the trip participants to hike along the riverbanks in this section. The staff lashed all the boats together, so as to create a single composite raft significantly larger than the crocodile and with many different buoyancy compartments, and we paddled this downriver to our final campsite and helicopter pick-up point.

In this section, however, one of our participants shot a large fish from the top of a high cliff, and called on the nearest person down on the riverbank, which happened to be myself, to jump in and retrieve it as it sank. 'I'll cover you', he added. I was dubious whether a rifle shot would stop a large crocodile, especially if it approached at depth, but I did jump in and pick up the fish none the less.

On the NOLS trip, there were several safety issues, though all within the instructors' capabilities. When I joined the group, one of the students was suffering from an eye infection, and though we had an appropriate antibiotic cream with us, the leader decided to use the helicopter to fly to Kununurra for a medical examination. In a legal sense this was indeed the correct procedure. Various participants later suffered infected wounds, but were able to treat themselves with antibiotics. Most of these were received whilst manhandling the collapsible canoes through steep or shallow sections. The instructor responsible for navigation mistook our location on one occasion, but this had no significant consequences. Subsequent courses have no doubt overcome these difficulties.

## Marketing

The first descent of the Drysdale by the Raleigh organization was marketed within 'Venturers' who had already signed up for the Australian sector. The NOLS semester courses in Australia are marketed by the NOLS organization in the USA, using its website (NOLS, 2005), catalogue, and school and university marketing networks.

# Jatapu River, Brazil: Fabio Bueno Neto and Carlos Colares

## Place

The Jatapu River is a fifth-order tributary of the Amazon River, accessible from Manaus by a 3-day journey on a local bus, a small riverboat and finally a dugout canoe. It is upstream of a stretch of rapids several kilometres long, where dugout canoes must be pushed upstream by wading alongside them. Since these rivers are inhabited by piranha and large razor-toothed catfish, as well as caiman, an experienced local guide is essential. At least in 1993, the area upstream of the rapids was essentially unvisited, since access was too difficult either for primary industry or subsistence agriculture. We had close encounters with a range of interesting local fauna, including army ants, caiman and piranha, as well as various snakes (Buckley, 1994), and jaguar are also not uncommon in the area. Again, a knowledgeable guide is essential.

## Operator

When I visited the area in 1993 I was fortunate to be guided by Señor Carlos Colares, a member of one of the local indigenous communities who had spent substantial time abroad and combined a very high level of local skills and knowledge with a very considerable level of international sophistication. Señor Colares has guided a wide range of international clients through this area. Bookings and logistic arrangements were handled by a Brazilian tour company run by Señor Fabio Bueno Neto. It is not clear if this company is still operational.

## Activity

Activities are considerably more varied than a typical river rafting trip. The core component is travel in a dugout canoe in a remote tributary of the Amazon River. To get there, we travelled first by bus, and then several days on a small local riverboat, to a point downstream of a stretch of rapids several kilometres in length. We stayed overnight in a small local homestead, where we swapped the riverboat for the dugout canoe. We were accompanied by the young son of the homestead family. We pushed the dugout canoe up the rapids and then travelled for several days along the river upstream, propelled either by paddles or a small outboard motor.

## Equipment

We used local transport, namely a scheduled bus service, a riverboat and crew hired on the riverbank, and a dugout canoe hired from the last subsistence homestead below the rapids. We slept in hammocks either in the riverboat, or slung between trees under a tarpaulin. We cooked on fires in a single, large black iron pot. Our only other equipment was a fishing line and hooks, and a machete.

## Accommodation

All accommodation was in hammocks slung between trees and protected by a tarpaulin slung above us. On the riverboat below the rapids we slept in the same hammocks slung across the boat. Above the rapids we ate fish caught in the river, mainly piranha; coarsely crushed cassava meal; flour and olive oil made into pancakes; and black coffee.

## Statistics

I was the only client on this trip. Others had booked but cancelled when they learned the details of the itinerary. There was one guide, Señor Colares. We also brought one local boy with us in the dugout above the rapids. His father was supposed to have come with us, but had disappeared into the forest. The boy spoke only a local dialect, which Señor Colares also spoke. The trip lasted about 10 days in total, with about half that time on the Jatapu River above the rapids. The cost per person per day was in the low price range.

## Access

We reached the Jatapu River from Manaus after a day on a local bus, several days on a riverboat and a day pushing a dugout canoe by hand up long rapids. Above the rapids we travelled in the dugout, propelled by paddles or a small outboard motor. There did not appear to be any active land management agency or any other organization requiring permits.

## Community

Everything on this trip was purchased and paid for locally. All food was locally supplied, principally fish from the river, and a large bag of coarse cassava meal was bought from one of the riverside smallholdings downstream in return for a coil of rope. There were very few of these smallholdings in the upper section of the riverboat trip; one immediately below the rapids on the Jatapu; and no sign at all of human habitation above the rapids.

## Experience

This trip was a very memorable experience. We spent several days in uninhabited and relatively pristine Amazonian rainforest. The area provides extremely good opportunities to see a range of uncommon Amazonian wildlife at close range in the wild. In the slow-flowing river sections downstream of the rapids, the pink and grey freshwater Amazon dolphin is relatively common, together with a considerable array of native bird species. In the narrower channels and denser forest upstream of the rapids, caiman are plentiful, and one can also see river otter, macaws and hoatzin, an unusual bird whose nestlings elude raptors by leaping into the water when disturbed, and subsequently climbing back up the trunk of the nest tree.

In addition, I learnt something of the various groups of people living in the area, including indigenous peoples, rubber tappers, gemstone prospectors and subsistence squatters; and I also learnt something of the broader attempts at industrial development, including a failed mine not far from the rapids, and the environmentally destructive Bilbao dam on the Jamari River downstream of the Jatapu. Finally, I learnt of Colares' efforts, largely single-handed, to have the Jatapu area declared a conservation reserve; an effort for which his guided tours provided support.

## Environment

All cooking was on small wood fires, using palm fronds to shield the fire from the frequent heavy rainfalls. We had nothing with us to generate litter, and the only sign of previous trips to the same area were saplings cut as poles to support the tarpaulin over the hammocks. In addition to learning about plants and animals, educational experiences included using lianas to provide drinking water, using tree buttresses as signal drums, catching (and releasing) caiman at night using string and a stick, and learning where it was safe to swim and where it was most emphatically not.

Perhaps one day the area that I visited with Colares will be a national park or World Heritage site, well known on the world's wildlife tourism itineraries. If so, I can only hope that whilst tourism may provide an economic justification for protecting the area from settlement and industrial activity, the number of tourists can be limited so that the otter, macaw and hoatzin continue to thrive, and perhaps also so that visitors may have an opportunity to see them in their natural state.

## Safety

Our safety was completely dependent on the local knowledge of Señor Colares. We were in an area inhabited by jaguar, though we did not see any. Snakes and on one occasion a column of army ants passed under our hammocks. In the river there were caiman, giant catfish and plentiful piranha. The freeboard of the dugout was only a few centimetres in calm water. We saw piranha around our feet as we pushed the dugout barefoot up the rapids, but Señor Colares assured me they would not bite in whitewater, and he proved correct. We washed in one selected spot that Señor Colares said was safe from catfish, caiman and piranha, and it was.

We caught (and released) a 2-m caiman at night using only string and a stick. Señor Colares said that once one had grabbed its jaws, it would not be able to open them, and he was right. Even so, it requires a degree of timing and concentration to grab a snapping caiman's jaws in the instant when they are closed. Señor Colares said that if we lay quiet in our hammocks whilst army ants passed about 50 cm below us, they would not climb the trees, and once again he proved correct.

At one point Señor Colares unluckily speared a large triple–triple barbed fishhook through his eye socket, and I had to perform surgery with a small but luckily sharp pocket knife. Fortunately this was successful. It did, however, show clearly how dependent we were on Señor Colares' skills, as I had to consider whether I could safely take the dugout back down river if he were incapacitated. Overall, this was not a trip that an insurance agency would gladly cover!

## Marketing

There is no routine advertising for this trip. It was organized by Señor Fabio Bueno Neto and marketed as a pre-conference tour. Señor Colares has apparently guided many such trips, but how people learn of the opportunity is not clear.

# 5 Whitewater Kayaking

Ralf Buckley, Maruia Falls, New Zealand. Photo RB collection.

# Futaleufu River, Chile: Expediciones Chile

## Place

The Rio Futaleufu runs from the mountains in the Patagonian region of southern Argentina and Chile, west across Chile to meet the sea at the small port of Chaiten. The Rio Futaleufu is considerably further south than the much better-known Rio Bio Bio, and because of the shape of the Chilean coastline there is no road access within Chile between the Futaleufu region and the main population centres in and around the capital city of Santiago.

The Futaleufu region is accessible only by air or boat to Chaiten, and a narrow dirt road that runs up the Futaleufu River and eventually through a mountain pass into Argentina. The lower stretches of the Rio Futaleufu are used extensively by commercial rafting and sportfishing companies. The river is reputed to offer some of the world's best fly-fishing for wild trout, one of the more expensive and upmarket forms of freshwater sportfishing.

## Operator

Expediciones Chile is a whitewater kayak company owned and operated by former whitewater rodeo champion Chris Spelius. The company also offers whitewater kayak safaris to a range of other rivers, such as the Rio Fuy in Chile, the Rio Manso in nearby Argentina and the Ottawa River in Canada, as well as rafting and sportfishing on the Rio Futaleufu. But the 'Club Futa' kayak camp on the Rio Futaleufu, established two decades ago, is its main operation. Originally, Expediciones Chile also offered kayak trips on Chile's other famous high-volume whitewater river, the Rio Bio Bio. Some years ago, however, the Bio Bio was dammed for hydroelectric power generation, flooding its most famous rapids.

Operating on an area of riverside land purchased from a local farmer, the Expediciones Chile camp has two principal buildings: a kitchen and dining area, and a sauna and hot water system. Clients bring their own tents for sleeping accommodation, but all meals are catered by Expediciones Chile. The sauna and hot water system make an enormous difference to the comfort of kayaking clients who have paddled all day in cold Class IV–V whitewater, sometimes in rather inclement weather. The camp is in an extremely scenic location, with views across the blue waters of the Rio Futaleufu to the snow-covered peaks of Tres Monjas. The core business of Expediciones Chile is to enable experienced kayakers to paddle the legendary whitewater of the Rio Futaleufu under the guidance of equally legendary kayakers such as Spelius and his staff.

## Activity

Expediciones Chile offers both fixed-base and safari-style trips. On the fixed-base trips, clients stay at the Club Futa camp every night, and paddle various sections of the Futaleufu, and some of its immediate tributaries. Half-week, one week and multi-week options are available. The safari-style trips start on creek-style rivers such as the Rio Fuy, famous for its runnable waterfalls up to 10 m in height, and finish on the Futaleufu. Currently, Expediciones Chile offers four different safari itineraries, each taking 1 or 2 weeks in total. All trips are accompanied by highly skilled kayaking guides and instructors.

## Equipment

Clients can bring their own boats, but most prefer to take advantage of the extensive range held by Expediciones Chile. The company owner and founder, Chris Spelius, is a former US whitewater rodeo champion who has for many years been sponsored by US kayak manufacturers, such as Dagger® Inc. Expediciones Chile therefore features these boats extensively, though not exclusively. Paddles may also be available on request. Clients bring their own sprayskirts, lifejackets, helmets and other safety equipment.

## Accommodation

At the Club Futa camp on the Rio Futaleufu, clients bring their own tents and sleeping bags, but eat in a communal dining room and kitchen equipped with a large cast-iron stove. The camp also has a sauna and an outdoor hot shower. Expediciones Chile employs a cook and masseuse, and serves local food, including traditional bread and locally made cheeses. On Rio Fuy safari trips in Chile, accommodation is in local hotels, both en route and on the shore of a lake that the Rio Fuy runs into. On Rio Manso safari trips into Argentina, accommodation is in a local estancia with a traditional asado, a form of spit barbecue used by the gauchos of the Argentinean pampas.

## Statistics

Group size can vary somewhat but is typically about six or eight plus instructors. The client-to-guide ratio is around 3:1. Eight-day Rio Futaleufu trips currently cost US$1595 per person, or US$200 per person per day. Thirteen-day trips on the Rio Fuy and Rio Futaleufu cost US$2495 per person, or US$190 per person per day.

## Access

Access to the Rio Futaleufu is by air to Chaiten on the south Chilean coast and thence by a 4-h drive in the Expediciones Chile shuttle bus on a dirt road up the Futaleufu valley. Access to the Rio Fuy is by road from Puerto Montt. Local access to the river is by agreement with landowners. The Expediciones Chile camp itself is on land owned by Chris Spelius.

## Community

Clients have several opportunities to meet local residents. Most notable is local landowner Don Washington, who visits the Expediciones Chile camp on occasion to share a glass or two of local wine. The neighbourhood football field is one of Don Washington's paddocks and it is quite a sight to see locals ride up, tether their horses, play a game and ride away. Expediciones Chile buys local produce and has helped to represent local residents against plans to dam the river.

Residents who currently occupy riverbank farms, run riverside guesthouses or simply have private homes along the river valley roadside would all be flooded if the river were to be dammed (see below). The local residents, accustomed to an independent gaucho lifestyle, had felt themselves to be powerless against a central government agency, an assessment that was probably perfectly accurate. Expediciones Chile has provided an avenue for their rights and concerns to be heard, though it remains to be seen if they will be taken into account.

The fate of the Rio Futaleufu and its valley will hence have considerable social and environmental implications for the Chaiten region and the northern Patagonian section of Chile.

## Experience

The Futaleufu River is justly famous for its whitewater; Expediciones Chile is justly famous for the expertise of its kayaking guides; and Club Futa, formerly known as Campo Tres Monjas, is justly famous for its location and scenic views. The water is cold and the wind can be bitter, but hot showers, the sauna and hearty dinners work wonders at maintaining enthusiasm, and the in-house masseuse restores weary frames for another day on the river. Even so, on some trips there is a significant dropout rate as the week goes by. I have made two trips to the Futalefu, and on both occasions the water level was too high to run Throne Room, the most famous rapid. But no matter: Infierno Canyon, Terminator and Casa de Piedro pushed my adrenalin levels to the top of the scale. On the second of these trips, the group included members of a European kayak manufacturer's 'extreme descents' team, and it was an education to watch just how skilled they were. The Expediciones Chile staff are equally skilled, and are also highly capable instructors, able to guide their kayaking clients through rapids at the limits of those clients' skills, and improve those skills in the process.

## Environment

The Expediciones Chile camp uses a local spring for water supply and local firewood for heating and cooking, and has a well-made outdoor composting toilet. The buildings are made of local timber and only the plumbing, stove and similar fittings were brought in. Expediciones Chile has minimal environmental impacts and makes a deliberate effort to educate its clients and others about environmental issues in the Futaleufu region.

Whilst Expediciones Chile was established simply as an adventure tourism operation, it has also had to act as an environmental advocate and lobbyist. ENDESA, the Chilean national electricity quango, has repeatedly tried to dam the Rio Futaleufu in order to sell power to Argentina. ENDESA had already dammed the Rio Bio Bio further north for hydropower, but the Futaleufu had previously seemed safe because the shape of the Chilean coastline cuts it off from electricity demand areas near Santiago.

With some preliminary assistance from an American river conservation group, American Rivers (2005), Expediciones Chile established a local conservation foundation, Futafriends, funded by client donations and sales of company merchandise; made and distributed a video, the *Plight of the Futaleufu*; and lobbied government officials in Santiago.

## Safety

Expediciones Chile's kayak trips are intended for skilled and experienced kayakers. Different trips are advertised as Class IV or Class V, depending on the season and the river sections run. Prospective clients provide information on their skills and recent experience.

The guides select appropriate sections of each river for the group to paddle each day, depending on water levels and client skills. They also advise individual clients whether to run or portage each rapid, what lines to take and how to paddle the chosen lines.

Ultimately, however, clients have to make their own decisions, and paddle their own kayaks as in any difficult whitewater. Even with the best will and skill, the guides may or may not be able to help them if they get into difficulties. Kayakers – though not Expediciones Chile clients – have drowned in Zeta and Infierno Canyon, two of the Futaleufu's Class V rapids.

Expeditiones Chile, however, has an excellent safety record, thanks principally to the guiding and instructing skills, and local knowledge, of Spelius and his staff.

## Marketing

Expediciones Chile is indelibly associated, in the kayaking world, with its owner Chris Spelius. 'Spe' is something of a legendary figure – as much for his recent efforts to save the Futaleufu from dams as for his earlier successes as a whitewater rodeo champion and for big-water first descents. Likewise, the Futaleufu is a famous river, known worldwide amongst kayaking aficionados. Whilst Expediciones Chile paved the way for commercial kayaking on the Futaleufu, there are now competing river camps and rafting operators. Kayakers can also paddle the river independently, and many do.

In the early days of Expediciones Chile, the marketing challenge was to let the kayaking world know that Patagonia has world-class whitewater. Currently, the challenge is to persuade kayakers that the company's local knowledge and kayak guiding skills are worth the price. Undoubtedly they are, and Expediciones Chile maintains a clientele of cash-rich, time-poor paddlers who value their own safety and comfort. Equally, however, the Futaleufu also attracts experienced kayakers with more time but less money, who are simply not in a position to pay a commercial operator.

# Reventazon, Pacuare, Pejibaye and Sarapiqui, Costa Rica: Endless River Adventures

## Place

Costa Rica lies in the wet tropics of Central America, with forested peaks to 4000 m, an extensive protected area system, abundant wildlife and a large nature, eco and adventure tourism industry. Its rivers offer a variety of warm whitewater, used extensively for raft and kayak tours. Best known are the higher volume rivers such as the Reventazon and Pacuare, but there are also a number of lower volume creeks such as the Pejibaye, Sarapiqui and San Lorenzo. The Reventazon can be run in three sections and is known for its big waves and almost continuous whitewater up to Class IV. The Pacuare has three sections, with the 15 km Class IV–V Middle Pacuare section the most difficult. The Pejibaye runs through spectacular dense forest with technical rapids to Class IV. The Sarapiqui and San Lorenzo are creek runs, Class IV and Class III respectively.

## Operator

Endless River Adventures (ERA) is based in North Carolina, USA. It has been operating for over 20 years and currently employs around a dozen kayak guides. It offers whitewater rafting on the Ocoee and Nantahala Rivers in North Carolina; guided kayak trips in Costa Rica, Ecuador and Mexico; and other activities such as rock climbing, fly-fishing, mountain biking and flatwater kayaking.

## Activity

In Costa Rica, Endless River Adventures runs 8-day guided kayak trips that tackle different sections of the rivers listed above, depending on water levels and client skills. When I took part in one of these trips it was shortly after a hurricane had flooded much of Central America, so the larger rivers were unrunnable and we were restricted to the creeks. These were technical but beautiful. These trips are intended for reasonably experienced, but not expert kayakers.

## Equipment

Clients have the option to use kayaks and paddles supplied by Endless River Adventures, or to bring their own. Clients bring their own sprayskirts, helmets, lifejackets, paddle jackets, throwbags, buoyancy bags and other accessories.

## Accommodation

During the tour, guides and clients stay in a variety of local accommodation, both en route to the river and when travelling between rivers. Camping is not necessary in ERA's Costa Rica kayak tours.

## Statistics

For the Costa Rica kayak trip in which I took part, ERA provided two guides for a group of five or six kayaking clients. The scheduled trips take 8 days in total and cost US$1375 in 2005, or a little over US$170 per day.

## Access

Access to Costa Rica is by air to the capital of San Jose. Access to the rivers is by road in the Endless Rivers Adventures' vehicles. Any permits or landholder agreements are arranged by the operator.

## Community

The group stays in a range of local accommodation and travels through a number of villages and townships. There are opportunities to talk to locals, but only if clients speak Spanish. Anglophone clients have little direct interaction with Costa Rican communities.

## Experience

The trip is well-organized and the logistics smooth. The usual itinerary was thrown into disarray by hurricane floods, but we would not have known this except for our guides' explanations. The river sections we paddled were very enjoyable, and chosen to be accessible to the less experienced paddlers in the group whilst still being interesting for the more skilled.

## Environment

The tour uses local accommodation, restaurants and cafés, whose environmental impacts are generally outside the operator's control. No litter was left on the rivers.

## Safety

Safety, guiding and informal instruction were excellent throughout. Indeed, by judicious planning our guides managed to stem or head off some domestic disputes amongst other members of our group, which could have spoiled the trip for all. The guides were familiar with all the rivers and hence able to choose routes even through blind sections, and to lead the clients through one at a time, drop-by-drop or eddy-by-eddy. There were no rapids where safety lines were required. We were unable to run the Reventazon Power House section because the floodwaters were so high that one could feel the ground shaking with the speed and power of the river. We did consider running a different section, but some clients were not keen and for safety reasons our guides therefore elected to stay on the smaller rivers.

## Marketing

Endless River Adventures has a good website and is based near the Nantahala River in Virginia, USA, one of North America's best-known whitewater kayaking areas. Much of its marketing, however, seems to be by word of mouth within the paddling community. Historically, ERA's owners also worked as kayak guides for Expediciones Chile, which no doubt brought them additional clients. One of the co-owners, herself an exceptionally skilled and smooth kayaker, is also the company videographer, and shoots videos of each trip for sale to clients. Such videos, replayed for other kayakers on the clients' return home, are no doubt also effective marketing tools.

# Karamea River, New Zealand: Ultimate Descents NZ

## Place

The Karamea River is one of the most northerly of the west coast rivers in New Zealand's South Island. It starts in the Tasman Mountains and reaches the sea at Karamea township. The upper sections are in Kahurangi National Park, and the lower stretches flow through sheep farms. As for most of this area, rainfall is relatively high and the landscape is green, at least in summer. As with other west coast rivers, some sections of the Karamea run through spectacular gorges.

## Operator

Ultimate Descents Whitewater Rafting, New Zealand (2005) is based at Murchison near the Buller River. Its main tourist attractions are 1-day whitewater raft trips on the Buller River. It also offers multi-day helicopter-access whitewater raft trips on the Karamea River and most recently, the Mokihinui River, and wilderness float trips on other rivers. The company has been operating since 1984. At the Murchison headquarters it also runs a café, and the retail-booking centre is inside the café. For Karamea trips it operates out of a tourist lodge in Karamea, The Last Resort.

## Activity

The Karamea raft trip is offered as either a 3- or 5-day tour. In either case the river section is 3 days. In the 3-day option, clients are shuttled to the put-in point by helicopter, along with rafts and other equipment. In the 5-day option they start 2 days early and hike cross-country to the put-in to join the rest of the group. Most of the river contains relatively straightforward rapids up to Class IV, but there is one long, technical and difficult Class V section known as Roaring Lion, which may be run or portaged depending on water level and clients.

## Equipment

The trip uses Incept® paddle rafts and inflatable kayaks. The company provides lifejackets and helmets; wetsuits, booties and spray jackets; dry bags, tents and sleeping mats; and cooking gear and food. Clients bring their own sleeping bags, and hardshell kayakers bring their own kayaks and gear.

## Accommodation

Accommodation on the river is in tents. Accommodation on the nights before and after the trip is not included, but the company recommends The Last Resort in Karamea, and the recommendation is well merited.

## Statistics

The heli-raft trip takes 3 days, as mentioned above, and costs NZD995 (US$700) per person for a minimum of four people, or about US$285 per person per day. The 5-day walk-in option costs NZD1050 (US$735). The client-to-guide ratio is 5:1.

## Access

Access to Karamea is by road. From Karamea to the put-in is by helicopter or on foot. The trip runs through Kahurangi National Park. Permits are arranged by the operator.

## Community

Farming, forestry and tourism are the main economic activities on the northwest coast of New Zealand's South Island. The Last Resort relies typically on self-drive tourists, and heli-rafting makes only a small contribution. Whitewater kayaking is a common recreational activity for local residents on the west coast.

## Experience

The area is very scenic and the wilderness aspect of the trip is probably as important to most clients as the whitewater. First-time rafters are unlikely to opt for a 3-day heli-raft tour unless they are relatively cash-rich, time-poor international travellers. Most clients are likely to be familiar with paddle rafting techniques and keen to experience a multi-day river trip. The Roaring Lion rapid, however, is sufficiently difficult to focus everyone's attention very strongly on the whitewater – kayakers included!

## Environment

Helicopters have significant environmental impacts through noise and high fuel consumption. Because of steep terrain and short distances, however, helicopters are used very extensively throughout this area for farming and especially logging, and heli-rafting makes only a small contribution. Choosing the hike-in option does not greatly reduce helicopter use since the rafts and equipment must be flown to the put-in point anyway. On the river, the tour operator used minimal-impact camping practices.

## Safety

The tour operator provides safety equipment, and clients are briefed both on safety around helicopters and safety on the river. There are numerous 'boulder garden' rapids but none of the rafting clients fell out. When I took part in this trip the rafts wisely portaged the crux section of the Roaring Lion rapid. The kayakers ran it, but one fell out just above a hole where the water poured under two narrow rocks, and was saved only by a timely safety rope. Without that rescue, the swim could easily have proved fatal.

## Marketing

Marketing is via the company's website, brochures at The Last Resort and elsewhere, retail shopfront marketing in Murchison, information in specialist whitewater magazines, and word-of-mouth.

# Colorado Grand Canyon, USA: Expeditions Inc. and Others

## Place

The Grand Canyon of the Colorado River separates Utah to the north from Arizona to the south. It is one of the world's best-known scenic wonders and the South Rim, in particular, is very heavily visited. The Grand Canyon is over 1.5 km deep from rim to river, and the main river section from Lee's Ferry to Diamond Creek is over 350 km in length. The river is dammed above Lee's Ferry by the Glen Canyon Dam, and water flow is controlled by dam releases, generally around 600 cubic metres per second. The releases are used in a hydroelectric power station and vary through the day to match the power demand from the electricity grid. This daily pulse travels down the river, gradually attenuating, so there is a small daily 'tide' at campsites.

Before the river was dammed, it was commonly red with suspended sediment, leading to its name. Water release from the dam, however, is green and cold. This looks scenic but has had major environmental impacts on native fish such as the humpback chub: their eggs are now eaten by introduced trout, which can survive in the cold, low-sediment waters. The Grand Canyon is a National Park and all access is managed by the US National Parks Service.

## Operator

There are at least 17 different commercial rafting companies operating on the Grand Canyon. Two of the largest and best-known are Arizona Raft Adventures (2005), known as AzRA, and Outdoor Adventure River Specialists (2005), known as OARS. Currently, a number of rafting operators offer 'kayak support trips'. When I took part in a commercial trip some years ago, however, the only company that was prepared to allocate some of its quota to kayakers was Expeditions Inc., based in Flagstaff, Arizona. This is a relatively small operator that apparently does not have its own website, but that ran an excellent trip with a mixture of oar rafts and kayakers.

## Activity

Rafting the Grand Canyon with a commercial tour operator is a relatively relaxing form of adventure tourism. Guides are responsible for cooking and cleaning and for loading and unloading rafts. Clients need only find a good site for their sleeping bags on summer trips, and put up tents on spring and autumn trips. Some campsites have sandy beaches, others have flat rocks and small overhangs. Most of the rafts use oar rigs where the guide does the rowing and the clients are purely passengers. In the main summer season, many of the rafts are motorized. In spring and autumn, motors are banned and only human-powered craft are permitted. Permits for these periods allow a longer time on the river, with greater opportunities to halt and hike along side canyons rather than simply rushing down the river.

Unlike many other raft-supported river trips, for kayakers on the Grand Canyon there is no need to stay with the rafts. Kayakers can stop and play in rapids as much as they want, as long as they catch up with the rafts by nightfall. There are relatively few surfable waves, so it makes sense to maximize the opportunities. There are also some long stretches of flat water, particularly in the lower sections, and there is a major advantage in being able to haul one's kayak on to the baggage raft and drift.

## Equipment

A wide range of different raft rigs are used on the Grand Canyon, from giant multi-raft motorized 'J-rigs' to smaller paddle rafts. The most common are large rafts with an outboard motor, or slightly smaller rafts with an oar frame. Experienced Grand

Canyon boaters also use dories, double-ended decked-in wooden or fibreglass boats with a single rower seated in a central well. Kayakers use a wide variety of hardshell boats, though since the trip lasts many days and involves extensive stretches of flat water, comfort is an important consideration, and the smaller playboats may prove painful. On the trip in which I took part, Expeditions Inc. had a range of kayaks available for hire, and kayakers brought their own spraydecks and other gear. All cooking and camping gear is provided by the outfitters.

## Accommodation

All accommodation is in campsites beside the river. There are only a limited number of accessible sites, and they are in heavy demand, especially in peak season. Indeed, the supply of campsites is ultimately the limiting factor on the total number of people who can run the river each season. Rafting outfitters provide tents and camping gear, and the guides do the cooking and cleaning. Campfires are permitted only in metal fire pits, which the rafters must bring with them. All firewood must be carried in, and all ashes taken out in the rafts. Portable toilets are also required. Historically, most commercial raft trips used army-surplus rocket boxes with a liner and – as a later concession to the clients' comfort – a toilet seat. More recently, because of changes in regulations, specially manufactured stainless-steel containers have been introduced, which can be flushed out into a conventional sewage system at the end of the trip.

## Statistics

The number of days a group can stay on the river is set as a condition of their launch permit, and so is the maximum size of the group. Given the demand for Grand Canyon trips, almost all groups take their full quota. A typical full-length summer trip, Lee's Ferry to Diamond Creek, might take 13 days, whereas spring and autumn trips can stay on the river up to 16 days. The total group size is typically around 23, including guides as well as clients. There is generally one guide per raft, plus one or more to row baggage boats, with a net client-to-guide ratio of around 4:1. Since supply is limited, raft tour operators can increase prices until the point where they can just fill their quota. Currently, 13-day trips cost from US$2900 to 3900 per person, or US$225–300 per person per day.

## Access

Access is tightly controlled by the US National Parks Service. Each operator has a defined quota of clients. The total numbers of launches and river-runners are also fixed, and the majority of the quota is allocated to commercial tour operators. Private raft and kayak groups must register on a waiting list, pay annual fees and take part in a lottery to allocate launch dates. Currently the wait is over 15 years from initial registration to a final permit to launch.

As noted above, there are limited campsites, and the number, size and spacing of raft groups launching must therefore be regulated for safety reasons as well as visitor satisfaction. When the quota system was first introduced, rafting outfitters operating at the time were allocated a 'grandfathered' quota set by their reported annual client numbers at that time. Unfortunately, this left only a small proportion of the total quota for private groups, a major bone of contention ever since and a severe lesson for natural resource managers worldwide.

One of the reasons why rafting operators are reluctant to take kayakers is that park regulations require them to send a kayaking guide on the trip, which reduces their paying clients by one. Of course, if the number of kayakers is more than one boatload of rafters, then the tour operator makes a net gain.

Physical access to the Grand Canyon is also limited. All groups launch at Lee's Ferry, immediately below Grand Canyon Dam, and most take out at the next road access, Diamond Creek. There is only one intermediate access point, Phantom Ranch, which can be reached on foot or mule back. Many raft operators offer the option for clients to leave or join the group at Phantom Ranch. Below Diamond Creek the Colorado River runs through a Hualapai Native American Indian Reservation, and only companies owned or licensed by the Hualapai are permitted on that section. There is a 1- or 2-day run from Diamond Creek to a lower take-out point at Lake Mead.

## Community

Whilst tourism to the Grand Canyon is very large-scale, rafting represents only a very small proportion of total visitation. There is a township at Diamond Creek, but rafting groups have little interaction with residents. Raft guides are generally respectful of Indian customs and traditions, for example, at sites on the Little Colorado River and various other sidestreams. The raft guides themselves form a relatively close-knit community, largely resident in Flagstaff and surrounding areas, which is dependent on commercial rafting clients.

## Experience

A rafting trip through the Grand Canyon, even a half-length trip in a motorized raft, involves several successive days drifting through the deep red-rock gorge and camping on the steep-cliffed riverbanks. No matter how citified the clients, they cannot avoid being splashed in the rapids and dried by the sun, coated by dust and chewing on sand, and learning to use a rather rudimentary portable toilet. If they take a trip with time enough, they will be able to hike into astonishingly beautiful side canyons and learn something of the Grand Canyon's geology and natural history.

Because the Grand Canyon is such a well-known destination, a Grand Canyon raft trip is an expensive once-in-a-lifetime experience for most commercial clients, and many of these clients have little or no previous outdoor experience. For such clients, simply living outdoors for several days, away from urban infrastructure and city noise, may be a more pervasive part of the experience than running the rapids. Indeed, especially in the lower sections of the river there are long flat stretches without significant rapids, when the raft guides row slowly or pass the oars to clients, and any kayakers haul their kayaks on to the baggage raft, rest their cramped legs and luxuriate in the sun.

## Environment

Environmental management issues in the Colorado Grand Canyon may be considered at two different scales. Largest-scale are the enormous impacts of a series of water storage dams, notably Glen Canyon Dam immediately upstream of the

Grand Canyon itself. An extensive environmental impact assessment of the dam was carried out by the US Bureau of Reclamation (1995), but not until after the dam was already built and operational.

The dam has two main direct physical impacts on the river. First, it changes the flow from a seasonally varying river to a dam-controlled fixed flow, with small variations to match electricity demand. In particular, there are no longer any seasonal floods. Secondly, the water is taken from penstocks at the base of Lake Powell, and as a result the river is cold, green and has low turbidity, rather than warm, red and turbid as it was before the dam was built. These changes to flow regime and water quality have equally major indirect biological impacts on aquatic and riparian ecosystems. Most significant, introduced trout are able to survive and breed successfully in the low-turbidity flows released from the dam. Only in undammed sidestreams such as the Little Colorado River, which still experience highly turbid seasonal floods, are trout still absent. This is critical for a number of native fish species, since trout prey on their eggs so severely that populations of native fish such as the humpback chub are now restricted to tiny sections at the confluences of sidestreams.

Riparian communities have also been affected by the changing flow regimes, notably the cessation of high-water flood flows. As a result, native fringing woodland dominated by open stands of large cottonwood trees has been replaced by a dense scrub of small tamarisks. In an attempt to reverse this, two artificial flood flows have been released from the dam, several thousand cubic metres per second for several days.

Compared to these large-scale effects, the environmental impacts of rafting are very localized, and more significant aesthetically than ecologically. They are concentrated at campsites, which receive very heavy use. They include erosion, cooking and cleaning wastes, litter, fire residue and human waste. To minimize these impacts, as noted earlier, raft tours must bring portable toilets, fuel stoves, firewood and firepits and must take out all waste, including litter, ashes and human waste.

## Safety

The rapids in the Grand Canyon, though large and powerful, are not technically difficult. Most of the rafts used in commercial trips are large, and the oarsmen are all experienced. The water flow is regulated by the dam upstream and conditions are predictable. It is hence very rare for rafts to flip or passengers to fall out, and even if they do, most of the rapids are safely swimmable by anyone wearing a lifejacket. At high flows, the risks are significantly higher, and there have been some dramatic incidents and rescues, but these are rare. Commercial rafting clients wear lifejackets, but helmets are not required since the river is broad and not rocky. Guides instruct passengers where to sit and how and when to hold on.

## Marketing

The Grand Canyon is such a well-known destination that rafting outfitters barely need to advertise it. Instead, each operator's marketing can concentrate on their particular perceived advantages relative to competitors. Several Grand Canyon rafting companies also operate on other rivers, both in the USA and in some cases in other countries.

# Franklin River, Australia: World Expeditions

## Place

The Franklin River runs through a large national park in southwest Tasmania, Australia. The area has World Heritage status and is largely wilderness, except for one access road. The vegetation is largely cool temperate rainforest, with high conservation value. The area is highly scenic, with rapids and deep pools amidst rocky gorges on the river, and mountain peaks such as Frenchman's Cap.

There was a large-scale and long-running environmental controversy in this area in the 1970s and 1980s, culminating in a 1983 High Court case between the Tasmanian state government and the Australian federal government. In brief, a quasi-autonomous subsidiary of the Tasmanian state government, the Hydro Electricity Commission (HEC), wanted to build a hydroelectric dam across the Franklin River and flood a large portion of the southwest wilderness area. Conservation groups in Tasmania and nationally, residents in the mainland states of Australia, and the Australian federal government opposed this project.

Australia is a federated nation, and the division of powers between the state and federal governments is defined in the Constitution. One of these is the so-called external affairs power, which essentially gives the federal government the power to represent Australia as a sovereign nation in its dealings with other nations. The critical issue was whether the fact that Australia is a signatory to the World Heritage Convention triggered the external affairs power in the Australian Constitution, and if so whether this gave the Commonwealth Government the power to halt the proposed dam development even if the state government had approved it. The High Court of Australia ruled that it did, and the Franklin River has remained undammed, though the HEC has built dams elsewhere. The so-called Franklin Dam case became a national controversy, and helped to raise public awareness of environmental issues throughout Australia.

At the time the area was almost completely unknown to most Australians, but one particular wilderness photographer had hiked and kayaked throughout the southwest of Tasmania for many years. His photographs illustrating the scenic beauty of the Franklin River area played a critical role in generating public interest in the controversy. Large numbers of people took the opportunity to travel down the Franklin River, mostly in small inflatable rafts of the type known as 'duckies', so as to see it for themselves. Effectively, these early raft and kayak descents were the forerunner of the commercial whitewater rafting industry on the Franklin River.

Many current commercial clients, however, particularly those from overseas, probably know little or nothing of this conservation history. The Franklin River and the southwest wilderness area are nature and adventure tourism destinations in their own rights, and the more famous scenic sections are well known from postcards and illustrated books available worldwide.

## Operator

Several different companies offer commercial rafting tours of the Franklin River. Best known of these is World Expeditions, a multi-activity adventure tourism retailer that is based in Australia but now offers over 140 small-group tours worldwide (Buckley, 2003a, pp. 112–114; World Expeditions, 2005b). At the time I took part in this tour, kayaking alongside the rafts, the World Expeditions group assembled in an outdoor goods store in Hobart, so presumably the company did not have a retail outlet in Tasmania.

## Activity

The Franklin River is a wilderness descent with no river access between put-in and take-out points, except for one road mentioned below. The put-in is on a bitumen road that crosses the Collingwood, a tributary of the Franklin, and the first 2 days of the trip are on this tributary. The Franklin is a relatively steep low-volume river with rapids ranging up to Class V in difficulty, and some mandatory portages. The descent is made in paddle rafts, so all clients must learn to paddle as a team and follow the instructions of their raft guide. All clients also help in carrying rafts and equipment during portages.

The banks are relatively narrow in many sections, and some of the campsites are in caves or relatively cramped rocky areas. All clients take part in loading and unloading rafts, setting up and breaking camp, and preparing food and cleaning up both at campsites and lunch stops. Interspersed with these activities, however, there are tranquil sections of the river where the rafters need only gaze at the scenery.

The trip includes a 2-day side hike to Frenchman's Cap, weather permitting, with 1 night's camping at a small lake below the Cap itself. At some campsites there are opportunities for clients to explore the riverbanks for a short distance, and at one site there is the opportunity for them to try their hands at bouldering above a deep pool.

At the end of the rafting section, the group may be flown out by seaplane from a landing on the Gordon River. On the trip in which I took part, I was paddling a hardshell kayak, which could not be carried out by a floatplane, so we continued downstream to a tour boat jetty, camped overnight and returned to the nearby town of Strahan in the tour boat the following day.

According to the World Expeditions (2005b) website, in the current itinerary rafting clients return to Strahan by sailboat.

## Equipment

The Franklin River is too narrow to be traversed by oar rafts or even by large paddle rafts. Commercial tour operators use small four-person paddle rafts, which have very limited load-carrying capacity. Rafts and rafting gear, tents and sleeping mats, dry bags for personal gear, and all food and cooking equipment are provided by the tour operator. Clients bring their own sleeping bags, outdoor clothing and personal equipment. Rain is not infrequent, and waterproof parkas are essential. The water is cold, and clients need wetsuits and paddling jackets. These are available for hire from World Expeditions for clients who do not have their own.

## Accommodation

All accommodation during the tour is in tents at riverside campsites. There are caves or overhangs at some of these sites. The tour starts from Hobart, and clients are responsible for their own accommodation in Hobart the previous night. At the end of the tour, the group stays overnight in Strahan, camping in the town campground.

## Statistics

The minimum group size is a single raft with four paddling clients and one guide. The client-to-guide ratio is hence generally 4:1. Larger groups simply take more rafts, with the same guide-to-client ratio, since the river is not wide enough to take larger boats. The maximum group size is limited by available space at campsites, and by the additional delay involved when rafts have to line up to run or portage the more difficult rapids. The total length of the trip is 9 days, including access to and from the river, or 11 days including the 2-day side hike to Frenchman's Cap. The current price is AUD2290 for 9 days or AUD2490 for 11 days, i.e. about US$190 per day.

## Access

Access to the river for most companies offering commercial tours on the Franklin is by road to the put-in described above. One company does offer trips on the lower section only, with access along the controversial McCall road (see below under Environment), but this is frowned upon by remaining operators, who would prefer that road were closed entirely. Departure from the river is by boat transfer to Strahan as outlined above, and then by road back to Hobart. Permits are required for all commercial tour operations in Tasmanian National Parks, and indeed also for private recreational visitors (Buckley, 2003c). These permits are obtained by the tour operator, and the fees are included in the trip price.

## Community

There are no local residents along the Franklin River within the South West Tasmania World Heritage Area. The closest settlements are at Derwent River on the road to the put-in point, and at Strahan, which is the gateway from the take-out point. Clients have very little interaction with residents of these communities. World Expeditions purchases equipment, food and other supplies in Hobart. Raft guides are not necessarily full-time residents in Tasmania, but most guides and shuttle drivers live locally at least during the tourist season, and contribute accordingly to the regional economy.

## Experience

A raft trip down the Franklin River is a relatively intense experience for most participants. It takes place in a wilderness setting with no outside intrusions. It involves a high degree of physical activity, often strenuous, and requires a high level of attention in order to maintain safety. This applies particularly during portages and the more difficult rapids, but care and vigilance are also needed on the river at all times and whilst moving around on the riverbanks, which are often wet and slippery.

Clients travel in small groups where each participant must pull their weight and all participants must work together, both on the river and in camp, almost constantly throughout the entire trip. For most trips, the guides and most of the clients will all be strangers to each other at the outset. There may be extended periods of cold, wet weather. All these factors combine to produce an experience very different from the normal working lives of most clients.

At the same time, participants get the opportunity to travel through an extremely beautiful forest and run some very exciting rapids, with experienced guides providing a high level of safety. The more tranquil sections of the lower gorge, such as the famed Irenabyss, are especially memorable. Weather permitting, the hike to Frenchman's Cap provides an altitudinal transect through a range of vegetation types, and outstanding views from the summit across the southwest wilderness. For groups that continue downstream to the tour boat landing point, the lower section of the river provides excellent opportunities to see platypus at close range.

## Environment

World Expeditions tours generally follow minimal-impact practices, and the company has its own code of environmental practice, *The Responsible Travel Guide Book*, which covers the social as well as the natural environment (Buykx, 2001).

Techniques and equipment to minimize environmental impacts of backcountry whitewater rafting have been examined extensively and are available as *Leave-No-Trace®* booklets in the USA, as a *Green Guide* in Australia (Buckley, 1999) and as minimal-impact guidelines produced by the Australian Alps National Parks. Whilst there are differences in detail between different ecosystems and different types of river, these guidelines are very similar in most regards and best practices are generally well established and agreed (Buckley, 2002a). Broadly, they may be divided into: access to the river; travel downriver; and camping beside the river. There are guidelines for: where to camp; cooking, cleaning, washing, heating and lighting; disposal of human waste, organic food scraps, greywater and garbage; minimizing noise and disturbance to wildlife, to other users, and to riverside heritage sites; avoiding the introduction of weeds and pathogens; and so on.

The World Expeditions Franklin River rafting trip followed accepted best practice in all aspects of its operations. The environmental interpretation component was focused principally on minimal-impact practices. Land-use history and environmental politics were discussed briefly. The natural history component, such as identification of plants and animals, was rather limited.

In addition, World Expeditions has on occasion taken an active political role in conservation disputes (Buckley, 2003a, pp. 112–114). In particular, there was a long-running controversy over an antecedent 4WD track in the southwest Tasmania World Heritage Area, through which the Franklin River flows. This track, the so-called McCall road, provides access half-way down the wilderness section of the river. Conservation groups had long argued either that it should be closed entirely and rehabilitated, or that it should be closed to commercial and recreational use, and maintained only as a management access track. In addition to concerns over wilderness quality, continued access by non-quarantined vehicles increases the risk that visitors may start fires or introduce weed species. Most importantly, it risks dispersing the cinnamon fungus *Phytophthora cinnamomi*, the causal agent of the virulent jarrah dieback disease, which attacks a wide range of native Australian plants species and currently causes major problems for protected area management in Tasmania.

Several commercial tour operators run whitewater rafting trips on the Franklin River, and they were divided over the use of this access track. One major operator uses the track for access, so as to run shorter trips. This operator lobbied to keep the track open. The others offer only full-length rafting trips through the wilderness area, and do not use the midway access track. These operators, including World Expeditions, were generally in favour of closing the track. Only World Expeditions, however, lobbied actively in support of the conservation viewpoint, even though this made it unpopular with larger-scale tourism interests who were against closing any recreational access anywhere. Of course, it could be argued that World Expeditions had commercial interests in seeing the road closed, since the company using it was a competitor. It would, however, have been equally possible for World Expeditions to offer short-duration trips using the access road, as well as the full-length trips. On balance, therefore, it does seem that their actions were driven by conservation concerns rather than commercial competition.

### Safety

Some of the rapids on the Franklin are not safe to run and must be portaged. Others are runnable, but require considerable care. Much of the river is relatively steep, narrow and boulder-choked, so even in the less difficult rapids, there are significant risks if rafts flip or participants fall out. In addition, if gear should become wet through a capsize, there may be little opportunity to dry it. Unlike many 1-day raft trips elsewhere, therefore, where guides may deliberately flip rafts at the end of the day to add to the excitement, on the Franklin River it is particularly important that the rafts remain right side up. The skill and experience of the raft guides is hence of paramount importance. Guides also need to be expert in manoeuvring rafts through tight gaps, with or without paddlers onboard, and in using throw-ropes very quickly and accurately to rescue anyone who falls overboard, before they reach the next rapid. The World Expeditions guides on the trip in which I took part were indeed skilled in all these areas. The company also provides a first aid kit and an emergency satellite phone.

### Marketing

The Franklin River raft trip is marketed as part of the World Expeditions Australia tour portfolio, through Australian and international brochures and tour catalogues, the World Expeditions (2005) website, and the company's retail sales operations in Sydney. The Franklin River is a well-known rafting trip, but World Expeditions is in competition with other tour operators.

## Upper Zambezi, Zimbabwe: Various Operators

### Place

Victoria Falls is 80 km downstream from Kazungula on the border with Botswana. Above Victoria Falls the Zambezi River is relatively broad and calm, with large open pools, reed fringes and occasional narrows with small rapids up to Class II. A wealth of birdlife can be seen from the water, especially in sections with fringing gallery woodlands. Crocodiles can be seen on the banks and there are pods of hippo in the pools.

## Operator

Several tour companies offer 1-day, 2-day 1-night, and 2-day 2-night kayak tours on the Zambezi upstream of Victoria Falls. In most cases these companies are probably all agents for the same local operators. To judge from illustrations and text, however, there must be at least two different local operators, one using inflatable kayaks and the other using rigid two-seater touring kayaks. Different websites also quote different distances travelled, different take-out points and different accommodation options, so there may be more than two operators.

When I took part in this trip some years ago it was a 2-day 2-night fully supported tour run by Shearwater Adventures for a group of South African bird-watchers. They paddled dark green, two-seater touring kayaks, and I acted as an additional safety kayaker in return for the opportunity to kayak the section below the Falls with Shearwater's 1-day whitewater raft trip.

It is not clear whether Shearwater still offer this kayak tour upstream of the Falls, since the company has now expanded into a range of other adventure activities such as riverboarding, bungee jumping, jetboating, helicopter flights and elephant-back safaris, as well as 1-day and multi-day raft trips. The current website for Shearwater Adventures (2005) does not seem to list kayak tours on the upper Zambezi. In July 2005, the website for African Adrenalin (2005) did still list the Shearwater tour, but as of September 2005 it did not. As of July 2005, the website for Wildlife Africa (2005) showed the dark green touring kayaks used by Shearwater, but as of September 2005 this trip was no longer listed on that site.

Other tour operators such as Safari Par Excellence (2005) offer a 1-day trip in two-person inflatable kayaks starting 25 km upstream of Victoria Falls and taking out 4 km upstream. This seems to be the only trip currently advertised on this stretch of the river, perhaps because of security considerations so close to the border. Until recently, Siyabona Africa (2005) offered a similar tour in almost the same words, except that it said the trip is only 15 km. As of September 2005, several operators were offering 3-night canoe tours on the lower Zambezi, on one of three 'canoe trails' known respectively as the Great Zambezi Canoe Trail, the Island Canoe Trail and the Mana Pools Canoe Trail.

## Activity

The description here refers to the 2-day 2-night land-supported trip as it was offered by Shearwater Adventures some years ago. The tour as outlined by African Adrenalin (2005) seems somewhat more basic, but essentially similar. The trip advertised by Wildlife Africa (2005) appears to be the same. Those advertised by Safari Par Excellence (2005) and Siyabona Africa (2005) involve only 1 day's paddling, in inflatable rather than touring kayaks.

In the trip in which I took part, the itinerary was relaxed and much of the day was spent drifting downstream, watching birds and other wildlife through binoculars. Big game as well as birds can be seen at close quarters on the riverbank as the kayaks drift quietly by. Both guides and clients also kept a sharp lookout for hippo, since these must be given a wide berth. At numerous sections binoculars were packed away whilst the kayaks navigated the rapids, which were relatively innocuous. The tour included a support vehicle that met the kayakers for morning tea, lunch and at camp each afternoon. At each stop clients were greeted with a white tablecloth laden with delicacies. At the overnight camps the support crew put up large canvas safari tents and cooked dinner.

## Equipment

The clients paddled heavy, two-person fibreglass touring kayaks, dark green in colour. The trip leader and myself were in single whitewater kayaks of an old design. The support team drove a light truck with camping gear, food and drinks, tents and tables, and clients' personal equipment. The operator supplied lifejackets and also bedding and cutlery. Clients had only to bring a pair of shorts for the day and lightweight long-sleeved clothing for the evening, and binoculars and cameras. Some current operators, as noted above, now use inflatable canoes or kayaks.

## Accommodation

In the tour I experienced, we stayed in a mobile tented safari camp constructed by the support crew. Before and after the trip we stayed at Victoria Falls, which has a wide range of accommodation options. One of the current operators, Safari Par Excellence (2005), offers accommodation in its own lodge, The Zambezi Waterfront, 4 km upstream of the Falls.

## Statistics

On the trip in which I took part there were six clients, one guide and myself. Companies currently offering this tour do not specify client/guide ratios. The trip currently offered is a 1-day tour involving 21 km paddling. The 2-day 2-night option offered until recently by Wildlife Africa (2005), closest to the Shearwater Adventures trip I experienced, involved 2 days of 18 km each, and ran only with at least four clients. When costs were last quoted on the African Adrenalin (2005) website, the 2-day 2-night tour cost US$320 per person, or US$160 per person per day. One-day 1-night tours with Safari Par Excellence (2005) currently cost about US$140.

## Access

Physical access is by air to Victoria Falls and by road to the put-in and take-out. Tour participants are required to pay park permit fees in cash, separately from tour costs. These were recently quoted at US$10 by African Adrenalin (2005), but may have increased.

## Community

Victoria Falls is a major adventure tourism destination, and all tourist activities contribute to the local economy and employment. Most tour operators employ locals as well as Zimbabwe residents from elsewhere in the country, and expatriates. Political upheaval in Zimbabwe is apparently diverting much of its tourist clientele to Livingstone, on the other side of the river in Zambia. If this continues, there will presumably be economic losses to local communities on the Zimbabwe side.

## Environment

The environmental impacts of tourism at a destination such as Victoria Falls, in a country such as Zimbabwe, may be considered in several distinct categories. There are impacts: from tourist travel to the region; from tourist accommodation locally; from individual activities; and from the increase in local resident populations as people move to the area in search of economic opportunities. The upper Zambezi canoe trip contributes pro rata to all the indirect impacts. The direct impacts of the actual canoeing, however, are negligible in comparison. These trips also provide nature-based educational experiences, and contribute indirectly to conservation through political support for the continuing existence of national parks, which is of considerable significance in Zimbabwe.

## Experience

This description is derived from my own experience on the Shearwater Adventures tour, which may no longer operate in the same way. Even though our equipment was relatively rustic, the level of support and service was so high that the trip had the luxury air of a classic safari, where food and drink were always on time and always served with sparkling crystal and silverware on white tablecloths in the shade of a tall tree overlooking the river. We saw a variety of birds and other wildlife, and all the clients enjoyed the trip greatly. Indeed, some of the clients were repeat customers who were bringing friends to experience the tour.

## Safety

The reason I was able to take part in this tour was that, for safety reasons, the trip leader wanted the group to include a safety kayaker at the rear, as well as himself in front. All our equipment was sound and well-made. We had lifejackets and spraydecks, but wore hats rather than helmets, with sunstroke a greater risk than rapids. We had one capsize where two of the clients swam to a reed bed, potentially a dangerous area for hippo, and it was my responsibility to provide support while the trip leader rescued their kayak. Fortunately, however, neither hippos nor crocodiles appeared and all was well.

## Marketing

Marketing by tour operators who currently offer upper Zambezi kayak tours is rather low-key and uninformative. These companies seem to focus principally on lower Zambezi canoe trips in the Mana Pools area. As outlined above, it is difficult to determine just what trips are currently offered. This may well be due to political instabilities in Zimbabwe, leading to rapid changes in client preferences or tour company operating permits.

# 6  Whitewater Rafting

Expeditions Inc., Grand Canyon, USA. Photo Ralf Buckley.

Allardice's Ultimate Descents, Nepal. Photo Ralf Buckley.

# White Nile, Uganda: Adrift

## Place

The River Nile has two major branches, the Blue Nile and the White Nile. The White Nile flows through Uganda, not far from the capital Kampala, and a stretch of the river known as the Itanda Falls section is run regularly as a 1-day raft trip. The source of the White Nile is a very large lake, Lake Victoria, so even at its headwaters the river is very high volume, over 1000 cubic metres per second.

Unlike the Zambezi, the White Nile has multiple channels, and only some of these are safely runnable by commercial rafting trips, though all have now been run by expert kayakers (Kayak the Nile, 2005). Uganda is tropical and the water is warm despite the elevation. The surrounding landscape is used principally for subsistence agriculture, with numerous small villages linked by dirt roads.

## Operator

Only one company, Adrift (2005), offers rafting trips on the White Nile. Trips have been run since the late 1990s. The company was originally based in New Zealand with a Ugandan subsidiary, but the Ugandan operations are largely independent in operational terms and currently seem to be owned by or linked to a UK company of the same name. Based in Kampala, Adrift is best known for its 31 km, 1-day Itanda Falls whitewater raft trip. Adrift also offers an 18 km, half-day whitewater trip; 46 km, 2- or 3-day whitewater trips, a raft and bungee-jump combo, and 3 km or 18 km family float trips on easier sections of the river (Adrift, 2005). The 1-day trip is described here.

## Activity

Clients, principally backpackers, are collected from their accommodation in Kampala in the company bus and driven to the put-in point, Bujagali Falls. The rafts are rigged as paddle rafts, and clients receive paddling instructions and safety briefings before launching. The first major rapid is immediately downstream of the put-in point, and the rafts run a number of large named rapids before reaching Itanda Falls itself. This is a long and intense rapid with multiple drops and large hydraulics, most notably a river-wide weir ledge, known as the Pencil Sharpener, halfway down. Depending on water level, there is a runnable line through this drop near the centre of the channel and the entire rapid has in fact been run by kayakers. This line may not be easy to see from upstream, however, and the consequences of missing it could prove serious. Rafters therefore land on the river right above the Falls and portage at least the upper section of the rapid. Depending on water level, the guides may elect to launch again immediately below the weir drop and run the lower section. The rapid ends with a steep and unavoidable 'rooster-tail' wave that can easily flip a raft, followed by a large eddy pool. Once the rafters reach the take-out point, the clients help to load the rafts on a trailer, and are then driven back to Kampala in the company bus.

## Equipment

Most manufactured items are relatively difficult and expensive to obtain in Uganda, because all but the most basic items are imported and are subject to import charges and restrictions and to transport costs, delays and losses. These considerations apply not only to outdoor equipment such as whitewater rafts and kayaks, but also to vehicles such as tour buses. Even relatively small items such as raft paddles, lifejackets and helmets may be difficult to replace. Despite these difficulties, the rafts used by Adrift all seemed to be in good repair. I myself was able to borrow a kayak owned by one of the guides. It was an older model with replacement parts, such as a thigh brace, carved from local wood. This, however, may have been a spare boat kept at the company's warehouse, not one paddled routinely by the guides themselves. Illustrations on the company's website indicate that they now use current-model kayaks.

## Accommodation

The 1-day trips do not include accommodation. A range of accommodation is available in Kampala. Adrift now operates the Jinja Nile Resort, a B&B and camping area, at the Bujagali Falls put-in. Other websites refer to the Nile High Camp near Bujagali (Kayak the Nile, 2005). The multi-day trips camp on Hairy Lemon Island, apparently exclusive to Adrift.

## Statistics

The whitewater trips use paddle rafts, whilst the float trips use oar rigs. Illustrations on the Adrift (2005) website indicate that each paddle raft carries nine or ten clients and one guide. A typical day's trip may include five or six rafts. Total group size is restricted by the capacity of the shuttle bus, and the size of the bus is restricted by the roads it must traverse. The 1-day trip includes lunch only. The 2-day trip includes two lunches, one dinner and one breakfast. Current prices (Adrift, 2005) are US$85 per person for a half-day whitewater trip, US$95 for a full-day trip, US$199 for 2 days and US$285 for 3 days.

## Access

For the whitewater trips, access is by air or overland to Kampala, and by road to the river in the company bus that picks up clients at various hotels and backpacker accommodation in Kampala (Adrift, 2005). It also picks up clients from Jinja township and the Jinja Nile Resort. For the family float trips, clients must make their own way by car to Kangulamirra, 100 km from Kampala. It is not clear whether any permits are required for commercial tour operations on the river, but if they are, arrangements are handled directly by the company.

## Community

Adrift Uganda employs Ugandans as well as expatriate staff, contributing to local economic opportunities. The villagers along the take-out road seemed to be well acquainted with the company bus, as might be expected, and willingly helped to push it out of the mud when it became bogged. This is an adventure rather than a cultural tour, however, and clients do not have any significant interactions with local communities.

## Experience

For the clients this trip is a long, energetic and exciting day. On the day I took part, every raft capsized in the tail-wave of Itanda Falls, so every client's experience included an inadvertent swim. Some of them were not strong swimmers, and as the current carried them around in the large eddy pool, they were clearly distressed. On that particular occasion, since I was kayaking, I was able to ferry a number of them to the bank and rescue their abandoned paddles. Other than this, however, there were no raft flips and the clients seemed to have fun without undue fear.

Later in the day, the road back from the take-out point was very muddy, and the clients had to help push the bus through the worst sections, getting very muddy themselves in the process. They seemed quite cheerful about this, but in any event there was little choice if they wanted to get back to Kampala. The guides invited the clients to a party after the trip, at a house where several of them lived. I did not go myself, so I'm not sure if this was a special occasion or a routine part of the proceedings, perhaps a way for a relatively small and isolated group of expatriate guides to broaden their social circle temporarily.

## Environment

Relative to the impacts of surrounding villages and agricultural operations, the environmental impacts of rafting are negligible. There are toilets at the put-in point, which has a sealed access road and car park area, and seems to be intended for general visitor use, with raft tours making up only a small proportion of the total. The tours carry out or burn all non-biodegradable waste, use gas stoves rather than local firewood, hire local transport and tradespeople, and purchase supplies locally. Rubbish and litter are collected and taken out to Kampala on the bus.

## Safety

Relative to most commercial raft tours, at the time of my own trip safety precautions on the White Nile were rather basic. The rafts were in good repair, the guides were competent and the safety briefing was standard. As with many other commercial whitewater raft trips, the rafts were not routinely accompanied by safety kayakers, though this now seems to have changed.

Most commercial raft trips, however, are on narrow rivers where clients can swim to the banks; on high-flow but low-volume rivers where any swimmers can, if necessary, wash safely through the rapid into a calm pool downstream; or on rivers where clients thrown out of one raft can generally be picked up by another. The Itanda Falls section of the White Nile, in contrast, is wide and fast flowing, and swimmers could well be at risk.

In running the lower half of Itanda Falls itself, the guides took the rafts through one after the other without waiting, even though all the preceding rafts had flipped and their clients were swimming. Perhaps each of the guides thought they would be able to run the final wave without flipping, and assist the others. Perhaps this was an unlucky day, and multiple capsizes are unusual. Perhaps they capsized deliberately so as to make the experience more exciting for the clients, on the assumption that the large eddy would stop them washing downstream and they were therefore not at serious risk. Some of the clients, at least, seemed to feel otherwise.

Interestingly, at the initial safety briefing the clients were given a somewhat unorthodox definition of the distinction between Class V and Class VI rapids, namely, that 'in a Class V rapid, you're sure you're going to die, but you don't; in a Class VI rapid, you're sure you're going to die, and you do'. Overall, therefore, Adrift Uganda did seem a little more cavalier in its attitude to safety than rafting tour operators in Zimbabwe or Nepal, for example, let alone the USA. No one was actually injured, however, and since the clients were almost all backpackers, this approach may have been an intentional aspect of the company's client communication strategy. It is difficult to make such an assessment from a single day trip. In addition, judging from the company's website, safety practices seem to have improved since my trip, with a number of local safety boaters now available.

### Marketing

Rafting on the White Nile is not nearly so well known internationally as, for example, the Zambezi in Zimbabwe or the Sun Khosi in Nepal. Despite this, the 1-day trip in which I took part was well patronized, so information about the opportunity must circulate effectively. The Ugandan company advertises via its website (Adrift, 2005), which is linked to a site in the UK. In view of the clientele, however, it seems likely that the most effective marketing is through specialized backpacker communication channels. These include both relatively formal means such as backpacker magazines and guidebooks, less formal mechanisms such as Internet bulletin boards, and person-to-person communication by e-mail and mobile phone text messages.

## Zambezi River, Zimbabwe: Shearwater Adventures

### Place

The main whitewater section of the Zambezi River is immediately below Victoria Falls, where the river forms the border between Zimbabwe and Zambia. Averaged over the year, the flow rate is around 1200 cubic metres per second, but peak flows are apparently up to 8000 cubic metres per second. This is over three times larger than Nepal's Sun Khosi in monsoon floods, and almost eight to ten times larger than the Grand Canyon of the Colorado at normal dam-release flows. Indeed, it is advertised as 'the biggest commercially run whitewater in the world' (Shearwater Adventures, 2005). During the 1990s, Victoria Falls became a major international adventure tourism destination, though political instability in Zimbabwe has no doubt taken some toll subsequently.

### Operator

Shearwater is a long-established tour operator in Victoria Falls, Zimbabwe, specializing in raft, kayak and canoe trips on the Zambezi River. It is perhaps best known for its 1-day whitewater raft trips on the section of the Zambezi River downstream of Victoria Falls. The company started operations in 1982 with canoe trips in the Mana Pools area on the lower Zambezi, and began offering rafting trips in 1985 (Shearwater Adventures, 2005). It has gradually taken over most of the adventure tourism activities at the Falls, until it is now by far the dominant provider.

According to its website, it is 'now the leading adventure activity company in Africa'. The 1-day whitewater run below the Falls is still the mainstay of its business, but it also offers riverboarding, jetboating, bungee jumps, helicopter flights and elephant rides, in various combinations.

## Activity

The Zambezi 1-day raft run enjoys a reputation amongst the international backpacker and adventure tourism market as one of the world's archetypal whitewater raft trips. Whilst many species of wildlife, notably crocodiles and a variety of birds, can often be seen during this trip, it is very much an adrenaline experience, strictly adventure rather than nature tourism. And if travelling in a paddle raft is not exciting enough, there are also so-called river sledding trips where tourists run the rapids on specialist bodyboards. For those with appropriate kayaking skills and equipment, the raft tours can provide transport and support for kayakers to paddle the same section of the river.

Different sections of the river are used at different seasons for 1-day and half-day rafting tours. In the 'low' water season from mid-July until late January, clients can raft either rapids 4–10 or 11–19 as half-day trips or rapids 4–19 as a full-day trip. In the high-water season from early February to mid-July, there is only a full-day trip from rapids 11–24 inclusive. Since 2004 the company has also offered an additional option in the low-water season. A track has been built to the river above the rapid 1, the first rapid below the Falls themselves. Once the clients are in the rafts, the guides can row them up to the edge of the 'Boiling Pot', the maelstrom of whitewater below the Falls themselves. This option was not available on the three occasions when I have taken part on this trip, paddling a kayak alongside the rafts. We put in immediately above rapid 4. All the rapids in the 1-day section are Class IV or V, and rapid 9 is considered unraftable and is portaged. It has been run successfully by a number of kayakers, but I myself elected to portage! Clients must walk down into the gorge at the start of the trip – and up again at the end of the day.

## Equipment

Despite the high volume, paddle rather than oar rafts are used for maximum client participation, and perhaps also to manoeuvre if rafts become held up in stopper waves. All equipment is provided by the tour operator, and clients need bring only clothing and sunscreen.

## Accommodation

This is a 1-day tour and does not include accommodation. A range of accommodation options are available, with the Victoria Falls Hotel being perhaps best known, though not necessarily most favoured by adventure tour operators.

## Statistics

The tour takes from 7:30 am to 5:00 pm and costs US$95 per person, plus park fees. The client to guide ratio is generally 8:1, judging from photographs of the rafts on the company website.

## Access

Access to Victoria Falls is by road or air. Access to the put-in and take-out points is by road in the tour operator's minibus, and then on foot down tracks into the gorge. A park permit fee is payable in cash, in addition to the tour cost. This is currently US$10 per person.

## Community

Local porters are used to carry the rafts in and out of the gorge at the beginning and end of each day, providing ongoing employment. Local boys also wait at the take-out and offer to carry clients' personal gear for a small fee. Entrepreneurial locals sell cold drinks, souvenirs and artefacts on the take-out track, at the car park above, and on the roadside.

## Experience

The 1-day whitewater run downstream of Victoria Falls is one of the world's best-known high-volume, high-intensity raft trips. Most clients are so strongly focused on the rapids that they will see little else, even the crocodiles sunning themselves on the rocks. The 1-day tour is a long and full day, and for most clients, possibly the mostly highly charged experience of their visit to Victoria Falls. Many clients have no previous rafting experience, and the paddle training at the put-in, right above rapid 4, fills them with considerable trepidation. They have little time to contemplate, however, because almost immediately the rafts are under way and they have to concentrate on obeying the guide's paddle commands and hanging on to the raft. For other clients, however, there is also the opportunity to run some of the rapids on riverboards, like extra-large boogie boards, and to surf the stoppers and standing waves. At the end of the day, clients have to hike out of the gorge along a steep narrow trail in the afternoon sun. For most of them this is the low point of the day, even though they can walk unburdened while porters carry rafts, paddles and gear.

## Environment

Whitewater rafting clients contribute pro rata to the overall impact of tourism at Victoria Falls and to the impacts of tracks in and out of the river gorge. As in many developing countries, most international tourists and tour operators are careful not to leave litter, but local residents who bring food, drinks and artefacts to the river to sell to tourists are often much less particular. The hike-out from the 1-day Zambezi raft trip is much cleaner that corresponding tracks in many other developing nations.

## Safety

Clients receive safety briefings and instructions at the start of the trip, and are outfitted with lifejackets and helmets. When I first paddled the Zambezi many years ago, large crocodiles were considered a serious danger and the Shearwater raft guides were emphatic that anyone who fell into the water in a rapid must immediately get into a raft before the next major pool. Currently, however, clients are assured that crocodiles are not a threat to rafters or riverboarders. According to

Shearwater Adventure (2005), all their equipment complies with the recommendations of the International Rafting Federation and its South African, Zimbabwe and Zambian equivalents. Guides receive introductory training with 3-monthly refreshers, and fortnightly first-aid refreshers. All guides are qualified as Swiftwater Rescue Technicians, at least at level 1, and receive monthly refresher courses. The company has Medical Air Rescue Service cover for all its clients and US$1 million public liability coverage. The minimum client age is 15.

### Marketing

The current Shearwater Adventures (2005) website emphasizes the range of activities available and offers a range of combinations at discounted prices. The individual activities and non-discounted prices are: rafting at US$95, riverboarding at US$125, jetboating at US$70, helicopter flights at US$85, bungee jumping at US$75 and elephant-back safaris at US$90. The bungee jump is from the bridge between Zambia and Zimbabwe and the drop is 111 m. The company also offers 3- and 5-day rafting trips that continue further downstream.

## Nymboida River, Australia: World Expeditions, Wildwater Adventures and Others

### Place

The Nymboida River is one of Australia's better-known whitewater creeks, used by several commercial operators. It is a low-volume, technical pool-drop creek with rapids up to Class V, and lies inland from Coffs Harbour in mid-north New South Wales (NSW). Both its headwaters and its lower sections flow through farmland, but the main commercial whitewater section runs through the Nymboi-Binderay National Park. Much of this park was until recently a production forest, and logging roads provide access to the river. River flow is rainfall-dependent and hence seasonal. The area has a subtropical climate pattern, with summer rains providing a relatively consistent flow during the commercial rafting season. The river runs through some spectacular gorges, and unlike most of Australia, the water is clear rather than muddy. During summer it is also warm enough that commercial raft clients do not need wetsuits.

### Operator

Until an extended drought a few years ago, a number of different commercial rafting companies offered trips on the Nymboida. The largest of these, Wildwater Adventures and WOW Rafting, were based in Coffs Harbour and offered both 1-day and 2-day trips throughout summer. These were large-group, high-speed trips aimed principally at the backpacker market. There was a similar operator, Rapid Action, based in Queensland's Gold Coast. World Expeditions, in contrast, offered 4-day small-group trips that ran outside the peak season, typically over Easter. Operating from headquarters in Sydney, Australia, World Expeditions (2005b) offers a wide range of hiking, cycling, whitewater and seakayaking trips worldwide as well as throughout Australia. Currently, the Gold Coast operation no longer has an operational telephone number, the websites for the Coffs Harbour operators are inactive and World Expeditions no longer lists the Nymboida trip. Operations may recommence once rainfall recovers enough to re-establish historical flows on the Nymboida River.

## Activity

The principal adventure activity for any of the Nymboida raft tours is running the rapids. The river is relatively steep, narrow and low volume, and only paddle rafts can be used. Many of the rapids are tight and technical, and require good teamwork by the clients under the guide's directions. The World Expeditions trips spent a longer time on the river and took smaller groups than the larger operators based in Coffs Harbour. They could therefore run each section of the river at a different time of day than the large groups, and were able to experience the rapids on their own and at their own pace, instead of queuing up to run them conveyor-belt style, as could often occur on busy days. In addition, the World Expeditions groups could camp on their own in small and little-used campsites with no road access, rather than the very heavily visited road-access sites used by the larger overnight groups and the single day trips. Kayakers, incidentally, commonly run the entire 2-day rafting section in a single day or, alternatively, paddle a different section upstream of that used for rafting.

## Equipment

As with most World Expeditions tours, the 4-day Nymboida rafting trip was fully outfitted, including rafting, safety, camping and cooking equipment. Clients brought only their own personal gear.

## Accommodation

All accommodation on the tour was in tents at riverbank campsites. Unless they drive to the put-in in their own vehicles, clients would generally require accommodation in Coffs Harbour before and after the river trip. This was not included in the tour. On the river, cooking was done by the guides, with assistance from the clients.

## Statistics

The minimum group size for the World Expeditions 4-day trip was a single raft with four clients and one guide, though most trips would have two rafts. The local operators ran 1- or 2-day trips with much larger group sizes. No current prices are available.

## Access

The put-in point for most raft trips on the Nymboida, including these, is at a camping area known as Platypus Flat where a forestry road crosses the river. This is accessible via a steep dirt road from either the west or eastern side. Both the semi-permanent camping area for the high-volume 2-day trips, and the lower take-out point, are accessible via steep dirt roads from the eastern side only. Tour prices generally include transport to and from Coffs Harbour. Although clients could drive their own cars to the put-in point at Platypus Flat, there is then no mechanism for them to recover their vehicles at the end of the trip. The surrounding areas are owned and managed by the NSW State Government, formerly as State Forest and currently as part of Nymboi-Binderay National Park. Commercial permits are required for all raft tour operators, and daily access and camping fees are payable on behalf of each client (Buckley, 2003c; Buckley *et al.*, 2003). These are obtained by the company and included in the trip price.

## Community

The area around the Nymboida River is rural in character, with numerous small settlements and townships but no major towns except Coffs Harbour itself. Most of the landscapes are agricultural, and historically there was a large logging industry in this area. The area is also particularly popular with long-term semi-subsistence lifestyle residents, and more recently has become a significant destination for relatively well-off amenity migrants (Buckley *et al.*, 2006). Coffs Harbour and the surrounding region thus have a significant tourism sector, principally domestic self-drive visitors, and rafting on the Nymboida River is one of the icon attractions of the area. Since it is a seasonal business, however, and guides are not necessarily local residents, its economic contribution is relatively minor. Whilst on the river, World Expeditions clients and other rafters are unlikely to meet any locals, though they may meet campers at Platypus Flat.

## Experience

I have taken part in many trips on the Nymboida River, with both commercial raft crews and private kayaking groups. On holiday weekends the river can become very crowded. The World Expeditions trip, by taking slightly longer than most, provides participants with the opportunity to experience the river's scenery as well as its rapids, and to camp at quiet untrampled sites rather than amidst crowds. It appeals more to those who want to enjoy the river rather than those searching for social opportunities.

## Environment

World Expeditions generally follows minimal-impact practices on all its trips, and on the Nymboida River these are generally in line with guidelines such as Buckley (1999). Whilst the river section used for rafting lies within a National Park, the river originates in agricultural land upstream and water quality is therefore far from pristine. There are composting toilets, installed and maintained by the land management agency, at the major access points, but there are no requirements for raft tours to carry self-contained toilets on the river. Since its groups are small and its campsites only occasionally used, World Expeditions relies on individual catholes.

## Safety

The Nymboida River includes a number of Class V rapids where a person in the water could potentially be in serious danger. Even though the river is relatively low volume, there are chutes, drops and powerful recirculating holes where a swimmer could become trapped and drown. Safety is thus of high concern. World Expeditions has a particularly good safety record, and the same generally applies for other commercial raft tours on the river itself. Incidents do occur, but these are commonly associated either with off-river horseplay amongst larger groups, or with private club trips where there is no clear leadership.

When I took part in the World Expeditions trip, on an Easter long-weekend, two people from other groups apparently had to be helicoptered out following off-river injury. We also encountered inexperienced kayakers from a club in the southern part of NSW, apparently left to their own devices by the more experienced members of their own group. The people concerned did not have the skills or experience to paddle the more difficult rapids, and having never visited the river before did not know where they were, what rapids they faced or even where to portage. They were not equipped for self-supported overnight camping, and at least one was severely hypothermic.

Since other rafting groups had tight schedules to meet, and in any event apparently had very limited first-aid gear, it was left to the World Expeditions tour to provide assistance until a rescue could be organized. It was a tribute to the leadership of the World Expeditions guide that he not only stopped to provide this assistance, but that he also persuaded his own commercial clients to halt their own trip for several hours meanwhile.

### Marketing

World Expeditions is a large adventure tourism retailer that maintains its own shopfront and prints and distributes annual catalogues of tours, one Australian and one international. Whilst many of its on-ground operations, especially those involving an expensive equipment inventory, are actually run by local operators, World Expeditions provides quality control, branding reliability and retail marketing.

## Rio Toachi and Rio Blanco, Ecuador: Yacu Amu Rafting and Rios Ecuador

### Place

The Rios Blanco and Toachi are low- to medium-volume rivers on the western flanks of the Andes near Quito in Ecuador. Quito is at 2835 m, the lower Rio Toachi canyon at 2600 m. Though originally forested, much of the region is now cleared for agriculture. The put-in point is several hours drive from Quito.

### Operator

Yacu Amu Rafting is a relatively small and local commercial tour operator based in Quito, specializing in single and multi-day trips on local rivers, especially the Rios Blanco and Toachi. It is locally owned and all or most of its staff are Ecuadorian. According to the Yacu Amu website, in 2003 it merged with another operator, Rios Ecuador, based in Tena, and the merged company now operates from both towns. However, it appears that Rios Ecuador also advertises and operates separately out of Tena (Rios Ecuador, 2005).

## Activity

Clients are collected from accommodation in Quito and driven by minibus to the river. The rafting is quite leisurely, with medium-grade rapids, extended lunch stops and the opportunity to watch for birds in the riverbank forest or flying overhead. There is the opportunity to swim at lunchtime.

## Equipment

Whilst the riverbed is quite wide, the rivers are rocky and shallow, and only suitable for paddle rafts. SOTAR® brand rafts are featured. The climate is warm, and clients require only lifejackets and helmets, which are provided by the company. Paddle rafts carry six clients and one guide each. Wetsuits are available for rent for trips on the Upper Rio Blanco between March and May, but are not included in the trip price and are not needed at other times of year.

## Accommodation

Accommodation before and after the trip is at the clients' expense in Quito. For 2-day trips, overnight accommodation is in a small riverside tourist hosteria or lodge, which is accessible by road. The hosteria is an independent operation, not associated directly with Yacu Amu Rafting. Clients do not need to bring any camping equipment. Dinner and breakfast are provided. On the trip in which I took part, those who ate this dinner, including myself, suffered from extremely bad food poisoning for several days subsequently, but presumably this was an isolated incident.

## Statistics

Yacu Amu uses paddle rafts with six clients and one guide each. All trips have at least two guides or one guide and a safety kayaker. The trip described here lasts 2 days, but 1-day and multi-day trips are also available (Yacu Amu, 2005). The 2-day trip costs US$195 or about US$100 per person per day.

## Access

Access to and from the rivers is by road from Quito. All permits and landowner arrangements are made by the operating company.

## Community

Yacu Amu employs Ecuadorian ground staff in its offices in Quito and Tena, and both Ecuadorian and international rafting guides. Clients on the 2-day raft trip stay in a local hosteria, visit a local town and eat local food.

## Experience

The water flow varies seasonally. The trip is marketed as Class III–IV, but was lower grade than this when I ran it myself, kayaking alongside the rafts. The 1-day trip takes 13 h, leaving Quito at 6:30 am and returning at 7:30 pm. The 2-day trip returns to Quito in the evening of the second day, but includes a relaxed overnight stay in a riverbank hosteria. On the river, the experience combines whitewater and scenic forest, though much of the latter is cleared.

### Environment

Yacu Amu's website advertises a commitment to environmental management. In practice the only impacts from a raft trip in this area would be from litter, and the guides do ensure that no litter is left.

### Safety

According to the company's website, all raft guides meet standards recommended by the International Rafting Federation, and all kayak guides are qualified in Australia, the USA, Canada or the UK. As for most commercial raft trips, each trip starts with a short safety briefing and training session. According to the website, safety kayakers are used where necessary and there are always at least two guides on each trip.

### Marketing

The 1-day trip is advertised as 'probably the world's longest day trip – 47 km of non-stop Class III–IV whitewater in 4 hours'. The rapid rating may be an exaggeration during the drier parts of the year, though not during the wetter periods. The website advertises commitments to safety and the environment. It also advertises a drive through cloud forest, though rather little of this remains.

## 'Luva River, Fiji: Rivers Fiji

### Place

Only two rivers in Fiji are rafted commercially, both in the Namosi Highlands in southern Viti Levu, Fiji's largest island. They are the Upper Navua River, and the Wainikoroiluva, or 'Luva, a tributary to the Navua. The upper sections of the 'Luva run through a narrow slot canyon, a few metres wide and many tens of metres deep, cut through limestone. The gorge is apparently boulder-choked, broken by waterfalls and quite un-navigable. The navigable section, which starts immediately below this canyon, is a low-volume stream with Class II rapids, and runs through a broad gorge that opens gradually into a wider valley before it joins the Navua. In the upper reaches there are cliffs and caves, whilst the lower stretches are used for shifting cultivation. To reach the put-in involves driving on a winding dirt road, originally a logging road, first over hills and then along a narrow cultivable corridor between high crumbling rock cliffs. Only 100 years ago the Namosi Valley was famous for its undefeated cannibal warriors; currently, it is equally famous for its rugby players.

### Operator

Rivers Fiji (2005) is apparently the only commercial rafting operator in Fiji. The story of its establishment, negotiations with landowners, and eventual commercial success has been told in a number of tourism texts, including Buckley (2003a). Its founders have currently returned to the USA but retain ownership, and the company has an expatriate operations manager at its headquarters in Pacific Harbour on the south coast of Viti Levu. Rivers Fiji runs raft trips on the Upper Navua, and inflatable kayak trips on the 'Luva, on alternate days.

## Activity

Running the river itself is only a small part of the 1-day 'Luva trip, which combines a mixture of road, foot and river travel with spectacular scenery and interesting cultural interactions. The drive to the Namosi Valley zigzags up spurs and ridges, passing giant orchids flowering profusely by the roadside. Finally the road enters the Namosi Valley, with its towering walls wreathed in grey mists and tropical foliage, apparently featured in various movies. Passing the Namosi police post, the group stops at the main village to pay its respects to the chief in an extended and formal kava-drinking ceremony. The chief, whose son is one of the River Fiji guides, then seems glad to answer questions and engage in general conversation. During this meeting the other guides take the inflatables down to the river and get them ready for the trip. The guests are given spray jackets, helmets, lifejackets and paddles by the roadside, and hike down a steep muddy track to the river, where they can choose either a single or double 'ducky'. After a couple of straightforward Class II rapids the group stops for lunch in a riverside cave, and then continues downstream to the junction with the Navua, stopping at one point to hike to a waterfall on a side stream. On the lower Navua the duckies are deflated, rolled up and slung aboard a longtail boat with the clients, for an outboard-powered ride downstream to the next road access.

## Equipment

The inflatable kayaks are manufactured by SOTAR®. Rivers Fiji supplies all rafting gear as well as transport, lunch and kava for the 'sevusevu' – the formal gift to the chief. It also supplies each client with a small dry bag to take personal gear on the river. Clients are advised to bring closed-toe shoes, but on the trip in which I took part, most did not.

## Accommodation

This is a 1-day trip and does not include accommodation. Both the Navua and 'Luva trips start early, so clients must generally overnight in Pacific Harbour. The Rivers Fiji headquarters is in the grounds of the Pearl Hotel, the town's most expensive accommodation, but the company can recommend a range of budget and mid-priced accommodation options.

## Statistics

The Upper Navua trip costs FJD240 and 'Luva trip FJD180, about US$110. These costs include transport and lunch. On the trip in which I took part there were three clients and two guides, but it was raining heavily that day. The previous day's trip, on the Upper Navua, had 15 clients.

## Access

Pacific Harbour, which now advertises itself as the adventure capital of Fiji, lies on the south coast road west of Suva. Access to the Namosi Valley is on a dirt road north from Navua, a little east of Pacific Harbour. The drive takes a couple of hours. There is then a steep foot track down to the river. Access is available only with permission from the landowners, through the chief of the local village. This involves both a formal financial lease arrangement, and a formal ceremony on each trip as described earlier.

## Community

One of the Rivers Fiji guides is the son of the village chief, and it was his task to bring us to the chief's house, prepare the ceremonial kava for drinking and, as our guide, to ask the chief's permission for us to travel downriver. Our other guide also lives nearby, and he left the river at the confluence with the Navua and returned on foot. At the point where the group transfers from kayaks to longtail boats there is a tourist village, with buildings of traditional construction erected specifically for tourists who travel up the lower Navua on boat tours. The Rivers Fiji group did not stop there.

## Experience

On the particular day on which I took part in the 'Luva River trip, it rained all day. This made the Namosi Valley particularly beautiful, with its rock walls wreathed in mist, but the river somewhat less so. We had a very interesting day none the less, learning a little about local history and modern rural life, from shifting cultivation to cannibal grandfathers, pig-hunting dogs to village planning. The whitewater is more riffles than rapids, but the day as a whole is an adventurous mélange of activities.

## Environment

There are relatively few environmental management issues to be faced for a low-volume day trip such as this. The main one is simply litter. In a final briefing on the riverbank before boarding the kayaks, the guides specifically mentioned litter as an important concern. There were no signs of any previous litter on the access track, put-in point, lunch stop or waterfall hike.

## Safety

The inflatable kayaks were of a reputable brand and in good repair, though clearly well-used. Lifejackets were of a good design, and guides helped clients to adjust helmets and lifejackets properly. There was a safety briefing with a demonstration of the safe swimming position in case of a capsize. One client, paddling a double kayak with a guide, did in fact fall out in the second rapid, but was quickly rescued. Pre-trip information advised clients to bring closed-toe footwear, but many did not actually do so.

## Marketing

Rivers Fiji's colour brochure is displayed widely in Viti Levu's south coast tourism accommodation. Most clients probably book trips at short notice as a day's activity from their coastal holiday resort, rather than planning it in advance as part of a Fijian holiday. The company has been featured in airline in-flight magazines and is listed in the *Lonely Planet*® guide to Fiji.

# Tully River, Australia: Raging Thunder, R'n'R

## Place

The Tully River is in tropical Queensland, Australia, 160 km south of Cairns. Although it lies within the wet tropics of Queensland World Heritage Area, it is dammed for hydroelectric power. The section used for commercial whitewater rafting is below the dam and outside the protected area. Unless water is flowing over the dam spillway, water flows for rafting are provided by controlled releases from the dam, and the rafting companies pay fees for these releases. There is thus just one short pulse of water each day sufficient for rafting or kayaking, with low flows outside that period. Commercial rafts need to launch precisely on time, and maintain speed downstream, in order to stay with the high-water pulse.

## Operator

Several different commercial whitewater rafting companies offer 1-day trips on this section of the Tully River. Best known are R'n'R (Raft and Rainforest, 2005) and Raging Thunder (2005). Both these operators also offer half-day trips on the Barron River. R'n'R offers multi-day helicopter-access raft trips on the North Johnstone River. Raging Thunder also offers seakayak and balloon tours. Cairns is one of the principal adventure tourism destinations in Australia, and rafting is one of the principal backpacker tour activities. Others include snorkelling and diving on the Great Barrier Reef, tandem skydiving at Mission Beach and bus trips to the Daintree River and Cape Tribulation.

Both R'n'R and Raging Thunder have relatively large though localized operations. Each may take one or more busloads of tourists to the Tully each day. Raging Thunder (2005) claims to be 'the largest adventure tour company in Australia', with 150,000 clients in 2004. This includes other activities, but rafting is probably the major one. Many of their clients are walk-ins and may sign up as late as the previous evening. The rafting companies therefore have retail shopfronts in Cairns. Raging Thunder's retail outlet is strategically sited next door to McDonald's®. There are also many small travel agents along the waterfront esplanade who sell a variety of adventure tours on commission.

## Activity

For 1-day raft trips on the Tully River, participants meet at the shopfront or are collected from their accommodation in Cairns early in the morning and driven south to the Tully River, stopping once en route for the opportunity to buy coffee and/or breakfast. On arrival at the put-in, some of the guides get the boats and equipment ready, whilst others give a high-speed briefing to the clients. Each client is issued a helmet, lifejacket and paddle and the clients are divided into raft groups, largely on the basis of language. Most clients are either Japanese- or English-speaking, and the guides know a set of basic rafting commands in Japanese. Whilst on the bus, clients are required to complete a register of names and to sign liability waivers.

Many of the clients have no previous rafting experience, and there is a certain degree of confusion at first. The guides are in a hurry to get all the boats on the water and moving downstream before the water release from the dam comes to an end. The river is rafted in a single section so as to keep up with this release of water. In the lower reaches, where there is more standing water, the guides keep the clients amused with swims, water fights, waterfalls, and raft flips and tricks. At the take-out, the participants are given lunch whilst the guides pack the rafts back on to the trailers. The clients are then driven to the tour company cafés to buy food, alcohol, souvenirs and a video of the trip, and thence back to Cairns.

## Equipment

The Tully is a relatively low-volume river and all the commercial raft operators use paddle rafts, generally with seven clients and one guide in each raft. R'n'R advertises that it uses 'specially made' Dolphin® rafts. Clients are told to bring clothing that they are prepared to get wet, such as a t-shirt, boardshorts or bikini, and running shoes or river sandals. They are also advised to bring sunscreen, a hat, spare dry clothes and a towel. The operators issue lifejackets and helmets and will rent out rivershoes and spray jackets if needed. There is no need for wetsuits since the Tully is in the tropics. The bus remains near the river during the trip and clients can leave dry clothing and other possessions on board.

## Accommodation

The 1-day Tully raft trips do not include accommodation. Most clients stay in Cairns on the nights before and after the trip. Clients with their own transport may stop at the Tully River whilst driving between Townsville and Cairns or vice versa. Tourist accommodation is also available at Mission Beach, on the coast not far from Tully.

## Statistics

Group sizes can be quite large, with several busloads of clients per day. Clients are organized into individual raft groups, however, and each raft has one guide for each seven clients. This is a single-day trip, and prices range from AUD145 to 175 (US$112–135) per person per day, plus an AUD25 levy as below.

## Access

Physical access is by bus directly to and from the river. Tour operators must have commercial permits, and pay an additional fee for water releases. They charge clients a levy on top of the basic tour price to cover park fees, water releases and a contribution to insurance. As of late 2005 this levy is AUD25 (US$19).

## Community

The 1-day Tully raft trips have rather little interaction with local communities other than the company guides. Both companies operate their own cafés, the Rafters Café and the Raging Thunder Café respectively, where they take clients after the river trip to sell them food and drink, videos, souvenirs and other tours. As noted earlier, whitewater rafting is one of the principal adventure tourism activities out of Cairns, particularly for backpackers, and backpackers visiting the Cairns region for adventure tourism make a significant contribution to the Cairns and regional economy.

## Experience

Even though the Tully Gorge is quite scenic, the 1-day Tully raft trip is principally an adventure and social experience. Clients get a good view of the landscape south of Cairns from the bus driving to and from the Tully, including cane fields and forested mountains. Many of the clients, however, sleep on the way down after partying the night before, and sleep on the way back after a day of sun, exercise and excitement on the river.

Rafting is new and unfamiliar to most clients, and much of their attention is taken by learning how to paddle, how to obey the guide's instructions, how to balance the raft against flipping whilst passing through the larger rapids, and how to operate as a reasonably coherent team. Many of the clients, especially the backpackers, are also more interested in getting to know each other than in observing forest or wildlife. Because it is only a brief period on the river, training focuses on the most basic instructions, and clients rely entirely on the raft guide to read the river and direct manoeuvres. They do not learn much about either rivers or rafts, but that is not why they are there. They are there to have fun, and generally they do.

## Environment

Even though the area is within a World Heritage site, the Tully River itself is very heavily modified by the hydroelectric dam upstream, and the impacts of rafting are negligible compared to the impacts of the dam. Environmental management by the guides focuses principally on litter, instructing clients not to throw food wrappers or cigarette butts into the river.

## Safety

At the water flows associated with controlled releases for rafting, the Tully River is relatively safe. The greatest risk would be potential foot entrapment if clients were to fall out of the rafts in the upper sections of the river. As a result, briefings focus on how to obey the guide's paddling instructions so as to run the rapids safely; how to shift across the raft to the high side to avert the risk of a capsize; and the safe feet-downstream swimming position to adopt if thrown out of a raft. There are numerous rafts on the river at any one time, and any client who falls out inadvertently will generally be picked up quickly by another raft. In addition, the banks are never far away.

There is no mention of safety kayakers on tour operator websites, and there were no kayakers other than myself on the trip in which I took part. For safety reasons, both companies restrict Tully rafting trips to clients over 13 years old. R'n'R (2005) advertises that its guides are 'internationally trained', that they take part in the company's own 'in-house rigorous whitewater skills and safety training programs' and that they have up-to-date rescue and first aid skills. Raging Thunder (2005) advertises that its guides are trained in safety and rescue procedures by 'Rescue 3', a private US-based company that also carries out training in Australia and elsewhere (Rescue 3 International, 2005). Rescue 3 runs Australian courses at six different levels (Rescue 3 Australia, 2005), and the Raging Thunder website does not specify which of these its guides take. The Raging Thunder (2005) website says that Rescue 3 Australia is a subsidiary of Raging Thunder and a franchise of Rescue 3 International. Rescue 3 International (2005) lists three Australian instructors, including one in Cairns, who is indeed listed under Raging Thunder.

### Marketing

Whitewater rafting on the Tully is a heavily marketed 1-day adventure activity out of Cairns, which is itself a heavily marketed adventure tourism destination in Australia. As with most whitewater raft trips, marketing focuses on the larger rapids and aims to project an image of thrills and spills. Social components are also featured. Both companies advertise that the 1-day Tully River raft trip is 'Australia's best one-day rafting adventure' (R'n'R, 2005) or even that the Tully 'has a reputation as the best rafting river in Australia and New Zealand'. Commercial rafting operators elsewhere in Australia, however, and especially in New Zealand, would no doubt disagree quite strongly. This would therefore seem to be somewhat of an exaggeration. Both companies advertise their respective cafés, including oppor-tunities to purchase videos of the trip.

## Kawarau River, New Zealand: Various Operators

### Place

The Kawarau River runs out of Lake Wakatipu near Queenstown in New Zealand's South Island. The section used for commercial rafting and river sledging is close to Queenstown and contains only four named rapids, with names such as Chinese Dogleg and Do Little Do Nothing. The water is rather cold, and the surrounding area is farmland.

Below the commercial rafting section are several more difficult sections sometimes paddled by private recreational kayakers. The Roaring Meg section is notable for a whirlpool-filled gorge and rapids such as Maneater. The Citroen section has one major rapid, Citroen itself. Most fearsome is the Nevis Bluff section, run only by the most extreme of kayakers. Another very difficult rapid further downstream, Sargood's Weir, was flooded by a hydroelectric dam in 1993.

### Operator

The three main commercial raft tour operators on the Kawarau are Challenge Rafting (2005), Queenstown Rafting (2005) and Extreme Green Rafting (2005). All of these are based in Queenstown and are specialist raft companies. According to Cater (Chapter 24, this volume), since 1998 Challenge Rafting has acted only as a retail marketing company, with the actual rafting operations subcontracted to Queenstown Rafting. They do also offer other activities such as jetboating, bungee jumping and helicopter flights in 'combo' packages with rafting trips, but generally these other activities are actually operated by separate specialist companies. Challenge Rafting offers 1-day raft tours on the Kawarau and Shotover Rivers; Queenstown Rafting also offers a 3-day trip on the Landsborough River. Extreme Green also offers services to the film industry.

## Activity

The Kawarau raft trip is a half-day activity taking about 4 h, with departures from Queenstown twice daily. Clients are assembled at a riverside depot, kitted out with wetsuits and safety gear and driven to the put-in point. After the raft run they are driven back for showers and snacks.

## Equipment

The major companies use paddle rafts with seven clients and one guide per raft. They provide wetsuits and booties, spray jackets, lifejackets and helmets. Clients need bring only swimsuits and a towel.

## Accommodation

The tour does not include any accommodation. Clients stay in Queenstown. Clients on the morning tours are picked up from their hotels; those on afternoon tours assemble at the operators' Queenstown retail booking offices and retail shopfronts.

## Statistics

Each raft carries one guide and seven clients. Most trips include numerous rafts. The trip takes about 4 h in total. Cost is about NZD140 per person, currently around US$98.

## Access

Access to and from the river is by road, in the tour operators' buses from Queenstown. Any permits are arranged by the operators.

## Community

Many Queenstown residents make their living from tourism. The town is well supplied with tourist accommodation and restaurants. Winter activities focus on nearby ski resorts. Summer activities include a wide range of adventure tours, rafting included. Tourists interact with locals mostly where the latter are employed in the tour companies concerned – but that is quite a high proportion of the town's inhabitants.

## Experience

The half-day Kawarau raft trip is generally seen as a beginner's trip, promoted as an introduction to whitewater rafting. The run is classified on the Challenge Rafting website as Class III–V, and the Extreme Green website as III–IV, which seems more accurate. It would, perhaps, generally be considered as a high-volume Class III+. Even so, the final rapid, Chinese Dogleg, is 400 m long and contains some waves, holes and stoppers substantial enough to generate a considerable adrenalin burst for most rafting clients. The trip is taken at high speed from start to finish, including kit-out and safety briefing, and most clients are probably focused more on the rapids than the rest of the river experience.

## Environment

The Kawarau River flows through an agricultural landscape and is dammed downstream for hydroelectric power generation. Any environmental impacts from river rafting are negligible in comparison. The principal concern is to ensure that clients do not drop litter overboard. There is a toilet at the parking area near the put-in.

## Safety

All operators provide routine safety equipment, including wetsuits for warmth and buoyancy as well as lifejackets and helmets. All give safety briefings at the outset. Extreme Green, Challenge Rafting and probably also Queenstown Rafting, recommend that for safety reasons clients should be at least 13 years old. Safety kayakers are apparently not used, but the same section of the Kawarau is also run by river sledges, so it is probably reasonable to assume that anyone falling out will float well enough till rescued. The Extreme Green website contains more detailed safety information than the others.

## Marketing

Queenstown is marketed as 'the adventure capital of the world' (Challenge Rafting, 2005), and the Kawarau as 'the largest-volume river rafted commercially in New Zealand' (Queenstown Rafting, 2005). These claims may seem grandiose, but the latter is probably correct, and even the former is not unreasonable (Cater, Chapter 24). Both companies advertise their endorsement by Qualmark, the main New Zealand quality certification agency. Neither says much about the rafting experience except that it is exciting, which is accurate enough.

# Shotover River, New Zealand: Various Operators

### Place

The Shotover River is a fast medium-volume river near Queenstown. Its lower stretches, up to the Oxenbridge Tunnel and Cascade Rapid, are used by jetboat tours. The section above this, from the Skippers Canyon Bridge to the tunnel, is used for commercial rafting. It contains six major rapids, some of them with multiple and individually named components, and many smaller rapids. Most of the river runs through a gorge, and the water is cold.

## Operators

The same companies that offer commercial raft tips on the Kawarau River (as above) also offer trips on the Shotover: Queenstown Rafting (2005), Challenge Rafting (2005) and Extreme Green Rafting (2005).

## Activity

One-day raft trips on the Shotover are similar in structure to those on the Kawarau. The drive to the put-in is further and more difficult, down the steep Skippers Canyon dirt road cut originally for gold mining. The take-out is immediately below Cascade Falls at the exit of the Oxenbridge Tunnel, not far from town. Rapids are Class III–V, and include the infamous Mother section with individual rapids such as Toilet, a deep and remarkably retentive whirlpool.

## Equipment

Major tour companies use paddle rafts with seven clients and one guide per raft. They provide wetsuits and booties, spray jackets, lifejackets and helmets. Clients need bring only a swimsuit and a towel.

## Accommodation

This is a half-day trip and does not include accommodation. Clients stay in Queenstown.

## Statistics

The trip takes 4.5–5 h overall and there are two launches per day. Paddle rafts carry seven clients and one guide. There are generally many rafts on each trip. The price is about NZD150 per person (US$105). Heli-rafting costs about NZD260 (US$180) per person.

## Access

Access in summer is along a steep, narrow dirt road, the Skippers Canyon road. In winter this road is closed, but both operators offer helicopter access for only NZD60 more than the summer drive-in price. Helicopter access is also available in summer. The helicopter departs from the helipad at Coronet Peak ski field near Queenstown.

## Experience

Rafting on the Shotover River is a more extended experience than the Kawarau. The Skippers Canyon road itself is enough to raise adrenalin levels for most clients. There are more rapids than on the Kawarau, and the narrow, rock-lined gorge seems more forbidding than the wide, tree-fringed Kawarau. At the end of the run the river plunges into a long tunnel barely wider than the rafts, and at the end of the tunnel is a short, sloping waterfall, the Cascade, with a pinnacle rock in the middle that must be avoided. Falling out of the raft in the more difficult rapids could potentially have serious consequences. Overall the excitement level is higher than on the Kawarau. In one kayak run we found an entire goat skeleton caught in the rocks by its horns. This was a sober reminder!

## Environment

This section of the Shotover River suffered major impacts from past gold mining, and rafting has negligible impacts in comparison.

## Safety

There are more, and more varied, hazards on the Shotover than the Kawarau. Rafting operators generally have an excellent safety record, but there have been several deaths. Two rafting clients drowned in 1995, and another in 2001. Additional details on these deaths are provided by Cater (Chapter 24). The Extreme Green Rafting (2005) website specifies that 'all river trips operate in compliance with the *Code of Practice for the Safety of Commercial Rafting* as required by the *Maritime Safety Act*'. Presumably this is also required for the other commercial rafting operators on those rivers, but there is more emphasis on this issue in the Extreme Green website.

## Marketing

All three operators market Shotover River raft trips in almost identical terms to Kawarau River trips, with little changed but the names of the rapids.

# Rangitata River, New Zealand: Rangitata Rafts

### Place

The Rangitata River is about 2 h drive from Christchurch in New Zealand's South Island. It flows through sheep-farming country, starting in open gravel bars but also passing through a short gorge section known for its Class IV and V rapids.

### Operator

Rangitata Rafts (2005) operates from its own lodge near the take-out for the 1-day raft run. It specializes solely on this particular river.

## Activity

The Rangitata is run as a 1-day trip with around 3 h on the river. The company picks up its clients in Christchurch in the morning, reaching the river lodge in time for an early lunch. After running the river there is a barbecue and guests are back in Christchurch around 7 or 8 pm.

## Equipment

The company provides all equipment including wetsuits, spray jackets, lifejackets, booties, helmets and a polypropylene underlayer on colder days. Paddle rafts are used, with seven clients and one guide each.

## Accommodation

Accommodation is not included in the trip. Most clients stay in Christchurch. Self-drive clients, however, can stay in the Rangitata Rafts lodge, which costs NZD15 per person in the main dormitory or NZD19 per person in a double room.

## Statistics

The trip takes around 12 h in total, of which 3 h are on the river. The price is NZD162 (US$115) per person, including transport from Christchurch (Rangitata Rafts, 2005). Client-to-guide ratio is 7:1.

## Access

Access to the river base is by road, and from the base to the put-in in the operator's bus across a private farm, by special arrangement.

## Community

There is little interaction with the local farming community, except via supplies for the barbecue. Presumably the farmer also receives some compensation for access to the river across his land.

## Experience

This is a short, high-intensity trip focusing on paddling and rapids. There are also good opportunities for clients to socialize both before and after the rafting itself. The Rangitata Raft operation is particularly well organized and clients are ushered through the wetsuit fitting room and on to the river very quickly and efficiently.

## Environment

Impacts are minimal. The lodge is heated by a large wood fire.

## Safety

The company is registered with the New Zealand Rafting Association, supplies all necessary safety equipment and uses highly competent guides.

## Marketing

Rangitata Rafts is an independent operation, and its marketing relies largely on its own brochures, website and links and references in other New Zealand tourism marketing materials at regional and national scales. The Rangitata Valley was used to film one of the sites in the *Lord of the Rings* trilogy, and this has helped to promote the area recently. In addition, the Rangitata is accessible as a day trip directly from Christchurch, so tourists who do not plan to visit the adventure tourism destination of Queenstown can still enjoy a day's Class V rafting on the Rangitata.

# 7 Seakayaking

Ralf Buckley, Southern Sea Ventures, Svalbard. Photo Al Bakker.

Natural High, Abel Tasman, New Zealand. Photo Carl Cater.

## Sector Structure

Seakayaking has long been a popular activity in North America, perhaps because the fully decked kayak propelled with a double-bladed paddle was first invented by the Inuit peoples of the Arctic region. Over the past two decades, production-model seakayaks made from fibreglass, and later from various blow- or rotation-moulded plastics, have become easier and cheaper to obtain, and the popularity of recreational seakayaking has grown accordingly worldwide. Commercial seakayaking tours are available from Alaska to Australia and beyond, and range from half-day introductory paddles to extended trips lasting several weeks. They range from relatively relaxed and low-risk trips in the warm waters of Fiji or Samoa to Arctic areas such as Svalbard, Greenland and even Ellesmere Island.

Whilst seakayaks themselves are perhaps the epitome of human-powered ocean travel, almost everywhere that seakayak tours currently operate is also accessible to powered watercraft, and few if any seakayak tours can be treated as true wilderness experiences. Seakayaking areas along the coast of Abel Tasman National Park in New Zealand, for example, are constantly traversed by water taxis and private recreational boats, as well as several commercial seakayak companies. Waters around Hinchinbrook Island in subtropical Queensland, Australia are used widely by local recreational fishermen. Many of the San Juan Islands off the coast of Washington State in the Pacific Northwest of the USA, an area used by commercial seakayak tours searching for orcas, are also accessed by local residents with large speedboats who maintain residential houses or second homes on some of these islands.

In Samoa, Fiji or the Solomon Islands, there are far fewer motorized vessels, but there are local villagers along the coasts and island shores. Many of the seakayak areas of southwest Alaska are national parks, and seakayakers share the shores and small islets only with seals and bears. In Prince William Sound, however, there are also commercial and recreational fishing boats, and in Glacier Bay and Admiralty Sound there are large tour boats and scenic overflights. Even at Pond Inlet at the northern tip of Baffin Island in the Canadian High Arctic, seakayakers are passed at intervals by large speedboats owned by local Inuit residents out hunting. Only in the Arctic waters north of Norway's Svalbard are seakayakers completely undisturbed by local boats. To get to that area, however, seakayakers need support from their own expedition cruise vessel, which operates outboard-powered inflatables as well as seakayaks.

From a participant perspective, seakayaking in southwest Alaska certainly has a wilderness feel; and seakayaking in the High Arctic, where the weather is potentially more severe and drysuits are a standard safety precaution, seems even more remote. Even though summer weather is relatively benign, winds and waves can whip up suddenly, tidal currents and chop can be strong, kayakers can become trapped within large expanses of floating ice, and storms or poor visibility can potentially leave one confined to camp for several days.

Most of the time, seakayaking depends more on stamina than skill. There may indeed be moments when balance and timing are critical, such as surfing on a steep following sea, or landing and leaving a lee shore with breaking waves. Close encounters with whales can also raise adrenalin levels on occasion, depending on the whales' behaviour. Most of the time, however, the rewards of seakayaking are in quiet and contemplative access to remote coastlines, islands or ice floes, and the opportunities to see sea otters and seabird colonies, whales and walrus, islands and icebergs, coral reefs and crystal waters. Whilst seakayaking is certainly sold as an adventure tourism activity, therefore, as with most such activities there is a balance between challenge and contemplation that is dependent on the place and the participants.

Seakayak designs and technologies have diversified considerably over recent decades. Well-made and seaworthy two-person collapsible kayaks, with a wooden frame and a heavy-duty rubberized fabric skin, were available half a century or more ago from manufacturers such as Klepper®. Some of these, such as the Klepper Aerius®, were even equipped for sailing with a small gaff-rigged sail, leeboards, air-filled buoyancy tubes along the gunwales, and a sliding seat for balance, taking the place of a trapeze on sailing dinghy. My earliest kayaking experiences, at the age of about four, were in such a craft. Similar designs are still on sale, manufactured both by Klepper® and by the North American company Feathercraft®. The materials have been modernized somewhat, with aluminium frames and new plastic composites for the skin, but the basic design still follows that of the traditional Inuit kayak.

Once fibreglass mats, resins and lay-up moulding construction methods became available in the middle of the last century, hardshell fibreglass seakayaks gradually gained prominence, except in remote locations where collapsibility is essential for transport, e.g. in small aircraft. The details of fibreglass designs improved slowly, e.g. with the use of independent watertight compartments with waterproof hatches, bucket seats with backrests, gel coats for reduced hull drag, hinged rudders that can be raised and lowered with a cord, and efficient lightweight paddles with carbon-fibre construction and wing-style blade profiles.

In the late part of the 20th century, fibreglass seakayaks were gradually overtaken by mass-produced moulded plastic models. These are manufactured using similar methods and materials to modern whitewater kayaks, and often by the same companies. They are similar in shape to their fibreglass predecessors but easier to produce in quantity, to supply the much expanded market demand. Some manufacturers also began to produce so-called sit-on-top kayaks, where the paddler sits in a seat-shaped external well moulded into the boat's deck, rather than sitting inside the hull on a seat attached to the hull's floor.

Sit-on-top designs can be capsized and righted without taking water even if the paddler falls off. A conventional kayak can be rolled without taking water as long as it is fitted with a spraydeck, backrest, footrest and thigh braces, is not too wide or heavily laden, and its paddler or paddlers have sufficient skill. In practice, however, a double seakayak fully loaded for a multi-day expedition is so heavy that realistically it cannot be rolled even by experienced kayakers, so in the event of a capsize the paddlers must bail out, right the boat using their paddles and paddle floats, and then bale water out of the hull. Even with independent water-tight compartments or a paddling sock as described under the Prince William Sound case study below, this is a tedious and potentially risky process.

Until recently, sit-on-top seakayaks had three major disadvantages. First, the paddler is fully exposed to the elements rather than protected in the boat's hull, so sit-on-tops were seen as only suitable for warm tropical water. As drysuits have become more generally available and affordable in recent years, however, this no longer presents an insurmountable difficulty. Secondly, since they were seen as inexpert family fun craft for use on flat water, rather than serious seakayaks, the designs actually produced were short, stable and very slow. Racing surf skis, however, also have sit-on-top seats, but are extremely long, narrow and fast, so kayak manufacturers came to appreciate that a sit-on-top seat is not necessarily a barrier to performance.

Thirdly, it is only very recently that sit-on-top designs have begun to incorporate effective footrests, backrests and thigh straps that serve the same function as thigh braces. Waist straps have been fitted for some time, but these alone do not provide the degree of control needed for a paddler to brace a narrow kayak in a rough sea. With new hull and strap designs as well as drysuits, however, it seems quite possible that sit-on-top seakayaks could soon become a widespread alternative to conventional designs even at the high-performance and expedition end of the spectrum.

As with most forms of adventure tourism, the majority of the commercial market consists of short trips for unskilled clients at heavily frequented destinations. The case study on Abel Tasman National Park in New Zealand, described below, provides an example. At the other end of the market are low-volume, high-price, long-duration seakayak trips in remote areas such as the High Arctic. Intermediate between these extremes are multi-day seakayak camping trips in warmer parts of the world, exemplified here by the case studies from Hinchinbrook Island in Australia and the Yasawa Islands in Fiji. Comparable tours are offered in many other parts of the world.

## Baffin Island, Canada: Blackfeather Inc.

### Place

Baffin Island is a large island in northeastern Canada. It forms part of the Province of Nunavut, northwest of the Province of Quebec. Its northern end reaches to about 74°N, well north of the Arctic Circle. It is separated by a large channel, Lancaster Sound, from Devon and Ellesmere Islands to the north. The northern tip of Baffin Island is dissected by a number of smaller sounds that connect into Lancaster Sound. The northeastern corner forms a separate island, Bylot Island, separated from Baffin Island by Eclipse Sound. All of these Sounds are icebound for most of the year, and this ice was the major barrier to the search for a North-West Passage in historical times. The ice breaks up in summer and navigation is generally possible for a month or so in August, though caution is needed because of occasional drifting icebergs and 'growlers', which are small and almost completely submerged chunks of floating ice.

The main settlement on the north coast of Baffin Island is at Pond Inlet, a community of several hundred people with an airport, telecommunications, local government and municipal buildings, and a rather basic but highly expensive 'hotel'. Pond Inlet serves as the base for oil exploration companies and government agencies operating in the area, and the winter residence for local Inuit communities. In summer, however, many of the Inuit move out of town to camps on the shores of various sounds, accessed by boat. Many families own seaworthy 6–8 m outboard-powered half-cabin boats which are used for fishing and access to hunting sites. There are several tour operators based in Pond Inlet, offering snowmobile trips to the edge of the ice floe in spring, or boat trips during late summer. There is also a large food and equipment store.

### Operator

Blackfeather Inc., based at Parry Sound, Ontario, offers a range of canoeing and seakayaking tours throughout Canada (Blackfeather Inc., 2005). Their website previously listed several small-group seakayak itineraries out of Pond Inlet, but the trip described here is currently the only one featured in this area. It is billed as 'In Search of the Narwhal' (Blackfeather Inc., 2005).

## Activity

The starting point for the commercial seakayak tour is in Pond Inlet, but in practice guides, clients and gear take the same flights from and to Ottawa. Neither these flights, nor the overnight accommodation in the Pond Inlet 'hotel' at the beginning and end of the trip, are included in the trip price.

The day after arrival, guides and clients are ferried by chartered high-speed fishing boats, along with boats, gear and food, to a beach at the head of Koluctoo Bay in Eclipse Sound some 5 h away. The charter boats depart and the group assembles the seakayaks and camps overnight. Starting the following morning, the group paddles through the sounds back to Pond Inlet, choosing an appropriate campsite each evening. The itinerary allows for at most 2 lay-over days in case of bad weather. Most of each day is spent either in the kayaks, loading and unloading them, or making or breaking camp. The guides do most of the cooking, but the guests do the washing up.

## Equipment

The tour uses Feathercraft® collapsible kayaks, two-person boats for the clients and one-person for the guides. These are arguably the best, and certainly the most expensive, brand of collapsible seakayak which is commercially available worldwide. Assembly and disassembly is relatively complex and must be carried out in precisely the correct sequence to avoid damaging the skin and frame.

The kayaks, paddles, ancillary components, camping equipment, safety gear and clothing, and food and cooking equipment are flown to Pond Inlet specifically for the trip, carried as excess baggage by guides and clients. Since everything has to be carried in the boats whilst at sea, both weight and volume are in any event restricted to the minimum needed for safe survival. The operator provides cooking equipment and issues each guest with an insulated mug. Clients are responsible for their own tents, sleeping bags and other camping equipment, and all clothing, including that worn whilst paddling.

Drysuits are strongly recommended since the sea is extremely cold and the weather can include strong winds, rain, sleet and snow. One of the guides brought a rifle for protection against possible polar bear attacks whilst in camp. The guides also had a radio, though they did not use this in front of the clients. The operating company provides paddles and life-jackets, but clients may bring their own if they prefer, and some do.

## Accommodation

Accommodation is in the clients' own tents throughout the entire trip. Clients and guides must arrive at Pond Inlet the night before the trip starts, and are responsible for their own accommodation and food, for which there are rather limited options. In practice most clients stay at the Pond Inlet 'hotel', which is in fact a collection of demountable prefabricated trailers with very small double rooms, similar to the accommodation used in oil exploration camps.

The hotel is locally owned, and caters principally to staff and personnel from government agencies, construction and maintenance crews, and geological and geophysical exploration teams. It is probably used only for a short season, but even so, prices are exorbitant relative to the service provided, even in such a remote location. No doubt this is effectively a monopoly rent, and perceived as a subsidy to locals, but it is certainly a major disincentive for tourism. At the end of the Blackfeather seakayak tour, fortunately, it is possible to camp near a beach a little out of town, a much more pleasant location.

During the trip itself, campsites varied considerably. There were flat beaches of coarse gravel, terraces of dwarf tundra vegetation, but also a swamp and a narrow, sloping and irregular raised beach of round fist- to head-sized rocks. This last was somewhat of an emergency campsite. We were fortunate that the wind blew a small iceberg onshore overnight, since this grounded a small distance from the beach and provided a narrow sheltered channel where we could launch the boats in safety the next morning.

## Statistics

On the trip in which I took part there were four clients and two guides, a ratio of 2:1. The total length of the trip is 16 days, of which about 11 are spent kayaking. The current price is CAD3695 per person, or about US$175 per person per day. Flights from Ottawa, and accommodation in Pond Inlet, are in addition to this.

## Access

All permits are handled by the operating company. Permits are presumably needed both from the local community and the provincial government. Special permits may also be needed for the radio and firearms.

## Community

Tourism seems to be a very minor activity as yet for the majority of the Pond Inlet community. Resource extraction and government programmes, probably funded by both federal and provincial agencies, seem to provide the economic mainstay. There appears to be a considerable degree of autonomy for the local Inuit community, and hunting and fishing are still major activities. Pond Inlet itself, however, has schools, sporting facilities, a library with sponsored Internet-connected computers, and an indoor shopping mall which is relatively small but heavily patronized.

Economic inputs to the local community through the Blackfeather tour include: the costs of accommodation in town as outlined above; charter fees paid to two fishing boat operators for high-speed ferries to the put-in point; and direct expenditure by clients on souvenirs, film, meals and other food. In addition, tours such as these fill seats and cargo space in scheduled flights to and from Pond Inlet, which helps to maintain a commercially viable scheduled air service for local residents.

Some members of the local community still hunt narwhal, illegally as well as legally (Buckley, 2005b). Clearly, such hunting makes it much less likely that tourists will get good narwhal sightings. One might hence expect a degree of internal conflict between community members engaged in tourism and those engaged in hunting. In reality, however, it seems that it may well be the same individuals engaged in both, using the same boats, and even combining narwhal hunting into the same trip as a seakayaker tour shuttle. Hence it would appear that money and perhaps also social status associated with hunting narwhal, even illegally, outweigh income associated with tourism, at least for boat owners. Accommodation operators might feel differently, but as yet it appears that tourism makes up only a very small proportion of their total income.

## Experience

The comfort, excitement and satisfaction experienced by individual clients on any adventure tour depend on the clients' prior skills and experience, inter-group dynamics, the skills and personalities of the guides, and the vagaries of the weather. They are therefore likely to vary much more than most other aspects from one trip to the next. When I took part in this trip there were only four clients, including myself, and two guides. Initially there was also a fifth client who had brought his own kayak, a Feathercraft® single. This boat was rather old and in disrepair, however, and ultimately he decided not to take part in the main tour.

The weather was generally good, we did see narwhal and the clients appeared generally satisfied with their experiences. One of the clients, despite previous seakayaking experience in Greenland, seemed somewhat alarmed when we had to round a headland with a sizeable following sea. He was the only person without a drysuit. He was also alarmed on the one occasion where we were able to approach a narwhal closely, with extreme caution so as not to provoke it to dive. Two of the clients were an older couple who seemed relatively uninterested in narwhal but were determined to paddle right back to the township of Pond Inlet, even though the rest of us were perfectly satisfied with the take-out and campsite at a beach a few kilometres short of town.

Both of the guides were clearly competent, but the leader was remarkably dictatorial both to his colleague and the clients. For example, he insisted on stopping for lunch at a set time every day irrespective of weather and conditions, even though the clients repeatedly made it clear that they would prefer to remain in the boats until they reached camp for the day. The same guide also gave one of the clients what can only be described as a thinly veiled threat at one point. There was no excuse for this, particularly since it took place on shore, there was no emergency and no one was in danger. Other than this, the guides' judgement and navigation seemed fine, and their campsite selection and cooking generally were good. They were very quick, however, to accept a client offer to wash up, and this became part of the routine for all clients. Under Arctic conditions this is not a very enjoyable task, particularly after dark. Client satisfaction might hence have been increased if they were relieved of this task.

From my own perspective, but apparently not the other clients', the principal purpose of the trip was to watch narwhal, which are a rare and beautiful whale found only at very few sites worldwide. Paddling a seakayak day after day was a means to travel quietly through areas where narwhal might be found, and to approach them cautiously once we found them. Seakayaking was not an end in itself, since one can do that in lakes and oceans worldwide. For the other clients, however, it appears that paddling the boat was the principal goal, and seeing narwhal an incidental bonus. We did indeed see narwhal, but only near our first camp at the initial drop-off point. My own choice would certainly have been to remain in this area for several days, paddle half the way back to Pond Inlet, and then pay an extra US$100 per person for a fishing boat to ferry us back the remaining distance. The other clients, however, were not keen on this option. The trip thus became a marathon paddle, largely an exercise in hard labour rather than the opportunity to enjoy the High Arctic environment and its inhabitants.

Another factor of particular concern to myself, but perhaps not to the other clients, was that because of poaching, the narwhal were extremely wary of boats and were accordingly quite difficult to approach closely. We were able to do so only once, with considerable care. To see a narwhal at close quarters is certainly a lifetime experience, and I for one would repeat the entire trip, will all its deficiencies, in order to do so again. It is only regrettable that my paddling partner, finally seeing a narwhal so close, began to backpaddle in panic. Of course, the narwhal dived immediately and did not return.

## Environment

Minimal-impact camping practices such as those outlined by Buckley (1999) were followed routinely by the entire group. These include, for example, selecting low-impact campsites; minimizing trampling; using fuel stoves rather than fires; packing out all litter; and burying toilet waste in catholes. Relative to other human activities in this area, any direct impacts from this seakayaking tour were negligible. Like any such tour in a remote area, there was a significant indirect global environmental impact associated with air travel to the starting point.

Most significant for this particular tour, however, are issues associated with the conservation of Arctic marine mammals, particularly narwhal. Currently, it seems that tourism has little or no impact on narwhal poaching. On occasion, seakayak charters may cover fuel costs for narwhal hunts; but the hunts would probably take place in any event, given the extremely high cash value of narwhal tusks and the high social value of narwhal blubber amongst the Inuit.

In some parts of the world, wildlife tourism has helped to reduce the killing of wildlife by local communities, if tourism can generate more value for the individual locals concerned from a live animal than they can obtain from a dead one. Unless there is a very large tourism industry associated with well-enforced protection of endangered species, however, financial incentives from tourism are not sufficient to prevent poaching of species for which there is a high-value international black market in specific body parts, such as narwhal tusks.

## Safety

The High Arctic is a relatively risky environment, even in summer. A multi-day seakayak expedition needs to be fully self-contained and this was indeed the case for the Blackfeather tour. The allowance for bad-weather lay-over and rest days was relatively short, only 2 days, but this proved sufficient in practice. If we had been grounded by storms we could have survived much longer – we would only have missed our plane.

The equipment supplied by the tour operator, notably the kayaks themselves, was of high quality and well-maintained. Drysuits were recommended but not mandatory. Clients were expected to have clothing and camping equipment appropriate for Arctic conditions. Few participants, however, had neoprene or similar hoods, though these can be critical for survival in cold-water immersion such as an Arctic capsize.

The group had a rifle, flares and one radio, but did not have handheld radios to maintain contact between kayaks in case one was separated from the group in bad weather. The group did not practice capsize safety procedures. There was no briefing on what to do if we saw a polar bear, but they are apparently not common in this area and as it turned out, we did not see one. Given the small size of the group and the previous experience of the participants, safety procedures were probably sufficient and appropriate.

## Marketing

The main aspects of the tour which feature in the company's marketing materials (Blackfeather Inc., 2005) are: a fully guided and catered tour; a multi-day seakayaking expedition; the opportunity to experience High Arctic environments; and a good probability of seeing narwhal.

The principal distinguishing factor is the likelihood of seeing narwhal. There are many other commercial seakayaking tours in Arctic environments, including several in the High Arctic and some which take place at even higher latitudes than this one. Whilst several mention that narwhal may be seen on occasion (e.g. Whitney and Smith Expeditions, 2005), there seem to be only two well-known locations where narwhal sightings are relatively common: Scoresby Sund on the central eastern coast of Greenland, and Eclipse Sound, Lancaster Sound and nearby areas at the northern tip of Baffin Island.

Judging from my own experience of this tour, therefore, it does indeed fulfil the company's marketing claims, though as noted above, once we had sighted narwhal neither the guides nor the other clients seemed particularly interested in watching them for any extended period, which personally I found disappointing.

## Svalbard, Norway: Southern Sea Ventures and Aurora Expeditions

### Place

Svalbard is an archipelago in the High Arctic north of Norway. It is also known as Spitzbergen, though technically that is the name of the largest single island in the archipelago. Svalbard is part of Norway, though there are also some Russian settlements on the eastern side, remnants of a past period when it was largely in Russian hands. The principal economic activity is mining. The principal settlement, Longyearbyen on the southwestern corner, is accessible by air from Tromsø in northern Norway. Svalbard was apparently an adventure tourism destination for wealthy travellers throughout the late 19th century and subsequently (Marsh, 2000).

Because of the warmer waters of the north-flowing Gulf Stream, there is much more open ocean around Svalbard than around areas at corresponding latitudes north of Russia or Canada. This allows several tours to offer expedition-style cruises around the southern and western parts of the archipelago, including a circumnavigation of Spitzbergen, if ice conditions allow. At least one such company also offers a ship-supported seakayaking option, described here.

## Operator

Aurora Expeditions (2005) is based in Sydney, Australia but specializes in medium-scale expedition-style polar ship cruises. On their circumnavigation of Spitzbergen, they offer the opportunity to travel by seakayak instead of outboard-powered inflatables for local off-ship excursions during the day. This is an optional extra at additional cost. The seakayaking component is run by a separate company, Southern Sea Ventures (2005), which is based in Queensland, Australia and also offers seakayaking tours in various South Pacific nations. For the Svalbard tour, Aurora Expeditions sells the seakayaking option as part of its own package, even though the boats, equipment and guides are provided by Southern Sea Ventures. Southern Sea Ventures also sells the entire package, including the Aurora Expedition components, through its own website and under its own name.

## Activity

This case study focuses only on the seakayaking component. The ship-based component is described separately in Chapter 9. Clients on the seakayaking option also pay the full price for the Aurora Expeditions tour and enjoy the same itinerary and privileges as the other passengers. Indeed, each day they have the choice whether to take up their seakayaking option, or join the other passengers in the inflatables. In general, the inflatables can travel further and faster, whereas the kayaks travel more slowly but more quietly.

Seakayaks can approach some wildlife species more closely, notably swimming seabirds. For others, such as cliff-nesting seabirds or hauled-out walrus, however, inflatables can generally approach just as close, and certainly provide a more stable platform for telephoto photography. The principal advantage of the seakayaks, therefore, is the opportunity to travel silently through the Arctic landscape, and to choose one's own routes amidst the icebergs or along the shores.

Of course, only a proportion of participants perceive a net advantage in travelling under one's own pace and power; and in practice, because of the deck space required and the additional launching time, only about 20% of cruise clients (10 of 54) can be accommodated in seakayaks. In addition, whilst the main expedition cruise vessel, the inflatables, radio and GPS provide a much higher level of comfort and safety to the seakayakers than they would have in a self-supported seakayak expedition, a certain degree of fitness is still needed to be able to paddle a kayak for several hours a day, even slowly. In practice, most clients on the Aurora Expeditions tour would be able to paddle seakayaks if they chose, but only a small proportion have the inclination.

## Equipment

The seakayaks used are a rigid plastic production model. Most of the clients paddle in double kayaks, with the guide and sometimes one client in single kayaks. The boats are stacked on the stern deck of the expedition cruise vessel when not in use. To launch the kayaks, an inflatable boat is lowered from the main vessel using davits, and the kayaks are passed down one at a time. Two of the vessel's crew hold each kayak in position alongside the inflatable, and if necessary assist the clients to embark and fasten their sprayskirts. Once all the kayaks are launched, the group starts paddling under the direction of the guide. The guide and one client carry radios which are in contact with the ship and each other, and the group also has a GPS to assist in navigation, assessing distances and for safety in the event of fog or unexpectedly strong wind or currents. Southern Sea Ventures also provides all sea-kayakers with rubberized nylon drysuits, as well as lifejackets and other kayak gear.

## Accommodation

Accommodation is on board the expedition cruise vessel, a converted Russian polar research ship. Further detail is provided in the case study on the Aurora Expeditions cruise itself.

## Statistics

A maximum of ten seakayaking places are available. The limit is set by factors such as: demand for the seakayaking option; the additional time taken to launch the seakayaks; storage space on the stern deck; and cabin space for the seakayaking guide or guides. The client-to-guide ratio was 10:1. In practice, however, most trips probably have at least one relatively experienced seakayaker who acts as an informal guide. There are thus four double kayaks, with one single kayak ahead and one astern. The overall circumnavigation of Spitzbergen takes 11 days from Longyearbyen, with at least 1 day's additional travel to and from Oslo at either end, and additional days' travel for individual clients to and from Oslo.

Seakayaking is dependent on the main vessel's position, weather and other conditions, but is generally available on 7 or 8 days in total. The additional price for the seakayaking option is AUD1075 (approx. US$800) per person. Added to this, however, is the cost for the Aurora Expeditions tour, air travel to and from Longyearbyen, and overnight accommodation in Oslo and Longyearbyen, which is relatively expensive. The cruise component alone costs AUD4250–7250 per person, depending on the class of cabin. Including these components, the total daily cost is in the high price range, around US$400 per person per day.

## Access

The Svalbard coastline, particularly to the north, is accessible only in an ice-breaking or ice-strengthened vessel. An unsupported seakayak voyage in this area would be a great deal more difficult, because of distances, weather and the need to ship kayaks to Longyearbyen. For most of the circumnavigation, the vessel is close to the coastline, and hence within Norwegian territorial waters.

## Community

Most of the population of Svalbard lives at Longyearbyen. There are other isolated settlements, but the expedition cruise does not visit them. There are occasionally used hunting and fishing huts, but we did not see any occupied. Our only interactions with local residents were in Longyearbyen itself, where we found everyone to be extremely helpful and friendly.

Relatively little of the total expenditure associated with this trip is spent in Svalbard: the principal component is accommodation for 3 nights, one at the start of the trip and two at the end, since there is a lay-over day before the plane departs. Norway is a wealthy nation, and not dependent on tourism. Various 1-day tours are available from Longyearbyen, however, and one can also hike on to a nearby mountain directly from town.

Because of the potential risk of polar bear attack, there is a local municipal rule that hikers leaving town must carry a heavy-calibre rifle or a shotgun loaded with slugs. Rifles and ammunition are available for rent from the town's principal supermarket, on production of a valid gun licence. On our lay-over day, however, the supermarket was closed. Learning of this difficulty, the town's one taxi driver kindly loaned me one of his own guns so that I could still go hiking, asking me only to leave it at the restaurant in the principal hotel when I returned. Such generosity to a complete stranger is a remarkable recommendation for the friendliness of the local community.

## Experience

Most of the clients had apparently done little or no seakayaking previously, but all of them seemed to enjoy the experience very much. On 1 or 2 days, one or two of the clients opted to make excursions in the inflatables rather than the kayaks, but this was more for ease of photography rather than any dissatisfaction with seakayaking. On most days, the seakayaks were generally some distance from the inflatables, and were not bothered by the sound of the outboard motors.

There was one occasion when kayaks and inflatables were exploring the same inlet and sighted a polar bear on shore, and one of the Russian crewmembers drove an inflatable at speed past all the other boats, spoiling the experience somewhat for the other passengers. This, however, was an exception. We did not kayak in any rough seas or encounter any dangerous or threatening circumstances, and none of the clients seemed frightened or uncomfortable.

At the most northerly point of our circumnavigation, amidst floating ice at the floe edge of the main Arctic icecap, we had a day's paddling over glassy waters under calm sunny skies, threading our way between dazzling white icebergs, deep blue ice caves and overhangs, and smaller 'growlers' of shining transparent ice carved into fantastic fluted shapes. On that day in particular, the silence of the seakayaks provided clients with an unforgettable experience. We did not see any polar bears swimming near the seakayaks, which was probably just as well. We did see polar bears on shore, and seals and walruses in the water and, though by no means heart-stopping, these encounters certainly focused all the paddlers' attention.

## Environment

Environmental management for the support vessel is considered separately under the Aurora Expeditions case study. The seakayaking clients contributed pro rata to the impacts of the support vessel. Seakayaking itself has little or no impact on water quality and produces far less noise than the outboard motors of the inflatables. Kayakers may disturb seabirds and marine mammals through visual proximity or human voices. Smaller seabirds such as murres generally kept at least 5 m from the kayaks, and seals stayed a little further away. There was no indication that the seakayaks disrupted breeding by cliff-nesting birds, since the nest ledges were generally well above the sea surface. This issue was of particular potential concern, because even brief disturbances to colony-nesting seabirds have been shown elsewhere to cause large increases in egg and chick predation (Buckley, 2004b).

## Safety

Safety precautions and procedures were high throughout the tour. Procedures for clients to embark and disembark from the kayaks were as described above. All kayaks had sealed flotation compartments and carried spare paddles. The kayak group remained together and maintained visual contact at all times. Radio contact with the support vessel was also maintained at all times, and the group carried a GPS which could have provided distance and bearing if inflatables had to be sent from the support vessel for a rescue operation. The kayaks also carried a limited supply of food and water, marine flares etc. Sea and weather conditions and predictions were checked each day before deciding whether and where to launch the kayaks.

## Marketing

This seakayaking tour is sold both by Southern Sea Ventures and by Aurora Expeditions. Southern Sea Ventures (2005) lists an all-inclusive price from Longyearbyen, including both the expedition cruise in the most basic class of cabin and the seakayaking addition. The Norwegian Arctic is shown as one of their 11 destination areas worldwide. Aurora Expeditions (2005) sells the seakayaking option as an add-on to its 'Circumnavigation of Spitzbergen' cruise, costed as a surcharge to the various cruise prices. Of the three illustrations on the opening webpage for this cruise, one shows the kayaking option.

# Prince William Sound, Alaska: National Outdoor Leadership School (NOLS)

## Place

Prince William Sound is a large bay southeast of Anchorage in Alaska, USA. Its convoluted shoreline and numerous islands provide relatively protected waters suitable for multi-day, self-supported seakayaking expeditions (Twardock and Monz, 2000). It is also used extensively by commercial and recreational fishing boats, and in some areas there are privately owned huts and houses along the shoreline. It is large enough, however, that in most areas one encounters no other boats.

In 1989, parts of Prince William Sound were devastated by the infamous Exxon Valdez oil spill. Remaining areas, however, were unaffected. Since seakayakers see principally the water surface, beaches and islands, and since the spill is now 16 years ago, its effects are not apparent.

The Sound lies at 61°N, with a maritime Arctic environment which is very different from the icebound High Arctic. There is continual rain during the summer months, and vegetation on the rocky islets is quite green and lush. The area is renowned for its salmon, and commercial fisheries are heavily regulated since the number of boats far exceeds the potential catch available. Fresh water is available from streams on the mainland shores and the large islands, though caution is required because of bears fishing for salmon.

Most of the coastline is steep and rocky, and large-scale maps or charts are required in order to find protected gravel beaches suitable for camping. Fortunately, however, during summer the skies are light all night, so if one potential campsite proves unsuitable, kayakers can always continue to another.

## Operator

The National Outdoor Leadership School (2005) is based in Lander, Wyoming with permanent branches or seasonal subsidiary operations in various other states of the USA and various countries worldwide. NOLS sees itself as an outdoor education provider, but has many similarities with adventure tourism operators. Most of its clients are university students taking an entire semester at NOLS, for which they receive university credit. Shorter courses are offered for secondary-school students and for older clients. There is a strong focus on teaching wilderness travel, minimal-impact and group leadership skills.

Whilst the emphasis on minimal-impact practices and education is shared with many ecotourism products (Buckley, 2003a, p. 174), NOLS is differentiated by its practical training in outdoor recreation and wilderness travel skills. Similarly, whilst some commercial adventure tours also provide limited training and outdoor skills, this is rarely the main emphasis. Either the skills taught are very basic, just sufficient for unskilled clients to take part in a tour or, for more expert trips, clients are expected to have appropriate skills before they sign up. In addition, few commercial adventure tours teach either natural history or group leadership.

These distinctions do indeed confirm that NOLS is an educational organization rather than a tour operator. Even so, NOLS does provide many of the same adventure recreation activities and opportunities as commercial adventure tour companies, and its students take part on a commercial basis.

The Alaskan branch of NOLS is at Palmer, northeast of Anchorage, with a subsidiary at Fairbanks. Seakayaking in Prince William Sound is one of the major activities from Palmer. Other activities include mountaineering, hiking and whitewater rafting. Seakayaking trips start from Whittier, on the far western side of the Sound, and generally last for about 12 days.

Participation in NOLS courses is generally restricted to students and instructors only. This rule was relaxed on a later occasion for me to accompany the first NOLS course in Australia, which I had helped to set up as outlined in the Drysdale River canoeing case study (Chapter 4). In Prince William Sound, however, rather than accompanying a NOLS group directly, I followed a NOLS itinerary on an independent trip, using rented NOLS equipment, and NOLS charts marked with campsites and course-related information. To save 1 day's paddling through a major shipping area, I took advantage of a boat shuttle offered by Honey Charters (2005).

## Activity

The philosophy of NOLS trips in Prince William Sound may be summed up by an unofficial NOLS instructors' t-shirt which reads 'Eat. Sleep. Paddle.' The majority of the day is spent on the water, taking advantage of tidal currents where possible and hugging the coastline where not. Navigation is not difficult, but does require careful attention to distances, currents and paddling times in order to reach reasonable campsites and intermediate rest stops. There are few if any onshore side trips, and camp is moved every day or nearly every day. Seabirds and marine mammals are abundant, and bird and wildlife watching is a major subsidiary activity during the day. Murres and guillemots are the most common swimming seabirds, and seals and sea otters the most common marine mammals. Black bear are not uncommon on shore.

## Equipment

For its Prince William Sound trips, NOLS used fibreglass hardshell seakayaks, mainly doubles, of a beamy high-volume three-hatch design. These are stored in a locked shed at Whittier. Other than the boats themselves, kayaking equipment is stored at the Palmer branch. This includes breakdown paddles, paddle floats, flares, sprayskirts and camping equipment.

The kayaks used do not have separate watertight compartments. Instead, each kayaker sits inside a large waterproof rubberized nylon bag, known as a sock, which fits tightly over the cockpit coaming underneath the sprayskirt. The kayaker thus sits in the bag on the kayak seat rather than on the seat directly. Similarly, the rudder pedals are operated through the sock. It is generally not possible to roll large, wide and heavily laden seakayaks such as these, so if the boat capsizes, the paddlers must bail out into the ocean, right the boat using paddles and paddle floats, and climb back in. If this should occur, the socks are intended to remain sealed to the cockpit coamings even if the sprayskirts are removed, so that water can only enter the sock and not the hull. Once the boat is righted, water can be emptied from the sock by turning it inside out.

The boats are also equipped with handheld bilge pumps in case water does indeed leak into the hull. All food and camping equipment is packed inside waterproof bags. Synthetic rather than down sleeping bags are used since even with the best precautions the bags are liable to become at least slightly damp during any extended saltwater trip. Extra tarpaulins are carried to hang over the tents, since otherwise they would become soaked every night and there is rarely any opportunity to dry them out.

Unlike the High Arctic, where most seakayakers wear drysuits, in Prince William Sound it is common to paddle dressed in heavy-duty oilskins, rubber boots and a sou'wester hat. Oilskin trousers are of the bib and brace design. Oilskins and boots are relatively cumbersome, but allow one to move directly from boat to shore to camp without the need to change clothing.

## Accommodation

All accommodation on this trip is self-supported camping. Shuttles run directly between Palmer and Whittier on the first and final day, with no overnights in Whittier. As noted above, campsites are in limited supply and whilst a few are broad and flat, many are crammed into small spaces under trees on islands or coastal spits. On one occasion the only campsite we could find, late at night, was a steep narrow tombolo of round, fist-size gravel, joining a small rocky islet to a larger island. It was covered with coarse metre-high wet grass which we trampled down to put up the tent, and high tide came to within 1 m of the tent on each side. At low tide next morning, we also found fresh grizzly bear scat on the steep gravel beaches all around the tent, but fortunately we were not disturbed by the bear itself, though we had indeed heard its footsteps on the gravel.

Most of our cooking was on fuel stoves, but to conserve fuel we also used small campfires. Driftwood was in plentiful supply, but generally damp at best. At the advice of one of the NOLS instructors, we carried a supply of dry tinder in plastic bags, and this was invaluable for lighting fires. Most of our meals were from dry bulk foodstuffs purchased from NOLS, which has developed its own supply and cooking systems over countless courses (Pearson, 2004). On one occasion, however, we bought a salmon from a commercial fisherman and baked it over coals. Since this is the ocean phase of the salmon's lifecycle, it can generally be caught only with a net, not with a rod and line.

## Statistics

Whilst my own audit of this particular NOLS itinerary was undertaken independently, NOLS courses generally include around a dozen students and two or three instructors, with a student-to-instructor ratio of around 4:1 (NOLS, 2005). The students camp and cook in 'tent groups' of four students each. Whilst a NOLS semester course in Alaska or elsewhere lasts for around 3 months, any one activity section generally lasts only 2–3 weeks at most. Self-contained seakayaking trips in Prince William Sound, marketed either to clients aged 23 and over or 40 and over, typically last 12 days (NOLS, 2005) and cost US$2715 per person plus a US$200 equipment deposit, or about US$240 per person per day.

## Access

Whittier lies at the head of a steep-sided narrow inlet, and the only land access is by a dedicated railway through a tunnel from the west. Access to the railhead west of the tunnel is by road from Anchorage. Whittier is a port, with extensive facilities for fishing boats, but little else. Seakayaks can paddle directly from Whittier, but the first day's paddling is through one of the less scenic and more heavily used parts of Prince William Sound. Accordingly, many kayakers use a charter boat to shuttle them to their first night's campsite in a more scenic and less heavily used area. NOLS courses generally paddle directly from Seward, first because they have too many boats for one shuttle charter, secondly in order to keep costs down, and thirdly because the high level of boat traffic may provide an extra safety factor during the first day's paddling.

## Community

NOLS instructors and staff live at Palmer throughout the summer semester, except when they are in the field with students. Some are permanent residents of the area, and stay over during winter. Alaska has a very rich and well-supplied economy, and whilst NOLS buys all its food supplies locally, this would represent only a very small proportion of total tourist purchases in the area. In Whittier itself, NOLS maintains a small store for seakayaks and gear, and is a regular patron of charter boat operators. NOLS also runs trips and courses in many other parts of Alaska, making regular use of national parks, national forests, float plane charters and so on.

## Experience

From its original establishment, NOLS courses were intended to teach both leadership skills and environmental awareness to future leaders in industry and government. In practice, NOLS course graduates go on to many different careers, but generally with a particular degree of self-reliance. Some NOLS students, certainly, see a semester course as a major challenge or even ordeal, and graduation as a corresponding achievement or even victory. Other students, generally those with greater prior outdoor experience, may see a NOLS course as an excellent opportunity to gain university credit outside the classroom. Whilst NOLS instructors have very high technical capabilities, and are certainly able either to lead or teach as required, their philosophy also seems to be that where possible students should learn things for themselves or from their peers.

The actual seakayaking in Prince William Sound is not difficult technically, nor is the camping. The paddling can be relatively long and arduous on occasion, however, particularly if wind or currents are not favourable. Camping also requires some attention to detail, to prevent gear becoming wet in the continual rain. In addition, mosquitoes and biting black flies are prolific in many areas. Despite these discomforts, the area is very beautiful even in grey weather and sightings of seabirds, seals and sea otters are excellent. Several glaciers also calve into Prince William Sound, and their snouts can be approached by seakayak. Approach distances must be calculated carefully, since a large calving block can generate a wave which would swamp a seakayak too close to the glacier snout, especially if the water is shallow.

## Environment

NOLS places a particular emphasis on teaching minimal-impact backcountry skills, and NOLS is also the originator of the Leave-No-Trace® minimal-impact programme for visitors to public lands managed by the US National Parks Service and the US Forest Service. Not surprisingly, therefore, minimal-impact practices by NOLS courses are exemplary.

Of course, NOLS students and instructors travel to course locations in the same types of transport as any tourist, and NOLS students and instructors use the same types of equipment as for outdoor recreation and adventure tourism. For these off-site travel and manufacturing impacts, therefore, NOLS courses contribute per capita and pro rata in the same way as purely commercial adventure tourism.

For seakayaking in Prince William Sound, NOLS teaches minimal-impact practices in campsite selection and operation, cooking and clean-up, washing and washing up, and toilet and waste management practices. Compared to powered recreational boats, let alone commercial fishing, the impacts of the NOLS seakayaking course are negligible.

## Safety

NOLS instructors are highly skilled in safety and rescue techniques, and NOLS courses have an excellent safety record. The teaching curriculum includes use of safety equipment. As on all NOLS courses, students are expected to travel unaccompanied, without instructors, during some parts of the course. Although the seakayaks used are of an old design and do not have watertight buoyancy compartments, the cockpit socks described above are apparently sufficient to prevent swamping, and the paddle floats and bilge pumps are sufficient to right the kayaks and remove any water.

NOLS also teaches map reading and navigational skills, and the courses carry the most detailed charts available. When I visited the Prince William Sound operational area, NOLS seakayaking courses did not carry radios or global positioning systems (GPS), but this may have changed subsequently. I imagine that it would not be easy to swim dressed in full oilskins and rubber boots, but since I had only one set of dry gear, I did not put this to a practical test.

## Marketing

Current course descriptions for NOLS seakayaking courses in Prince William Sound (NOLS, 2005) specify that the courses will teach basic wilderness travel skills, seakayaking, navigation, safety and judgement, leadership and teamwork, outdoor living and environmental ethics. The specific seakayaking skills listed include safe launching and landing, paddle signals, paddle strokes, rescue techniques, coastal hazards, safety equipment and personal navigation. Although, as mentioned earlier, I did not accompany the students and instructors on this course, I have done so on another NOLS course and can confirm that the teaching curriculum is covered well.

The description of the Prince William Sound seakayaking courses (NOLS, 2005) mentions wildlife watching, tidewater glaciers and day hikes, but also emphasizes that rain is commonplace and that rain may continue for several days. It also mentions that the group may be grounded by storms on some occasions, and that a high level of personal responsibility is required. It thus provides an accurate picture of the likely experience.

# Yasawa Islands, Fiji: Southern Sea Ventures

## Place

The Yasawas form a narrow island chain running southwest to northeast off the northwestern coast of Viti Levu, the main southern island of Fiji. The islands are largely volcanic baserock, with spits and beaches of calcareous sand and coral rubble, and fringing reefs. There is also one uplifted limestone islet, which contains water-filled caves which have become a tourist attraction. The islands are all held under traditional ownership by local residents and villages. Most of the larger islands have one or more villages, but even the smaller uninhabited islands are privately owned. Like the neighbouring Mamanuca Islands immediately to the south, the southern Yasawa Islands are used quite intensively for tourism. Accommodation ranges from backpacker huts to the upmarket Turtle Island Lodge, described as a case study by Buckley (2003a, pp. 47–48). A fleet of cruise boats also plies the waters between the islands, capitalizing on the movie *Blue Lagoon*, which was filmed in the Yasawas. There are also a limited number of local commercial dive shops.

## Operator

Southern Sea Ventures (2005) is a specialist seakayak tour operator which offers trips in Australia, the Arctic and Antarctic, and in Fiji, Tonga and Turkey. Many of these are co-marketed with World Expeditions (2005a) or Aurora Expeditions (2005).

Based in Australia, the company has now been operating for 15 years, and has added new trips and destinations at intervals. It maintains separate seakayak fleets in each of the areas concerned. The Arctic and Antarctic trips operate as add-ons to expedition cruises. The Pacific and Australian trips are in tropical and subtropical environments and rely largely on camping.

## Activity

Seakayaking is the principal activity, but for no more than 4 h in any one day. Some of the clients are experienced seakayakers, but others are novices. The trip starts with a boat shuttle from Lautoka on Viti Levu to Tavewa Island in the Yasawas, where the company maintains a boat storage shed and camping area by arrangement with a local landowner.

On the second day the group paddles to the village of Navotua, where it spends 2 nights. During this stay there is a round-trip paddle to visit the limestone caves on a nearby island, a brief tour of the village by one of the seakayak guides who lives there, and a dance and kava-drinking ceremony in the evening. On the fourth day the group paddles to uninhabited Vawa Island, where it spends 2 nights. The rest day is available for snorkelling and hiking on the island. On the sixth day the group paddles back to the original campsite on Tavewa Island, in preparation for the boat shuttle back to Lautoka on the final day.

The tidal range is relatively low, only a metre or two, but the seas around the islands are shallow, and each day's paddling is planned to take advantage of tidal currents where possible. Winds can also be a significant consideration, especially where they generate a short steep chop in some sections. Overall, the paddling is relatively easy, but even so a support boat was used most days, to carry camping equipment and when necessary, tired clients and their kayaks. Only on the last day's paddling was all the equipment carried in the kayaks.

## Equipment

A variety of kayaks are used, some older fibreglass models and some new plastic production designs. On the trip in which I took part, the three guides and two clients paddled single kayaks and the other clients were in doubles. Designs ranged from rather slow and beamy to higher performance narrow hulls. The operator provided all kayak gear, including dry bags for personal equipment. Tents and sleeping mats were also provided. Clients brought their own clothing, a light sleeping bag or blanket, and mask and snorkel. The trip is fully catered and the operator provides group cooking gear and cutlery.

## Accommodation

Accommodation is in a waterfront hotel in Lautoka on the first and last night, and in tents for the remainder of the trip. The tents are pitched on mown grass lawn at Tavewa and Navotua, and on the beach above high tide on the uninhabited island of Vawa. At Tavewa and Navotua there are bures, thatched wooden huts, for cooking and eating; on Vawa the kitchen is set up under a large overhanging *Calophyllum* tree.

## Access

Access to the Yasawa Islands is by air to Nadi, by road to the nearby port city of Lautoka and by boat to Tavewa. Depending on the size of the group, the shuttle may be on a charter vessel or on the high-speed inter-island ferry, the *Yasawa Flyer*, which caters to the majority of the Yasawa tourist trade.

On the Yasawa Islands access to the individual islands, villages and sites is by private negotiation with the local landholders. These arrangements are made directly by the tour operator, on a routine basis, and are not immediately apparent to the client. At Tavewa, Southern Sea Ventures maintains a permanent base camp and storage area. At Navotua, the home village of one of the guides, the village charges SSV a camping fee per person per night. An additional fee is payable for the dance demonstration and kava-drinking ceremony. The support boats are also hired from this village.

The limestone caves are on an island owned by a different village, and separate entrance fees are charged. Again, these are included in the SSV trip price. The caves are a popular tourist destination, and many other tourists arrive in a variety of boats. The access track is closed off by a locked gate except when open for business. Similarly, the large cruise boats visit the village of Navotua for a craft market and dance exhibition.

## Statistics

The Yasawa Islands seakayak tour lasts 7 days in total and currently costs AUD1920, or about US$205 per person per day. The minimum group size is four, or two by special arrangement, and the maximum is advertised as ten. In fact there were three guides and 11 other clients on the trip in which I took part. The client-to-guide ratio is hence generally around 3:1.

## Experience

This is as much a cultural as an adventure experience, with two of five island days spent in the middle of Fijian villages where local customs must be observed, and there is a combination of real and staged authenticity. The total distance paddled each day is relatively short, but even so, some clients were unable to keep up at the beginning of the trip. Several had no previous kayaking experience. All the clients, however, seemed well satisfied with the experience, and keen to continue seakayaking in future.

Many of the clients on this particular trip were over 50, with the eldest being close to 80, and according to the guides this was not atypical. The trip immediately after ours, however, included a family with young children. The Yasawas are currently a popular backpacker destination, but this multi-day seakayak trip does not attract that particular market segment.

## Community

There are many interactions with local communities on the Yasawa Islands seakayak tour. One of the regular seakayak guides lives at Navotua on Nathuia Island. The group camps in this village for 2 nights and sees various aspects of a day-to-day life in a small Fijian village. Village life combines a traditional social structure with strong Christian church practices. Traditional small-scale food gardens, fruit trees, pigpens and chickens are still important, but so is cash-based tourism and fishing using outboard-powered boats.

The tour group does not join in with any of the village activities, and sees only certain aspects. For example, the drums for church services and the voices of the choir are audible to all, but the visitors do not enter the church. Individual residents sometimes invite individual visitors briefly into their houses or bures, and they are all very friendly and welcoming to the Southern Sea Ventures group.

The company and its clients have made significant contributions to the village. These include endowments for facilities and school scholarship funds, and donations to the village kindergarten. Perhaps more importantly, however, the seakayak groups pay cash fees to the village for permission to camp there, and additional fees for a dance exhibition and kava ceremony. They also charter boats from members of the village, and provide permanent employment for one and contract work for others.

The village stay includes two formal components, which are, if not staged, at least choreographed. The first is a brief village tour, with a commentary on social structures. This is interesting, but the main aim of the tour is to take visitors to the kindergarten building and ask them to donate teaching materials or money. This exercise was slightly marred by the way in which the children were leafing quickly through children's books without looking at the pages, which in some cases were upside down.

The second and formal component is the dance exhibition and kava ceremony, held on the second evening. This is heavily staged, and indeed had also been staged for visitors from a cruise boat earlier in the day, and probably most days. The cruise boat visitors, as well as the seakayak group, also got the opportunity to buy various Fijian souvenirs from local residents, including home-made necklaces, printed cloth sulus (sarongs) which are bought in from Viti Levu, and various carved shells of species which may or may not be rare.

In addition to the main village stay, the group met local residents briefly on Tavewa Island on the first and last night, where the camp is on private land. Payments are also made to camp on the uninhibited Vawa Island, but without the kayakers meeting the landowners.

Before entering the village of Navotua, the guides briefed the clients on the most critical aspects of social protocol. Men must wear long shorts rather than swimming trunks, and women must keep their shoulders and torsos covered and wear a sulu or trousers. In the village one may not wear any sort of headgear, such as a hat, headband or even a headlamp. One may not touch any person on the head. Similarly, before the dance exhibition and kava ceremony, the guides briefed the clients on protocol for entering the bure and for drinking kava.

## Environment

Most of the areas visited have been occupied by Fijian villages for a long time, and many have also been used by fishing boats and tourist cruises for several decades. Seakayaking itself has negligible impacts in comparison. Even the support boats are locally owned craft which are used for fishing when not chartered by Southern Sea Ventures. The uninhabited island, Vawa, has been populated by goats and its native woodland vegetation has also been modified by fire and invading weeds, including lantana. The reefs are used for harvesting octopus and shells, and the sand-dwelling ghost crabs are caught for fishing bait.

Southern Sea Ventures is, however, careful to collect all rubbish, separating food scraps, burnables and durable litter. Scraps are fed to village pigs, burnables are burnt with other village rubbish and other types of rubbish are taken to the villages. It was also noteworthy that none of the seakayaking clients bought any shells at the village market, though they were on sale to cruise boat passengers. This, however, was a choice by the clients: there was no guide briefing on these issues.

### Safety

Many of the clients were inexperienced, and safety is a significant concern. All kayaking equipment was in good repair, old as well as new. All clients and guides wore lifejackets whenever kayaking. Hats, sunscreen, long-sleeved shirts and lightweight paddling gloves were recommended for sun protection and most clients had these. Support boats were used on the first few days. On the crossing to the uninhabited island, two clients became tired and were in fact picked up, with their kayaks, by the support boat. There was a safety briefing on the first evening of the trip, before leaving for the islands.

Only in the water-filled cave were safety procedures a little confused. There was a safety briefing, and guides stationed to help clients under a rock ledge into a darker second cave, which was fine – but the guides also started whooping and shining torches to display echoes, and some of the clients became disorientated and panicked. However, no harm was done.

### Marketing

This trip is apparently marketed both by Southern Sea Ventures (2005) and World Expeditions (2005). Some confusion arose as clients who had purchased the trip through World Expeditions had received slightly different information, e.g. as regards which meals were included and which were not. Compared to other international seakayak tours featured in Southern Sea Ventures' (2005) brochures and website, the Yasawa trip is readily accessible and undemanding for Australian clients. Its price puts it beyond the backpacker market, however, and in practice most clients are middle aged or older. Some own their own seakayaks at home or have other prior experience, but some have none. The SSV Yasawa trip is featured in the *Lonely Planet*® guide to Fiji.

## Hinchinbrook Island, Australia: Southern Sea Ventures and World Expeditions

### Place

Hinchinbrook Island is a large, mountainous and densely forested bedrock island close to the central northern coast of Queensland, Australia. It includes a large area of mangroves and a number of sandy beaches. Most of the island is a national park, but there is a small resort in one area. The park is part of the Wet Tropics of Queensland World Heritage Area. The surrounding seas are part of the Great Barrier Reef Marine

Park, also World Heritage listed. The area is subtropical, with sunburn a higher risk than hypothermia.

## Operator

Multi-day seakayak tours around Hinchinbrook Island are retailed by World Expeditions (2005a) in Sydney and operated by Southern Sea Ventures (2005). SSV also markets these tours independently. World Expeditions is a large international retailer of outdoor nature, eco and adventure tourism products (Buckley, 2003a, pp. 112–113) that started operations as an Australian trekking company in Nepal, but now offers a wide range of outdoor activities in destinations worldwide. Southern Sea Ventures is a small specialist seakayaking operator which offers tours in various polar and tropical destinations. The Arctic tour, carried out as part of the Aurora Expeditions circumnavigation of Spitzbergen, is described in the Svalbard case study. The company owns all its own boats, equipment and paddling clothing.

## Activity

The Hinchinbrook seakayaking tour is a relatively low-key multi-day trip, paddling from beach to beach around the island. Particular beaches are preferred by the guides for campsites and lunch stops, but there is considerable flexibility to modify the detailed itinerary if weather conditions or group capabilities require it. The itinerary is designed for inexperienced paddlers, though one of our group was so uncoordinated that their only contribution to forward propulsion was to knock the paddle from their partner's hands at frequent intervals. The trip is oriented principally to kayaking rather than side hikes on shore, and the main attractions are scenic rather than wildlife. The itinerary includes 2 days' paddling to nearby Goold Island and the Family Islands.

## Equipment

Southern Sea Ventures provides stable two-seater production seakayaks and appropriate accessories. It also provides tents, group shelter, cooking equipment, cutlery and crockery etc. Of particular note is a custom-made toilet, for use when camping on beaches. This is described under the Environment heading below.

## Accommodation

All accommodation during the seakayak trip is in tents at beach campsites on the islands. The company provides two-person tents. Clients must bring their own sleeping bags. All cooking is done by the guides. There is a pre-trip briefing at Mission Beach on the evening before the trip, so clients must stay overnight in Mission Beach. This is not included in the trip package. On the last day the group returns to Mission Beach in time for clients to travel back to Cairns, the nearest airport, on the same day if they wish.

## Statistics

Maximum group size is ten clients and two guides, a 5:1 ratio. On the trip in which I took part there were eight clients and two guides. The Hinchinbrook circuit paddle takes 7 days in total, including arrival and departure days and the Goold and Family Islands component. Total price is AUD1650 per person or about US$180 per person per day.

## Access

Guests must make their own way to Mission Beach the afternoon before the trip. On the first day's kayaking, physical access to the put-in and take-out points is straightforward: clients are driven from Mission Beach to Lucinda and the kayaks are launched from the beach. Some of the beach landings on Hinchinbrook Island itself potentially could be difficult, since the eastern beaches face directly into the Pacific Ocean. They are protected from ocean swell by the outer reef of the Great Barrier Reef. Some of them are lee shores when the southeasterly tradewinds are blowing, but the windward fetch is short and the windchop relatively small. Caution is needed in landing and launching the double kayaks with relatively inexperienced paddlers, but beach access is still possible. Hinchinbrook Island is a national park, and permits are required both for overnight camping and for commercial tour operations.

## Community

The coastal town of Lucinda is quite small, and many businesses on the main road rely on drive-through tourists for business. There is a large-scale resort residential development at nearby Cardwell, incorporating a marina, and this caused widespread controversy because of its likely impacts on World Heritage Areas. In addition, relations between the developer and local subcontractors were apparently not always cordial. Small-scale low-impact tours such as seakayaking trips, however, do not fall under the same stigma and are generally welcomed. Indeed, these seakayaking tours have very little interaction with residents, who probably do not even know they are taking place. Local residents use the area around Hinchinbrook Island for recreational fishing using small outboard-powered dinghies, but fishermen and kayakers do not interact to any noticeable degree.

## Experience

The trip in which I took part was the first seakayaking experience for all the other clients involved. None of them had any difficulties, and the tour does indeed seem to be suitable for unskilled clients with little outdoor experience. The weather is benign, the itinerary is relaxed, the scenery is pleasant, the campsites are comfortable, the guides competent and the clients well looked after. For the main part of the trip around the outside of Hinchinbrook Island, the prevailing wind is from behind, so the kayaks make good speed on the small ocean swells without any great effort.

## Environment

Most of the beaches are relatively small, and used for camping throughout most of the year. Management of trampling, litter, cooking and cleaning and human waste is hence critical, if only to maintain recreational amenity. The tours follow minimal impact camping practices (Buckley, 1999). These campsites are within Hinchinbrook National Park, so there are environmental regulations in force.

In particular, at some sites all human waste must be removed. Seakayak groups must therefore carry portable toilets. Most commonly available models, however, are heavy, bulky and box-shaped, designed to be carried either in vehicles or rafts, but not in kayaks. Accordingly, Southern Sea Ventures uses an ingenious design consisting of a metre-long length of polypropylene piping, of the type used for gutter downpipes, with screw cap fittings at both ends. A toilet seat is attached to a large funnel which in turn is attached to a screw-on pipe fitting. In camp, the lower half of the pipe is buried vertically in the sand, and the upper cap is replaced by the screw-on seat, providing a stable and comfortable toilet at a convenient height. In transit, screw caps are sealed, the seat arrangement is packed in one of the kayaks, and the capped tube is strapped on to the stern deck of another using elastic cords. According to the owner of Southern Sea Ventures, he did not invent this design himself, but I have never seen it elsewhere. It works well.

### Safety

The Hinchinbrook Island circumnavigation is a relatively low-risk area for seakayakers. The water is warm, the waves are small, the boats are close to shore, and there are numerous recreational powerboats in the area in case an emergency evacuation may be required – as did in fact happen on the trip in which I took part. Client safety briefings focus on assisted rather than self-rescue, and the client seakayaks carry little safety or emergency equipment.

### Marketing

Southern Sea Ventures (2005) markets this trip directly via its own website, with nine departures in 2005. World Expeditions (2005a), which also sells the SSV trips, advertises only two departures. A Google® search for 'seakayak Hinchinbrook Island' identifies several tour operators. SSV and one other appear to be local operators, with the remainder being international packagers.

## Abel Tasman National Park, New Zealand: Ocean River and Natural High

### Place

Abel Tasman National Park lies at the northwest corner of the South Island of New Zealand. Its northern coastline, running westward from the township of Marahau, consists of tree-covered headlands and islets separated by bays with golden sand beaches. The tidal range is low, tidal currents relatively gentle, and the weather is generally dryer and more sunny than most of New Zealand's South Island. The water is relatively warm, at least in summer, and the area is thus well suited to low-key seakayaking trips by relatively inexperienced paddlers.

The national park has a heavily used coastal hiking track with well-maintained campsites, which are also accessible from the sea. Several operators run high-speed water taxis to and from these campsites for hikers who do not have the time or inclination to hike the entire track. Several companies rent seakayaks and associated equipment, and/or operate guided seakayak tours with full or partial catering.

Seakayakers generally use the same designated campsites as hikers, and because of heavy use campsites must be booked well ahead during the summer season. The campsite areas have water, toilets and day shelters, and some also have overnight storage racks for seakayaks. The shoreline is highly scenic, and seakayakers can generally also expect to see seals and seabirds in certain areas.

## Operators

A number of different commercial operators offer seakayaking tours along the northern coast of Abel Tasman National Park. I have carried out case studies of two of these: Ocean River (2005) and Natural High (2005). Ocean River is a small specialist company which focuses entirely on Abel Tasman seakayaking tours. It is based in Marahau. Natural High offers a range of outdoor recreation activities, with a focus on seakayaking and mountain biking. It is based in Nelson.

## Activity

Both of these companies offer multi-day guided seakayaking tours, with overnight camps at coastal camping areas in the national park. Half and 1-day seakayaking excursions, and packages which combine seakayaking with other activities, are also available. For multi-day seakayaking tours, these and other operators offer a range of itineraries including round-trip, one-way with a water-taxi shuttle, or a combination of seakayaking and hiking. In addition, the same companies offer seakayaks for so-called freedom rentals, where similar options are available but without a guide. For guided trips, either catered or self-catering options are available. For the former, food is actually delivered to the overnight campsites by the water taxis, with only lunch and snacks being carried in the kayaks.

All of the operators provide basic training in seakayaking skills before leaving the beach, and even the multi-day tours are perfectly suitable for complete beginners. The Abel Tasman area is the most popular place for backpackers to experience seakayaking as part of a New Zealand itinerary, and is also used by school groups and international university classes. As a result, the number and size of seakayaking groups is quite large, and popular lunch beaches can become quite crowded. There is also a continual traffic of water taxis ferrying people and equipment for hiking and seakayaking trips and general sightseeing, and the campsites are heavily used by hikers. Overall, therefore, the activity is a rather low-key and social form of adventure tourism, with an emphasis on scenery, nature and social interactions rather than skills or wilderness.

## Equipment

Most companies use production model two-seater plastic seakayaks of intermediate design. Some operators, including Natural High, use so many boats that they import them in bulk from manufacturers overseas and sell them second-hand at the end of the season. Others use locally manufactured brands such as those made by Current Craft Perception®. In general, New Zealand is well supplied with outdoor equipment manufacturers, and New Zealand gear has an excellent international reputation for design and reliability.

As well as kayaks, paddles and sprayskirts, the seakayak tour operators can provide tents and other camping equipment if clients require it. The campsites in Abel Tasman National Park are equipped with cooking facilities, but the tours also bring small fuel stoves for making hot drinks, especially during bad weather. The park campgrounds also have running water, toilets, day-use shelters etc., so seakayaking tours do not need to carry portable toilets, group cooking tarpaulins or large water containers.

## Accommodation

Accommodation during the tour is in national park campsites as outlined above. During almost the entire summer season, campsites must be booked well in advance, especially for large groups. Campsites are well managed and maintained by the New Zealand Department of Conservation, which is responsible for national parks. A variety of commercial accommodation options are available in Marahau and Nelson. These are not included in seakayak tour packages, but the tour operators run shuttle buses to collect clients from overnight accommodation.

## Statistics

Group sizes vary, but groups of 20 people or more are not uncommon. When I joined a commercial tour with Ocean River a few years ago there were six or eight clients and one guide. In January 2004 I took a group of 16 university students on a commercial trip with Natural High, and the company provided two guides, but the group also included two university staff with previous seakayaking experience.

Trips of various durations are offered, but the longest generally involve three overnight camps in the national park, since this is ample time to paddle along most of its northern coastline. Most groups paddle one way only, returning either by water taxi or, as in our own case, by hiking along the coastal trail. Exact price depends on the construction of the package, i.e. number of days, whether catered or not, whether guided or not and whether water taxis are included. Currently, prices range from NZD245–265 for a 2-day guided but uncatered trip, to NZD410–450 for a 3-day fully catered trip (Natural High, 2005; Ocean River, 2005). These correspond to US$90–105 per person per day.

## Access

Commercial tour operators require permits to offer tours in Abel Tasman National Park, and per capita camping fees are also charged. There are a number of small islands close to the coastline, and some of these are in a marine park with restricted access and regulations for wildlife watching. Physically, access is straightforward, with seakayaks and clients brought by road to the beach at Marahau, and the kayaks launched directly from the beach. All the campsites are very close to the beach, and easily accessible.

## Community

Abel Tasman National Park is a significant tourist attraction. There are many local businesses catering to tourists, and many local residents rely heavily on tourism. Visitation patterns, however, are quite strongly seasonal. As in other such areas, residents not actively involved in tourism are probably less enthusiastic about the high number of visitors. There are a number of enclaves of private land along the coastal trail, and warning signs and keep-out notices are prominent and plentiful. Broadly, however, local communities in this area are very friendly towards tourists, as elsewhere in New Zealand.

## Experience

As noted earlier, this is a relatively easy, safe and low-skilled seakayaking experience. It emphasizes scenery, seabirds, marine mammals and social interactions more than skills, risk or wilderness – at least during the crowded summer season. No doubt it would look rather different during a winter storm, but the seakayak tour companies do not operate at that time.

The coastline of Abel Tasman National Park is very scenic, with temperate treefern forest running right to shoreline, and golden sand beaches between rocky headlands. In some places, kayakers paddle close to shore where the seafloor is clearly visible through clear water. Birdcalls can be heard from the forest, and seabirds perch on rocks. Seals are often seen at some points, and some of them are habituated to seakayaks and will follow the kayaks for some distance, swimming alongside and diving under the boats. Even during rain, the summer weather is relatively warm and kayaking is not unpleasant. Rain is certainly a disadvantage when putting up tents or packing them away, but the campsites have shelters which provide protection from rain while cooking.

I noticed that the Ocean River guides have favourite camping sites at the edge of the camping areas, which they like to secure for their groups. They bring their own cooking stoves, light their own campfires and generally keep their clients as a coherent group separate from other campsite users. The Natural High guides, in contrast, use the main shelter areas for cooking and generally encouraged conversations between their clients and other groups. This, however, may reflect individual guide personalities or their interpretation of particular clients' preferences, rather than any general company policy.

## Environment

Abel Tasman National Park is heavily used and intensively managed. Overnight seakayakers contribute pro rata to impacts at campsites, but these are managed principally by hardening these sites using lawns, formed tracks, shelters, gas-fired cookers, toilets, etc. Seakayakers do also use some beaches which are not frequented by hikers, but these beaches are also accessed by water taxis and in some cases by private yachts and recreational powerboats. Some are even used for water skiing.

Compared to the other users, the impacts of seakayakers are negligible. Both Ocean River and Natural High made sure that clients left no litter at lunch stops or campsites. Seakayakers could potentially disturb seals and seabirds resting or nesting on rocky islets, but group sizes and approach distances are governed by a regulated code of conduct, which seakayak tour companies seem to adhere to. Guides from both seakayak tour companies provided ongoing briefings about the natural environment during the tour, including park regulations and codes of conduct.

## Safety

Seakayak tour groups are relatively large and conditions are relatively calm in Abel Tasman National Park, so risks are generally low. The clients' kayaks do not carry spare paddles, paddle floats or other safety equipment. The guides did give safety briefings, and these focused on assisted rather than self-rescue techniques. Essentially, clients were told that if they capsized, they should make sure they were on the upwind side of their boat or the side away from rocks, and wait for assistance. In the event of a capsize, the technique used would be to empty the capsized boat by raising it over the stern deck of a second boat. This is generally feasible only in relatively calm water, but would indeed be possible around Abel Tasman. In the event of any more serious difficulty, loss of equipment, or injury to guides or clients, the groups rely on the ever-present water taxis to transport gear or, if necessary, people.

## Marketing

Seakayak tours along Abel Tasman National Park are marketed both through websites and through leaflets distributed locally. Not surprisingly, marketing imagery nearly always portrays the area as sunny and calm. Marketing materials generally emphasize the flexibility and range of options; the relatively low level of skill required; and the scenery and wildlife, particularly marine wildlife. Easy access, shuttle-bus pick-ups and accommodation options at the start and end of the trips are also mentioned. These marketing materials do generally provide an accurate picture of what clients can expect.

One aspect which is not mentioned, however, and which many of our students commented upon in 2004, is the high level of crowding, the number of other sea-kayak groups, and the number of other users, including powered boats. Those with expectations of a wilderness experience were somewhat disappointed in this regard.

# Phang Nga Bay, Thailand: John Gray's Sea Canoe

### Place

Phang Nga Bay lies near Phuket in southeast Thailand. The bay is dotted by numerous tall, steep-sided limestone islands. Some of these contain large caves occupied by birdsnest swiftlets, accessible by boat through openings at around high-tide level. These nests have been harvested for generations by particular local families. Because the birdsnest material is such a valuable commodity, these families have heavily armed guards living permanently at the mouths of the caves, in bamboo platforms suspended above the cave entrances. Some of the limestone islands are also hollow, but open to the sky above and contain internal lagoons known as *hongs*, which are accessible only through narrow intertidal tunnels. These are the principal attraction in the Sea Canoe tours.

### Operator

SeaCanoe is a company started by John 'Caveman' Gray, expatriate from Hawaii, in Phang Nga Bay, off Phuket on the eastern coast of Thailand. Because of copycat tours with similar names, John Gray's original company (SeaCanoe) now operates under the new name of John Gray's Sea Canoe (2005). The company has expanded to offer sit-on-top kayak tours amidst mangroves, and a variety of tours in Vietnam, the Philippines and Fiji, with less emphasis on the *hongs* of Phang Nga Bay.

## Activity

The principal activity for which John Gray's Sea Canoe is famous, and indeed the activity which John Gray himself first invented, is to make one's way into the *hongs*, the central lagoons of the hollow open-topped islands, by pushing inflatable canoes through narrow intertidal tunnels. The canoes are narrow, flat and low to the water. Where space allows, they are propelled with conventional paddles. In the tighter sections of the tunnels, however, the passengers lie down flat, holding torches, and the guide pushes the canoe through the tunnel by walking his hands along its roof.

Most of the tunnels are quite long and curved so that one cannot see the exit from the entrance. At high tide they are underwater, so there is only a relatively brief window of time in each tidal cycle for all the canoes to make their way through the tunnels, around the *hongs* and back out of the tunnels. Some of the islands have multiple *hongs* which are themselves joined by intertidal tunnels, so to reach the innermost section the canoes have to pass through several tunnels in succession. This is straightforward if there are only a few canoes, but can create significant delays if there are many, especially if one group is trying to get out whilst another is still getting in. The interior walls of the hollow islands are tens or hundreds of metres high and near-vertical, and a few minutes searching with binoculars generally reveals a range of birds and wildlife.

Exploring these hollow islands, though certainly the core attraction, is by no means the only activity on John Gray's tours. Rather than being open at the top, some of the islands have giant interior caves inhabited by birdsnest swallows or swiftlets. These caves are controlled by particular families, who have built elaborate structures made of tree branches lashed together with ropes, so that skilled climbers can reach the upper sections of the cave walls, where the birds make their nests. These structures are precarious and slippery, and the only light is from torches carried in the climbers' teeth, so this is not a job for the faint-hearted. The nests, which are essentially cups of dried bird saliva, are stripped from the wall before the birds lay their eggs, and sold to Chinese buyers at exorbitant prices, to be used in birdsnest soup. The birds then build a replacement nest where they are left in peace to raise the next generation. The families which control the birdsnest islands appear to operate in a somewhat mafia-like manner, but John Gray has established cordial relations with some of these families at least, so his guests can visit one of these islands unscathed.

Elsewhere, there are islands with small sandy beaches used by local fishermen, where passengers can swim or go ashore; and there are large expanses of mangrove woodland, outside the islands, where passengers can paddle slowly through a maze of small channels, looking out for a variety of colourful birdlife.

## Equipment

Gray developed the special narrow, low-profile inflatable canoes, now known as sea canoes, which can be threaded through the tunnels during a short period in the middle of each tidal cycle.

## Accommodation

John Gray's Sea Canoe currently offers four different trips in Phang Nga Bay: a single-day trip to the *hongs*, which of course does not include accommodation; an overnight trip, camping on one of the island beaches; a 'starlight' trip to the *hongs* at night; and a coastal seakayaking trip. The overnight trip has several major advantages. Most importantly, it allows John Gray's clients to visit the islands early or late in the day, when day trips have returned to Phuket. This can be particularly significant as some of the entrance tunnels to some of the *hongs* may be flooded by high tides in the middle of the day. In addition, 2-day trips include seakayaking through mangroves and a visit to the birdsnest caves. The sea canoe trips are supported by a local 'longtail' boat.

## Statistics

Costs range from THB2900 (US$70) for a 1-day trip and THB5450 (US$133) for the starlight trip, to THB8775 (US$215) for an overnight camping trip (John Gray's Sea Canoe, 2005).

## Access

Access to the tour is via Phuket, which can be reached directly by air, or by road from within Thailand or Malaysia. Access to the *hong* islands is via a longtail boat, a long wooden local boat powered by a car motor with a propeller on the driveshaft.

## Community

John Gray made a particular effort from the outset to establish partnerships with local communities, giving local people active roles in the management of his company as well as simply hiring them as employees. Even so, through no fault of his own he fell afoul of local politics. After years of efforts and investment perfecting the sea canoes and promoting the *hongs* internationally, his business became quite successful. At that point, wealthy businessmen from outside the Phang Nga Bay area began copying the SeaCanoe product, using the same boats and almost identical business names.

Not only did this create problems of crowding, poor management and local competition; it also brought the whole sea canoe industry to the attention of the birdsnest families, who demanded a cut. When John Gray refused to pay what was essentially protection money, his manager, a local Thai man, was gunned down. Thanks to Gray's international contacts, this assault and associated circumstances became well-known worldwide, and sparked a series of letters to the Thai Royal Family by representatives of the international tourism industry. Gray attempted to form a local industry association of tour operators to establish agreed quotas and safety and environmental standards, but some of the other operators formed a competing association with messy and confusing results.

Subsequently, the company continued operating, but changed its name to John Gray's Sea Canoe to differentiate itself more clearly from the many copycat operators. It also expanded its product so it was less dependent on access to particular *hongs* and expanded its geographical sphere of operations to include similar terrain in other countries such as Vietnam and the Philippines.

## Experience

Because the interior walls of the hollow islands had previously been inaccessible, these hollow islands still support diverse plant and animal communities, including monkeys and birds which tourists can no longer see on the nearby mainland. To emerge from a long, dark seawater tunnel into a fully enclosed *hong*, lit by sunlight from above and surrounded by hundred-metre vertical walls of limestone, is certainly an astonishing experience.

## Environment

From the outset, John Gray's Sea Canoe attempted to maintain the conservation value of the *hongs*, limiting numbers and ensuring that visitors remained quiet and did not discard any litter or waste.

When I took part in one of Gray's multi-day tours some years ago, several copycat companies had already started operations and left litter inside the *hongs*. The major concerns at that time, however, were pollution of the Bay from coastal prawn farms and industrial development. By demonstrating the economic potential of ecotourism, and by Gray's own lobbying efforts, John Gray's Sea Canoe was instrumental in reducing these threats.

Some years later, however, Gray expressed concerns that by promoting his discoveries to tourists, he may inadvertently have triggered a chain of events which threatened the conservation value of the *hongs*. These problems were not of Gray's making, but illustrate the difficulties which may face even the best-intentioned and successful eco- and adventure tourism ventures.

## Safety

For a tourist keen to visit the famous islands of Phang Nga Bay, the single most important safety consideration is to identify John Gray's Sea Canoe from the maelstrom of competing touts on the dockside. Fortunately, most of Gray's clients already have an advanced booking. Once on the tour, the most significant safety concern is an accurate knowledge of the islands and tunnels, and of the day's tidal range and tide times, since these are the factors that determine which islands one can safely go in and out of, and exactly when. As noted earlier, the biggest risk is due to overcrowding, as too many groups try to get in and out of the same *hongs*.

## Marketing

John Gray's Sea Canoe is internationally synonymous with the *hongs* of Phang Nga Bay, thanks to innumerable illustrated magazine articles in many different languages. If readers remember only Sea Canoe rather than John Gray, however, they will soon be confused by the morass of copycat operators. When the company was first established, the main focus of Gray's marketing was simply to show people that the *hongs* existed and that his company could take people inside them. Currently, his principal marketing issue is to differentiate his own company from copycat operators, whilst the copycat operators aim to confuse this distinction and hang their business from his international marketing investments.

# 8 Sailing

Mirrabooka, Australia. Photo Gayle Jennings.

## Sector Structure

Sailing has a long and distinguished history, and a wide variety of sailboats are still in use worldwide for subsistence and small-scale cash fisheries. Sailing is also a popular activity for private recreation in many developed nations, both in lakes and oceans. Much of this is competitive. There is a wide variety of one-design racing dinghy classes, some of them represented at the Olympics. There are also well-known races for ocean-going yachts, including the Admiral's Cup, the America's Cup, the Sydney-to-Hobart race and the Whitbread Round the World race. In countries where outdoor education is part of the school curriculum, dinghy sailing is often one of the components.

The number of sailboats used in commercial tourism is small relative to the number used for sport, competition, education and recreation. In addition, tax laws in some countries may lead to yachts being listed for commercial charter, even where they are used principally for private recreation. Recreational sailing has indeed spawned a large commercial industry, but one that relies principally on the sale of boats, equipment, moorings, marina berths and water-front property. Indeed, the main financial link between sailing and tourism is through coastal resort-residential developments that incorporate marinas. Many beach and island resorts also offer small dinghies or catamarans for hire on an hourly basis.

Yachts are also available for hire in various parts of the world, commonly on a charter basis either with or without skipper and/or crew. Charters that do not include crew are referred to as bareboat charters, and are a popular part of the tourism portfolio in some sheltered coastal destinations. Whilst bareboat charters may be a significant tourist activity at such destinations, they are essentially equipment rentals rather than tours as such, corresponding, for example, to the so-called freedom rentals offered by seakayak tour operators in some areas.

Products that could reasonably be considered as sailing adventure tours fall into three main categories. First, there are yacht charters. These may have a skipper or a full crew; they may be self-catering or fully catered; and they may have a fixed or flexible itinerary. For any of these options, however, they are distinguished by the requirement to charter the entire vessel for a fixed period. Second, there are yacht tours with fixed itineraries where commercial clients can purchase a place onboard. These range from a half-day cruise as a passenger aboard a fully crewed ship, usually with food and drink included, to long-distance voyages in ocean-going yachts, where the clients train as crew over a period of weeks or months. And third, there are some organizations that offer adventure trips or training that includes smaller sailboats as a means of wilderness travel.

Sailboarding tours, in contrast, generally operate from a fixed base, with the activity itself providing the adventure component. In this sense, they are perhaps more akin to surfing than to sailing tours, except that it is wind rather than surf conditions that determines the destinations. As with surfing, many recreational sail-boarders may take their holidays in places known for their sailboarding opportunities, bringing all their own equipment with them and using commercial tourism providers only for transport and accommodation, if at all. There are, however, a relatively small number of commercial tour operators that specialize in travel packages for sailboarders, sometimes including equipment hire and/or instruction. The Yahoo® directory of sailboard and windsurfing tour operators, for example, lists ten sailboard operators based in, or offering tours to, places such as Hawaii, USA, the Caribbean, Mexico, Venezuela, Brazil, the Canary Islands, Europe, Egypt, Morocco, Fiji, Australia and New Zealand. Similar considerations apply for kiteboarding tours, such as those offered by Planet Kitesurf (2005) in the UK, which runs trips to 17 destination resorts.

Unlike adventure activities such as heliskiing or whitewater rafting, for example, only a very small component of the recreational sailing industry is associated with adventure tourism. The three case studies outlined below indicate the range of products on offer. Unlike the other activity sectors considered in this volume, only one of these case studies has been audited in person.

## Scotland to Faeroes: Private Yacht

### Place

The Faeroe Islands are a group of 18 islands in the North Atlantic Ocean, midway between Scotland and Iceland, with a total land area of about 1400 km$^2$ and a population of round 50,000. The Faeroe Islands were settled by Vikings in the 8th century and became part of Denmark in 1386, with autonomous home rule since 1948. The main economic activity is fishing, with fish products making up all but a few per cent of total exports, but the inhabitants also farm sheep for wool and local consumption. There is now a small but significant tourism industry.

### Operator

I sailed from Scotland to the Faeroe Islands several decades ago, in a privately owned yacht run commercially out of Tobermory on the island of Mull off the west coast of Scotland. The yacht was owned and operated directly by its skipper, with no company structure. As with many small adventure tour companies, the dates of voyages were determined by the preferences of the first clients to book, and the remaining places on the trip were then filled by direct advertising. The vessel was an ocean-going cruising yacht, with sufficient berths only for active crew, not inactive passengers. The paying clients hence formed the crew, under the direction of the skipper.

This particular vessel, not surprisingly, no longer seems to be operating commercial voyages to the Faeroe Islands. Indeed, only one sailing yacht tour operator is currently listed in tourism promotional material for Tobermory on the Isle of Mull. This vessel, the *Corryvreckan*, sails the west coast of Scotland and sometimes to Ireland, but apparently not to the Faeroes. Tourist promotional material for the Faeroe Islands themselves does not mention sailing yachts at all. The yacht in which I made this voyage was a great deal smaller than the *Corryvreckan*, with a total crew of five, including the skipper.

### Activity

This trip was very much a full-time sailing voyage, with most of the time at sea and several nights sailing under relatively severe weather conditions. There was half a day to hike on one of the outer islands of west Scotland on the voyage out, and 1 day to hike on the Faeroe Islands before the return voyage.

## Equipment

The yacht we sailed on in the 1970s was a carvel-built wooden-hulled vessel of traditional design. We had navigational instruments but not self-steering gear. The wheel was very close to the stern and unsheltered from the weather.

## Accommodation

All accommodation was on board. There were four bunks in the fo'c'sle and two in the saloon, plus a small galley and a table that did double duty for charts or dining. The yacht *Corryvreckan*, which currently operates out of Tobermory, offers five double cabins for passengers.

## Statistics

On the voyage in which I took part there were five people on board, the captain plus four paying crew members, including myself. All were experienced sailors. The trip was scheduled to take a week, but was extended slightly through bad weather.

## Access

Access to Tobermory in Mull is by ferry from Oban on the west coast of Scotland. Access to Oban is by road. Other than by yacht, the Faeroe Islands can be reached by car and passenger ferry from Denmark, or by air from the UK, Denmark or Iceland. When we landed in the Faeroes we were required to provide our passports for formal immigration, but other than that there were no formalities. However, that was 35 years ago.

## Community

During our brief visit to the Faeroes, I spoke to a number of local residents whilst hiking and hitchhiking around the main island. They were all very hospitable and happy to discuss the practical economics of life on the islands – for example, that luxury European cars were available but rusted out within two years in the constant sea spray.

## Experience

On the voyage in which I took part, there was a strong wind and the principal activity for all on board was sailing the ship. On the first night we anchored off one of the west coast islands and took the opportunity to scramble to the top and enjoy the view. Once we left Scotland, we divided into two watches to sail through the night. We had a strong following wind and made very good time, but constant vigilance was needed to avoid breaching in a strong and steep following sea. We had one full day on the largest of the Faeroe Islands themselves, where I hiked and hitchhiked around to see something of the landscape. We also sailed around some of the smaller islands. We might have stayed longer, but the wind had risen to Force 9 – and of course, on the way back to Scotland it was a headwind. We were forced to heave to north of the Orkneys for 2 days before we were able to make landfall. From the Orkney Islands I took the ferry back to the mainland while the others, less pressed for time, waited for the wind to abate so they could sail back to Tobermory. Since this did not require sailing overnight, the reduction in crew did not create any difficulty.

## Environment

The yacht was equipped with a standard marine 'head' or pump-out toilet, but given the high biological productivity of the North Atlantic, this is unlikely to have produced any significant environmental impact. All waste and litter was held on board until we returned to Scotland, and disposed of on land. The boat had an auxiliary motor, but we travelled almost entirely under sail, with negligible environmental impacts.

## Safety

The yacht proved herself very seaworthy in severe gale conditions far from land. All crew members wore lifejackets, but we did not have harnesses, even at night. Commercial yacht tours currently would be subject to much more stringent safety standards.

## Marketing

This trip was marketed initially by word of mouth by former clients, and subsequently through a very small advertisement in a national UK newspaper in order to fill the last crew place (mine). A full crew was needed for the crossing to the Faeroes, so there would be two two-person crew watches, plus the skipper if needed, for sailing at night. It was purely fortuitous that I saw the ad, and since the boat was departing the next day but one, I had only 1 day to hitchhike from Cambridge to Oban. Modern-day yacht tours out of Tobermory and nearby areas are marketed via tourism promotion websites and Internet directories.

# Bay of Islands, New Zealand: Various Operators

## Place

The Bay of Islands lies on the northeastern coast of New Zealand's North Island, in one of the drier, warmer and sunnier parts of the country. It is a popular holiday destination with a variety of tourist accommodation, tours and activities. These include hiking, horse riding, quad biking, diving, dolphin watching, sailing, speedboats, seakayaking and scenic flights.

## Operators

There are at least 11 operators offering skippered, fully crewed and/or catered sailing yacht cruises and charters in the Bay of Islands (Table 8.1). There are additional companies, not listed, offering bareboat charters only. I have not audited any of these operations in person, though I have sailed in the Bay of Islands in a privately owned racing catamaran.

## Activity

The various operators listed in Table 8.1 offer a range of sailing activities from full crew participation and/or instruction to luxury, relaxation and gourmet food. Some also offer diving, snorkelling, seakayaking, dolphin swims or dolphin watching whilst on board.

## Equipment

The yachts used range from 12 to 26 m length overall with a variety of sailing rigs (Table 8.1). At least one has a dive compressor, at least one carries six seakayaks and at least one carries a guitar.

## Accommodation

Of the 11 yachts listed in Table 8.1, four apparently operate only day cruises, with accommodation on shore. There are over 100 different tourist lodges, B&Bs and hotels in the Bay of Islands area. The other seven yachts offer overnight and/or longer cruises, with accommodation on board ship. Some of the larger yachts offer either a bunk berth or a twin cabin.

## Statistics

Advertised cruises last from 1 to 7 days or longer. Some of these yachts operate in the Bay of Islands only during October to May, and sail longer voyages in the Pacific during the rest of the year. The various yachts can carry from 4 to 15 passengers, and one can carry up to 45 for day sailing only. The smaller yachts may operate with only a skipper, using passengers as crew on a charter basis. The larger yachts, especially

**Table 8.1.** Sailing cruises in the Bay of Islands, New Zealand.

| Operator[1] | Yacht LOA[2] | Days | Max no. passengers | Price[4] (pppd NZD) | Special features |
|---|---|---|---|---|---|
| Atair | 22 | 3–7 | 4 | 320 | Square-rigger |
| Gungha II | 20 | 1 | 8? | 85 | Speed |
| Carino | Cat, 15 | 1 | 10? | 80 | Dolphin swim |
| Chelsea Bride | 13 | 2–3 | 6 | 130–180 | Honeymoons |
| Deliverance | 16 | Var. | 8 | 75–160 | Diving |
| Ecocruz | 22 | 3 | 10 | 165–200 | Seakayaks |
| Fairwind | 15 | >7 | 6 | 195 | Several yachts |
| Kingfisher | 12 | 1–3 | 8 | 90 | Two yachts |
| Phantom | 15 | 1 | 10 | 90 | Ocean racer |
| Tucker Thompson | 26 | 1 | 15/45[3] | 110 | Tall ship |
| Woodwind | 15 | 1–5 | ? | 70–200 | Live music |

Notes: [1]Listings from http://www.bay-of-islands.com.nz/charters.htm. Data from individual operators' websites. Operator names abbreviated. [2]LOA = length overall. [3]15 overnight, 45 day charter. [4]Approximate advertised prices per person per day, NZD including boat, skipper, crew and, in some cases, food; rates may vary with season and number of passengers.

those offering scheduled 1-day cruises, carry their own crew so the clients are solely passengers. For these boats, client-to-crew ratios are typically about 3:1 or 4:1. Prices range from NZD70 to 320 (US$50–225) per person per day. In general, most day cruises cost NZD80–110 (US$56–77) per person, and most multi-day cruises cost NZD150–220 (US$105–140) per person per day.

## Access

The various operators are based in Russell, Kerikeri, Paihia and Opua. Access to these townships is by road, or there are domestic flights from Auckland to Kerikeri. International access is via Auckland.

## Community

The Bay of Islands is part of New Zealand's North Island Region, which has an economy based on sheep farming, orchard crops, timber and tourism. The Bay of Islands is described as the 'tourist hub' and is also a domestic amenity migration destination.

## Experience

I have not taken part in any of these cruises. I sailed in the Bay of Islands over four decades ago. The weather was fine and sunny, the wind was a good strength, the scenery was beautiful and I and two others were sailing a custom-built 15 m racing catamaran. The boat had no superstructure at all – just the hulls, curved deck, mast and sails and two giant daggerboards. It was fast. I took the 'Cream Boat' ferry, so named because historically it was used to collect the cream from the island dairies every day, out into the centre of the Bay of Islands. The catamaran sailed alongside, I climbed down from the ferry, and we departed in a flurry of sails and a cloud of spray. Not quite at record speed (currently 48.7 knots, 90 km/h), but fast enough for me to remember the day well.

## Environment

Sailing cruises are generally a low-impact activity. I have not audited any of those listed in Table 8.1 personally and cannot comment directly. Those that offer dolphin swims or dolphin watching usually advertise minimal-impact practices on their websites.

## Safety

In the 1960s we had no safety equipment at all. We were sailing in swimming trunks only, because the boat threw up so much spray. Interestingly, illustrations on websites for the yachts listed in Table 8.1 do not show passengers wearing lifejackets, even under way; and only one of the charter operators lists lifejackets as part of the charter. Presumably, however, New Zealand maritime law requires all commercial sailing yachts to carry lifejackets, flares, navigation and communication equipment. For recreational vessels, at least, Maritime New Zealand (2005) lists 'essential equipment' as including compass and/or GPS; at least two means of communication; first aid; fire extinguisher; bailing system; anchor; torch; tow rope; and lifejackets. Only lifejackets, however, are listed as mandatory. Flares are not mentioned.

## Marketing

New Zealand has a range of effective interlinked tourism marketing websites. The Bay-of-Islands site is linked into regional and national sites. Websites for individual yachts and sailing tour operators are linked into the Bay of Islands site. Not surprisingly, the images on these sites almost all show sun and fine weather. Some of the photographs show sailors in foul-weather gear, but others show them in bikinis. This may not be entirely representative.

## Baja Peninsula, Mexico: NOLS Mexico

### Place

The Baja Peninsula, also known as Baja California, is a peninsula running south from California, west of the Gulf of California, and connected to the rest of Mexico at the head of the Gulf. It is a popular holiday destination, known for boating, diving, fishing and off-road driving, and for surfing and whalewatching off the ocean coastline. The NOLS Mexico base is on Concepcion Bay, about two-thirds of the way down the Peninsula on the Gulf side. Baja California is generally dry, hot and sunny.

### Operator

NOLS (National Outdoor Leadership School, 2005) is described under the Drysdale River kayaking (Chapter 4) and Prince William Sound seakayaking (Chapter 7) case studies. It is a US outdoor education organization that offers a variety of commercial adventure activities. NOLS Mexico offers sailing and seakayaking courses only.

### Activity

The Baja Coastal Sailing course runs for 3 weeks, three times a year. The main emphasis is on learning to sail; coastal navigation; and camping, expedition and leadership skills. The group sails about 120–250 km in total, with some lay-over days to hike on land, but most days spent on water.

### Equipment

The boats used are open two-masted Drascombe® Longboats, a little under 7 m in length. The NOLS groups use two to four boats depending on the number of participants. The boats are two-masted, with a jib, a gunter-rigged boomless mainsail and a small mizzen. NOLS provides group equipment, including lifejackets and cooking gear, and issues course participants with very detailed lists of the personal gear that they must bring themselves. Most of this gear is available for rent from NOLS.

## Accommodation

All accommodation is camping, including the first and last night at the NOLS Mexico branch base. Most camps are on remote beaches and coves. The boats are pulled ashore at sites where anchoring is unreliable. It appears that tents are not used, as participants are instructed to bring a bivouac bag or groundsheet as well as a sleeping bag and mat.

## Statistics

The course lasts 3 weeks and costs US$3225, or approximately US$150 per person per day. Gear rental is additional. Average group size is 14 (NOLS, 2005) with four instructors, a ratio of 3.5:1. Minimum age is 16, average age 21.

## Access

Participants arrive via Loreto, the nearest airport to the NOLS Mexico branch base at Mulege. Transport from Loreto to Mulege, and during the course, is arranged by NOLS. Loreto can be reached by air directly from San Diego or Los Angeles; by air from within Mexico; or by road. All permits and access arrangements are made by NOLS and are included in the course fee.

## Community

The NOLS Mexico branch was acquired from a local landowner in 1971. The base employs ten local Mexicans, most from Mulege families (NOLS, 2005). Once on the water, the course participants have little interaction with local communities.

## Experience

I have not audited this course or visited this site in person, but I have audited other NOLS courses and visited other bases and have found that NOLS is a highly pro-fessional organization and that its course advertising is generally accurate. According to the course description, the daily experience is centred around winds and tides, with long days on the water but also lay-over days on land and oppor-tunities to snorkel over coral reefs and watch whales and sea lions. On most days the group sails 10–20 nautical miles, about 18–37 km, but occasionally up to twice this distance. According to the course description (NOLS, 2005), participants are expected to demonstrate an understanding of coastal hazards and navigation; sailing skills; boat safety procedures; and anchoring and beaching procedures.

## Environment

NOLS has a very strong minimal-impact philosophy, and minimal-impact backcountry skills are part of its core curriculum. The published description for this course (NOLS, 2005) also specifies that participants are expected to 'show an interest in pertinent environmental issues; demonstrate basic knowledge and respect for local cultures; show understanding, appreciation and respect for the natural world above and below the water; and know characteristic flora and fauna of the area'.

## Safety

Safety is one of the prime areas of instruction in this course, starting with the boats used. In addition to knowledge of tides, weather and navigation, participants are taught how to use safety equipment, radio and signal flags; how to rescue someone fallen overboard; how to handle the boat in heavy weather; how to right and bail a swamped boat; how to avoid hazards under water and on land; how to apply first aid techniques; and how to operate effectively as a team leader and team member.

## Marketing

The course is marketed via the NOLS website and course catalogue. The information provided is quite detailed, especially regarding activities and equipment.

# 9     Expedition Cruises

King penguins, MV *Explorer*, Antarctica. Photo Ralf Buckley.

Zodiac group, MV *Explorer*, Antarctica. Photo Ralf Buckley.

## Sector Structure

The giant modern cruise liner industry is almost the epitome of mass tourism and the antithesis of adventure tourism. Travelling to remote parts of the world as a commercial passenger on an expedition or other working vessel, however, was a well-established historical practice in the days before liability laws rendered such practices uneconomic.

Indeed, when I was still at primary school, my family travelled from England to New Zealand as passengers on a cargo boat, and back a year later. On the way we passed places such as Pitcairn Island, famous as the refuge of mutineers from the *Bounty*. We did not land, but the modern inhabitants came out to visit us in their own boats, selling fruit and wood carvings.

Building boats specifically as commercial expedition cruise vessels, to operate a business taking paying passengers to remote tropical and polar parts of the globe, seems to have started with construction of the *Lindblad Explorer* in 1969. For a long time, the *Explorer* was the world's only ice-strengthened commercial expedition cruise vessel, so she effectively enjoyed a monopoly on Arctic and Antarctic tours.

With the break-up of the former USSR, however, a number of former Russian polar research vessels became available for private charter, triggering a considerable expansion in this sector of the expedition cruise industry. Originally named after famous Russian academicians, these vessels now have highly flexible names depending on the particular tour company they are chartered to at the time. They are certainly not luxury cruise liners, but they are comfortable enough and more importantly, they are built to travel safely through the polar ice floes, and skippered by highly competent Russian captains and crew.

Expedition cruises are not restricted to the Arctic and Antarctic. These same vessels also visit mid-Atlantic islands and steam far up the equatorial Amazon River in the season between their Arctic and Antarctic voyages each year. There are also specialist tour boats that operate only in tropical areas. In addition to the tourist riverboats on the Amazon itself, there are expedition vessels that travel far up other broad, slow-flowing tropical rivers such as the Sepik in Papua New Guinea. Some of these, including the MTS *Discoverer* described in the Papua New Guinea case study, are equipped as dive boats and also operate dive tours to coral reef areas around the countries concerned.

The opportunity to offer multi-activity adventure cruises from a single, well-equipped expedition vessel, taking paying passengers to uncrowded oceans where they can choose to dive, surf, seakayak or perhaps even kiteboard away from the crowds, does not yet seem to have been exploited. Many island resorts do indeed offer such a range of activities, however, as outlined under the surfing and diving chapters of this volume, so perhaps tropical adventure cruises are the next step. If so, they may well be assisted by the publicity surrounding professional marketing exploits such as the Quicksilver® Crossing, an extended boat-based surfing safari featuring a succession of sponsored surfers and aimed ultimately to sell Quicksilver® brand clothing (Buckley, 2003b).

# South Georgia and Antarctic Peninsula: Abercrombie and Kent, Explorer Shipping

## Place

Only a tiny fraction of the Antarctic is available for tourism by any means of access (Splettstoesser *et al.*, 2004). All but a very few of these tourists arrive by ship, in cruises that visit the northernmost tip of the Antarctic Peninsula. As the least ice-bound part of the continent, this area is used both by penguin breeding colonies and for scientific bases such as the British base at Port Lockroy. Most Antarctic cruises ply fairly directly between Ushuaia, on the southernmost tip of the South American continent, and the Antarctic Peninsula.

A few, including the early season *Explorer* cruise in which I took part, also visit a variety of sub-Antarctic islands. Since these islands are both further north and surrounded by ocean, they have much milder climates than the Antarctic Peninsula and indeed support permanent vegetation of various types. As the only oases of land in the vast Southern Ocean, they are also used very heavily by breeding colonies of otherwise pelagic seabirds and marine mammals. It is on these sub-Antarctic islands that one can see breeding colonies of seals, including elephant seal; seabirds such as the giant skua and various species of albatross; and penguins, including king penguins.

These sub-Antarctic cruises commonly visit the Falkland Islands, most of which are regrettably still inaccessible because of Argentinean minefields; some also visit Grytviken in South Georgia, once the base for the former Antarctic whaling industry and now abandoned save for a British military garrison and a single family who maintain a small museum amidst the rusting wreckage of industrial whaling. Populations of the many whale species may take centuries or more to recover, and then only if they are protected from future whaling. Elephant seals, however, can be seen along the shores of Grytviken Bay.

## Operator

When I took part in this tour it was operated by Explorer Shipping, which was then a subsidiary of the large international nature tourism company Abercrombie and Kent. Explorer Shipping operated three consecutive seasons each year, in the Arctic, Amazon and Antarctic, respectively. The first Antarctic tour each year started from the Falkland Islands and visited South Georgia and other sub-Antarctic islands before proceeding to the Antarctic Peninsula. Subsequent cruises shuttled more directly between the port of Ushuaia, at the southern tip of South America, and the Antarctic Peninsula. These, or similar itineraries, are now offered by companies such as GAP Adventures (2005) and Intrepid Expeditions (2005). Similar itineraries are also currently offered by Abercrombie and Kent (2005), using a different and larger vessel, the *Explorer II*.

## Activity

Much of each voyage is necessarily spent at sea, but landings are made on a number of islands as well as the Antarctic Peninsula itself. Most of these landings are for wildlife watching, focusing on marine mammals and nesting seabirds, but the history of whaling at Grytviken in South Georgia, of Shackleton's astonishing voyage, of the Antarctic research bases, and even of the Falklands war are also covered. Interpretation is delivered through a series of illustrated lectures by relevant experts whilst the vessel is at sea, and by knowledgeable guides during landings. Landings are made in small inflatable boats.

## Equipment

The *Lindblad Explorer* was built in 1969 as the world's first purpose-built expeditionary passenger ship. She is 73 m in length and originally carried 98 passengers in 53 cabins, and ten inflatables that could transport up to 15 people each. She was commissioned by Lars-Erik Lindblad for his pioneering worldwide nature tourism company, Lindblad Expeditions (2005), which is still operational but no longer owns this vessel.

Some years ago, the vessel was taken over by an independent company, Explorer Shipping, and renamed *Explorer*. At the time when I took part in this tour, Explorer Shipping had been taken over by Abercrombie and Kent. Subsequently, Abercrombie and Kent replaced her with a larger vessel, *Explorer II*, built in 1996. *Explorer II* carries up to 198 passengers, 146 crew and 12 inflatables.

The original *Explorer* was refitted extensively in 2004 and now carries up to 108 passengers. She is currently owned by the GAP Shipping Co. Ltd and managed by V Ships Leisure, both based in Monaco. She is still captained by the legendary Captain Uli Demel. Cruises on the *Explorer* are now offered both by GAP Adventures (2005) and by Intrepid Expeditions (2005). Throughout these vicissitudes she has apparently maintained a faithful clientele of repeat passengers as well as crew, to whom she is still known as the Little Red Ship.

## Accommodation

Accommodation during the cruise itself was on board the expedition vessel, the *Explorer*, and ranged from small two-berth, lower-deck cabins to luxurious upper-deck suites. There was one night's hotel accommodation in Buenos Aires before the charter flight to the Falkland Islands to join the *Explorer*. Currently, itineraries offered on the *Explorer* by GAP Adventures (2005) and Intrepid Expeditions (2005) connect via Buenos Aires, and those offered by Abercombie and Kent (2005) on *Explorer II* connect via Santiago, Chile. When the vessel returned to Ushuaia at the end of the trip, passengers could proceed directly to connecting flights with no need for hotel accommodation, unless they planned to extend their stay for local tours.

## Statistics

The original *Explorer* carried up to 98 passengers if all beds were full, and 60 crew. The refurbished *Explorer* carries up to 108 passengers and 53 crew. *Explorer II* can carry twice that number of passengers and 2.5 times as many crew and staff. Staff include: the boat's crew, responsible for sailing the vessel; a separate hospitality crew responsible for the cabins and catering; guides employed full-time by the tour operator; and naturalists and scientists contracted trip by trip. Generally, only guides and scientists accompany the clients ashore, unless boat crew are needed to drive some of the inflatables. While the overall client-to-staff ratio is around 2:1 in the *Explorer*, the effective client-to-guide ratio is perhaps 10:1 or higher.

The closest current equivalent to the expedition cruise I experienced is the 'Full Spirit of Shackleton' tour offered by Intrepid Expeditions (2005) using the *Explorer*. This takes 23 days in total, of which 18 are on board the ship, and costs US$6630–12,730 per person depending on the class of cabin, plus a local port fee of US$400 per person. This represents a price range of around US$300 to over US$500 per person per day.

Expedition cruises to Antarctica, South Georgia and the Falkland Islands currently offered by Abercrombie and Kent (2005) in *Explorer II* take 18 or 19 days in total, including 5 days for transfers between Miami, USA and Ushuaia at the southern tip of Argentina. Costs for the various cruise dates in the 2005/06 southern hemisphere summer season range from US$6370 to US$20,770 per person twinshare, depending on the deck and class of cabin, plus US$475 per person for air transfers and US$995–17,595 single supplement. These include port charges of US$275 per person at Ushuaia. These prices thus correspond to costs ranging from US$380 to over US$2000 per person per day.

## Access

The trip in which I took part was the first trip of the Antarctic season in that year, and the *Explorer* had just arrived at the Falkland Islands after steaming south through the Atlantic. We joined the vessel by a charter flight from Buenos Aires to Port Stanley. At the end of this trip the *Explorer* returned to Ushuaia.

Current itineraries offered on the *Explorer* by Intrepid Expeditions all include sub-Antarctic islands as well as the Antarctic Peninsula. Access is via Buenos Aires. For Abercrombie and Kent's current cruises to the Antarctic and sub-Antarctic islands, passengers join and leave the *Explorer II* in Ushuaia, reached by air from Miami via Santiago, Chile.

Access from either vessel to shore is in outboard-powered inflatables. On the trip in which I took part, on the original *Explorer*, the inflatables were stacked on deck when not in use, swung overboard using davits, and brought alongside the *Explorer* one at a time, where a set of steps was lowered from deck to allow passengers to disembark into the inflatables. On shore, the inflatables were simply run aground for passengers to disembark over the bows. The only exception was on the Antarctic Peninsula itself, where the *Explorer* steamed slowly into thin pack ice until passengers could disembark directly.

The Antarctic itself has no government and no laws except the Antarctic Treaty, but various sectors of the Antarctic continent are claimed by different nations and in some instances these nations apply their own domestic legislation, or have enacted specific legislation for their Antarctic territories. The June 2005 meeting of the 45 Antarctic Treaty nations also agreed on new environmental rules for pollution control. The various sub-Antarctic islands are claimed by a number of different countries. The Falkland Islands, South Georgia and associated islands nearby remain under British control. Any landing permits that may be required are obtained by the tour operator. Port fees at Ushuaia are charged separately to the basic tour cost as summarized above.

## Community

Community might seem a strange term to use in connection with the Antarctic, but in fact we met a number of local inhabitants, starting with the man who drove us from the Falkland Island airport to the port with a running commentary on the Falklands wars. At Grytviken we met a small detachment from the British garrison, and a family who had arrived in their own yacht and were living in the old whaling station maintaining a small museum. At the British scientific base on the Antarctic Peninsula we met someone who had sailed a yacht single-handed from Australia and anchored near the station so that his boat froze into the ice over winter. He had lived onboard by himself throughout the continuous dark of the Antarctic winter, with just enough fuel to turn his heater on once a week. Not surprisingly, he was very keen to talk.

## Experience

For most clients, highlights of the product include colonies of various seals, including elephant seals; large colonies of various penguin species, including breeding king penguins; and an enormous variety of seabirds seen at short range, including breeding colonies of several species of albatross. Icebergs and Antarctic landscapes are also an important scenic attraction. The *Explorer* is well fitted out, especially after its 2004 refurbishment, and the *Explorer II* appears to be even more so. Even so, crossing the Drake Passage from Argentina to Antarctica seems to induce seasickness in all but the hardiest and best-medicated passengers.

## Environment

Whilst at sea the vessel appears to follow the requirements of the MARPOL Convention. For example, we observed garbage being bagged and stored in a hold under the aft deck. Similarly, passengers were briefed not to throw cigarette butts or any other litter overboard.

By far the most significant potential impacts on the natural environment, however, are during landings, and particularly during interactions with breeding birds and animals. Passengers were advised repeatedly of minimal allowable approach distances to various species, and these restrictions were generally observed by passengers and diplomatically enforced by staff. Passengers were also advised of the types of impacts that can occur, for example the very rapid attacks by skuas and other predators on seabird eggs and chicks if the parent birds are disturbed or distracted for even a very short period. Similarly, passengers were told how to recognize symptoms of stress in penguins, and how seal pups may be crushed if tourists disturb the territorial balance between dominant males (Buckley, 2003a, pp. 188–190).

There were several instances, however, where nesting seabirds, although not leaving the nest, did show signs of stress even at the approved approach distances, particularly when a number of tourists approached with cameras at the same time. This suggests that these approach distances, which are set in guidelines applying for all Antarctic tour operators in this category, may need revision; and to be sure of minimal impact meanwhile, the *Explorer* may wish to set a somewhat greater margin for its own passengers (Buckley, 2003a). In terms of total impact on the populations of the species concerned, it seems likely that the early season landings by relatively small numbers of well-behaved passengers from the *Explorer* have little impact as compared to the much larger numbers of tourists landing from cruise liners later in the season. Since the *Explorer* lands at a number of sites that are not accessible to the liners, however, minimal-impact behaviour by its guides and guests is particularly critical (Buckley, 2003a).

## Safety

For a voyage such as this in Antarctic waters well away from normal shipping lanes, and involving frequent passenger disembarkation, there are a wide range of ever-present safety considerations. Foremost of these is the safety of the vessel itself. The *Explorer*, and presumably also *Explorer II*, is a highly seaworthy purpose-built ice-strengthened expedition boat. Her crew, particularly her captain, are highly experienced in Antarctic waters. In the initial passenger briefing on the first day of the voyage, he was careful to point out that whilst he and his crew can keep the ship safe from storms and icebergs, the passengers as well as the crew have a respon-sibility to keep the vessel safe from fire. As with any seagoing ship, there are briefings on emergency signals and procedures, and lifeboat drills.

When passengers go ashore in the inflatables, there is a system for each individual passenger to mark when they leave the main vessel and when they return, to make sure no one is inadvertently left behind. In boarding the inflatables, passengers are called down the stepped gangway one at a time and assisted into the inflatable by two crewmembers, one standing at the base of the steps and one in the boat. Passengers are also assisted in disembarking from the inflatables onshore. These precautions are necessary since some of the passengers are relatively elderly.

## Marketing

Originally built as a special-purpose expedition vessel for Lindblad Expeditions, the *Explorer* was well ahead of her time. Subsequently, she was operated by a stand-alone company, Explorer Shipping, which carried out its own marketing. Some years ago, Explorer Shipping was taken over by the large international nature tour operator Abercrombie and Kent, which marketed expedition cruises on the *Explorer* as part of its overall portfolio. These cruises are now offered on the *Explorer II*. Cruises are offered in the Arctic, the Amazon and the Antarctic at different seasons each year. Abercrombie and Kent is a long-established and very well-known tour operator with an extensive clientele and a wide range of tours worldwide, so many passengers on the *Explorer II*'s Antarctic cruises are also likely to have taken part in their trips before. Cruises on the original *Explorer* are currently marketed by GAP Adventures (2005) and Intrepid Expeditions (2005). These companies also offer a portfolio of other adventure tours.

# Svalbard: Aurora Expeditions

## Place

Information on Svalbard is provided under the Svalbard seakayaking case study in Chapter 7. Since the Gulf Stream brings warmer water north of the Arctic Circle in this area, the ocean is navigable for ice-strengthened vessels much further north than in the Canadian Arctic. Except for trips to the North Pole by icebreaker or helicopter, therefore, boat cruises around Spitzbergen are probably the most northerly commercial tours in the world.

## Operator

Aurora Expeditions runs expedition cruises to the Arctic and Antarctic, and the Kimberley coast of Australia. The company headquarters is in Sydney, and tour guides are principally Australian and American.

## Activity

During the northern hemisphere summer, Aurora offers Arctic voyages in the Svalbard area north of Norway, and the eastern coastline of Greenland. One of these voyages is a circumnavigation of Spitzbergen, the principal island of the Svalbard Archipelago.

## Equipment

Aurora's Arctic and Antarctic cruises use ice-strengthened Russian vessels, refitted from research to commercial passenger configurations and operated by Russian crews. The circumnavigation of Spitzbergen by Aurora Expeditions is an 8-day voyage departing and returning to Longyearbyen, the principal settlement in Svalbard. The boat used is a 72 m Class-A, ice-strengthened vessel, the *Polar Pioneer*, with around 30 crew and staff and cabins for 54 passengers. She is powered by twin diesel turbines driving a single variable-pitch propeller, and is equipped with bow, stern and side thrusters for manoeuvring in ice. The *Polar Pioneer* was built in 1985 and refurbished for commercial use in 2000.

## Accommodation

Accommodation during the tour is in cabins aboard the vessel. Clients also need to stay overnight at Longyearbyen in Svalbard for at least 1 night before the vessel departs, and 1 night when it returns. These are not included in the tour price. There are two principal hotels available. One is designed and constructed in a rustic style, supposedly mimicking a polar expedition base in historical times. The other has a more conventional layout. Both are comfortable, and expensive. Most clients also need to stay overnight in Oslo on the way to Longyearbyen.

## Statistics

The *Polar Pioneer* can take up to 54 passengers. There are generally around four to five guides and lecturers excluding the ship's crew. This hence gives a ratio of around 10–12 clients per guide. The voyage takes 8 days, plus 2 or 3 days staying in Longyearbyen and another 2 days or more reaching it. The total cost of the boat trip, ex Longyearbyen, is AUD4250, or about US$300 per day. Airfares, and hotel costs in Longyearbyen, are additional.

## Access

Access is via Longyearbyen in Svalbard, which is reached by air from mainland Norway. All permits are arranged by the tour operator.

## Community

Interactions with the Svalbard community are as described for the Svalbard seakayaking case study.

## Experience

Svalbard is a beautiful but rugged place, and an ice-strengthened expedition cruise boat is one of the few ways to see it. The opportunity to go ashore and walk across the tundra is a critical part of the experience, even though reindeer stay far away, presumably keeping out of rifleshot. We did see polar bear, though not close; but the best sightings were of Arctic fox, apparently undisturbed by a line of camera-wielding tourists lying on their bellies. Also memorable was a still, sunny day amongst the edges of the pack ice at almost 82°N.

## Environment

Environmental management issues and practices for this tour are described by Buckley (2003a, pp. 191–193). Non-biodegradable wastes were apparently bagged and later taken ashore. Food scraps were dumped overboard. Sewage is treated on board and the treated effluent discharged. As with other expeditionary cruise boats, passengers are taken ashore once or twice each day in Zodiacs, inflatable rubber boats powered by outboard engines. Potential impacts from the inflatables include noise disturbance and two-stroke fuel and oil residues. Both of these are unavoidable, as with outboard-powered recreational boats worldwide. They can be reduced by the choice of engine, good maintenance procedures, and cautious driving when close to wildlife (Rainbow *et al.*, 2000). In general, the Aurora staff did indeed drive with care and discretion around seabird colonies and marine mammals.

The most significant potential impacts were onshore, through tramp-ling of Arctic vegetation and disturbance to birds and wildlife. The guides were careful to keep passengers far enough away from wildlife that the latter seemed undisturbed, albeit alert. We were even able to watch Arctic fox at close range, for an extended period. Svalbard residents hunt wildlife, and the impacts of tourism are presumably low relative to those of hunting.

## Safety

The overriding safety concern for this tour is when guests and guides are onshore in areas frequented by polar bears. Public notices in Svalbard itself and in incoming flights warn visitors to take the danger of polar bear attacks seriously, and visitors and residents alike are warned not to leave the settled area without a firearm of adequate calibre. Parties going ashore from the *Polar Pioneer* are accompanied by several armed guides and crew, who check the terrain and guard the perimeter unobtrusively. Except in very open flat terrain with good visibility, therefore, the passengers are kept together in relatively tight groups where they can be managed quite closely by the guides.

## Marketing

This tour is marketed as part of Aurora's overall portfolio, which includes both Arctic and Antarctic voyages. In addition to its website (Aurora Expeditions, 2005), the company produces and distributes catalogues and brochures, and sends out newsletters to previous clients.

# Sepik River, Papua New Guinea: Various Operators

## Place

The Sepik River is the largest river on the northern side of Papua New Guinea, flowing from the mountains north of Mt Wilhelm to its estuary between Wewak and Madang on the north coast. For most of its length it flows through tropical lowland rainforest inhabited by local villagers whose lifestyle is still largely traditional. In particular, it flows past the small townships of Ambunti and Angoram, known for their ornate village longhouses, *haus tambaran*. Local communities in this area are also famous for their woodcarvings.

The river itself is slow-moving and sinuous, broad and muddy. Upstream from the townships there are some large lakes connected to the river, the Chambri Lakes. As with much of Papua New Guinea, large areas have been logged. I have not visited this particular region since the mid-1970s, so I cannot comment on the current status of these forests. A general description of current conservation issues in Papua New Guinea rainforests has been provided recently by Primack and Corlett (2004).

## Operators

A number of different tour boats currently operate on the Sepik River. The MV *Sepik Spirit* runs a 4-day, 3-night tour between Karawari Lodge on the Karawari River and Timbunke on the middle Sepik (PNG Tours, 2005). The MTS *Discoverer* operates 4-day cruises between Madang and Timbunke, including a side trip to the Chambri Lakes; and 5-day, 4-night cruises on the Middle Sepik, starting and ending at Timbunke (Melanesian Tourist Services, 2005). There are also tours based at Ambunti that take clients on the river in outboard-powered canoes (Diversion Oz, 2005). When I visited in the 1970s there were no tour boats, and I travelled in a small local boat going upriver to fish and trade. Information presented here on place, community, etc., is derived from my own experience; information on tours and operators is derived from current websites.

## Activity

These are essentially remote-area sightseeing tours, but provide opportunities for clients to go ashore at various villages and to paddle on the river in canoes or local dugouts. The vessels can travel close to the riverbanks in some stretches, and clients can watch birds, wildlife and local villagers from the decks. The MTS *Discoverer*'s 5-day Sepik cruise visits Angoram, the Keram River, Kambaramba, Tambanum, Timbunke and the Chambri Lakes, returning to Timbunke at the end of the trip. Passengers generally fly back from Timbunke to Madang. This flight is not included as part of the tour package.

## Equipment

The *Sepik Spirit* is a shallow-draft expeditionary vessel built in 1989 to American Bureau of Shipping standards. She carries 18 passengers in nine two-berth cabins, each with bathrooms en suite. The MTS *Discoverer* is a large vessel with a total passenger capacity of 42. Cabins are equipped with satellite phones. It has a dive shop, a helipad and five tenders. This contrasts rather strongly with the dugout canoes used by local villagers, which are generally too narrow to sit in and are propelled by a single-bladed paddle.

## Accommodation

On the MTS *Discoverer*, accommodation is on board, and the same applies for the *Sepik Spirit* whilst on the water. Other tours are based out of Ambunti Lodge (2005), and trips on the *Sepik Spirit* start or end at Karawari Lodge. Overnight stays at Karawari, if needed, are not included in *Sepik Spirit* tour costs.

## Statistics

The MV *Sepik Spirit* offers a 3-night, 4-day tour at a price of US$1545 twinshare or US$2300 single, plus US$270 per person each way for air travel from Mt Hagen (Trans-Niugini Tours, 2005). This corresponds to over US$500 per day in total. The 4-day Sepik cruises on the MTS *Discoverer* cost US$1400 per person twinshare, and the 5-day cruises cost US$1750 per person twinshare. Airfares between Madang and Timbunke are additional. This corresponds to about US$400 per person per day. These tours are also marketed by a wide range of agents and tour packaging companies, under their own names, with different transport and accommodation options and at widely different prices.

## Access

Timbunke, Ambunti and Karawari are all accessible by air. For the MV *Sepik Spirit*, access is via Karawari. Flights between Karawari and Mt Hagen in the New Guinea Highlands operate 3 days per week. For the MTS *Discoverer*, access is via Timbunke, reached by air from Madang. Madang and Mt Hagen are major internal airports in Papua New Guinea.

## Community

Local communities and their arts, traditions and artefacts are one of the major attractions for most international tourists to Papua New Guinea, so interactions with local communities are generally an important part of any trip package. A passenger on the MTS *Discoverer* clearly has the option to remain in the comfort of the boat and see everything at a distance, but most passengers take opportunities to disembark and visit local villages and markets. Such opportunities are probably even greater on the smaller MV *Sepik Spirit*, though since I have not travelled on either, I cannot comment directly.

Trips that involve canoe travel are likely to use local boatmen and involve a high degree of interaction with villagers. When I visited the area several decades ago I encountered only two other white people, an American couple there to buy carvings for their art store in New York. Apart from them, all my dealings were with local communities.

## Experience

When I visited, locals carried on with their day-to-day activities without paying any attention to me or the boat I was in. Hand-hewn dugout canoes were plentiful, used for fishing and local transport. Convention was that men paddled standing and women sitting. I learnt this when I was offered the opportunity to take one out, and tried to sit in it as if it were a flatwater racing kayak. In that way I was able to paddle it without falling in, but I did not last for long once I stood up, so my skills were judged deficient even in comparison to the youngest local boys.

The river surface is generally glassy, and back then there were very few motorboats of any type to create wash or wake. When our riverboat passed by it created a set of low ripples that tipped most of the boys into the water, but the older men were able to balance gracefully. Falling in is not a trivial matter, since the Sepik is famous for its crocodiles, and crocodile emblems are carved everywhere. I do not know how much circumstances have changed subsequently.

Mosquitoes were very abundant, but modern tour boats have air conditioning and presumably also screened windows on cabins and observation decks. I was able to visit the *haus tambaran*, with appropriate respect, and saw numerous carvings, but did not attempt to buy any. At that time, these were original artworks with a semi-religious significance, not artefacts made to sell to tourists. I was therefore somewhat concerned that art buyers were trying to buy such large quantities and bargain down prices so severely. Their knowledge of New Guinea pidgin, now known as Tok Pisin, was rudimentary, so they were not very successful.

## Environment

Environmental management practices by the tour boats mentioned above are not known. Direct impacts might include discharge of sewage, food residues and litter, noise and bank erosion from wash. The river is already nutrient-rich, however, and already receives human wastes from riverbank villages, so the addition of organic matter from tour boats is likely to have little impact. Large dive boats are likely to be equipped with holding tanks, though these may not always be used.

Indirect impacts are likely to be of greater ecological significance. These may be either positive or negative. Positive impacts might include the potential role of tourism as a counterpart or alternative to logging. Negative impacts might include increased hunting, capture or collection of native birds, animals or plants to make artefacts for sale or display to tourists. No quantitative information is available.

## Safety

The river is relatively placid and the tour boats are generally not at risk from waves or storms. Passengers are unlikely to fall overboard and, if they do, can readily be rescued as long as they are not injured or attacked. The risk of illness from contaminated food is low as long as passengers eat only on board tour boats or in lodges. Eating local food always carries a somewhat greater risk, especially for tourists whose digestive systems may not be used to it. The greatest risk to tourists in Papua New Guinea, however, is the potential of small-scale violence from local 'rascals'. Again, this risk is probably lower for organized tour groups than for individual travellers, both because there is safety in numbers and because guides are better able to judge conditions and hazards.

## Marketing

Marketing of these boat trips on the Sepik River, as for most tours anywhere in Papua New Guinea, is somewhat confusing and changes frequently. Numerous agents and tour companies based in many different countries offer the same basic trip under different names, packaged in different ways, and with different pricing structures. For example, trips run from another country may include airfares, accommodation in gateway towns, and international guide costs as well as local transport, accommodation and food, activities and guides. Sometimes the only way to tell whether two trips use the same vessel is to compare photographs on their respective websites, since they may use different names for the same boat. This issue is not unique to Papua New Guinea (PNG) – the same practice, for example, occurs for Russian vessels used by polar tour companies – but it does seem to be particularly prevalent in PNG.

# 10 Diving

Walindi Resort, Papua New Guinea. Photo Peter Lange. By permission.

Walindi Resort, Papua New Guinea. Photo Darek Sepioto. By permission.

## Sector Structure

Scuba diving is now a major recreational activity worldwide. In popular dive tourism destinations such as Australia's Great Barrier Reef, commercial tour operators have installed large permanent pontoon structures with giant underwater cages (Quicksilver Cruises, 2005). In these, day tourists with no previous diving practice or qualifications can learn to use a tethered regulator under supervision, either as a stand-alone experience or as a first step in gaining basic dive qualifications (Buckley, 2003a). There are dive resorts and dive charter boats operating throughout the tropics and subtropics.

Indeed, as a commercial tourism activity, diving has a number of advantages over other recreational water sports. Most importantly, since compressors are large, expensive and heavy so that very few divers own one, divers rely completely on commercial dive shops to fill their tanks. Unlike many other adventure tourism activities, therefore, almost all dive tourists are tied in to commercial providers at least for air, even if they have their own equipment, local knowledge and transport. Of course, most dive shops also have an extensive range of equipment and accessories for sale, including high-priced items such as dive computers and underwater photographic gear. In practice, most dive resorts and charter boats now offer standard packages that include guides, equipment rental and even wetsuits as well as air and local transport. Clients can hence arrive completely unequipped, as long as they are appropriately qualified.

The commercial dive tourism industry also benefits from the internation-alization of recreational diving qualifications. The international systems operated by PADI, the Professional Association of Dive Instructors (2005), and its US counterpart NAUI, the National Association of Underwater Instructors (2005), are now recognized almost universally for divers and instructors alike. These act as safety certification systems, both for tour operators accepting clients and for divers seeking reputable tour operators. Dive shops and tour operators are classified by facilities offered and instructor capabilities up to 5-star; and individual divers are certified according to capabilities and experience, from basic open-water up to various advanced instructor levels.

As the number of recreational divers has grown, at least partly because of introductory dive tourism, the number of highly experienced recreational divers has also grown. Many of these are constantly seeking new dive locations and experiences as well as specialist diving qualifications. In particular, these include the use of EANx, Enhanced Air Nitrox, for longer deep dives. EANx, commonly referred to simply as Nitrox, is a nitrogen–oxygen mixture with a higher proportion of oxygen than normal air. Many higher-ranked dive shops now offer Nitrox facilities and new dive tourism operations are constantly exploring increasingly deep and remote des-tinations. Whereas most commercial dive tours remain above 25 m depth, for example, there are now operators who will lead dives to considerably greater depths at some sites.

Various commercial operators offer dives with sharks, using shark cages for some species and circumstances, but relying on behavioural understanding for other species. Open-water night dives are commonplace, even on completely submerged coral pinnacles far from land.

The most recent addition, perhaps representing the current edge of dive tourism, is diving under the edge of the Arctic and Antarctic ice. Whilst marine scientists have undertaken such dives for decades, it is only recently that logistical support, suitably skilled clients and sufficient demand have been available for such tours to be offered commercially (Aurora Expeditions, 2005; Smith Diving, 2005; Victory Adventure Expeditions, 2005). Perhaps in future, as deep-diving submersible vessels become more commonplace and hence cheaper, these too will be offered as a commercial tourism experience.

## Great Barrier Reef, Australia: Taka Dive

### Place

The Great Barrier Reef, the world's largest coral reef system, runs for over 2000 km down the northeast coast of Australia, covering a total area of 350,000 km$^2$. It is not a single reef but a complex of some 3400 individual reefs, in three main types. The outer ribbon reefs are narrow linear reefs that run along the outer margin of the continental shelf. The eastern slopes, subject to open ocean swell, are solid and massive and fall steeply away to the deep ocean seabed over 1000 m below. The western edges are shallow and ragged, flanked by the shallow sandy seabed and protected waters of the Great Barrier Reef lagoon. At the narrowest point, near Cape Melville, the outer ribbon reefs are only 25 km from the mainland. At its widest point, Swains Reefs at the southern end stretch to almost 300 km offshore.

Scattered throughout the length and breadth of the Great Barrier Reef Province are large platform reefs, most of them broadly oval in shape but highly variable in detailed topography. Some of these support small coral islands, whereas others are entirely beneath the water surface. There are also a relatively small number of baserock islands, and most of these are surrounded by narrow fringing reefs, the third major type of reef in the region.

For much of the year the area is subject to southeasterly trade winds, which set the direction of surface chop and hence exert a major influence on the shape and structure of the platform reefs and islands. During midsummer the trade winds cease, but there are occasional cyclones that can cause extensive local damage to shallow branching corals. The biological diversity of the reefs generally increases from south to north. The area is managed by the Great Barrier Reef Marine Park Authority (GBRMPA). Only part of the area is zoned for full protection, with the remainder open for fishing.

### Operator

Taka Dive (2005) is a specialist dive tour operator that runs a single, 30 m, live-aboard dive boat out of Cairns, the principal tourist gateway to the Great Barrier Reef. It offers 4-day, 5-day and 7-day dive cruises to sections of the Great Barrier Reef north of Cairns.

### Activity

The flagship tour product from Taka Dive is a 5-day, 4-night live-aboard trip to Osprey Reef, several days steaming northeast of Cairns. The trip visits a number of other dive sites en route, including famous and highly frequented dives such as Cod Hole and the North Horn shark dive, and more remote and little-visited locations such as Steve's Bommie. The trip includes four dives each day on most days. At some sites, some of these are night dives. Clients should generally have at least Advanced Open Water or equivalent qualifications and appropriate experience, and in fact many clients are highly qualified.

Prior to each individual dive the divemaster provides a briefing on underwater topography, points of interest and maximum depths, and also displays a sketch of the dive site on a small whiteboard. Clients dive in pairs or buddy groups and are generally not accompanied by a guide or instructor, but the divers are generally within visual contact so as to maximize the chances that everyone will see as many interesting marine plants and animals as possible. At some dive sites there are particular marine species that are regularly sighted at or near the same precise location, and one of the Taka dive staff or videographer will help clients find it. The vessel's crew includes a cook and all meals are provided, with timing adjusted if necessary to fit around the dive schedule.

## Equipment

The company's current live-aboard dive boat is a 30 m, purpose-built vessel launched in 2003, with a cruising speed of 11 knots, a cruising range of 5000 nautical miles, a 5 m custom-built dive tender, and accommodation for 30 passengers and 12 crew. Prior to 2003 the company used a purpose-built 24 m diving vessel, *Taka III*, which was the one I travelled in. The rear deck was fitted out as diving platform, with sockets and retaining straps for dive cylinders and backpacks, compressed air hoses from an overhead gantry, drying racks for wetsuits and other clothing, and freshwater bins to wash and store masks and snorkels. This layout allows all divers to get kitted up simultaneously and quickly before each dive, so they can all enter and leave the water at about the same time. This is important for the overall scheduling of the trip, since the time between dives is needed to travel from one dive site to the next, by day as well as overnight.

Taka Dive can provide its clients with a full set of diving equipment, including a dive computer, at a price of AUD140 (US$105) for the 5-day trip. Computers are essential for the intensive repetitive diving over a multi-day period, since decompression requirements are too complicated to calculate using dive tables or analogue multiple-dive decompression calculators. Clients may bring their own diving equipment, but these must comply with Queensland Government regulations, e.g. a requirement for a double octopus/regulator system.

## Accommodation

The trip is a live-aboard tour package that includes a shared cabin and all meals on the boat, but not accommodation or meals in Cairns before or after the trip. Taka Dive's current vessel has a variety of cabin classes, seven of them twin-berth and four quad-berth. In the vessel I experienced, the quad cabins each held two two-storey bunks. The bunks barely fitted in the cabin and the people barely fitted in the bunks, but this was a specialist dive tour and the clients were there to dive, so this was to be expected. Fresh water is limited to what the boat can carry, so whilst showers are available, water use is restricted. The current vessel has 12 showers and can carry 30,000 litres of water. The vessel in which I travelled was not luxurious, but it was perfectly comfortable, well-designed to carry as many divers as possible in the relatively calm waters of the Great Barrier Reef. The current vessel offers a greater degree of luxury.

## Statistics

The current vessel, still named the *Taka*, carries a total of 30 dive clients and 12 crew (Taka Dive, 2005). The Osprey Reef trip described here includes a total of 5 days and 4 nights port-to-port. Prices range from AUD1180 to 1680, depending on cabin class, plus AUD140 for a full set of dive gear including computer, and an additional levy of AUD25. This is around US$250–350 per person per day in total.

## Access

Cairns is accessible by road or air, with some international flights connecting directly to Cairns and others arriving via Brisbane. On *Taka III*, access to the dive sites was directly from the stern deck. The current vessel uses a 5 m diving tender. As a commercial tour operator within the Great Barrier Reef Marine Park, Taka Dive has an operating permit from the Great Barrier Reef Marine Park Authority. The Authority levies user fees for all recreational use of the Marine Park, currently AUD4.50 (US$3.40) per person per day. One-day trips at the lower end of the dive tourism market, competing principally for the highly price-conscious backpacker clientele, commonly charge this user fee as a separate add-on, not quoted in the tour price. Those at the upper end of the market, including multiple-day live-aboard specialist dive trips such as those offered by Taka Dive, are competing principally on product and service quality for a well-informed international specialist market, so it is simpler for them to include the user fee in the tour package price, and this was Taka's practice when I took part in this trip. Currently, however, Taka Dive (2005) charges an AUD25 levy on top of tour prices, described as an 'environmental management charge, port levy and fuel surcharge'.

## Community

Whilst regional landscapes are largely agricultural, the Cairns economy relies principally on tourism: perhaps more so, in proportional terms, than any other Australian city. A wide range of nature and adventure tourism products are available out of Cairns, but the Great Barrier Reef is the principal icon attraction that most tourists want to visit, whether from the underwater observatory at Green Island, a 1-day snorkelling or introductory dive trip, or a specialist dive tour such as that offered by Taka Dive. Taka's clients also contribute to the income and employment in the Cairns community. The tour itself, however, does not include any direct interaction with local community members other than boat crew and dive staff, who are not necessarily local residents.

## Experience

This is an intensive diving tour for qualified and experienced divers keen to dive at as many high-quality sites as possible in a short period of time. The logistics work smoothly, the scheduling is efficient, the equipment is well maintained, the briefings are informative and the divemasters are knowledgeable. Different dive sites have widely different highlights. At Cod Hole, divers are approached closely by individual large fish that have been habituated by feeding over many years. At North Horn, divers can watch hammerheads and other sharks. At the other end of the scale are tiny near-transparent nocturnal shrimp, and spectacular rarities such as the red file clam. Other notable sightings commonly include sand eels, mantis shrimp, manta rays and turtles.

## Environment

Environmental management issues and practices for the Great Barrier Reef in general, dive operators more specifically, and Taka Dive in particular have been examined in some detail in Buckley (2003a, p. 114). Taka Dive generally follows industry best practice both on the boat and in the water. This includes, for example: complying with Marine Park regulations that restrict pumping out of marine toilets at sea; making use of permanent mooring points at heavily visited dive sites; anchoring in sand rather than corals at sites without permanent moorings; and diving with care and buoyancy adjustments so as not to break or damage corals or stir up sediment. Other relevant environmental management measures are listed in Rainbow *et al.* (2000, 2002). The Taka Dive crew, particularly the videographer, are well informed on the natural history of the principal dive sites, and routinely pass this knowledge on in an informal way to clients that express interest.

As required for all licensed tour boats of this size in the Great Barrier Reef Marine Park, the vessel is fitted with holding tanks, and must bring all garbage except food scraps back to port for disposal on land. Sewage and greywater, however, are not pumped out on land, but macerated and pumped out when the vessel is well offshore and in motion. Passengers are told not to throw any litter overboard, including cigarette butts; how to separate garbage for recycling; and how to avoid damaging the reef while diving. Since in general only experienced divers would take a specialized trip of this nature, these instructions are readily followed.

There is a briefing before each dive, which covers animal species of particular interest at the site, as well as safety and navigation aspects. The boat carries a video photographer who is also a highly competent marine naturalist, and video from each dive is played back in the evening with an accompanying commentary. Broader environmental issues, however, are not discussed. These could include: management of the Great Barrier Reef Marine Park; the environmental impacts of tour boats and other activities in the area; or local or global environmental threats to coral reefs, such as the crown-of-thorns starfish or coral bleaching associated with global warming.

## Safety

Taka Dive follows the standard safety precautions used by live-aboard tour operators. These include, for example: a general safety briefing at the beginning of each trip; a site-specific briefing at each dive site; well-maintained dive equipment; issue of dive computers to all clients, with a briefing on how to use them; instructions on maximum depths for each dive; all dives in buddy pairs or buddy groups; head counts and individual sign-in by every diver after every dive; and ship-to-shore radio contact in case of emergency. Most of these measures are standard, but not all dive tour operators follow them as rigorously as Taka.

## Marketing

Taka Dive maintains a retail shopfront in Cairns, which sells dive clothing and equipment, dive computers and underwater photographic gear, etc., as well as booking tours. In addition to this shopfront, Taka Dive uses three main marketing strategies: local promotions around Cairns; its website; and advertisements in specialist diving journals. Most of the clients on the trip on which I took part had either learnt of the company by word-of-mouth, or had decided to take a live-aboard dive trip on the Great Barrier Reef and had selected Taka on the basis of the material on its website.

# Kimbe Bay, Papua New Guinea: Walindi Plantation Resort

### Place

Kimbe Bay lies on the northern shore of the island of West New Britain in Papua New Guinea. The seafloor is sandy or muddy, but there are numerous fringing reefs around islets, isolated reefs that reach the ocean surface and isolated bombora reefs that extend to a shallow depth below surface. The area is a well-known international diving destination, featured in specialist diving magazines worldwide. The coastline is forested, except where cleared for villages and plantations, principally oil palm.

### Operator

Diving in Kimbe Bay is available on a day-by-day basis from Walindi Plantation Resort, travelling in dive tenders to the nearer reefs up to 40 km from the Resort. Walindi Plantation Resort (2005) is part of Walindi Plantation, one of the longest-established plantations on the northern coastline of West New Britain. The Resort operates as a separate business from the plantation. It caters principally but not entirely to divers. Live-aboard trips to more distant areas are available on the MV *FeBrina*, a 22 m specialist dive boat with seven twinshare cabins.

### Activity

Day dives leave the Resort after breakfast and proceed by boat to the first dive site. Following the first dive, the boat proceeds to the lee of one of the small islands for lunch and a break between dives. The second dive takes place as soon as repetitive-dive requirements allow, and would generally be a shallower dive. Divers may dive in a single group or two separate groups, with at least one dive guide per group. The boat returns to the Resort mid- or late afternoon, depending on wind conditions. A range of other activities are also available from the Resort, including forest hikes, visits to local villages and visits to a warm-water river flowing from a nearby volcanic thermal source.

There are 25 regularly visited dive sites in Kimbe Bay that are accessible on a day trip from Walindi Plantation Resort. These range from 5 to 75 min away by boat, up to 40 km from the Resort. Dive sites around Walindi are famous worldwide for their diversity of small, colourful and unusual marine creatures, as well as the larger and more common species. Perhaps most famous is the pygmy seahorse, only millimetres in length, and so well camouflaged that it is barely visible even straight in front of one's eyes.

## Equipment

Divers can bring their own equipment, but dive equipment is also available from the Resort's dive shop. The Resort has dive tables, but no diving computers. Since there are no particularly deep dives, however, and most divers do bring computers, there is no difficulty if divers arrive without equipment, as I did. The Resort has three well-outfitted dive tenders, one 10 m in length and the others slightly smaller.

## Accommodation

Accommodation is at Walindi Plantation Resort, a beachfront resort with 12 individual beachfront bungalows and a central dining and lounge area. It also has a boat dock, a dive shop and an independent photo shop that offers underwater photographic equipment for rent.

## Statistics

Dive groups generally comprise up to eight divers with two dive instructors and a boat captain. Up to three dive tenders may operate simultaneously. Official daily rates are available only on request from the Resort, but agent sites list rates of around US$100–150 per person per night, plus US$130 for two dives per day from the Resort, i.e. about US$230–280 per person per day. Most guests would stay for around a week.

## Access

Access to the Walindi Plantation Resort is by air to the town of Hoskins in West New Britain, and by road to the Resort. Access to the dive sites is in the Resort's dive tenders, or in the MV *FeBrina* for live-aboard tours. This can potentially be curtailed through high winds or poor visibility, but that did not happen during my own visit.

## Community

Walindi Plantation Resort employs local residents, both in the resort itself and in the dive shop. It also supports a range of local community activities. Guests at the Resort have opportunities to visit local villages and meet local artists. The local environmental organization Mahonia na Dari (see below) is engaged in negotiation with a landowner from the local village to establish a half-day guided natural history trail through rainforest on a hill behind Walindi Plantation.

Approximately 6000 divers visit PNG each year, spending a total of PGK50 million each year (US$17 million): 40% with Air Niugini, 33% in local towns, 12% in major cities and 9% in local villages (Lawrence, 2004). There are 22 dive operators in PNG, including six dive shops, seven dive resorts and nine live-aboard dive boats. There are also 350 fixed moorings at heavily used dive sites.

## Environment

Walindi Plantation Resort supports a non-governmental environmental research organization, Mahonia na Dari, Guardians of the Sea. Mahonia na Dari occupies land provided by Walindi Plantation Resort at a peppercorn rent. Its buildings were funded by the European Union.

The Resort has its own water supply on site. It has septic sewage treatment systems and on-site sullage drains. Waste oil from the generators and boat maintenance area is collected in barrels and is used as a lubricant by local sawmills and as a furnace fuel, together with oil palm prunings, by New Britain Palm Oil Ltd.

Electricity is currently provided by three generators, of 90, 100 and 130 kW capacity, respectively. The main demand for electricity is to power the dive tank compressors. To reduce generator noise and fuel consumption, the owners are installing a 50 kW generator for low-demand periods when the compressors are not running. They are also installing battery banks, energy-efficient lighting and solar-powered hot water heaters in the accommodation bungalows, so that the batteries will be charged by the main 130 kW generator when the compressors are running, and the generator systems can then be turned off completely overnight.

At the main dive sites the Resort has also installed fixed moorings with buoys that do not reach the ocean surface, so that the Resort's guides can find them but local fisherman do not. This avoids the potential for damage to reefs from anchor flukes and chains, which commonly occurs with repeated anchoring.

Websites for both Walindi Plantation Resort and MV *FeBrina* emphasize minimal-impact diving practices, noting particular species that are especially sensitive to breakage even from air bubbles, let alone sudden currents or contact. To add to the emphasis the website states that 'we will take as good care of your cameras as you take of our reefs'.

## Safety

Normal dive safety procedures are followed. In particular, the time spent on the surface between morning and afternoon dives is examined carefully by divers as well as dive instructors so as to comply with safety requirements for repetitive dives.

As elsewhere in New Guinea there is a small but non-negligible risk of being held up by 'rascals' during road travel around the area, but the area is one of the safest in the country, and the Resort owners and staff are well respected in the local community and well informed about potential problems.

## Marketing

The owner of Walindi Plantation Resort also chairs the PNG Dive Association, one of the corporate members of the PNG Tourism Industry Association. PNG dive operators spend a total of PGK2.4 million per year in international marketing. Kimbe Bay, and Walindi in particular, are well-known in international diving circles and often featured in specialist dive magazines. According to the company's website, reader surveys in such magazines have voted Walindi the best dive resort in the world. Detailed information is available on the Resort's website (Walindi Plantation Resort, 2005).

# Mnemba Island, Zanzibar: Conservation Corporation Africa

## Place

Mnemba Island is a small sand cay on a reef just off the northeastern tip of Zanzibar in Tanzania. It supports typical vegetation for small subtropical reef islets; open woodland dominated by beach casuarinas; salt-tolerant trees such as the cannonball mangrove; and pantropical sandy-beach shrub species. The island's position moves slightly on the reef top from season to season as wind and wave patterns change. It is reached by boat from the nearest beach on Zanzibar. The reef around the island is a marine park, protected from fishing.

## Operator

There is a small luxury resort on Mnemba Island, owned and operated by Conservation Corporation Africa (2005). It forms part of CCAfrica's East African portfolio, which also includes safari lodges such as Klein's Camp, Grumeti River Lodge, Lake Manyara Tree Lodge and Ngorongoro Crater Lodge described in the wildlife chapter. CCAfrica is a very well-known operator of game lodges, many in private reserves. Its environmental successes and tourism distinctions are outlined in Buckley (2003a, pp. 9–11).

## Activity

Mnemba Island Resort offers a range of water-based activities such as sailing, snorkelling and dive instruction. For qualified divers it offers two dives a day on the Mnemba Reef itself, reached by a small dive tender from the resort's beach.

There are a number of other dive operators based on Zanzibar itself, and Mnemba Reef is a popular destination since it is one of the few protected as a marine park. The reef was declared a reserve after lobbying from CCAfrica, but competing dive tour operators also benefit.

The dives are relatively shallow, but there are rather few dive resorts in this part of the world, so even highly experienced and well-travelled divers are likely to see species that are new to them. Currents can be strong and many of the dives are drift dives.

## Equipment

Mnemba Lodge has a full complement of diving equipment, including wetsuits and dive computers. Guests can bring their own equipment but need not do so. The dive tender is an outboard-powered inflatable.

## Accommodation

Accommodation is in Mnemba Island Resort itself, which eminently deserves CCAfrica's reputation for low-key luxury. A series of private and well-appointed beach houses, built of local materials, runs along the sheltered west-facing beach either side of a central lounge and dining area. Each has a spacious ocean-facing veranda as well as a luxurious four-poster bedroom and a well-designed bathroom. Service meets the high standards set by CCAfrica's other lodges. In fine weather, tables are set up on the beach for dinner. This may be one reason why the lodge is often listed as one of the world's most romantic destinations. Indeed, when I visited, all the guests except myself were couples, but many were qualified divers for whom the diving was the primary attraction.

## Statistics

There are ten beach houses, and maximum occupancy is hence 20. There is only one dive tender and a limited number of dive computers, so not everyone can dive at once. Since many guests are not there to dive, however, or only want to take an introductory course, in practice I was able to dive twice a day without difficulty, generally with five or six other divers each time. The average length of stay is about 2 or 3 days and the cost, all-found, is about US$585–730 per person per day. Diving and other activities are included in this cost. Overall client-to-staff ratio is about 1:3. During dives it is about 3:1.

## Access

Mnemba Island itself is privately owned by CCAfrica, but the reefs are not. Access to the island is by a CCAfrica road transfer from Zanzibar airport to the northeast coast and by boat to the island. Access to the reef is in the lodge's dive tender.

## Community

Most of the lodge's staff and boatmen are locals, who live in the island's staff quarters whilst at work. The lodge also buys fresh foods from the Zanzibar markets and fish from local fishermen.

## Experience

Mnemba Island is a very beautiful and relaxing place, where the chance to watch terns on a sandspit at dawn, drift in a dhow at sunset or enjoy an outstanding dinner by candlelight on the beach is as much a part of the experience as the diving itself. The diving is certainly very much worthwhile, however, with the opportunity to see species that are not common in the Pacific or even the north and east Indian Oceans.

## Environment

CCAfrica has a well-deserved reputation for contributing effectively to conservation, and for minimizing the environmental impacts of its lodges through design and management (Buckley, 2003a, pp. 9–11). Mnemba Island Lodge is no exception. In particular, it was CCAfrica's efforts that led to the establishment of the marine park surrounding the island. All the accommodation and facilities are built of local materials and rely on good design and ventilation for cooling. Water is drawn from a well near the eastern beach and desalinated on site.

## Safety

Standard dive safety practices are followed. Particular attention is paid to currents and underwater navigation. The lodge's dive instructors know the Mnemba reefs very well and can generally find an interesting dive away from other dive boats, no matter where the latter may have anchored.

## Marketing

Mnemba Island Lodge is marketed principally as a relaxing and romantic place to spend a few days after a game safari in the famous national parks of Tanzania, such as the Serengeti. Its marketing does also feature the diving, however. All expectations are more than met.

# Maldive Islands: Various Operators

### Place

The Republic of Maldives is a group of atolls in the Indian Ocean southwest of India, stretching over a total area of 900,000 km$^2$ but with a total land area of 298 km$^2$. There are 26 atolls containing 1190 individual islands. All of the islands are low sand and coral cays, with an average area of 16 ha and maximum elevation of 1.5 m above sea level. Most of them are less than 1 m above high tide level, but the tidal range is small and the islands are protected by fringing reefs. A variety of breakwaters and beach protection works have been constructed in some areas.

### Operator

Tourism in the Maldives is largely concentrated in enclave resorts on particular islands, most of them in the North and South Male atolls. Most or all of the resort islands currently incorporate commercial diving operations, typically run by a separate company from the resort itself. These diving operations differ greatly in the level of services provided, but some at least have a PADI 5-star rating. These have facilities and instructors accredited to certify individual divers at an advanced level, including the use of specialist equipment such as Nitrox.

With shallow lagoon waters adjacent to each of the resort islands, dive schools in the Maldives are also well placed to offer introductory dive training and base-level certification, and this appears to form a major component of the overall dive tourism market. Although diving and more recently surfing are the advertising icons for tourism in the Maldives, at many of the resorts the principal clientele appear to be city dwellers escaping the northern hemisphere winter and seeking only the sun, the beach and the warm water.

### Activity

The resorts generally offer two dives per day to qualified divers, one in the morning and one in the afternoon, with sign-ups a few hours beforehand. The dive-shop staff prepare the tanks, and place them ready in the dive boats. Clients are kitted out with wetsuits and other gear that they can keep in a designated place in the dive shop during the duration of their stay, to save time on subsequent dives. All dives are accompanied by qualified instructors who provide pre-dive briefings and oversee safety.

## Equipment

All essential diving equipment is available from the resort dive lodges. Clients do not need to own or bring their own gear. The dive shops generally do not provide dive computers, but since they only offer two shallow and well-separated dives a day, computers are not critical. Dive sites are reached in small dive tenders directly from the resort.

## Accommodation

There are 87 tourist resorts on nine atolls in the Maldives, with a total of about 16,000 beds. The resorts differ in size, but most have between 100 and 500 tourist rooms. In general they follow similar designs, incorporating a line of beachfront rooms encircling much of the island concerned; overwater rooms built on pylons from the reef and accessed by raised walkways; a limited number of lower-priced garden rooms in the island interior; central reception, dining and associated facilities; and a boat harbour, landing jetty and dive school on the lagoon side of the island. A small number also have local airstrips or floatplane landing areas.

## Statistics

The average length of stay at most of the island resorts is 5–10 days, though guests do not necessarily dive every day. A typical dive might include 5–10 divers and an instructor. Prices for room and board at the dive resort where I stayed are around US$260 per person per night twinshare, US$400 single, plus US$80 per dive: i.e. about US$420–560 for accommodation, meals and two dives per day.

## Access

Access to the Maldives is by air to the international airport at Male and then by air or sea to the individual atolls. Four of the atolls have local airstrips. Access to dive sites is by boat from each resort. Permits are arranged by the resort.

## Community

Approximately 200, or about one in six, of the Maldive Islands are inhabited, with a total population of 260,000. One-quarter of the total population lives in Male, the capital island. Tourism provides 60% of foreign exchange earnings, 20% of GNP and 10% of employment. The Maldives government adopted a deliberate strategy to develop tourism only in upmarket enclave resorts on previously uninhabited islands, keeping tourists and local communities away from each other. To do this, the government laid claim to all the uninhabited islands, and leased some of them to private entrepreneurs for resort development. Residents of nearby inhabited islands were apparently not consulted (Robinson, 2001).

This strategy has been successful in earning revenue for the government and generating wealth for the entrepreneurs and employment for those working at the resorts. The distribution of benefits, however, is apparently rather inequitable (Robinson, 2001). Some of the entrepreneurs now own several resorts and vessels, whilst the average salary for resort employees is around US$1200 per annum (Robinson, 2001).

Government revenue has helped fund schools, health care, water supplies and telecommunications in Male itself, and the concentration of resorts and hence employment in North Male atoll has given many local residents funds for their children's education. Residents in more remote atolls, however, have apparently gained little (Robinson, 2001). Residents living near the resorts have lost access to those particular islands, which were used traditionally as a source of timber and a base for local fisheries. Traditional arts, crafts, customs and architecture are on the decline and so also is family structure when parents work at resorts (Robinson, 2001).

Officially, tourists are allowed only on resort islands, and Maldivian nationals may live only on so-called local islands (Firag, 2001). In practice, however, this is clearly not the case (Buckley, 2003a, pp. 199–203). At the islands I visited, part of the island was walled off from visitors, and these areas were used for staff accommodation as well as for services such as generators, sewage treatment, supply jetties, desalination plants, workshops, etc. Whilst some staff apparently live in unoccupied guest rooms, others live in considerably more ramshackle dwellings inside the walled-off areas.

One major reason for this is that people do not necessarily find themselves offered employment at a resort immediately adjacent to their home island. In many cases, individuals may move first from an outer atoll to the capital, and subsequently from the capital to a resort island. It is, of course, not necessarily a problem that local staff live on resort islands, but it might be better if it were acknowledged openly, so that staff quarters and facilities could be planned as an integral part of resort design (Buckley, 2003a, pp. 199–203).

## Experience

When I dived in the Maldives, the reefs were recovering from an unusually warm year, where the high water temperature had led to the death of most of the shallow-water corals. The underwater landscape was hence rather brown and heavily grazed and scraped by fish. At greater depth, and especially under overhangs, the corals were intact. Interestingly, fish were still abundant and diverse, so the diving was still very enjoyable. We also had the opportunity to dive at a site with a sandy bottom where manta rays swam close overhead. I stayed at Paradise Island, which has a PADI 5-star dive shop run by Delphis Diving Centre. The resort was pleasant enough, but very expensive, and to find oneself surrounded by huge numbers of honeymooners can be an unnerving experience.

## Environment

The economic potential of dive tourism apparently helped to persuade the Maldives government to protect 25 sites as marine parks in the late 1990s (Riza, 2000). The sites were selected principally on economic rather than ecological criteria, however; they were all within a designated tourism zone, close to resort islands and outside areas currently or potentially used for fishing (Riza, 2000).

Officially, tourist resorts are subject to a wide range of regulations that specify, for example, that: at least 80% of each island's area and one-third of its beach must remain free from development; buildings may only be 1–2 storeys high; no large or rare trees may be felled; no engineering works may be undertaken without environmental impact assessment; coral and sand may not be mined; fishing is restricted; and recycling facilities, desalinators and sewage treatment systems are required. In practice, however, these regulations are not always followed (Buckley, 2003a, pp. 199–203). Engineering works are commonplace, as are non-native plant species in garden landscaping. Garbage is sometimes simply taken to landfill on a neighbouring inhabited island, and sewage effluents have caused deterioration of reef systems in some areas.

## Safety

Normal commercial dive safety procedures were followed, with safety briefings, instructors and divemasters, and inspections of dive certification cards and logbooks.

## Marketing

The Maldives are marketed heavily as a tropical island destination, particularly for European clientele. Diving is one of the icon attractions, but the majority of visitors buy package tours to one of the resorts and may then take an introductory dive course or, if already qualified, buy dives day-by-day from the resort dive operations.

# Bega Island and Lagoon, Fiji: Lalati Resort

### Place

Bega Lagoon is an area of shallow seas about 20 km offshore from Pacific Harbour on the south coast of Fiji's main island of Viti Levu. Bega Lagoon is a well-known dive destination, famous especially for its soft corals. It is protected to the south, east and west by a narrow barrier reef, which encloses the large islands of Bega and Yanuca, and several small islets. Bega Island is occupied by several villages and hosts several resorts. Lalati Resort lies near the mouth of a long, protected inlet at the northeastern end of Bega Island, with views across the water to the mountains of Viti Levu.

### Operator

Lalati Resort is a small and well-appointed establishment with its own dive boats, catering particularly, but by no means exclusively, to divers. It is run by a couple, originally from Minnesota, who welcome their guests individually, join them at the communal dining table, arrange their diving and other activities, and generally act as gracious hosts.

### Activity

The principal activity for most of Lalati's guests is diving in Bega Lagoon. Dives are available either directly from shore or, more commonly, from the resort's main dive boat. The boat leaves at 8:30 am each day for two consecutive single-tank dives, returning in time for lunch. There are dive sites around Bega Island, on pinnacles within Bega Lagoon and, if the seas permit, on the Bega barrier reef. Night dives are also available.

Frigates Passage, an opening in the western section of the Bega barrier reef, is one of Fiji's most famous surf breaks, and Lalati Resort will take surfers there for the day on request. There are apparently no exclusive surf rights at Frigates and it is visited daily by boats from Waidroka on mainland Viti Levu, as well as two surf camps on nearby Yanuca Island. Lalati is about 45 min by boat from Frigates, and budget-conscious visitors who come solely to surf would be unlikely to stay at Lalati. Surfers staying at Lalati are commonly travelling with their partners, keen to surf if opportunity permits, but not to the exclusion of other activities.

Paddling sit-on-top kayaks around the Lalati is another popular activity. At high tide it is possible to thread a kayak along a narrow channel through the mangroves at the head of the inlet, out to the ocean, and back around the head of the island, stopping to snorkel en route. Alternatively, there is excellent snorkelling immediately offshore from the resort itself. Guests can also take guided hikes, visit the nearby village and, on occasion, watch firewalking displays.

## Equipment

The resort has an aluminium catamaran about 8 m in length, powered by two 225 HP outboards, which is used to ferry guests to and from the mainland. It also has a slightly smaller vessel outfitted as a dive boat. There are several smaller runabouts, and a small fleet of sit-on-top kayaks. The resort has its own well-equipped dive shop and compressors, and can provide a full set of rental dive equipment if required, including wetsuits and dive computers.

## Accommodation

There are five large waterfront bures, each accommodating one couple or family, and two older-style hillside or garden bures behind them. All are spacious, well-built and well-appointed, with full en suite facilities, large balconies, outdoor furniture and hammocks. The central bar, lounge and dining area is built to a similar design. The resort has its own residential chef and all meals are gourmet. All buildings are non-smoking, and shoes are left outside in Fijian style. There is a swimming pool, an outdoor open pool and an indoor therapeutic spa, exercise room and library. All the buildings are set in well-maintained lawns and gardens.

## Statistics

Daily rates are currently FJD450 per person (US$280) and include full board. Guided two-tank boat dives cost FJD190 (US$115), but unguided shore dives, for certified divers, are free. Full board plus two single-tank boat dives therefore costs US$395 per person per day. To take the boat to the surf at Frigates Passage costs FJD360 (US$215), divided between the number of passengers. There is no fixed length of visit, but most guests seem to stay either a week or a weekend. Maximum guest capacity is 12 and there are 36 staff in total, an overall ratio of 1:3. On the dive boat there were two diving guides for three guests, a ratio of 1:1.5.

## Access

Transfers to Lalati are in the resort's own boat, from Pacific Harbour on the south coast of Viti Levu. Access to dive sites is in the resort's dive boat. There is a village fee of FJD30 (US$18) per person per day for diving or surfing, included in the tariffs listed above. This is a relatively high fee.

## Community

All the resort's staff, other than its managers, are Fijian, and many but not all are from the local village. In addition to the lease on the resort's land, the activity fees and employment, the village presumably receives payments for tours, dances and displays. The staff are very friendly to guests: they will share life stories at the slightest invitation and ask guests about their own. This seems to be characteristic of Fiji in general. The resort also hosts a medical clinic for the island, with a doctor and pharmaceuticals provided by a US charitable foundation, and loans its boats for emergency transport to Suva Hospital.

## Experience

My own experience of Lalati was marred by a bout of severe fever shortly after I arrived. This must have been contracted elsewhere, but it certainly robbed me of the ability to take full advantage of Lalati's opportunities. It did, however, give me a particular appreciation for the generosity of my hosts, who looked after me diligently and very kindly extended my stay until I was well enough to travel again.

Fortunately I did have the opportunity to kayak around the Lalati inlet and enjoy a couple of boat-based dives before I succumbed to fever, and after 5 days my appetite returned sufficiently to submit the chef's creations to a critical (and entirely favourable) evaluation. I can only hope to return in full health on another occasion.

## Environment

Lalati advertises itself as a sustainable resort, and the guest information kits contain an explanation. Most important are the composting toilets, an ingenious design with a low-consumption pedal-operated freshwater flushing system, which drains to a large replaceable plastic composting bin. The bins contain crushed coconut husks suspended in plastic netting. They drain to a perforated underground drain, with air vents, which also receives greywater. They also have an electrically operated vent fan. When the composting bins are full they are exchanged, and the full bins are left to complete digestion. The system combines an odour-free and comfortable en suite flush toilet with the environmental advantages of a composting system.

Fresh water is collected from the roofs of the buildings, which are metal, steep-sloping and surrounded by extra-large gutters. It is pumped into the bathrooms by electrical pressure pumps. Hot water is heated by gas. Electrical power is provided by diesel generators, which run continuously. There are limited maintenance facilities for boat engines and other equipment, with major maintenance being carried out in Pacific Harbour on the mainland.

## Safety

Guests receive their first safety briefing as they board the boat at Pacific Harbour. On the dive boat, the divemaster checks all the equipment before each dive and provides a safety briefing on each site. This includes a site diagram and information on currents and maximum depths and durations. With only three guests and two guides diving, we descended as a single group and remained in visual contact. Rental dive gear included knives, whistles and computers as standard. Each diver was required to sign back in on returning to the boat, with co-signature by the skipper.

## Marketing

According to the resort's owners, most of Lalati's guests come to dive, and clients find out about the resort via their website. When I visited Lalati, most of the other guests were American honeymoon couples, not all of them divers or surfers. This particular clientele, however, apparently arrives only in August, reflecting the 'wedding season' in the northern hemisphere summer. During the rest of the year, most clients are experienced divers. Bega Lagoon is certainly featured in specialist diving magazines, and perhaps Lalati has gained a particular reputation since its owners, and also their son, are themselves keen divers and expert underwater photographers, who have published their work extensively.

# Rocktail Bay, South Africa: Wilderness Safaris

### Place

Rocktail Bay is on the northeast coast of South Africa, not far from the border with Mozambique. It lies midway between Kosi Bay and Sodwana Bay in Northern KwaZulu-Natal. There is a local township, and a lodge operated by Wilderness Safaris (2005). The ocean is relatively warm and the area is one of the better-known habitats for grey nurse shark, also known as ragged-tooth sharks. It is also known as a corridor for seasonal migration by humpback whales. Diving is on nearshore reefs where the water is relatively turbid through sediment resuspension. Rocktail Bay Lodge lies within the Maputaland Coastal Forest Reserve at the northern end of the World Heritage listed Greater St Lucia National Park. Offshore lies Maputaland Marine Reserve.

### Operator

Wilderness Safaris (2005) is a large southern African wildlife safari company that operates a range of lodges in six different African nations (Buckley, 2003a, pp. 23–24). Rocktail Bay is its only coastal lodge and hence the only one offering diving. The diving operation is based a little distance from the lodge and may be a separate company, but dives are sold directly by Wilderness Safaris either prior to arrival or from the lodge.

## Activity

Rocktail Bay Dive Centre is at Manzengwenya, about 10 km from the lodge. It is listed on the operator's website as an accredited dive centre. It does not appear to be included in listings for either PADI or NAUI, but perhaps there is a South African dive accreditation programme. The area is a resting site for pregnant female ragged-tooth sharks, which can be seen routinely in summer. Both leatherback and loggerhead turtles also breed on the beach here. At the time I visited, all dives were early in the morning because of wind later in the day. The area is famous for its sightings of whales, whalesharks, leatherback turtles and pregnant ragged-tooth sharks, depending on season.

## Equipment

All diving equipment is available on site, including wetsuits. Dive computers are not provided, since only a single dive is offered each day. There is no harbour and the dive boat leaves and lands directly on the beach, so if the surf is of any size, diving may be difficult or impossible.

## Accommodation

Accommodation is at the Rocktail Bay Lodge, operated by Wilderness Safaris (2005). This lodge won a South African Imvelo tourism award in 2003. The lodge has 11 well-built, free-standing wooden cabins, each containing sleeping quarters, a living area, en suite facilities and an outdoor balcony. There is a central lounge and dining room. Full board is provided, and includes other local activities such as guided wildflower walks through the heath vegetation immediately inland, and vehicle drop-offs some kilometres down the beach so that guests can walk back along the shore to the lodge. The lodge itself is immediately behind a large vegetated coastal dune, and even when there is a strong wind on the beach, the area around the lodge itself is sheltered and calm. The woodland around the lodge offers sightings of a number of unusual bird species, including green twinspot, purple-crested lowrie, pink-throated longclaw and the oddly named buff-spotted flufftail.

## Statistics

Rocktail Bay Lodge has 11 chalets and can accommodate up to 24 guests at any one time. Because the dive boat has to be launched from the beach, however, only a small craft can be used, with a maximum of ten divers together with a dive instructor and the boat captain. There are one or two dives per day, depending on weather conditions. Accommodation at Rocktail Bay Lodge costs ZAR1810–2170 (US$285–340) per person per day twinshare, and ZAR2685–3015 (US$420–475) per person per day single, varying with season. Diving costs are additional.

## Access

Access to Rocktail Bay Lodge is by road, or by light plane to a nearby airstrip, with a 4WD shuttle to the lodge. Access by air is either to the 800 m Manzengwenya strip 30 min from the lodge, or to the 1300 m Sappi strip 60 min away. Since the site is within a national park, access to the lodge itself is restricted to park opening hours. Park permits are also required. Access to the dive sites is in an outboard-powered, semi-rigid inflatable boat that launches and lands on the beach. This is only possible when the tide is low, and dives must therefore be timed around low tide.

## Community

The lodge employs local staff and also offers its guests the opportunity to visit local communities. Perhaps most importantly, the local Rocktail Bay community has an equity shareholding in the lodge itself (Wilderness Safaris, 2005). Rocktail Bay Lodge is owned by a non-profit company called Isivuno, whose shareholders are the parks agency and the local community of Nqobela. Operating rights are leased to Wilderness Safaris in return for an annual fee and a percentage of turnover.

## Experience

Rocktail Bay Lodge itself is a very relaxing place, with excellent food, friendly staff and the opportunity to explore on foot. The diving area is wind-affected, at least during the season when I visited, and visibility is limited. Despite this, we had excellent sightings of large marine fauna, including a whale swimming under the boat, close views of sleeping ragged-tooth sharks and several marine turtles. Beach launches and landings were managed with aplomb. I would gladly dive there again.

## Environment

The Maputaland Marine Reserve is a migratory rest area for pregnant female ragged-tooth or grey nurse sharks, an endangered species. Sharks may occasionally be encountered sleeping in underwater caverns. There is a strict code of conduct regarding minimum approach distances to sleeping sharks, so as not to disturb them. Of course, if one suddenly encounters a waving shark tail whilst drifting along a coral wall, this code may be difficult to observe to the letter. None the less, it does provide protection against deliberate crowding or close approach. Before entering the boat all divers are instructed to observe routine minimal-impact practices, notably proper buoyancy adjustment so as not to kick or touch live coral, or stir up seafloor sediment. Rocktail Bay Lodge itself is designed and operated with minimal impacts in mind, in keeping with the approach used for all Wilderness Safaris lodges.

## Safety

Normal diving safety practices are followed. Computers are not used since there are only one or two dives per day. Clients are briefed on safe practices for entering and exiting the dive tender, including the beach launching and landing. They are also briefed on potential risks associated with open-water drift diving.

## Marketing

Diving at Rocktail Bay is marketed principally as an activity available from Rocktail Bay Lodge, which in turn is marketed as part of the Wilderness Safaris portfolio. The

Wilderness Safaris (2005) website for Rocktail Bay features diving as one of a range of activities available at additional cost. The website includes monthly diving newsletters for the past year, which focus principally on notable sightings and guest comments, with notes on visibility. The website also features very positive comments taken from letters sent to Wilderness Safaris by visitors from diving equipment manufacturer Mares®, and a *Lonely Planet*® investigative team.

## Great Barrier Reef, Australia: Quicksilver Cruises

### Place

This tour takes place on a section of the Great Barrier Reef near Cairns and Port Douglas. This is one of the most heavily used and intensively managed sections of the Great Barrier Reef, with a wide variety of 1-day boat trips. There are a number of platform reefs with small sand and mangrove islands in this section, and the ribbon reefs are approximately 70 km offshore. A more general description of the Great Barrier Reef Marine Park is given in the Taka Dive case study.

### Operator

Perhaps the best-known of the large-scale reef tours on Australia's Great Barrier Reef is operated by Quicksilver Cruises out of Port Douglas, north of Cairns. Started in 1979 as a small family business, by the mid-1990s it employed 156 staff and catered for around 200,000 clients annually (Harris and Leiper, 1995).

The company's principal product is a single-day trip to a permanent pontoon structure on the inner edge of one of the outer reefs, using a high-speed, wave-piercing catamaran. The company also operates multi-day dive trips in a smaller vessel (Quicksilver Dive, 2005). In addition, the pontoon can be reached by helicopter for those not wishing to travel by sea. Several other tour operators offer trips to permanent pontoons, but Quicksilver was the first to use large, high-speed catamarans, and is still the largest operator. Only a proportion of its clients on any given day, however, are qualified divers. The remainder take the trip either to snorkel in an enclosed area adjacent to the pontoon, or to take an introductory tethered dive. These take place in a large purpose-built cage under the pontoon, using hookah-style breathing apparatus where the breathing regulator is attached to a long air hose from a compressor at the surface, rather than a tank attached to the diver.

A subsidiary company, Reef Biosearch, carries out interpretation on the tours, and also conducts monitoring and research as required by the Great Barrier Reef Marine Park Authority, which is the management and permitting agency for the area.

### Activity

Clients are collected in the high-speed catamarans in the morning, first from Cairns and then from Port Douglas. From Port Douglas, the boat makes its way directly to the pontoon, which it moors alongside. The guests then have several hours to enjoy the facilities on the pontoon, returning in the catamaran in the late afternoon. Food and drink are available both on the catamaran and the pontoon. Snorkel equipment is also available on the pontoon, and disposable underwater cameras are for sale.

There is a glass-bottom boat that takes tourists on short coral-viewing tours near the pontoon. For qualified divers, a single dive is available on the same reef, but some distance from the pontoon, reached by a small dive tender.

## Equipment

Quicksilver currently runs three tour boats: a 45-m high-speed wave-piercing catamaran with a speed of 35 knots, which transports passengers to permanent pontoons at Agencourt Reef; a 30-m sailing catamaran; and a 24-m specialist dive boat (Quicksilver Cruises, 2005). The tour described here uses the largest vessel, the *Quicksilver VIII*. The pontoons incorporate underwater observatories, underwater communication facilities, and high-pressure air and diving platforms for scuba diving. Helicopter overflights are also available.

Both the pontoon and the high-speed, wave-piercing catamaran are critical to the Quicksilver operation, allowing an underwater tour to be offered as a single-day high-volume tourism product to tourists with no previous experience. The large, wave-piercing catamaran provides a very stable ride even in high winds, so very few passengers experience seasickness. In addition, its rapid transit time means that clients can spend several hours at the outer reef without having to stay overnight. Smaller and slower vessels, in contrast, can only reach the less diverse reefs close to Cairns in a day trip, and multi-day live-aboard trips are only economically viable for specialist diving tours.

The pontoon structure is equally critical to the Quicksilver operation, because it is much larger than the catamaran and allows the passengers to spread out and take part in various different activities at their leisure. It would be very difficult, in contrast, for all the passengers on the catamaran to snorkel around the boat, since: the high-speed hull is not well-suited for passengers to climb directly in and out of the water; there are too many passengers to watch them all safely at once; there is not enough space on the catamaran to carry all the equipment needed; and issue and recovery of gear from passengers would be too slow.

By simply mooring at the pontoon, in the sheltered lee of the reef, and disgorging all its passengers en masse on to the large fixed structure, all these problems are overcome. In addition, the pontoon has a large fixed enclosed area for guests to snorkel in under the watchful eye of lifeguards, and a large underwater cage where clients can get a firsthand experience of diving by climbing slowly down the walls of the cage whilst breathing from a hookah. This has far fewer risks than learning to dive using scuba. Clients who are qualified to dive and want to do so have a separate area to get kitted up in, and a separate small dive tender to travel out from the pontoon to an appropriate dive site nearby, with a qualified divemaster. Additional equipment, such as the glass-bottomed boat, can be kept safely at the pontoon when not in use. And finally, staff can live on the pontoon and maintain all the equipment ready for the daily influx of clients. Large, wave-piercing catamarans can seat several hundred passengers, all in enclosed cabins with large picture windows.

## Accommodation

This is a 1-day tour that does not include accommodation. A variety of tourist accommodation is available in Cairns and Port Douglas. The trip starts as the guests board the catamaran at the docks in Cairns or Port Douglas.

## Statistics

For the 1-day trip to Agincourt Reef on *Quicksilver VIII*, the basic cost is AUD189 (US$140) from Port Douglas or AUD199 (US$150) from Cairns. This includes lunch and the use of snorkelling gear and a glass-bottomed boat. For certified divers, a single dive costs an additional AUD92 (US$69), and two dives cost AUD134 (US$103). A full day trip including two dives thus costs about US$250 per person.

## Access

The pontoon is owned and operated exclusively by Quicksilver, with a permit from the Great Barrier Reef Marine Park Authority. Access is only by the Quicksilver high-speed catamarans, or helicopter. Access to Cairns is by air or road, and to Port Douglas by road from Cairns.

## Community

Quicksilver is a relatively large company, and it is a significant employer in the Cairns region. Employees include a variety of management, sales, hospitality, catering and maintenance staff, as well as specialists such as divemasters and boat captains. The trips are, of course, intended principally for tourists, but as a relatively straightforward single-day activity, they are also patronized by Cairns residents accompanying visiting relatives and friends, so there is some opportunity for interactions between locals and long-distance tourists. In addition, since Quicksilver's clients must generally spend at least 2 nights in either Cairns or Port Douglas, the company makes a significant indirect contribution to total hotel and restaurant expenditure in these destinations.

## Experience

This is a high-volume tour that operates to a tight schedule and therefore follows a set system. During the trip from Cairns to the pontoon, the various activities available on the pontoon are explained through videos and staff briefings, and associated paperwork and payment transactions completed where necessary. Clients planning to dive are introduced to their divemaster, and their dive cards and, if necessary, log books are inspected. Tea and coffee are available and a variety of snacks and souvenirs are on sale. Once the catamaran is docked at the pontoon and all passengers have disembarked, the divers assemble in a fitting room and then board the dive tender for a short journey to the day's selected dive site. On the day that I took part on this trip, it was unusually windy, so there was a strong current across the reef flat and through the shallow dissected patches of reef on the lee side of the main reef, which is where we were diving. The water was turbid with suspended sediment and visibility was poor. Perhaps for safety reasons the divemaster cut the dive short, although I personally was perfectly happy searching for small critters in the muck and would gladly have stayed underwater much longer. Lunch was provided once we returned to the pontoon, and we were then free to join the other passengers in the enclosed snorkel area until it was time for the catamaran to depart.

## Environment

Environmental management issues and practices by Quicksilver are described in Buckley (2003a, p. 115). All sewage and rubbish is held on board the catamaran or pontoon and taken ashore. Videos outlining environmental issues and management practices in the Great Barrier Reef Marine Park are shown on board the catamaran on the way to the pontoon, and leaflets distributed. The same messages are reiterated by dive and snorkel guides. The pre-dive briefing includes instruction to avoid touching any coral or marine organisms.

## Safety

The high-speed catamaran is a large, stable vessel with fully enclosed passenger areas and a full complement of navigation and safety equipment. The fixed pontoon on the reefs provides a safe base and platform for inexperienced tourists to enter the water in an enclosed area under the watch of lifeguards, for as long or as brief a period as they wish. The diving cage and tethered hookah regulators provide a safe way for tourists without dive qualifications to gain a first experience of watching fish underwater whilst breathing from a regulator. The scuba dive follows normal dive safety precautions, though buddy pair arrangements were lax since most of the divers were inexperienced. The dive site is shallow, the dive tender remains nearby and additional safety facilities are available on the pontoon if needed.

## Marketing

The Quicksilver 1-day trip is heavily marketed in the Cairns destination area and internationally, through a wide range of avenues. It is listed in many travel agent brochures, promotional material produced by Tourism Queensland and directories produced by Ecotourism Australia, and is mentioned in many books on Australian tourism. Quicksilver is also represented directly at tourism trade shows.

# Ningaloo, Australia, Whaleshark Snorkel: Various Operators

### Place

Ningaloo is a small coastal township near Exmouth at about 22°S on the mid-coast of Western Australia, just north of the Tropic of Capricorn. Exmouth provides access to Cape Range National Park and Ningaloo Marine Park. Ningaloo is known for its subtropical reefs and most particularly for its whalesharks, which congregate to feed each year for a brief period, commonly April to June (Western Australia Department of Conservation and Land Management, 2005). The life history of whalesharks is little known, but there are very few places worldwide where they can be seen regularly in shallow water, and Exmouth is one of those places. Whalesharks are the largest species of shark, commonly 12 m and up to 18 m in length, but they are plankton feeders and not aggressive to humans.

### Operator

A number of different companies offer day tours from Exmouth to snorkel with whalesharks. Tours have been running since 1993, with over 1000 clients per year in total, shared between over a dozen boats (Davis *et al.*, 1997). There are also boats operating out of Coral Bay a little further south. Examples include the Exmouth Diving Centre (2005), Ningaloo Blue (2005) and King Dive (2005), but there are at least half a dozen in all. Some of these operators also offer dives for qualified divers, on the reef edge not far from the whaleshark area. Most operators offer a second-day guarantee: if you don't get the opportunity to swim with whalesharks on the first day, you can come back again another day free of charge.

## Activity

Rules set by the parks agency, Western Australia Department of Conservation and Land Management (WACALM) prohibit scuba diving with whalesharks in Ningaloo Marine Park. The rationale is that the sharks should be able to leave the swimmers, if they choose, simply by sinking deeper. There may also be concern that divers would be tempted to exceed safe depth limits in their excitement. Tour operators hence offer snorkel trips only.

There are rules as to how the sharks should be approached, in the same way as for whalewatching. Tour boats take turns to put their clients in the water. If only one shark or one group is located, then to maximize the chance for everyone to see the whalesharks – and minimize the chance clients will claim the second-day guarantee – each boat puts its clients in the water for 10 min initially. Once everyone has had a 10-min swim with the sharks, the clients from the first boat can take a second turn in the water. Alternatively, if several boats are lined up waiting, the first boat might choose to go in search of more sharks. This 10-min rule is an agreement between tour operators, not a requirement of the management agency, WACALM (2005), which allows each boat up to 90 min.

## Equipment

Most boats are dive boats or converted fishing boats. They carry masks and snorkels for their clients. Many of the clients have disposable underwater cameras, and a few bring diving cameras or video recorders. Flash photography, however, is not allowed (WACALM, 2005).

The whalesharks are blue-water ocean creatures, and generally do not breach even when swimming near the surface. Since the whalesharks are underwater and not visible from the boats, the tour operators form syndicates which hire spotter planes or microlight aircraft to search on their behalf, since shallow-swimming sharks can be seen from above. Within the syndicate they communicate by radio, and plan which boat will go where. When I visited this area nearly all the operators except one seemed to belong to a single syndicate. The other operator had a spotter plane of its own. Of course, boats can also watch their rivals' planes, and search for agglomerations of other boats.

## Accommodation

Accommodation is in Exmouth or nearby Coral Bay and does not form part of the tour. Various options are available, from an enormous campground to relatively upmarket motels.

## Statistics

Most of the whaleshark boats can carry up to 20 or more clients. Ningaloo Blue's *Venture III*, for example, is a 15 m vessel. The boats are crewed by a skipper, a guide or host, and a deckhand. Some boats also bring commercial videographers. The tour is a 1-day activity, including the reef dive or snorkel. The tour is not cheap, AUD320 (US$240) per day for most operators, plus an additional AUD40–50 (US$30–37) for a reef dive away from the whalesharks. This, however, takes into account the costs of spotter planes, the second-day guarantees and the relatively short operating season.

## Access

Physical access to the whaleshark area is only by ocean-going boat. The area is a marine park and permits are required by WACALM. The operators sell the permits on board. They are provided in books like lottery or raffle tickets, each with a stapled stub and a tear-off permit. Supposedly, the operators give the tear-off receipt to the client, and hand in the stubs monthly to the WACALM rangers together with the fees collected. In practice, however, it may be that clients paying in cash do not always receive the tear-off permit receipts unless they specifically ask for them, so the numbers of clients may well be under-reported. I am not sure whether clients exercising their second-day guarantee from the tour operator are expected to pay for a second day's permit or not.

## Community

Tourism now makes a significant contribution to the economies of Exmouth and Coral Bay, and whalesharks are the icon attraction, even though they are only around for part of the year. Crew and staff of the whaleshark boats are not necessarily local residents.

## Experience

Once in the water, clients swim towards the whalesharks, which may be still or swimming slowly. If the sharks swim at speed it is quite impossible for swimmers to keep up. Most clients have underwater cameras and everyone is trying to take photographs. The result is a kind of reverse feeding frenzy, snorkellers milling around the whalesharks, trying to maintain the regulation 3–4 m minimum distance, and often kicking each other as they try to get in position for a good shot. The whalesharks themselves are in dignified contrast to this disorganization, cruising slowly with giant letterbox mouths agape, their blue-and-white rippled skin pattern like sunlight over sand. Surveys carried out by Davis *et al.* (1997) found that many snorkellers complained about crowding.

## Environment

WACALM has a regulated code of conduct for boats approaching whalesharks, comparable to but different from that for whalewatching. Broadly, the boats must approach slowly, must approach from ahead rather than behind the sharks, and must drop their snorkellers off where the whalesharks are likely to swim toward the snorkellers, rather than the reverse (WACALM, 2005). The boats must not approach closer than 30 m, or encircle the sharks. The intention is to avoid causing any change to the sharks' behaviour, especially whilst feeding. Nobody knows how important this period of feeding in warm shallow water may be to the year-long energetics of individual whalesharks. If it is critical, then any disruption could affect whaleshark populations. WACALM also produces illustrated minimal-impact guides for the snorkellers themselves. The main rule is to maintain at least 3 m distance from the sharks, or 4 m if one is near the tail.

## Safety

The minimum-distance rule is as much for the snorkellers' own safety as to protect the whalesharks. An accidental slap from a whaleshark's tail would be no light matter. As with any boat-based diving or snorkelling activity offshore, it is a critical safety requirement that everyone is checked back on board after the swim. There is less risk than with diving, since snorkellers must surface to breathe, and the water surface is generally calm so they can easily be spotted. Even so, skippers need to count and recount heads before setting course for port or another whaleshark. All boats also carry lifejackets, marine flares, radios and rescue equipment as required under maritime safety law. For additional safety some tour boats also put an inflatable dinghy in the water with the snorkellers.

## Marketing

Whalesharks are a major theme in marketing for the entire Exmouth region, and brochures and boat operators' websites feature them extensively. In general the websites do point out that the whalesharks are only there for a few months, though they may perhaps exaggerate the likelihood of early arrivals and late departures. Most of them mention their spotter planes and their second-day guarantee.

# 11 Surfing

Surfing, Nagigia Island Surf Resort, Fiji. Photo Kimoto.

Surfing, Mentawai Sanctuary, Indonesia. Photo courtesy of Freedom Charters.

## Sector Structure

Surf tourism is a relatively recent addition to the commercial adventure sector (Buckley, 2002a). Currently, a number of specialist tour operators take experienced surfers to a variety of relatively remote and hence uncrowded surfing destinations, especially in South Pacific island nations (Buckley, 2002b). The surf at these sites ranges from relatively mellow to highly challenging, with most being coral reef breaks where a wipeout, especially in big surf at low tide, carries a significant risk of injury. Most of these tours are based in live-aboard charter boats, and more recently also in small specialist surf lodges on various islands (Buckley, 2002a, b, 2003a). Surfing is a highly skilled activity, and these tours certainly qualify as skilled commercial adventure recreation in remote areas, SCARRA (Buckley, 2004a).

Examples include: Mentawai Sanctuary (2005), Indies Trader (2005) and the Surf Travel Company (2005) in the Mentawai Islands of Sumatra, Indonesia; surf resorts in Samoa (Salani Surf Resort, 2005; Samoana Resort, 2005; Savaii Surfaris, 2005), Tonga (Ha'atafu Beach Resort, 2005) and Fiji (Nagigia Surf Resort, 2005; Lalati Resort, 2005; Tavarua Island Resort, 2005); tours to Dhonveli (Tari) and Lohifushi Islands in the Maldives by Atoll Adventures (2005); and more.

The world population of surfers is growing, ageing and becoming wealthier. This is increasing crowding at mainland continental surf breaks, fuelling demand for surf tours. The limiting factors are largely social: the response of local communities in the destination areas, and the interactions between surfers themselves, both tour clients and independent surfers, as the more remote destinations become more crowded (Buckley, 2002a, b).

As with other forms of outdoor recreation, it is generally private groups and professional teams that first discover new surf breaks, ride larger and more difficult waves, and develop new techniques and variations such as tow-in surfing, hydrofoil surfing and kitesurfing (Buckley, 2004a). To date, for example, the giant waves of the Cortez Bank, in the Pacific Ocean 170 km west of San Diego, have been ridden only by professional surfers in boats chartered by their sponsors, not by clients of surf tour companies.

Reasons for this certainly include skill, safety and cost. Additionally, however, these waves break only occasionally, when weather conditions generate particularly large ocean swells. And when they do, they are much too large for a surfer to catch by paddling on to the wave. The only option is to be towed on to it with a jetski, and this requires not only a jetski but an experienced tow-in surfing partner to drive it, and special surfboards with footstraps to maintain full speed over a choppy water surface. Only professional surfers, in general, have both the resources and the flexibility to join a charter boat to the Cortez Bank at short notice. I have little doubt, however, that commercial surf charter boats will soon start offering trips to Cortez Bank for suitably skilled and well-heeled clients.

The economic significance of surf tourism depends on how it is defined. Broadly, there are perhaps four major components. Probably largest in traditional travel-industry terms, but not identified specifically as surf tourism, are experienced surfers who travel to surf, but using mainstream transport and accommodation. Relatively small, but still part of the surf tourism sector, are low-budget surf safaris that take organized groups of surfers to a series of sites, typically by bus. Also small, but perhaps significant for the future of the industry, are surf schools where backpackers can take a day's surfing lesson as part of their travel experience, even though few will subsequently become serious surfers.

Icons of the surf tourism industry, however, are specialist surf tour companies that run scheduled tours to prime surfing locations worldwide, often using charter live-aboard boats and/or specialist surf resorts. These companies form the core of the surf tourism industry, and it is this sector that links most closely with clothing manufacturers and competition surfing. Companies with names such as Atoll Adventures (2005), Indies Trader (2005), Mentawai Sanctuary (2005), Surf The Earth (2005), Surf Travel Company (2005), World Surfaris (2005), and more take so-called cash-rich, time-poor surfers to relatively inaccessible and hence uncrowded waves worldwide, especially in the islands of the Pacific and Indian oceans. It is these companies that take pro teams and photographers on magazine photo shoots. It is these that contribute most to the clothing, fashion and entertainment sector of the surf industry (Buckley, 2004b), by providing its marketing materials. It is also these that gain most from that sector, which indirectly markets their destinations and attractions.

## Maldive Islands: Dhonveli Beach Resort and Others

### Place

Surfing in the Maldives is available from two specialist island surf resorts and a number of live-aboard surf charter boats. The resorts also operate boats to take surfers to additional breaks nearby. I have visited one of the two surf resort islands. This resort has exclusive access to one of the better-known breaks, and close proximity to two more. Some of the surf charters visit the same breaks as those used by the resorts, whilst others visit the more remote outer atolls in the far southern part of the country. Broadly, the boat-based tours appeal more to younger and perhaps more competitive surfers travelling alone or with other surfers, whereas the surf lodges appeal more to older surfers travelling with non-surfing partners or dependents. In particular, one of the key surf lodges limits the total number of surfers on the island at any one time, so that all its clients have a good opportunity to surf its exclusive-access local break. This is a significant consideration for clients who live in areas that have either very crowded surf, or no surf at all. The other surf resort also has an exclusive break, but does not limit the proportion of surfers amongst its guests.

Dhonveli Beach Resort, formerly known as Tari Village, occupies one of the numerous small islands in North Male atoll in the Republic of the Maldives, described in the diving chapter (Chapter 10). It is one of the two islands in North Male atoll that is known for having a good surfable wave breaking directly on the island reef, easily accessible by paddling straight from shore. The windward reef flat is a relatively level and continuous pavement of eroded and concreted limestone, which allows a well-shaped wave to form even when the surf is relatively small. On the lee side of the island there is a long sand-spit with a protected, shallow swimming lagoon, and a boat dock constructed of coral rock and concrete. The central oval section of the island supports open woodland, with guest housing and facilities scattered through it as independent two-storey buildings.

### Operator

The island resort itself is currently operated by a company known as Yacht Tours Maldives, which also owns several charter vessels. It operates a dive shop on

Dhonveli Island as well as surfing, fishing and holiday accommodation. The company is based in Male, the capital of the Maldives. Surfers planning to spend some time at Dhonveli, however, generally can not deal directly with this Maldive-based operating company. Rather, they buy a surf tour to this destination through one of the outbound surf tourism operators in their country of origin. For my own visit, this was Atoll Adventures (2005), based in Melbourne, which also offers surf tours to a variety of other Pacific and Indian Ocean destinations.

## Activity

Dhonveli caters principally to surfers, and surfers want to spend their time surfing. At Dhonveli they have exclusive access to the island's own break, known as Pasta Point. There is a bar, freshwater showers and a shaded board rack right near the point, and guests can and do paddle out and paddle in at any time of day, with conditions depending on wind and tide.

If the home break is small, or for variety, the resort will shuttle surfers on demand to two well-known breaks on the next-door island. This is a local island without a resort, with surf wrapping left and right around its windward end, often forming several different sections that can accommodate a larger number of surfers. These breaks are also often visited by live-aboard surf charter vessels. On another island further north there is another well-known break, but it takes an hour or so to reach it by boat from Dhonveli, so it is generally an all-day trip. This break, which is also visited by live-aboard surf charter boats, was working particularly well during my own visit, being longer and faster than the other breaks.

As an alternative to surfing, the island also operates a dive shop and dive boat, run by a dive instructor who is prepared to lead deep dives to 60 m for suitably experienced divers, unlike most commercial diving operations. On days with particularly small surf there is good snorkelling off the windward side of the island. And of course, this is a beautiful tropical island with aquamarine waters, golden sands and warm breezes. There is no compulsion to be active all the time. Indeed, some of the guests visiting at the same time as myself seemed entirely happy to alternate all day between the bar and the beach. And why not?

## Equipment

The island has a speedboat used to ferry clients from the capital and take them to more distant surf breaks, and a number of small outboard-powered dinghies for local use. Surfers bring their own boards and other equipment. Masks and snorkels are available for loan on the island.

## Accommodation

Guest accommodation is in a number of separate two-storey guesthouses with bedrooms, bathrooms, a small lounge and an outside veranda. There is a communal dining area where meals are served, a small shop, a day-bar near the surfing point, and a lounge, games room and evening bar in the reception area. At the time of my own visit, operations were low-key but very comfortable and friendly. It appears that the accommodation may have been refurbished subsequently.

## Statistics

Total accommodation capacity is currently 100 guests, of whom no more than 30 may be surfers so as to avoid crowding on the home break. There are two local surf guides. Prices depend on the package, but are currently around UKP1067 (US$1920) per week twinshare or UKP1310 (US$2360) single, including meals and boat shuttle, i.e. about US$275–340 per person per day.

## Access

Access to the Republic of Maldives is by air to the capital city at Male. Some of the more distant atolls have their own airstrips with domestic connections to Male. For islands within the atolls of South Male and North Male, however, access is by boat from the capital city. There is a dock immediately outside the airport terminal building and the island resorts send speedboats to pick up their guests. From Dhonveli Resort to other surf breaks, access is on one of the resort's own local boats.

## Community

The interactions between tourists and Maldives locals are considered under the Paradise Island case study in the diving chapter. The issues are similar for the surfing resorts. One additional factor is that at least some of the local staff are keen surfers.

## Experience

When I visited the Maldives, there was a sizeable swell when I first arrived, but I was staying on a diving resort island and though I had my surfboards I had no access to islands with surf breaks, despite trying hard to charter a local boat. By the time I reached the surf break at Dhonveli (then known as Tari Village), the swell had dropped off considerably. Apparently, during the larger swell of the previous days, nobody had surfed at all. During my own stay, the surf at Pasta Point was rather small and scrappy, though still rideable. The two breaks on the nearby island were much better, but rather soft and slow. The break on the island an hour's boat ride further north was better still, though only of moderate size. The reefs were well-shaped and it is clear that the surf could be extremely good during the right conditions.

One interesting opportunity which I was able to take advantage of occurred when a small clean swell was running in. By snorkelling out beyond the windward reef, swimming up some small gullies cut into the reef flat, and holding on to the bottom, I could watch a small but glassy wave breaking into a perfectly formed barrel, a long silvery cylindrical bubble of air spiralling off into the distance. It was a wonderful sight, but marred slightly by the very persistent attentions of a small reef shark some 2 m in length, which remained close and inquisitive despite the very shallow water. Eventually I simply stood up and walked ashore.

## Environment

Environmental management issues for the resort islands of the Maldives have been considered under the Paradise Island case study in the diving chapter, and are similar for Dhonveli.

## Safety

As with other surfing destinations, safety on the waves is principally the responsibility of the individual surfer. In the event of injury the resort has radio contact to
the capital and can transport people there by speedboat, either to the local hospital
or for evacuation. Some surfers bring helmets and reef booties, whilst others do not.

## Marketing

At least for surfers, visits to the Maldives are sold principally through specialist surf
tour companies, which advertise principally in specialist recreational surfing
magazines. It appears that access to Dhonveli is currently controlled and sold
entirely through Atoll Adventures (2005). Surfing is also promoted, along with
diving, in general tourist promotional materials of the Maldives.

# Savaii Island, Samoa: Savaii Surfaris

### Place

The South Pacific nation of Samoa consists of two main islands, Savaii to the west
and Upolu to the east. There are surfable breaks on both the north and south
coastline of Savaii, with different breaks working at different seasons depending on
the predominant wind direction. The southern coast is better-known, especially the
area around Aganoa Point (sometimes spelled Akanoa Point). Inland, the terrain is
mostly steep and heavily dissected, with forested ridges, valleys and rivers; and
much of the coastline is cliffed. Samoa is well placed to receive Pacific Ocean swells,
but there are relatively few accessible sites with well-formed and rideable surf
breaks.

### Operator

Savaii Surfaris is the only surf tour operator on the western island of Samoa. The
company has been operating successfully for a number of years, making use of local
accommodation, guiding visitors through the niceties of Samoan culture, and taking
clients to the best breaks on any given day, either onshore or by boat. In an era when
surf resorts with exclusive, and hence expensive, access to particular famous breaks
are becoming increasingly common throughout the Indo-Pacific region, Savaii
Surfaris has achieved a particular reputation for welcoming independent travelling
surfers and sharing local knowledge and logistic support.

### Activity

Surf breaks in Samoa are generally suitable for experienced surfers only, with fast
hollow waves, shallow reefs and very tight takeoff zones. The better-known breaks
in the Aganoa area on the south cost of Savaii can be reached by paddling directly
from shore, but it is certainly much easier to be ferried out in a small boat, and this
is the usual practice at Savaii Surfaris. If there is no surf, there are various rivers and
waterfalls, forests and cultural sights that can be reached in a day trip from the
Aganoa area.

## Accommodation

Depending on the season, the best surf might be either on the north or the south coast of Savaii, and different accommodation is used accordingly. When I visited Savaii Surfaris, we stayed in independently owned beach fales in the village nearest to Aganoa. These are small single-room huts or cabins built on poles about head-high above the beach. They have wooden floors, thatched roofs and walls made from hanging straw mats that can be rolled up or down to adjust ventilation. The fales themselves have no facilities except a mattress: there is a separate shower and toilet block, and a separate bar and dining area. This is a semi-traditional design, low-key but very comfortable. More recently, it appears that Savaii Surfaris (2005) has completed construction of its own purpose-built accommodation, Aganoa Beach Fales at Aganoa Point itself, with ten fales equipped with freestanding beds, and a central amenities block with hot showers. Four of the cabins are air-conditioned doubles. The remainder are naturally ventilated triples.

## Statistics

There does not appear to be any fixed group size for Savaii Surfaris. Maximum capacity in the new accommodation would seem to be about 25 guests. When I surfed there, there were about eight surfers in total. There was no guide with us, but none was needed since only one break was rideable at the time, a short dinghy-ride from the beach fales. Even with only eight surfers, this break showed symptoms of crowding. There is no fixed length of stay. Current prices are around SAT167 (US$65) per person per day, including accommodation at the new fales, meals, and car and boat transfers to surf breaks (Savaii Surfaris, 2005).

## Access

International access to Samoa is by air to Apia on the eastern island of Upolu. There are internal domestic flights between Upolu and Savaii, but the planes are generally too small to carry surfboards, so the local inter-island ferry provides a more reliable option. Samoa's infrastructure is currently not designed for, nor capable of handling, a large influx of tourists, but visitor numbers are growing and infrastructure is likely to be improved. Within the island of Savaii, transport is by road in a Savaii Surfaris vehicle. Access to individual surf breaks is either directly from shore, or in a small dinghy from the nearby beach.

Land in Samoa is under traditional ownership and access generally requires, at the very least, permission from the chief of the nearest village. Custom dictates a gift as part of this process. For areas visited frequently by tourists, this has evolved into standardized entry fees, payable in cash, for tourists to visit individual beaches, waterfalls, forests, etc., or undertake specific activities, such as swimming or surfing. Currently these amounts are small and provide a means for local landowners to gain revenue from tourism. From a tourist's perspective, however, it is not easy to know what is reasonable and what is not. For the independent traveller, there can be some uncertainty as to who is delegated to collect such fees and how much they should be, and this uncertainty also creates the possibilities of causing offence.

In addition, there are a range of Samoan customs that visitors must not infringe. Both these aspects provide particular opportunities for Samoan tour operators and guides, who can assist tourists in maintaining protocol without being taken advantage of. To visit with a local resident who is familiar with people and protocols avoids the possibility of any discourtesy, and this applies for surfing as much as for land tours.

## Community

Samoan society has a strong and distinctive structure, an amalgam of traditional tribal ways and modern Christianity. The former, for example, decrees that visitors must follow certain local customs; the latter, that one of these customs is now no sport on Sundays, including surfing. Similarly, one may not walk through a village between 5 and 6 pm. This amalgam of custom ancient and modern is known as *faaSamoa*, the Samoan way of life.

Surfers visiting Samoa with Savaii Surfaris must quickly learn at least the basic rules and courtesies, and this alone is one good reason to have a local guide. Savaii Surfaris (2005) contributes to an education fund for the local village schools. At least when I visited, we stayed in beach fales whose bars and restaurants were both run and patronized by local villagers. Some of these locals were keen to share extended conversations, though of course such interactions provide little insight into details of daily Samoan lifestyle or society. I also met an expatriate volunteer teaching at a local village school and engaged to a Samoan. Conversations with her gave at least an inkling of the complexities of living in a Samoan village.

## Experience

According to the locals, the surf was not at its best whilst I was there, and in fact only one break was working, immediately in front of the village church. This break produced a fast hollow wave over shallow live coral, so that one could see the colours of the reef and fish through the face of the wave whilst surfing. It was a beautiful wave and none of Savaii's clients had any complaints whatsoever. Since we were staying on the beach right next to this village, we could surf at our own convenience, taking advantage of a small outboard-powered dinghy kept on the beach. At other times we visited various local historic and scenic sights, including the Tafua canopy walk described by Buckley (2003a, p. 61).

## Environment

The beachfront fales used previously are effectively just part of a local Samoan village and contribute pro rata to all its impacts. I have not visited the new Aganoa Beach Fales and cannot comment on environmental management practices.

## Safety

For shore-based surfing, such as that at Savaii Surfaris, safety is largely the responsibility of the individual surfers, who must make their own judgements of surf conditions and their own capabilities. Local knowledge can help find the best breaks for surfers with different abilities under different conditions, and can provide information on any particular features such as the underwater reef topography, currents, wave behaviour and useful landmarks on shore. A local surf guide can also paddle out with clients, or stand by in a small boat in the nearest channel. None of these, however, can substitute for the skill, experience and judgement of each individual surfer.

## Marketing

Savaii Surfaris advertises in the end pages of various specialist surfing magazines, and these probably provide the majority of its clients. It also maintains close links with other tour operators within Samoa to assist in packaging and cross-marketing. Total client numbers are relatively small, and word-of-mouth referrals are also likely to be important.

# Upolu, Samoa: Salani Surf Resort

### Place

Upolu is the more easterly of Samoa's two main islands. It is also somewhat more developed, with the country's international airport and its capital and principal port at Apia on the north coast. Most of the island's interior, and much of the coastline, is steep and rugged, but there are sandy beaches and small coastal plains in some areas. Along the south coast there are several surfable breaks, principally at river mouths and the fringing reefs of small offshore islets. The surf breaks in Samoa are powerful reef breaks of high wave quality, which attract experienced surfers from around the world. There are relatively few surfable breaks, however, and even with relatively few surfers the waves can quickly become crowded.

### Operator

Salani Surf Resort is a dedicated surf resort behind an uninhabited beach on the southeastern coast of Upolu, at the mouth of the Mulivai Fagatoloa River, immediately opposite Salani Village (Salani Surf Resort, 2005). Salani enjoys direct and privileged access to two breaks immediately offshore from the river mouth. Two more, accessible in a small open boat, are also used by surfing clients of a beach resort further west, and by independent surfers.

Salani Surf Resort is a specialist surf lodge that caters principally for skilled surfers coming to Samoa specifically to surf. It is also well set up to cater for non-surfing partners in surfing couples, with comfortable accommodation and a range of activities available either directly from the resort or from independent tour operators such as Ecotour Samoa (2005). The same applies for non-surfing visitors who want Samoan south-coast accommodation with Western-style amenities. Salani's owner has been active in establishing links between different tourism operators in this area, including joint marketing and promotional activities.

Surfers are taken by boat to whichever break is working best in the light of prevailing surf, wind and tide conditions. Typically they would have one surf session in the morning and one in the afternoon, returning to the lodge for lunch and a rest in the middle of the day. The two breaks at the Salani river mouth are only a few minutes offshore and are generally surfed only by guests at Salani. Other breaks are further away and may also be accessed by surfers from the other main surf resort. The two operations maintain contact and generally plan their surfing sessions so as to avoid taking clients to the same break at the same time, since this could lead to crowding and potential conflict.

## Activity

Salani is known and advertised for its surfing, and this is certainly the principal activity for most visitors. There are four good surf breaks within 25 min by boat, two of them immediately offshore from Salani itself. The swells are generally larger from May to September, but cleaner from November to March. In addition to surfing, there are opportunities to fish; to paddle sit-on-top kayaks; to walk, swim or lie on the beach; or to travel inland to see the rest of Samoa.

## Equipment

Surfers bring their own boards and gear. Salani has three open outboard-powered runabouts that take surfers to the various breaks as above. Snorkelling and fishing equipment are available for loan to guests who are not surfing.

## Accommodation

Salani Surf Resort incorporates eight individual bungalows, a separate amenities block, and a central bar, lounge and dining area where meals are served. A maximum of 12 surfing guests are accepted at any one time.

## Statistics

Maximum visitor capacity at Salani is 16, with a maximum of 12 surfers at any one time. Commonly, only a proportion of visitors are active surfers. When I visited there were no surfing guides as such, but the locals driving the boat were knowledgeable about surf breaks and conditions. Currently, Salani Surf Resort (2005) advertises that the boats are 'piloted by skilled, expatriate surf guides'. There is no fixed length of stay, but most surfers would probably stay at least 3 or 4 days, and commonly for a week or so. Prices vary somewhat with season, but are around US$90–130 per person per day.

Prices on offer as of 26 August 2005 were substantially lower for clients from the USA than those from Australia or New Zealand (Salani Surf Resort, 2005), which probably contravenes international trade agreements, but only if the Australian or New Zealand government complains to the World Trade Organization.

## Access

Access to Salani is by air to Apia and by road to the resort. Access to the surf breaks is in a small, open outboard-powered dinghy from the beach or river mouth. The two surf breaks at Salani itself can also be reached by paddling directly from the beach, but it would be a long paddle and the boat is certainly much more convenient. Relations between Salani and local communities are good, and use of the reef, beach and river mouth does not seem to be an issue.

## Community

Modern Samoan society combines strong Christian religious practices with traditional social structures, including extended families, traditional matai or chiefs, and traditional customs or *faaSamoa*. Within village areas, for example, dress codes are very conservative, curfews are observed at dusk, and sports are strongly discouraged on Sundays.

Maintaining good relations with local villages is an essential prerequisite to business survival – and perhaps even personal safety – in Samoa, and surf resorts and tour operators must therefore ensure that their clients observe local customs. In practice, this means no walking through villages in boardshorts, or between 5 and 6 pm, and no surfing on Sundays no matter how good the wave.

Salani Surf Resort contributes to its local village community both as an employer and through initiatives such as the clean-up programme described below. The village itself has no tourist facilities and is not adapted or modified for tourism, though guests at Salani are welcome to walk through it.

## Experience

Salani is a relaxed and self-contained place, enjoyable irrespective of surfing conditions. My visit was brief and we surfed principally at an offshore island reef some distance away, as the Salani home breaks were somewhat wind-affected. Photographs of these breaks, however, indicated that under good conditions they can shape up extremely well. The owner of Salani was particularly helpful during my visit, arranging opportunities to carry out detailed inspections of the site's facilities and also to visit other operators on Upolu's south coast. Several young couples were staying at Salani whilst I was there, and the non-surfing partners seemed to enjoy themselves as much as the surfers.

## Environment

Salani has made a particular effort to construct and operate its facilities for minimal environmental impact (Buckley, 2003a, pp. 49–50). Broadly speaking, it is constructed to Western design standards, e.g. in regards to sewage treatment, in an area where such standards do not always apply.

Salani has also sponsored clean-up campaigns in the local village, providing gloves, implements, wheelbarrows, etc., and vehicles to haul off trash for permanent disposal. As in most traditional South Pacific societies, historically all material goods were made from local materials and were hence rapidly biodegradable, so used items could be discarded on the spot without impact. Customs have not yet adapted to the advent of Western manufacturing practices and the availability of imported consumer goods, and litter has hence become a significant aesthetic and pollution problem in populated areas. At the village near Salani, for example, discarded items are commonly thrown over the riverbank, creating a hazard as well as an eyesore. Salani's clean-up campaigns have aimed to provide both the equipment and the leadership to improve these practices.

## Safety

The major concern facing surf resort operators in Samoa is the risk of overcrowding. Under normal – i.e. less-than-perfect – surfing conditions, crowding already occurs at the best surf breaks even though the three main commercial surf tour operators already limit their numbers, by agreement with local villages. On the main island of

Upolu, two major south-coast surf resorts have adopted an informal system to avoid taking their clients to the same breaks at the same time on the same day, but a non-resort operator apparently also takes surfers to the same breaks.

Crowding produces two problems from a tourism perspective. First, commercial surf tour clients tend to be older surfers who may not be as competent as they once were, or as young independent surfers still are. One reason they pay for surf tours is to avoid crowded breaks at home. If independent surfers take all the best waves at tour destinations and the commercial tour clients miss out, they will lose the incentive to buy a tour. Second, the Samoan reef breaks are relatively difficult and dangerous to surf. Crowding leads surfers to incur higher risks of injury.

The surf breaks accessible from Salani are all reef breaks suitable for experienced surfers only, and the Salani website says rightly that 'beginner surfers should look at other surf destinations'. As elsewhere, the single main determinant of safety whilst surfing is the individual's ability to assess their own skills accurately in relation to the difficulty and danger of the particular place and conditions. Local knowledge contributes to safety by helping to select the best break on any given day, predict how conditions are likely to change, and provide site-specific information on tides and currents, underwater topography and wave behaviour.

## Marketing

Salani Surf Resort seems to have a two-pronged marketing strategy. There are now a number of international surf tour packaging companies that act as retail marketing arms for a wide range of local surf resorts and boat charters in different parts of the world. These companies advertise in specialist surfing magazines, offering a range of destinations, and surfers can book surfing holidays at any of these sites through a single retail organization. Most of these companies are based either in Australia or the USA, and offer a range of Indo-Pacific surfing options in Indonesia, the Maldives, Hawaii, Fiji, Tahiti, Tonga and Samoa. Salani Surf Resort is featured by a number of these tour-packaging companies, which presumably use a commission structure as in other sectors of the tourism industry. Currently, Salani is marketed in the USA by Waterways Surf Adventures (2005), and in Australia by Atoll Adventures (2005), previously known as Atoll Travel. Salani is also active at a local level, helping to create Samoan tourism marketing alliances across a range of different activities.

# Kadavu Island, Fiji: Nagigia Surf Resort

## Place

Kadavu is the southernmost of Fiji's larger islands, lying about 80 km south of the main island of Viti Levu. Kadavu itself is about 50 km long, narrow and mountainous, with few roads, and villages dotted along the coastline. Its native flora and fauna differ somewhat from Fiji's other islands, with characteristic species such as the distinctive Kadavu Parrot. Kadavu is a well-known international diving destination, especially famous for the drop-offs of Great Astrolabe Reef on its southern side.

In recent years it has also become known for its surf, notably a left-hand reef break near Cape Washington at the far western end of Kadavu. The break is called King Kong Left, apparently since the original 1935 version of the movie King Kong was filmed, in part, on the mountain behind Cape Washington. The surfing potential was first recognized several decades ago by Nagigia's current manager, from a casual visit by cargo boat, and for many years he surfed it alone. A few years ago, however, a lodge was built on 13 ha Nagigia Island, immediately adjacent to King Kong Left, and Nagigia is now known as one of Fiji's prime surfing destinations.

## Operator

Nagigia Island itself, and exclusive surfing rights to the various Nagigia surf breaks, are leased from the local landowners by a company known as Nagigia Island Ltd. Development of Nagigia Surf Resort was made possible using capital from a New Zealand investor based in Kadavu, who now owns Nagigia Island Ltd and the fixed assets. Further expansion is planned, by selling house sites to new investors who will be able to build their own residences adjacent to the existing facilities. Presumably they will have the option to have these residences managed commercially by the resort, if they wish. The entire lease, including 34 individual lots, is apparently also up for sale.

## Activity

Nagigia advertises a range of activities, but in practice it seems that most clients come principally to surf, and other options are used only as back-ups if surf conditions are poor. Diving is available through Dive Kadavu (2005), but people who come principally to dive would probably stay at Dive Kadavu's own resort. To dive from Nagigia requires a boat shuttle to Dive Kadavu, taking an hour each way and costing US$64 in addition to dive costs.

At Nagigia there is also excellent snorkelling, sit-on-top kayaks to paddle to a nearby sandy beach, and the opportunity to walk on the reef flat at low tide, along with villagers collecting seafoods. The resort also offers local fishing excursions and sizeable wahoo can be landed: up to 42 kg during my own visit.

During my visit, however, everyone was there principally to surf, and most of the clients were experienced surfers from Australia's Gold and Sunshine Coasts. This created a certain degree of crowding, since the surf was rather mediocre at the time, sets were few, everyone wanted the same waves, and there were up to 15 surfers on site. The break is directly visible from the main deck of the lodge, however, and it is only a 5 min boat shuttle from lodge to surf, so the surfers were able to take turns during the day and everyone got waves with only a little reasonably good-natured grumbling. If the waves had been more consistent there would have been more than enough for everyone. During my visit the winds were variable and the swell was generally rather small and crumbly, rather than the powerful hollow swell we were hoping for. The Nagigia website displays photographs of the surf almost every day for the past 5 years, so prospective visitors can make their own assessment of when might be the best time of year to visit.

## Equipment

Nagigia does have one or two surfboards available for rent, but on condition that a broken board must be replaced at a cost of US$600. Surfing clients bring their own boards, generally several each. A few brought shortie wetsuits, which proved very useful as the water was not as warm as expected. Rash vests and sunscreen were also critical. One or two wore helmets and reef booties, but most did not. The resort provides snorkelling gear and sit-on-top kayaks on loan and fishing gear as part of a fishing package.

## Accommodation

Nagigia can accommodate up to 25–30 guests in two styles of accommodation. There are ten individual bures or cabins, most with one double and one single bed. These have an outdoor cold-water shower but no other facilities, except that one also has an en suite toilet. There is also one slightly larger building that operates dormitory style. The showers and toilets are in a central block, which helps to conserve freshwater. The bures are along the waterfront, with a central kitchen and dining area on a low hill behind.

Rather unusually, the residential tariff is for room only, and meals are charged separately. Since the bures have no kitchens or refrigerators, there is no other local source of food, and clients would not even be able to bring fuel for camping stoves on the plane to the island, there is not really much choice about paying up for three meals per day. Perhaps this division is made for marketing reasons.

## Statistics

Prices for residential accommodation alone range from US$50 to 110, depending on the bure and length of stay, plus US$32 per person per day for three meals. Transfers from Kadavu's airport at Vunisea cost US$32 per person each way. Surfing costs US$15 per person per day, of which about half is paid to the village landowners as a resource use fee. The daily surfing price includes local boat shuttles from Nagigia to King Kong Left, on demand, as often as required. Shuttles to more distant breaks cost more. There is no fixed length of stay, but most clients seem to stay about a week. Total costs per day for surfers staying a week are hence about US$100 per person per day.

## Access

Nagigia can be reached by private yacht, but most visitor access is by air from Nadi or Suva to Vunisea, and in an open boat to the resort. The surf can be reached by walking and/or paddling out across the reef flat, but it is much quicker, easier and safer to take the boat shuttle. Guests at Nagigia have exclusive access to the break in return for the fee as above.

## Community

Except for the managers, all staff at Nagigia are local, most of them from the adjacent village. Other villagers forage routinely on the reef flat at low tide and are very friendly to guests, but only staff come on to the island. The villagers receive several sources of support from the resort. The main one is the annual rental for the overall lease, which is shared between the relevant landholders. Nagigia also pays for daily deliveries of fresh water, with payments supposedly divided between the local village, and another village 8 km away that supplies the water via a pipeline. The resort is the major source of local employment, and also charters up to five local boats each day for surfing, transfers, fishing and supply runs. Village tours are available at a price, and artefacts such as mats are on sale. The village thus operates a subsistence economy for food, but relies on the resort for its cash income.

## Experience

Nagigia Island is a beautiful place, especially when the sun is shining. The snorkelling is excellent. The surf can also be excellent, though during my own visit it was not especially memorable. Of course, this can happen at any surf break anywhere, especially during a brief visit. The resort and facilities are low-key but pleasant, the bures basic but comfortable, the food more than adequate, and the staff laid-back but very helpful and friendly.

## Environment

Fresh water is in short supply, as noted above. Rainwater is collected from roofs, but more must be brought over every day, by boat, in tanks. Drinking water is filtered in the kitchens. Greywater drains directly into the ground, which is eroded porous coral rubble and rampart rock. Sewage is treated in septic tanks and french drains. Lighting is provided by a generator that runs 16 h/day, and hot water is heated by gas. Organic catering scraps are taken to the village by staff, to feed their pigs. Plastic bottles and containers are re-used in the village. Cans are crushed and buried in landfill on Kandavu. Glass is crushed and dumped in deep water (600 m) well outside the reef.

## Safety

There are no safety briefings or procedures as such. Presumably anyone who takes the effort to travel to Nagigia to surf knows enough about surfing to look out for themselves. There is a permanent buoy near King Kong Left and apparently the normal procedure is for a boat to remain near this buoy whenever anyone is surfing. In practice this did not happen, even on one occasion when I was surfing on my own. There does not seem to be any way to signal a boat to come and fetch surfers, except to wave surfboards and hope someone on shore happens to be looking. On one or two occasions, surfers decided to paddle in across the reef rather than wait.

There are various tracks around the island, and one of these goes to a lookout at the point near the break. The final 100 m of this track is unformed and crosses very sharp, jagged, eroded limestone rampant rock. A fall could cause significant injury. One can also clamber down from this point to the reef flat, which requires considerable care. Of course, villagers do it all the time with the utmost nonchalance. There is a helipad on Nagigia Island, but apparently no helicopter on Kadavu. Normal medical evacuation requires an hour by boat to the nearest doctor at Vunisea, and the once-a-day flight to Nadi or Suva.

## Marketing

Nagigia's website name is well designed to reach surfers looking for options in Fiji: http://www.fijisurf.com. The island features occasionally in specialist surfing magazines, though it is not nearly as well known as Tavarua in the Mamanuca

Group, west of Viti Levu. Word-of-mouth and repeat visitors seem to be important. The majority of clients are experienced surfers from Australia. This may change if the proposed expansion proceeds or the island is sold.

## Mentawai Islands, Indonesia: Great Breaks International and Mentawai Sanctuary

### Place

The Mentawais are a chain of small islands off the western coast of Sumatra at the northwestern end of Indonesia. Though less than 100 km from the mainland coastline, the Mentawais are separated from it by an ocean trench over 1000 m deep. In consequence, even during past geological epochs when sea level was much lower than at present and many of the islands in this region were connected by land bridges, the Mentawais have always been surrounded by water.

Whilst the southern islands in the Mentawai chain are low reef-top islands formed of sand and coral rubble, the largest island of Pulau Siberut is a high baserock island that supports dense tropical forest. Because of their geological separation from the Sumatran mainland, the forests of Siberut support endemic wildlife, including primates such as the Kloss gibbon, and are therefore of considerable global con-servation significance (Sproule and Suhandi, 1998; Buckley, 2002a). The island of Siberut is also famous for its forest villages, which practise a shamanistic religion. To the southwest, the Mentawais face directly into the full fetch of the Indian Ocean, which delivers a powerful and consistent swell throughout year, though generally larger mid year. There are at least 30 named major surf breaks (Buckley, 2002a, b), most of them shallow reef breaks suitable for experienced surfers only.

### Operator

At least a dozen different vessels operate surf charters in the Mentawai Islands. Each boat is independently owned and skippered, but they operate in retail syndicates to sell surf tours. There is now apparently one syndicated surf tour operation that spe-cializes in the Mentawais. Martin Daly's Indies Trader®, with three boats, also operates mainly in the Mentawais but independently of the syndicates; and one of his vessels is in use elsewhere in the Quicksilver Crossing®, a round-the-world surf tour.

The specialist Mentawais syndicate seems to have traded under various names at different times, though using the same fleet of boats throughout. Groups can book one of the boats in its entirety, or buy individual places on weeks where bookings are available. For many years the company was known as Great Breaks International, but currently it is listed on its website as Mentawai Sanctuary (2005). Since the tsunami damage to these regions of Indonesia and elsewhere in southeast Asia in late 2004, it is also running a relief operation under the name of Electric Lamb Mission.

### Activity

Surfers meet their boat in Padang on the Sumatran coast. The islands and surf breaks visited, and the precise route, are at the discretion of the ship's skipper and are likely to reflect actual and forecast swell, weather and positions of other vessels, where known. It takes a full day or night to travel between the most northerly and the most southerly surf breaks.

Any of the breaks becomes crowded by one boatload of surfers, so boats will generally try to spread out. Some breaks, however, are particularly famous, and everyone wants to surf there, so competition between boats is not unknown. The best time of day for surfing varies depending on tide times, accessible breaks and the skill of the surfers. The water is warm and the sun can be very hot, so given the choice most surfers would probably choose to surf morning and evening, avoiding the midday heat. Apart from surfing, surfers spend most of their time on the boat, eating, resting, fishing and waiting for the next surf. Those interested may also land on the islands.

## Equipment

The Mentawais Sanctuary syndicate currently lists three boats: the 25 m *Sanssouci*, the 17 m *Saranya* and the 17 m *Electric Lamb*. Surfers must bring their own boards and boardshorts, spare fins and leashes, board repair kit, wax and zinc. Reef booties are strongly recommended to guard against coral cuts on the feet, and a long-sleeve rash vest to protect against sunburn. A lightweight 'short john' wetsuit with thin neoprene and short arms and legs is an alternative. Most surfers would bring at least two, and generally three boards, with different lengths for different sizes of surf, and to provide spares in case of snapped boards, since there is no way to replace them.

## Accommodation

The trip generally involves one night's overnight accommodation in Padang at the start and end of the trip, to meet up with connecting flights. For the rest of the time, accommodation is on board. The various boats differ considerably in the layout, size and luxury of cabins and living spaces (Mentawai Sanctuary, 2005). The *Sanssouci* can carry ten clients, the *Saranya* and *Electric Lamb* six or eight each. Cabins are generally shared. On most trips the vessels are booked by groups rather than individual clients. Fresh water must be carried onboard and is in limited supply. All boats carry fresh food and catch fresh fish, either by trawling or using handlines whilst anchored. Cooking and washing up is done by the crew.

## Statistics

Most surf tours by the Mentawai Sanctuary boats last 11 days in total. The tours generally do not include surfing guides as such, but most of the boat skippers are expert surfers themselves, and the *Sanssouci*'s crew also includes surf videographers. Prices depend principally on the boat, and to some degree on the season. For *Sanssouci* the currently quoted price is US$2750 per person for 11 nights; for the *Saranya*, US$2450; and for *Electric Lamb*, US$1550. These prices correspond to US$140–250 per person per day. Group size while actually surfing is determined by the boat's capacity, unless the skipper is able to drop half his surfing passengers at one break and the other half at a nearby break. Boat capacities range from six to ten passengers, as noted above.

## Access

Access to the Mentawais is by air to Padang in Sumatra, and by boat from the Padang Harbour to the Mentawai Islands and then to the individual breaks. Padang is accessible by air directly from Singapore, which provides a considerable advantage for many international clients. There is a public ferry from Padang to Pulau Siberut, and it is possible for independent travelling surfers, with plenty of time at their disposal, to surf the breaks on Siberut and its immediate surroundings using only local transport as available. To reach the more distant islands and breaks, however, especially if one has little time available, a surf charter boat is the only option. These range from local fishing boats to luxury specialist surf charters such as those described here.

Land on any of the Mentawai Islands is generally owned by local villages and local villagers, and permission is required for anything more than a brief visit. A number of surf tour operators have contemplated the construction of small lodges on one or other of these islands, so as to offer shore-based surf holidays. To date, it appears that only one of these has actually been built, at a break named Macaronis. Another is apparently under construction, by the Mentawai Sanctuary group at a site known as E-Bay on the southwestern corner of Pulau Siberut. Damage from wave surge associated with the tsunami in late 2004, and a submarine earthquake in 2005, led to reassessment of many potential beachfront sites that were previously under consideration.

Access to the surf breaks of the Mentawai Islands in live-aboard boats has been a somewhat contested issue for a number of years (Buckley, 2002a, b). Technically there is a system of access permits, and these are operated under concession by a Padang-based organization, and supposedly enforced by the Indonesian navy. The merits or otherwise of this approach were debated fiercely in specialist surf magazines in the first few years of this millennium, with accusations of exploiting the locals traded off against accusations of heavy-handed enforcement. The situation did appear to have stabilized in 2004, but it is not clear whether it has survived the disruption caused by the earthquake and tsunami.

## Community

Live-aboard surf charters employ Indonesian crew, but these are unlikely to be local villagers. At some of the Mentawai breaks, surfers have opportunities to land and meet local villagers. Such contacts have become more frequent recently, in part because of a medical assistance programme known as SurfAid, which is sponsored by most of the major surf charter operators in the area and also by surf clothing man-ufacturers. There do not seem to be many local surfers on the islands, but experience from elsewhere in Indonesia and the rest of the Pacific indicates that locals will learn as soon as they can get hold of surfboards.

## Experience

I have made two visits to the Mentawai in surf charter boats. Neither of these were full 11-day tours, but we were able to visit and surf most of the best-known breaks none the less, from Pulau Siberut to the southernmost tip of the Mentawai archipelago. On the first visit we had an engine breakdown, apparently caused by sabotage, which delayed us in Padang Harbour for 2 days. Some of the Mentawai breaks are supposedly amongst the best surf in the world, and even though conditions were far from perfect during my own visit, the surf certainly lived up to its reputation of high quality. We also gained a glimpse into the complexities of local politics.

## Environment

A live-aboard charter boat in ocean waters, such as those around the Mentawais, will generally collect all garbage to take back to port but will throw food scraps and organic waste overboard. Toilets are likely to be of the saltwater marine type that pump out directly after each use, or if holding tanks are fitted they would generally be pumped out whilst the vessel is travelling from one site to another. Fresh water may be carried in tanks, or produced by desalination, as in *Sanssouci* and *Saranya*.

As island resorts are constructed, environmental management issues will become accordingly more complex. To a degree, these are inseparable from the gradual import of Western material cultures into traditional societies that are unused to dealing with non-biodegradable litter.

Overall, however, the impacts of surfers are negligible compared to the impacts of locals fishing with dynamite, which has led to widespread destruction of reefs in this area. Equally, any impacts on land are negligible compared to the past clearance of the lower reef islets for coconut plantations, and the current clearance of the larger baserock islands for industrial logging and oil-palm plantations. Similarly, the potential cultural impacts of surfers are negligible compared to those of tourists visiting the traditional hill villages in the interior of Pulau Siberut, as described briefly by Buckley (2002a, b). If surf charter boats can catalyse the construction of permanent surf lodges, which lead in turn to growth of marine tourism and terrestrial nature tourism more broadly in this area, this may potentially counteract the economic pressures for continued clearing of native forest of high conservation value.

## Safety

Surfing in the Mentawais Islands potentially involves a number of risks, and joining an organized group on a live-aboard charter boat reduces most of these. In particular, travelling with local guides reduces the risks from the less scrupulous local residents; and travelling in a vessel built and maintained to Australian or equivalent service standards will generally be much safer than travelling in a local fishing boat. In addition, if a passenger becomes injured, a surf charter boat can take steps to get them to the best medical care as quickly as possible, which may not otherwise be feasible.

The skippers of most of the expatriate-owned surf charter boats know the islands and the surf breaks very well, and can choose safe passages, safe anchorages and safe surf breaks in line with the ability of their clients. They will drop surfers off immediately outside the breaks so there is no need to walk or paddle across the reef from shore, though of course this may happen in any event if a surfer is caught inside a wave and washed over the reef flat.

Despite precautions, however, some risks remain. On my first visit, for example, one of the group decided to visit a local village in the evening, travelling by boat along narrow passages through mangroves. He was rewarded with a bout of dengue fever. On my second visit, whilst the boat's owner and skipper was ashore at one surf break, we noticed that the boat appeared to be dragging anchor to a point where it was at severe risk from set waves. Fortunately, one of those remaining aboard was also a very experienced skipper and we were able to move the vessel to safety.

## Marketing

Surf in the Mentawais is well-known to surfers worldwide because of extensive coverage in specialist surf magazines and movies. There is thus a strong demand for live-aboard surf charters in this area. The principal marketing issue for the various tour operators is thus competition between the different syndicates, which is inextricably entangled with local politics and access issues. A selection of relevant material is available on the website of Mentawai Sanctuary (2005).

# 12  Heliski and Snowboard

Ralf Buckley, Tyax Heliski, Canada. RB collection.

Ralf Buckley, CMH Galena, Canada. RB collection.

## Sector Structure

Despite their relatively high cost, heliskiing and heliboarding are established forms of adventure tourism in many parts of the world. The heliski industry seems to be most heavily developed in the Rocky Mountains ranges of southwestern Canada, but there are also well-established heliski operations in New Zealand, Russia, India and in Alaska, Utah and Colorado, USA.

The level of skill required differs between countries and operators, depending partly on terrain and partly on target markets. Advertising by Harris Mountains Heli-ski (2005) out of Queenstown, New Zealand, for example, aims to sell single-day three- or four-run heliski packages to intermediate-level skiers who are already visiting ski resorts in the area. The heliskiing package does not include accom-modation or meals, except for lunches on the slopes.

Operators such as Canadian Mountain Holidays (2005) or Mike Wiegele Helicopter Skiing (2005) in Canada's British Columbia, in contrast, sell only 1-week all-inclusive packages based in their own lodges, aimed principally at advanced skiers and boarders, and relying strongly on multiple repeat business from long-established clients. Clients of CMH, MWHS and local competitors such as Selkirk-Tangiers (2005) need to be quite fit, strong and skilled skiers or snowboarders simply to keep up with the rest of their helicopter group.

In all except the most expensive group charters, heliski tour packages use a single helicopter to shuttle three, four or five groups of skiers and snowboarders in succession. For this system to work safely and efficiently, all the clients need to be able to ski or ride similar terrain at similar speed. If any skier causes their group to miss its place in the lift cycle, they will not be popular!

Different heliski operations involve different degrees of skill and remoteness. Not surprisingly, these are reflected in pricing structures; though overall, the single most important determinant of price is the number of groups sharing each helicopter. Heliskiing is expensive, but for many heliskiers price is not a significant barrier. For these individuals, more important factors include: political stability and ease of access for the area concerned; quality and reliability of snowpack; skills and safety qualifications of guides and helicopter pilots and mechanics; and finally, facilities on the ground. In the longer term, the most limiting of these is the quality of the terrain and snow. Given sufficient market demand and hence funds available, tour operators can provide, control or bypass all the other factors; but clients will only pay this price if the rewards are greater than at established heliski areas.

Very broadly, the main marketing advantages for heliski operations in the Canadian Rockies are reliable snow and ready access for American clients. In Alaska the principal attraction is particularly steep terrain, not available elsewhere because of avalanche risks. New Zealand is generally less expensive than elsewhere because of currency exchange rates, is easily accessible from Japan without significant jetlag, and is available in the off-season for northern hemisphere clients.

In the Himalayas the principal attraction is the possibility, though by no means the guarantee, of particularly deep, light and dry high-altitude snow, with some of the runs starting at above 5000 m. Russian operations (Heli Ski Russia, 2005; High Sky Adventures, 2005; Yak and Yeti, 2005) are readily accessible to the European markets; though in perception at least, facilities and safety may not be at the same standards as elsewhere. A new heliski destination, such as Greenland, has to compete with all of these. Initially it can do so simply as somewhere different and unknown, and hence attractive to experienced heliskiers looking for a new experience. In the longer term, however, this attraction can only be maintained if Greenland establishes a reputation for high-quality snow at a price comparable to existing destinations.

## Manali, India: Himachal Helicopter Skiing

### Place

India's only heliski company operates from a hotel in the hill town of Manali. Well-known in India for its hot springs, temples and orchards, Manali is a well-established summer holiday destination for Indian domestic tourists, and is reputed to be particularly popular amongst honeymoon couples. During winter, however, there are very few domestic visitors, and most of the tourist shops are closed. During the heliski season, heliskiers provide the bulk of the clientele for Manali's major hotel, the Manali Holiday Inn.

The main road to Manali continues over a high mountain pass to Kashmir and the border with Pakistan, and there is a substantial Indian army garrison on the outskirts of Manali, responsible for opening the road during spring thaw every year and running convoys to the border posts. In addition to any direct economic impact through local purchases, the garrison is important to the Manali economy since it maintains the access road at a much higher standard than would otherwise be anticipated, at no expense to the town. Holiday accommodation in Manali is therefore much more easily accessible for domestic tourists than would otherwise be the case.

Heliskiing and snowboarding in the Himalayas is a recent innovation. The terrain is eminently suitable, but because of the latitude and relatively low precipitation, skiable snow is generally only available in alpine areas at 3500–5000 m elevation, which is close to the practical operational limits for most skiers as well as most helicopters. In addition, relatively few areas have the necessary access and infrastructure to support a safe and commercially viable heliski business.

### Operator

To date there is only one commercial heliski operator in the Himalayas, namely Himachal Helicopter Skiing (HHS, 2005). HHS was established in Himachal Pradesh in India because of concerns over political instability in Nepal, which did indeed prove well-founded.

### Activity

Even from the breakfast table, guests and guides can see the snow-covered peaks across the Kullu valley and make a first assessment of weather conditions. Helicopter groups, and the time and order of take-offs, are posted at the dining room door. Skis, snowboards, avalanche transceivers and safety packs are stored in drying rooms on the lower terrace of the hotel, close to the radio operations centre. There are two helipads in a dedicated area immediately outside the hotel walls, accessible by a gate from the lower terrace. Ski groups remain behind this gate until it is their turn to board.

The first flight of the day takes heliskiers out of the green terraced fields and orchards around Manali, high above the tree line to peaks and ridges up to 5000 m elevation. The altitude is certainly noticeable; even bending down to fasten snowboard bindings requires unusual effort. In a good season the Himalayan snow is legendary for its lightness, though of course conditions vary here as they do everywhere. A typical run starts with a steep short drop from a ridgeline or sometimes a cornice, big sweeping turns in the upper bowls, then a traverse to the lower slopes and a final run through open trees to the pick-up point. At the end of the day all the guests and guides reassemble at the lower terrace of the hotel for a drink in the afternoon sun.

## Equipment

Himachal uses two helicopters in its Manali operation, a Bell 407, which carries five passengers plus the guide and pilot, and an Aerospatiale Lama, which carries three passengers plus the guide and pilot. Three pilots and three mechanics are onsite at any time during the operating season.

The helicopters are supplied by the Swiss helicopter charter operator Helibernina, with Swiss pilots and mechanics. The helipads are on small terraces directly outside the guest accommodation. The charter operator Deccan has also been used.

## Accommodation

Himachal Helicopter Skiing operates out of the Manali Holiday Inn during the heliski season. When I visited, HHS also operated out of a lodge in Patlikul, further down the Kullu Valley, but this has now been moved to Manali, though kept as a separate operation (Himachal Helicopter Skiing, 2005).

## Statistics

HHS uses two helicopters for the main Manali operation, as above. The total number of heliskiers at any one time depends on the number of groups per helicopter. Currently, the HHS website offers two different products with different numbers of groups per helicopter, but no quantitative details are provided. Because of the rather long and difficult access to Manali, the standard product is a 1-week package, which costs US$5950–7900, including all accommodation and meals, powder skis and safety equipment, and helicopter access from Chandigarh. There is an additional single supplement of US$300. Total costs are hence around US$1000 per person per day.

## Access

To reach Manali by road takes most of a day's driving from Chandigarh. Weather conditions permitting, the usual access is by a very scenic 1-h helicopter flight from Chandigarh airport directly to the Manali Holiday Inn. Access to Chandigarh is by air or rail from Delhi. The rail connection is considered more reliable. The provincial government of Himachal Pradesh charges a US$300 heliskiing fee per person per week. This is charged separately, in addition to the package price.

## Community

The most significant social and environmental aspects of the HHS operations are through indirect contributions. Employment of hotel staff and suppliers in the off season has already been mentioned. In addition, as noted above, each client is required to pay a heliski tax of US$300 to the Himachal Pradesh State Government, though this money is not necessarily earmarked for expenditure in the Manali–Patlikul area.

## Experience

Because of its small scale, isolation and remote location, heliskiing with HHS is relatively expensive. To maintain its clientele despite relatively high prices, HHS relies on the Himalayan terrain and climate, which produce an extremely light, dry powder snow. Blue skies and spectacular terrain are additional natural attractions.

## Environment

Since Himachal Helicopter Skiing uses existing hotels rather than running its own backcountry lodges, it has relatively little control over environmental management practices associated with tourist accommodation. As with most heliski operations, HHS is careful not to leave any litter in operational areas, notably at lunch sites. Except when immediately above the base hotel at the beginning and end of the day, almost all the helicopter operations are in high montane areas above the tree line, where the impacts of rotor noise on wildlife are less likely to be significant. The actual wildlife species present, their population sizes and their reactions to helicopter overflights, however, do not appear to have been examined.

HHS has sponsored a major clean-up of village litter in the area around the base hotel at Manali, and has assisted in the provision of a safe drinking water supply. Most importantly, HHS has commenced negotiations with villages in high montane areas at the margins of their operational area, in relation to conservation of endangered wildlife species. If these prove successful, HHS will have made a significant contribution to conservation of the natural environment.

## Safety

HHS operates in a very large area of remote and rugged high-altitude terrain, with no other operators, limited meteorological information, little opportunity for avalanche control and little information on snowpack except for what they collect themselves. Safety is thus an extremely high priority, and HHS goes well beyond the standard safety practices of the heliski industry elsewhere in the world. In addition to all the usual safety equipment, briefings and procedures as used, e.g. by heliski operators in Canada or New Zealand, the owner of HHS has developed three new pieces of technology to improve skier safety.

All skiers carry specialized backpacks that contain not only a snow shovel and avalanche probe, but also an avalanche flotation device consisting of two large wing-shaped airbags that are deployed from the backpack by pulling a handle mounted on the full-body harness. The device uses a small refillable bottle of compressed air, and an entrainment valve that sucks in additional ambient air to fill the flotation bags in seconds or less. If a skier or snowboarder can successfully deploy the bags in the first moments of an avalanche, the bags will help to keep the person afloat amidst the sliding snow rather than sinking underneath it.

The second safety device that all Himachal clients carry is a tiny individually coded radio beacon attached to the avalanche transceiver, which continuously transmits that skier's location. If someone is trapped in an avalanche, therefore, then in addition to the conventional ground search where a group of other skiers close in gradually on their buried companion using directional and grid searching strategies, the helicopter pilot can pinpoint the buried person's location accurately and immediately.

The third special safety device is not attached to the skier or snowboarder directly, but helps Himachal's guides and staff analyse snowpack conditions much more quickly and comprehensively than can be achieved by digging a necessarily limited number of test pits. Himachal's owner, a talented inventor, has developed a new design of recording multi-parameter penetrometer that can quickly provide a full profile of snow temperature and density from the snow surface right down to ground level. Instead of a single pit, guides can quickly create a map of snow profiles across an entire bowl or snowfield.

There is certainly some steep terrain and unstable snow in the Himalayas, and it is not uncommon to see several very large avalanches in a day, on the opposite side of the valley. Himachal's guides choose their skiing terrain very conservatively, and safety precautions seem particularly thorough. Indeed, the only significant safety incident seems to have been a much-publicized occasion some years ago when a high-altitude helicopter landing pushed out a Perspex panel and filled the cockpit with snow, closing down operations until an investigation could be completed. Apparently no one was injured. There was also one occasion when a rotor blade struck the snow, causing some damage to the helicopter but no injuries. Considering the conditions under which HHS operates, its overall safety record is thus excellent.

### Marketing

Marketing by Himachal Helicopter Skiing is highly targeted. Many HHS guides also work at other heliski operations around the world, and they often bring clients to HHS as an additional experience. In Calgary in the Canadian Rockies, surely the world's highest-volume heliski gateway airport, HHS has an advertising poster that can be seen by all resort, backcountry and heliskiers and snowboarders as they arrive. HHS also runs successful e-mail campaigns to past clients to maintain repeat bookings.

## Galena and Monashees, Canada: Canadian Mountain Holidays

### Place

The world's most heavily used heliski area, measured in total skier-days, must surely be the mountain ranges immediately west of the Canadian Rockies in south-eastern British Columbia, Canada. Whilst the well-known National Parks of the Rocky Mountains themselves, such as Waterton, Yoho, Banff and Jasper are generally restricted to lower-impact recreational activities, the mountain ranges immediately to the west, such as the Selkirk, Monashee, Cariboo and Bugaboo ranges, are largely under provincial forest tenure and are open to a range of motorized activity. In winter this includes both snowmobiles and heliski operations, the latter under concession agreements.

Over 3000 m in elevation, these ranges can receive over 10 m of snow in some years and are known worldwide for their powder-skiing opportunities. The terrain is heavily dissected and many of the ridges are asymmetric, with cliffs on one side. The lower slopes are forested, and these treed areas provide the best skiing after heavy snowfall when there is a higher risk of avalanche in gullies and open slopes. Whilst December and April can have good snow some years, the reliable heliskiing season is from January to March.

## Operator

Canadian Mountain Holidays, CMH, operates heliski lodges in concession areas throughout the southern section of the Canadian Rockies. The lodges offer 1-week packages that include bus transfers from Calgary to the nearest staging point, helicopter shuttles to the lodges, full board and a nominal 30,500 m vertical elevation skied (CMH, 2005). Shorter packages are also offered from a hotel base in the town of Revelstoke. The company's headquarters are in Banff.

CMH has a total of 11 heliski lodges throughout this region, and measured in total client days, terrain area or number of helicopters, CMH is the world's largest heliski operator. Each individual lodge has its own exclusive operating area and helicopters, and a maximum capacity of around 44 guests, so the experience remains exclusive and uncrowded. Indeed, some of the lodges are open only for private charter groups. Some of the CMH lodges stay open in summer for heli-hiking operations, whereas others are open only in winter. Because of the terrain, one or two of the lodges are marketed to experienced heliskiers only, and CMH generally suggests that clients should visit one of their other lodges first. This applies particularly to the Galena and Monashees Lodges.

I have visited two of the CMH lodges: Galena (twice) and Monashees (once). These descriptions and analyses apply particularly for those lodges.

## Activity

Many of CMH's lodges have no road access during winter, and clients and staff are shuttled in and out by helicopter on Saturdays each week. The standard CMH heliskiing product is thus an all-inclusive 1-week package, from Saturday to Saturday. The package includes: 6 full days and one half day of guided heliskiing; lodge accommodation; all meals; and bus and/or helicopter transport to and from the lodge. The package also includes use of powder skis and lodge facilities, including tuning and waxing of clients' skis and snowboards, guest laundry, etc.

Clients arrive at the lodges around lunchtime on Saturdays, either all at once if there is bus access, or in small groups if there is a helicopter shuttle. Safety briefings and avalanche transceiver practices are carried out on the Saturday afternoon, so there are no delays on the following morning. Clients are allocated to helicopter groups by the guides, based on a combination of relative skills and client preferences. Most of the lodges have a maximum capacity of 44 guests, with four groups assigned to each helicopter.

The lodges are not always completely full, because twinshare rooms are sometimes occupied by single clients. Some clients do not always ski the full day, so at times there are only three groups per helicopter. The day's activities are quite intensive. There is a morning wake-up call followed by a 30-min stretch class before breakfast, and the first helicopter load lifts immediately after breakfast. The helipad is directly outside the lodge. The order of the helicopter groups is rotated during the week, so that different guides and groups take the lead on different days. In addition to the main machine, each lodge also has a smaller helicopter that is used to bring lunch out to the slopes and, when necessary, to bring guests back to the lodge, so that the cycle of lifts using the main helicopter is not interrupted.

## Equipment

CMH lodges use Bell 212 helicopters that can carry up to 11 skiers plus the guide and pilot, and the smaller Bell 206 as shuttle vehicles to bring guests, staff and lunches from the lodges to the operating area and back during the day. Powder skis are provided for all clients who require them, but they must bring their own ski boots. Clients may also bring their own skis or snowboards. CMH (2005) does not provide snowboards and clients must bring their own, though a limited supply of snowboards may be available for loan at some lodges. These are demonstration models provided by the local Burton® dealer. All clients are supplied with Ortovox® avalanche transceivers. Clients may bring their own transceivers if they use the same frequencies and are otherwise compatible. Some clients, but not many, carry Avalung® sub-snow emergency breathing equipment, and these are also available for sale in the lodge sports stores. The guide and one client in each heliski group carry safety packs equipped with snow shovels, avalanche probes, radios, etc. Some of the clients wear helmets, but this is not compulsory and many do not, even for high-speed tree skiing. Helmets seem to be more common among snowboarders than skiers.

## Accommodation

All accommodation is within the heliski lodges. Different lodges were constructed at different times, but the older lodges are refurbished or rebuilt at intervals to maintain a high quality of accommodation and service. Galena Lodge is one of the older lodges, whereas the Monashees Lodge has recently been rebuilt. In general the bulk of the accommodation at each lodge is in the form of en suite twinshare rooms. The newer lodges, however, have been deliberately designed to include a number of single rooms as well as a full complement of doubles. Under this design the total guest capacity of the accommodation is greater than the total guest capacity of the heliski groups, so the accommodation is never completely full.

In the older lodges, where all accommodation is twinshare and total guest capacity of the accommodation is matched exactly to total guest capacity of the heliski groups, every guest that requests single accommodation effectively reduces the total guest capacity for the week by one. Even with the payment of a substantial single supplement, this reduces the lodge's overall financial yield for that week. As long as the demand for heliskiing continues to exceed supply, and as long as the company has secure long-term tenure over the lodge site, it is worth investing extra capital to construct lodges with a limited number of extra rooms, so as to maintain a full complement of heliskiing clients every week of the season. For those lodges that are also kept open for heli-hiking and other activities in summer, the additional summer income also forms part of the financial equation.

## Statistics

CMH's standard operations use 12-seater helicopters with 11 clients and one guide per group, and four groups in each lodge. The standard product is an all-inclusive 1-week package including 6.5 days' heliskiing. The price structure includes an additional charge for single rather than twinshare accommodation in the lodge, and additional charges also apply for vertical elevation skied beyond a predefined threshold. As with most heliski operators, there is a guaranteed minimum vertical elevation for the week, and if this threshold is not reached, clients receive a limited refund, calculated at the same rate as the charge for extra vertical elevation. At CMH these thresholds are both the same, 30,500 m for a one-week package. Additional vertical is charged at around CAD100 per 1000 m. Prices depend on season and also differ slightly between lodges. During peak season, 1-week packages at Galena and Monashees Lodges cost CAD8466 twinshare, CAD9166 single, or about US$1050–1130 per person per day.

## Access

CMH's various lodges operate in a variety of land tenures, with lease and concession arrangements with the landholders and land management agencies. Most of the terrain is managed by the provincial government forestry agency and is used for logging. The lodges and their immediate surrounds, however, are generally on freehold land. The ski concession areas include clear-cut and densely wooded areas, as well as alpine areas above tree line. The terms of the leases allow CMH to carry out glading in some of the wooded areas, according to plans agreed with the forestry agency. Glading is restricted to smaller trees of low timber value, and effectively doubles as thinning for forestry operations. Within the heliski concession areas, the shape of logging coupes is modified to improve their value for skiing. CMH pays a per capita fee to the forestry agency for each of its clients. Permit arrangements and fees are handled by the company and are included in the price of the heliski package.

Physical access to the Monashees Lodge is by road, commonly in a CMH bus from Calgary airport. Physical access to Galena Lodge is by a helicopter shuttle from a roadside helipad near Lake Galena, reached in a CMH bus from Calgary. A forestry road to the Galena Lodge is traversable only in summer.

## Community

The CMH lodges are generally self-contained, and clients have little or no interaction with locals other than the lodge staff. Most of the staff live in the region, and CMH provides a significant source of winter employment. The company has also made a number of direct investments in local communities, such as endowing a Chair in Snow and Avalanche Research at the local university.

## Experience

Snow and weather conditions change from hour to hour, day to day, week to week and during the course of the ski season. Helicopter operations can be restricted by high winds or low visibility, especially dense valley clouds. During the warmer weather and the later part of the season, they may also be restricted by icing on the rotor blades. The pilots are highly experienced, however, and can fly safely even during heavy snowfalls as long as it is not too windy. When there is low-lying cloud the pilots can fly up side valleys below the clouds and search for holes in the cloud cover where they can safely fly up above the cloud.

Depending on the weather and snowfall patterns, the guides may decide to ski either within the trees or on the open terrain above the tree line. From my own experience, most of the skiing at Galena and Monashees Lodges is on the forested slopes and lower down, through open logged areas. This, however, is no disadvantage: the lightest snow and the steepest safely skiable terrain is generally within the trees.

On the few days when the helicopter cannot fly safely, a variety of alternative activities are available. At the Monashees Lodge there is a three-storey indoor climbing wall, and also a communication room with phones and Internet hook-ups. Cross-country skis are available for loan at Galena, with easy access to snow-covered forestry trails along the main valley. This, however, is not really an option until relatively late in the day, since any improvements in weather conditions earlier in the day has everyone scrambling for the helicopter, which waits for nobody. Of course, on the rare occasions when flying is definitely called off for the day, the lodges have both bars and saunas. These are also much frequented at the end of heliskiing days, both before and after dinner in the main lodge dining room. It is also a tradition at Galena Lodge to hold a fancy-dress party on Friday nights, with a theme chosen by the staff at short notice.

## Environment

A detailed discussion on environmental issues associated with heliskiing, and CMH's environmental practices in particular, is available in Buckley (2003a, pp. 204–206). The company also publishes its own report on environmental and community initiatives under the title *Second Nature* (CMH, 2005). CMH was one of the founding members of BCHSSOA, the British Columbia Helicopter and Snowcat Ski Operators Association, which addresses environmental management issues amongst others.

Individual lodges have adopted various approaches to reduce energy consumption and the impacts of waste disposal. Such measures include energy-saving appliances in the kitchen and laundry, energy-saving light globes, water-saving showerheads, and guest programmes to reduce laundry. Biodegradable soaps, shampoos and other cleaning products are used in most lodges. Glass, aluminium, used tyres and paper are recycled at head office and some lodges. Measures to minimize soil and water contamination include: bunding on fuel storages; drip trays under fuel transfer areas; recycling of waste oils and lubricants, grease and sludge traps in kitchen and greywater drains; and use of biodegradable detergents, cleaning agents, soaps and shampoos. Some of the lodges use basic septic systems to treat sewage, some have small-scale secondary treatment and a few use tertiary treatment or self-contained integrated digestion systems.

Most of the heliskiing terrain, as noted earlier, is leased from the provincial forestry agency, British Columbia Forests and Lands, and is otherwise used for logging. The environmental impacts of logging are considerably greater than those of heliskiing. It is not clear whether heliskiing affects logging operations in any significant way, but it seems unlikely.

The principal environmental concern associated with heliskiing operations is the likely impact of helicopter noise disturbance on caribou, as discussed by Buckley (2003a, pp. 204–206). Heliski operators have argued that caribou may also be affected by noise and in some cases deliberate harassment by snowmobiles. Both helicopters and snowmobiles have been shown elsewhere to cause significant behavioural impacts on a variety of animal species, including large grazing ungulates such as caribou. The precise significance of heliski operations for caribou populations in southeastern British Columbia, relative to other sources of impact, does not yet appear to have been quantified. Such measurement would be very valuable in evaluating the environmental significance of heliski operations, but would require a detailed ecological field study over several generations and a wide area.

## Safety

The CMH heliski group is a company run by skilled and experienced guides who are familiar with the entire terrain and are experts in avalanche safety procedures. Throughout the season, the guides maintain a close watch on snow and weather conditions, digging snow profile pits at intervals and reassessing safe and unsafe terrain every morning.

Each run is led by the guide, who selects a route within the clients' capabilities in terms of terrain and that has been assessed as low in avalanche hazard. On each individual run, the guide will instruct the clients which lines are safe. For example, the guide may tell all clients to ski on the same side of the guide's own track. Guides will also specify a safe spacing, and in some cases will instruct the clients to ski a particular slope one at a time, signalling each individually when it is safe to start. In treed areas, where one cannot see far and the principal hazard is falling into a tree well, clients are supposed to pair up and ski or snowboard with a buddy, watching out for each other. To do this while skiing at speed requires a certain degree of skill. At the top of a tree run, the guide will generally let clients know if there are any particular terrain features they should watch out for, such as cliffs or logging roads.

Skiing as a tight group through dense trees also requires skill and teamwork. The usual strategy is to ski in an arrowhead formation, with each successive pair skiing an untracked route just outside the tracks of the previous pair, and keeping them in sight. In practice this is not always straightforward, particularly if there are previous tracks from other groups that may have taken a different line, or if someone gets tangled in a tree well and has to be helped out.

On the afternoon of the Saturday at the beginning of each week, before any skiing, all clients receive a safety briefing that covers tree-well hazards in addition to helicopter safety and avalanche rescue procedures. Clients also receive training or re-training in the use of the avalanche transceivers, followed by practical exercises in locating buried transceivers.

CMH groups ski with one guide per group, but two safety packs. In addition to the main pack carried by the guide, there is a client safety pack carried by one of the clients on each run. It is the responsibility of this client to ski at the rear of the group throughout the run and as far as possible to watch out for the other clients, be ready to render assistance and generally act as a tail guide. The client's safety pack contains a snow shovel and avalanche probe, and also a radio to contact groups or guides if necessary. If the situation warrants it, the group guide can contact other guides and the helicopter pilot to bring in assistance from upslope.

## Marketing

Outside Canada, CMH's sales and marketing are franchised to exclusive agents in individual countries. Even if a client first learns of CMH through the company's Canadian website or by word of mouth, as is commonly the case, bookings must generally be made through the agent in the client's country of residence. Each agent has a quota of places to sell for the season, though dates and availability must presumably be coordinated centrally from CMH headquarters in Banff, Canada. A certain degree of informal trading of quota seems to take place between agents. For example, if an agent in one country has used its entire quota, but another has not, then the latter may book clients on behalf of the former. Since it is in CMH's interest for all quotas to be used, such arrangements are presumably beneficial for all concerned.

## Blue River, Canada: Mike Wiegele Helicopter Skiing

### Place

Mike Wiegele Helicopter Skiing (MWHS) operates out of Blue River in British Columbia, Canada, between the Monashee and Cariboo Ranges. The company's operating terrain includes large sections of each of these ranges, facing in to the central valley. This is part of Canada's prime heliskiing country, and adjacent areas are used by other well-known heliski operators. Snowfall is heavy, and the season lasts from December until April. The peaks and ridge lines are at elevations of around 3000–3500 m. A range of terrain is available, with access limited principally by avalanche risk. There are wide bowls above tree line, and steeper tree skiing at lower elevations. As in most of this area, the forests are subject to logging, and some of the runs pass through cut blocks or cross logging roads. These areas also provide most of the helicopter pick-up points. Some of the slopes are cliffed or rocky, and skilled and experienced guides are needed to select a safe line to an accessible pick-up point. There are well over 100 individual named runs within the MWHS concessions, though the more remote areas can generally only be skied during fine and settled weather.

### Operator

The Mike Wiegele Helicopter Skiing village at Blue River is apparently the world's single largest individual heliski operation, measured in client capacity, though there are multi-base operators that have higher total capacity and total terrain area. The company is well-known because of its charismatic owner, Mike Wiegele himself, who lives on-site and frequently skis with private charter groups. It is also well-known for hosting the World Powder Eight Championships each year.

The Blue River base village contains 24 guest chalets, a central dining and facilities area, a reception and operations building, a sports and equipment store, a guides' house and several helipads. Helicopter hardstand areas, hangars and maintenance bays are at the Blue River airstrip nearby. Maximum guest capacity is over 150. Staff include pilots, guides, reception and radio operators, equipment technicians, chefs and kitchen staff, bar staff and waiters, housekeepers and masseuses. The company also maintains a smaller separate lodge, Albreda Lodge further up the valley, with a guest capacity of 20. It is currently considering the construction of a private ski lift and residential estate.

## Activity

The company advertises two main types of heliski package: private and semi-private charter groups, marketed under the title 'Elite', and 1-week inclusive packages where one helicopter is shared between three groups, marketed under the title 'Deluxe'. The majority of clients purchase the latter. Each ski group consists of eight clients with two guides. These packages include: bus transfers from Kamloops airport; 7 nights' accommodation in one of the chalets; all meals, namely breakfasts and dinners in the main lodge and lunches on the slopes; use of skis or Burton® snowboards; and of course, six full days and one half day heliskiing, depending on weather.

Depending on the area skied each day, all three ski groups with each helicopter may lift off directly from the lodge; or alternatively, the first group may lift off in the helicopter and the other two may be shuttled by road to a point closer to the runs being skied. The same applies at the end of the day. The same individual guide acts as lead guide throughout the entire week, and the three groups take off in the same order every day, rather than rotating. Depending on availability, it is also possible to purchase individual day's heliskiing, with or without the accommodation package. This option does not seem to be advertised, however, and may be an ad hoc arrangement. A professional videographer is available to accompany the 'Elite' groups, and occasionally the 'Deluxe' groups. A collage of stills and video footage from the week's skiing is shown in the bar each Friday night, and individual stills are available for purchase.

## Equipment

The helicopters are Bell 212 ten-seaters for the 'Deluxe' groups and Bell A-Stars for the smaller 'Elite' groups. The company provides powder skis or snowboards as part of the package, or clients can bring their own. In particular, specialist and semi-specialist powder snowboards from the Burton® range, the Fish® and Malolo® respectively, are available for use by clients. Having tried both, I can confirm that the Fish in particular is considerably easier to ride in powder snow than the much longer all-mountain boards. The latter need a lot more work to make tight linked turns around trees, particularly when the snow is wet and heavy. All clients are supplied with avalanche transceivers. Some, but not all, clients wear helmets, and a few clients carry Avalung® sub-snow emergency breathing devices.

## Accommodation

Accommodation is in the chalets at the Blue River base village, or in Albreda Lodge further up the valley. The Blue River chalets are constructed in log-cabin style, and are very spacious and well appointed. Each chalet has two bedrooms with large en suite bathrooms, a small kitchen and a large lounge area with a fireplace and cable TV. Each chalet also has its own telephone with an external line. Albreda Lodge is constructed in a deliberately rustic style, but is large and luxurious and includes a three-storey climbing wall. The central facilities area at Blue River Village include a gym, stretch room and sauna. Both the Blue River Village and Albreda Lodge also have games rooms.

## Statistics

Group size is eight clients plus two guides in the Bell 212 helicopters, and four clients in the A-Star. The price for the 1-week 'Deluxe' package in the 2005/06 main season is CAD9212. The corresponding price for the 'Elite' package is CAD10,451 (US$9000). These prices correspond to about US$1100–1300 per person per day. Unlike most heliski operators, the package price includes unlimited vertical, i.e. there is no extra charge no matter how many runs are skied. Unlike most other heliski operators, however, charges are made for tuning and waxing clients' own skis or boards at the sports store, and for guest laundry – perhaps to encourage clients to use the washing machines in the chalets. Most importantly, however, unlike other operators there are two guides in every heli-group, with a client-to-guide ratio of 4:1.

## Access

Access is generally by air to Kamloops airport and thence by bus to Blue River, but there is also an airstrip at Blue River and a once-a-week connecting flight to Vancouver airport, timed to coincide with the end of the week's heliski package. Clients who take this charter flight can connect to long-distance and international flights on the same day, without having to overnight in Vancouver, but they miss the final Saturday morning's skiing. Clients can also drive to Blue River in their own vehicles, though not many do so in winter. Like other heliski providers in British Columbia, the company operates in a concession area owned by the Province and otherwise managed principally for logging. All permit arrangements are managed by MWHS and no additional fees are payable by clients.

## Community

Blue River is a small town in its own right. It lies on the main north–south transport link through British Columbia, and provides services for long-distance haulage contractors and for self-drive summer tourists. During winter, these activities are much reduced. One restaurant and one bar remain operational near the heliski village. Some of the regular heliski guides and other staff rent or own houses in Blue River and most of them spend money in the local community one way or another. The clients themselves have little interaction with Blue River residents other than MWHS staff, unless they decide to visit the town bar. Indirectly, however, heliski clients provide the main economic support for Blue River during winter. Indeed, as summer heli-hiking continues to increase in popularity, the company makes an increasing contribution to the town in summer as well as winter. According to its website (MWHS, 2005), the company hosts an annual Christmas party for Blue River children, and is taking part in development of a high school in the township.

## Experience

I have only visited Mike Wiegele Helicopter Skiing once, and it is difficult to generalize from a single week since the heliskiing experience is so strongly dependent on weather and snow conditions. Considerable new snow fell in the early days of the week concerned, and temperatures were relatively warm, so the snow was quite wet and heavy in the lower sections of each run. Because of wind gusts and snow flurries, areas above tree line were inaccessible on 5 out of 6 days. On the one sunny day, we had excellent conditions on the upper slopes, with the opportunity to jump from one or two small cornices, windlips and rock drops. At the end of the week, when temperatures had dropped somewhat and the snow was drier, we had some fast and reasonably steep tree runs. These variations in conditions, however, are part and parcel of all heliskiing operations, and guides and clients adapt to them routinely. Service and safety were outstanding throughout the entire week and no complaints were heard!

For southern hemisphere visitors who visit Canada specifically for a 'week at Wiegele's' a few days' warm-up is a critical component of the experience, before boarding the helicopter with northern hemisphere skiers and boarders who have been on the slopes every day for months. Of course, the same applies in reverse for northerners heliskiing in New Zealand. Fortunately, the southern sections of the Canadian Rockies are well supplied with ski resorts. On this occasion I visited Sun Peaks for several days, staying at Delta Sun Peaks (2005). It was late in the season and snow cover had already declined considerably, but fortunately there were new snowfalls shortly before I arrived.

## Environment

Environmental management issues were not mentioned during any client briefing, but in fact seem very similar to other heliski operations in British Columbia. The company's website (MWHS, 2005) mentions various environmental programmes, including the use of geothermal power for on-site heating. There is also a map of the entire concession area downstairs in the main facilities building, with the locations of wildlife sightings marked. No mention of this map was made to clients, and there is no information on the map about the dates of the sightings or what is done about them, but the company's website (MWHS, 2005) says that wildlife sightings are taken into account in planning ski runs and flight paths. Because the base village is in an existing township and accessible by major road, there is presumably no need for stand-alone water supply, power generation or waste disposal facilities. The village does, however, appear to have its own sewage treatment or at least sewage collection facilities associated with each of the chalets.

## Safety

Unlike most heliski operators, where each ski group is accompanied by a single guide, MWHS provides both a lead and tail guide for each group. Both guides carry radios and full avalanche safety packs. Clients receive briefings on avalanche safety, helicopter safety, and avalanche search and rescue techniques on the morning of the first day's heliskiing, with practical training in the use of avalanche safety transceivers. Each group's guides check each morning that all transceivers are functioning properly in both transmit and receive mode. Guides maintain radio contact with each other, the helicopter pilots and the base station throughout the day, and meet morning and evening to plan and recap the day's programme.

## Marketing

Mike Wiegele Helicopter Skiing seems to receive more frequent editorial coverage in outdoor magazines than most other heliski operators, so presumably it has been par-

ticularly successful in maintaining close links with these industry publications, e.g.
by providing promotional trips for ski journalists. The World Powder Eight
Championships, run each year at the end of the season, also receive significant media
coverage and help to promote the company. MWHS differentiates itself from its
major competitors by pricing its 1-week packages to include unlimited vertical, and
also by its practice of providing two guides for every ski group.

## Harris Mountains, New Zealand: Harris Mountains Heli-ski

### Place

Harris Mountains Heli-ski (2005) operates throughout the South, Central and
Northern Harris Mountains in the South Island of New Zealand, and also in the
North and South Buchanans nearby. These are the mountain ranges around
Queenstown and Wanaka, which are the main gateway towns to resort skiing areas
such as Coronet Peak, Treble Cone and Cardrona. Outside the towns themselves,
this is an agricultural area used principally for sheep farming. The terrain is heavily
dissected, with relatively level but narrow valley floors between steep-sided ridges
and ranges. Even in midwinter, sheep can survive outdoors on the valley floors,
which are generally free of snow, though farmers must provide feed.

Most of the ridgelines are sharp or even knife-edged, but many of the slopes
have a shallow ledge halfway down. During peak ski season, heliskiers can ski the
steep upper section, the lower-gradient central section and the steep lower section
almost to the valley floor. During shoulder seasons or in poor snow years, only the
upper and central sections are accessible. The dominant vegetation on the ridges and
slopes is tussock grassland and low shrubs, which are completely covered with snow
in winter. Many of the slopes are cut by small side gullies, however, and these
commonly support dense cool temperate rainforest. These forested gullies provide
winter habitat for a number of bird species.

### Operator

Harris Mountains Heli-ski is a subsidiary of The Helicopter Line (2005). It is the
principal though not the only heliski operator in the Queenstown and Wanaka area,
and is probably New Zealand's largest heliski operator. The company maintains full-
time retail offices in both Queenstown and Wanaka. It also operates helicopters out
of both towns, and can shuttle clients between the two areas if required by operating
logistics, weather conditions or client requests. It runs a minibus shuttle to pick up
clients from tourist accommodation every morning. In Wanaka at least, the company
maintains special arrangements with the principal upmarket tourist hotel, which has
a helipad in its grounds so that clients can be picked up by helicopter from directly
outside their rooms.

### Activity

Heliskiing in the Harris and Buchanan Mountains is heavily dependent upon
weather conditions, particularly wind speed. In a typical week, the helicopter might
only be able to fly on 3 or 4 days out of 7. Weather conditions are unpredictable, and
the company contacts every client each morning to advise on the day's activities. On

good days, a full day's heliskiing is possible. On other days, clients may have to wait on standby in the hope that weather conditions may change. On the windiest days, when heliskiing is clearly not possible, the company will take clients to one of the ski resorts instead. If the wind then drops unexpectedly, the company will send the helicopter to pick the clients up from the resort for a half day's heliskiing. If there are enough clients on any given day, the company will operate separate helicopters out of Queenstown and Wanaka. If not, they will operate only out of one, and shuttle clients by road to the other operating area.

Whilst Harris Mountains Heli-ski does sell 1-week packages under the title of 'Odyssey', the majority of its business is single-day trips purchased at short notice by skiers visiting the resorts at Queenstown or Wanaka. Many of these clients have little or no previous heliskiing experience, and the company sells relatively inexpensive three- or four-run days as an introductory heliski package. Lunch is provided on the slopes after the first three or four runs, and during lunch clients are given the option of extending to a more expensive seven-run package. This is only possible, however, if a large enough number of clients select the seven-run option, so that the helicopter can continue to run profitably. Also available is a so-called 'Max Vert' option, when clients continue skiing after seven runs for as long as they want or the guides consider safe, paying for the extra runs on the basis of additional vertical elevation skied. In general, the more runs skied on any given day, the cheaper the cost per run, so experienced heliskiers will generally select this option if available.

## Equipment

The Helicopter Line uses Aerospatiale AS350 and AS355 Twin Engine Squirrels, with seating for four clients plus one guide and the pilot. Powder skis are available for rent, or clients can bring their own. At least when I audited this company's operations, snowboarders had to bring their own boards. Many of the guides also ride snowboards, however, and if enough of the clients on any given day are snowboarders, one of the guides may elect to snowboard rather than ski. Lunch is provided. Only the guide carries an avalanche pack.

## Accommodation

Except in the 'Odyssey' package, heliskiing trips with Harris Mountains Heli-ski do not include accommodation. Clients stay in hotels or lodges in Queenstown or Wanaka, and are collected in the morning in the Harris Mountains Heli-ski shuttle bus. The 'Odyssey' package is a flexible set of 'Max Vert' heliskiing days, extra vertical, resort skiing days, helishuttles and minibus shuttles, and accommodation. The package has to be flexible because of uncertainty over weather conditions, and also because of uncertainty over the number of other heliski clients on any given day, which affects the day's logistics. The unit prices of each component are fixed in advance, together with a notional bundle of components, and the final price is adjusted later to reflect the week's actual activities.

## Statistics

The client to guide ratio is 4:1, reflecting the capacity of the helicopters used. A minimum of three groups is needed for the helicopter to operate on any given day, so the minimum group size is 12. A single helicopter can service up to five groups, especially if the clients have only selected three or four-run packages. As noted earlier, most clients buy packages of only a single day's duration, but a few buy the 'Odyssey' package that stretches over a full week. Prices range from NZD695 (US$490) for a three-run package to NZD945 (US$660) for a seven-run package, plus an additional NZD85 (US$60) per extra run. The basic 'Odyssey' package, including 4 days heliskiing, is offered at a base price of NZD3500 (US$2450) (Harris Mountains Heli-ski, 2005). This corresponds to about US$600 per person per day's heliskiing, including accommodation but not meals.

## Access

Access is via Queenstown, which is accessible by road, or by air either from Christchurch or, on some days, directly from Brisbane in Australia. Access to Wanaka is by road from Queenstown, and there is a commercial shuttle bus between Queenstown airport and Wanaka accommodation. The helicopter staging points in the valley floors are generally on private farmland. There are also helicopter landing sites in the commercial ski resorts. Much of the mountain slope area is also owned by sheep farmers and used for summer grazing. There are also extensive areas of public land managed by the New Zealand Department of Conservation. All permit and access arrangements are made by the operator, and heliski clients do not have to pay any separate permit fees in addition to the heliskiing prices.

## Community

Both Queenstown and Wanaka are major tourism destinations, and in recent years have also become major amenity migration destinations. Skiing is the principal tourist activity in winter, and the area attracts skiers from all over the world. There are far fewer ski areas in the southern hemisphere than the north, and New Zealand is not only English-speaking, but easily accessible from Japan and North America. Heliskiing is marketed as a mass tourism activity, rather than an elite activity as in Canada and the USA, so there is a considerable overlap between the resort skiing and heliskiing markets. In addition, both resort skiers and heliskiers use the same accommodation, restaurants and other tourist facilities. Though much smaller in total client-days than the resort skiing market, therefore, heliskiing contributes to local communities as a significant component of the winter tourism economy. Most of the heliski guides live locally, even though they may also work overseas during the northern hemisphere ski season.

## Experience

Because weather conditions in the Harris and Buchanan Mountains are uncertain and heliski clients differ greatly in ability, the Harris Mountains Heli-ski experience may be very different for different clients on different days. At peak season in a good year, with an expert group keen to ski as much as possible, the experience can be as good as anywhere. The terrain is varied and interesting and a strong group can fit in a dozen runs in a day. Charter groups with a dedicated helicopter have been known to make 20 or more runs in a day. When snow or weather conditions are poor, however, or when most of the day's clients are inexperienced and have chosen only a three-run package so that the guides choose only the safest and easiest terrain, it can be a frustrating experience for a more experienced heliskier or snowboarder.

## Environment

The mountain vegetation is largely snow-covered during the heliski season, and New Zealand has hardly any native mammals, so the skiers themselves have negligible environmental impacts. The principal impacts from the helicopter operation are first, the risk of fuel spills from refuelling depots; and secondly, the potential impact of helicopter noise on bird species wintering in the forest gullies. The former can be minimized through safe and careful refuelling practices, by bunding fuel tanks where possible, and by parking refuelling tankers well away from creek lines. This is not always straightforward in practice, since side valleys are often narrow and farm roads are often close to creeks.

The impacts of helicopter noise on birds can be minimized by choosing helicopter routes well away from wooded areas. Unfortunately, the forested gullies often form the quickest way up and down the mountain for a helicopter, so to minimize noise impacts the helicopter pilot must deliberately fly along ridges and stay away from forested areas. This requires a conscious decision on the part of the pilot, and may also increase fuel costs slightly, so in practice it will only happen if the company is aware of the issue and adopts a deliberate policy to protect the environment.

## Safety

All of the guides employed by Harris Mountains Heli-ski are certified either by the New Zealand Mountain Guides Association (NZMGA) or its international equivalent the Union internationale des associations de guide de montagne (UIAGM) (now the International Federation of Mountain Guides Associations (IFMGA)), or both. During the day's heliskiing, they remind clients constantly about safety issues and procedures. As with most heliski companies worldwide, all clients receive briefings on helicopter safety, skislope safety and avalanche search and rescue procedures before boarding the helicopter for the first time. Over the past decade I have spent 3 separate weeks snowboarding with Harris Mountains Heli-ski, totalling perhaps a dozen days in the mountains, and we experienced avalanches on 2 of those days. Nobody was injured on either occasion. Two clients were caught in a small knee-deep slide on one occasion, but neither lost their footing and neither were injured, though both were shaken. On the other occasion, I was snowboarding with a group of skiers who had all descended a broad bowl in the steep upper section and were waiting in a safe position to one side. When I started my own descent, it triggered a significant and potentially lethal avalanche, but fortunately I was able to escape from the side just as the snow surface began to crack into blocks.

## Marketing

Marketing by Harris Mountains Heli-ski (2005), and indeed by other heliski operators in New Zealand, tends to emphasize that heliskiing need not be an expert activity, but is available to all reasonably competent skiers. Certainly, the pleasures of untracked powder and a day in the mountains far from the madding crowds at the resorts are also featured, as they are for heliski operators worldwide. The opportunity to try out heliskiing for a day, especially by selecting the relatively inexpensive three-run option, provides a point of differentiation from most of the heliski operations in Canada or elsewhere worldwide, where the basic product is a relatively expensive all-inclusive 1-week package including accommodation in a remote lodge and 6.5 days' heliskiing, intended principally for expert skiers.

## Methven, New Zealand: Methven Heliskiing

### Place

Methven is a small town about an hour's drive west of Christchurch in New Zealand's South Island, not far from the Mt Hutt ski area. Methven Heliskiing (2005) runs a retail sales outlet in Methven and operates in the Arrowsmith, Ragged and Palmer Ranges further west. The skiable terrain is relatively steep and varied and makes for excellent skiing and snowboarding. The areas used are above tree line and includes some steep chutes, snow-filled gullies and jumpable windlips. Surrounding areas are used largely for sheep farming, and the base station for helicopter operations is on a privately owned sheep station, Glenfalloch Station.

### Operator

Methven Heliskiing is co-owned with Mt Cook Heliski, which is based at Mt Cook itself. The two operations are too far apart to run joint logistics, and function independently. The heliski operations are also associated with Alpine Guides, which offers summer and winter climbing and backcountry skiing tours and training.

### Activity

Heliskiing out of Methven is heavily weather-dependent, with wind velocities often too high for safe helicopter operation. On windy days, skiers can visit Mt Hutt instead. The company offers three-run, four-run and seven-run basic packages with the option to purchase additional runs on the day if conditions are good and the group is keen to continue. Skiers are picked up from accommodation in Methven in the morning and driven by minibus to the helicopter base. Lunch is provided on the slopes.

### Accommodation

Accommodation is not included, but the company can recommend options in Methven. There are a number of well-appointed B&B establishments. Clients can also drive from Christchurch for the day.

### Equipment

Methven Heliskiing uses Aerospatiale AS350 and AS355 Squirrels that carry the pilot, one guide and four passengers. Clients bring their own skis or snowboards. There are ski stores in Methven that can sell or rent gear and tune and wax skis and boards.

## Statistics

Each group consists of four skiers or boarders plus one guide, and the helicopter can support three to six groups at once. Heliskiing is sold day-by-day with payment on the morning of each day, because of uncertainties over weather conditions. The standard day's package is five runs, at a cost of NZD770 (US$540), plus NZD110 (US$77) per 1000 vertical metres for any additional runs. Most runs are 700–1100 m, so a seven-run day would cost around US$680 per person. This does not include accommodation.

## Access

Access to Methven is by air to Christchurch airport and by road to Methven. A shuttle bus is available. Access from Methven to the helicopter base is in the company's minibus, or by private car. Permission for access to the base and the slopes is arranged by the company and included in the day's heliski price.

## Community

The economy of Methven and surrounding areas appears to depend jointly on farming and tourism. Accommodation, restaurants and outdoor stores in Methven depend on tourists, including skiers and snowboarders visiting Mt Hutt. Heliskiers probably make up a relatively small but by no means insignificant proportion of total winter visitors. Particular B&Bs and restaurants recommended by Methven Heliskiing seem to earn a substantial component of total income from the company's clients, who are perhaps more likely than most tourists to rely on restaurants rather than catering for themselves.

## Experience

I have only spent 1 day snowboarding with Methven Heliskiing, but it included some excellent terrain. Operations were somewhat restricted by winds, and the day before and after winds were so strong that even the Mt Hutt ski lifts closed down at midday. I would certainly return.

## Environment

The skiable areas are above the tree line and completely snow-covered, the operating base is farmland and the helicopter crosses the intervening valley at altitude. Noise impacts are hence low relative to most heliski operations. Refuelling is at the base, so spill risks are slight.

## Safety

Clients are issued with avalanche transceivers at the helicopter base and receive briefings on helicopter safety and avalanche search techniques before boarding the helicopter. Guides lead each group from the front and instruct clients on any particular safety procedures before each run. Such procedures may include, for example, minimum spacing, or a requirement to descend a particular slope or section one person at a time. Since the groups are small and the skiing is above tree line, guides and clients can nearly always remain in visual and audio contact throughout each run.

## Marketing

The Methven Heliskiing (2005) website features Mt Cook Heliski and Alpine Guides as well as Methven Heliskiing itself. Easy access from Christchurch and varied terrain are particular selling points. Helicopters for Methven Heliskiing are supplied by The Helicopter Line, which owns Harris Mountains Heli-ski, but this is not immediately obvious from their website, i.e. there does not seem to be deliberate cross-marketing.

# 13 Cross-country Skiing

Ice feather, Jasper Canada. Photo Ralf Buckley.

Snowcamp, Mt Kosciuszko, Australia. Photo Ralf Buckley.

## Sector Structure

Cross-country skiing is a popular and widespread outdoor activity in the temperate developed nations, but there are relatively few commercial cross-country ski tour operators. Downhill skiers and boarders are largely tied to expensive lifts, tows, ski resort infrastructure and the associated social interactions. One major appeal of cross-country skiing, in contrast, is the opportunity to ski under one's own leg power, far from the crowds, with no costs except one's own equipment and vehicle.

Certainly, there are overlaps. Many Nordic skiers like best to race on groomed trails, often associated with downhill ski resorts. Many resort skiers use free-heel boots and bindings and are adept at telemark as well as parallel turns. Some individual skiers are equally comfortable on lightweight stepped back-country touring skis, heavy-duty telemark skis with skins, or downhill skis. Some snowboarders have split boards that can be separated to travel cross-country and joined to ride downhill. A few – very few – skiers can ride steep powder and perform jumps and aerial manoeuvres even on narrow touring skis with highly flexible 'rat-trap' or three-pin bindings. But despite these overlaps, there is a broad distinction between downhill skiers who routinely use commercial suppliers either at their local ski hill or for a travel and ski package, and cross-country skiers who commonly prefer to travel quietly at their own pace in their own snow-covered neighbourhoods, enjoying the scenery more than the adrenalin.

Similar considerations, of course, apply for many adventure activities, including hiking, mountain biking, surfing and kayaking: most of the time, most people travel in their own transport and use their own gear. There are commercial tour providers for all these activities, and the same applies for cross-country skiing. This seems to be a relatively small subsector of the adventure tourism industry, however, and accordingly only three case studies are described.

## North Pole, from Norway: Global Expedition Adventures
(Not audited in person)

### Place

The North Pole is now accessible, both by icebreaker and, in the northern hemisphere summer, by air. The polar ice cap is only 2 m thick, though the ocean beneath is 4200 m deep. The ice cap is constantly drifting through the action of wind and currents. During April each year, there is enough daylight and sufficiently consistent ice cover for an approach on cross-country skis. Earlier it is too dark and later the ice floes become unstable. I have not visited the North Pole and this case study is taken entirely from secondary materials.

### Operator

Several tour companies offer trips to the North Pole by various means. At least one of these, Global Expedition Adventures (2005), offers the opportunity to cover the last degree of latitude, from 89° to 90°N, on cross-country skis. These trips have been offered for the past 8 years. I have not had any direct dealings with this company and all information presented below is from their website. This case study is included because in many ways it exemplifies trends within the adventure tourism sector: a relatively short, intense and very expensive experience at a remote location, requiring a degree of fitness and experience but not a high level of skill, and with logistic support to minimize risk.

## Activity

The trip starts at Longyearbyen in Svalbard (Spitzbergen), accessible by scheduled flights from mainland Norway. In March each year the company establishes a base camp on pack ice in the polar ice floe. This ice typically drifts 5–15 km per day, and the camp is established in an area where the drift is northerly, towards the pole. Hence the camp may be closer to the North Pole than 89°.

At the start of the trip, clients are flown by charter aircraft from Svalbard to the base camp on the ice floe. According to the company's website, non-skiers can be accommodated at base camp and join skiers at the Pole for caviar and champagne on arrival, so presumably the operator maintains a helicopter at the base camp, perhaps shared with other tour companies or scientific expeditions. Presumably the helicopter is used to ferry skiers from base camp to 89°N at the start of the skiing phase.

The group spends 1 day at the base camp to check equipment and get used to conditions, and on this day the company flies group leaders over the intended route to check conditions, especially pressure ridges and leads that could impede progress. The group spends 5 days skiing 8–10 h per day, dragging sleds with tents and equipment and covering about 10–20 km per day. The total distance skied is about 80 km. The sixth day is spent at the North Pole, returning by helicopter to base camp and the next day by charter flight to Svalbard.

## Equipment

The company provides skis and sledges; tents and cooking equipment; and communications, navigation and emergency gear. The base camp also has heaters. The clients are required to bring all their own polar clothing and sleeping bags.

## Accommodation

Accommodation in Svalbard is in one of the hotels in Longyearbyen. At the base camp it is in fixed tents set up for the season. During the skiing phase it is in tents on the ice, set up each evening.

## Statistics

The entire trip takes 11 days, including 5 days' skiing and 1 day at the North Pole. Group sizes are not specified, but the illustration on the company's website shows ten people, two of whom are guides. The cost is US$15,500, or close to US$1500 per person per day. This includes charter flights to and from Svalbard, and helicopter flights to and from the base camp on the ice.

## Access

As noted before, physical access is by scheduled air services to Svalbard, charter plane to the base camp on the ice, helicopter to the 89°N start point and back from the North Pole, and cross-country skis from 89°N to 90°N. No information is provided about any permits that may be required.

## Community

There are no resident communities at this latitude. These trips, like other tourist activities based out of Longyearbyen, contribute to the Svalbard economy.

## Experience

Not having taken part in this tour, I cannot comment on the experience. The company's website says it is hard work but worth it, and that psychological attitude is as important as physical fitness.

## Environment

No information is available. Presumably all wastes are flown out.

## Safety

Not surprisingly, safety is a major concern for operators and clients alike. The group is accompanied by two guides during the skiing phase. There is a medical technician at the ice base. The group carries a satellite phone, whose signal is also used to track the skiers' position. Any clients unable to continue skiing are returned to base camp by helicopter and flown to the North Pole on the final day. The operator's website states that no one has been injured on any of its previous trips.

## Marketing

The website for Global Expedition Adventures (2005) markets this trip as 'the adventure of your life' and emphasizes the calculated risks as a contrast to 'the doldrums of everyday life' or 'playing your life safe and not taking any risks, and then dying of cancer'. Clearly, for the clients this is pitched at, cost is not a consideration, but bragging rights may well be.

# Snowy Mountains, Australia: Paddy Pallin

### Place

Skiable terrain in Australia is relatively restricted. The main areas with significant snowfall are the peaks and high plains of the Australian Alps, spanning the border between the States of Victoria and New South Wales, and a smaller area in central Tasmania. Most of Australia's ski resorts are in the southern section of the Snowy Mountains in New South Wales, and adjacent areas in the Victorian Alps. By international standards the snow quality at Australia's downhill skiing resorts is often rather mediocre.

The backcountry skiing areas, however, are remarkably beautiful, with the gnarled and many-coloured trunks of snow gums dusted with fresh-fallen snow, or ice crystals stacked against the windward sides of their twigs and branches. The terrain varies from steep slopes and narrow valleys to broad rolling uplands. Even near its source, the Snowy River generally keeps flowing all winter, but the high lakes freeze over and are soon covered with drifted snow. The weather can change rapidly and multi-day whiteouts are not uncommon. There are a few well-known sites where deep drifts form year after year and ice climbers routinely dig extensive snow caves. Throughout most of the Snowy Mountains, however, snow cover is relatively thin and the terrain is much better suited to camping in snow tents. In some parts of Mt Kosciuszko National Park, there are well-known cross-country skiing routes along old roadways, with historic wooden huts at intervals. In the section of the Main Range used for commercial multi-day ski camping tours, however, there are no roads, no huts and few if any other visitors, even though the area is not far from the nearest ski resort.

## Operator

Paddy Pallin's, named after its founder, is believed to be Australia's first outdoor equipment manufacturer, and is still going strong despite continued competition against imports from around the world. Its branch at Jindabyne, principal tourist gateway to the Snowy Mountains, also offers a range of backcountry tours including cross-country skiing trips in winter. These include day trips from their purpose-built cross-country skiing lodge, and multi-day camping trips on the Main Range (Paddy Pallin, 2005). The principal offering is a 5-day fully equipped, guided and catered tour known as the Main Range Explorer. The Jindabyne branch is also one of the main rental outlets for day visitors who need to hire cross-country skis for the groomed racing and touring trails at the NSW ski resorts, as well as a retail outlet for a wide variety of outdoor equipment.

## Activity

The 5-day ski camping tour starts from the Paddy Pallin lodge, with a car shuttle to a convenient roadhead. Carrying backpacks, the guides and clients ski to a convenient site a few kilometres away from heavily visited areas, and establish a base camp in a small stand of snow gums. The ski-in route starts along a defined trail and then heads off trail through open subalpine forest. One of the guides drags a pulk, a fully enclosed plastic sledge loaded with food and equipment. At the base camp site, the guides check that the clients have put up their tents correctly, and then construct a snow enclosure and bench area for cooking, and another for eating. Clients are invited to assist, in order to practise their skills with snow shovels. As soon as the cooking area is set up, the guides brew hot drinks and hand out food.

The group camps at this site throughout the tour, i.e. it does not strike and pitch camp at a different place each day. Instead, guides and clients make relatively short day trips out from the base camp, carrying only food, stoves and emergency gear. This makes for easier skiing, so even relatively inexperienced clients can practise skiing in varied snow conditions, up and downhill, and navigating through open woodland. For example, the group can ski out to the edge of the plateau and look down the steep slopes into a neighbouring valley.

## Equipment

Snow tents, group cooking gear and food are provided as part of the tour. Clients bring their own skis, backpacks, sleeping bags and maps, and ski clothing, or they can hire most of these items from the Paddy Pallin store at Jindabyne. The company does also provide booties to wear in the tents. As well as keeping the clients' feet warm, this helps to protect the tent floors, since clients might otherwise keep their ski boots on inside the tents. Cooking is carried out on small backcountry fuel stoves, e.g. of the MSR® type.

Minimum temperatures in the Australian Alps are significantly warmer than those in, e.g. the backcountry skiing areas of the northern USA and southern Canada, so ski clothing and sleeping bags are relatively lightweight in comparison. Aluminium tent pegs and cooking pots can be handled directly, without the need for glove liners.

The tour group skis only on relatively easy slopes below tree line, avoiding both the steep valley sides and the cliffs and icy patches in the alpine zone. Narrow lightweight skis with stepped or fishscale bases, and soft lightweight runner-style ski boots with toe-clamp or three-pin bindings, are therefore adequate. Hardshell telemark boots and heavyweight metal-edge backcountry skis with skins are not needed for this tour, though certainly invaluable for the steeper backcountry ski routes and chutes elsewhere in Kosciuszko National Park.

## Accommodation

Accommodation is in the Paddy Pallin Jindabyne Lodge at the beginning and end of the tour, and in tents otherwise. The lodge is fitted out to accommodate cross-country skiers in comfort but not in luxury. The rooms are fitted out with bunk beds, and there are communal bathroom areas, a communal lounge and dining area, and a kitchen with resident cook. The tents are two-person domes, designed as four-season hiking and mountaineering tents rather than specifically as snow tents, but more than adequate for the conditions.

## Statistics

The 5-day backcountry camping tour is offered only twice each season, at a cost of AUD780 per person or about US$117 per person per day. On the trip in which I took part there were two guides and half a dozen clients in the group. The trip price includes National Park fees.

## Access

Access to the lodge is by private vehicle. Transport from the lodge to the skiing roadhead is in a Paddy Pallin shuttle bus. The area is within Mt Kosciuszko National Park, and daily park entry and camping fees apply. These are paid by the tour operator and included in the trip price.

## Community

Tourism is the principal mainstay of the regional economy in this area, but commercial cross-country ski camping tours contribute only a very small proportion in comparison to the major downhill ski resorts and associated accommodation. The Paddy Pallin store in Jindabyne has been open for many years and contributes to local employment. Food and fuel supplies for the lodge and the camping component of the tour are purchased locally. Once on the tour itself, clients generally will not meet anyone apart from their guides.

## Experience

For a reasonably skilled cross-country skier with previous snow camping experience, this tour is very straightforward, even if the weather deteriorates. The distances covered are small, the terrain is relatively level, the guides are responsible for navigation, and tents and equipment remain at the base camp so that skiers do not need to carry heavy backpacks during the day. For someone used to operating their own cooking stove in the vestibule of their tent, it is an unusual experience to sit on a snow bench and be served hot food cooked by someone else. The trip logistics allow for significantly more fresh food than one could generally carry on an independent backcountry ski trip.

The subalpine woodland area used for the base camp is not as beautiful as the small patches of older snowgums perched on the higher slopes above the main tree line, but it is safer for a large group, and better able to accommodate the large amount of local traffic between tents and cooking area without creating environmental impacts. On the one occasion in which I participated in this tour, the highlight of the trip was a couple of hours spent practising telemark turns by moonlight on a small slope of steep soft snow near the base camp, at around 2 am, accompanied only by one of the guides.

## Environment

Cross-country skiing and snow camping can be very low-impact activities if carried out with appropriate care. Unlike snow grooming at ski resorts, cross-country skiing generally does not crush the undersnow burrows of small mountain mammals or damage plants under the snow. If skiers move quietly there is little or no noise disturbance, and if they are careful not to drop litter or food scraps there need be no impacts associated with supplementary food sources. The area immediately under each tent must generally be trampled down to provide a supporting surface, but the degree of compaction is generally not enough to affect snowmelt in spring. The principal impacts are those associated with human waste, since there is no toilet at the base camp. Such concerns, of course, apply equally to bushwalkers in summer.

## Safety

The design of this trip ensures a high level of safety. The group is never far from a road, and one of the guides or indeed clients could easily ski out to get assistance if needed, at least if they were confident of the right direction. The terrain chosen is relatively level and skiers can stop safely at any point. The area is below tree line so landmarks are plentiful and route-finding easy even during falling snow. The entire group and both guides ski together at all times, providing additional safety. The camp is set up on the first day with plenty of time before dark, and in an area well known to the guides, so there are never any concerns about finding a suitable campsite before the end of the skiing day.

## Marketing

These tours do not seem to be marketed heavily. They are not advertised on the main Paddy Pallin website, but only on the local site for the Paddy Pallin Jindabyne branch. Information about the tours is also available in the Paddy Pallin Jindabyne store. Since there are only two departures each season, it would appear that demand is not high, and that most clients prefer to stay at the lodge and ski one day at a time. Perhaps the main purpose of the multi-day ski camping tours is to introduce clients to snow camping gently and safely, so that they may then buy their own snow camping equipment for future private trips. Thus, the tours may be principally a marketing device for retail equipment sales. This, however, is merely a speculative suggestion.

# Yellowstone National Park, USA: Yellowstone Expeditions

## Place

Yellowstone National Park lies largely in Wyoming USA, extending into southern Montana and eastern Idaho. It is one of America's icon parks, very heavily visited indeed, and the focus of numerous management controversies over issues such as prescribed burning, predator reintroductions, wolf and bison kills by neighbouring ranchers, and snowmobile use. Because of the high visitation rate in summer, it has long since ceased to be a wilderness or adventure experience for all but a few backcountry travellers. Increasing snowmobile use in winter is having similar impacts, but cross-country ski camping trips are still possible.

## Operator

My own backcountry skiing experience in Yellowstone National Park was as an independent visitor, with one colleague. Several commercial organizations offer cross-country ski tours in the region. The US National Outdoor Leadership School (NOLS, 2005) offers a Yellowstone Winter Natural History course, which includes 9 days' backcountry skiing and snowcamping, building iglus, snow caves or quinzhees. Various ranches around the area offer short cross-country ski tours. The main commercial tour providers, however, seems to be Yellowstone Expeditions (2005), which has operated a winter basecamp in West Yellowstone since 1983. The company does not appear to offer any other tour products.

## Activity

For an independent backcountry ski tourer, issues such as skiing safely, navigation and the mechanics of camping with reasonable comfort at 20°C below zero consume most of one's time and attention. Watching wildlife may also be a major aim. In practice, however, we found that most animals are smart enough to wander along cleared roads rather than pushing through deep crusted snow at far higher energetic cost, so the wildlife viewing opportunities are actually rather limited.

## Equipment

Snow conditions vary widely and some trails are steep, narrow and icy. Metal-edged skis are preferable. Most of the terrain is relatively level, and the snow is often crusted or heavy, so lightweight patterned skis and soft boots with three-pin or rat-trap bindings are preferable to heavyweight skis with skins, hardshell boots and cable bindings. Temperatures commonly fall to –20°C overnight and may drop much lower, to –40°C or even lower during blizzards. Backcountry ski campers need to be prepared for such conditions. At these temperatures, for example, one cannot touch bare metal such as a camping stove with bare hands, but must use glove liners. Similarly, clothing and sleeping bags must be warm enough, and skiers need snow shovels as well as snow tents.

## Accommodation

Accommodation is available at Mammoth, the northwest gateway to the park, throughout the winter season. Backcountry accommodation requires a four-season tent or a snow tent. At least in the areas I have visited, there is generally not enough snow to dig snow caves. The Canyon Skier's Camp operated by Yellowstone Expeditions consists of eight individual 'yurtlets', heated by propane and supplied with beds and bedding; a central shower and sauna; and a central dining area. It is dismantled in summer.

## Statistics

Yellowstone Expeditions (2005) offers 4 day/3 night, 5 day/4 night and 8 day/7 night packages, including accommodation, food and guided skiing during the day. Costs are around US$160–200 per person per day twinshare, plus US$15 per day single supplement.

## Access

Winter access to Yellowstone National Park is generally via Mammoth Springs, reached by road from Bozeman, Montana. The Canyon Skier's Camp is reached from West Yellowstone. Bozeman is accessible by air or road.

## Community

The Greater Yellowstone area has undergone major social change over recent decades (Johnson, 2004) and local communities contain a mixture of ranchers, amenity migrants, tourism industry staff and parks staff. Backcountry skiers generally interact only with tourism industry personnel, to get information, equipment and/or tours; and parks personnel to get permits.

## Experience

When I visited Yellowstone National Park in winter, we were camped in a four-season tent of New Zealand manufacture, but it was not a snow tent as such. In addition, our sleeping bags were designed for the Snowy Mountains in Australia rather than for the northern USA. So we were cold. We knew what to expect, however, and were adequately equipped with glove liners and boot warmers, so our extremities survived intact and we were certainly able to appreciate the astonishing beauty of landscapes covered by inch-high feathered ice crystals. We had also hoped to see wildlife. In practice, however, the snow was crusted: not quite strongly enough to bear a loaded ski, but enough to trap an unloaded ski underneath the crust; so the going was rather slow. The larger wildlife had adapted well to such circumstances, by walking along the snowploughed road rather than cross-country. So the wildlife-watching part of the exercise was not quite as planned. Perhaps it would be different from the Canyon Skier's Camp.

## Environment

I have not visited the Yellowstone Expeditions camp or operations in person and so cannot comment on their environmental management. In general, cross-country ski camping can be carried out with negligible impact if appropriate care is taken. If not, however, sub-snow vegetation may be damaged, and litter and human waste left buried in snow for exposure in spring.

## Safety

The main potential risks in an independent backcountry ski camping trip are injury while skiing with a heavy load, and exposure and/or hypothermia if lost or caught out ill-prepared in extreme weather conditions. These risks are greatly reduced by skiing in a guided group and returning to a heated camp each night.

## Marketing

My only information on Yellowstone Expeditions (2005) is from its website. Information on the park itself is also available from the US Parks Service.

# 14 Ice Climbing

*Contributed by Jerry Johnson and Ian Godwin*

Conrad Anker, Hyalite Canyon, Montana, USA. Photo Kristoffer Erickson.

## Introduction

Ascending spectacular, frozen waterfalls of vertical, blue ice finds its roots in the sport of mountaineering; in order to climb the great peaks of the Alps and elsewhere, Victorian-era climbers frequently ascended glaciers and frozen gullies of summer snow and water ice. Ice climbing, as a sport removed from general mountaineering, really began in 1959 with Jimmy Marshall, a Scotsman. It was Marshall, and others who climbed in the Scottish Highlands, who conceptualized and then realized the potential of iced-up chimney-gullies as a sport worthy of specialized techniques and equipment. Ben Nevis, the highest mountain in the UK (1344 m) presented hundreds of such gullies, smears and icy faces on which the foundations of modern ice climbing techniques were developed.

Contemporary ice climbing remains a relatively obscure sport. The number of consistent practitioners is probably under 10,000. For the past few years, global industry sales have been about US$7–8 million per year (C. Bacasa, Black Diamond Equipment, personal communication, 2005). The equipment is expensive, highly specialized and becoming more so. Typically, two technical ice axes, ice screws, crampons, rigid-soled boots and warm but water resistant winter clothing round out the normal rock climbing or mountaineering kit of ropes, hardware, harness, etc.

Within the context of adventure sports, ice climbing is somewhat dangerous, but usually not fatal. Puncture injuries, broken ankles and legs, facial lacerations and head injury are the most common injuries. Additionally, avalanches threaten many locations where the sport is practised. While modern clothing, especially boots, has made the sport almost comfortable to practise in the coldest conditions, 'almost' remains the operative word, so much so that the warmer blooded amongst us are typically discouraged from participating.

Compounding the cost, consequence and comfort issues identified above, high-quality ice climbing is found in just a few places around the world. The Scottish Highlands – Ben Nevis, Cairngorm Mountains; Iceland, only 35 min from Reykjavik; Norway – most notably the Gol Valley located 3 h north of Oslo; the European Alps all the way from Chamonix to Slovenia and Northern Spain; and the North American locations discussed below, all offer high quality experiences. In the developed alpine destinations of Scotland and Europe, high-quality guides are available. The UK in particular has a well-developed system of schools and outdoor centres where the full range of outdoor skills can be learned. Perhaps the best location for ice climbing instruction in that system is Glenmore Lodge Scotland's National Outdoor Training Centre, located in the heart of Cairngorms National Park. In Europe, where guiding has a long and respected tradition, the best contacts can be made through the International Federation of Mountain Guides Associations (IFMGA) or the Compagnie des Guides de Chamonix in France.

Commercial services dedicated to guiding and providing ice climbing instruction are few in number. Seasons can be short and are obviously weather dependent, and good climbing conditions are not necessarily conducive to maintaining the comfort and morale of clients. Risks of cold-related injuries such as frostbite or hypothermia are real concerns.

The North American locations below comprise many of the best destination ice climbing opportunities on the continent and attest to the sometimes limited opportunities for contracting with commercial vendors for instruction and guided climbing. None of the purely commercial guide services described below offers ice climbing as their primary guiding activity. Rather, it is typically marketed as an interesting add-on to a winter visit to a destination ski area or novelty activity for winter tourists. Two of the organizations described below operate as not-for-profit enterprises. The Ouray Ice Park and the Chicks with Picks programme exist specifically to offer ice climbing instruction and training.

The authors have climbed and guided extensively in Canada and the Rockies, and so have personal experience with those locations and the services referenced. Additional knowledgeable persons were also contacted for their input and verification regarding the selection of the areas profiled (M. Feduschak, Gore Range Natural Science School, personal communication, 2005; J. Bicknell, Colorado Mountain School, personal communication, 2005; K. Erickson, professional alpinist/climber/photographer, personal communication, 2005). The east coast locations were researched via websites and communication with area guides (L. Des Rochers, Coopérative des guides d'escalade du Québec, personal communication, 2005). In the case of Ouray we interviewed the manager of the Ice Park (E. Eddy, Ouray Ice Park Inc., personal communication, 2005). The director of the Chicks with Picks programme was also interviewed regarding the specifics of that programme (K. Reynolds, Chicks with Picks, personal communication, 2005).

## Banff, Alberta, Canada

### Place

The Canadian Rockies may be the best destination worldwide for climbing ice: a lifetime of climbs amid dramatic vertical relief, some of the most spectacular mountain vistas to be seen, and cold winters that make for reliably good conditions from November through to April. The limestone geology of the Canadian Rockies offers the permeability needed to ensure countless waterfalls, drips, seeps and other sources of water found on rock walls throughout the region.

One hundred and thirty kilometres west of Calgary in Alberta, the resort community of Banff is located in the heart of Banff National Park. Canmore, 18 km to the south, and Lake Louise, 60 km to the north, make up the bulk of the Bow Valley Parkway. These three towns located in the Bow Valley are rightly called the 'world capital of ice climbing'. The region is surrounded by thousands of square miles of National and Provincial Park land, including Banff, Kootenay, Yoho, Jasper, Mount Assiniboine, Kananaskis and Yamnuska. World-renowned ski resorts like Lake Louise and Sunshine are only a 30–45 min drive away.

Mountaineering here began with ascents of Lefroy and Victoria in 1894. It was not until around 1972 though, with the advent of modern ice climbing gear, that the potential of the Rockies ice was fully appreciated. Throughout the 1970s, the ice lines climbed here were at the forefront of the world climbing endeavours in terms of length and difficulty. Perhaps the most famous route in the Rockies is Polar Circus – the 700 m path of blue ice first climbed in 1975. It remains a sought-after test piece.

First class amenities abound in the region. Banff (elevation 1475 m) contains plentiful accommodation, restaurants and pubs across the price spectrum. Every service, including more than a dozen commercial guide services, needed by year-round tourists is available. Canmore is a rapidly growing town (pop. 12,000) with an expanding list of accommodation and tourist services. The Lake Louise area is a destination resort encompassing the village of Lake Louise (1536 m), Lake Louise itself,

Moraine Lake, and the Lake Louise gondola and ski area. Accommodation ranges from the upscale Chateau Lake Louise to simple lakeside resorts and public campgrounds. In any case, accommodation is in shorter supply than in Banff.

Climbing in the region is typically 'roadside', with short drives and approaches anywhere from 10 to 60 min. The climbs range from easy for beginners to multi-pitch extreme classics as hard as anything in the world.

The Banff area is similar to other notable alpine destinations like Chamonix, France; Zermatt, Switzerland; or Jackson, Wyoming, where a wide range of high-quality services are available. The product range is broad – from highly structured package tours to custom guiding. Because of the importance of the region to the sports of climbing and mountaineering, many of the guide services are based globally. Europeans, Americans, Japanese and Canadian firms (among others), list ice climbing in Banff on their itineraries. Regulation of guiding is via the Association of Canadian Mountain Guides (ACMG). They assist members of the IFMGA to obtain legal access to Canadian mountains. Virtually all firms provide the basic ice climbing kit – ice axes, crampons, helmets, harness, ropes, etc. Because of Canadian liability concerns, many small firms are not able to transport clients to the destination. Rather, the client is expected to meet the guide at the venue or transport the guide. A spectrum of the firms operating in this area is summarized below.

Current avalanche conditions for the region can be found at the Canadian Avalanche Association (2005) website. *Waterfall Ice: Climbs in the Canadian Rockies* (Josephson, 2002) is the most current guide for the region.

## On Top Private Guide Service

On Top Private Guide Service is an international mountain ski and guide service specializing in mountaineering, trekking, backcountry skiing in Europe and North America and custom guiding globally. They are certified by the International Federation of Mountain Guide Associations and the Association of Canadian Mountain Guides. They offer only two ice-related packages – a 3-day ice climbing course for CAN560 (US$480) and personalized custom guiding. Rates are CAN380 (US$325) for one client to CAN480 (US$410) for a group of three. Ancillary winter activities include skiing, alpine climbing and snowshoeing. This very small firm provides small client-to-guide ratios (2:1 is typical) and can offer a highly customized 'boutique' experience. It is similar in both philosophy and programmes to the alpine guides of the European Alps.

## Banff Adventures Unlimited

Banff Adventures Unlimited is a 'one-stop adventure shop'. They tend to cater to the tourist interested in new experiences while on holiday rather than those focused primarily on ice climbing. They market a variety of winter activities that complement each other – i.e. ice climbing in the morning and dog sledding in the afternoon. They also offer backcountry ski touring, heliskiing, snowmobile tours, snowshoe walks and hockey tickets. Costs for a full day of introductory ice climbing range from CAN400 (US$340), for one, to CAN150 (US$130) per person for a group of four or more. Banff Adventures is very much the package tour option for summer or winter visitors to the region; those interested in a broad array of experiences rather than in-depth technical training.

## Yamnuska Mountain School and Guide Service

The Yamnuska Mountain School and Guide Service has had a presence in the Canadian Rockies since 1977. It began as an adult 'Wilderness' programme at the YMCA Yamnuska Center in Canmore. The Yamnuska Mountain School later split from the wilderness programme as a non-profit service. In the mid-1980s it was reorganized into a limited partnership owned and operated by the guides. The school is certified by the ACMG and the IFMGA and some of their courses can be used for professional guide training.

The school offers a full complement of courses:

- Weekend course for beginners and rock climbers. Prices range from CAN400 (US$340) for singles to CAN140 (US$120) for groups of four or more.
- Five-day course for beginners and rock climbers. Cost CAN800 (US$685) with a client-to-guide ratio of 2:1.
- Ice Safety Refresher Day. A low cost, CAN100 (US$85), 'demo day' intended as a get together to try new gear and 'tune' skills.
- Advanced Ice Systems – a weekend course focusing on technical protection and gear skills for leading and multi-pitch climbing at CAN1250 (US$1070) per person.
- Mixed climbing camps. Cost CAN620 (US$530) for 4 days' instruction, with student to instructor ratios not exceeding 5:1.
- Custom guiding at all levels for individuals, families, groups.

Yamnuska bundles other winter activities including backcountry skiing, hut to hut tours and avalanche courses.

'Yam' is perhaps the best-known source of guided experiences in the region. If one's interest is in learning foundation skills that can be expanded, Yamnuska is the place of choice. They possess the capacity to teach to all levels and experiences.

# Ouray, Colorado, USA

## Place

Prior to the winter of 1994–1995, the town of Ouray, Colorado was probably best known for its hot springs. Since that winter, this diminutive town of 800 year-round inhabitants settled in a pristine river valley has become the most accessible and used ice climbing site on the globe. Located about 129 km and two mountain passes north of Durango, this town (elevation 2381 m) is often referred to by visitors as the 'Switzerland of America'. Discovered in 1875 and developed into a mining town, Ouray, like many other western mountain towns, has been rediscovered several times in various incarnations.

## Ouray Ice Park

While limited ice climbing test pieces had been climbed in the Umcompahgre Gorge in Ouray for nearly two decades, the origin of the Ouray Ice Park (San Juan Mountain Guides, 2003a) only dates back to 1992 when Ouray Hydroelectric's operator, Eric Jacobsen, purchased the gorge property in a bankruptcy auction. With the sole condition that he and his company have liability insurance provided,

Jacobsen was more than willing to allow climbing access to the site. An interesting cooperative agreement between Jacobsen and Ouray County provided him and his company insurance under the county's policy in exchange for a US$1.00 land lease for recreational purposes that extends until 2008.

With insurance provided and access assured, the groundwork for 'artificial' ice making was laid in the fall of 1994 with the installation of the pipes, hoses and sprinkler heads required to develop lines of ice on the rocky walls of the gorge. Just over 2 years later, Ouray Ice Park, Inc. (OIPI) was formed to provide structure to the previous grassroots efforts. Since its formation in 1997, the not-for-profit OIPI corporation has provided the vision and developed the resources to expand the park into a facility with 175 designated ice climbs of all grades (currently utilizing a mix of private, US Forest Service, County and City land) that has also proven to be a substantial boon to the local economy.

According to Erin Eddy (Ouray Ice Park Inc., personal communication, 2005), economic impact of the park is currently measured in two ways: through sales taxes collected in town, and from estimated expenditures for the season's allocation of guided clients. In terms of the sales tax, those expenditures are tracked for the 3 months each winter that the park is open and compared to sales tax expenditures for those same 3 months prior to the park's existence. Part of the assumed economic impact of the park has thus been calculated to be a gain of approximately US$4 million for that 3-month period. The other method used to calculate direct economic impact on the town has been to estimate conservatively that 1000 persons use the park for a given winter season and that each of those spent US$500 in town on food, lodging, transportation, etc. This results in a gross direct impact of US$500,000 each winter.

Cost for patrons wishing to use the park, staffed principally by volunteer labour, is zero. Funding for the development, expansion and maintenance of the facility has come from donations, corporate sponsorships, the annual Ouray Ice Festival and voluntary memberships. The principal donors to date are The Access Fund, the Ouray Chamber Resort Association and an anonymous donor. Currently, over half of the annual expenditures are raised by the Ice Festival. The US$40 membership (US$35 if purchased early season) is essentially a donation that provides members with preferential participation in festival clinics, discounts at local businesses and lodgings, and 'an annual refill of good climbing karma'. Finally, the list of lodging, local business and corporate sponsors (available at their website) is expansive and inclusive.

Given that the park is managed by a not-for-profit organization and free to patrons, the management of guide services is necessary to prevent a 'tragedy of the commons'. Accordingly, the OIPI and the Ouray County Commissioners voted to designate the San Juan Mountain Guides (SJMG) as the principal concessionaire within the park. The OIPI board defines the number of guide/client days for each season based on previous use, expansion and planned special events. The San Juan Mountain Guides have guides in the park on a daily basis who monitor for and report any abuses of park rules by other approved concessionaires, if necessary. The San Juan Mountain Guides is also responsible for managing the application process for all guiding vendors (services and individual guides) wishing to operate in the park (E. Eddy, Ouray Ice Park Inc., personal communication, 2005).

The application process is required because the demand for commercial use in the park exceeds the resource supply. Accordingly, even those who do get selected as sub-contracting guide services have limited service days allocated to them. The Ouray Ice Park Guiding Operation Plan (Ouray Ice Park, 2005a) defines the eligibility requirements, selection criteria, allocation of service days, fee structure, application document requirements and rules of compliance for all potential subcontracting guides. For the 2002/2003 ice season the following guides and/or services were allowed commercial access to the park: San Juan Mountain Guides, American Alpine Institute, Southwest Adventures, Skyward Mountaineering, Chicks with Picks, International Mountain Guides, Crested Butte Mountain Guides, Gunnison Valley Adventure Guides and Mountain Madness. Three of the above services are briefly profiled below.

A developing online, interactive map to the Ouray Ice Park (2005b) is available. Virtually no avalanche danger threatens the Park, making it a safe place to learn to climb or to simply visit and watch.

## San Juan Mountain Guides

In addition to being the managing concessionaire of the Ouray Ice Park, the San Juan Mountain Guides, LLC (San Juan Mountain Guides, 2003b) is based in Ouray and provides instruction and guiding services for rock climbing, ice climbing (identified on the website as a specialty), alpine mountaineering, backcountry skiing, avalanche training and international expeditions. The San Juan guides offer both private guiding and courses of instruction. The private guiding, which may or may not include climbing in the ice park, costs US$285 per person per day for one-on-one guiding, and US$195, US$160 and US$135 per person per day for 2:1, 3:1 and 4:1 student-to-instructor ratios, respectively. The courses offered by SJMG are based on a 2-day format and are available at the beginner and intermediate levels. These courses are typically held on Saturday and Sunday. During the 2005/2006 season, 12 weekends are scheduled for beginning instruction. The maximum student-to-instructor ratio for the beginner programmes is 4:1 and costs US$305 per person. The intermediate courses cost US$340 per person and have a maximum student-to-instructor ratio of 3:1. There are five intermediate classes scheduled for the 2005/2006 season. Both course types typically convene at the Ouray Ice Park. For both private guiding and courses, all ice climbing equipment is provided. As a setting and opportunity for learning the necessary skills of climbing ice, the experience cannot be matched.

## Chicks with Picks

The Chicks with Picks (CWP) clinics (Chicks with Picks, 2005) were created by Kim Reynolds in 2000 to encourage 'women climbing with women, for women'. At the time, Kim, a long-time instructor and course director for the Colorado Outward Bound School, was guiding for San Juan Mountain Guides. There were two principal and supporting goals for the clinics; the first was 'to teach self-reliance through the development of skills in a safe, non-competitive environment' and the second was to raise funds for women's shelters. Thus far, CWP has raised approximately US$75,000 for women's shelters. For the 2005/2006 season, CWP has five clinics planned. Three will take place at the Ouray Ice Park and the other two will take place in North Conway, New Hampshire. Typical clinics last from 2 days, including meals, lodging, demo gear and a 4:1 student-to-guide ratio (for US$626 person, double occupancy), to 4 days, including meals, lodging, demo gear and a 4:1 student-to-guide ratio (for US$1250 per person, double occupancy). There is also a special 4-day clinic with a 2:1 student-to-guide ratio, available for US$1550, which emphasizes the development of backcountry ice skills.

While CWP is not the only women-only guide service, it may be the only one in North America that has received numerous awards for community service and helping other women in need.

## Mountain Madness

Mountain Madness (2004) is a guide company based out of Seattle, Washington. It is accredited by the American Mountain Guides Association and was founded in 1984 by the late Scott Fischer. With 'Client Care', 'Fabulous Cuisine' and 'Customized Itineraries to Meet Your Goals' identified as reasons to choose them to venture with, Mountain Madness can probably be considered one of the highest end guiding companies available. In addition to ice climbing, other activities offered by this company include: guiding the Seven Summits, guiding expeditions on every continent, mountaineering (in North and South America), rock climbing, backcountry skiing, canyoneering, avalanche programmes, women's programmes, trekking (in Africa, Asia, Europe and South America) and custom trips. It should be noted that the 'Waterfall Ice Climbing Courses' that they offer are a very small portion of their programme. They offer three 2-day, basic ice climbing courses, all held in the Ouray Ice Park and costing (for both days) US$650 (1:1 student-to-instructor ratio), US$450 (2:1 ratio), US$380 (3:1 ratio) and US$330 (4:1 ratio). Their other structured ice climbing opportunity is a 2-day 'San Juan Backcountry Sampler'. This programme takes place in the backcountry in and about the Ouray and Telluride areas. Again, only three dates are offered and the cost is US$650 (1:1 student-to-instructor ratio) and US$450 (2:1 ratio). Finally, they do offer an option for private/custom guiding and instruction that has open dates and costs US$325 per day (1:1 ratio), US$225 per day (2:1 ratio), US$190 per day (3:1 ratio) and US$165 per day (4:1 ratio).

# North Conway, New Hampshire, USA

## Place

The 'Granite State' of New Hampshire with its thinly developed soils, shallow bedrock, cold winter temperatures, humidity and limited snowfall (generally, when compared to the Rocky Mountain region) provides a reasonably centralized ice climbing resource. While multiple, distinct ice climbing areas exist in the White Mountains (Cathedral Ledge, Crawford Notch, Ethan Pond/Mt Willey, Franconia Notch, Frankenstein Cliff, Lake Willoughby, Mount Washington and Trollville or Duck's Head), it is telling that the locations of most of the areas are typically referenced relative to the town of North Conway.

With its resident population hovering just over 2000 and elevation of 162 m above mean sea level, North Conway has been the traditional centre of rock and ice climbing in Northern New England, principally due to the big granite walls of Cathedral Ledge (183 m) and Whitehorse Ledge (244 m), both of which are within a few of kilometres of the town centre. While other 'destination' sport climbing areas have captured the minds and souls (not to mention tattoos and piercings) of New England's 'bolt clipping' crowd, North Conway continues to fuel the fires of the traditional climbers and more masochistic ice fiends in the region and beyond.

While North Conway is known within the climbing community as one of the northeast's venerable climbing areas, and sees a fair amount of traffic for that reason, it pales in comparison to the traffic jams created by the town's real industry: outlet stores. North Conway has been drawing in the outlet shops and associated throng of bargain shoppers for over 25 years. Shopping aside, North Conway serves as a stepping-off point for the various snow sports for people from Boston to Montreal. There is alpine skiing at Attitash, Cranmore, Black, Wildcat, Bretton Woods, King Pine, Shawnee Peak and Sunday River, and cross-country skiing at the Jackson Ski Touring Foundation and along the hiking trails throughout that area of the White Mountains. Ultimately, the economic impact of climbing (both ice and rock) in the North Conway area is miniscule. Still, there are several guide services, from those provided by the national outdoor retailer shops, to the local rock/ice specialty shop to the individual, independent guides ready to accommodate the market. The three guide services below represent some of the variability that does exist.

The regional guidebook is *An Ice Climber's Guide to Northern New England* (Lewis and Wilcox, 2002).

**International Mountain Climbing School**

The International Mountain Climbing School (IMCS) (2005), an offshoot of the International Mountain Equipment (IME) store in North Conway, has provided climbing instruction in New England and beyond for 31 years. Their mission is to provide people of all ages and all abilities with a 'safe, enjoyable and worthwhile climbing experience' all the time. In addition to organizing the annual Mount Washington Valley Ice Festival (13th this year) and winter climbing programmes, IMCS also provides rock climbing programmes, a climbing trip to Ecuador, ski mountaineering programmes, youth climbing programmes and an annual women's rock day.

The IMCS runs three levels of ice climbing course and clinics through the winter: novice/beginner, intermediate and advanced. The offerings for novice/beginner ice climbers include an Introduction to Waterfall Ice Climbing that is run six times over the season at a cost of US$100 each for four climbers; the Early Season Ice actually services all levels of climbers by taking them into Tuckerman's Ravine on Mount Washington any day between November 24 and December 20 for US$200, US$145 or US$115 (per person per day for private guiding, group of two or group of three, respectively); the Three-Day Basic Ice Climbing Skills is run eight times at a per person cost of US$650 (private weekend), US$600 (private midweek), US$480 (group of two) or US$390 (group of three). Intermediate level offerings include a 2-day Alpine Snow and Ice Climbing Skills course run six times through the winter with a per person price of US$450 (private), US$320 (group of two) or US$260 (group of three) and a 2-day Vertical Ice Climbing Skills session run seven times with the same per person cost as the Alpine Snow and Ice Climbing Skills course. The advanced level courses include a 2-day Mixing It Up: Advanced Rock and Ice Climbing Skills course run six times during the season at the same cost as the intermediate offerings, and their Advanced: Three-Day Ice Leader Course that is run five times in the winter at a per person cost of US$650 (private), US$480 (group of two) and US$390 (group of three). The International Mountain Climbing School also offers privately arranged courses and guiding services at the following rates: US$225 private (weekend) 1:1 climber-to-guide ratio, US$200 private (midweek) 1:1 ratio, US$160 for a 2:1 ratio, US$130 for a 3:1 ratio, US$110 for a 5:1 ratio and US$95 for a group of five.

Of particular note in regards to IMCS and IME is their organization, as mentioned above, of the Mount Washington Valley Ice Festival. This 4-day event provides opportunities for climbers to participate in skill-based clinics, guided climbs, view slide shows presented by various ice climbing glitterati, and test the latest gear. Of further interest are the partnerships that IMCS has forged with the American Alpine Club and the Cranmore Mountain Ski Resort to host the event. Additionally, Patagonia, the softgoods manufacturer, is the title sponsor with two other companies, Asolo USA and Mammut, also listed as major sponsors. Lastly, Chicks with Picks (further information provided in the Ouray section), for the seventh year, is an integral part of the Ice Festival. All told, there are 98 possible activities available for people to register for, with costs ranging from US$8 (breakfast buffet) to US$525 (for a 3-day Presidential Range Traverse with an IMCS guide).

## Eastern Mountain Sports

Eastern Mountain Sports (EMS) was founded in 1967 in Wellesley, Massachusetts. Since that time, the EMS chain has grown to more than 80 stores and considers itself 'one of the nation's leading outdoor specialty retailers' (Eastern Mountain Sports, 2005). Now based in Peterborough, New Hampshire, the majority of the stores are located in the northeast region of the USA, with stores as far south as Washington, DC and extending west with three stores in Michigan and three in Colorado.

The EMS Climbing School (2005) has been in operation since 1968 and is fully accredited by the American Mountain Guides Association (AMGA). Claiming to have 'more AMGA Certified Guides on our staff, than any other Eastern School' and providing more than 3000 lessons each year, this school is probably one of the largest retail-based guide services in the country. In addition to operating climbing schools in the following locations: North Conway, New Hampshire; New Paltz, New York; Lake Placid, New York; West Hartford, Connecticut; Boston, Massachusetts; and Rumney, New Hampshire, EMS also operates two kayaking schools in Hingham, Massachusetts and Portland, Maine.

The North Conway school, identified as the 'main office' for the store's climbing schools, runs multiple ice climbing programmes (in fact, all of the EMS climbing schools except the Boston location run ice climbing programmes). The programme offerings are subdivided into Introductory, Advanced and Specialized programmes.

Both the Introductory and Advanced offerings include the following programmes:

- Single Day Ice Climbing Programme (per person price: US$195 for a single, US$185 for a single in a group of two or three, US$185 for a party of two and US$175 for a party of three).
- Three-Day Ice Climbing Programme (per person price: US$550 for a single, US$520 for a single in a group of two or three, US$520 for a party of two and US$490 for a party of three).
- Private and Semi-Private Ice Climbing (per person price for 1 day: US$245 for a single, US$205 for a party of two and US$175 for a party of three).

- All courses are available every day of the winter season and are booked through a reservation line.
- The maximum client-to-instructor ratio is 3:1 and all technical equipment is provided at no additional cost.

The Specialized programmes include:

- Guided Ice Climbs (US$295 for a single, US$235 for a party of two and US$195 for a party of three).
- A 2-Day Self-Rescue Course (no additional information available).
- Alpine Gully Climbs (US$295 for a single, US$235 for a party of two).

### Synnott Mountain Guides

Synnott Mountain Guides (SMG) (2005) is Mark Synnott of Jackson, New Hampshire (approximately 16 km north of North Conway). In addition to being the owner/operator of SMG, Synnott works as a freelance photojournalist, senior contributing editor of *Climbing* magazine and professional climber/technical consultant for The North Face. When not on an expedition or otherwise working for The North Face, Synnott operates SMG as a year-round guiding service. In addition to guiding ice, SMG guides on rock, mixed climbs, mountaineering, big wall/aid climbs, ski mountaineering and self-rescue. In the waterfall ice arena, Synnott is prepared to guide and/or teach beginners to advanced practitioners. The daily rates charged by SMG are: US$220 private (one person); US$160 per person for two; US$130 per person for three; and US$110 per person for four. In addition to the technical guiding services, SMG offers to take care of the logistical arrangements for client visits, including lodging, transportation, all equipment needs and pick up and drop off at the nearest airports. Synnott's operation is unique because it is an opportunity to learn from one of a few professional climbers pushing the limits of the possible as well as guiding at the pedestrian level.

## Quebec, Canada

### Place

In contrast to most other locations in North America, ice climbing in the province of Quebec radiates from its two major metropolitan centres, Montreal and Quebec City. Mont Tremblant (124 km northwest of Montreal) and Shawbridge (40 km north of the city) in the Laurentide region are the two 'best bets' for climbing Canadian ice in proximity to Montreal. Other opportunities also exist south of the border in Vermont at Smugglers' Notch and Lake Willoughby. The area around the city of Quebec is said to be second only to the Rockies for its variety, quantity and quality of ice climbing. Montmorency Falls, a 10-min drive from the city's downtown and taller than its famous cousin to the south, Niagara Falls, is almost too accessible not to climb. Roughly 30 km to the east of Quebec City, the town of Pont-Rouge hosts the annual Festiglas du Québec (2005), sponsored by The North Face and said to draw up to 5000 participants and onlookers for the 3-day event. North and east of the city, the numerous routes of the Charlevoix area beckon those looking for a less urbanized experience. Because of the proximity of the ice to major urban areas, with its associated accessibility to beginning ice climbers, the level of participation and link to commercial guiding seem more prominent in this region of the continent. Three such service providers are profiled below.

There is a new guidebook to ice and mixed climbs in Quebec, the *Guide des cascades de glace et voies mixtes du Quebec* (Lapierre and Gagnon, 2004). This is written in French, with a bi-lingual introduction, and covers every area in Quebec. The Centre d'Avalanche de La Haute-Gaspésie (2005) website has information on avalanche conditions for the region.

## École d'Escalade L'Ascensation

L'École d'Escalade L'Ascensation (2005) is a guide/school/professional development programme that has been in existence since 1989 and is associated and co-located with the Roc Gyms in Quebec City. This symbiotic arrangement provides them with access to a facility suitable for use with all levels of clientele and a potential client base for their myriad programmes. In addition to their ice climbing programmes, L'Ascensation emphasizes group and corporate programmes, rock climbing, indoor climbing, alpine mountaineering, avalanche workshops and via ferrata excursions. While L'Ascensation is a complete guide service that operates throughout the province, the most significant aspect of this company in regards to ice climbing is that it has the exclusive licence to guide in the Montmorency Park. Cost for their 1-day standard group ice climbing experience ranges from CAD89 (US$75) + tax per person for the minimum four adult clients to CAD75 (US$65) + tax per person for the maximum 40 clients. The per person cost for students for the same experience is CAD20 (US$17) less across the range. In addition to their 'Discovery of Ice' half-day programme (1:1 customer-to-guide ratio CAD175 (US$150) + tax; 2:1 ratio CAD200 (US$170) + tax; 3:1 ratio CAD250 (US$214) + tax), L'Ascensation also provides guiding throughout the province (1 client CAD250 + tax; 2 clients CAD150 (US$130) + tax per person; 3 clients CAD125 (US$110) + tax per person) and several introductory through to advanced courses offered throughout the winter.

## Cooperative des Guides D'Escalade du Quebec

The Cooperative des Guides D'Escalade du Quebec (COGEQ) (2005) is structured as a cooperative of guides in the province of Québec. The various guides are accredited at different levels by l'ÉNEQ (École Nationale d'Escalade du Québec), which is an associate member of the Union Internationale des Associations d'Alpinisme (UIAA). L'ÉNEQ's mission is to conceive and offer training courses for people wanting to either guide or instruct in mountaineering activities. Some members of the COGEQ may also have other accreditations such as the ACMG (Association of Canadian Mountain Guides). They must all have certification from l'ENEQ and an RCR and first aid course both up to date. All guides carry a US$5 million insurance policy.

COGEQ offers a comprehensive mix of six types of ice-related programmes: an introduction to ice, lead climbing, guided climbs, a self-rescue programme, an ascent of the Charlevoix classic, La Pomme d'Or and a dry tooling programme. The per person per day prices for all but the Pomme d'Or programmes are identical: CAD200 (US$171) for 1 person, CAD125 (US$107) for 2 people, CAD100 (US$85) for 3 people and CAD75 (CAD65 for students) (US$64 and $56) for 4 or more. Other than pro-grammatic goals, the differences between the offerings include the duration of the various programmes and the maximum acceptable student-to-guide ratio.

- Introduction to Ice: 1 day, 6:1 student-to-guide ratio.
- Leading Ice: 2–4 days, 4:1 ratio.
- Guided Climbs: 1 day (repeatable), 3:1 ratio.
- Self-Rescue: 2 days, 4:1 ratio.
- Dry Tooling: 2 days, 6:1 ratio.

The Pomme d'Or trip is different in that its objective is a 330 m, grade IV, WI5+. The maximum student-to-guide ratio for this trip is 2:1. The cost is CAD500 (US$428) for one and CAD650 (US$556) for two, and includes transportation from Quebec, a night's lodging, food and transportation via snowmobile to and from the climb.

### Mt Tremblant Resort

An interesting 'guide' service for the Mont Tremblant ice is the Mt Tremblant Resort (2005). This year-round, full-service resort with its golf course, shopping, movie theatres, spas, horseback riding, snowshoeing, sleigh rides, skiing and multitude of other offerings makes a half-day and full-day ice climbing experience available. The climbing takes place on resort property and is oriented towards the beginners interested in a new and different experience (though advanced lessons are also available). Cost for the experience is CAD79 (US$65) per person for a half-day and CAD119 (US$100) per person for a full day.

# Bozeman, Montana, USA

Bozeman, Montana is one of many rapidly growing amenity communities throughout the Rockies. The town is home to a mid-size university, a high-quality airport and almost limitless year-round outdoor recreation; including outstanding ice climbing. Hyalite Canyon is the largest grouping of natural water ice in Montana. The canyon and its drainages support over 70 ice climbs from short top-ropable climbs to climbs that have seen few ascents. A combination of relatively easy access and good tourist services means Bozeman and Hyalite are rapidly becoming a global destination for climbers. Currently, only one guide service is operating under a special use permit to offer professionally guided ice climbing. Montana Alpine Guides (2005), based in Bozeman, is a small full-service summer operation that offers ice climbing in winter. Special use permits to guide on ice usually requires a group of three or more and then the price is US$150 per person per day.

Hyalite Canyon features one ice festival and one 'Demo Days' weekend in December. Each of the local outdoor shops in town sponsors one of the events. In addition to climbing instruction from featured experts, evening activities typically include slide talks and equipment demos.

Avalanche conditions in the Hyalite area can be highly variable and dangerous. Local conditions are updated daily at the Gallatin National Forest Avalanche Center (2000) website and the Hyalite Canyon Ice Climbing Guide. An online guide to the Hyalite area (Hyalite Canyon Ice Climbing Guide, 2005) is available and a printed guidebook, *Winter Dance: Select Ice Climbs in Southern Montana & Northern Wyoming* (Josephson, 2004), covering Bozeman and surrounding area ice climbs, is also available.

## Cody, Wyoming and Valdez, Alaska, USA

Finally, two areas must be mentioned as premier ice climbing destinations for the truly adventuresome. Based on geographical location neither Valdez, Alaska nor Cody, Wyoming would appear to be destinations for a sport requiring long cold winters. Valdez, 120 air miles east of Anchorage, is at sea level on the north shore of Port Valdez, a deepwater fjord in Prince William Sound and the southern terminus of the Trans-Alaska oil pipeline. Its maritime weather results in mild winters with record snowfall. Cody lies at the eastern gateway to Yellowstone National Park and is a small western town on the edge of the Wyoming desert country.

Both locations boast wilderness ice climbing of unexpected quantity and quality. Unfortunately, you are on your own because neither location has a local guiding service. Both locations offer full service food and lodging accommodation as well as other winter pursuits, such as dog sledding, snowmobile tours, backcountry and heliskiing.

The small town of Cody, Wyoming is home to some of the best ice climbing in the USA. The valley hosts the highest concentration of ice in the lower 48 states. The season begins as early as October and can run into the long sunny days of April. Cody attracts a small group of climbers each year; steep approaches, long routes and untouched ice ensure that Cody will remain a destination for those few willing to share climbs in a remote wilderness setting with grizzly bears and bighorn sheep. Local conditions can be researched at the Coldfear (2005) website. There is only one guidebook to the region but it is very good: *Winter Dance: Select Ice Climbs in Southern Montana & Northern Wyoming* (Josephson, 2004).

Valdez, Alaska has several local canyons with very large ice features. The climbing is close to town and access tends to be easy and short. In February the locals hold an Ice Festival in the region (Valdez Ice Climbing Festival, 2005). An online guide to the area is also available (Valdez Ice, 2005).

Mooney Mountain Guides (2005) located in New Hampton, New Hampshire offers an 8-day programme in Valdez on an 'as needed' basis for US$3000. The programme cost includes guide (AMGA certified), 6 nights' lodging on a shared basis in Valdez, all transportation in and around Valdez and group climbing gear. It does not include airfare to Valdez, food, personal equipment or insurance.

## Future Trends

Given the extreme winter conditions and locations for good ice climbing, it is difficult to believe that the traditional form of the sport will recruit new participants at a high rate or become a mainstream activity. Rather, it will be an expansion activity for rock climbers hoping not to hang up their harness when the cold weather arrives, or as a training activity for mountaineers. From a commercial aspect, it is a niche market at best, for those who want a novel outdoor experience as part of a traditional winter holiday. It is relatively difficult to find commercial guide services that teach the sport, and the expensive specialized equipment creates a large start-up cost. Currently, the most common introduction to the sport is via the festivals that take place at popular climbing locations; virtually every location profiled here holds at least one festival each season. The festivals are low cost and essentially risk and discomfort free. They are also good introductions to the guide services in a region, as well as to active climbers.

Manufactured destinations such as Ouray in Colorado are clearly a dominant trend for the sport. They create a friendly setting in a safe and controlled environment where beginners can have a semi-artificial experience without high risk. Following the trend of indoor rock climbing, which has evolved into a sport unto itself, one firm, EntrePrises USA, has designed a foam wall specifically for simulating ice climbing. The climbing takes place indoors under highly controlled conditions. The sport is safe and easy to organize and low temperature isn't an issue. The implications for courses and lessons are obvious. Artificial destinations may be the best path for non-climbers to participate in the sport on a one-time basis.

Mixed climbing has emerged as the new frontier of technical ice climbing. Climbing on rock using ice tools in a method known as 'dry tooling' is allowing the sport to grow and diversify. In the process, more rock climbers are discovering a new and different sport for the vertical world. The implications for guided climbing are probably not important since practitioners are typically already proficient climbing enthusiasts.

# 15 Mountaineering

## Contributed by Robert Hales

Rob Hales, Shishapangma, Tibet, an 8000 m peak. RH collection.

# Introduction

The history of mountaineering adventure tourism is more extensive than the casual observer may realize. Indeed, commercial mountain-guiding commenced long before the term 'adventure tourism' was coined. Commercial interests have spurred development in mountaineering from both a guiding and technological perspective. Early ascents of peaks in the European Alps and elsewhere were driven by experienced clients seeking guidance from local experts to scale hitherto unclimbed peaks. One of the best examples of this was the first ascent of the Matterhorn by Edward Whymper's party in 1865. This successful and tragic trip led to the popularity and notoriety of that peak, as a result of an accident during their descent from the summit. Clients Douglas Hadow, Charles Hudson and Lord Francis Douglas, as well as a guide named Michael Croz, fell to their deaths during the descent.

Whilst guiding has had a long tradition in the history of mountaineering, there have been recent changes in this form of commercialization in the mountains. Historically, mountaineering was the preserve of an experienced elite, who had the skills, self-reliance and independence needed to travel in the mountains. In the past, clients served their own apprenticeship on smaller peaks, before tackling larger iconic peaks with a guide. More recently, however, increased social engagement in mountaineering has changed the typical scene in mountaineering. Increased leisure opportunities, and changes to the essential ingredients of what it means to be a mountaineer, have facilitated commercial developments in mountaineering adventure tourism in ways that seem quite different to Whymper's era (Beedie and Hudson, 2003).

This chapter examines recent developments in mountaineering adventure tourism. To start with, comments from some notable mountain-guiding companies set the scene on contemporary participation trends. The next section details many of the operators that currently provide guiding services around the world. These are profiled on a continent-by-continent basis, to examine trends in service provision and participation rates. Lastly, a number of case studies are discussed to explore some recent issues and trends. These include: the so-called Everest phenomenon; some explanations of the popularity of mountaineering adventure tourism; and the issue of risk in mountaineering adventure tourism.

This is a large task, and it is difficult to do justice to all involved: the commercial operators who provide services throughout the world; the guides and clients who engage in mountain experiences; and the local people and their environment that afford the opportunity to participate in this challenging and rewarding activity. No one author can hope to be familiar with them all in person. For this chapter, therefore, I have drawn information from a wide variety of websites, and added my own perspective as a (part-time) mountaineer who has visited and climbed in many of the mountain regions described in this chapter. Most of these climbs were in private groups, but a few as a member of a guide team.

# Trends in Mountaineering Adventure Tourism

There are apparently no reliable published statistics on the total number of people taking part each year in commercial guided mountaineering tours worldwide. The perception of major guiding companies is of a large increase during the past quarter century. In the view of Alpine Ascents (2005), for example:

We have seen a large increase in the numbers of people wanting to go mountaineering since the mid 1980s. The big increases were in the early 90s and then in 1996–1999. I think one of the main reasons for the last increase was the public appeal of the films *Into Thin Air* and *Everest Imax*.

(G. Janow, Alpine Ascents International, personal communication, 2005)

Alpine Ascents is a long-established company that has run ascents of Mount Everest since 1990. Indeed, much of its early reputation was built on these trips. It currently offers 'Seven Summits' trips, to climb the highest peaks in each of the seven continents; and claims to be the first company to market this theme commercially. Its main climbing bases are in the North Cascade Range in Washington State, USA, and on Denali in Alaska. They run mountaineering schools at both sites.

## Case Studies from Around the World

There are hundreds of different commercial mountaineering tour and guiding companies around the world. Some operate worldwide, but most specialize in one particular mountain range, or the ranges of one particular continent. There are differences in the types of commercial mountaineering services available in different mountain ranges. These depend on market demand; local climbing conditions; the depth of guiding knowledge in each company; transport, services and infrastructure; and political stability in the countries concerned, for example.

In addition, during recent years a number of companies have developed international portfolios of trips and tours that take place in several different continents, not necessarily near the company's home base.

The aim of this analysis is not to compare individual companies from different continents and mountain ranges, but to describe how mountaineering adventure tourism operations differ across the globe. There are distinguishable patterns in the services provided in different regions, depending on local cultural and physical characteristics. The following sections summarize the scope of mountaineering adventure tourism, and tour operators, for each of the major continental regions. Companies that operate worldwide are reviewed first. For North America, Europe and the Himalayas there are so many different operators that it is not feasible even to list them all individually. The relevant tables thus include only the better-known companies.

For each continent or region, mountaineering adventure tour providers are tabulated in the following format, using data derived from website searches.

- *Country* refers to the country of origin or home base of the company.
- *Instruction* indicates whether or not they offer tuition in climbing techniques through mountaineering instruction schools.
- *Guiding* indicates whether or not they offer guided mountaineering trips.
- *Expeditions* indicates the level of support they provide to and from the mountain, including base-camp support.
- *Domestic* and *International* refer to the destinations of the trips offered.
- *Certification* refers to types of qualification possessed by individual guides. Many of the companies also have accreditation with mountaineering guiding associations but this is not shown.
- *Environment* refers to environmental principles or practices described in company

websites. No audited information was available on what guides actually do, which is a critical component of environmental management.

\* means that the site indicates the company is aware of environmental issues;

\*\* means that the company claims to have adopted minimal impact strategies;

\*\*\* means the website specifies what measures the company takes to implement these strategies;

\*\*\*\* means the company claims to contribute to local environmental and community organizations;

\*\*\*\*\* indicates a high standard in all of the above.

Although the UIAA (Union Internationale des Associations d'Alpinisme) Environment Label exists to promote high standards of conduct and responsible access for climbing and mountain activities, there were very few companies that advertised their affiliation. As an Environmental Label holder, companies agree to follow the UIAA environmental objectives and guidelines, including providing participants in activities with a briefing of minimal impact strategies and a final evaluation by participants of guided activities.

## Companies that operate internationally

These companies focus on guiding trips to iconic mountain destinations throughout the world. They offer technical guiding expertise and/or expedition support at a level that is not generally available locally at the destinations concerned. Their main market edge, however, seems to be that their clients prefer to trust companies based in their own country of origin, or in other developed countries that have a particular emphasis on safety.

The destinations offered by these companies include the high altitude peaks of the Himalaya, Patagonia, Central Asian countries, and other Seven Summits destinations.

All of the companies listed in Table 15.1 are based in developed countries where there is a strong tradition of mountaineering. Some companies have been operating for over 20 years, and were established well before the growth spurt in general rock climbing and mountaineering that occurred in the early 1990s. This means that these companies have been well positioned to take advantage of this trend. Other companies have jumped on to the wave of interest in international iconic mountaineering packages.

The number of clients on international trips offered by these companies are commonly lower than on local trips offered in the USA and the European Alps; but the trip prices and potential profits are considerably higher.

## Andes

The Andes Range of South America contains the largest mountains outside of the Himalayas. Mountaineering adventure tourism in this region is characterized by relatively low interest from local climbers, but an increasing interest from international clients. Spectacular peaks with little regulation and easy access have made these ranges attractive to operators promoting more adventurous mountaineering tourism packages (Table 15.2).

The predominant countries where trips are run include Ecuador, Bolivia, Peru,

**Table 15.1.** International mountaineering adventure tour operators.

| | Country | Instruction | Guiding | Expeditions | Destination[1] | Certification[2] | Environment |
|---|---|---|---|---|---|---|---|
| Aventuras Patagonicas | USA | No | Yes | Yes | Global HA | Various | |
| Adventure Consultants | NZ | Yes | Yes | Yes | Global HA | Various | |
| Adventure Dynamics | S. Africa | No | Yes | Yes | Global | | |
| Adventure Peaks | Wales | Yes | Yes | Yes | Global HA | | |
| Alpine Guides International | UK | Yes | Yes | Yes | Global HA | IFMGA | * |
| Andean Trails | Scotland | Yes | Yes | Yes | Andes | | **** |
| DCXP | Australia | No | Yes | Yes | Global | | |
| EWP | UK | No | Yes | Yes | Global | | |
| Field Touring | Australia | No | Yes | Yes | Global | | |
| International Mountain Climbing School | USA | Yes | Yes | Yes | Global HA | AMGA | |
| International Mountain Guides | USA | Yes | Yes | Yes | Global HA | AMGA | |
| International School of Mountaineering | UK | Yes | Yes | Yes | Global HA | IFMGA | |
| Jagged Globe | UK | Yes | Yes | Yes | Global HA | BMG, AMGA | *** |
| Mountain Experience | USA | No | Yes | Yes | Global HA | AMGA | ** |
| Patagonia Mountain Agency | USA | No | Yes | Yes | Global HA | | |
| San Juan Mountain Guides | USA | Yes | Yes | Some | HA | AMGA | |
| Sherpa Ascent International | USA | No | Yes | Yes | HA | | ** |
| World Expeditions | Australia | No | Yes | Yes | HA Antarc. | | **** |

Notes: [1]Global: runs trips to all parts of the globe. HA: high altitude trips. [2]IFMGA: International Federation of Mountain Guides Associations. AMGA: American Mountain Guides Association. BMG: British Mountain Guides.

Chile and Argentina. Some countries have been more popular than others. This depends on the aesthetic appeal of the mountains on offer, the ease of logistics, exchange rates and the possibility of civil unrest.

Aconcagua is one the most visited mountains in the Andes. It is the only mountain above 7000 m outside the Himalayas, other than in the Pamirs. Several companies offer guided ascents and expedition-style support for this peak, which is by far the most popular climbing destination in this mountain range.

In the 2001/02 season, the total number of people entering the provincial park to

**Table 15.2.** Mountaineering adventure tour operators in the Andes.

| | Country | Instruction | Guiding | Expedition logistics | Domestic | International | Certification | Environment |
|---|---|---|---|---|---|---|---|---|
| Aconcagua Adventures | Argentina | No | Yes | Yes | Yes | No | No | ** |
| Aconcagua Expeditions | Argentina | No | Yes | Yes | Yes | No | AAMG | |
| Adventurismo | Chile | No | Yes | Yes | Yes | No | No | |
| Andean Summits | Bolivia | No | Yes | Yes | Yes | Yes | IFMGA | ** |
| Aymara Adventures and Expeditions Mendoza | Argentina | No | Yes | Yes | Yes | Yes | No | |
| Rudy Para–Aconcagua Trek | Argentina | No | Yes | Yes | Yes | No | No | |
| Santa Cruz Expeditions | Peru | No | Yes | Yes | Yes | No | PMGA | |

Notes: AAMG: Argentinean Association of Mountain Guides. IFMGA: International Federation of Mountain Guides Associations. PMGA: Peruvian Mountain Guides Association.

climb to the summit was 3378 (Para, 2005). Only 12% of these were from Argentina. The other 88% were visiting from other countries, mostly the USA. About two-thirds of these climbing groups succeeded in placing at least one person on the summit.

Similar services are provided for other Andean peaks, but these are less popular than Aconcagua. The southern areas of the Andes, with their spectacular summits, also attract many climbers; but guided ascents in this region are fewer in number because of the extreme weather conditions.

Commercial mountaineering operators in the Andes accredit their own guides through their own national schemes, such as those run by the Argentinean Association of Mountain Guides and the Peruvian Mountain Guides Association. Some difficulty was experienced in attempting to profile operators from this region. Many companies do not have websites, or do not have English language sites.

## Antarctica

Commercial climbing operations in Antarctica (Table 15.3) fall into two main categories. One company, Adventure Network International, has for many years offered fully supported climbing trips on the Vinson Massif in the interior of the continent. Access is by charter flight from Punta Arenas in Chile, to a blue ice landing strip at their Patriot Hills base camp in the southern Ellsworth Mountains. The Vinson Massif has Antarctica's highest peaks, up to 4897 m. The base camp is dismantled and reconstructed annually. Historically, about 150 climbers per year have taken part in these expeditions (Splettstoesser, 1999).

**Table 15.3.** Mountaineering adventure tour operators in Antarctica.

| | Country | Instruction | Guiding | Expedition logistics | Domestic | International | Certification | Environment |
|---|---|---|---|---|---|---|---|---|
| Aurora Expeditions | Aust. | Yes | Yes | No | No | Yes | No | *** |
| Adventure Network International | Chile | No | Yes | Yes | No | Yes | No | ** |
| DCXP Mountain Journeys | Aust. | No | Yes | Yes | No | Yes | No | ** |
| Antarctic Horizons | Aust. | Yes | Yes | No | No | Yes | No | * |

The majority of commercial climbing clients visiting Antarctica, however, arrive by ship from Ushuaia and climb the lower peaks on the Antarctic Peninsula. Some of these tour operators are international climbing specialists; others specialize in polar expedition cruises, with climbing as just one of the activities provided.

For all these trips, costs are high because of the logistic difficulties and expense, and the extreme weather conditions. The journey by ship across Drake Passage from Ushuaia to the Antarctic Peninsula takes at least 4 days, and an ice-strengthened vessel is needed to make landfall safely.

Unlike most of the world, Antarctica has no government to regulate tourism activities. Most of the nations with any presence in Antarctica are signatories to the Antarctic Treaty. This treaty, however, relies on the individual nations to apply and enforce their own environmental and other laws, and in practice few have the will or the resources to do so. This deficiency has been compensated for to some degree by a relatively strong and environmentally concerned tourism industry association, the

International Association of Antarctica Tour Operators (IAATO) (2005). Most, but not all of the specialist commercial tour operators in Antarctica are members of IAATO, and generally follow the environmental guidelines it produces.

Trends in mountaineering adventure tourism in Antarctica, and issues facing the sector, have been summarized recently by Greg Mortimer, owner of Aurora Expeditions and a full member of the IAATO. Note, however, that whilst the rules and regulations he refers to below do indeed apply to Australian-based companies such as Aurora Expeditions, companies based in other countries do not necessarily have any such legal requirements.

> Antarctica is a climbing Mecca that could become one of the most exciting climbing destinations in the world during the 21st century. In the Antarctic Peninsula and Ross Sea region alone there are literally thousands of kilometres of unclimbed mountains. The highest mountains around Vinson Massif are within 600 nautical miles of the South Pole.
>
> In recent years an increasing number of yachts with climbing parties onboard have ventured into the relatively warmer areas of the northern Antarctic Peninsula after braving the infamous Drake Passage. Looking into the future this trend is likely to continue. The more easily accessible and technically varied peaks of the Peninsula are likely to become the focus of mountaineers' attention. The cost is likely to remain high so the numbers can be expected to remain low compared to the great peaks of the Himalayas or the intensely used European Alps. However we may see the advent of climbing base camps and perhaps a change in transport methods whereby climbers fly into the region and move around via small vessels.
>
> Two significant elements apart from cost may restrict the numbers: first, the need for each party to present an Environmental Impact Statement of their activities to their national authorities; and secondly the expected requirement of the Antarctic Treaty system for each climbing party to be insured for rescue and potential environmental damage.
>
> To that end the current regulatory framework is generally more restrictive in Antarctica than in other mountain regions of the world. As an avid 'Antarctican' and Antarctic climber it is my view that the current environmental management systems are more than adequate to deal with a significant increase in numbers within reasonable limits. It is an interesting paradox about Antarctica – the rules came first then the people came.
>
> (Mortimer, Aurora Expeditions, personal communication, 2005)

In general, commercial climbing companies operating in Antarctica do seem to feature their environmental management practices in their promotional material more prominently than for companies operating in other regions. This is likely to reflect their perception of client expectations as well as any regulatory requirements.

## Central Asia

Climbers from the former USSR have a proud history of mountain-climbing in the ranges of central Asia. During the Soviet era, mountaineers were supported by the State, and the strong community of climbers that developed around 'climbing for their country' expanded the limits of climbing in these regions. With the disintegration of the former USSR, these climbers lost their government support and many turned to adventure tourism for a new livelihood or income supplement. This was possible because the opening of the former Soviet borders allowed Westerners the opportunity to climb in ranges such as the Caucasus, Tien Shan and Pamirs, and other mountain areas such as Kamchatka, with far fewer restrictions that previously – though climbers must still be sponsored by a local company. Some regions of Central Asia still experience civil unrest, which can create significant safety problems for the climbing tourist. This causes corresponding difficulties for international and local companies attempting to package climbing itineraries that promise adequate tourist safety.

Many companies from North America, the UK and Europe also run climbing tours in the same mountains as these companies. In some instances, the operators listed in Table 15.4 act as local providers for these international tour companies. The companies listed specialize in the logistic, political and cultural support needed to get international mountaineers to their climbing destinations. One notable characteristic of climbing tour operators in this region is that guides expect clients to be highly proficient and self-directed climbers. Reflecting this cultural difference from Western nations, companies in this region generally do not offer instructional courses. Likewise, environmental management issues are not mentioned at all in their promotional materials.

**Table 15.4.** Mountaineering adventure tour operators in Central Asia.

| | Country | Instruction | Guiding | Expedition logistics | Domestic | International | Certification | Environment |
|---|---|---|---|---|---|---|---|---|
| Explorer (Turkey) | Turkey | Yes | Yes | Yes | Yes | Yes | No | No |
| International Travel and Mountaineering Centre Tien Shan | Kyrgyzstan | No | Yes | Yes | Yes | Yes | No | No |
| Tien Shan Travel | Kyrgyzstan | No | Yes | Yes | Yes | Yes | No | No |
| Ullutau | Russia | No | Yes | Yes | Yes | Yes | No | No |
| Top Sport Travel | Russia | No | Yes | Yes | Yes | Yes | No | No |
| Alptour | Russia | No | Yes | Yes | Yes | No | No | No |

# Europe

The European Alps are the birthplace of mountaineering, and remain a major focus for commercial mountaineering worldwide. The Alps have numerous high peaks, and extensive tourist and resource infrastructure nearby, and indeed even within the mountains. This provides easier access, refuge and safety for mountaineering adventure tourism operations.

Mountain guiding in the Alps is a family tradition as well as a commercial enterprise. Individual families in particular regions have been guiding visiting climbers from generation to generation. Strong relationships with particular mountains, and adherence to local cultural traditions, are hence characteristic of many of these guiding operations.

A selection of Alpine guiding companies is compared in Table 15.5. As indicated in this table, most Alpine guides are accredited with the IFMGA, the International Federation of Mountain Guides Associations. These companies focus almost entirely on on-mountain guiding, leaving climbers to arrange their own travel and accom-

**Table 15.5.** Mountaineering adventure tour operators in Europe.

| | Country | Instruction | Guiding | Expedition logistics | Domestic | International[1] | Certification | Environment |
|---|---|---|---|---|---|---|---|---|
| Alpes Exploration | France | No | Yes | No | Yes | Yes | ? | No |
| Alpine Adventures | France | No | Yes | No | Yes | Yes | IFMGA | No |
| Alpine Guides School of Trentino | Italy | Yes | Yes | No | Yes | Yes | IFMGA | No |
| Association Internationale des Guides du Mt Blanc | France | Yes | Yes | No | Yes | Yes | IFMGA | No |
| Cham Adventures | France | Yes | Yes | No | Yes | Yes | | No |
| Chamonix Alpine Adventures | France | No | Yes | No | Yes | Yes | No | No |
| Chamonix Experience | France | Yes | Yes | No | Yes | Yes | No | No |
| Chamonix Guiding | France | Yes | Yes | No | Yes | Yes | IFMGA | No |
| Christian Cesa | Italy | No | Yes | No | Yes | Yes | IFMGA | No |
| Compagnie des Guides de Chamonix | France | Yes | Yes | No | Yes | Yes | No | No |
| Evolution 2 | France | Yes | Yes | No | Yes | Yes | No | No |
| Icicle Mountaineering | France | Yes | Yes | No | Yes | Yes | IFMGA | **** |
| Interlaken Swiss Alpine Guides, Mountaineering School | Switz | Yes | Yes | No | Yes | Yes | IFMGA | No |
| Kailash Adventures | France | Yes | Yes | No | Yes | Yes | Various | No |
| Mountain Guides | Switz | No | Yes | No | Yes | Yes | IFMGA | No |
| Mt Blanc Guides | France | No | Yes | No | Yes | Yes | IFMGA | No |
| Murray Hamilton Mountain Guide | France | No | Yes | No | Yes | No | IFMGA | No |
| Swiss Rock Guides | Switz | No | Yes | No | Yes | Yes | IFMGA | No |

Notes: IFMGA: International Federation of Mountain Guides Associations. [1]All guides work across borders in the European Alps but have limited trips to other regions.

modation. They do not offer instruction. Some do offer international trips as well as Alpine guiding.

The strong culture of guiding is reflected in public expectations. More people hire guides in Europe than in the USA or in New Zealand, where there is less deference to expertise or local knowledge. Guiding operations thus developed earlier in Europe than elsewhere, and this European influence has persisted worldwide. The Union Internationale des Associations d'Alpinisme (UIAA), for example, was formed in 1932 as the international peak mountaineering association; and the internationally accepted guiding qualifications of the International Federation of Mountain Guides Association (IFMGA) are derived from that organization.

Despite this strong tradition of guided mountain ascents, even in Europe there are changes in the portfolio of adventure activities offered to alpine tourists. Recent trends in the European Alps suggest that short, intensive itineraries featuring rock- and ice climbing, snowboarding, canyoning and rafting are now patronized more than mountain ascents, which require greater resources, time and expertise. To meet these new demands, mountaineering companies have changed their operations to offer more tightly packaged, easily identifiable tours that place value for money above traditional local knowledge.

**Table 15.6.** Selected mountaineering adventure tour operators in the Himalayas.

| | Country | Instruction | Guiding | Expedition logistics | Domestic | International | Certification | Environment |
|---|---|---|---|---|---|---|---|---|
| Abode Himalayan Adventure Treks | Nepal | No | Yes | Yes | Yes | Yes | No | No |
| Adventure Everest Vision | Nepal | No | Yes | Yes | Yes | Yes | No | No |
| Adventure Third Pole Treks and Expeditions | Nepal | No | Yes | Yes | Yes | Yes | No | No |
| Adventure Tours Pakistan | Pakis | No | Yes | Yes | Yes | No | No | ** |
| Apex Mountain Nepal Treks and Expeditions A151 | Nepal | No | Yes | Yes | Yes | No | No | No |
| Arun Expeditions | Nepal | No | Yes | Yes | Yes | Yes | No | * |
| Askole Treks and Tours | Pakis | No | Yes | Yes | Yes | No | No | No |
| Climb High Himalaya | Nepal | Yes | Yes | Yes | Yes | Yes | No | *** |
| Himalaya Expeditions | Nepal | No | Yes | Yes | Yes | No | No | *** |
| Himalayan Journey Treks and Expedition Nepal | Nepal | No | Yes | Yes | Yes | No | No | No |
| India Adventure | India | No | Yes | Yes | Yes | No | No | * |
| Jasmine Tours | Pakis | No | Yes | Yes | Yes | No | No | No |
| Makalu Adventure Treks | Nepal | No | Yes | Yes | Yes | No | No | No |
| Mountain Monarch Adventures | Nepal | No | Yes | Yes | Yes | No | No | *** |
| Nazir Sabir Expeditions | Pakis | No | Yes | Yes | Yes | No | No | ** |
| Nepal Mountain Trekking | Nepal | No | Yes | Yes | Yes | No | No | ** |
| Nomad Nepal Treks and Mountaineering | Nepal | No | Yes | Yes | Yes | Yes | No | * |
| Overland Escape | India | No | Yes | Yes | Yes | No | No | No |
| Peak Adventure Tours PL | India | No | No | Yes | Yes | No | No | * |
| Rucksack Tours | India | No | No | Yes | Yes | No | No | No |
| Shikar Travels | India | No | Yes | Yes | Yes | No | No | * |
| Skyline Treks and Expeditions | Nepal | No | Yes | Yes | Yes | No | No | No |
| SuSwagatam Treks | Nepal | No | Yes | Yes | Yes | Yes | No | * |

# Himalayas

The Himalayas contain the largest mountains in the world, and these attract climbers from all over the world. The main climbing countries in the Himalayas are Nepal, India, Pakistan and Tibet. Table 15.6 lists selected mountaineering tour operators in these countries. It is not a complete survey of all operators. In Nepal alone there are at least 491 companies that are members of the Nepal Mountaineering Association. In India and Pakistan the numbers are not as high, but the list of companies numbers in the hundreds. Many of these Himalayan companies also offer other adventure tourism packages that include trekking, cultural tours, whitewater rafting and wildlife safaris.

Today, most mountaineering adventure tourism activities based in these regions take on aspects of service similar to the pioneering expeditions of yesteryear. Climbing Sherpa and porter support still form the backbone of these companies. However, there are some changes to this general pattern. Increasingly, these companies have had to adapt to the development of infrastructure that has allowed easier access to the peaks. Typically their response has been to offer more specialist services. Locally based companies have gradually adopted values, objectives and strategies similar to international tour companies, including guiding practices. They have also promoted guided climbs on smaller peaks, led solely by local guides.

Interestingly, mountaineering adventure tour companies in the Himalayas have tended to promote their environmental management credentials more than corresponding companies from developed nations. Many of the Himalayan mountaineering companies also offer tours with nature and cultural components, ecotours in the broad sense of the word, and social and environmental considerations may perhaps cross over to their climbing activities. Alternatively, it may represent a reaction to poor environmental management practices in the past, including littering Mt Everest and deforesting the Annapurna area.

One interesting development in this region, perhaps an indicator of future trends, is the establishment of base-camp huts near many of the smaller peaks of Nepal. Seasonal guides and equipment for rent are stationed in these huts, allowing trekkers the opportunity to experience these smaller Himalayan peaks without the logistic problems of yesteryear's expedition-style trips.

Mountaineering adventure tourism operations in the Himalayas have come a long way from being just the middle-man between the foreigner and the mountain. Despite the changes, one feature that is likely to continue into the future is that assistance from porters and climbing Sherpas will be combined with foreign guides to deliver mountaineering tour packages on the larger peaks. This alliance allows the combination of attributes from local and international operators, to satisfy the requirements of expedition-style trips.

## New Zealand

Most of the climbing opportunities in New Zealand are in the Southern Alps on the South Island, where there is an extensive hut system managed by the New Zealand Department of Conservation and local climbing groups. This allows climbers to take refuge from the bad weather often encountered in this region. In the past only those qualified under New Zealand's own system of mountain guiding certification were permitted to guide in New Zealand's mountains. Currently, to operate as a commercial guide in New Zealand, individuals may be a certified member of either the New Zealand Mountains Guides Association (NZMGA) or the International Federation of Mountain Guides Associations. This is to maintain the tradition of mountain guiding in a country which, though small, has produced a number of successful local companies with world-class guides.

Some of the mountaineering tour companies in New Zealand are summarized in Table 15.7. The Australian School of Mountaineering is also included for comparison.

Most mountaineering adventure tour companies in New Zealand feature some form of environmental management principles and practices in their marketing materials. This is probably due to the requirements of the New Zealand Department of Conservation (NZDOC), which controls access to many mountaineering areas and facilities throughout New Zealand, and liaises closely with tour companies operating in parks and reserves.

Another feature of New Zealand companies is that fewer offer international trips than their North American or European counterparts. This might be due to the high cost of international travel from New Zealand, or to the (past) existence of a largely captive market for domestic New Zealand (and Australian) clients.

NZDOC maintains statistics on visitors staying in some of its huts, so it is possible to compare the number of commercial clients with the total number of

**Table 15.7.** Mountaineering adventure tour operators in New Zealand.

| | Instruction | Guiding | Expedition logistics | Domestic | International | Certification | Environment |
|---|---|---|---|---|---|---|---|
| Alpine Guides New Zealand | Yes | Yes | Yes | Yes | No | NZMGA | ** |
| Alpine Recreation | Yes | Yes | No | Yes | No | NZMGA, IFMGA | * |
| Alpinism and Ski | Yes | Yes | No | Yes | No | IFMGA | * |
| New Zealand Snow Safety Institute | Yes | No | No | Yes | No | – | |
| Summits Etc | Yes | Yes | Yes | Yes | Yes | NZMGA | |
| Wild Walks | Yes | Yes | No | Yes | No | IFMGA | *** |
| Australian School of Mountaineering (Australia) | Yes | Yes | No | Yes | Yes | | ** |

recreational visitors. Data for huts in Aoraki/Mt Cook National Park are summarized in Fig. 15.1.

Guided climbing clients make up little more than one-third of total visitors. The proportion of climbers who are on guided tours is higher than these figures might indicate, however, because hikers are also included in hut use figures.

## North America

Mountaineering adventure tourism in North America has several distinct characteristics: large mountainous regions close to large population centres; well-developed transport infrastructure and emergency facilities; an affluent society where many people have time and money; and a culture that embraces the achievements and experiences gained through mountaineering. These characteristics allow mountaineering operators to provide services such as mountaineering skill courses, as well as guiding experiences, and many local companies based near significant peaks do indeed offer instruction in techniques as well as guided

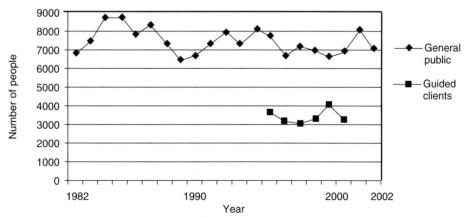

**Fig. 15.1.** Hut usage in Aoraki/Mt Cook National Park, New Zealand. Source: New Zealand Department of Conservation (2004).

**Table 15.8.** Mountaineering adventure tour operators in North America.

| | Country | Instruction | Guiding | International | Certification | Environment |
|---|---|---|---|---|---|---|
| Alaska Mountain Guides | USA | Yes | Yes | Yes | | **** |
| Alaska Mountaineering School | USA | Yes | Yes | Yes | | ** |
| Alpineadventures | USA | Yes | Yes | No | | *** |
| Alpine Ascents International | USA | Yes | Yes | Yes | AMGA | **** |
| Alpine Skills International | USA | Yes | Yes | No | AMGA | |
| American Alpine Institute | USA | Yes | Yes | Yes | AMGA | **** |
| Bob Culp Climbing School | USA | Yes | Yes | Yes | AMGA | |
| Chauvin Guides International | USA | Yes | Yes | No | AMGA | |
| Colorado Mountain School | USA | Yes | Yes | Yes | AMGA | |
| Cosley and Houston Alpine Guides | USA | No | Yes | Yes | AMGA, ACMG | |
| Earth Treks | USA | Yes | Yes | Yes | AMGA | |
| Eastern Mountain Sports | USA | Yes | Yes | Yes | AMGA | |
| Exum Mountain Guides | USA | Yes | Yes | Yes | AMGA | |
| Hood Mountain Adventures | USA | No | Yes | Yes | | |
| International Mountain School | USA | No | Yes | Yes | AMGA | |
| Jackson Hole Mountain Guides and Climbing School | USA | Yes | Yes | Yes | AMGA | *** |
| Mount Rainier Alpine Guides | USA | No | Yes | No | AMGA[a] | |
| Mountain Experience | USA | No | Yes | Yes | AMGA[a] | |
| Mountain Madness | USA | Yes | Yes | Yes | AMGA | **** |
| Mountain Trip Alaska | USA | No | Yes | Yes | AMGA[a] | |
| Pike Peak Alpine School | USA | Yes | Yes | No | AMGA[a] | |
| Rainier Mountaineering | USA | Yes | Yes | Yes | AMGA[a] | *** |
| Rhinoceros Mountain Guides | USA | No | Yes | Yes | | |
| Shasta Mountain Guides | USA | Yes | Yes | No | AMGA[a] | **** |
| Sierra Mountain Centre | USA | Yes | Yes | No | AMGA[a] | **** |
| Sierra Mountain Guides | USA | Yes | Yes | No | AMGA[a] | |
| Sierra Wilderness Seminars | USA | Yes | Yes | Yes | AMGA[a] | *** |
| South West Adventure Guides | USA | Yes | Yes | Yes | AMGA[a] | |
| St Elias Alpine Guides | USA | No | Yes | No | AMGA[a] | **** |
| Summit Expeditions International | USA | Yes | Yes | Yes | AMGA[a] | |
| The Mountain Guide Alliance | USA | No | Yes | Yes | AMGA[a] | |
| The North West Mountain School | USA | Yes | Yes | Yes | AMGA[a] | *** |
| Timberline Mountain Guides | USA | Yes | Yes | Yes | AMGA | |
| Canada West Mountain School | Canada | Yes | Yes | Yes | ACMG | |
| OnTop | Canada | Yes | Yes | Yes | IFMGA | |
| Slip Stream | Canada | Yes | Yes | Yes | | *** |
| West Coast Mountain Guides | Canada | Yes | Yes | No | ACMG, AMGA | |
| Yamnuska | Canada | Yes | Yes | Yes | Unsure | |

Notes: AMGA: American Mountain Guides Association. ACMG: Association of Canadian Mountain Guides. [a]Unsure if all individual guides are AMGA qualified.

ascents. Most of the trips in Canada and the Lower 48 States of the USA can be experienced within a short time-frame, but climbing in Alaska, the Northern Canadian Rockies and Mexico needs more time for acclimatization, logistics and travel.

Many of these companies were started well before 1990, and benefited from the rise in participation rates in the early 1990s. Information on the number of mountaineering participants for this region is limited, but Roper ASW (2003) estimates that 8.8 million people engaged in rock climbing in the USA in the year prior to June 2003. This is 3% of the total population of the USA. This proportion has not changed significantly since outdoor recreation surveys were first started in 1994. Although rock climbing is not the same as mountaineering, a small percentage of rock climbers do also participate in some form of mountaineering. Rock climbers are also one of the main target markets for mountaineering operators, as is indicated by the large number of mountaineering advertisements in climbing magazines such as *Rock and Ice* and *Climbing*. These mountaineering operators offer courses and guided experiences to provide the mountaineering skills and judgement commonly lacking in inexperienced aspirant mountaineers.

Relatively few of the companies listed in Table 15.8 advertise their environmental management practices. Those that do, however, seem to treat it seriously, claiming contributions to communities and conservation as well as measures to minimize impacts.

As one example of recent trends in mountaineering, Fig. 15.2 shows increases in the numbers of climbers attempting peaks in Denali National Park, USA, from 1979 to 2004. Denali is the original name of the mountain otherwise known as Mt McKinley in Alaska. It is a popular destination for mountaineers from all over the world. The higher altitude sections are not technically difficult, though weather conditions can be severe. The ascent is challenging but achievable for a wide range of mountaineers.

There was a marked increase in the number of climbers in the late 1980s, in line with the generally increased popularity of mountaineering during that period. Summit attempts were also frequent before that period, however, and have remained popular subsequently.

## Great Britain

Despite the relatively low mountains, mountaineering is very popular in Great Britain and there are numerous mountain guiding companies (Table 15.9). The

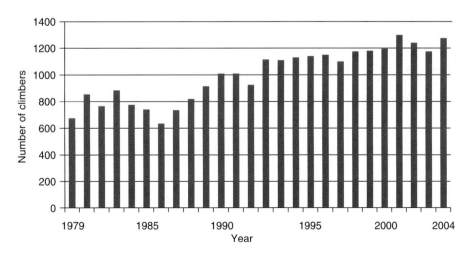

**Fig. 15.2.** Numbers of climbers in Denali National Park, Alaska, 1979–2004. Source: US National Park Service (2005).

**Table 15.9.** Mountaineering adventure tour operators in Great Britain.

| | Country | Instruction | Guiding | Expedition logistics | Domestic | International | Certification | Environment |
|---|---|---|---|---|---|---|---|---|
| Adventure Expeditions | UK | Yes | No | No | Yes | No | | |
| Alpineadventures | UK | Yes | Yes | No | Yes | Yes | IFMGA[a] | |
| Capricorn Mountaineering | UK | Yes | Yes | No | Yes | No | | |
| Ecosse Mountains | UK | Yes | Yes | No | Yes | Yes | AMI | |
| Graham McMahon | UK | Yes | Yes | No | Yes | Yes | IFMGA | |
| Guiding Light Mountain Guides | UK | Yes | Yes | Yes | No | Yes | | |
| Harold Edwards Mountaineering | UK | Yes | Yes | Yes | Yes | Yes | IFMGA | |
| Icicle Mountaineering | UK | Yes | Yes | Yes | Yes | Yes | IFMGA | |
| Martin Moran Mountaineering | UK | Yes | Yes | Yes | Yes | Yes | BMGA | |
| Mountain Dream | UK | No | Yes | Yes | No | Yes | | ** |
| Mountain Tracks | UK | Yes | Yes | Yes | No | Yes | IFMGA | |
| Neil Hitchings Mountain Guide | UK | Yes | Yes | No | Yes | Yes | IFMGA | |
| Rock and Ice | UK | Yes | Yes | No | Yes | No | | |
| Cirrus Outdoors | Wales | Yes | Yes | No | Yes | No | | |
| Dragon Mountain Skils | Wales | Yes | No | No | Yes | No | AMI | |
| Rob Collister | Wales | No | Yes | No | Yes | Yes | IFMGA | |
| Bob Barton Mountain Guide | Scotland | No | Yes | No | Yes | Yes | IFMGA | |
| Glenmore Lodge | Scotland | Yes | Yes | No | Yes | No | IFMGA[a] | *** |
| Mountain Options | Scotland | Yes | Yes | No | Yes | Yes | IFMGA? | |
| Stuart Johnston Mountaineering | Scotland | Yes | Yes | No | Yes | No | | |
| Team Ascent | Scotland | Yes | Yes | No | Yes | Yes | IFMGA | |

Notes: AMI: Association of Mountain Instructors. BMGA: British Mountain Guides Association. [a]Unsure if all guides are IFMGA qualified.

mountains are only snow-covered in winter, so in summer these companies offer rock climbing courses, other outdoor activities or trips to climb overseas. Indeed, some former UK companies have now moved their operations to the Alps. Companies based in Great Britain commonly offer climbing instruction, local guided climbs in the UK and a series of progressively harder trips overseas. Companies that operate internationally have IFMGA-certified guides, whereas those operating only in the United Kingdom are generally certified only with the AMI or BMGA. According to the Mintel Report (2002) and the British Mountaineering Council (2005), there are around 1.25 million active climbers in the UK, with a large increase over the previous decade. Clearly, therefore, there is a large potential clientele for international mountaineering tours. Indeed, two-thirds of the operators listed in Table 15.9 offer overseas climbing trips.

## The Everest Phenomenon and the Seven Summits Quest

The influence of Dick Bass and his friend Frank Wells on the increasing popularity of mountaineering and mountaineering guiding should not be underestimated. Their achievement heralded the start of the modern mountaineering guiding era because they proved that with assistance from experienced guides, 50-year-olds with no previous experience and only average fitness could climb the major summits of the world. In addition, their story linked their achievements in mountaineering to their personal and business goals and capabilities, which led people to see a broader purpose to mountaineering. Shrewd marketing by adventure companies has capitalized on this. Their achievement had such strong influence on the mountaineering sector that it is worth quoting at length from the book *Seven Summits* (Bass *et al.*, 1987).

Their goal was to climb the highest mountain on each of the seven continents. It was an imposing list: Aconcagua in South America, Everest in Asia, McKinley in North America, Kilimanjaro in Africa, Elbrus in Europe, Vinson in Antarctica, Kosciusko in Australia.

Everest would be the most difficult because of the extreme altitude, over 29,000 feet. Vinson would be the greatest logistical challenge because of its location deep in the interior of frozen Antarctica. But the other peaks were not to be discounted. McKinley, for example, at over 20,000 feet and close to the Arctic Circle, has some of the most severe weather on earth.

No one had ever scaled all seven summits. To do so would be an accomplishment coveted by the world's best mountaineers. Thus it was even more improbable that Frank Wells and Dick Bass proposed to try it, both of them having so little climbing experience they could hardly be ranked amateur, much less world-class. And if that wasn't enough, Frank was a few months from his 50th birthday, and Dick had already reached 51.

What made them think they had a chance? Part of it was naivety: they knew so little about high altitude mountaineering that they didn't realize just how preposterous their proposal was. But part was also their strong conviction that with enough hard work and perseverance they could accomplish anything they set their minds to. It was a conviction that for both of them had led to successful business careers: Frank was the president of Warner Brothers Studios, Dick an entrepreneur with an oil business in Texas, a ski resort in Utah, and coal interests in Alaska. They figured that if it worked in business, why not in mountain climbing.

So with the attitude that anything is possible, the two set out to accomplish the impossible. But why? Why risk their lives on the frozen, barren slopes of the world's most remote mountains? Especially when both could justifiably take pride and pleasure in their success in the business world? When they first started their adventure, Frank and Dick weren't that sure themselves. By the time they had finished their Seven Summit odyssey, however, they had no doubt. They were so charged from their experiences they were eager to share them with anyone willing to listen.

Dick told his friends how in his business it often took years before he could enjoy the successful completion of a project. 'Look at my Snowbird Ski Resort. I've been in it fourteen years, and I've got at least that many more before I see it reach its manifest destiny. And when you're involved in long-term projects, sometimes you feel you're on a treadmill in a dark tunnel and you don't know when you're ever going to break out into the sunlight.'

'With mountain climbing, I've discovered a tangible, short-term goal. It's me and the mountain, and that's it. There are no bankers or regulatory officials telling me what I can and can't do. It's just me and my own two feet, my own physical strength and my own mental resolve. At the same time it's only rewarding if the mountain is a real one. Podunk hills don't count. I'm trying to make up for the frustration I face in the lowlands, and to do that I've got to have a challenge, something to gut up for, something that forces me to strain. There has to be a spirit of adventure to it, too, and an element of uncertainty and risk. Then when I persevere and prevail, when I overcome and make it, I come back down to the lowlands, back to the bankers and the regulatory officials, and by golly I'm recharged and ready to take them all on.'

Today there are numerous websites that herald the achievements of participants in the quest for the Seven Summits. So far there are 95 people who have summited the highest peaks on all seven continents. This number is quite small compared to other adventure tourism participation rates. However, the iconic nature of this quest also inspires many others to attempt peaks of all shapes and sizes. Additionally, the popularity of Mt Everest is partly due to the fact that these previously inexperienced individuals have achieved success on the highest mountain of the world as part of their Seven Summits quest.

Everest has become an extremely popular mountaineering destination. At the end of 2004 the total number of people who had successfully summited Mt Everest was 2249. Figure 15.3 shows the historical record of ascents on Mt Everest since the first climb by Sir Edmund Hillary and Tenzing Norgay in 1953.

The small rise in successful ascents from 1973 to 1986 may be attributed to: increased access to the southern side of the mountain; improvements in technology; lower costs; and media coverage of significant mountaineering achievements. These included the first ascent by a woman, Junko Tabei from Japan who reached the summit in 1975, and the first oxygen-less ascent of the peak in 1978 by Reinhold Messner and Peter Habler.

The largest increase occurred after Dick Bass and his team made the first guided ascent of the peak in 1985. The continued increase in the number of climbers can be attributed directly to the success of guided climbing. This trend has been maintained even though substantial increases in the peak fees charged by the Government of Nepal have priced out most climbers.

The much publicized accident in 1996, where many clients and guides lost their lives, has not discouraged potential customers. In fact, the two companies involved, Mountain Madness from the USA and Adventure Consultants from New Zealand, have increased business after this incident. The notion of safety in the mountains, whilst being paramount to both the participants and guides, is characterized as an inherent aspect of mountaineering. Risk is an inherent part of the business.

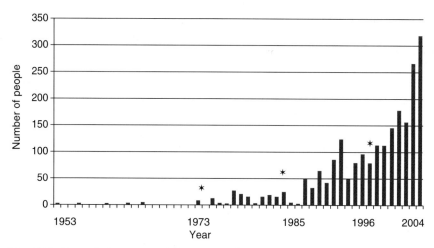

**Fig. 15.3.** Recorded ascents of Mt Everest. Source: Hawley and Salisbury (2004).
*, key dates mentioned in text.

## Popularity of Mountaineering Adventure Tourism

There are three main reasons why mountaineering adventure tourism has become so popular. Broadly, these are: the democratization of leisure opportunities; improvements in technology and know-how; and the embodiment of leisure in personal identity.

Most mountaineers have relatively high disposable income and few commitments, i.e. they are largely from developed nations. Access to cheap international air travel over recent decades has provided more leisure opportunities for more people. This process has been referred to as democratization of the leisure and tourism market (Gartner and Lime, 2000; Bourdeau *et al.*, 2002). This is an ambiguous term that may be construed in a political as well as an economic or structural sense. Local communities in the relatively impoverished and politically tumultuous nation of Nepal may question whether the increasing numbers of tourists in their mountains play any significant role in their process of democratization.

The increasing popularity of climbing and mountaineering has led to many new developments in equipment, and mountaineering adventure tourism has benefited as a result. There have also been advances in know-how, e.g. in relation to avalanche safety, physiological effects of altitude and rope-work techniques.

As leisure opportunities increase and technologies and knowledge improve, more people want to climb directly at icon sites without an apprenticeship in mountaineering skills. Many people think they can substitute technology for experience and do not want to learn the ropes (Ewert, 2000). This creates problems for both land managers and commercial guides. For land managers the critical issue is that many people climbing in high-risk areas simply do not have the requisite skills and hence place themselves and others in danger. As a result, land managers such as the US National Park Service at Denali have introduced screening and education programmes to filter out mountaineers who overrate their capacities.

Guides must be aware that many clients overestimate their own abilities, in mountaineering as in many other adventure activities. Guiding companies have responded by offering efficient training packages to school clients in mountaineering techniques before they enrol for expedition-style trips. These training opportunities may be sold separately or jointly, but must be advertised in such a way as to attract customers who in their own minds are already competent climbers. To ensure the safety of guides and clients, commercial operators must therefore understand the psychology of their clients before their expeditions commence, not only on the mountain itself.

A different aspect of human psychology is used to promote mountaineering adventure tours to an increasingly broad clientele. People's own perceptions of themselves include success in leisure as well as work, family and other aspects of their lives. Mountaineering adventure tours provide an opportunity for people to become mountaineers and to succeed in summit ascents without the long apprenticeship needed historically. The choice of activity is linked to the search for identity. Tour operators foster this link by incorporating legendary features of mountaineering history, and sometimes also contemporary climbing icons, in their marketing material. Effectively the marketing of mountaineering links the literal meaning of 'getting to the top' with its social meaning.

## Safety in Mountaineering Adventure Tourism

Although risk and uncertainty are important elements in the mountaineering experience, the purpose of the activity is to stay in control, climb high and come home. However, objective dangers in mountaineering necessitate good judgement about situations that are difficult for participants and guides to predict, in order for them to stay in control of such situations. Even though technology and mountaineering know-how has increased, the ability to make judgements about local conditions, the requirements of the climb and the ability of participants is still a difficult task for the guide. A critical question for adventure tourism operators is how to keep such risks in balance.

The levels of risk accepted by mountaineers are different to those in many other forms of outdoor recreation. Some mountaineers rationalize this risk by claiming, for example, that climbing is less risky than driving a car. In reality, however, this belief seems incorrect. British mountaineer Doug Scott has apparently stated that he knows far more people who died from climbing than from driving (Anderson, 2000). Several noted mountaineers have also stated that they personally know many people who died through mountaineering accidents: Mark Twight, 49; Steph Davis, eight; and Joe Simpson, one every year (Coffey, 2003). Such quotes do not take the place of formal accident statistics calculated as, e.g. deaths per thousand participant hours, but they do indicate that mountaineering, at least at the expert level, is indeed a high-risk activity.

Most mountaineering accidents and deaths involve either: (i) misjudgements about objective elements of the environment, such as avalanches, rockfall or altitude complications; or (ii) individual mistakes, such as falling. Guides can reduce risk through: their own training and experience; local knowledge of the site; and skills in understanding client ability and psychology. Even with these skills, it requires continual good judgement to provide clients with a safe, successful and enjoyable experience in a constantly changing physical environment.

Risks in mountaineering adventure tourism vary with the region and altitude, the type of climbing, and the expectations of the guides and clients. Both the likelihood and severity of potential events vary widely.

The risk of fatalities depends more on altitude, weather extremes and remoteness than on the technical difficulty of the climbs. In Aoraki/Mt Cook National Park, New Zealand, there have been proportionally more deaths on the higher and more committing peaks than on lower and less committing peaks (Malcolm, 2001). Death rates on the higher NZ peaks are similar to those in the Himalaya. Judgements made by guides in remote, high-altitude areas are hence more critical for safety that at lower-altitude sites.

Inexperienced mountaineers may not assess risks accurately, since they are likely to be influenced more by mass-media reports of mountaineering accidents than by their own experience. In other high-risk recreational activities, it appears that inexperienced participants focused on the expected emotional rewards and in the process underestimated the associated risks (Creves, personal communication, 2003). Mountaineering clients are thus encouraged, rather than dissuaded, by mass-media reports of mountaineering accidents, since these commonly convey the rewards as well as the risks.

In recent years, the number of clients for commercial mountaineering trips has increased, and their average experience has perhaps decreased. The number of accidents has increased in proportion to total participant numbers, but the accident rate does not seem to have increased. In the European Alps, Lischke *et al.* (2001) found that the number of accidents and rescue missions had increased over preceding years, but the number of deaths had not. The British Mountaineering Council (2005) reports similar results. There are two possible reasons for these patterns. Either climbers have grown better at avoiding life-threatening accidents; or rescue and emergency services have grown better at keeping injured climbers alive. In either case, the improved statistics are helpful to mountaineering adventure tourism operators.

The inherent risks in mountaineering provide a major drawcard for climbers and commercial clients, but a potential nemesis for adventure tour operators. The ways in which each company negotiates the real risks in commercial mountaineering will continue to be a critical and confronting aspect of their business operations.

The relationship between guides and clients in commercial mountaineering adventure tours must necessarily continue to acknowledge the inherent risks in climbing and mountaineering, even embracing the technological and social changes outlined above. Clients do indeed seem to appreciate these issues. The two companies involved in the 1996 Mount Everest tragedy, for example, are still operating successfully. Perhaps more so than for many other types of adventure tourism, in mountaineering the expectations of business have had to adapt to the serious literal meaning of adventure.

## Chamonix, France: Evolution 2

### Place

Chamonix is one of the major centres of guided mountaineering in the European Alps, and is reputed to be the birthplace of mountaineering. The town is situated on the northern boundary of the European Alps, and is thus close to Paris and the UK. Chamonix affords easy access to many high mountains including Mt Blanc, the highest mountain in Western Europe. The area is noted for alpinism and is also a premier ski destination. The region thus has a year-round tourism season that takes advantage of all its natural features.

### Operator

Evolution 2 (2005) has a number of adventure tourism operations throughout France. Guided mountaineering is its mainstay, but it also offers skiing, snowboarding, rafting, hiking and treks to Nepal. The Chamonix operation has been operating since 1987, and in 1997 diversified the range and locations offered.

### Activity

The starting point for most tours is the town of Chamonix. From the town centre it is a short distance via road to the trip starting points. Many of the mountaineering trips are accessed via cable car. This makes it easier to ascend the peaks, by decreasing the approach times to the base of the technical climbing sections. Trips include tailored climbs on a number of notable routes, standard guided climbs of Mt Blanc, hikes and glacial walks including the so-called Haute Route. Also offered are instructional courses in rock and ice climbing, mountaineering, and avalanche safety and rescue.

Mt Blanc is commonly climbed guided using one of two routes, the Aiguille du Gouter or the Aiguille du Midi. There is a cable car to Aiguille du Midi, and climbers need climb only the last 970 m to gain the summit. On the Aiguille du Gouter route, clients start at the bottom of the valley and descend again after the climb. The first day of the trip is spent in preparation for the climb, including training in technique. The following 2 days are allowed for climbing the mountain.

## Equipment

Standard mountaineering equipment is available to clients as part of the package. This includes boots, ropes, harnesses and ice axes. Clothing and other personal gear can be hired for additional charges.

## Accommodation

Ascending via the Aiguille du Gouter allows clients to stay overnight at the Gouter refuge, which provides beds and basic services similar to a small hostel, including cooked meals. This is included in the Evolution 2 package. Accommodation on the first night, however, is in Chamonix at the clients' choice and expense. Accommodation options and rates in Chamonix are as might be expected for a ski resort in summer in France.

## Statistics

The client-to-guide ratio during ascents is 2:1. For the 3 days needed to climb Mt Blanc, Evolution 2 charges €980 per person (US$1150). The cost of accommodation in Chamonix, from UKP37 (US$65) and upward, is additional. Realistically, a minimum of 3 nights' accommodation is required, bringing the total cost to at least US$450 per person per day.

## Access

Chamonix is 612 km by road from Paris. Once in Chamonix, the routes start literally from the town centre. Hut booking is handled by the company. No permits are needed to climb the mountain.

## Community

Mountain experiences have played a large part in shaping the community of Chamonix. Since the 1940s the population has doubled to well over 10,000. This increase has seen mixed outcomes in terms of economic development and sustainability. Economic development can largely be attributed to the development of the ski industry. Development of the ski fields has meant that skiing now contributes more to the local economy than mountaineering. However, the links between the two activities are stronger here than in most other places, because the steep terrain means that skiing in the valley takes on objective risks normally associated with mountaineering. The tradition of people and adventure in the mountains is strong.

The Chamonix Alpine Museum, for example, is dedicated to documenting the history of the mountain experience and the natural history of the mountains of the Chamonix region.

## Experience

The prerequisite experience needed to climb Mt Blanc is minimal. More important is physical fitness. The route is not technical, i.e. it is not so steep that specific mountaineering techniques need to be honed before attempting the peak. The peak has regular ski descents. In many respects climbing Mt Blanc is easier than climbing most other similar-size peaks at similar latitudes because the refuges supply catering, which decreases the weight that clients and guides need to carry in their packs. Nevertheless, the high altitude does make this peak a significant undertaking.

## Environment

Since the majority of mountaineering occurs on snow and ice, minimizing impacts seems to be of lesser concern than safety of clients.

## Safety

Good preparation is critical to safety in mountaineering. Evolution 2 screens its clients for fitness and provides briefing documents. Its guides are locals with excellent knowledge of weather and route conditions. They are certified through the French national scheme rather than IFMGA, putting local knowledge above international recognition. Once a trip commences, the company refuses to issue refunds if the trip is aborted through bad weather. This policy places guides under considerable pressure to make advance judgements on likely weather conditions.

## Marketing

Evolution 2 (2005) is a relatively large and diverse ski and mountaineering operator, based in Chamonix, but with branches elsewhere. The website provides detailed information on specific trips. They are also well-known within the local Chamonix ski and climbing community. The company's ski school has received awards for excellence, which also helps marketing.

## Trekking Peaks in the Khumbu Valley, Nepal: World Expeditions

### Place

The Khumbu is the name of the region on the Nepalese side of Mt Everest. At the base of Mt Everest there are a number of smaller 6000 m peaks that provide challenging Himalayan climbs and outstanding views of the larger peaks. Since Nepal was opened to foreigners in the 1950s, there has been a steady growth in infrastructure for large climbing expeditions such as Everest ascents. This includes heavily used trekking routes up the Khumbu Valley, well-supplied with food and accommodation in the form of local tea houses or guesthouses. As a result, climbers can now reach the base of these lower peaks with far less difficulty than formerly.

This has led to a secondary climbing industry where climbers aim not at the principal peaks such as Mt Everest itself, but the so-called trekking peaks where altitudes and permit fees are less extreme.

The preferred seasons for climbing are the periods between the monsoon and midwinter: either March to May or October to November. The pre-monsoon period in March to May has the advantage that the snow is more compacted than post-monsoon. This can be a very significant consideration for climbers plugging knee-deep steps up a slope at 6000 m where there is 50% less available oxygen.

## Operator

World Expeditions advertises itself as one of the world's oldest adventure travel companies. Originally formed as Australian Himalayan Expeditions in 1975, the company has developed into one of the world's leading exponents in adventure tourism. The headquarters are in Australia, but the company has branches worldwide. Their products are offered on all continents, and include adventure touring, trekking, cycling, seakayaking and mountaineering. On the mountaineering trips, the guides come from Western backgrounds.

In this case study I have profiled a World Expeditions trip to a number of trekking peaks in Nepal. Whilst I have not joined their tour, I have co-guided a trip that had an almost identical itinerary, when I owned my own mountaineering company. This profile is based on a combination of my own experience, and materials produced by World Expeditions.

## Activity

World Expeditions (2005a) offer a package where climbers can attempt three trekking peaks in the Khumbu Valley. The peaks are Lobuche, Imja Tse (Island Peak) and Pokalde. This type of package maximizes the time spent climbing after the slow process of acclimatization during the approach. It also offers more chances to summit, in case clients become sick or do not acclimatize in time. A number of other companies offer similar style packages in this region and other parts of Nepal.

The trip starts in Kathmandu. A short plane flight brings guides and clients to the steep runway of Lukla. From here the trek goes through the town of Namche Bazar and then to Gokyo Lakes for the views of Mt Everest and acclimatization. Whilst crossing Cho La pass to Lobuche Base Camp some technical training is undertaken on the glacier. The climb ascends the south ridge to a high snow camp where clients gain commanding views of Everest and are ideally placed to climb to the summit the following morning.

Following the ascent of Lobuche, the trip then continues to Island Peak (Imja Tse) and Pokalde. The success rate of summiting these two peaks are higher because these peaks are not as difficult as Lobuche and further acclimatization has occurred as a result of attempting Lobuche. The weather is generally fine during the climbing season. On one similar trip which I was guiding, however, a storm dumped 50 cm of new snow in 24 h, so the routes that I was to guide on were out of condition for the remainder of our tour.

## Equipment

Most equipment is supplied by World Expeditions. The following items are provided: group medical kit; a portable emergency altitude chamber; individual trek packs including sleeping bag, down- or fibre-filled jacket, and insulated mat; and individual climbing packs including ice axe, crampons and harness. Porters are employed to carry all personal and group equipment.

Individual items such as mountaineering boots, sunglasses, gloves and similar personal items of clothing are the responsibility of clients. These items can be bought or hired at relatively cheap rates in Kathmandu.

## Accommodation

Accommodation at the start and end of the trip in Kathmandu is part of the World Expeditions package. On the trekking and climbing portions of the trip, clients use tents supplied by the company. However, when staying near local teahouses, the group camps in the grounds of the teahouse so that clients can use the dining room at meal times, and also the bathroom facilities. The standard of the guesthouse depends on their remoteness. Teahouses at higher altitudes cost more to run and have harsher conditions to deal with, so the aesthetic appeal of the establishments decreases with altitude. However, the spectacular views at higher altitudes provide more than adequate compensation.

## Statistics

In 2005 the package costs AUD4900 (US$3675) per person. This includes: airport transfers in Kathmandu; flights between Kathmandu and Lukla; an expatriate climbing guide; all meals whilst on the tour; and the equipment as listed above.

## Access

The climbs start at Lobuche Base Camp, reached by trekking from Lukla via Namche Bazar. Lukla is reached by plane from Kathmandu, which is an international airport accessible directly from Europe, India or South-East Asian cities.

Trekking peak fees apply to groups attempting these peaks. These fees are included in the package cost. These fees are: US$350 for groups with 1–4 members; US$350 plus US$40 per person for groups with 5–8 members; and US$510 plus US$25 per person for groups with 9–12 members. The maximum number of members permitted in one group is 12.

In addition to these fees, there is the Sagamartha National Park Entrance fee. At the time of writing this was US$9.30 per person. Charges levied by local teahouses for the right to camp on their grounds and use their facilities are also included in the package price.

## Community

The link between tourism and community development is strong in many regions of Nepal. The total number of international tourists visiting Nepal collapsed from a high of 500,000 in 1998 to under 200,000 in 2002, but recovered slightly to 258,000 in

2004. Internal civil unrest, as well as a downturn in the international tourism sector, has been the blamed for the slump. The recovery has been welcomed in the Khumbu region, where tourism is the major economic sector.

The Khumbu Valley has fared much better in terms of economic development than surrounding valleys. The popularity of this valley, as the principal route to Mt Everest, has generated social and economic prosperity for the Sherpa people who live there. The Sherpas have lived in the Khumbu for more than 500 years, farming the terraced slopes and herding yaks in the higher pastures in summer.

Communities in the Khumbu have changed greatly as a result of tourism. People rely more and more on the cash economy created by trekkers and climbers. Many young men, and some women, have become climbing and trekking guides as well as porters. This means they are away from their families and farming responsibilities for much of the year. As a result, less land is being used for farming than in the past. In addition, if local guides or porters are injured or killed on climbing trips, their families may be left without a primary income source. The effects of this are severe if the family does not have life insurance or other insurance to cover loss of earnings.

To address these issues, World Expeditions has adopted a Porter Protection policy that aims to ensure the safety and welfare of its porters. The company supports the International Porter Protection Group (IPPG), which urges companies to adopt insurance and appropriate working conditions for porters. World Expeditions also supports the Himalayan Trust, a fund that aims to improve school and medical facilities for the Sherpa people of the Everest region.

## Experience

What people get out of any adventure tour depends on the prior skills and experience of individuals, inter-group dynamics, and the skills and personalities of the guides, as well as local environmental conditions. In a mountain environment where there are definite objectives and schedules, the chance that difficulties or disagreements may arise is high. To minimize such risks, individuals need to be well prepared both in physical fitness and in appropriate expectations. As noted on the World Expeditions (2005a) website, its trips may involve trekking on remote trails in variable weather conditions for up to 8 h a day.

> This may include spending successive days at altitudes not generally exceeding 5,500m. These treks may often be over three weeks in duration. You will need an excellent level of fitness, be prepared to carry a daypack weighing up to 8kg and be completely comfortable in adverse weather conditions. Suggested preparation: One hour of aerobic type exercise, four to five times a week for three to six months before your trek. Hill walking with a pack in variable weather conditions is also recommended.
>
> (World Expeditions, 2005a)

## Environment

World Expeditions claims to have earned its reputation through: the unique experiences it provides, its environmental philosophy of minimal impact travel and the community contributions it makes. As detailed above, at a local level these claims do seem well founded. For example, World Expeditions' practices of using tents for their clients even if staying in villages, and using kerosene stoves for cooking, decrease consumption of fuelwood in the park. The instigation and impetus for much of the environmental and community work can be credited to the guides themselves.

There may, however, be some exaggeration in the company's claims of 'true sustainability in all of our business planning and operations' and 'minimal environmental impact at all stages of the business' (World Expeditions, 2005a). If all aspects were addressed, then measures to offset greenhouse gas emissions from clients and guides travelling across the world would be needed, as well as measures to minimize impacts of local tour activities (Simmons and Becken, 2004). This issue, of course, applies not only to this particular company, but to the tourism industry as a whole.

## Safety

The commercial routes on the trekking peaks of Nepal pose only moderate risks in mountaineering terms. They do not have the risks associated with high altitude mountaineering in the same region. Safety has also improved somewhat through the routine use of satellite phones, and the installation of ground telephone lines, though ground telephone installations are often a target for civil insurgents.

The two greatest risks for guided climbs of the Khumbu trekking peaks are first, inadequate acclimatization; and secondly, slips and falls on relatively easy ground. Although appropriate acclimatization schedules are followed, there is always a chance that an individual will not conform to physiological norms, or that they will not be honest about their own condition. This can lead to serious complications. As a back-up, therefore, the group carries a Gamov Bag. This bag allows the person who is inside it to experience the higher pressure of lower altitudes, created by a foot pump apparatus outside the bag.

## Marketing

World Expeditions promote their Lobuche–Island Peak trip as one of the most challenging 'trekkers' peaks' trips in the Everest region, and one that is more demanding technically, and requires greater commitment and climbing expertise, than other more commonly guided peaks in the Himalayas. They also state that on some sections of the climb, clients will get superb views of Mt Everest.

The features that distinguish this company from others offering similar trips are: its endorsement by conservation groups; its extra financial contributions to local communities; its minimal-impact philosophies and practices; and its promotion of responsible-travel philosophies and practices to its clients. The company also has highly experienced guides who lead its mountaineering trips in the Himalayas.

This particular trip provides excellent value for money, with a well-constructed itinerary and the extra cultural dimensions of the Khumbu Valley.

# 16 Hiking and Bushwalking

View from Annapurna Circuit, Nepal. Photo Ralf Buckley.

Campsite in Pacific Northwest, USA. Photo Ralf Buckley.

## Sector Structure

Travelling on foot through the backcountry carrying all one's own supplies and equipment is a popular recreational activity in many developed nations. It is variously known, in different countries, as hiking, bushwalking, tramping, trekking or simply walking; and it may take hours, days or weeks, on or off trail. In sparsely populated areas in some developing nations, travelling by foot with one's own supplies and possessions is simply part of a normal daily livelihood. In other areas, locals can now make a living guiding or otherwise assisting foreign hikers.

The practice of hiring a guide while travelling on foot in an unfamiliar area has a long tradition, whether for navigation, local customs and culture, language and livelihood, or safety and security. The practice of using local porters to carry supplies and equipment also has a long history in international explorations and expeditions, whether climbing mountain peaks or searching for the source of remote rivers. Porters are still routinely used for climbing, trekking and river trips in many areas.

The packaging of guided trekking trips as a tourism product, with porters to carry tents and food and cooks to prepare meals, seems to be only a few decades old. Nepal, in particular, became well known as a trekking destination in the 1970s, promoted by companies such as the former Australian Himalayan Expeditions, now World Expeditions (2005b), and others. Subsequently these tour operators diversified into other activities and areas, and at the same time guided trekking or hiking tours in other continents became more popular in the international markets. Guides and porters had been available previously for local hire in many of these areas; what was new was the design and marketing of tours with predefined departure dates and itineraries.

Examples include ascents of Mt Kilimanjaro in Tanzania, and traverses of the Inca Trail in Peru or the Milford Track in New Zealand. These routes were also hiked by independent travellers carrying their own equipment, and this is still the case. Increasingly, however, national and international adventure tourism providers began to offer a broader range of hiking options, from walking safaris in southern Africa to guided hikes up Mt Wilhelm in Papua New Guinea. Most recently, tour operators have successfully sold the advantages of guides and logistic support for walking tours in developed nations. Some of these are off-track in relatively remote and rugged national parks and wilderness areas, such as Australia's Kakadu and Kimberley regions. Others, however, are along heavily used tracks in popular parks, such as parts of the Pacific Northwest in Oregon and Washington State, USA, the Cradle Mountain Track in Tasmania, or the recently constructed Bibbulmun Track in coastal southwest Western Australia.

Another recent innovation is the advent of heli-hiking, where hikers are flown by helicopter from a luxury lodge to a wilderness hiking area for day hikes, and flown back at the end of each day. These are marketed mainly by heliski companies such as Canadian Mountain Holidays (2005), as a way to fill their lodges during summer. The popularity of such products indicates that there is now a significant market sector of well-off clients who are prepared to pay quite heavily to enjoy a few days' hiking in scenic areas, but in luxury. They may be driven by shortage of time; by lack of fitness or strength (e.g. through age or young children); by the desire to avoid discomfort; or by inexperience in backcountry hiking and camping.

Unlike some other adventure activity sectors, there does not seem to be a strong global hiking tour industry in the same sense as, for example, the horse riding or heliski sectors. Perhaps this is because most hikers travel without commercial assistance. Recent market reports by the Sporting Goods Manufacturers Association (SGMA International) (2005), the Outdoor Industry Association (2005), and outdoor equipment and clothing retailers such as Recreational Equipment Inc. (REI) (2005), L.L. Bean (2005) in the USA, and Mountain Equipment Co-op (MEC) (2005) in Canada, indicate that in North America at least, sales of hiking boots, clothing, tents and other equipment continue very strongly.

According to SGMA (2005), for example, sales of camping gear in the USA alone, for the preceding year, totalled US$1.7 billion, of which US$275 million was on tents, US$435 million on hiking boots and US$555 million on walking shoes. These figures compare with US$277 million for skis and US$240 million for dive gear – but over US$2 billion for firearms and hunting. The US *Outdoor Recreation Participation Study* in 2004 found that two-thirds of the US population had taken part in some form of outdoor recreation in 2003, with hiking and backpacking among the most common activities (Outdoor Industry Association, 2005).

It remains to be seen whether, in years to come, hiking and back-country camping will follow other adventure tourism sectors, with unskilled city dwellers purchasing fully guided and catered tour packages rather than acquiring experience and equipment themselves. Currently, there is certainly a commercial hiking tour sector, albeit small relative to private recreational hiking, and some case studies are described below.

## Podocarpus National Park, Ecuador: Surtrek

### Place

Podocarpus National Park is an area of montane forest in southern Ecuador, part of the Andean cordillera. It includes five different major ecosystems, ranging from rainforest in the valleys to low heaths and grasslands above the tree line. It provides habitat for a number of endangered or other icon species, including woolly mountain tapir, spectacled bear, condor and cock-of-the-rock. Whilst lower in elevation than the 5000 m peaks of northern Ecuador, the ridges extend to altitudes around 4000 m, with passes around 3500 m.

### Operator

Multi-day hiking tours in Podocarpus National Park are offered by an Ecuadorian company, Surtrek (2005). Based in Quito, Surtrek offers a portfolio of adventure tours throughout Ecuador, including mountain biking, horse riding, climbing, rafting and diving as well as trekking.

### Activity

Surtrek's hiking tour of Podocarpus National Park is a 4-day guided walk that starts from a roadhead near Cerro Toledo. The first day's hiking takes the group downhill to the village of Esmeralda, walking principally through open pastures along eroded mule trails. The second day continues to a stream known as Las Penas. The third and most interesting day involves a steep hike through forest and up on to alpine grassland with a small lake, Lagunas Margaritas. The trail crosses a pass at 3400 m and descends to Capamaco Refuge for the third night. On the fourth day, the group rides on horseback down a long valley, mainly agricultural, to the township of Vilcabamba, ready to fly out to Loja and Quito the following morning.

## Equipment

According to Surtrek (2005) the trip price now includes use of tents, pack animals and rubber boots, though when I took part in this trek some years ago we had none of these. Clients bring their own clothing and raingear and, presumably, their own hiking boots and sleeping bags.

## Accommodation

The current trip description (Surtrek, 2005) says that accommodation at Esmeralda and Las Penas, on the first and second day, is in tents carried by pack mules; on the third day it is at Capamaco Refuge, and on the fourth and final night, at the Hostel Madre Tierra Spa Lodge in Vilcabamba, all included. When I took part, however, we stayed in a small farmer's cottage on the first night, a half-collapsed single-room hut on the second and on the veranda of an operating farmhouse on the third. We were scheduled to stay at Capamaco Refuge, but took a different route and missed it. The guide went to retrieve the horses on the fourth day, but I simply walked out rather than wait.

## Statistics

The tour is advertised as a 5-day trip, but the final day is only for flights back to Quito. There are 3.5 days hiking, of which 1.5 days are through areas without any agricultural clearance. The client-to-guide ratio is variable. When I took part I was the only client, so there were three of us in all: the company owner and guide, a friend of his and myself. The current listed price is US$778 (Surtrek, 2005), but this includes return flights from Quito to Loja.

## Access

Access is by air from Quito to Loja and by 4WD vehicle from Loja to Cerro Toledo. Park fees are payable on the spot at the start of the trek.

## Community

Local residents immediately around the national park appear to be principally small-scale or subsistence farmers. On the first day we met mules laden with timber that had been cut from the valley forest, whether inside or outside the park being unclear. The current trek description refers to pack mules to carry tents between Esmeralda and Las Penas, and presumably these are hired locally. Similarly, horses for the final day are probably hired at Vilcabamba, which is a small-scale tourist town on the backpacker circuit. When I took part we stayed 1 night inadvertently in a local farmhouse, eating a late dinner and early breakfast with the family and getting a chance to sample some of their local fruit.

## Experience

When I took part in this trip about a decade ago there was a certain degree of confusion, but it was a very interesting experience none the less. I expect that arrangements are now more routine. Our first night's accommodation was rustic but functional. Our second night was simply a small and leaky lean-to hut roofed with a piece of plastic sheeting. There was strong wind and heavy rain, and emergency repairs were needed. We made a fire on the earthen floor. I slept on a small shelf of sticks over the woodpile, the others on the floor. In the middle of the night the shelf collapsed, leaving me wedged half upright in a pile of sticks, but I was too tired to care. We heard a booming call at night which was apparently a rare animal or perhaps bird. I never did find out. The next day, however, the hike up through the forest and over a roadless pass was spectacularly beautiful and well worth the effort. We swam in the mountain lake amidst drifts of cloud and gleams of sunlight. Staying in the local farmhouse, though unplanned, was also an interesting experience.

## Environment

The trek itself produced minimal impacts. We were hiking along trails, many of them cut down over head height by mules. Only the ascent through the forest and over the pass were along little-used foot trails. The area around the park, however, and perhaps within it – there was no way to identify its borders – was largely or completely cleared for grazing, and this clearance was continuing through timber cutting either for firewood or construction. On the first day we stopped at a farmhouse on the way downhill, and the owner showed us a condor he had recently shot. The area hence suffers significant environmental impacts from local residents. Whether tourism will reduce or increase these impacts it was too soon to say.

## Safety

There were no particular hazards and no particular safety precautions. Without a guide it could well have been difficult to identify access trails, to cross pasturelands, and to navigate through dense forest and over an open pass. Indeed, even the guide mistook the way, though this did not cause any significant problems. We were within a day's hike of habitation and horses at all times, in case anyone had been injured too badly too walk.

## Marketing

The Surtrek (2005) website claims that 'woolly mountain tapir, spectacled bears and cock-of-the-rock … are common', but we saw no trace of any of them, though the hope of seeing such wildlife was the main reason I chose this trek. The website also says that clients will 'encounter harmony and silence … singing birds and the rushing of the rivers'. This was more accurate. It notes that this is a 'moderate' trek, but 'can be very strenuous … cross-country through mud and forest'. This is true.

# Annapurna Trek, Nepal: World Expeditions

## Place

Annapurna is one of the well-known Himalayan peaks in the Gandaki region of central Nepal. At 8078 m elevation, it lies between the Kali Gandaki River to the west and south, and the Marsyangdi to the north and east. The Kali Gandaki is used for commercial rafting, and the Marsyangdi is popular with kayakers. Further west lies Dhaulagiri, further east is Manaslu, north is the Mustang region against the Tibetan border, and south is the town of Pokhara and its lake.

The steeply stepped trail from Pokhara to the mountain villages around Annapurna is heavily used by traders and local traffic, as well as trekkers and other tourists. There are numerous side trails and circuit routes, many used by commercial trekking tour operators. The areas used for trekking include significant stretches of subalpine forest, with pine, fir, rhododendron, oak and bamboo. Many sections have been cut heavily for fuelwood.

The area has been managed very successfully for the past two decades (since 1987) by a specialist NGO, the King Mahendra Trust for Nature Conservation (KMTNC), under the name of the Annapurna Conservation Area Project (ACAP). Additional detail is provided in Buckley (2003a, pp. 70–74). There are numerous villages within ACAP, and several hundred trekking lodges and guesthouses. Until recent political upheavals in Nepal, the area received over 50,000 visitors per year, contributing over US$800,000 per annum in fees in the mid-1990s (Nepal, 2000). KMTNC was renamed in 2006.

## Operator

World Expeditions offers a wide range of multi-day trekking, mountaineering, rafting, cycling and seakayaking trips in many countries worldwide, some led directly by its own guides and others subcontracted to local operators. The company's core expertise is in Himalayan mountaineering and, typically, trekking and mountain trips are led directly by World Expeditions' guides, whereas river and ocean trips involving an expensive specialist equipment inventory are more likely to be subcontracted to local operators. Currently, the company offers several dozen different trekking options and combinations in Nepal.

## Activity

Some years ago I took part in one of World Expeditions' shorter Himalayan treks in the Annapurna region. It was led by a local Sherpa who lived along the trekking route and gave us the unexpected privilege of visiting his home and meeting his family. It was a fully catered trip, with all camping equipment, cooking equipment, fuel and food carried by porters because of concerns over deforestation in areas around village guesthouses. The guide was very conscientious about minimal-impact behaviour. The trip I took part in was the company's most basic introductory trek, and consisted mostly of hiking and looking at the view. The closest equivalent currently on offer is listed as the 'Annapurna Trek' (World Expeditions, 2005b).

## Equipment

World Expeditions supplies tents, backpacks, sleeping mats, sleeping bags, down or fibre parkas, and all cooking gear and cutlery. Most of the gear is carried by porters. Guests carry only their own clothing and personal gear. All necessary equipment that is not supplied by World Expeditions can be hired or purchased in Kathmandu. Care is needed in selecting such items, since many of them are unlikely to be genuine. Even such basic items as wide-mouthed plastic bottles, supposedly manufactured by Nalgene®, turn out on close inspection to be cheap bootlegs. They still hold water, however.

## Accommodation

Except in Kathmandu itself, at the start and end of the trip, all accommodation is in tents. This applies even in Pokhara, where our group stayed in a campground before starting its trek. The tents are carried and put up by porters. The sites chosen for overnight camps are near, but not within, local villages. The trek does not rely on the local guesthouses for its client accommodation, but these lodges are used by the porters – or at least they were during the trip I experienced. Similarly, though all cooking for the clients is done by a cook who hikes with the group, using aluminium utensils carried by himself and his assistant and food carried by the group's porters, the porters themselves do also make use of facilities in local village lodges. From most clients' perspective, camping in a quiet and private site in a clean tent, with a reliable supply of hygienic and slightly Westernized food, is generally preferable to staying in local lodges.

## Statistics

The Annapurna Trek offered by World Expeditions takes 11 days in total, of which 6 days are spent actually trekking. Fifteen departure dates are listed for this trip in 2006. The current price is AUD1490 per person, or about US$110 per person per day.

## Access

The trekking route to Jomson starts from Pokhara, which is reached by air or road from Kathmandu. All trekkers in Nepal require a trekking permit from the Nepali government, available on arrival at the international airport. Visitors to the Annapurna Conservation Area also require a special permit issued by the former KMTNC, which manages the ACA. For commercial tour clients, these permits are generally obtained by the tour operator.

## Community

The complex interactions of social and environmental issues and impacts for commercial trekking tours in the Himalayas are considered in detail for Annapurna, Mustang and Makalu-Barun National Parks by Buckley (2003a, pp. 68–76, 82–84).

On the World Expeditions trek in which I took part, over a decade ago, tent and fuel stoves were carried for the clients, but porters apparently stayed and ate in local village guesthouses using fuelwood. On this trek, in addition to the porters and cook, we had a local Nepali leader. He did an excellent job, even though it was his first trip as leader.

According to its *Responsible Travel Guide Book*, World Expeditions aims to: employ local staff, use local suppliers and assist local businesses; avoid diversion of resources away from local communities; provide opportunities for cultural exchange; contribute to the welfare of host communities; and educate its travellers about destinations, local cultures and minimal-impact behaviour (Buykx, 2001).

World Expeditions provides its Himalayan trekking clients with quite detailed guidelines for interactions with local residents, including: appropriate and inappropriate forms of public behaviour both within the tour and between travellers and locals; what to buy, what not to buy and when to bargain or not; when and how one should respond to individual requests for assistance, e.g. for money, medicine or school supplies; what to wear and what not to wear under various circumstances; and when it may or may not be appropriate to take photographs. Clients are also given opportunities to provide donations, e.g. to the Child Haven Orphanage in Kathmandu.

World Expeditions is also a major sponsor of the Fred Hollows Foundation, an international charitable organization that provides medical expertise and equipment for cataract surgery in developing nations. World Expeditions raises funds for the Foundation through the 'See Nepal Challenge', which started in 1999, and the 'See the World Challenge', which has been added subsequently. World Expeditions runs special treks for participants who have raised AUD4500 each for the Foundation. As of mid-2002, over AUD410,000 (currently US$235,000) had been raised (Fred Hollows Foundation, 2005).

## Experience

It is 20 years since I took part in this trek, and the experience may well have changed. From my recollection, the trail out of Pokhara was heavily used by mules, and heavily besplattered with mule dung, somewhat spoiling the hiking experience through smell as well as competition for space. The side trails at higher altitude, however, around Jomson Pass itself and the Annapurna Sanctuary, are apparently not major trading thoroughfares and are hence much less used and much more pleasant to hike along, with clear mountain air and astonishing views. The locals were very friendly, the food was excellent, and hiking up and down endless stone steps gave us plenty of exercise. That particular trek was the first guided hike in which I ever took part, and moved rather more slowly than I should have preferred, but that was two decades ago and no doubt it would seem different now.

## Environment

World Expeditions promotes a minimal-impact philosophy through its *Responsible Travel Guide Book*, which is endorsed by The Wilderness Society and received an environmental tourism award in 2001 (World Expeditions, 2005b).

*The Responsible Travel Guide Book* incorporates a set of minimal-impact instructions for travellers. These include, for example: stick to the trail, even if it is wet or muddy; don't tread on vegetation, even lichens; don't pick plants or collect souvenirs; pack out all rubbish and pick up other rubbish along the trail; use toilet facilities where provided, and otherwise dig a 15 cm hole at least 100 m from any water course; pack out sanitary items; bring only biodegradable and phosphorus-free soaps, shampoos, etc.; wash at least 50 m from any water course and scatter any wastewater the same distance away; and use hot water provided by World Expeditions, which is heated by kerosene, rather than taking showers at local establishments where fuelwood consumption contributes to deforestation (Buykx, 2001). Instructions are also provided for use of campfires, where these are appropriate, and for watching and photographing wildlife.

### Safety

At the time of writing in late 2005, there are security considerations for tourists in Nepal, associated with political instability. These, however, are relatively recent. For most of the past 20 years and longer, Nepal has been a very safe country to visit. At the time of my own visits, both for this trek and for various subsequent kayaking trips, the risks were much more minor. In urban areas one had to be on guard against thieves and pickpockets; on local buses there is the ever-present risk of road accidents, but little one can do about them; and as in many countries, there is the risk of gastrointestinal infection from unhygienic food preparation. Trekking with an organized tour such as World Expeditions reduces all of these risks: they have local guides, their own buses and their own cooks.

### Marketing

World Expeditions does indeed operate worldwide and produces annual catalogues of trips and tours covering a wide range of activities and countries. When the company started operations it was initially known as Australian Himalayan Expeditions, and Himalayan treks such as this one were its core business. They remain an important component of the company's overall marketing.

## Purnululu, Australia: Willis's Walkabouts

### Place

The Bungle Bungle Ranges in Purnululu National Park form part of the Kimberley region of northern Western Australia. They are famous for their beehive-shaped eroded sandstone rocks and for their deep narrow clefts and gorges, some water-filled. The park has been a World Heritage site since 2003, and is managed by the Western Australia Department of Conservation and Land Management (WACALM). Off-road vehicles are allowed only on the one formed track, and hiking is permitted in the gorges but not on the easily damaged beehive rocks.

Most tourists visit by air, either in fixed-wing overflights from the town of Kununurra, or helicopter overflights from a local commercial helipad. Particularly in the morning and evening when the low sun angle gives the most scenic views, helicopter and aircraft noise is almost continuous. These overflights earn substantial permit fees for WACALM, but destroy any sense of wilderness for backcountry hikers and produce unknown impacts on wildlife, including endemic and uncommon species such as great bowerbirds.

## Operator

Willis's Walkabouts organizes and guides backcountry hiking and bushcamping trips in various parts of northern Australia (Willis's Walkabouts, 2005). The company is based in Darwin and offers trips in Kakadu National Park and Central Australia as well as the Kimberleys. It has been operating since 1986.

## Activity

I have not taken part directly in this tour but have hiked independently in the area concerned on several occasions. I also have an independent report from a colleague who took part as a commercial client.

Willis's Walkabouts offers guided walks where clients carry their own backpacks and bring their own camping equipment. They also bring their own food for breakfasts, lunches and snacks. The company provides food for dinners, cooked by the guide. This food is divided up to be carried by the clients. Routes go well away from roadheads to areas rarely reached by independent hikers unfamiliar with the area. There are generally opportunities to camp by, and swim in, crocodile-free waterholes.

## Equipment

Willis's Walkabouts supplies transport to the hiking areas, but all hiking, camping and cooking gear is brought by the clients themselves. The company rents or sells some items. Mosquitoes can be common, so a tent or mosquito net is needed. Most walks take place in the tropical winter, so the weather can be hot but not unbearable. Warm clothes are not needed, but strong hiking books and heavy-duty gaiters are important in the rocky sandstone country, because of loose footing, spinifex grass and the possibility of snakes. A broad-brimmed hat, torch, first-aid kit and a large waterbottle or waterbag are also essential. The company also recommends that clients bring swimming goggles so as to see underwater in swimming holes.

## Accommodation

All accommodation on the trip is in the clients' own tents or mosquito nets, at campsites selected by the guides.

## Statistics

Group sizes range from 4 to 12 (Willis's Walkabouts, 2005) and client-to-guide ratios are around 4:1 or 6:1. Purnululu trips are run in three 1-week sections that can be purchased jointly or separately. Prices range from AUD1475–1725 per section, i.e. about AUD215 (US$160) per person per day; or AUD2995 for all three, i.e. about AUD145 (US$110) per person per day.

## Access

Clients assemble in Kununurra and are driven to the park. Beyond the main parking lot, all access within the park is on foot. Park entrance and camping permits are required and are obtained by the tour operator, which also needs a commercial permit to run tours in a Western Australian park.

## Community

The first of the three hiking sections at Purnululu is in an area managed by traditional Aboriginal owners adjacent to the national park. I have not visited this area and it is not clear how much interaction with Aboriginal residents is expected. Fees are no doubt payable.

## Experience

The main part of Piccaninny Gorge, especially that reachable in a return day walk from the parking area, is heavily visited. The easily reached sections in the main gorge are used by bushwalkers, but not intensively. The hidden gorges, waterfilled gorges, caves and hanging chasms, and tortuous routes to the plateau above are very rarely visited and include some remarkably beautiful scenery. I particularly remember a vast hanging side gorge high above the main gorge, with huge sculpted red rock overhangs, a sandy floor and its own palm fringed creek.

## Environment

Willis's Walkabouts has its own *Bushwalking Guide*. The Guide includes a code of environmental conduct and is sent in advance to paid-up clients. A text-only copy of the *Bushwalking Guide* is also downloadable from the company's website (Willis's Walkabouts, 2005). The code covers all the basics of minimal-impact hiking and bush camping in tropical savanna ecosystems. Cooking on some trips is on campfires, but in Purnululu cooking is on camp stoves only because of park regulations. The *Bushwalking Guide* also covers washing up, washing and human waste disposal, including packing out toilet paper. Indeed, it states categorically that: 'If you are not willing to make the effort to dispose of your waste properly, do not consider coming on any Walkabout'.

## Safety

I have not taken part in a Willis's Walkabout tour myself, though I have several times independently hiked the same routes and areas that they use in the Piccaninny Gorge section of Purnululu National Park. I have also received favourable reports from one of their former clients, a colleague at Griffith University. Their website emphasizes safety aspects, but with a focus on the need for potential clients to be competent, fit, appropriately equipped and self-reliant. As the website says, there is rarely any radio or phone communication and medical evacuation may take many days, so 'if you receive an injury which requires immediate hospitalisation, you will die'.

## Marketing

The company's website (Willis's Walkabouts, 2005) contains extensive illustrations of northern Australian scenery looking its best, but does also mention the less pleasant aspects such as insect pests. The detailed descriptions of each hike include lowlights as well as highlights. Indeed, for the Purnululu hike the website mentions quite rightly that helicopter noise is 'intrusive most of the day'. The company is clearly proud of its *Bushwalking Guide*, which it describes as 'one of the most comprehensive pre-trip information booklets offered by any tour operator anywhere in the world'. It does indeed include considerable detail, though perhaps not particularly more than other remote-area tour operators. It emphasizes safety and self-reliance, and the need for potential clients to assess whether or not they are really keen and capable to take part in an experience of this type. According to the company website, 50% of its clients in 2004 were repeat customers.

## Teleki Valley, Mt Kenya, Kenya: Various Operators

### Place

Mt Kenya (5200 m) is an extinct volcano that lies astride the Equator in central Kenya. Its topmost summits, Batian and Nelion, require technical climbing skills, but the third peak, Point Lenana (at 4985 m) can be reached by hikers. Its highest huts, Austrian Hut and Top Hut, lie above snowline in a saddle below the summits. Teleki Valley lies a little lower, below snowline and south of the peaks.

There are at least four main routes up the flanks of Mt Kenya to a loop track, the Top Circuit around the peaks. There are also several other routes without defined tracks. The best-known routes are the Naro Moru route from the southwest, the Sirimon route from the northwest, the Chogoria route from the east and the Ithanguni route from the northeast. The last two intersect below Hall Tarns east of the summits.

### Operators

There are commercial alpine guiding companies that will lead ascents of the peaks (e.g. Cosley and Houston Alpine Guides, 2005). There are also a number of commercial tour companies such as EWP (2005), which offer guided hikes, usually up one of the major routes and down another, linking the two either via Austrian Hut and Point Lenana, or by hiking part of the Top Circuit. EWP (2005) advise hikers to 'beware of bogus operators', especially in Nairobi. I have not audited or taken part in any of these commercial tours and cannot comment on their operations. I visited the area independently some decades ago and this case study is based on that visit and current operator websites.

Some operators also offer guided hikes that ascend and descend via the same route, so that there is no pressure on clients to cross the higher-altitude sections. Wild Frontiers (2005), for example, offers 6-day trips by either the Sirimon or Chogoria routes. Many visitors hike these routes independently, as I did myself in 1974. Relevant information is available from the Kenya Wildlife Society (2005).

### Activity

There is a broad distinction between mountain hikers and technical climbers. For climbers, the main activity is an ascent of Batian or Nelion peaks, and Teleki Valley is simply the first day's staging point. For hikers the main activity is hiking up, across and/or around the mountain, enjoying scenery and views. The highest point reachable without technical climbing skills and equipment is Point Lenana at 4985 m. This is 1 h from Top Hut and Austrian Hut, themselves at 4790 m, and 3–4 h from Mackinder Camp in the Teleki Valley. Many hikers are perfectly content to remain at slightly lower elevations. The most heavily used route is from the Naro Moru roadhead at 3050 m, through the so-called Vertical Bog to Teleki Valley, which takes about 4–6 h. Circumnavigation of the Top Circuit takes 2 days.

## Equipment

Equipment required depends whether the clients are climbing or hiking, whether they will go above snowline and whether they are camping or not. Independent hikers need to be fully equipped for mountain weather and the possibility of extended storms. In my own case in 1974, since the trip was unplanned, I was very poorly equipped. In fact I had a pair of tennis shoes, a cheap nylon sleeping bag and a 5 kg bag of peppermints which was all I could buy at the one local store that morning. I traded handfuls of peppermints for more nourishing food with other hikers and climbers I passed en route. However, that was 30 years ago!

## Accommodation

There are now numerous huts and camping areas at high elevation on Mt Kenya. In Teleki Valley there is a commercially operated tented camp, Mackinder Camp, at 4200 m, and a hut and camping area known as American Hut or American Camp a little further up the valley at 4320 m (EWP, 2005). When I visited in 1974 there was a small wooden climbers' hut in Teleki Valley, with strongboxes to protect food from hyraxes and a raised communal sleeping platform. It is not clear from current websites whether this hut is still there, but it may be the Mountain Club of Kenya hut referred to by EWP (2005). According to EWP (2005), however, 'unmanned huts on the mountain are generally small and dirty ... camping is recommended'.

Apparently, there is now a park ranger station and rescue post in the upper section of Teleki Valley (EWP, 2005). In 1974 there was also a shelter at the point now occupied by Austrian Hut and Top Hut, at 4790 m. Other routes up Mount Kenya also have huts and camping areas. On the Sirimon route, for example, there are two camps known as Judmeier and Shipton's (EWP, 2005). Outside the park there is accommodation at the Naro Moru River Lodge on the southwest; some unnamed bandas or cabins near the meteorological station at the Naro Moru roadhead; and cabins on the eastern side along the access to the Chogoria and Ithanguni routes.

## Statistics

From the roadhead above Naro Moru to Teleki Valley is a day's hike. One needs to overnight at Teleki before returning, and most people would stay at least 1 day in the Teleki Valley so as to hike further up towards Austrian Hut. Many hikers also continue around the mountain and descend via another track on the eastern or northern slope, or vice versa. Hiking tours offered by commercial operators take at least 5–6 days and cost around US$1200 per person, or about US$200–240 per person per day. Guided climbs are more expensive, US$3400–5600 per person depending on client-to-guide ratios (Cosley and Houston Alpine Guides, 2005).

## Access

As noted above, Teleki Valley can be reached along several different trails, with the western direct trail from Naro Moru being most heavily used. Naro Moru is accessible by road from Nairobi. Mt Kenya is a national park, and permits are required, currently costing US$15 per day for entrance and US$8 per day for camping (EWP, 2005).

## Community

There are no local residents on the upper slopes of Mt Kenya itself, though the lower flanks are heavily settled. Hikers pass through local towns and villages such as Naro Moru and may purchase food, supplies and accommodation. EWP (2005), however, advise that 'food should be brought from Nairobi'. Some commercial trips hire local porters to carry clients' gear.

## Experience

Teleki Valley can be an extraordinarily beautiful place, with sunbirds darting between giant groundsels, moss-fringed pools and rock hyrax waiting to steal food from unwary climbers. Of course, when sun and calm skies are replaced by scudding clouds and snow blizzards, the landscape looks less inviting. The altitude is not insignificant and most people feel its effects during the climb. An area on the approach route known as the Vertical Bog has a reputation as the most tiring section.

## Environment

East African mountains support a very specific altitudinal series of ecosystems, not found elsewhere. In particular, above tree line there are areas dominated by giant lobelias and further up, tree groundsels. These ecosystems are small in area and could very easily be subject to human impact. The ground cover is often wet, especially in the Vertical Bog, and easily damaged by trampling.

At the time of my own visit there were no toilet facilities in the Teleki Valley, and human waste may well be a significant source of water pollution in the moss ponds. According to Mt Kenya Clean Up (2005), litter left by hikers has become an increasing problem over recent decades, though identifiable litter at Austrian Hut dates back to at least 1963. Around 20,000 people currently make the hike or climb each year. From 1 to 8 August 1988, 15 young local climbers carried out 420 kg of litter, including 60 kg from Teleki Valley (Mt Kenya Clean Up, 2005).

## Safety

The principal risks in hiking to the Teleki Valley are related to weather. Indeed, in 1974 I and others made a precipitate descent as a large storm blew in. The western route from Naro Moru to Teleki is the most popular, and anyone who stays on the track is soon likely to receive assistance. Away from the tracks, however, or further up the peaks, there would be much less chance of receiving assistance.

## Marketing

Information on the tour operators mentioned above is from their websites, but presumably they also advertise locally within Kenya.

# Routeburn Track, New Zealand: Ultimate Hikes

### Place

The Routeburn Track runs through Fiordland and Mount Aspiring National Parks in the Southwest of New Zealand World Heritage Area. It crosses part of the Southern Alps, between the Hollyford and Dart Valleys. The higher elevation sections are open, with mountain lakes and rocky outcrops. The lower sections are dense beech forest. Weather is often wet and highly variable, but the scenery is beautiful none the less.

### Operator

The Routeburn Track is used principally by independent hikers, and this is how I visited it many years ago. A number of operators, however, offer commercial hiking tours along the Track, including transfers to and from Queenstown. One example is Ultimate Hikes (2005), which offers a 3-day, 2-night guided walk including accommodation in private 'luxury lodges'. The national parks huts, though well built, are too basic and crowded to be described in these terms.

### Activity

Ultimate Hikes (2005) describes its Routeburn Track tour as follows. On the first day the group travels by coach from Queenstown through Te Anau to a road pass, The Divide, where the track starts. The group climbs to Key Summit and to the first lodge at Lake Mackenzie. Total distance is 14 km, taking 5–6 h. On the second day the group traverses a section known as the Hollyford Face and then descends to a lodge in the Routeburn Valley. Total distance is 15 km, taking 5–7 h. The final day involves a 10 km descent through beech forest, and the coach ride back to Queenstown.

### Equipment

This is not a difficult hike and whilst hikers should generally be equipped for changeable mountain weather and be able to navigate in cloud, in practice the only absolutely essential item is a rainproof parka. Ultimate Hikes (2005) provides its clients with all food and bedding, including sleeping liners. Clients only need to bring personal clothing.

### Accommodation

There are three accommodation options on the track itself: tents, parks service huts or private lodges. Ultimate Hikes (2005) uses private lodges. For independent hikes the New Zealand Department of Conservation (NZDOC) charges NZD10 per person per night for camping, and NZD40 to stay in NZDOC huts.

## Statistics

It is in fact quite possible to run the entire length of the Routeburn Track in 1 day, but most hikers camp 2 nights and hike 1 full day and two half days. Tour operators provide one guide per group. Ultimate Hikes' (2005) current price for a 3-day trip out of Queenstown, including transport, private lodge accommodation and a guide is approximately US$250 per person per day, depending on season.

## Access

Access to either end of the Routeburn Track is by road. The southern end starts at The Divide, a pass through hills between Te Anau and Milford Sound. The northern end is in the lower valley of the Routeburn River. For clients of Ultimate Hikes (2005) the road journeys are made in a coach, from Queenstown. There are also scheduled bus services. Queenstown is accessible by road or air.

Permits are required from the New Zealand Department of Conservation (NZDOC) in order to camp or stay in huts on the Routeburn Track. The Ultimate Hikes tour uses private lodges and presumably has a special agreement with NZDOC. Clients do not have to pay separate fees.

## Community

Tourism is one of the economic mainstays of this region of New Zealand, along with farming, and many local residents are involved one way or another in the tourism industry. In addition, many New Zealanders hike the Routeburn Track independently, staying in the NZDOC huts or camping. Clients of commercial tours such as that offered by Ultimate Hikes (2005) would have opportunities to converse with any of these, if they wish, or to remain apart in their guided groups and private lodges, if they prefer.

## Experience

I have not taken part in any commercial tour on the Routeburn Track, but I hiked it independently many years ago. The weather was changeable at the time, cold wind and rain alternating with flashes of brilliant sunshine and occasional but highly scenic views. On that occasion I ended up simply running from one end to the other, complete with backpack and camping gear. It is a beautiful area, however, and I shall gladly return in a more leisurely manner one day when time allows.

## Environment

I have not visited the Ultimate Hikes (2005) lodges and it is many years since I examined the NZDOC huts, so I cannot comment on current environmental management practices. The area is controlled by NZDOC, however, which generally has an excellent reputation for park and visitor management, so it is likely that there are toilets installed at huts and campsites, and regulations regarding litter, soap and shampoo, and fires.

## Safety

Navigation, hypothermia and falls are the main safety concerns. Guided groups are unlikely to become lost, even in poor weather. Ultimate Hikes (2005) can provide rain parkas for those without their own. The tracks are well marked.

## Marketing

The Routeburn Track is well known both in New Zealand and overseas, and often featured in a variety of outdoor magazines. Information is also available from NZDOC. Ultimate Hikes (2005) advertises via its website and no doubt also local brochures.

# Pacific Northwest USA: Various Operators

## Place

The forests and mountains of north-central Oregon and south-central Washington State, USA, are known nationally for their outdoor recreation opportunities, which include whitewater kayaking, skiing and snowboarding, climbing and horse riding as well as hiking. Best known of the hiking trails is the PCT, the Pacific Crest Trail, but there is an extensive network of other trails, some through various national parks and others through wilderness areas managed by the US Forest Service. The national parks such as Mt Rainier in Washington are heavily frequented, and provide the best access to the alpine ecosystems.

US Forest Service (USFS) Wilderness Areas such as Bull of the Woods, Mt Hood, Mt Adams, Indian Heaven and Salmon Huckleberry, however, contain spectacular salmon rivers, old-growth Douglas fir and hemlock forests, blueberry heaths and mountain lakes (Great Outdoor Recreation Pages (GORP), 2005a; USDA Forest Service, 2005). Bull of the Woods Wilderness Area, for example, is over 13,000 ha in area and contains over a dozen lakes as well as Bagby Hot Springs.

## Operators

A number of local outfitters offer guided hikes in the Pacific Northwest. I have not taken part in any of these commercial tours, though I have hiked through these areas extensively with private groups. Described here is a hike offered by Oregon Peak Adventures (2005). The description is based on information from their website. I have visited all the sites mentioned.

## Activity

The Indian Heaven Backpack tour offered by Oregon Peak Adventures (2005) is advertised as a 3-day trip covering about 25 km in total. It starts at Cultus trailhead, visits Elk Lake and Lake Wapitki, and ends at the Filloon trailhead. It is a guided hike. Clients carry backpacks with their personal gear and a share of group gear. Porter support is available if required, for an extra charge, to carry clients' shares of group gear. The trails are well-formed and the distances and grades relatively easy, so the trip gives clients the opportunity to enjoy the scenery.

## Equipment

The outfitter provides tents, food, cooking gear, water filter and trekking poles. Clients bring their own sleeping bags and mats and their own cutlery and clothing.

## Accommodation

The trip includes 2 nights' camping, one at Elk Lake (about 1450 m) and the other at Lake Wapitki (about 1600 m). The company provides the food and the guides do the cooking.

## Statistics

The trip takes 3 days. It seems to be offered only once a year, though the company also offers a range of other hikes elsewhere. The trip runs during blueberry season. Cost is US$300 per person for groups of 3–6 clients or US$600 per person for a single client. This includes the drive from Portland and back. The usual price is hence about US$100 per person per day.

## Access

Access is by road from Portland, the 'Rose City' in Oregon. Indian Heaven is in southern Washington near Mt Adams. Permits are required and are obtained by the outfitter and included in the trip price.

## Community

Rural communities in the Pacific Northwest depend heavily on tourism, which has taken over from a former economy based largely on logging. Most tourists are domestic self-drive visitors who purchase food, fuel, accommodation, maps and equipment locally. There are relatively few commercial tour clients.

## Experience

Since I have not taken part in this particular guided hike I cannot comment on the service component of the experience. The scenery and environment, however, are extremely beautiful. The area has relatively high rainfall, but when this guided hike is run the weather is likely to be dry. Clients can swim in the lakes and gorge themselves on blueberries, whilst guides keep a lookout for bears – which also enjoy blueberries.

## Environment

The parks and wilderness areas of the Pacific Northwest are generally well regulated and subject to relatively intensive management and education campaigns. There are track signs and trailhead notices, and the principles of Leave-No-Trace® hiking are printed on USFS wilderness maps. The principal impacts, other than wildfires, are from high visitation. These include erosion of trails and litter around campsites. Even GORP (2005b), for example, acknowledges that Twin Lakes in Bull of the

Woods wilderness area 'shows the impacts of poor camping habits'. Some of these areas are open for fishing, and lakeshores are often strewn with old line. Others are open to horse riding and packhorse outfitters, and these suffer additional track erosion, and in some cases, introduction of weeds in feed and dung (Newsome *et al.*, 2004a).

## Safety

Safety procedures are not described in the Oregon Peak Adventures (2005) website. Most of these areas do potentially contain bears, though these are not common and the precautions needed in Alaska, or even in Glacier National Park in Montana, do not seem to be needed.

## Marketing

There are many sources of information about the parks and wilderness areas, including recreational opportunities, but relatively few about commercial tour operations.

# 17 Horse Riding

*Contributed by Claudia Ollenburg*

Claudia Ollenburg, Boojum Expeditions, Mongolia. CO collection.

Claudia and horse, Boojum Expeditions, Mongolia. CO collection.

## Sector Structure

Horse riding adventure tourism products are similar in many ways to other types of adventure tourism, but there is one critical difference: the horse. Horses are animals, not equipment. Tour guides or other staff must have the skills to train, ride and manage the horses, as well as managing the tour clients and the interaction between the two. Tour operators must have facilities and staff to care for the horses year-round, not only during tours. This is very different from mechanized adventure tourism where equipment can be turned off when not in use, serviced or replaced when broken, and stored in the off season.

As with many types of adventure tourism, commercial equestrian adventure tourism is effectively a small offshoot of the recreational horse riding sector. The distinction between private recreational horse riding, commercial recreational horse riding and horse riding tourism depends on the precise financial arrangements involved, and on whether or not the rider is based at home or travelling as a tourist on the days concerned. To understand the structure of the equestrian tourism industry it is therefore useful to start by reviewing the recreational activities.

In addition, many commercial horse tourism products require considerable riding skills, and are hence only available to clients who are already skilled recreational riders. This applies especially to many multi-day horse treks and horse-packing trips.

The total number of recreational horse riders worldwide does not seem to have been subject to detailed study, but it has been suggested that there may be around 20 million active recreational horse riders in the developed world, principally in Europe and North America (Lancaster, personal communication, 2004, cited in Ollenburg, 2005). Most horses in developed Western nations are kept solely for recreation.

A number of different competitive riding disciplines are recognized, some of them with military or agricultural antecedents. They include the so-called classical riding disciplines such as dressage, show-jumping and 3-day events; racing, over various distances and courses; and specialized styles such as endurance and western riding. Different horse breeds are commonly used for different riding disciplines. Only a few of these recreational disciplines feature in commercial horse-tourism products, and fewer still in adventure products.

Commercial equestrian tours may be classified into four main categories (Ollenburg, 2005): guided commercial horse treks and trail rides; fixed-site farmstays, guest and working ranches; expert riding clinics and children's riding camps; and horse-drawn carriages, commonly in urban areas. Of these, clinics, camps and carriages do not qualify as adventure; and nor do the short trail and pony rides offered at many low-key family farmstays. The principal equestrian adventure tour products are hence: (i) guest ranches that focus on horse riding; and (ii) horse treks, especially multi-day treks in remote areas.

As with other types of adventure tourism, different equestrian tourism products are available at different prices, in different places, for clients with a wide range of different prior skills and experience. At the high-volume, low-price, low-skill, short-duration 'soft' end of the spectrum, there are rides that offer tourists with no previous riding experience the opportunity to sit briefly on a placid horse or pony being led at a gentle walk on level ground.

At the low-volume, high-price, high-skill, longer-duration 'hard' end of the spectrum, there are international multi-day or multi-week horse treks for expert riders. These are guided and generally catered, and in many cases involve off-trail travel through remote mountain or desert terrain (Ollenburg, 2005).

In these trips, small groups ride at speed for many hours a day through relatively difficult terrain. Clients must have substantial prior experience, good riding skills and good fitness, stamina and endurance. From an adventure tourism perspective, this is the key subsector in commercial equestrian tourism, and the case studies presented in this chapter will therefore focus on tours of this type.

More localized and generally shorter backcountry horse treks and horse-packing tours are also offered in some countries by local ranchers and outfitters. There is often some overlap between fixed-site ranches and mobile horse treks. Some treks take place on private ranches, stations, estancias or their equivalent in other countries, which are large enough to travel around on horseback for many days. Equally, horse treks in remote areas do not always move camp every day, but may establish a base camp for several days and ride out in different directions, before moving on.

## Guest Ranches

Farms and ranches in many countries have a variety of commercial and semi-commercial arrangements to take in paying guests as an adjunct to agricultural production. In addition, there are dude and guest ranches that are purely tourism businesses with no working agricultural component. These seem to be particularly widespread in the USA (Table 17.1).

The types of tourism opportunities offered on farms, working ranches and guest ranches vary widely (Ollenburg, 2006). Rarely are guests allowed to take part in the actual working life of the farm, but often they can watch, and sometimes take part in

**Table 17.1.** Horse riding options at selected North American guest ranches.

| Operator | Place | Activity | Pack trips/area, length | Group size | US$ per person, per day, overnight | US$ per person, per day, weekly |
|---|---|---|---|---|---|---|
| 63 Ranch | Montana, USA | Half- and full-day rides, 6 days a week | Absaroka Beartooth Wilderness, 2 days | 4–6 | 200 | 195 |
| 7 Lazy P Deep Canyon Guest Ranch | Montana, USA | Half- and full-day rides, 6 days a week | Bob Marshall Wilderness, up to 10 days | 2–11 | 250 | 165 |
| 7 D Ranch | Montana, USA | Half- and full-day rides | Custom pack trips | 1–6 | 275–350 | 205–230 |
| Colorado Trails Ranch | Colorado, USA | Half- and full-day rides, 6 guests per wrangler | Not offered | | | 250–280 |
| Diamond D Ranch | Idaho, USA | Half-day rides twice daily, 1.5–2.5 h | Not offered | | | 160–195 |
| Big Creek Lodge | British Columbia, Canada | Daily guided and unguided trail rides | Not offered | | | 140 |

staged components. Some working farms and ranches do use suitably skilled visitors to help in farm work, and this may include highly skilled horse work such as cattle mustering. Such participation, however, is rarely offered as a tourism product.

The principal horse riding opportunities for tourists are hence at guest ranches, and most tourists who visit guest ranches do so principally in order to ride. Such ranches typically offer a range of different riding opportunities. These may include, for example: short trail rides for independent self-drive customers; an overnight rate including accommodation, meals and a ride; a 1-week price including a half- or full-day trail ride every day; and multi-day backcountry horse-packing trips that start and finish at the ranch.

Guided on-farm trail rides are commonly offered to guests at all levels of riding skill, though typically with a minimum age of 6 years, and are often designed to appeal to family groups. These would not generally be considered as adventure tourism.

The multi-day backcountry horse-packing trips offered by some ranches, however, do indeed qualify as adventurous for most participants. Such trips range in length from overnight to 10 days or more, and are commonly offered only during an appropriate season, generally summer.

In North America at least, these trips typically operate in adjacent wilderness areas or national forests accessible from the ranch. Unlike the horse treks described in the following section, these ranch-based horse-packing trips involve only a short ride each day, with ample time for other activities such as hiking and fishing, and do not require prior riding skills and experience.

Camping equipment and horse riding tack are provided by the operator, though clients are sometimes expected to supply their own sleeping bags. Multi-day trips are accompanied by packers, wranglers and a cook.

## Horse Treks

Commercial adventure horse treks are offered in a wide range of destinations worldwide (Ollenburg, 2005). Typically, they involve 5–7 h riding every day for 1–2 weeks or longer, averaging 20–40 km per day. Prices typically range from US$120 to 500 per person per day.

Clients for tours of this type should be: experienced in long-distance endurance riding; able to control an unfamiliar horse in difficult terrain; and able to adapt to local horse breeds, riding gear and other customs. This last may include, for example, different saddle and bridle designs, different techniques for tethering, picketing, hobbling or yarding horses during stops and at night; and different signals and commands to communicate from rider to horse.

In practice, most clients on these trips do have some riding experience, but often overestimate their skills. This is a significant safety concern for tour operators. Operators usually specify required riding skills for particular tours, ranging from intermediate to highly experienced, but there is no international certification scheme for riding skills, so it is difficult for them to verify clients' claims prior to the trip. As one common example, riders may not realize that the ability to compete in short-duration events on their own horse in a familiar level showground does not necessarily give them the ability to ride an unfamiliar horse at speed over rough terrain all day, every day for a fortnight.

International equestrian tour agents commonly have arrangements with local residents to provide the horses, guides and on-ground logistics in destination areas.

They may do this through inbound horse riding tour operators, through local ranches or outfitters, or though their own networks of local guides and wranglers.

The horses are generally of local breeds or crossbreeds and used to the terrain, which is a significant safety aspect. Examples of local horse breeds used in commercial trekking include the Connemara pony, the Mongolian horse and the Criollo. There are several advantages to using local tack. First, particularly in remote areas in developing nations, the horses and local guides are hired together as a package. They are used to their own local equipment and they know it fits the horses, which is important for safety. Secondly, to use local tack is simply part of the experience. And thirdly, it is an enormous challenge to transport horse equipment on commercial flights and even more so to bring it back, especially into countries with strict quarantine requirements.

Different operators and different treks use different types of accommodation. For example, in areas that are inaccessible to vehicles either because of terrain or tenure, the group may carry its own camping equipment on pack horses that accompany the riders. In areas with road access, the camp may be sent ahead in a 4WD vehicle whilst the clients ride via a more picturesque route. In areas with established local populations, horse trekkers may stay in local accommodation, which may range from simple huts or tents to luxurious lodges, guesthouses or private estancias.

The principal destination areas for adventure horse trekking are in southern Europe, southern and eastern Africa, North and South America, and central Asia. Mountains, steppes and savannas are particularly favoured. In some countries, notably the USA and Canada, many horse treks operate in national parks. In others, national parks are closed to horses, and tours operate in other public or private land. The impacts of horse riding and their relevance for management of national parks have been reviewed by Newsome *et al.* (2004a).

There is a specialized international horse-trekking industry, with an oligopoly of specialist outbound horse tourism agents, based principally in North America and Europe; and a plethora of small local operators in destination areas, who own the horses, employ the local guides and other staff, and make arrangements for local accommodation and transport as required.

Most of the international outbound agents offer a similar portfolio of treks, though some of the smaller companies specialize in particularly remote areas or in treks with extended cultural interactions. Different outbound packagers commonly use the same local operators in particular destination regions, as also occurs in other forms of adventure tourism.

In all save the most basic tours, the local operators provide staff to groom, feed, saddle and unsaddle the horses; to pitch and strike camp as required; and to do the cooking and look after camp logistics. In addition to the staff, the local operators will generally provide one or more local guides, and the outbound packager may also provide a guide fluent in the native language or languages of the clients. Local guides are particularly critical in remote areas, where their local knowledge of the terrain, people, customs and wildlife is indispensable for safe travel.

Trekking groups are commonly rather small, typically from two to twelve riders, with one local guide for every four to six clients, plus support crew as outlined above. The horses provided are generally local breeds or cross breeds, and weight limits commonly apply for riders, varying from 85 to 95 kg depending on the local horse breed.

Horse-trekking operators in African nations commonly use Arab crosses,

Kalahari crosses, Hanoverians and part Thoroughbreds. In South America, Peruvian Paso and local Criollo breeds are commonly used, often crossed with Andalucians or Thoroughbreds. In Asia, particularly in the mountainous areas of Central Asia, local Kazakh and Mongolian ponies are used because they are particularly sure-footed and sturdy, and used to the rough mountain terrain. Irrespective of the particular breeds, local tour operators will select individual horses that are well-schooled and forgiving, able to adapt to different riders, forward-going but controllable, and used to local conditions and wildlife.

In general, the commercial horse treks offered in African and South American nations require riders with advanced or at least intermediate riding skills. Horse treks offered in Asian, North America and European nations, and in Australia and New Zealand, include options available for less experienced as well as highly skilled riders. Irrespective of skill, however, all riders must be prepared to spend 4–7 h in the saddle every day. In addition, whilst some multi-day treks use luxurious accommodation, others involve many nights camping in remote areas, generally without hot showers or other such creature comforts.

Typical prices for multi-day adventure horse treks range from about US$120 to 180 per person per day, depending largely on the type of accommodation offered, but with African trips tending to be more expensive than those in Asia.

There appear to be about 15 specialist international equestrian tour operators that offer commercial treks at a retail level. Information on destinations, markets and clientele for eight of these operators is available from a survey conducted in November 2004 (Ollenburg, 2005). Of these eight major operators, those based in the USA have largely (95%) American clients, with the remainder being Europeans. Operators based in the UK have largely (73%) European clients, and around 10% American clients. One agency, with branches in both America and the UK, has 45% American clients and 45% European.

There are internationally famous horse treks in, for example: Kenya, Botswana and South Africa; Australia and New Zealand; Chile, Argentina and Uruguay; India, Mongolia and Tibet; Canada and the USA; and in France, Spain, Italy, Austria, Wales and Iceland. The American clients prefer European destinations, especially Ireland, Italy and Spain. European clients choose mainly African and South American destinations. Some examples of the major outbound operators, and some of the specific trips they offer, are summarized in Table 17.2.

Marketing for these trips relies on: individual company websites; links and listings in more general tourism websites; advertisements in specialist equestrian journals; and printed catalogues distributed by riding stables and equipment stores. About half of the clients for commercial horse-trek companies also own their own horses at home: the proportion ranges from 20 to 100%. Most of these operators have a high level of repeat business, ranging from 18 to 75% with a mean of 42%.

Major management issues identified by the survey respondents include: the ongoing need to keep identifying both new destinations and new clients; difficulties experienced when clients over-estimate their fitness and riding skills; and clients' unfamiliarity with riding styles, riding tack, and horse breaking and training techniques in different parts of the world.

Interestingly, none of the respondents mentioned insurance as a particular problem for their businesses, though this is often identified as a critical issue by other adventure tourism operators, and many liability lawsuits involve injuries sustained while riding (McDonald, 2003).

**Table 17.2.** Selected multi-day horse-trekking tours worldwide.

| Operator | Country of origin | Destination | Days (riding) | Accommodation | Group size | Features |
|---|---|---|---|---|---|---|
| Cross Country International | USA | Ireland: Kerry, Killarney | 8 (6) | B&B | 10–12 | MacGillycuddy Reeks, Ross Island |
| | | Morocco: Atlas Mts | 6 (4) | 5-star hotel | > 4 | Atlas Mountains |
| Equitours | USA | USA: Wyoming | 8 (6) | Camp, ranch | 4–8 | Yellowstone NP, 4000 m passes |
| | | Kenya: Masai Mara | 14 (10) | Safari camps | 4–12 | Maasai Mara NP wildlife |
| In The Saddle | UK | South Africa: Lapalala | 10 (8) | Cottage, camp | 6 | rhino sanctuary, Waterberg |
| | | South America: Andes | 11 (10) | Camping | | Andes |
| Ride World Wide | UK | Kyrgyzstan: Tien Shan | 13 (10) | Camp, yurts | 2–8 | Tien Shan Mountains |
| | | Chile: Patagonia | 12 (8) | Camping | 2–12 | Torres del Paine National Park |
| Tiger Paw Adventures | Canada, UK | Tibet: Damshung | 14 (6) | Hotel, camp | | Horse festival, 5000 m passes |
| | | Nepal: Mustang | 19 (12) | Camp, hotels | 4–6 | High altitude, mountains |
| Unicorn Trails | UK | Chile: Patagonia | 10 (8) | Camping | 12 | Wilderness ride along glaciers |
| | | France: Provence | 7 (6) | Country house | 2–8 | Forest, hills |
| Adventures on Horseback | USA | India: Rajasthan | 17 (9) | Hotels, camping | | Animal fairs |
| | | Brazil: Pantanal | 12 (6) | Hotel, fazendas | 2–8 | Pantanal |
| Boojum Expeditions | USA | Mongolia: Khovsgol, Gobi | 11 | Ger camps, hotels | 5–8 | Naadam Festival |
| | | Uruguay: Coastal | 8 | Estancias, hotels | >2 | *National Geographic* and *Outside* awards |

# Lake Khovsgol, Mongolia: Boojum Expeditions

## Place

Khovsgol is the northernmost province of Mongolia, immediately south of the border with Russia. Lake Khovsgol itself, Khovsgol Nuur, is Mongolia's largest and deepest lake. Its outflow joins the largest tributary stream of Lake Baikal in Russia. It is 136 km long, 36 km wide, 262 m deep, 1645 m above sea level and holds 1–2% of the world's freshwater supply. The surrounding terrain includes mountains, steppes and subarctic coniferous taiga forests of larch and pine. The area is home to argali sheep, ibex, bear, sable and moose, as well as over 250 species of birds, including Baikal teal, barheaded goose, black stork and Altai snowcock. The lake is now part of the Khovsgol Nuur National Park, established in 1992 and 8380 km$^2$ in area. Almost one-third of the park is forested, over 2500 km$^2$, though tree cover is now starting to disappear around the lakeshore. Khovsgol Nuur freezes over completely in winter, with ice cover 1.2 m thick, and may not thaw out completely until early June. The frozen lake is crossed by huge trucks carrying fuel from Siberia. Occasionally, these fall through the ice. Several different ethnic groups, including the Darkhad, Buryat and Tsaatan, live in the Lake Khovsgol area. The Tsaatan people are reindeer herders and part of the Tuvan ethnic group, which also occupies adjacent areas of Siberia on the northern slopes of the Sayan Mountains. There are 60 Tsaatan families, about 200 people in all, spread over an area of 100,000 km$^2$.

## Operator

Based in Bozeman, Montana, USA, Boojum Expeditions has been operating since 1984, and offers horse treks in Mongolia, Tibet, Patagonia and Uruguay. The company is owned by Kent Madin and his wife Linda Svendsen, who have 30 years' experience in this activity. When Mongolia became accessible to international visitors in 1994, Boojum's owners were amongst the first to explore the country with a view to adventure tourism. In 1998 they established a wholly owned Mongolian tourism company, Khovsgol Lodge Management Company, in the capital of Ulan Bator. Since that date, Boojum has maintained a permanent office base in Ulan Bator and runs several trips each season. These include specialist horse riding expeditions 8–10 days in length, and custom itineraries for travel in Mongolia with or without horse riding. In 2004, Kent Madin received an award from the Mongolian Government as an 'Outstanding Leader in Tourism Development'. He is one of only two foreigners to have received this award.

## Activity

Boojum Expedition's flagship tour is a 19-day trip that includes: a 150 km horseback journey through the vast Darkhad Valley, near Lake Khovsgol and Saridag Mountains; a visit to the summer camp of the Tsaatan reindeer herders near the Siberian border; and participation in the annual Naadam Festival at Renchinlkhumbe. I took part in this trip in July–August 2005.

The trip started with a sightseeing tour of Ulan Bator on the first day; a domestic flight to the gateway township of Moron on the second day; and a ferry trip on Lake Khovsgol on day three, to reach Jigleg Pass, the access point for the main horseback journey. This 150 km journey took 6 days, with 5 or 6 h riding each day. Each day's riding started at about 8 am, with a lunch stop of at least 1.5 h in the main heat of the day.

The seventh day of this trip was a rest day, camped near a small lodge owed by Boojum's Mongolian partner company. Clients had the opportunity to go hiking, do their laundry, and visit a local summer school and a Shaman demonstration.

The following 2.5 days were again spent riding, to reach Renchinl-khumbe, where we took part in the 2-day Naadam Festival. This festival is a world-famous annual get-together of northern peoples and their horses; with races, wrestling and archery competitions, and markets and concerts. After the Naadam Festival we travelled by truck to the airport of Moron, a 1.5 day trip, and took a flight back to Ulan Bator where the trip concluded.

## Equipment

All riding equipment is provided by Boojum Expeditions, though clients may bring their own if they prefer. Modified Russian saddles were used in preference to Mongolian saddles, which are made out of wood and make the long hours spent in the saddle very uncomfortable. These Russian saddles are fitted with saddle pads that are made specially for Boojum Expeditions.

The horses used are all of local Mongolian breed. These are small and very hardy horses with an incredible endurance, well used to the terrain, conditions and altitude. Mongolian horses possess remarkable working ability and can easily walk 50–60 km a day. The Mongolian horse is one of the most important and numerous breeds found among the indigenous horse breeds of Central Asia. It is distributed widely throughout the highland areas of northern China, Mongolia and adjacent areas of Russia and the independent central Asian republics. It is a dual-purpose breed, used primarily for riding and carting, but also for meat and milk production. The average wither height is 127–128 cm, but body size varies with environmental conditions.

Most of the horses used on this trip are supplied by local wranglers, who accompany the clients on the riding journey. A few of the individual horses are owned by Boojum Expeditions directly, but cared for year-round by the same wranglers, who have worked for Boojum every season for a number of years.

The operator provided group camping equipment, including tents. Clients brought sleeping bags and mats, or these were available for rent from Boojum Expeditions at additional charge. Boojum Expeditions sends out a detailed gear list to every participant well before the trip. For most of the trip the camping equipment was transported in a Russian 4WD truck, but there is a 3-day roadless section in the Saridag Mountains where packhorses were used instead.

## Accommodation

In Ulan Bator the accommodation was in twinshare rooms in a hotel. Single rooms were available at additional charge. During the horse trek the group was accommodated either in tents or in local gers. Gers are the traditional Mongolian dwelling, large circular transportable tents made from poles and felt, with a wood-fired metal stove for heating and cooking, and beds for sleeping. Local nomadic Mongolian families in this area live in gers. Each family unit generally has its own ger. On this trip, the Boojum clients stayed in guest gers, with 2–5 people in each ger. In areas away from the summer encampments, the Boojum group stayed in standard two-person backpacking tents. The clients were responsible for putting up and taking down their own tents each day.

All cooking was carried out by a Mongolian cook who was employed for the season. She travelled in the truck and prepared all the group meals, either in the vehicle using a gas stove or in local gers and homes along the way, using their kitchen facilities. She cooked Westernized food for the clients, and traditional food for the wranglers. Given the very limited supplies of food in the countryside, most of the food was bought in Ulan Bator before the trip. On one occasion during the trip, we ate a locally slaughtered sheep prepared in a traditional Mongolian way, cooked in the ground with hot rocks.

## Statistics

Groups may include 2–12 clients, who are accompanied by two or three guides, two wranglers, the cook and a truck driver. The 19-day trip costs US$3100, or about US$165 per person per day, including airfares within Mongolia.

## Access

International access to Mongolia is by air to the capital at Ulan Bator. Air carriers that fly to Ulan Bator include Korean Air, Air Mongolia and China Airlines. Access to the riding area at Khovsgol is via a domestic flight to the gateway town of Moron, followed by a 3-h 4WD trip on a dirt road to Khatgal, on the shores of Lake Khovsgol. From Khatgal, a 4-h ferry trip across Lake Khovsgol brought us to the Jigleg Pass, the starting point for the horse riding component of the tour. Jigleg Pass is halfway up the western shore of Lake Khovsgol. Trails further north along the lakeshore or west from Jiglegyn Am to Renchinlkhumbe, on the way to Tsagaan Nuur, can be traversed only on foot or on horseback. From Renchinlkhumbe there is road access, away from the lake, to the airport at Moron.

The mountain areas traversed during the horseback journey are used for summer grazing by the local nomadic peoples. We were able to travel unhindered through these areas because of the good relationship established with these families over many years, by Kent Madin and his Mongolian partner and wranglers. To operate tours in Mongolia, Boojum Expeditions established a local tour company, the Khovsgol Lodge Management Company. All these arrangements are made by the tour operator and are invisible to the clients.

## Community

Interaction with Mongolian nomadic culture is a major component of this tour. Mongolian culture and horse riding are inextricably connected. Before the trip, Boojum Expeditions sends each participant a set of DVDs that feature the Mongolian lifestyle and culture, and a CD with useful Mongolian phrases and pronunciations.

For the clients on this tour, the highlights of the trip were of cultural significance. Indeed, this trip is specifically designed to visit the Reindeer people and take part in the Naadam Festival, Mongolia's celebration of its ancient culture through wrestling, archery, horse racing, song and food.

During the horse riding section of the tour, the group had many interactions with local nomadic families. Most of the lunch and camping locations were close to the nomads' herds and encampments. Clients often purchased craft articles and spent time playing with local children.

Boojum Expeditions has a well-established network of local contractors who provide the truck, the passenger 4WD and the horses, and local seasonal staff who act as guides, wranglers and cook. At the end of each working season, the company flies its guides to a group meeting either at the Montana headquarters or elsewhere, to review the season's trips in detail. This has helped to establish strong loyalty to the company and its founder, and many staff have worked for Boojum for 4 years or more.

Boojum Expeditions also shows a strong commitment to the community of Renchinlkhumbe, and has initiated and supported several local projects. Kent Madin and an American colleague are currently paying the salaries for two teachers at the summer school near Tsagaan Nuur. This project is in its first year and provides 2 months of full-day school lessons for 20 students aged 3–15, who had not had any previous opportunity to visit a school.

## Experience

For this particular tour product, it is not possible to separate the adventure and cultural aspects. Horses are the medium of transport, an expression of wealth and the passion of every Mongolian in rural Mongolia. It is this cultural environment that makes this horse riding adventure tour such a special experience.

This trip is not intended for beginners, or for clients inexperienced at camping. To enjoy this trip, it is essential that clients have previous riding experience and are familiar with backcountry camping. Parts of the trip are physically strenuous: not so much from the exercise as from the heat, the flies and the long hours in the saddle. For an inexperienced rider, this is a tiring combination, and if fatigue affects concentration, this may reduce the rider's margin of safety.

For experienced riders, however, particularly those passionate about horses, familiar with camping and interested in other cultures and environments, this trip certainly qualifies as a 'lifetime experience'.

## Environment

Mongolia is at the ecological crossroads of Asia, where the Siberian coniferous taiga forests meet the Asian high-altitude grassland steppes and the arid expanses of the Gobi Desert. From north to south, Mongolia can be divided into four main zones: mountain-forest steppe and mountain steppe in the north and centre, and smaller areas of semi-desert and desert in the far south.

The horseback journey crosses one of the country's most fragile freshwater ecosystems: the Darkhad Depression and Lake Khovsgol itself. The Shishigt River, which runs through the Darkhad Depression, feeds into the Arctic Drainage Basin. As noted earlier, Khovsgol Lake itself is the second largest freshwater lake in Asia.

Relative to local populations and their herds, the Boojum group has negligible environmental impacts. Even so, the company follows best practices in minimal-impact environmental management. The guides ensured that all rubbish was collected and taken out. Clients were instructed to use only biodegradable soaps. A pit toilet was dug at every camp and every lunch stop.

## Safety

To ensure that all participants are physically capable of extended endurance riding, have adequate backcountry camping experience, and understand the challenge of the unfamiliar environment in Mongolia, the owner of the company calls every participant personally before each trip.

Boojum has more than 10 years of tourism experience in Mongolia, and has gradually improved the design of this trip so as to minimize risks. A satellite phone is carried for emergency communications. Extreme care is taken in purifying water for drinking and cooking: even though the steppes are surrounded by significant volumes of fresh water, the streams and waterholes in the steppe itself are of very poor quality. Water for hand washing is also provided at all stops.

Rides are accompanied by two or three guides and two wranglers. The guides have basic riding skills, but their main roles are to manage logistics and act as interpreters. The wranglers are responsible for the horses, and for the safety of the clients while on horseback. They saddle the horses, lead the group whilst riding and take care of the horses at the end of the day. Boojum Expeditions has employed the same wranglers for several years and has therefore been able to provide training in what the company and the clients expect. The horses are well-behaved, and experienced with the route and tours. The only potential safety problems I encountered were associated with differences in culture and language. The wranglers did not speak English so all communication had to be through the guides, not directly with the wranglers. This made it difficult to quickly exchange information about any problems with the horses or equipment whilst riding, or even to consult about the pace.

Clients are required to sign a three-page insurance disclaimer before the ride. This protects the operator from liability for any injury including death. Hard riding helmets and boots, designated safety equipment for horse riding, are recommended, though the choice to wear one is entirely up to the client. On this trip everyone wore riding boots, as recommended by Boojum, and most of the clients wore riding helmets.

### Marketing

The majority of Boojum's clients use the Internet as their main information source, and contact the office in Bozeman to enquire about the company's tours. Because of Boojum Expeditions' long-term involvement and experience in the Mongolian travel industry, the company is often commissioned to organize tours and logistics for journalists and television crews. As a result, Boojum Expeditions' Mongolian trips have been featured in articles in *National Geographic*®, *Outside*® and the *New York Times*®, and in documentaries by the British Broadcasting Corporation. These have helped greatly in publicizing Boojum internationally.

## Snowy Mountains, Australia: Reynella Station

### Place

The Snowy Mountains form part of Australia's Great Divide, a low mountain spine running the entire north–south length of the continent a little inland from the eastern coastline. The highest point on the Great Divide, and indeed in Australia, is Mt Kosciuszko in the Snowy Mountains in southern NSW, part of an area also known as the Australian Alps. Mt Kosciuszko is 2228 m in elevation, and together with nearby Mt Townsend and Mt Twynam, forms the core area of Mt Kosciuszko National Park. The higher slopes support a treeless alpine vegetation, grading to patches of gnarled snow gums and down to increasingly dense and tall stands of mountain gums in the subalpine zones. Within the subalpine there are also large open grassy areas.

The Snowy River, famous from the film *The Man from Snowy River*, has its source here, and so does the River Murray. Before Kosciuszko National Park was dedicated, the upland areas were used for seasonal cattle grazing. This no longer happens within the NSW portion of the Australian Alps National Parks, but it is still permitted even in parks in the adjacent state of Victoria, amidst ongoing controversy. From an economic perspective, tourism is by far the principal industry in the region, which has most of Australia's ski resorts, a large summer tourism industry and growing amenity migration (Buckley *et al.*, 2006).

### Operator

Reynella Rides is based at Reynella Station near Adaminaby, just outside Kosciuszko National Park. Established 35 years ago, Reynella is now Australia's oldest continuously operating commercial horse riding outfitter. Since it first started, the business has been run by the landowners, John and Roslyn Rudd, with up to five additional seasonal staff. Reynella Station operates a guest lodge and farmstay operation as well as the horse-trekking business. The family also runs 5000 sheep and cattle on an 800 ha property.

The tourism business at Reynella Station started as a farmstay operation with guided local trail rides, but soon began to offer multi-day rides into Kosciuszko National Park. The earliest trips were up to 12 days long, and access to the National Park was almost unrestricted. Current trips are less than half this length, carried out under a permit.

John Rudd's knowledge of this area, known locally as the High Country, began in the 1940s when he joined his uncle in leading trail-riding trips into the National Park. This gave him a broad knowledge of the area and a lifetime affinity with the High Country. Not surprisingly, he is a highly accomplished horseman and knows the area very well. In 2004, he received the Order of Australia for his services to ecotourism.

## Activity

The icon tour product from Reynella Rides is the Reynella Alpine Horseback Safari, a multi-day horse trek into Kosciuszko National Park. The trips are run either for 3 days and 4 nights or 5 days and 6 nights, and operate from October to April each year.

In addition to the multi-day camping horse treks, Reynella Rides offers single-day rides from Reynella Station, with riders staying at the guest lodge near the homestead. This is a popular weekend getaway activity.

In winter, Reynella Station also provides accommodation for skiers. The ski areas are about 40 min away from the homestead, but Reynella has arranged packages with local ski operators and offers all-inclusive ski holidays.

The multi-day horse-trekking trips start either at the homestead itself, or at a leased property 20 min drive away, depending on where the horses are being grazed at the time. The 3-day and 5-day groups start their rides together. After 3 days, the former return to the station by road, the latter on horseback.

The guests arrive at the homestead for dinner the night before the trek starts. After breakfast next morning, the horses are caught and yarded, and each rider is allocated a horse according to the level of experience claimed by the rider. This is a particularly critical issue for the operator, because people often overestimate their riding ability. All the horses at Reynella are experienced, however, and so are most of the clients, which helps to minimize risk. Over the following days, participants are encouraged to ride different horses on different days. Two or three spare horses, one pack horse and often one young inexperienced horse are taken with the trekking group, running free alongside the riders.

The trek starts with an extended climb into the alpine areas of the park at 1400–1800 m elevation, where the group constructs a temporary camp. On average, the group rides for 5 or 6 h each day, covering 25–30 km. The day's riding starts at about 10 am each day, after breakfast, feeding and saddling the horses. The group stops for a 1–2 h lunch break around a campfire in the middle of the day.

## Equipment

All riding equipment is provided by Reynella, though clients may bring their own if they prefer. Reynella also provides all group camping equipment, individual tents, sleeping mats and extra blankets. Clients are expected to bring their own riding clothes, sleeping bags and personal gear. Sleeping bags are available for rent from Reynella for a small additional charge. Waterproof oilcloth riding coats of traditional design are also available for rent.

Reynella's horses are Arabians, Thoroughbreds and crossbreeds. Most critically, all of them are well-trained, experienced, reliable, used to the conditions and willing to go forward. In particular, they are accustomed to crossing creeks and climbing steep mountain areas without demur, so there are no difficulties for riders when such conditions are encountered.

Camping equipment is transported using a truck and 4WD vehicle. Two different sites are used for the base camp, and on some trips, the camp is moved between these sites so that clients spend time at both. The camps are set up by the staff, with clients responsible only for their own tents. At the end of the trip, everyone lends a hand in cleaning, dismantling and packing up the tents.

## Accommodation

The first and last night of each trip are spent in the homestead, and either 2 or 4 nights camping. The tents are spacious and thick mats or mattresses are provided. The kitchen is set up around a campfire, and all cooking is on the fire. Reynella provides a cook, employed on a casual basis. Guests usually help with the washing up. A shower and a toilet tent are provided, and the toilet is moved every day. The camp is accessible by 4WD, and fresh food is delivered every second day. Reynella recently bought a campervan that is used to store the food and kitchen equipment. The food is very wholesome, with fresh vegetables and fruit every day, and a country-style breakfast with bacon, eggs and sausages.

## Statistics

Group size varies from 15 to 30 clients. Three-day trips cost AUD890 (US$630) per person and 5-day trips cost AUD1350 (US$950). Costs are thus around US$190–210 per person per day. Clients can also rent a sleeping bag and an oilskin parka for an additional charge of AUD33 (US$23). Soft drinks and alcoholic beverages are not included in the trip price, but are available for purchase at the campsite.

## Access

Most clients drive directly to Reynella Homestead in their own vehicles. The station can also be reached by air from Canberra or Sydney, and then by car or public bus from Cooma. A bus transfer from Canberra takes 1 h 40 min, and clients can be picked up in Cooma by Reynella staff and driven to the homestead for an additional charge of AUD19 (US$13).

Relatively few national parks in Australia permit horse riding. This contrasts with North America, where horse riding in national parks is much more commonplace. Reynella is one of only two commercial operators who have permits to operate in Kosciuszko National Park. Access, however, has been increasingly restricted over the past decade.

## Community

Cooma and Adaminaby are the closest towns. Both towns have been enjoying an increase in population recently, because of the recreational opportunities in the area. This region is one of the most famous Australian ski destinations in winter, and offers great hiking opportunities in summer.

As mentioned above, long-term High Country residents identify the area strongly with Banjo Paterson's famous poem 'The Man from Snowy River', and the modern tourism industry uses this theme extensively in marketing and souvenirs. In fact, however, there are now only about three horse riding outfitters in this area, and only Reynella can claim a long experience in the sector.

On the trip itself, given the remoteness of the area, there was no interaction with local residents. The guides, however, were local residents themselves and the clients showed an interest in their lifestyle and were keen to learn about the history of the area.

All food supplies were purchased in Cooma, the closest town. Reynella has arrangements with the local butcher and bakery to ensure the quality of their supplies.

## Experience

I have visited Reynella only once and it is difficult to make generalizations about the tour, since the horse riding experience depends on the similarity of the skills of the group. I was lucky to take part in a group that consisted mainly of skilled riders, so we had opportunities to ride at speed through vast plains, to jump logs and to make steep climbs. For beginners the rides are modified slightly and are generally slower. Fifty per cent of the clients who participated in this trip are repeat customers. Some of them were taking part in their third ride in this season alone, and one of them has been visiting repeatedly for 17 years.

The trip provides an authentic Australian bush experience, with cooking over a campfire and bathing in cold mountain streams. Many of the clients mentioned how much they enjoyed the open spaces, the peaceful environment and a feeling of freedom.

## Environment

As in many places in Australia, the High Country environment is characterized by extreme conditions: flood, drought and bushfires. In fact, the business suffered for 2 years after a major bushfire in 2002, which led to the temporary closure of some parts of the national park. The impacts of horse riding in national parks have been debated extensively (Newsome *et al.*, 2004a).

Reynella Rides followed best minimal-impact practices. The horses were fed with nose bags, so that no feed was placed on the ground. They were held in temporary yards, with no visible impact on the vegetation. Vegetation damage whilst riding was minimal, since the horses were on established tracks most of the time, and clients spread out widely for fast riding on the plains. The destruction of vegetation by wild pigs was by far the most obvious environmental impact in the area.

## Safety

In general two experienced guides accompany each ride. The rides are designed to suit beginners as well as skilled riders. This is arranged by allocating horses of appropriate temperament to each rider and is possible because all the horses are well trained, used to the local environment and familiar with the rides, so that beginners can take part safely.

The night before the ride starts, everyone takes part in a safety briefing about the main rules of the ride. The overriding rule is that whoever is riding in front always travels at a walk. On the tracks the horses always walk. Experienced riders, however, are encouraged to leave the tracks and ride at whatever pace they feel comfortable with and the terrain allows.

This increases potential risks for Reynella, but is one major reason for its success and the high percentage of repeat clients. The opportunity to ride independently, off track but within sight, allows experienced riders to enjoy the scenery and the riding simultaneously. Beginners, who may prefer a slower pace, can stay on the track where they can enjoy the horseback perspective without having to worry about hazards.

Issues of safety and liability have become critical for horse riding businesses in Australia in recent years. Indeed, over the past 4 years many such businesses have closed because of the high costs and restrictive conditions required to obtain insurance. As with other horse riding operators, and indeed other forms of adventure tourism, Reynella's clients are required to sign a three-page indemnity and insurance waiver before the ride. This relieves the operator of any responsibilities for client injury or even death.

Reynella provides hard riding helmets and boots, designated safety equipment for horse riding. It is up to each client whether or not to use them, but this choice is recorded and confirmed by a client signature on the waiver document. In practice, all clients wore riding boots, but only 50% wore hard riding helmets. The riders who chose not to wear helmets were not necessarily the most experienced riders.

## Marketing

Most of Reynella's clients are Australian, and after 34 years of successful operation Reynella has a high proportion of repeat clients and word-of-mouth referrals. In addition, international horse tourism agencies send several groups each year. Reynella Rides has established an international reputation for a reliable and consistently high-quality operation that gives riders an authentic experience of the 'Man from Snowy River' country. Indeed, it has been featured in several international adventure travel shows.

Even so, to keep the Reynella name visible to its horse riding clientele, a significant part of its overall budget is devoted to advertising. This includes print advertisements in specialist riding magazines internationally, and in 'outback' and 'high country' tourism and lifestyle magazines in Australia. Reynella also produces a printed brochure that is distributed through local visitor centres.

Horse riding in the Kosciuszko region of the Snowy Mountains has longstanding historical associations for many Australians, and also for most of Reynella's international clients. Several of the famous 19th-century bush poems penned by Banjo Paterson are inspired by this rugged environment. Best known of these, 'The Man from Snowy River', provides a reflection on the tough life of the early farmers in the High Country, the free-ranging herds of horses, and the trusting relationship between man and horse. Links to this historic legacy provide Reynella's key marketing advantage.

## Torres del Paine, Patagonia, Chile: Ride World Wide

### Place

Torres del Paine National Park is a well-known and highly scenic conservation area in Patagonia, southern Chile. It was declared a UNESCO Biosphere Reserve in 1978. The main attraction is the Paine Massif itself, with three peaks known as the Torres or Towers, and three more known as the Cuernos or Horns. The peaks are snowbound for much of the year, and the area is known for its scenic beauty, its lakes and cliffs, and its strong winds. The park provides habitat for a number of endangered and iconic plant and animal species, including condor, puma, guanaco and grey fox.

### Operator

Ride World Wide (2005) is a specialist equestrian tour operator based in the UK and operating globally since 1995. It does not run the riding trips itself, but markets trips in 25 different countries, having first sent its staff to meet the local operators and their guides, wranglers and horses, and to take part in the tours concerned. Riding tours are currently offered in France, Spain, Portugal, Greece and Romania; Jordan, Georgia, Mongolia, Kyrgyzstan and India; Morocco, Kenya, Tanzania, Malawi, Botswana and South Africa; the USA, Mexico, Ecuador, Peru, Uruguay, Chile and Argentina; and New Zealand, but apparently not Australia.

### Activity

The company's main tour product in Patagonia is a 12-day tour of the Paine Massif, staying either in camps or local estancias. Participants need to be skilled and experienced, able to control a horse at all paces in open terrain. They also need to be comfortable with backcountry conditions and have some camping experience. The trip involves 4–6 h on horseback each day, covering 20–40 km, including steep slopes, rough terrain, open and forested areas, and creek and river crossings. At one crossing the riders are ferried across whilst the horses swim. There are views of glaciers, lakes, waterfalls and both the Towers and the Horns of the Paine Massif.

### Equipment

All camping equipment except sleeping bags is provided by Ride World Wide and carried by packhorses. Vehicles are used on one occasion, to shuttle clients to a campsite whilst the horses are left with wranglers, known as baqueanos. The horses are medium-build crossbreeds, generally Chilean Horse crosses or Criollo mix. Some have Percheron blood. They are bred locally on the surrounding estancias, principally for working cattle and sheep. Most range from about 14.2 to 16 hands in height. Saddles are Chilean style with a comfortable sheepskin on top. The horses are trained western-style and are used to neck reining (Ride World Wide, 2005).

## Accommodation

There are two versions of this tour. In the camping option, the trip includes 11 nights' accommodation; 2 in a hotel in Punta Arenas, 1 in a local estancia, and 8 camping. Some of the campsites are close to estancias; some are run by the parks service and have showers; and the remainder are in more remote locations with no vehicle access or facilities. Camping is twinshare in weatherproof three-person dome tents, which are moved ahead of the riders each day. Clients put up their own tents, but guides assist if needed.

On the estancia version of this tour, guests stay the first night in an estancia on Skyring Sound, the last night in a hotel and the others in twinshare, en suite guest rooms either on working estancias or in estancias converted to guest lodges.

## Statistics

The trip lasts 12 days and runs at intervals between November and March each year. It starts and ends at Punta Arenas and includes 8 days' horse riding. Group sizes range from 2 to 12 riders. For a trip with two clients, the camping trip costs UKP1590 per person; with 3–6 clients UKP1490; and with 7–12 clients UKP1420. This includes twinshare accommodation, riding and guiding equipment, vehicle transfers and park fees. There is a single supplement of UKP150 for the camping rides. The estancia option costs UKP1780 per person with only two clients, UKP1660 per person with 3–6 and UKP1595 per person with 7–12 clients. The single supplement for the estancia ride is UKP200. These prices correspond to US$210–255 per person per day for the camping option and US$230–290 per person per day for the estancia option.

## Access

The departure point for these tours is Punta Arenas at the southern tip of Chilean Patagonia. Punta Arenas can be reached on a domestic flight from Santiago, the capital of Chile. Access to the southern entrance of the park where the ride starts, and from the last night's camp back to Punta Arenas, is by vehicle. The entrance fee for the park is included in the price, and is organized by the operator in advance.

## Community

The entire tour is locally run with accommodation on local estancias, horses and tack provided by local owners, and local guides and wranglers. Participants have opportunities to meet estancia owners at a traditional barbecue or asado.

## Experience

Participants spend 8 days on horseback, most of them camping. Highlights include access to remote areas of the national park such as the Cascada Zamora waterfall, as well as visits to more accessible areas such as Lago Grey and Rio de Los Perros, and classic views of the Paine Horns and Towers. There are visits to a colony of Magellan penguins, a barbeque with the local baqueanos, river crossings and an optional boat ride.

## Environment

No specific details are available, but Ride World Wide is a reputable operator and complies with normal minimal impact practices. At campsites within the national park, park rules apply. On estancias, environmental management issues are handled by the estancias themselves.

## Safety

Similar considerations apply for safety issues. Both pack and riding horses are locally owned and bred, familiar with and suited to the terrain and climate, used to commercial tours, and handled by their own local wranglers and guides. Clients are expected to be experienced riders, familiar with backcountry riding for long hours each day, and this requirement is made clear in the company's trip information materials.

## Marketing

This trip is marketed through Ride World Wide headquarters in the UK, principally through the website.

# 18 Mountain Biking

*Contributed by Julie Schaefers*

Julie Schaefers, Colorado, USA. Photo Chris Rowe.

## Sector Structure

Mountain biking is a large and diverse sport (Cessford, 1995; Bowker and English, 2002; Cordell *et al.*, 2004). Over the past decade it has grown in popularity and fragmented into distinct categories. Mountain biking as a whole is defined by the bike, whose heavy-duty frame, shock absorbers and fat studded tyres distinguish it from thin-framed, skinny-tyred racers.

Different people, however, ride their mountain bikes in different ways and places. At one extreme are those who ride in a largely upright position, on paved bike paths, either for exercise or transport, e.g. to commute to work. At the other extreme are the free-riders who enjoy the thrills and skills in riding at all angles on all surfaces: half-pipes or terrain parks; streetscapes and urban obstacles; or jumps, tippers and log rides in peri-urban parks and peaks.

Between these extremes are the adventure mountain bikers, who typically like to ride backcountry trails where the technical challenge derives from natural rather than built features. Surveys of these riders show that they want scenery and social interaction as well as speed and exercise (Cessford, 1995; Bowker and English, 2002). More skilled riders want more technical trails, with obstacles such as rocks, tree roots and switchbacks to challenge their skills and physical condition and provide speed, excitement and risk (Cessford, 1995). It is this style of riding that has given rise to mountain biking adventure tours.

According to various rider surveys, the typical adventure mountain bike rider is a physically active college-educated professional about 30 years old, who enjoys the outdoors (Cessford, 1995; Bowker and English, 2002; Green, 2003; National Sporting Goods Association (NSGA), 2005). About one-third of these riders are female and two-thirds male.

There was a period in the early 1990s when sales of mountain bikes grew rapidly, but since then sales have levelled off as riders wait for new advances in mountain bike technology. This pattern is reported both in Europe (Bicycle Business, 2005) and the USA (NSGA, 2005). There were about 8 million mountain bikes in the USA in 2004 (NSGA, 2005), down 2.3% from 2003. Participation by female riders, however, continues to grow (NSGA, 2005), as bike manufacturers, training camps and tour operators have catered more to the female half of the population.

Besides a bike and some physical endurance, an adventure mountain biker needs access to a trail system. Options include a bike-width single track, a trail several feet wide, or roads, which can be paved, gravelled, dirt or 4WD routes. Preferences vary by skill level, but generally paved and gravelled roads are least desirable and single track trails provide the best riding experience (Cessford, 1995).

Mountain biking is a relatively new use in existing trail systems. In the USA in the late 1980s, many communities closed their local open space and urban park trails to all mountain biking, owing to conflicts with more traditional horse and hiking users, as well as concerns over resource damage caused by mountain bikes. With the conflict between users' groups continuing to escalate, several mountain biking groups formed to protect trail access. In California, the International Mountain Bicycling Association (IMBA) was one such group. They have grown over the years and have been successful in working with land management agencies to protect and increase access for mountain biking on existing trail systems, building new trail systems, increasing safety and protecting resources. At the same time, IMBA pushed mountain bikers toward a trail etiquette to ride safely, yield the trail to other users, and to prevent trail and resource damage. There are similar issues in Australia (Goeft and Alder, 2001).

Despite the efforts of groups like IMBA, many trails remain closed to mountain bikes. The US National Parks Service has closed the majority of Park trails to mountain biking, restricting riding to paved roads. Many urban areas continue to maintain a ban on mountain bikes in local parks. These closures attempt to address the social conflicts between horse and hikers and mountain bikers, as well as safety issues associated with mixed use on some trails. The US Code of Federal Regulations for Wilderness Designated Lands and Wilderness Study Areas closed these designated lands to all motorized and mechanized modes of transportation, which is interpreted to include bicycles. Many groups, including the IMBA, continue to challenge these regulations in order to gain additional access to trails for mountain biking.

Although some areas are closed to biking, there are many more areas that are open. Moab, Utah may be the quintessential mountain bike community. The region is packed with 'must ride' trails, and local land managers work with a variety of user groups to keep the trails open, maintained, safe and accessible to the public. The terrain in the region offers challenges for all levels of riders, along with incredible scenery and infrastructure needed to enjoy a mountain bike trip. Currently, the majority of 'mountain bike meccas' are in the Western US and Canada. As communities interested in expanding their tourism opportunities work to encourage mountain biking in their region, however, the list of icon sites will continue to grow. Other areas where mountain bikers congregate include: Whistler in British Columbia, Canada; Durango and Fruita in Colorado; Mount Tamalpais State Park in California; Tsali in North Carolina; and Markara Peak in New Zealand.

Surveys of mountain bikers indicate that they are willing to travel long distances and spend several nights in a destination area in order to ride good terrain. Overall, they tend to be a fairly self-sufficient group, bringing their own equipment, rarely booking tours and selecting places to bike based on word-of-mouth recommendations rather than outside advertising (Reiter and Blahna, 2002; Green, 2003). Less experienced riders in particular, however, take advantage of the opportunities provided by adventure tour companies. In addition to tour operators, there are other tourism industries that benefit from mountain biking: rental, gear and repair shops; lodging and dining; and other infrastructure such as ski areas, shuttle services and trail systems. Some of these services are highlighted in the following sections.

## Ski Areas

Ski areas are opening their lifts and terrain to mountain bikers during the summer off-season (Blumenthal, 2001). Access to lifts offers a day of downhill riding without too much of the uphill pedalling. The ski areas develop trail systems, meaning that bikers are not just headed straight down the hill through vegetation. These trail systems create excellent trail riding opportunities while protecting the area from resource damage or erosion. As with the ski slopes, the trail systems are rated for beginners, intermediates and advanced riders (Frost and McCullough, 1995). Lifts are modified to carry bikes on the back, and there are attendants to assist you and your bike on and off the lifts. Only a few lifts are open, so not all the skiable terrain is open for biking. Often, lift tickets cost significantly less than a winter ticket (Table 18.1).

I have ridden at Vail Associates' Keystone, Breckenridge and Vail ski areas and found the riding to be well worth the lift tickets. Unlike ski runs, the bike trails link

**Table 18.1.** Selected North American ski resorts open for mountain biking.

| Ski area | Location | Lift ticket (US$) |
|---|---|---|
| Vail | Colorado, USA | 29 |
| Whistler | British Columbia, Canada | 33 |
| Deer Valley | Utah, USA | 20 |
| Winter Park | Colorado, USA | 22 |
| Mount Snow | Vermont, USA | 30 |
| Mammoth Mountain | California, USA | 32 |

up all across the mountain, with lots of riding through the trees. The runs were long enough that I never felt I was spending more time on the lift that in the saddle. The services at the bottom were similar to ski season – plenty of food and drink, as well as a bike rental and service shop. A service shop is a valuable asset just in case something goes wrong, so that the whole day would not be wasted by broken parts! Luckily I did not have reason to visit the first aid station, but the ski areas are leaving these open too, to service those who get a little too much downhill.

## Hut Systems

Hut systems, popular with backcountry skiers and backpackers, can also be used by mountain bikers. These hut systems require riders to be self-sufficient. They must be able to plan an extended trip and act as their own guide, cook, doctor and bike mechanic. Most huts have little or no equipment, so biking up to them requires panniers or riding with a full pack. Recently, however, several hut systems have been set up specifically for mountain bikers. These huts are stocked with food and bedding, so only minimal weight needs to be carried from hut to hut. The riding to and around the huts varies: some are forest access roads, others have single track trails accessible from the huts and others have single track trails connecting to other huts.

The San Juan Hut System (2005), for example, allows groups of up to eight mountain bikers of intermediate skill to ride from either Telluride or Durango in Colorado to Moab in Utah, stopping at seven huts along the way in each case. Total distance is about 330 km along the Telluride route, and 345 km along the Durango route. The routes include a mixture of forest roads and single-track trails, and the prices are currently US$553 per person along either route.

Tenth Mountain Division Huts (2005) maintains a set of huts in Colorado that are accessible by mountain bike and can accommodate from six to 20 people in different huts, at a price of US$28–41 per person per night. All of the huts are accessible by mountain bike, but some of the trails between them traverse Wilderness Areas where bikes are not permitted.

The Alpine Club of Canada (2005) maintains a similar system of huts in southwestern British Columbia, Canada, accessible to mountain bikers at a cost of CAD18–30 per person per night, i.e. US$13–24.

## Courses, Camps and Competitions

Camps have been established in many areas where mountain bike riders congregate. The options range from 1-day, one-on-one sessions, to multiple-day group tours with instruction throughout. Different camps offer different instructor-to-client ratios, and some focus on providing instruction from an Olympic or other well-known rider. These multiple-day courses or camps vary in costs and location, but generally meals and accommodation are included in the prices, as well as transportation during the class and instruction. Clients bring their own bikes. Many of the ski areas open for the summer season now offer biking classes, comparable to ski school. These are generally 1-day courses, and prices include lift tickets and bike rental as well as instruction.

Competitions are important for many adventure mountain bikers, allowing them to test their abilities and skills in a friendly atmosphere. There is a wide variety of competitions, some more serious than others. Mountain biking is an official sport of the Olympics, so there are several competitions for people wanting to qualify for their Olympic team. At the more casual end, there are competitions in communities throughout the world, for people to try out their skills and speed against others. For example, teams of four can grab their headlights and ride in the 24 Hours of Moab – a relay race in which each team member rides a set circuit as many times as possible in an hour and then hands over to the next team member for the next hour, for a total of 24 h in a row. Some communities have set up competitions during larger festival weekends, such as the Fat Tire Festival in Fruita, Colorado. Winter Park, Colorado holds a series of hill-climbing, cross-country and mountain circuit races throughout the summer.

## Day Trips

Half-day or full-day guided mountain bike tours are offered commercially in many parts of the world. These range from the introductory to the extreme. Most common are tours that cater for people who know how to ride a bike and look forward to a day out pedalling, but are generally not experienced in trail riding. Rather than focusing on the skills and endurance of mountain biking, these tours focus on historic, scenic, wine tasting or specific landscapes of an area. The bike is just the mode of transportation. Other day tours combine mountain biking with other activities such as rafting or fly-fishing. Tours such as this are available from Africa to Alaska, Thailand to Tibet.

In other areas companies offer single-day trips that provide a much more extreme biking opportunity. In New Zealand, for example, there are several heli-biking tours where a helicopter drops clients off with their bike at the top of a mountain, and a guide navigates the trip down. Even these tours, however, do not advertise any particular need for physical endurance or biking skills.

In some areas, such as Moab in Utah, 1-day introductory tours are offered specifically for those who have not ridden mountain bikes before, but are interested in trying out the sport. In these cases, the guide also acts as instructor to assist clients in getting down the trail and back up. Such a tour may be the first step to converting someone into a full-fledged adventure mountain biker.

For these 1-day tours, bikes are generally supplied as well as transportation to and from the starting point, helmet, water bottle, food and a local guide. These operations tend to market their tours through traditional means, attracting tourists looking for fun activities for the day. Websites offer clients discounts for advance bookings, and flyers and brochures are available to those planning on site.

A classic example of these tours is the sunrise ride down Haleakala in Maui, Hawaii. The tour begins long before sunrise. The operator takes clients up in a van, gives them a tour of the crater and positions the group for maximum exposure to the sunrise on Haleakala. After that, clients are given a bike, some gear and a map. Some tours then leave clients to make their own way down the volcano and back to the bike shop. Other operators guide their clients downhill as a group, with stops along the way to learn about the island. Either way, the day is a fun and downhill way to see the island.

## Multi-day Tours

Multiple day tours generally cater to those who have solid biking skills and enjoy it enough to focus a longer vacation on riding with family and friends. Operators of multiple day tours set up a series of all-day rides within a region, as well as accommodation and transportation in between these rides. These packages allow those who have limited time, do not have trip planning skills or are not familiar with the area, to get out riding the best trails for the group's skill level without worrying about setting up logistics. These tours focus on mountain biking as the primary activity, but comfort is also considered, with fully catered lodgings rather than camping and cooking out. Depending on the tour length and location, additional activities such as rafting, hiking or fishing may be scheduled through the operator.

Multiple day tours are available throughout the world. Depending on the location and size of group, some tours can be customized to fit the skill level of the clients. Many advertise that they are family friendly; others focus on single-track riding and apply to more advanced riders. Bikes and other needed equipment are also provided to increase the 'show and go' factor: i.e. clients just need to arrive and the rest of the trip is taken care of by the operator. The length of these trips also varies greatly, from a few days to a few weeks.

I have not ridden on any multiple day tours, but I have taken part in private trips on the same route and encountered commercial tours along the way. In Chugach National Forest in South-Central Alaska, I met eight visitors and a guide riding through temperate rainforest, in rain, mist, fog, clouds and occasional sunshine. As long as the mud is not too deep, Alaska offers excellent biking temperatures and uncrowded conditions. In addition to spectacular scenery, visitors are likely to encounter a variety of wildlife including moose, Sitka deer, brown bear, bald eagle, raven and mountain goat. Safety briefings from the guide included important information on getting along in bear country, especially important when riding quietly on a bike through the forest.

Alaska Backcountry Bike Tours (2005), for example, offers a 9-day intermediate-level tour in Chugach National Forest in South-Central Alaska, with a combination of single-track and forest-road riding, bikes provided, and a mixture of inns and camping for accommodation. The cost is US$1795 per person, or just under US$200 per person per day.

Recreational Equipment Inc. Adventures (2005) offers a 9-day tour through Copper Canyon in northern Mexico at a price of US$1599 per person or approximately US$180 per person per day. This includes accommodation in lodges, cabins and hotels; most meals; bike rental and gear; local transport; and a bilingual guide.

In Grand Teton National Park, Wyoming, Teton Mountain Bike Tours (2005) offers a 5-day trip with 3 days single-track mountain biking and 1 day whitewater rafting. The total cost is US$1795 per person, which includes accommodation in B&B or lodges, all meals, local transport, bike rental and gear, and a guide. This price corresponds to around US$360 per person per day.

In the southern hemisphere, Down Under Dirt (2005) in New Zealand offers 6-

day mountain bike tours, including technical training with routes, itineraries and prices customized to individual groups.

Generally, these tour operators have good quality bikes in good working condition and are efficient at getting their clients out of the door and on to the trails. Guides accompany the group on the trails, and depending on the skill level of the clients, can offer tips and techniques throughout the trip to improve riding skills. Clients seem pleased with the selection of trails and the service given. These trips seem to work best if all members of the group are at similar riding skill level. Otherwise, a beginner in a group of advanced riders may find themselves well outside their comfort level, or an advanced rider in a group of beginners may be bored with the terrain.

Some tour operators now also offer multi-day mountain bike trips with vehicle support. The support vehicle carries camping equipment and food, leaving the clients free to enjoy an unencumbered ride. Generally, these tours focus on trails through the backcountry not easily accessible by day trips. Facilities are limited and primitive – although the tour companies excel at bringing basic comforts to their clients in the backcountry. Most tours supply guides, vehicles, food, water, first aid, basic bike support and shared camp equipment. Clients provide their own bike, tent and sleeping bag/pad. The White Rim Trail in Utah, profiled below, provides one example.

## White Rim Trail, Utah

The White Rim Trail outside of Moab, Utah, rated as an intermediate or moderate ride, is considered a rite of passage by many in the adventure mountain biking community. The 145 km trail is actually a jeep road, with 1830 m of vertical as the trail winds along a layer of white sandstone in Canyonlands National Park (US National Park Service, 2005). The trail is not technical, but the length of the trip, and the stiff climbs encountered each day, require endurance and physical condition. The trip starts on top of the Mesa, switchbacks down into the canyon along the Colorado River, passes by the confluence of the Colorado and the Green Rivers, follows the Green River and then finishes with a climb back out on to the Mesa. There are several companies offering the tour throughout the spring, summer and autumn season under special use permits with the National Park Service. The National Park Service regulates use and requires all parties to obtain a permit and be assigned campgrounds for the 3–4 day trip.

Each day holds a solid climb, some outrageous downhill and slickrock sections, as well as some riding through the flats. The scenery is incredible, as you are completely surrounded by the red rocks and desert sandstone arches, spires, slot canyons and mesas. I have ridden the White Rim several times, but always as a private trip. With assigned campsites, I have had opportunities to interact with the commercial trips, and on one occasion was able to borrow a working derailleur from a guide for the rest of our trip. On private trips everyone wants to ride and no one wants to drive the support vehicle. Private groups therefore travel light and fit everything for nine people into a single vehicle, so each person has to drive only one 15 km section. Clients on the commercial trips do not have this constraint, so they get better food, colder drinks, better bike repair services and more comfortable camps with chairs, tables and shade tents.

Some of the tour companies offering the White Rim trip are summarized in Table 18.2 below. Generally, the cost of the tour includes guides and cooks, meals, snacks, non-alcoholic beverages, water, group kitchen and camp gear, National Park Service fees and reservations, first aid for you and your bike, and a 4WD support vehicle and driver. Clients must bring their own bikes, tents, sleeping bags and pads, or can rent them from the tour company for an additional daily fee. Overall, prices range from US$170 to 205 per person per day.

**Table 18.2.** Supported mountain bike tours on the White Rim Trail.

| Company (website) | Days | Cost (US$) | Other tours offered |
|---|---|---|---|
| Rim Tours (www.rimtours.com) | 3, 4 | 615, 725 | Hiking, rafting, kayaking, canoeing |
| Escape Adventures (www.escapeadventures.com) | 4 | 699 | Hiking, rafting |
| Holiday Expeditions (www.bikeraft.com) | 3, 4 | 585, 685 | Rafting, various multi-day tours |
| Kaibab Tours (www.kaibabtours.com) | 4 | 699 | Road and mountain bike trips, western USA |

## Mountain Biking Resorts

Resorts catering toward those interested in adventure mountain biking as their primary activity are becoming more prevalent around the world. As those interested in mountain biking vacations settle down with families and children, or 'anchors' as they are affectionately known in the biking community, resorts that have good terrain for biking, as well as other recreational opportunities and facilities for non-mountain bikers, become particularly appealing. Serviced rooms and restaurants have advantages over camping and cooking out when one has a family to cater for.

I have not stayed at a mountain bike resort, but as my usual biking group continues to gain more 'anchors' in recent years, I can see the appeal of such an arrangement. Ciclo Montaña (2005), for example, is surrounded by trails, so there are many hiking options for those not biking. The resort is about 1 h from the Mediterranean, so there are also opportunities for fishing, snorkelling, diving, surfing and relaxing. The standard mountain biking package offered by Ciclo Montaña includes: a 1-week stay in a traditional guesthouse in Mecina-Fondales in Andalucia; airport transfers; five guided 1-day rides; evening meals and supplies for breakfast. Clients must bring their own mountain bikes. The cost is €446 per person for mountain bikers and €363 for non-riders accompanying them. This corresponds to approximately US$75 per person per day.

Sri Lanka has long been a vacation destination for those drawn to sandy beaches and water sports. RideLanka (2005) will now guide mountain bikers on single track trails throughout the island. Three different price options are offered depending on the length of the tour and the level of accommodation. A 10-day trip staying in lodges costs US$695 per person, or about US$70 per person per day. A 10-day tour in more upmarket accommodation, listed as 'semi-luxury' by RideLanka (2005), costs US$995 per person, or approximately US$100 per person per day. A 12-day tour with a mixture of inns and camping costs US$1075 per person, or approximately US$90 per person per day. Each of these prices includes twinshare accommodation, meals, guides, local transport and bike rental. Non-riders can enjoy the beach, surf and beauty of the island. The non-mountain bike activities available at these resorts are intriguing enough that even I might be persuaded to take a day off from the trail.

# 19 Off-road Safaris

Sand dunes in Taklamakan, China. Photo Ralf Buckley.

Simpson Desert, Australia. Photo Ralf Buckley.

## Sector Structure

Even in countries such as the USA and Australia, where a significant proportion of the population owns 4WD vehicles, most of these vehicles are driven only in town, and most of the vehicles visiting remote areas are driven by their owners on private recreational trips. Even so, the commercial adventure tourism industry in these countries does make extensive use of 4WD and other off-road or all-terrain vehicles (ATVs).

Fully equipped, guided and catered tours, where participants purchase a place on an all-inclusive product package are one option, but there are several others. There are so-called tagalong tours, where participants drive their own fully equipped 4WD vehicles behind a lead or guide vehicle, whose driver knows the terrain and is equipped to help rescue any other vehicles if need be. Tagalong tours are particularly popular for multi-day traverses in relatively remote areas, where a single vehicle could be at significant risk.

In some countries, 4WD vehicles are permitted on formed tracks in some national parks and other public lands. The environmental impacts and management of such use have been considered on a number of occasions (e.g. Hornby and Sheate, 2001; Buckley, 2004d). In many parks, off-road vehicles are banned.

People will also pay to drive their own vehicles on privately owned off-road areas, sometimes set up as challenge courses to test the capabilities of vehicles and drivers. In relatively easy and heavily frequented off-road areas, there are companies that simply rent 4WD vehicles to tourists, generally with heavy insurance and a large deposit. And finally, there are many commercial tours that, though not centred around the 4WD experience, use 4WD vehicles to reach a particular area such as a put-in or take-out site for a river rafting trip.

In many developing countries, in contrast, 4WD vehicles are not readily available for general or recreational use. Short of mounting a major international expedition and importing all one's own vehicles, with the associated taxes and permit problems, the only way to travel by 4WD is to hire vehicle and driver together. In the past this was often in the nature of a charter that could only be arranged through local contacts on arrival. Such arrangements have generally now been formalized into internationally bookable commercial tours, where the local contacts and charter arrangements are made by the tour operator rather than the individual traveller.

In this chapter, only the first of these categories is considered: tours in the conventional sense that they are packaged products available for sale at a retail level, and an individual customer can purchase a place irrespective of any other participants. In particular, the focus is on off-road safaris in desert and semi-desert areas where there are few if any people, little or no shade or water supply, and soft sandy or clay soils that require skills in off-road driving and sometimes also a winch.

There are now commercial 4WD tours in arid steppes and sand-dune deserts around the world, from Africa to Australia, Chile to China. Most of my experiences in these areas were for scientific research on desert sand dunes and their vegetation, long before any commercial tours commenced operation. In Australia's Great Sandy, Great Victoria, Gibson, Simpson and Strzelecki Deserts I drove my own 4WD. In the Namib and Kalahari Deserts of Southern Africa, the Atacama Desert in northern Chile, the Ordos Desert of Mongolia, the Taklamakan Desert in far western China and the Qinghai Plateau north of Tibet, I travelled with scientific colleagues, sharing driving where the country's laws permitted. The case studies in this chapter combine advertised information on commercial tour products currently available with my own previous experiences in the areas concerned.

For most of the case studies described in this chapter, I have driven independently along the routes concerned, not with the specific commercial tour(s) referred to. Further details of relevant dates, and differences between private and commercial trips, are given under the case studies concerned. Many of my own off-road journeys were simply to provide access to the areas concerned, for scientific research projects.

Over the years these off-road journeys have included a number of additional experiences that might well qualify as 'adventurous'. In various 4WD vehicles I have, on occasion, been either airborne or submerged, sometimes intentionally and sometimes inadvertently. Jumping a long-wheelbase Landcruiser® off a ramp to cross even a small ditch, let alone a collapsed section in a narrow cliffside track, is certainly an adrenalin-charged activity. The same applies to a 100-m river crossing on a shifting gravel bed where the vehicle is almost afloat, or winching and driving simultaneously up a steep diagonal bank from a deep waterhole. These tales, however, are not part of a tourism text!

## Southern Taklamakan Desert, China: Various Operators

### Place

The Taklamakan Desert lies in the far west of China, between the Himalayas to the south and the Tien Shan ranges to the north. It stretches west to Kashgar (Kashi) on the border between China, Pakistan and Afghanistan; north to Aksu; and south to Hotian and Yutian. The ancient Silk Road between Europe and China ran along the margins of the Taklamakan. The desert area is hyperarid, with a mean annual rainfall of around 10 mm.

Rivers fed by glaciers to the south run out into the desert and evaporate. Where these rivers enter the desert there are oasis towns famous for agricultural produce such as silk and melons. Whilst small relative to major Chinese cities, towns such as Hotian number over 1 million inhabitants. From each of these major towns, roads run north along or parallel to the riverbeds, to a series of successively smaller villages. Beyond the roads, villagers journey further up dry riverbeds to collect donkey-loads of firewood. The central part of the Taklamakan is a shifting sand desert with little or no vegetation and some of the world's tallest dunes, including giant star-shaped and pyramidal dunes whose mode of formation is still not entirely clear.

### Operator

A number of tour operators, most of them German, Italian, French and Chinese, offer tours across the Taklamakan. Many more offer tours that supposedly include such a crossing, but on close inspection of itineraries clearly include only a vehicle trip along the southern fringing road, the southern branch of the former Silk Road. Most of those that do actually cross the desert take one of two routes. The most adventurous travel by 4WD from Yutian in the south, up the Keriya River to Daheyan; from there on foot, with camel trains carrying baggage, west to the ancient 8th-century fortified hill of Mazar-tagh; and from there by jeep again north to Aksu. Of course, the same route can also be taken in reverse.

Other trips travel due south from Aksu to Hotian along the Hotian riverbed, with a side trip to Mazar-tagh. These travel the entire distance by 4WD. And a few take a loop route, from Yutian by 4WD to Daheyan West; by camel and foot to Mazar-tagh; and south by 4WD to Hotian. One company, Golden Bridge (2005) mentions a route from Daheyan West via Arzhan and Alar to Aksu.

Some of the tour operators who offer such trips include Shaolin Viaggi (2005) in Italy; China Tours (2005), Auf und Davon Reisen (2005) in Germany; Horizons Nouveaux (2005) in France and See Xinjiang (2005) in China.

I have not taken part in any of these tours. I have travelled along much of the route as part of a scientific reconnaissance trip in the early 1980s with colleagues from the China Academy of Sciences based at the Desert Research Institute in Lanzhou. We travelled by 4WD up the Hotian River valley, back down to the southern fringing road, and again into the desert north from Yutian. We did not travel the central section by camel, although my Chinese colleagues had explored that area, and many others, in previous decades.

As far as we could establish, our trip in the 1980s was the first access into the central Taklamakan by any Westerner since the Swedish explorer Sven Hedin almost a century earlier, but this may simply reflect lack of historical records. Whilst we were there, an all-Chinese expedition made a crossing of the desert north to south. Silk and carpet merchants were also well established in the towns along the desert borders. If I understood correctly, they were already weaving carpets on commission for international clients, as well as continuing to produce traditional designs.

## Activity

Tour operator websites provide day-by-day itineraries, but rather little information about activities along the way. Most tours depart from Beijing and fly to Urumqi and thence Aksu in the north or Hotian in the south. From there they spend several days driving in jeeps or trucks, 6–8 days hiking with camel support and several more days driving out, before flying back to Urumqi and Beijing or Guangzhou. It seems likely that most of the day is spent travelling and making and breaking camp. Photo galleries on the tour operator websites indicate that there are also opportunities to walk near camp, to examine the old fortifications at Mazar-tagh, and to visit local residents' houses in the riverbed villages.

Our aim in the 1980s was a reconnaissance mission for geomorphologic research on sand dune dynamics, so we set out to explore as far into the desert as possible in view of our vehicles' capabilities, our ability to carry fuel and the time available. We drove on and off roads and tracks, hiked or rode camels to climb up dunes, slept in communal huts or by communal campfires in the smaller villages, and ate whatever we could buy along the way or brought with us.

## Equipment

In the 1980s we travelled in two vehicles, a Toyota® Landcruiser and the Chinese equivalent of a short-wheelbase Jeep®.

## Accommodation

In the 1980s there was a hotel in Hotian and basic guesthouses on the main road along the southern margin of the sands. In the villages along the riverbeds there were communal huts for travellers, but these had little to recommend them. In a bazaar I had bought a greatcoat stuffed with the discarded outer shells of silk cocoons, and a sheepskin hat. Wearing these, I slept on the ground by a communal campfire used by donkey herders, firewood collectors and other travellers.

## Statistics

Costs for commercial tours currently offered are around US$5000 per person. Golden Bridge (2005) for example, quotes prices of US$3723–5293 depending on group size, with a single supplement of US$451. This price includes travel from Beijing and back to Hong Kong, with 12 days in the Taklamakan itself. The German operator Auf und Davon Reisen (2005) charges €4083 per person for groups of ten or more, plus a €390 single supplement. These prices are hence around US$350 per person per day. On our trip in the 1980s there were eight people including myself, my colleagues from Lanzhou, some of their local colleagues from Hotien and the drivers. We spent several weeks in the area altogether, with our longest trip into the desert dunes taking 4 or 5 days.

## Access

Access to western China is heavily dependent on the political situation at the time. My trip to the Taklamakan in the 1980s was not long after China was first opened to outsiders following the long closure during the Cultural Revolution. During my first visit to the Chinese Academy of Sciences Desert Research Institute (DRI) in 1983, to visit the Tengger (Tenggri) Desert of the Ordos Region in Inner Mongolia, I was accompanied by party cadres at all times, as well as scientists. By the time I visited Hotien, one could travel alone through much of China, but the far west was still a restricted area. The borders at Kashgar were closed and the only point of entry into China was through Beijing.

I flew to Lanzhou and then on to Urumqi, Aksu and Hotian. From there we drove. The main road along the desert margin was a well-formed dirt road when near the major towns but not elsewhere. The tracks along the dry riverbeds were donkey trails or non-existent. There were no commercial facilities such as rental vehicles, and I was entirely dependent on my colleagues from the DRI for all logistical arrangements. In particular, we were travelling as scientists, not tourists.

## Community

At the time of my visit, Chinese government policy had led to a wave of migration by Han people into the region around Urumqi and south, and this was not popular with local people of different ethnic descent. The main such people were the Uygur or Uighur, who look more Caucasian than Mongolian and whose language is more similar to European than to tonal Chinese languages. Many Uygur words contain strings of consonants not separated by vowels, unlike Chinese languages. The Uygur word for 'thank you' for example, is a somewhat guttural 'rachmat' with a hard 'ch'. This is easy for an English speaker to pronounce, but the closest a Chinese speaker can manage is 'ra ha me ta.' Many of these local peoples are Muslim, which separates them further from the Han Chinese. At night in the smoky local bazaars, clad in greatcoat and sheepskin cap, I was unremarkable to the locals except for my height, as long as I kept silent. I was hence able to observe local customs, but not to communicate.

## Experience

Tour operator websites speak of the silence of the sands and the beauty of the dunes. Web logs by individual travellers and groups also mention sandstorms and interesting cultural interactions. In the 1980s, I was certainly an object of interest to local residents, children particularly. Our local translator asked at one stage why I only photographed rich children. In fact I had photographed children wearing bright clothes, assuming them to be traditional costume, in contrast to others who wore miniature versions of the stereotypical Red Army overalls, in green or blue denim. It turned out that the latter were simply less well off.

There were no other cars, and everyone in the villages was either on foot or on bicycles. Donkeys and donkey carts were the universal means of transport. We were welcomed everywhere, and bought local food as we went along. This consisted principally of boiled or roast mutton and boiled bread. In the villages furthest into the desert we found flat bread similar to Indian naan. We also ate rice on occasion but not routinely. It was a particular variety with very short plump grains and a black eye. It was by far the most delicious rice I have ever tasted.

## Environment

The river-corridor ecosystems experience major environmental impacts from firewood collectors who cut the poplar trees that line the major watercourses. The principal demand and market for firewood, however, is in the major towns. The more remote villages, and occasional tour groups, consume only a small proportion. 4WD vehicles may cause noise disturbance to local wildlife. Tourists may cause impacts on the ancient heritage buildings at Mazar-tagh, and probably cause some social and cultural impacts in the villages. However, I have not visited the area recently to check.

## Safety

The central Taklamakan is a relatively forbidding environment, with very low rainfall and shifting sands. Tour routes, however, stick to watercourses where possible, and the camel route through the centre seems to cross relatively low dunes, at least in comparison to the giant star and pyramidal dunes in some of the Taklamakan. Tour operator websites made no mention of navigation, communications or safety, but presumably the vehicles carry GPS, radio, and winches and sand anchors. Or perhaps not.

My trip in the 1980s took place during a transitional period in Chinese politics when vehicles still belonged nominally to the State, but individual drivers were held 'responsible' for them as a step in taking on private ownership. This so-called responsibility system produced some strange quirks. Our drivers were fanatical about keeping their vehicles clean, but quite inexperienced in off-road recovery techniques. As a consequence, our vehicles did not have winches, sand anchors, sand ladders or even spades. But they did have feather dusters. They did not carry water, but we did have crates of beer.

Of course, we got bogged, and that was when we discovered that the freewheeling hubs were destroyed, since the vehicle had been driven in 4WD with hubs unlocked, until the locking mechanism was worn down to shiny stubs. We walked many kilometres to find wood to put under the wheels, and once we were unbogged I stored the wood in the vehicle for next time. But next time we got stuck I found the driver had secretly thrown the wood out, apparently because it was 'dirty'.

## Marketing

Tour operator websites are relatively uninformative. Brochures may contain more detail.

## Simpson Desert, Australia: Various Operators

### Place

Most of Australia is flat and dry. Large areas in central Australia are covered by sand dunes. The lower slopes of the dunes are stabilized by grasses and shrubs, but the dune crests are unstable and windblown. The dunes are of the type known as parallel or longitudinal, i.e. in line with the prevailing wind. They are over 25 m high in some areas, though generally lower, and some individual dunes run unbroken for over 100 km. The flatter areas between the dunes, known as swales, support spiny hummock grasses and patches of an acacia species known as mulga. The bases of dead mulga trees remain as sharp and sometimes hidden stumps that can easily puncture the tyres of 4WD vehicles. To cross the sand dune crests off-road, vehicles must first gain speed on the lower flanks, risking punctures in the process.

The dune crests are quite wide and often have secondary dunes and hollows that are not visible from below, so a 4WD vehicle can easily become bogged in soft sand on the crest. There are few trees on the dune crests, so winching requires a sand anchor. All in all, driving cross-country across the larger dunes is difficult and time-consuming. The summer heat is intense and there is no surface water. During the day one is pestered by bushflies, and during the night by mosquitoes.

There are several distinct regions: the Great Sandy Desert in the northwest, the Gibson Desert in the central west, the Great Victoria Desert in the southwest and south, and the Simpson and Strzelecki Deserts in the central east. Between these lies the town of Alice Springs, a number of low rocky ranges, some ephemeral rivers, and flatter and less sandy areas occupied by large cattle stations. Water for cattle is from groundwater bores. In some areas groundwater is at several thousand metres depth, but subartesian: i.e. it will rise up a bore shaft to within a hundred metres or so depth, and can then be pumped to the surface.

Large areas have been subject to geophysical exploration for oil, and this generally includes cutting tracks for access by seismic exploration vehicles. There are a number of salt lakes, such as Lake Amadeus in the central west, Lake Eyre in the southeast and Lake Peera Peera Poolanna in the central east. There is also one small marginal area with freshwater lakes, the Coongie Lakes, fed by the Coopers Creek system that is replenished by rainfall outside the desert area.

### Operator

Tourism in central Australia focuses principally on Uluru or Ayers Rock, accessible by road or air from Alice Springs and supplied with a range of tourist accommodation and facilities. There are also tours to rocky gorges west and east of Alice Springs itself. During the 1970s, when I worked in the central deserts, there was little or no tourism in the more remote sand dune areas.

Since then, however, it has become commonplace for off-road 4WD clubs to carry out traverses of the better-known routes. These include: the Canning Stock Route in the northwest, which links waterholes and was once used to drive cattle; the Gunbarrel Highway, a formed but eroded dirt road running west across the Gibson Desert; the Birdsville and Strzelecki Tracks running north–south along the eastern margins of the Simpson Desert sand dunes; and the so-called French Line running west to east across the central Simpson Desert itself. The French Line is the supply road built to support oil exploration in the 1970s. It is a wide, bulldozed road that cleared vegetation from the swales and slopes and cut through the soft dune crests, and can thus be driven at speed by a laden 4WD vehicle. This is enormously easier than driving across dunes off-track.

Currently, a number of commercial tour operators offer trips to these areas, mostly on a so-called tagalong basis: i.e. clients bring their own off-road vehicles and follow a lead guide vehicle. Examples of such tour operators include: Swagman Tours (2005), which offers both passenger and tagalong options; and Duncans Off-Road (2005), which offers tagalong only. Swagman Tours offers trips from west to east, and Duncan's from east to west. Most of the crossing is on the main French Line, but a number of the other former geophysical exploration tracks are also used. At least one tour operator also offers commercial camel treks across the Simpson Desert (Outback Camel Company, 2005).

I have not taken part in any of these commercial tours but have driven their routes, and many others throughout central Australia, whilst carrying out ecological research in the mid-1970s. I also led commercial tours to central Australia in the 1980s, but these were natural history rather than adventure trips.

## Activity

The main activity during the desert crossing is simply driving. Stops are made at scenic areas such as Dalhouse Springs, an artesian hot spring and pool on the western margin. Stops are also made at various historic sites such as Poeppel's Corner, a survey point making the boundary between three States. Walks across the sand dunes or along the salt lakes are also possible where time permits. For vehicles that stay on the main tracks there should be no need to dig or winch, unless wet areas are encountered.

## Equipment

A 4WD vehicle with good clearance is the basic prerequisite. For tours that stay on formed tracks, wide tyres are an advantage, since they can be run at low pressure on soft sand. For driving off-track, standard narrow tyres are less likely to suffer punctures, but have more difficulty crossing dunes. Winch, sand anchor, jack, long-handled spade, spares and puncture repair kit are essential. This includes levers to remove split rims from light truck tyres in some 4WD vehicles, as well as tyre levers. Radio, maps and GPS are also important. Sufficient fuel for detours or even a return trip, and sufficient water to survive an extended breakdown are strongly advisable, even though commercial tours always have multiple vehicles for safety. On tagalong tours, every vehicle is expected to be fully equipped.

## Accommodation

All accommodation in the Simpson Desert itself is in tents or swags, the local name for a canvas bedroll with a blanket and thin mattress. Rain is rare and local stockmen use swags. Overnight temperatures can fall below freezing in winter, however, and tents are also valuable in screening out mosquitoes. Commercial accommodation is available at the legendary Birdsville Hotel at the eastern edge of the desert, and at Mt Dare Station Homestead on the western edge.

## Statistics

Group sizes vary, but tagalong tours may easily have 8–10 vehicles or more, each commonly with only two occupants, though occasionally four or five. Vehicles provided by 4WD tour operators will generally carry as many passengers as possible, for economic reasons: typically four or five. The crossing of the central sand dune section typically takes 3 days, but is usually offered as one section of more extended 4WD tours that may take 8–20 days in total. Costs are around AUD2500 per person for fully equipped tours, i.e. AUD200 (US$140) per person per day; and around AUD100 (US$70) per person per day for tagalongs.

## Access

Most of the main tracks in the Simpson Desert lie within South Australia and are part of the Simpson Desert National Park. A parks pass is required for access and camping (South Australia, 2005). Access from Alice Springs via Finke, New Crown and Andado Stations on the northwest is within the Northern Territory, and access via Birdsville on the eastern side is within Queensland. Access via Oodnadatta, Marree and Mt Dare Station on the south and west is within South Australia.

## Community

There are no permanent inhabitants in the central Simpson Desert dunefields, Aborigines included. The few areas with permanent water, such as Coopers Creek on the southeast margin, certainly have traditional owners and a wealth of pre-European artefacts such as grindstones. Aboriginal peoples currently living in this area, however, are more likely to work on cattle stations or even in tourism than to live traditional lifestyles. Tourists taking a 4WD trip across the Simpson Desert are more likely to encounter local European residents, whether at the Birdsville pub on the eastern margin or at the cattle stations of New Crown, Andado or Mount Dare on the northwest.

## Experience

In the early 1970s, the central Simpson Desert was one of the most remote parts of Australia. The first vehicle crossing was apparently made by geologist Reg Sprigg in 1962. In the early 1970s nobody went there except oil exploration crews, and they stayed on their bulldozed tracks. Any other visitors, including scientists such as myself, were entirely dependent on their own resources. I made a number of solo trips on- and off-track, some taking several weeks. I had no communications until the last of these trips. If stuck or incapacitated so that I was unable to drive out on my own, therefore, there was little likelihood of rescue. I had several narrow escapes.

Participants in modern tagalong tours, however, report that a large part of the day's experience is dust from vehicles travelling ahead in the same group. The sandy dune crossings on the French Line are no longer difficult for 4WD vehicles, but some of the other tracks are heavily eroded. Rain is unusual, but tour operator websites show vehicles bogged in mud on some trips. Potential difficulties such as these, however, are part of the challenge for most off-road drivers.

In addition, once the vehicles are stopped, the Simpson Desert can be extremely beautiful, especially in spring when the desert wildflowers bloom against a backdrop of red sand, and especially in mornings or evenings when the sun is low. During midsummer midday there is rather less to recommend it.

There is quite a wide variety of wildlife, including the world's second largest lizard species, the 2–3 m perentie. There are kangaroos, many snakes and lizards, and some rare and beautiful birds such as Major Mitchell's cockatoo and the plains turkey. There are also camels, through these are feral rather than native.

## Environment

The various sources of human impact on the Simpson Desert region have been controversial. Broadly speaking, they include: the spread of weeds and feral animals; modifications to fire regimes; farming around the margins; oil exploration and production; and tourism at specific sites. Foxes, feral cats, and introduced rabbits and house mice, for example, have apparently produced major impacts on particular endangered species in the central Australian arid zone. A variety of weeds have also spread into the area, particularly around watercourses (Buckley, 1981). Most of these introductions are linked, at least indirectly, with the history of farming in the area.

More recently, during the 1960s and 1970s there was extensive oil exploration in the Simpson Desert area, and this led to the bulldozing of roads and extensive grids of seismic lines across large areas of the arid zone. In addition to immediate impacts in clearing major vegetation and modifying soil and topography, these tracks created secondary impacts by providing easier access for 4WD vehicles, including those of tourists.

Tourists have since been blamed for starting fires, leaving litter at campsite areas such as Coongie Lakes, leaving gates open on cattle stations, and causing pollution at heavily frequented waterholes such as Dalhousie Springs. Compared to the large-scale ecological changes associated with the pastoral industry, the intensive activity at the Moomba oil and gas production facilities, or the drying up of the artesian mound springs caused by the massive dewatering carried out by the Roxby Downs uranium mine, however, the impacts of tourism seem relatively insignificant. A more detailed analysis is available in Schmiechen (2004).

## Safety

Travelling on an organized multi-vehicle commercial or tagalong 4WD tour across the Simpson Desert is a relatively safe proceeding. The tracks used are well-formed, compacted by heavy use and cut through dune crests so that low-range gear ratios are not needed. The tracks are smooth sand with no tree roots or other obstructions to puncture tyres. Drivers can travel at speed and there is no difficulty in carrying enough fuel and water. Most vehicles are prepared for punctures and minor breakdowns, and if one vehicle does become undriveable, there are others in the group to rescue its passengers.

The greatest risk is perhaps that of possible collision with another vehicle coming in the other direction through a narrow dune-crest cutting. To reduce this risk, most vehicles carry a tall flexible mast known as a whoopee stick, similar to a surfcasting fishing rod, so they can be seen over the crest of the dune. These flags were first used by oil crews in areas of heavy traffic around oil production facilities.

Travelling off-track in the central Australian desert, especially alone as I did in the early 1970s, is a somewhat different proposition. Even highly experienced off-road drivers can become irremediably stuck: as happened, for example, to a group of very skilled park rangers on an off-road expedition to a large salt lake in central Australia at the same time as I was working there.

For Simpson Desert off-road trips I used an old Toyota® Landcruiser trayback truck and carried: two 44-gallon drums of fuel and one of water; a manually operated Toyo® winch and a specially made sand anchor; long-handled shovels; four spare tyres; extra-heavyweight screwdrivers to take the split rims off the wheels, which were of the light truck type; tyre levers and patching gear; tool kits and spare parts. On my last trip, though not previously, I also carried a Codan® radio transceiver with a call sign for the Royal Flying Doctor Service radio base in Alice Springs.

At one time or another I used and needed almost all of these items. The only one which proved useless was a supposedly old-style soldering iron designed to be heated directly in a charcoal fire rather than by electricity. This had a large heavyweight head with high thermal mass designed to hold heat, which it did. Unfortunately it also had a plastic handle over its metal shaft. When the working end heated to operating temperature, the handle melted, rendering the entire contraption useless. Luckily I was only testing it out, not using it in anger.

### Marketing

Four-wheel-drive tours across the Simpson Desert are marketed principally within Australia, to domestic rather than international clients. As noted earlier, many of them are tagalong tours where participants must have their own off-road vehicles and appropriate driving skills. In addition to websites, these operators rely on low-key printed brochures and mailouts. The overall structure of the tourism industry in the Lake Eyre basin, including the Simpson Desert, has been reviewed recently by Schmiechen (2004). One significant factor is that the region overlaps four different States and is hence not a core component in any of their tourism marketing strategies.

## Chalbi Desert Crossing, Kenya: Various Operators

### Place

The Chalbi Desert lies in the far northern region of Kenya, north of Marsabit National Park, east of Lake Turkana, and south of the border with Somalia and

Ethiopia. Rainfall is 200–400 mm per annum. The lake is seasonally flooded, and traversable only during the dry season. The first vehicle to cross each season hence has no tracks to follow. Nowadays a GPS can be used, but when I took part in the season's first crossing in 1974 we navigated by compass bearing and dead reckoning.

The bed of an ancient lake, the central Chalbi Desert is almost completely flat and level, with very few discernible landmarks, and only 50 m variation in elevation. Mirages are intense throughout most of the day, so one has the impression of travelling at speed in a small bright pool surrounded by a shimmering circular wall. An occasional shrub or herd of gazelles appears through the dust and heat haze as a distant tower or citadel, confusingly realistic. There are both north–south and east–west routes across the desert, intersecting at a point known as North Horr.

During 2005 there were local newspaper reports of armed fighting near North Horr, with several deaths. The area may therefore be temporarily off-limits for tourism.

## Operator

A number of African safari operators advertise trips that include a crossing of the Chalbi Desert. Their websites all seem to use identical sentences to describe the Chalbi crossing, but since they depart from different points of origin, and run trips of different duration using a variety of different vehicles, presumably they are in fact independent operators.

I took part in a Chalbi crossing in 1974 as the guest of a safari company exploring new routes, on the condition that if anyone had to walk out, it would be me. Since I would have done so in any event, this was no great price to pay, and in any event it proved unnecessary. The crossing was apparently not being offered as part of any commercial safari at that time.

## Activity

Chalbi crossings are offered as one component of driving safaris, typically round trips starting from Samburu, Nairobi or even Mombasa. These trips commonly feature visits to Samburu and Marsabit National Parks; the Singing Wells at Sarana; the drive either across or around the Chalbi, depending on rainfall; a visit to Lake Turkana; and the return trip, south from the lake.

## Equipment

Different operators advertise trips in 4WD station wagons or in 'overland' trucks. In 1974 we travelled in three vehicles: a new 4WD for the company directors, a minibus for their support staff, and a very old, battered, but reliable short-wheelbase Landrover® for the chief guide and myself.

## Accommodation

On the trip I experienced, accommodation was in lodges on the rim of Marsabit Crater and again at Lake Turkana, and camping elsewhere as required. There are now, apparently, several lodges at Lake Turkana, a luxury lodge at the Sarana Singing Wells and a well-appointed lodge at Kalacha Camp, an oasis within the

Chalbi Desert itself, near the eastern edge. This has been in operation since 1999. There does not appear to be any tourist accommodation at North Horr.

## Statistics

On the exploratory trip in which I took part, there were about eight people, all of them company staff except myself. Currently, the Chalbi crossing takes only 1 or 2 days, but is typically carried out as part of a tour lasting 8–10 days in total. Prices for 8- or 9-day trips from Nairobi are around US$520–675 per person twinshare, or US$65–85 per person per day. These prices include park entrance fees totalling US$75 per person.

## Access

The Chalbi Desert crossing is an off-road trip as outlined above. Access is by 4WD vehicle along dirt roads. There are airstrips at Lake Turkana and Kalacha. Permits are required to enter national parks in Kenya, including Marsabit and Lake Turkana.

## Community

The principal livelihood in northeastern Kenya is subsistence pastoralism, with mixed herds of cattle and goats as in much of sub-Saharan Africa. Some of the peoples living around Lake Turkana, but not all, also catch fish from the lake. Tourism does provide employment for Kenyans as well as expatriates, but as in most countries employees are not necessarily from the immediate locality. There are tourist lodges in this region, the Northern Frontier District of Kenya, which are advertised as ecolodges and may make a particular effort to provide employment for locals, but I have not visited them to check.

## Experience

When I visited the area in 1974, our group spent the day at Marsabit National Park, a large extinct volcanic crater containing a crater lake and forested slopes, where I was able to hike down to the lake and watch the country's heaviest-tusked elephant from very short range amidst the trees. This, however, was not an officially sanctioned part of any tour. A French film crew was filming the same elephant herd from the crater rim, using long telephoto lenses.

We visited the Singing Wells of Sarana, where I was persuaded to climb down into the well and take my turn in a chain of local men passing water up to their cattle in rhinoceros-hide buckets. This process involved four men standing one above the other on a slippery and ramshackle frame of branches, each passing the bucket above their head to the next in line, without looking up. The timing is coordinated by a four-part song, which gives the wells their name. Fortunately, the parts are not complicated.

From the Singing Wells we drove to the southeastern end of Lake Turkana, passing through an area of volcanic lava bombs, pitted round boulders the size of footballs. The Chalbi crossing itself is from Lake Turkana eastwards, eventually intersecting the international highway south from Moyale in Ethiopia. In 1974 this highway was a single-track dirt road. Since then it may have been upgraded, but there is no guarantee of this.

## Environment

The main human impacts on this region are from grazing cattle and goats. A few decades ago, this area was part of a major zone of desertification, and this is still the case (Worldwide Fund for Nature, 2005). In any event, the impacts of tourist safaris are likely to be minimal relative to factors such as these. Tourist lodges may possibly produce localized pollution through sewage discharge, but on-site investigations would be needed to check.

## Safety

I have not audited safety procedures for any of the current tour operators. Airstrips and telecommunications are now available both near and within the Chalbi Desert, e.g. at Lake Turkana and at Kalacha Camp. As noted above, in July 2005 there were reports of two deaths from fighting at North Horr, and many more at Marsabit.

## Marketing

A considerable number of tour operators and agents offer tours through this region of northern Kenya, including a Chalbi Desert crossing. They all describe the crossing in similar or identical terms. The level of detail is rather low.

# Namib Desert, Namibia: Various Operators

### Place

The Namib Desert occupies a large part of Namibia, on the west coast of southern Africa. It is known for its large, bare and sinuous parallel dunes, most of them red. It is bisected from east to west by the intermittently flowing Gobabeb River. On the coast itself there are two former fishing towns that have now also become tourist destinations, Walvisbaai and Swakopmund. To the north of the sand dune desert is an area known as the Skeleton Coast, and inland from that lie the Welwitschiavlakte, home to the giant, rare, unusual and endemic welwitschia plant. To the south, across the border with South Africa, is another area of coastal desert occupied by alluvial diamond mines.

On the banks of the Gobabeb River is the Desert Ecological Research Unit, a permanent base for a wide variety of Namib Desert research. To the south, and accessible only from the inland side of the desert, lies Sossus Vlei, a large pan hidden amongst the dunes. Sossus Vlei provides easy access for tourists to walk up some of the larger dunes, and also provides reliable sighting of the desert gemsbok, a remarkably beautiful species of oryx.

### Operators

A wide variety of local and international tour operators offer road, air or fly/drive trips in and around the Namib Desert and Skeleton Coast. I have visited these areas on various occasions over the past decades, but I have not taken part in any of the commercial tours and cannot comment on any one in particular. Conservation Corporation Africa (CCAfrica) (2005) operates the Sossusvlei Mountain Lodge in the Namib Rand Nature Reserve, a private reserve adjacent to Namib Naukluft National

Park. CCAfrica has an excellent reputation throughout Africa and worldwide. Sossusvlei Mountain Lodge is not actually at Sossusvlei, but it offers excursions there. It also offers quad-biking on sand dunes, guided so as to minimize impacts. Quad-biking is also offered commercially on dunes near Swakopmund, though this is highly controversial because of impacts and unlicensed bikers.

There is an official 4WD trail through Namib Naukluft National Park, 73 km in length, but this is through mountainous areas rather than sand dunes. Itineraries offered for commercial tours in Namibia seem to include the Namib Desert itself only in the form of a brief half-day visit to Sossus Vlei. No operators seem to offer 4WD tours in the dunes themselves, though a few offer excursions by quad bike. This may be because 4WD vehicles are not permitted on dune areas inside Namib Naukluft National Park, or it may be because the terrain is considered too difficult, or it may be through lack of demand.

## Activity

Most tour operators in this region simply offer road trips that start from Windhoek, the capital of Namibia, and visit a range of sites including wineries, farmstays, mountains, the coastal towns and Sossuss Vlei. No off-road driving is required. To drive through the sand dunes south of the Gobabeb River, as I did in 1974 as a passenger with the scientists from the Desert Ecological Research Unit, requires a high level of off-road driving skill. This skill is needed first to cross the broad, sandy riverbed; secondly to cut through an eroded vertical sand cliff on the southern side of the riverbed; and thirdly, to pick a route through and over the sand dunes that minimizes the gradient and maximizes speed, so that the vehicle does not bog in soft sand, roll down an unstable dune face, or become trapped in a steep-sided depression with no way out.

## Equipment

Illustrations on the website for Siyabona Africa (2005) indicate that its Namibian safaris use an open-topped 4WD, probably a Landrover®. The site also refers, however, to safari trucks, larger 4WD vehicles. The itinerary refers to 2 days at Sossus Vlei, and 1 day in Swakopmund with the opportunity to try quad-biking.

## Accommodation

Siyabona Africa (2005) offers a 16-day tour with 11 nights camping and 4 nights in guesthouses. CCAfrica (2005) offers a 'Namibia in Style' guided lodge-accommodated safari with 6 days in lodges, 2 days in tented camps and 2 days in hotels in town, Windhoek and Swakopmund.

## Statistics

The Namibia Safari offered by Siyabona Africa (2005) apparently has a maximum group size of ten. A 15-day camping trip is advertised at US$2200 per person, or about US$150 per person per day. An 11-day Namibian safari advertised by CCAfrica Expeditions, including 2 days at CCAfrica's Sossusvlei Mountain Lodge and a 1-day ATV excursion, costs NAD24,300 (US$3684) per person twinshare, or around US$335 per person per day. Quad-biking from Swakopmund costs about US$85 for a 6-h trip.

## Access

Access to Namibia is generally by air to Windhoek, and travel within Namibia is largely by road or 4WD track.

## Community

There are many different people living in the Namib area, but off-road tours do not necessarily involve interactions with any of them. Guests at upmarket establishments that offer quad-bike tours, such as CCAfrica's lodge at Sossus Vlei, will generally also be offered opportunities to visit local communities if they wish, though typically as a separate exercise.

## Experience

When I have visited the Namib Desert on various occasions, I was travelling either on my own or with colleagues from research organizations, rather than commercial tours. I have visited the areas traversed by the multi-day 4WD tours, including Sossus Vlei, Gobabeb and Kaiser River, the Skeleton Coast and the Welwitschiavlakte. I have driven through and over the large and almost bare dunefield on the southern side of the Kuiseb River near Gobabeb in a conventional 4WD vehicle. I have not, however, driven a quad bike in the areas used by commercial tour operators near Swakopmund or Sossus Vlei. The experience reported here hence reflects the places more than the products.

Terrain in the Namib region includes extremely slippery salt clay soils on the Skeleton Coast, and steep rocky trails through mountain areas, as well as the shifting sand dunes for which it is famous. It was in the sandy riverbed near Gobabeb, however, that I witnessed one of the most memorable manoeuvres I have ever seen in over four decades of off-road driving. The vehicle was an old Landrover® and the driver was a scientist from the Desert Research Institute at Gobabeb. Having driven across the dry riverbed, we found our way blocked by a metre-high wall of sand, an erosion scarp from the last time this intermittent river flowed. I was expecting to get out and dig a ramp, but he had a different technique. In low ratio low gear, he nosed the vehicle solidly up against the sand scarp, wound the engine up to a scream and popped the clutch. There was a giant explosion of sand, and the vehicle simply burrowed straight through the wall in a cloud of airborne sediment. What it did to the air filter, let alone the engine, one hesitates to contemplate. Many field ecologists in sub-Saharan Africa, however, are quite used to driving full tilt through everything from trees to aardvark burrows, so a pile of sand is not likely to slow them down.

## Environment

The environmental impacts of off-road driving are very heavily dependent on the place and ecosystem, the frequency and type of use, and the skill and attitude of the driver (Buckley, 2004d). In particular, aggregate impacts are generally lower if all vehicles follow the same route than if they spread out over the entire landscape (Priskin, 2004). Thus on the one hand, the Namib Naukluft National Park can promote its 4WD trail as a good way to see the park without destroying its conservation values; whilst on the other, concerns have been expressed in Namibian newspapers about the environmental damage caused by all-terrain vehicles near Swakopmund. The off-road tours operated by Conservation Corporation Africa, in contrast, almost certainly use minimal-impact driving techniques in line with CCAfrica's overall corporate practices. I have not, however, audited any commercial off-road operations in the Namib recently.

### Safety

Quad bikes generally have a relatively high accident rate (see Chapter 2), but of course, this depends on where and how they are driven. Large mobile dunefields such as those in the southern Namib Desert can occasionally contain large hollows or depressions that are completely surrounded by steep dunes. If a vehicle once gets into such a depression, particularly if it then loses speed, it can be very difficult to get out again. The recommended technique is to drive in an ever-widening spiral similar to a 'wall-of-death' manoeuvre, but this does not always work. Between the need to maintain momentum on steep soft sand slopes, and the risk of becoming stuck in such a terrain trap, therefore, off-road driving through irregularly shaped mobile sand dunes is in itself a significant hazard.

### Marketing

The various commercial operators referred to in this case study all carry out marketing through their websites. Some package tours also include a 4WD safari component or a day's quad-bike riding. Independent ATV rentals such as those from Swakopmund also advertise locally.

## Qinghai, China: Various Operators

### Place

Qinghai is a high-mountain province in western China. It lies immediately northeast of Tibet, or Xizang as Tibet is known within China. It lies south-east of Xinjiang, the province which contains the Taklamakan Desert, the Tarim Basin, the giant salt lake of Lop Nor and the mountains of the Altun Shan. Qinghai is known for its mountain peaks, high grassy plateaux, yaks and horses, and a very large lake, Qinghai Lake, at 3200 m elevation in the eastern section of the province. Further west lies the Qaidam Basin, and to the south the mountains of the eastern Kunlun Shan. Qinghai Lake is known for its birdlife, but during 2005 this has apparently been affected badly by Asian bird flu.

### Operator

There seem to be relatively few commercial operators with tours specifically to Qinghai, and most of those focus on specialist birdwatching opportunities at Qinghai Lake rather than the broader opportunities available through off-road travel. Travel China Guide (2005), for example, lists Bird Island in Qinghai Lake as a primary attraction. Dreams Travel (2005), however, offer 12-day overland tours through the Qinghai–Tibet Plateau. I have not investigated any of these in person and cannot comment on particular operators, only on the destination. I visited eastern Qinghai in the late 1980s with colleagues from the China Academy of Sciences, principally to study the giant climbing dune at the eastern end of Qinghai Lake, and dune stabilization works further south and west.

## Activity

Commercial overland tours currently operating aim to cover 2000 km in 10 days' driving, which probably allows rather little time for other activities en route. My own trip in the 1980s started from Xining in eastern Qinghai. We travelled on a variety of roads, some well-made and others rutted dirt tracks or less. We visited the Yellow River, already a very large and silt-laden river even so early in its course. We visited Qinghai Lake, far from the sea but home to a variety of cormorants and other birds. I climbed an unnamed 5000 m mountain or, to be more accurate, walked up it through yak herds and found two small boys sitting on the summit. We walked through high grassy plateaux rich with short-toed larks and plateau pikas. And we visited dune stabilization programmes and took part in various ceremonial events.

## Equipment

In the 1980s we travelled in a Chinese 4WD, a short-wheelbase canvas-topped copy of a Jeep®. Battered and dilapidated, it none the less survived the journey well. Modern overland tours probably use minibuses or trucks, though their websites are not explicit.

## Accommodation

In the 1980s we stayed in local accommodation throughout. In Xining this was a commercial hotel. In the smaller villages it was considerably more rustic. At Qinghai Lake we stayed in a small lodge built principally for birdwatchers. Its straw mattresses were particularly flea-infested, but its location was unparalleled.

## Statistics

The overland tours offered currently take 10–12 days and drive 2000 km. The Qinghai–Tibet Plateau 12-day overland tour offered by Dreams Travel (2005), which starts in Xining and ends in Lhasa, costs US$160–275 per person per day, with the lower prices for groups of 7–10 clients and the higher for groups of two or three. Our trip in the 1980s consisted of one jeep load, namely one Chinese scientist, one interpreter, one driver and myself. It took about 10 days.

## Access

All access was by 4WD vehicle. In the 1980s, travel permits were required and we were able to obtain them only for scientific purposes. Roadblocks were frequent, apparently because of an outbreak of bubonic plague. Currently, it appears that there is a park permit fee of RMB60 (US$7.50) (Travel China Guide, 2005) and a Tibet travelling permit fee of RMB500 (US$60).

## Community

Everyone we met in the 1980s was friendly, but we were very tightly tied into a predetermined programme and though we did succeed in making some modifications, this required extensive negotiation. We were required to sit through a long and elaborate welcome ceremony at the dune stabilization village, with many official speeches. The translator, thankfully, summarized each 20-min Chinese presentation in a single laconic English sentence. Hopefully, commercial tours currently involve less ceremony.

## Experience

Qinghai has some very beautiful landscapes, and our 1980s trip was very memorable. Indeed, of the areas I have visited in China I would rate Qinghai as more beautiful than better-known tourist sights such as the karst landscapes of Guilin or the Stone Forest of Kunming. Rural roads and accommodation are much the same anywhere in China. Qinghai food featured yak meat, which is excellent; and tomatoes and cucumbers with sugar rather than salt, which are surprising.

## Environment

The environmental pros and cons of large-scale landscape manipulations such as dune stabilization depend on historical context. It was not clear to me whether these particular dunes had been created by human activities such as deforestation and overgrazing, in which case stabilization would be considered as restoration and rehabilitation; or whether the dunes were natural, in which case stabilization would represent large-scale landscape modification.

All of China has a long history of human habitation, but the peaks and plateaux of Qinghai appeared relatively undisturbed, being used principally to graze yaks and horses. Whether the meadows would have looked different without grazing livestock, I do not know. The turf included a very diverse range of small herbaceous plant species, however, not only grasses, and there seemed to be many small native mammals. Chinese agricultural practices make use of all animal waste as fertilizer, human waste included, but in this area the tilled fields are small in area relative to grazing pastures. Relative to human agriculture and forestry in the region, our impacts as visitors were negligible.

## Safety

We took no particular safety precautions.

## Marketing

At the time of my visit, this was not marketed as a commercial tour. Tours currently offered, at least those with websites, provide rather little information except an approximate itinerary.

# 20 Wildlife

Leopard, Conservation Corporation Africa. Photo Ralf Buckley.

Polar bear cubs, Natural Habit Adventures, Canada. Photo Ralf Buckley.

# Sector Structure

Wildlife tourism is generally treated as part of the nature tourism sector (Newsome *et al.*, 2002) or indeed as a sector of its own (Shackley, 1996a; Newsome *et al.*, 2005). Wildlife-watching opportunities, however, may equally well be classified as adventure tours either because of the remoteness of the area, the mode of access or risks from the animals themselves.

These characteristics commonly apply, for example, to watching large and potentially dangerous wildlife species at close range in relatively remote areas. The mode of access commonly depends both on the weather and the wildlife. To approach a group of hungry polar bears on foot, for example, especially at night, would probably be a cold and short-lived experience. To see a mountain gorilla or a well-fed grizzly bear on foot, however, with a guide who can interpret its intentions and avoid an attack, is a memorable and adrenalin-charged experience.

As with many other outdoor activities, commercial tour products can differ considerably in the various components that create the perception of adventure for different participants. To watch polar bears playing in the Arctic night, even through the windows of a heated tundra buggy, seems adventurous enough for most tourists. Others, however, would treat such an experience as tame, preferring instead to meet the polar bear face to face on the edge of an Arctic ice floe.

For myself at least, to lock eyes with a lion from less than a metre away is certainly an exciting experience, even if one is sitting in an open safari vehicle at the time. The same applies when an elephant walks by close enough to touch, easily able to pluck one from the seat with a single swing of its trunk, if it decided to do so. To cling to a charging elephant's back, Indian rather than African, as it trumpets at a tiger is also likely to raise the adrenalin level beyond the norm for placid forms of wildlife watching.

This is by no means to belittle the enjoyment of wildlife tourism more generally, including watching the many beautiful, fascinating and sometimes rare species that are small and shy rather than large and fierce. A leopard or a tiger is liquid magnificence, but a striped possum is equally astonishing. To be charged by a black panther in Kenya's Aberdare Mountains is heart-stopping, but to have a baby Pels fishing owl land silently on a branch next to one's head in the Okavango Delta is almost a religious experience, at least for a biologist.

Some of the more adventurous wildlife-watching experiences form one component of adventure safaris, whether on foot, on horseback, in 4WD vehicles or by boat. For such tour products the principal focus may be on the activity, with wildlife as one component of the scenery and setting; or it may be on the wildlife, with the mode of access seen as a way to improve viewing opportunities. The distinction is rarely clear-cut, and different participants may be more interested in different aspects of the same tour.

In other wildlife-watching tours, there are known sites where particular species can be seen at particular times of year, and commercial tour operators offer access, accommodation and local guiding and interpretation. Tour packages commonly link several such sites into a single retail tour product, but travel between the sites is then treated as part of the logistics rather than part of the attraction. For these safari-style tours, the adventure component is derived from the activity as a whole. For fixed-site options, the adventure component is commonly derived mainly from interactions with individual animals.

# Northern Circuit Wildlife, Tanzania: Conservation Corporation Africa

## Place

East Africa is perhaps the world's most famous and long-standing wildlife-watching destination. It has long been known for the so-called Big Five: lion, leopard, elephant, rhino and buffalo. Named initially as the most dangerous and challenging quarries for hunters, these species became the most desirable target for photographers and wildlife-watching safaris. Indeed, East African 'big five' bus tours have long since become a mass-market tourism attraction. Equally popular is the annual migration of wildebeest, zebra and other large grazing herds through the plains of the Serengeti in northern Tanzania and the Masai Mara in southern Kenya.

East African ecosystems, however, are far more diverse than mass tourism marketing materials would suggest. The broad grassy plains are only one of many landscapes. There are also high mountains and low rocky outcrops, rivers and swamps, gallery forest and open savannah woodlands.

Likewise, the great migratory herds and the Big Five are by no means the only wildlife. There is an enormous variety of other species including birds, reptiles and invertebrates as well as mammals, not to mention the wealth of plant life. For the seasoned wildlife tourist, the chance to watch an aardwolf or a caracal, a pearl-spotted owl or a narina trogon, or a sunbird on a giant tree groundsel is far more fascinating than brief sightings of better-known species between tour buses. And to watch a tiny dikdik antelope on foot whilst walking quietly in the midday heat, or to stare into a lion's torch-lit face from arm's length, moves wildlife watching well into the realm of adventure tourism. For both safety and conservation reasons, however, these options are generally available only in private reserves, not in the major national parks; and only with highly experienced guides who can interpret and anticipate every nuance of animal behaviour.

## Operator

Conservation Corporation Africa (CCAfrica) is a remarkable organization, dedicated to conservation of Africa's wildlife and ecosystems in both private and public reserves, and privately funded through highly successful upmarket game lodges and safaris (Buckley, 2003a; CCAfrica, 2005). CCAfrica (2005) currently operates 37 lodges and camps in six African countries, including four in Tanzania and one in Kenya. Its lodges in South Africa and Botswana are described in Buckley (2003a, pp. 19–23).

The Tanzanian lodges are all in locations that allow their guests to escape the crowds. Klein's Camp is in a private reserve on the border between Tanzania and Kenya, next to the Serengeti. Grumeti River Camp is in a little-visited corner of northwestern Tanzania. Lake Manyara Tree Lodge is in a park open to the public, but too far from the park gates to be reached by day visitors, and hence accessible only to the Lodge's guests. And Ngorongoro Crater Lodge, perched on the edge of one of East Africa's most famous and heavily visited wildlife tourist destinations, provides unparalleled views over Ngorongoro Crater, access to the cloud forests of the crater rim and trips to the crater floor in early mornings and late afternoons, outside the rush hours for tour buses based in Arusha. CCAfrica is known for the expertise of its guides and the standard of its service, and its East African lodges certainly maintain its reputation.

## Activity

All of CCAfrica's Tanzanian game lodges offer wildlife watching as the principal activity. The opportunities certainly include the Big Five and the migratory herds, but many other species besides. Klein's Camp lies in its own 10,000 ha reserve, where night drives and daytime bushwalks are possible, as well as day-long game drives in the Serengeti. The Camp itself is built on the flanks of the Kuka Hills, which overlook one of the main valleys traversed by the annual migrations. The concession area includes a tree-lined river much frequented by leopard, and an open grassy valley with good sightings of cheetah.

Grumeti River Camp also offers spectacular wildlife viewing when the migrating herds cross the Grumeti River itself. The Camp is located right next to a backwater channel of the river, and hippo are frequently seen – and heard – browsing close to the tents at night and early morning. The river is flanked by tall gallery forest that supports a resident population of black and white colobus monkeys.

Lake Manyara Tree Lodge lies in a mahogany forest on a narrow strip of low land fringing Lake Manyara itself, backed by the escarpment of the Great Rift Valley. As one leaves the forest a short distance from the lodge, there are extensive views across the lake and its surrounding mudflats, with large herds of buffalo and elephant. Indeed, at one point during my visit we waited in an open 4WD whilst several elephant walked by within touching distance, so close that we were looking up at their bellies. Lake Manyara is also known for its unusual tree-climbing lions. Within the forest there are excellent sightings of birds and smaller antelopes.

Ngorongoro Crater Lodge provides the opportunity to visit the crater floor when the national park gates first open at dawn and to linger there until they close at dusk, avoiding the midday crush of minibus tours from the nearby town of Arusha. And since the lodge is right on the crater rim and provides an unparalleled aerial view, CCAfrica's guides can often give their guests sightings of individual animals that are far from obvious to a casually passing vehicle.

In addition, there are opportunities to drive to less commonly visited areas along the crater rim, and to clamber on foot through the dry forest, wary of the buffalo that often come into camp. And in the mornings one can sit with a cup of tea while sunbirds flit between the flowers, and cloud drifts cool between moss-covered trees or breaks clear to show the sunlit crater floor far beneath. Who needs to drive anywhere?

## Equipment

Open 4WD safari vehicles, converted Landrovers® with tiered seats so everyone has an uninterrupted view forward and to both sides, are standard in CCAfrica's private concession areas such as Klein's and are also used at Grumeti and Lake Manyara. For excursions into the central Ngorongoro Crater, closed vehicles are used to comply with park regulations. The open vehicles also have tracker seats on the front bonnet, and a rifle rack across the dashboard. All CCAfrica's vehicles are equipped with radios and maintain contact with their lodge and other vehicles. Bush walks are accompanied by guides with rifles and radios.

## Accommodation

Klein's Camp consists of ten individual stone cottages and a central lodge area with a spacious open lounge overlooking the valley, and a separate dining area. Each of the cottages has an independent view over Klein's private wildlife concession. There is also a swimming pool. The centrepiece of the lounge area is an enormous fireplace with a bar on the uphill side.

At Grumeti River Camp, guest accommodation is in ten large permanent tents with en suite bathrooms and verandas. The central lodge area incorporates a dining room and lounge built around a tree-studded lawn that slopes to the river.

Lake Manyara Tree Lodge, recently rebuilt, consists of ten very large timber tree houses, each with bathroom, bedroom, balcony and living area and each perched well above the ground amongst the mahogany trees. The central area includes a raised bar and lounge, and a ground-level open display kitchen and dining area. Even though the lodge is set within the mahogany forest and views are limited, the very large raised and open tree houses, with no interior walls, provide a spacious ambience.

Ngorongoro Crater Lodge consists of three separate safari camps at the same site, each run independently with its own manager, kitchen, lounge and dining area. North and South Camp, with 12 suites each, have the more opulent lounge areas, but the smaller six-suite Tree Camp has picture-postcard views to the crater floor and beautifully designed timber cottages with their own fireplaces and four-posters, private butlers and baths perched in oval annexes with their own views across Ngorongoro. Tea at dawn from a bone china cup and silver teapot, sitting on a timber balcony amidst drifting cloud, is a memorable experience in itself.

## Statistics

Most visitors to CCAfrica's northern Tanzania lodges will make a circuit, staying 2 or 3 nights at each lodge so as to experience the variety of wildlife and ecosystems. They may also visit Mnemba Island off the coast of Zanzibar, usually at the end of their stay. Maximum capacities are around 20 guests at each lodge, except for Ngorongoro Crater Lodge, which has a higher total capacity in its three separate camps. Prices at the lodges vary seasonally and range from US$445–595 per person per night twinshare.

## Access

All of CCAfrica's Northern Circuit lodges are accessible either by air or by road. Most guests travel by air using either of two local airlines. The lodges run 4WD shuttle services from the airstrips. At Grumeti the airstrip is right next to the lodge. At Klein's it is on the opposite side of the concession area, providing an opportunity for a game drive on the way across. Ngorongoro and Lake Manyara use the same airstrip, on a plateau above the Lake Manyara escarpment. The drive to Lake Manyara Tree Lodge is through Lake Manyara National Park, with a pause for refreshment en route and ample opportunities to watch birds and wildlife. The road to Ngorongoro Crater Lodge passes first through a densely settled agricultural area and then through the park gates into the forested crater slopes of the extinct volcano.

Klein's is a private wildlife concession leased from the local Masai community, and entry is restricted to CCAfrica's guests. The other lodges are in national parks, and park fees are charged. The same applies when guests at Klein's drive into the Serengeti. Klein's Camp charges a daily conservation management fee that is used either to cover park fees or to contribute to wildlife management in the concession area.

## Community

As in most African wildlife lodges, relations with local communities are close. The Klein's concession is leased from a local Masai community, who have a village downriver and run cattle in the upper parts of the valley. The whole of Ngorongoro National Park is run in conjunction with local communities, who drive cattle down the inner slopes of the crater every day. Local residents are employed at all the lodges, as well as staff from other parts of Tanzania.

## Experience

Conservation Corporation Africa (CCAfrica) has a well-deserved reputation as one of the world's pre-eminent operators of private game reserves and wildlife safaris, and the lodges in the northern Tanzania circuit live up to this reputation. Each lodge or camp is different, and each has particular features that take advantage of the terrain. At the Ngorongoro Crater Lodge, for example, one can breakfast on a balcony hanging out over the wall of the crater, with what amounts to an aerial view of the wildlife below. One can be first to the crater floor in the morning, when the resident bateleur eagle, icon of CCAfrica, is still perched on his favourite trackside branch. One can be last to leave in the evening, when the tour buses from Arusha have headed home and the rhino emerge from their hidden hollow in a seemingly flat landscape.

Likewise, at Lake Manyara Lodge one has privileged access to the southern parts of the western scarp in the morning and evening, when the light slants low and Manyara's famous lions loiter on the rocks.

At Grumeti we saw the vanguard of the migrating herds prancing in the earliest fall of the rains, lit by brilliant sunshine on a new-grassed plain, against a black sky behind. We also saw a large female leopard strolling quietly in front of us, tail twitching indolently, and an unusually large and pale-coloured lioness with cubs.

At Klein's Camp the guest rooms are stone rondavels perched amongst the rocks with a view across the valley and river below. There are cheetah in the valley and leopards in the trees lining the river. With an armed guide one can climb up to the crest of the hill behind the lodge and look north to the Masai Mara and south and west to the Serengeti, whilst keeping a careful watch and a safe distance from wandering files of buffalo and the occasional solitary but irascible male.

Overall, the experience of visiting Conservation Corporation Africa's northern Tanzanian lodges is one of distinctive luxury, outstanding service and adventurous encounters with wildlife both large and small in a series of beautiful natural settings.

## Environment

In keeping with its name, best practice environmental management is a critical component of the company's operations. As reported previously (Buckley, 2003a, pp. 19–23, 245) for the company's southern African operations, CCAfrica has made significant contributions to wildlife and nature conservation and can justifiably claim to generate a positive triple bottom line. Besides buying private land and rehabilitating it to game reserves, it has successfully developed breeding and translocation programmes and techniques for a number of endangered species, which have been taken up more broadly beyond the company.

In Tanzania, the lodges are on leasehold concessions rather than private lands, so there are limitations on direct contributions to conservation. As elsewhere, however, the individual lodge managers have taken various steps to identify and act on any local environmental issues.

At the Ngorongoro Crater Lodge, CCAfrica took over the site from a large international tour operator that had occupied it previously and had disposed of a range of solid wastes, including potentially toxic items such as batteries, by burying them in large unlined pits. In addition to proper treatment of its own greywater, sewage and kitchen waste on a small and steeply sloping site, therefore, CCAfrica is faced with potential excavation and re-treatment of residues from a previous occupant. Besides these localized on-site waste treatment issues, CCAfrica is closely involved in broader-scale processes to improve the management of visitors and wildlife in the crater itself, as well as access to the crater by cattle from neighbouring communities. These are politically sensitive issues.

At Lake Manyara Lodge, sewage and solids are treated onsite, but other wastes are taken to a nearby village for recycling or disposal. Similar procedures are followed at Grumeti Camp, which also saves power by keeping vegetables cool in an evaporative cool room with water-sprinkled charcoal walls. The managers at Klein's Camp have paid particular attention to environmental issues, using a combination of different energy sources including some renewables, recycling glass at the nearest town and reusing waste oil to treat timber in the local village. Environmental audits of all lodges have been carried out progressively by the group's environmental manager in conjunction with the individual lodge managers.

## Safety

As with all Conservation Corporation Africa's private game reserves, guests are taken to watch wildlife in open-topped 4WD safari vehicles. This contrasts with tours in publicly owned national parks, which must use closed vehicles to protect passengers from potential attacks by the larger and more dangerous wildlife. In CCAfrica's open vehicles, the safety of the guests depends on the skills of the drivers and trackers in locating individual animals, understanding and predicting their behaviour, positioning and moving the vehicles accordingly, and ensuring that guests behave in ways that do not provoke attack, either for food or defence.

This expertise is even more critical when guests are on guided walks. The ability of guests to move quietly, and to obey the instructions of their guides promptly, is essential for safety. Indeed, since the lodges are unfenced, even guests moving between buildings can encounter potentially dangerous animals. When guests first arrive, therefore, their introductory briefings include issues such as how to move safely around camp. After dark, it is a strict requirement at all lodges that guests may only walk around camp in the company of an armed guard.

## Marketing

Conservation Corporation Africa is already well known worldwide and has an established clientele. In addition to its website, it produces brochures for each individual lodge and for the portfolio as a whole. These brochures are provided within the lodges to encourage a low-key cross-marketing. CCAfrica has won a number of environmental and tourism awards, and these also assist in promoting the company worldwide.

## Tigers, Bardia National Park, Nepal: Tiger Tops Karnali

### Place

Bardia National Park is an area of flat, low-lying land near the southern border of Western Nepal, in an area known as the Terai. It is close to the point where the Karnali River runs out of its gorge in the foothills of the Himalayas, on to the Terai plains. The park is partly dry open forest, and partly swamps and tall grasses dissected by multiple narrow river channels. It is surrounded by agricultural land and villages. Originally gazetted in 1976 as a 368 km$^2$ hunting reserve, it was extended to 968 km$^2$ in 1988 and re-gazetted as a national park. It is the largest and least disturbed wilderness area in the Terai (Nepal Tourist Board, 2005), and provides habitat for a range of endangered animal species such as Bengal tiger, rhinoceros, elephant, gharial, Gangetic dolphin, swamp deer and black buck. Other wildlife species include leopard, jungle cat, civets, mongoose, hyena, sloth bear, langur, otter and nilgai, as well as over 400 bird species. The park is known particularly for the opportunity it provides to see Bengal tiger in the wild, from elephant-back.

### Operator

Tiger-watching tours are run directly by the main tourist lodge, Tiger Tops Karnali. The tours are run on elephant-back. This is probably the only safe way to travel through the high swampy grass, which in places is higher than an elephant. Tour clients mount and dismount from the elephant using a specially constructed platform in the grounds of the lodge.

### Activity

The tour starts with a relaxed ride through open forest, with a guide pointing out plants, birds and other wildlife. The tigers tend to frequent the tall grass and low scrub around the river channels. The clients are asked to remain silent, and the guides look and listen intently for any sign of tiger. They probably also know the tigers' preferred resting places. Once a tiger has been located, the elephants spread out and surround the point where the guides think it is. If the tigers run, the elephants chase after it, trumpeting furiously. The tigers seem to have no difficulty escaping, though they probably do not appreciate being harassed. If the elephants are not actively chasing them, the tigers seem to be relatively relaxed, watching the tourists unconcernedly. The elephants wade or swim across the river channels and heave themselves up the steep muddy banks. The best views of tigers are across the narrow channels, when they can be seen lying quietly in the open.

### Equipment

The opportunity to search for and see tigers in this environment is dependent entirely on the elephants. There is no mechanical vehicle that could successfully traverse the range of different terrain types, from tall grass to swamps and steep river banks. To travel on foot would be slow and potentially dangerous, and would not provide the raised vantage point that is critical to tiger sightings. Each elephant has its own mahout, who sits on its neck and gives it directions partly by voice and partly by pushing with his bare feet behind the elephant's ears.

The passengers ride on a flat, square wooden tray attached to the elephant's back with a giant girth and crupper. Guides and trackers commonly stand on the crupper, holding on to the back edge of the tray. The wooden trays are rather poorly designed, precarious and uncomfortable. Each is essentially a small square of planking, with wooden stanchions at the corners supporting a thin horizontal wooden rail. The rail is just high enough above the platform for passengers to wedge their legs underneath, and this is what the guides suggest, but this position becomes very painful if the elephant starts running. In addition, if there are four passengers on a single elephant, each is forced to look in a different direction. If the passengers do not wedge their legs under the rail, however, then first there is not enough space for four people on the tray, and secondly they risk being flung off when the elephant runs. This design could be greatly improved with very little effort and at minimal cost.

At the beginning and the end of the elephant ride, clients climb on and off the elephant from a fixed platform at an appropriate height, reached by a set of steps. The platform is large enough for four or five people, so the passengers can board one elephant-load at a time. If individual guests want to climb down from the elephants at some intermediate point during the trip, the mahout will give the elephant an instruction to place its trunk as a step, and then move it up or down like a forklift.

## Accommodation

Tourist accommodation is available at a number of local lodges. These include Tiger Tops Karnali, a member of the Small Luxury Hotels of the World; and Bardia Jungle Cottage, established in 1994 by a retired employee from the national parks service. Bardia Jungle Cottage consists of a set of bungalows using solar power, kerosene lamps and candles. My recollection of Tiger Tops Karnali is that though perhaps not particularly luxurious, the rooms were clean, spacious and comfortable, and the main lobby area featured large expanses of dark carved wood panelling.

## Statistics

As noted above, each elephant can carry a maximum of four clients on tiger-watching excursions, in addition to its own mahout. When I took part in this tour, there was only one English-speaking guide, three elephants and eight or nine passengers. Including the mahouts, therefore, the effective client-to-guide ratio was about 2:1. The elephant-back trip itself takes only a few hours, but most visitors would probably stay several nights and take several trips into the National Park so as to maximize the chance of good tiger sightings. Daily rates at Tiger Tops Karnali range from US$76 to 150 for accommodation only. Bardia Jungle Cottages (2005) offer 3-night visits including food and local tours for US$150 per person twinshare, or US$50 per person per day.

## Access

The usual access to Bardia National Park is by air from Kathmandu to the town of Nepalganj, and then by road to the park. The road is in relatively poor condition and the journey takes several hours. Some visitors arrive by rafting the Karnali River immediately west of the park and then travelling by road to the main entrance.

## Community

The area around Bardia National Park is occupied by small farms and villages. There have apparently been some conflicts between villagers and park management, over two main issues. The first is that native mammals may leave the park and raid crops in nearby fields. This leads to loss of livelihood, and if the villagers kill the animals in retaliation, also to loss of endangered wildlife. The second is that the villagers have apparently relied on the forest area within the park to cut poles for construction, and on the grass swamps for thatching material.

Tiger-watching tourism has apparently alleviated these conflicts to some degree by providing additional employment and economic opportunities, and resources to protect crops. Perhaps more importantly, however, in the interest of good community relations the park management agency has apparently allowed seasonal harvesting of poles and thatch within the park. Issues such as these, of course, are by no means restricted to Bardia, but are commonplace worldwide wherever protected areas adjoin agricultural landholdings.

## Experience

Watching tigers from elephant-back is a rather different experience from traditional wildlife safaris in an enclosed 4WD vehicle, or even an open vehicle as used in some private game reserves. The most significant aspect is, of course, the elephant itself. Although one is not formally introduced, the elephants appear to inspect their passengers with some care. Except at the beginning and end of the trip, one is dependent on the elephant's goodwill and behaviour in order to climb on and off its back.

Not surprisingly, the elephants seem to be very much at home in the forests and swamps, wandering with ease through dense vegetation that would be hard going for a human, or swimming across channels with their trunks raised as periscopes. The contrast is thus all the more noticeable when the elephants surround a tiger and start charging about and trumpeting excitedly.

Of course, chivvying tigers through the undergrowth on a charging elephant is hardly the ideal low-impact wildlife-watching experience. The tigers seem to have no difficulty taking evasive action, but no doubt it is still annoying to be disturbed, particularly if one happens to be stalking one's dinner, or perhaps digesting it. The only time we saw an apparently undisturbed tiger was across a river channel where the tiger occupied a commanding position, could see us as clearly as we could see him and had an easy advantage in case we might start to cross. Whether across a river or skulking through the undergrowth, a fully-grown tiger is an extremely impressive animal, and to see one from elephant-back is a memorable experience. The rest of the ride, and the other wildlife and ecosystems we saw, also made a major contribution.

## Environment

As with many other examples of wildlife tourism, tiger-watching elephant safaris in Bardia National Park may have both positive and negative consequences. On the one hand, as noted above, tourism may have led both to closer scrutiny of land-use practices in and around the park, and to economic and employment incentives for local villagers to contribute to conserving the park and its wildlife.

On the negative side, the guide and mahouts are clearly concerned to make sure that their clients do in fact see tigers, either because this is critical to customer satisfaction, or perhaps because they see this as a challenge to their professional skills as trackers. It seems likely that these searches do disrupt tiger behaviour for at least a short period almost every day. How significant this may be for individual tigers or the future tiger population in Bardia National Park remains unknown.

## Safety

Since elephants are in general larger and stronger than tigers, tigers do not generally attack elephants, and passengers riding on elephant-back are hence relatively safe. The greatest danger is perhaps the risk of injury from the poorly designed elephant-back passenger platforms, and perhaps also the risk of falling off completely. The platform used to get on and off the elephant at beginning and end of the ride improves safety as well as comfort.

## Marketing

Until a decade or so ago, Bardia National Park was little known in comparison to Chitwan National Park. As Chitwan became more and more heavily visited, Bardia began to be promoted as a less crowded alternative. Recognition of Tiger Tops Karnali in the Small Luxury Hotels of the World, a prestigious portfolio marketed worldwide, has no doubt also increased the international visibility of Bardia and its tigers. The elephant-back ride itself does not seem to be marketed as a separate tour, but as part of a package visit to Bardia.

# Mountain Gorillas, Mgahinga National Park, Uganda: Various Operators

## Place

Mgahinga National Park lies in the Virunga Mountains at the southern edge of Uganda, at the border with Rwanda and Zaire and a little to the east of the larger and better-known Bwindi Impenetrable Forest (Hamilton *et al.*, 2000). The Virunga Mountains support wet tropical montane rainforest and provide the last remaining habitat for mountain gorillas, a highly endangered species of which only small populations still exist: only a few hundred individuals in total. Mgahinga National Park is about 34 km$^2$ in area and is managed by the Uganda Wildlife Authority (2005). Because of international concern over the gorillas, there are various research and conservation projects funded by international aid and donors, which supplement on-the-ground management by the parks service itself (McNeilage, 1996; Buckley, 2003a, pp. 38–41).

## Operator

Once visitors are within the park itself, gorilla tracking is managed, controlled and guided by parks service staff as described below. Various tour operators, however, sell gorilla-watching tours either independently or more commonly as part of a Ugandan or East African wildlife safari package. Some of these companies, such as Abercrombie and Kent (2005) have their own tourist accommodation at the park and operate the entire tour logistics themselves. Others assemble a package using local tour and minibus operators based in Kampala, and local guesthouses at Mgahinga. International tour operators such as these obtain gorilla-watching permits for their clients on a specific day before finalizing their itineraries.

So-called overland tour buses also stop at Mgahinga on various long-distance trans-Africa routes. These operators, however, do not have gorilla-watching permits in advance. Instead, they will typically stay at Mgahinga for several days, long enough for interested passengers to buy permits on site, as outlined below.

## Activity

Gorilla-watching relies on extended family groups of gorillas, known as troupes, which have been habituated to the presence of humans. These groups are habituated gradually over a period of years by the parks service trackers, to the point where they can be approached safely by small guided groups of tourists. According to Adams and Infield (2003), there are eight gorilla troupes in all that use Mgahinga part of the time, but also cross into Rwanda and the Democratic Republic of Congo.

Only a very restricted number of tourists may visit each gorilla troupe each day, for a maximum of 1 h, and this quota is enforced through the permit system as described below. According to the Uganda Wildlife Authority (2005), the maximum number of tourists per troupe per day is six. In my own experience this limit was sometimes relaxed slightly, at least in the past.

The habituated troupes are followed each day by the parks service trackers, so their general whereabouts within the park are always known from one day to the next. The only exception occurs if the gorillas cross the Ugandan border, in which case the trackers are not permitted to follow but must wait for them to return, sometimes several weeks later.

Whilst a maximum of 1 h close to the gorillas is permitted, the experience as a whole takes most of the day. When I visited, tourists assembled at the parks service office early in the morning. Some already had pre-allocated permits, and others queued for permits sold on the day. The groups were accompanied by an English-speaking guide and several trackers. Before leaving the parks service office, the guide gave a general briefing on what to expect during the day, including how to behave in the forest and near the gorillas, and safety procedures to protect both the gorillas and the gorilla watchers.

In particular, the guide checked that nobody had a potentially infectious respiratory ailment, since even a cold can be passed to the gorillas with severe consequences. The guide also noted that the day would involve 4–6 h of strenuous climbing up and down densely vegetated muddy slopes in the midday heat, and checked to make sure this was within the capabilities of all the tourists. If any of those who had pre-allocated permits decided they were unfit to proceed, their permit was re-sold on the spot to anyone waiting.

At the time of my own visit, there were two habituated gorilla troupes at Mgahinga, in different parts of the park. To reach the usual territory of one group required a 2–3 h walk directly from the parks office, first uphill along the park boundary, and then down a river gully and into dense forest. To get to the other group required an hour or so's drive on a narrow dirt road, but a shorter walk. The Uganda Wildlife Authority (2005) currently advertises that there is only one troupe available for viewing in Mgahinga.

The trackers go first to the point where they left the gorillas on the previous day, and then find them simply by following their tracks. In some areas these are readily apparent even to an unskilled observer, as the gorillas break and trample soft-leaved understorey plants. Where the gorillas travel through tall open forest, however, their tracks are much more difficult to follow and the skills of the trackers are critical.

Once the troupe has been located, the guides hold the clients back initially and remind them quietly to keep silent, stay well back and make sure that their camera flashes are turned off. As long as these rules are followed, the gorillas seem to pay little attention to the watching humans, but continue with apparently normal feeding and social behaviours. Once they have checked that the gorillas are undisturbed, the guides allow the tourists to approach closer. When an hour is up, the guides signal quietly and lead the tourists back the way they came.

## Equipment

No special equipment is required. Most tourists wear hiking boots, most carry cameras and some bring binoculars. None of these, however, is essential, though some kind of sturdy footwear is needed for all but the hardiest of feet.

## Accommodation

Several different accommodation options are available, and the choice depends largely on how the trip was packaged. When I visited, I stayed in a small, privately owned local guesthouse a small distance inside the park gates. This was essentially a private house with a few rather basic extra rooms, cramped but clean, added on for tourists. Meals were served in a small dining room. At the time I was apparently the only guest. At that time, the well-known international nature tourism company Abercrombie and Kent was building an upmarket private lodge a little further into the park, but this is not currently listed on their website (Abercrombie and Kent, 2005). There was apparently another tourist lodge some 5 km outside the park gates. This may possibly be the lodge currently advertised as Mt Gahinga Lodge.

Most visitors arriving with their own transport or in overland buses, however, stayed in rondavels operated by the parks service at the park entrance, and ate in a small, locally owned restaurant nearby. This restaurant, incidentally, was apparently one of the few mechanisms by which tourism expenditure reached local communities directly. The rondavels were well-built, clean and comfortable, and excellent value for money, and I should certainly have been quite content to stay there if I had not already made other arrangements. The principal difference from the rooms in the guesthouse is that the rondavels relied on a single centralized ablution block, whereas the guesthouse had small en suite bathrooms.

## Statistics

If the gorillas are around, there is a very high probability that the trackers will find them. Most international tourists on gorilla package tours hence spend only 1 day at Mgahinga, particularly since it can be difficult to be sure of another gorilla-watching permit on a second consecutive day. Visitors arriving in their own vehicles, overland buses or local transport will typically stay at least 3 days, to maximize the chance of being able to buy a gorilla-watching permit on site for at least 1 day during their stay. I spent 3 days, 1 day watching each of the two habituated gorilla troupes and 1 day hiking to a river in the forest. No more than six people may visit each troupe at once, so the group size is six, with an effective client-to-guide ratio of about 2:1.

Prices vary enormously, depending exactly what the package contains in the way of travel and accommodation. The actual walk to see the gorillas, led by the parks service staff, is paid for via the gorilla-watching permit, as outlined below. Currently the base cost for the permit alone appears to be US$360 per person, which includes a US$20 park entrance fee (Uganda Wildlife Authority, 2005). Prices for an entire gorilla-watching tour package purchased outside Uganda are a great deal higher, typically several thousand US dollars. Abercombie and Kent (2005) currently offer a 4-day tour out of Nairobi, with 2 days' gorilla tracking at Bwindi, for UKP2189 per person, or around US$975 per person per day. Eastern and Southern Safaris (2005) offer a 5-day trip out of Kampala, with 2 days at Bwindi, for US$2153 per person twinshare, i.e. US$440 per person per day.

## Access

For international travellers, direct access to Uganda is by air to Kampala. Overland buses and some upmarket 4WD safaris arrive by road. From Kampala to Mgahinga is a full day's drive. The final sections are on red dirt village roads, which are fine when dry but could be problematic when wet. Within the park, access is on foot, or in a parks vehicle and then on foot, as outlined above.

To watch the gorillas requires a permit from the Mgahinga parks office, and only a limited number of permits are sold for each day of the year. When I visited, ten permits a day were issued, but for two troupes of gorillas (i.e. five tourists per troupe). According to the parks staff at that time, seven of these permits were sold in advance to tour operators once a month, and the remaining three were sold on site on the day concerned. Some tour operators claimed to have a permanent allocation of permits, but the park rangers denied this, and it may be that this was a matter of custom more than contract.

In practice, international tour operators sold gorilla tours subject to being able to obtain a permit for the day concerned. Presumably they then contacted the parks service, other tour operators or permit brokers to obtain the permits. It seems likely that certain local tour operators based in Kampala routinely purchased permits speculatively and then either sold them on to international operators, or used them as a tool in selling an entire domestic gorilla-watching tour package to an international tour retailer. Information I was able to obtain about this system (Buckley, 2003a, pp. 38–41) was not consistent.

When I visited Mgahinga, I had an advance-purchase permit for 1 day, bought as part of a tour package. Almost everyone else, however, apparently bought their permits on site, and I did likewise for my second day. The price charged on site was less than half that charged for advanced purchase. This suggests that either the international tour operator, or more probably the domestic operator or broker in Uganda, charged a significant premium for obtaining permits. This was possible since the demand for gorilla-watching tours exceeds the total quota of places available; since most international travellers have tight schedules so they want a permit for a particular day; and since the price of the permit, though high relative to park entrance and activity fees worldwide, is still only a small proportion of the total trip cost for international visitors who buy a gorilla tour or Uganda safari package.

According to the current website of Uganda Wildlife Authority (2005), the permit system is now somewhat different, perhaps because of past 'permit scalping' practices. Currently, permits can be booked by various organizations as below, but can only be sold by UWA, and can only be sold at face value. Payments must be made directly to UWA. Permits can be booked through UWA headquarters in Kampala. Up to 80% of all permits available each month can be booked up to 2 years in advance on payment of a 30% deposit, but only by members of the Association of Uganda Tour Operators (AUTO). International tour operators must book through local operators. AUTO members may book up to 20 permits each month on the first business day of that month, and more on subsequent days if still available. Individual visitors can also book permits, but only up to 3 months in advance, and for no more than 2 days per month.

Permit fees may be refunded if individual visitors are forbidden to track gorillas because of illness, or if the gorillas have moved across the border and hence out of Uganda.

Differential fees apply for Ugandan citizens, other East African residents and international visitors from the rest of the world. Park entry fees are USH5000 (US$2.75), US$10 and US$20 respectively for a single day and night, and USH7500 (US$4), US$20 and US$35 respectively for 2 nights. Gorilla tracking fees, which include park entry fees and a community levy as well as the guide fees, are USH100,000 (US$55), US$340 and US$360 per person per day, respectively (Uganda Wildlife Authority, 2005).

## Community

Interactions between the parks service, tourists and local communities around Mgahinga and Bwindi National Parks have been studied in some detail (Archabald and Naughton-Treves, 2001; Adams and Infield, 2003; Buckley, 2003a, pp. 38–41). In summary, local communities were supposed to receive part of the funds from the gorilla-watching permit fees as compensation for losses to their subsistence crops immediately around the park boundaries. This system did not work well initially, and locals to whom I spoke during my own visit claimed not to have received any funds from the parks or tourism. Of course, I had no way to check whether these claims were accurate or representative. According to Archabald and Naughton-Treves (2001) some funds had been distributed by that date, but by a mechanism that would not necessarily compensate individual subsistence farmers. According to Adams and Infield (2003), local communities have received some funds, but not enough to compensate them fully for lost agricultural production. Even so, during my visit the locals did not seem to be antagonistic to the park; though again, since I could only talk to people who spoke English and they are likely to be involved in tourism, their opinions may not be representative.

According to Archabald and Naughton-Treves (2001) all three of the neighbouring parishes at Mgahinga had received community development funding from tourism revenues. They also received funds from the International Gorilla Conservation Programme (IGCP), an international non-government organization. Funds have been used to build schools, health clinics and roads. Local residents have expressed concerns over loss of land and raiding of crops. Funding of US$4 million has also been provided by the Global Environment Facility (Adams and Infield, 2003). This is about 20 times the total annual revenue from park and tracking fees.

## Experience

To see mountain gorillas in the wild is certainly a privilege. We were able to watch babies at play, young adults grooming and an old male lying back and chewing idly on a grass stem, whilst keeping an eye on us meanwhile. This expressiveness is probably their most memorable feature. Though clearly powerful, they do not give the same impression of enormous strength as, for example, a bear. I was able to visit both of the Mgahinga troupes which were habituated at that time, and in each case would gladly have stayed longer than an hour, if this had been permitted.

## Environment

Mountain gorillas are a highly endangered species that survive only in this area of the Virunga Mountains. Their only remaining habitat is in Bwindi and Mgahinga National Parks and adjacent areas of forest in Zaire and Rwanda, and these are under increasing pressure as surrounding areas continue to be cleared for agriculture. Individual gorillas are killed by local farmers, by poachers and by soldiers in various local wars.

There are various international efforts to conserve the remaining populations and habitats, and the tourist permit fees were supposed to play a part in this. In practice, however, it appears that Mgahinga relies principally on donor funding, and the permit fees are used to support the Uganda Wildlife Authority more generally. The practice of using funds from icon parks to support other parts of the conservation estate, of course, is widespread worldwide. Since the trackers follow the habituated gorilla troupes day by day, they presumably act effectively as guardians of those particular gorillas. It is possible, however, that habituated individuals are at particular risk when they leave the protection of the park.

As elsewhere, it seems likely that at least some of the international visitors who are able to see the gorillas for themselves may subsequently contribute to international awareness of their plight and to international efforts to conserve them. There does not yet seem to be any documented evidence, however, that this necessarily occurs in practice as well as theory. Meanwhile, tourists themselves may potentially produce impacts on gorilla populations. On one occasion in 1988, and another in 1990, a total of 61 lowland gorillas in the Democratic Republic of Congo suffered a respiratory infection, apparently transmitted by visiting tourists, which caused the death of eight gorillas before the remainder could be treated (Butynski and Kalina, 1998). It is for this reason that tourists with colds, and children under 15 who are more prone to such infections, are not allowed to take part in the gorilla-watching walks.

## Safety

The reason that tourists are taken to watch only habituated gorilla troupes is that habituation dampens the so-called fight-or-flight response. As long as the visiting tour groups are small, stay quiet, keep well back and behave submissively if challenged, habituated gorillas will neither run away nor attack the humans, but simply ignore them. Such neutral behaviour, however, requires that the approaching tourists behave appropriately. For the sake of safety, therefore, it is critical that the tourists understand and follow the guides' instructions, especially when close to the gorillas.

The trackers approach first and alert the gorillas to their presence. Once the guides are confident the gorillas are sufficiently relaxed, the tourists can approach, a few at a time, crouching down once they are in position. If the gorillas move towards the tourists, the tourists must move back accordingly. If the gorillas behave assertively, the people must behave submissively, e.g. by crouching slightly and looking down. It seems that these approaches are successful, since tourists have apparently not been attacked by any of the habituated gorillas. Indeed, during my own visit one of the tourists lost his footing on a steep slope and rolled downhill into the midst of the troupe, but they ignored him even so. Guides must hence be highly knowledgeable in interpreting and anticipating gorilla behaviour, and must be able to speak the language of the tourists in their group, and control tourist movement and behaviour tightly, to protect the tourists as much as the gorillas. For example, the guides decide from which direction to approach the gorillas, and when photography is permissible.

With appropriate precautions, therefore, the gorillas themselves do not seem to pose a significant threat to tourist safety. Of greater concern, perhaps, are the possibilities of traffic accidents or civil unrest. Not long after my own visit, a group of gorilla-watching tourists was kidnapped and killed. Not surprisingly, this caused a serious downturn in visitor numbers for some years.

## Marketing

The gorilla-watching trips are marketed by a range of international nature tourism and safari operators, typically in conjunction with other destinations in Uganda and nearby countries, and generally as part of a portfolio of tour products. These large operators advertise by traditional tourism distribution channels such as brochures and catalogues, inbound and outbound agents, and travel and trade shows, as well as their own websites, newsletters, mail out, specialist slide show nights and retail sale offices.

# Jack's Camp, Botswana: Uncharted Africa and Wilderness Safaris

### Place

Jack's Camp lies at the edge of the Makgadigadi Pans, a vast expanse of seasonally flooded salt flats at the edge of the Kalahari Desert dune fields. Accessible by air from Maun in northern Botswana, Jack's Camp provides the only permanent upmarket tourist accommodation in the Makgadigadi area. It has a subsidiary camp, San Camp, which is open only seasonally. The bare white salt pans are dotted by low vegetated sand islands, and the camps are on these. When the pans are dry, they can be traversed by quad bikes, small, fat-tyred all-terrain vehicles kept at Jack's Camp.

### Operator

When I visited Jack's Camp a few years ago, it was owned and operated by Uncharted Africa Safaris (Buckley, 2003a, pp. 20–22). The Camp apparently still has the same owners, Catherine Raphaely and Ralph Bousfield, and Uncharted Africa has an operating website that includes Jack's Camp. The latest prices shown, however, are for 2004. Jack's is now advertised through Wilderness Safaris (2005), which runs a portfolio of game lodges and safaris throughout southern and eastern Africa. Wilderness Safaris currently offers a total of 48 camps and lodges in seven different countries. Within Botswana, Wilderness Safaris operate 20 lodges in the Okavango area. The company recently received a *National Geographic*® Legacy Award for its environmental management practices.

## Activity

Game drives are the principal visitor activity, as with most private game lodges in sub-Saharan Africa. Some of the game viewing areas are also used by local village communities for grazing cattle and other livestock. Jack's Camp is on the route of one of the last remaining major African wildlife migrations, and provides visitors with a rare opportunity to watch large herds on the move, unimpeded by fences. It is also one of the few areas where brown hyenas are seen routinely (Uncharted Africa Safaris, 2005).

## Equipment

Jack's Camp is in a hot desert environment and guests need only bring binoculars, cameras and a hat. In addition to game drives in an open 4WD safari vehicle, and guided walks led by Kalahari Bushmen, one of the principal guest activities at Jack's Camp is to drive a small distance on to the giant salt flats of the Makgadigadi. For these drives, Jack's keeps a small fleet of four-wheeler all-terrain vehicles, commonly known as quad bikes. These have two-stroke motors, a motorbike-style transmission system and clutch, and are steered by handlebars. They are single-person vehicles and are therefore driven by the guests themselves, following line astern behind a guide from the lodge.

## Accommodation

Jack's is a tented camp in very traditional style. There are nine guest tents and one additional guide tent, spaced around the edge of the vegetated area at one end of the sand island, together with large and sumptuous lounge and dining tents, and another that is used as a tea tent at times. The view over the pans to distant sand islets is spectacular, especially at dawn and dusk. At the front of each guest tent is a low wooden platform bearing the accoutrements of a traditional safari camp: folding chairs, a tripod supporting a beaten copper basin, and a large copper water jug. A hardwood dresser and small chest next to the beds complete the fitout.

At the back of each guest tent are two open-topped enclosures fenced in by close-set stakes. One of these contains a porcelain flush toilet, a little out of keeping with the safari ambience, but a welcome addition for most guests. In the other enclosure, an old-style bucket shower hangs from a pulley attached to a dead tree. A shaving mirror and soap container hang off the fence, the latter with a sliding wooden lid to prevent birds absconding with the soap! The camp staff carry warm water to the copper jug in the early morning, and to the bucket shower in the afternoon.

Cold water is in fact reticulated to each guest tent, to supply the flush toilet cisterns, but the copper basin and bucket shower allow the guests to experience traditional style, and serve to remind them of the arid climate and sparse water supply. The reticulated water supplies run only to the toilet cisterns, and are not accessible to the guests. Sewerage piping is also reticulated to the individual guest toilets, running to a central, self-contained septic tank system. Even though the camp has a generator, the guest areas use candles and lanterns in keeping with the traditional safari theme. Similarly, drinks in the central lounge and dining tent are kept cool in a modernized version of the traditional wooden ice chest.

## Statistics

There is no fixed duration for stays at Jack's Camp, but since it is a relatively unusual destination that takes time to reach, most guests would stay at least 3 nights. At some times of year a fly camp known as San Camp also operates, and guests can stay additional days in order to visit it. Even in the midsummer heat, when I visited, the Makgadigadi Pans are a fascinating area and I would willingly have extended my stay for a week or more. Jack's Camp is relatively small, and even at full capacity would not have more than 18 guests. On game drives there would rarely be more than five guests and one guide in the vehicle. When I was there, I was the only person to take the guided walks at night, or the guided walk with one of the local resident Bushman guides, so for these activities there was a client-to-guide ratio of 1:1. Current prices at Jack's Camp are not advertised by Wilderness Safaris, which refers potential clients to travel agents. The Uncharted Africa Safaris (2005) site advertises 2004 rates as US$375–640 per person per night twinshare, depending on season, plus a US$150 single supplement. A UK operator, Botswana Odyssey (2005), which markets all of the Wilderness Safari camps, advertises current rates at US$675 per person per night.

## Access

Jack's Camp is accessible in a 4WD vehicle for most of the year, but guests generally arrive by air from Maun at the southern edge of the Okavango. Most international tourists will combine a visit to Jack's with stays at one or more lodges in the Okavango for the Botswana portion of their safari. Maun itself is accessible by air from Gaborone, the capital of Botswana. The flight from Maun takes about an hour and lands at Tsigaro airstrip, 20 min drive from the camp.

## Community

Uncharted Africa Safaris, the parent company for Jack's Camp, has provided support for the non-profit Green Cross Wildlife Orphanage and Education Centre (Uncharted Africa Safaris, 2005). Wilderness Safaris (2005) also operates a range of community support programmes.

## Experience

In addition to the wildlife migrations and the scenery of the Makgadigadi Pans, Jack's Camp offers its guests the opportunity to learn about local ecosystems through the eyes of their earliest inhabitants, the Kalahari Bushmen. For myself at least, this was the most interesting and intense interpretive experience it has ever been my privilege to take part in. In an hour's walk, straight from the camp, I received an astonishing wealth of information and demonstration covering an enormous range of skills and knowledge. These included, for example, the design and manufacture of traditional Bushman weapons and other implements, including the precise plant and animal species used in each case, and why; how to read tracks and set snares of various kinds; how to recognize and prepare various edible and medicinal plants; how to make arrow poison and how to dig up scorpions; and how to seal up a wound using ant jaws and plant latex. Other guides are also highly skilled at finding, identifying and describing plants and wildlife, but to be introduced to the Kalahari by one of its own Bushmen sets Jack's Camp apart.

## Environment

Overall, maintenance and environmental management at Jack's Camp seem to be of a particularly high standard, perhaps because some of their staff have worked there for many years (Buckley, 2003a, pp. 20–22).

## Safety

As at most upmarket African game and safari lodges, guests at Jack's Camp are always accompanied by a guide outside the camp boundaries, and the guide is generally armed. This applies for game drives as well as walks. When one is walking with a Bushman guide, he carries a traditional Kalahari Bushman bow and poisoned arrows. Guides from Jack's Camp itself carry rifles. Safety briefings are provided for all activities, and for the quad-bike ride, guests are given instructions in driving and steering technique, and practise near the lodge before heading out across the salt flats.

## Marketing

Jack's Camp is currently marketed as part of the Wilderness Safaris portfolio, generally in conjunction with other lodges in Botswana and elsewhere in southern Africa. Wilderness Safaris (2005) produces its own annual catalogues and brochures that are distributed through traditional tourism marketing networks such as trade shows and inbound and outbound packages and agents. It also maintains an informative website.

# Polar Bears, Churchill, Canada: Natural Habitat Adventures

## Place

Churchill, Manitoba, on the west coast of Hudson Bay, is the world's prime site to see polar bears at close range. The bears congregate at Churchill in October and November to await freeze-up of the sea ice, and this is the most southerly and accessible part of their range. Hudson Bay provides habitat for seals, the polar bear's principal prey. It is also large enough for its maritime influence to affect the local climate and hence the latitude of the local tree line. The tree line separating treeless tundra from the boreal forest or taiga is much further south in areas near Hudson Bay than it is elsewhere in Canada or indeed Russia. In fact the tree line runs immediately south of Churchill itself, so that the Churchill coastal plains provide suitable habitat for polar bears.

Unlike more northerly populations of polar bears, which remain on the polar ice year-round, the population of the Churchill area must come ashore when the sea ice melts in spring, and remain ashore until it re-forms for winter (Lunn and Stirling, 1985; Derocher and Stirling, 1990a, b, 1995). On the ice, the bears eat seals, but whilst ashore they have very little food and they are therefore very keen to get back on the winter ice as soon as it forms.

Because of the Churchill River and the shape of the coast, the sea ice forms first at Churchill. Every year, therefore, no matter where they may have come ashore from the ice in spring, the bears gradually congregate around Churchill in the last few weeks before freeze-up. And once they have arrived in the area, they have little to do but wait, so they are easily watched. It is these factors that give Churchill its unparalleled opportunities for tourists to see polar bears.

## Operator

Natural Habitat Adventures (NHA) (2005) is a natural history tour company based in Boulder, Colorado. It has been operating since 1985, has 25 full-time staff, and offers 160 itineraries in 30 countries, including bear-watching in Alaska and Canada. It is a retail-level packaging and guiding operator that uses local operators on-site. A number of operators provide tourist transport and accommodation in and around Churchill to watch bears in winter and whales in summer. These include hotels and lodges, charter buses, helicopter operations and so-called tundra buggies, specialized vehicles with a raised chassis and oversized tyres that take tourists to see polar bears at close range.

Two companies have permits to operate a total of 18 tundra buggies in the Churchill area, one with 12 buggies and the other with 6. Each of these also operates a bear-viewing lodge in the tour area, where tourists can stay overnight in a complex of tundra buggies linked end to end and modified with sleeping and catering facilities as well as bear viewing areas. These two operators also carry out their own marketing and organize their own inbound tours (International Wildlife Adventures, 2005; Great White Bear Tours, 2005). The majority of bear-watching tourists to Churchill, however, arrive in groups with inbound operators that subcontract local facilities and services. NHA is the largest of these, locally estimated to bring between 50 and 75% of the polar bear tourists.

## Activity

NHA's flagship polar bear tour, billed as the 'Ultimate Polar Bear Adventure', includes: 2 nights in a lodge on the northern side of the Churchill River, in an area adapted for ground-level viewing of polar bear cubs and their mothers; 2 days and 1 evening in tundra buggies in the main bear-viewing area east of Churchill town on the southern side of the river; a day by helicopter, viewing bears from the air along the ice edge south of Cape Churchill; and 2 days available for other local activities.

The principal attraction is, of course, the polar bears, but a range of other Arctic wildlife species may also be seen, including wolf, Arctic fox, red fox, Arctic hare, snowy owl and ptarmigan. The tundra vegetation is snow-covered during polar bear season, but willows, tamarack (larch) and spruces along the tree line are visible.

Interpretation throughout the tour is provided by an NHA guide. On the tour which I audited, the guide had a university degree in wildlife biology and was clearly knowledgeable about the broader aspects of bear management and the Arctic environment, adding significantly to the value of the tour. In addition, the tour includes evening video presentations at the White Whale Lodge, and evening lectures from local Churchill residents whilst staying in town. These lectures, however, do not address any of the controversial aspects of current bear management practices.

## Equipment

As noted above, many of the bear-watching tours at Churchill rely on specialized vehicles known as tundra buggies. These are effectively large buses raised high above the ground so the windows are beyond a polar bear's reach, and running on broad, large-diameter tyres with low operating pressure so as to spread the weight of the bus wide and avoid the wheels digging into the tundra. The buses are heated, and passengers board them from a heated building, so tourists do not need cold-weather gear. Tundra buggy tours operate at night as well as by day. Whilst they are designed to travel off-road, they are restricted to operating on formed tracks, because of the large number of buggies and their potential impacts.

In addition to tundra buggy tours, different operators use conventional buses for local tours around the Churchill area, and helicopters to visit an area of the Hudson Bay coastline east of Churchill. Other activities, unrelated to polar bears, include riding in a racing dogsled. In general, tourists need to bring no specialized equipment except cameras, binoculars and reasonably warm clothing.

## Accommodation

Three types of accommodation are available for polar bear tours around Churchill. Tourists booked into tundra-buggy, helicopter or local town tours generally stay in hotels or motels in Churchill itself. One operator has assembled a group of tundra buggies into the so-called Tundra Buggy Hotel, at a site some distance out of town which the tundra buggy tours visit. This enables tourists to stay at that site overnight. Since the mobile tundra buggies now offer night tours to the same location, however, there is perhaps little advantage in this.

The third accommodation option is a lodge on the far side of the river from Churchill itself, an area used by female bears with cubs so as to provide some protection from male bears, which commonly attack cubs. An old and somewhat rustic-style lodge has been converted into tourist accommodation, officially named the White Whale Lodge, but known locally as the mothers-and-cubs lodge. It is a single-storey wooden building with a deck on one side. The deck and the windows have been protected with bars, so that tourists can watch bears safely at very short range when the bears come up to the building. An open viewing deck, and an enclosed and heated viewing room, have also been constructed on the roof to provide unobstructed views of bears a little further away.

These modifications provide excellent viewing opportunities, which certainly outweigh the relatively basically nature of the accommodation. There are three rooms filled with bunks, one for male guests, one for female and one for staff. The volume of snoring is quite impressive. There is a small central lounge, a kitchen and dining area and a food storage space. Water is in very short supply, with a tank that is sufficient for drinking and cooking, but not for guest showers. Guests therefore generally stay only for 2 nights. There is a minimalist shower for on-site staff who have to stay a lot longer.

## Statistics

This particular tour, known as the 'Ultimate Polar Bear Adventure' (Natural Habitat Adventures, 2005), is NHA's premium polar bear product. It is positioned at the upper end of the market and caters for relatively small groups, a maximum of 14 clients with one NHA guide. The tour takes 8 days and 9 nights, of which 5 days are spent watching the bears. The current price, not including flights between Winnipeg and Churchill, is US$4395 per person twinshare with an additional US$420 single supplement and an additional US$795 for the helicopter component (Natural Habitat Adventures, 2005). This corresponds to US$650–700 per person per day. On the tour in which I took part, the group met in Winnipeg and flew together to Churchill.

## Access

Churchill is accessible by air, generally from Winnipeg. There are local roads around Churchill, and access beyond that is in tundra buggies or by helicopter. The various components of the NHA tour are provided by local operators who have their own operating permits, e.g. for the tundra buggies. The number of tundra buggy operators, and the number of buggies each can operate, are regulated as outlined above. All permits are included in the overall trip price.

## Community

Churchill is a regional administrative centre and a port, but for many residents tourism seems to be the economic mainstay, at least in season. The port is connected by rail to the central Canadian wheat-growing provinces, and was built to service bulk grain carriers. In recent years, however, it appears to have fallen somewhat into disuse and according to locals only eight carriers had loaded during the preceding year.

The economic significance of tourism has increased in both absolute and relative terms as the rail and port industries have declined. The entire tourism industry is based on polar bear watching, and the bears are hence of very considerable importance to the town's economy. Tourists have ample opportunity to discuss these issues with local residents, from helicopter pilots and tundra buggy drivers to supermarket staff and people working at the port.

## Experience

Polar bears are very impressive animals and certainly awe-inspiring to watch. Bear behaviour in the Churchill environs does, however, appear to be modified significantly by a variety of human disturbances. Some of these are due simply to the town itself, whereas others are more specific to tourism. There are still polar bears at the town dump, even though this is no longer the principal tourist port of call. Some of the bears one can see from the tundra buggies are simply wandering about or lying in the snow, but others are investigating the buggies themselves, either reaching up to the windows or drinking water draining out of the Tundra Buggy Hotel, perhaps from a sink.

In the helicopter section, a few bears remained unperturbed, but most seemed to be highly disturbed by the helicopter noise, and either ran away or ran in circles. At the White Whale Lodge, we had excellent views of a mother bear and two small cubs snoozing peacefully, but at other times the same mother bear pushed her snout between the bars on the kitchen window or the front deck. Given that the bears have not eaten for months, it is of course not surprising that they should investigate anything that smells even potentially of food, and the 'reverse zoo' arrangement at this lodge does seem like a good way to limit the impacts of bear watching.

Certainly it is much better than a property close to Churchill where the owner charges tour buses to drive in, nominally to see his sled dogs, which are tethered outside, but apparently also to watch bears who are attracted by the meat on which the dogs are fed.

All of these local tours, of course, are run by local tour operators. Natural Habitat Adventures simply packages them together and has no direct control over any of them. Besides, given how hungry the bears are at this time of year, and how powerful they are, facilities such as tundra buggies and barred windows are essential to provide a safe viewing opportunity. One certainly does see bears, one sees them up close, and many of them seem to be quite relaxed and ignore the intrusions. The NHA package provides opportunities to see polar bears in a range of different settings. We certainly appreciated this variety and the NHA 'Ultimate Polar Bear Adventure' deserves its name and reputation.

Of course, I should have been greatly disappointed if we had not got good opportunities to watch the bears. Even so, however, the single most memorable part of the experience for me was to see a snowy owl, its white feathers barely flecked with grey, surveying the landscape from a small hummock of snow.

## Environment

Historically, management of interactions between people and bears around Churchill was apparently rather poor, with hungry bears foraging in an open tip and then being confined in a so-called bear jail or in some cases shot. Whilst this situation has now improved, largely in response to the growth in tourism, there is still conflict and criticism of current practices (Pilkington, 2002; Dyck and Baydack, 2004). A more detailed discussion is given in Buckley (2003a, pp. 176–181).

The practicalities of on-ground environmental management for NHA's polar bear tours are handled by the individual local suppliers, namely hotels and charter bus companies in town; the tundra buggy and helicopter operators; and the self-contained White Whale Lodge. The tundra buggies travel mainly on old roads, but do cross tundra when turning or manoeuvring. The buggies have bus-style toilets.

Natural Habitat Adventures itself was named in 2001 by the World Wide Fund for Nature as a 'Conservation Travel Provider'. It was one of only two companies worldwide to receive this distinction (NHA, 2005).

## Safety

Polar bears are undoubtedly dangerous to humans even when well fed, and after several months of fasting they are clearly a significant threat. One can walk through town unhindered, even at night, and though locals apparently do encounter bears on occasion, the interactions generally prove to be harmless. This, however, is in town: out on the tundra the result might prove rather different. Whenever bears were around, therefore, we were protected either inside a bus, a tundra buggy, a building or a barrier. We did also have the opportunity to walk on various occasions, but only after checking that no bears were nearby. On one occasion we were even able to climb into a bear's den, but only after checking it had been abandoned for the season.

## Marketing

Natural Habitat Adventures (2005) is a large nature tour company based in North America but offering trips worldwide. It produces its own brochures, newsletters and other marketing materials and circulates them through trade shows and targeted mailing lists so as to maximize word-of-mouth referrals. Indeed, this was how I first learnt of the company, though I went to its website for more detailed information. NHA is a member of the 'Adventure Collection', an upmarket adventure tourism marketing syndicate.

# Brown Bears, Kamchatka, Russia: Explore Kamchatka

## Place

The Kamchatka Peninsula forms part of Russia's eastern seaboard, a large peninsula running north–south and attached at its northern end. It is famous for its volcanoes and volcanic landscapes, its salmon, its marine wildlife and its brown bears. The bears are the same species as the grizzlies of North America. During most of the year the bears are widely dispersed and not easy to see, but at the beginning of the salmon run each year they congregate to catch salmon swimming upriver to spawn. In particular, at the southern tip of the peninsula there are several lakes that are known for their bear populations and bear-watching opportunities. One of these is Lake Kurilskoye, a sizeable lake with several small inflowing streams and a substantial outflowing river. Within the lake there is also an island used as a breeding site by various seabird species. The surrounding vegetation consists principally of grasslands and low open woodlands.

## Operator

Explore Kamchatka (2005) is a small specialist tour company based in Yelizovo. It is owned and operated by a Russian-American couple. It offers a range of sightseeing, fishing, skiing, hiking and bear-watching tours, generally for small groups, and principally for American and Japanese clients. Local logistic arrangements are made in conjunction with a local Russian firm and travel agency. The owners also run their house as a guesthouse, providing a base for the tour operations. When I visited, the bear-watching tours were led by a specialist, Swiss-born, bear guide experienced with the grizzly populations in the Canadian Rockies, but this is not always the case.

## Activity

The principal activity for this tour is watching brown bears from a purpose-built pavilion overlooking the mouth of a small creek that flows into the lake. This pavilion is reached by a short walk from a rustic lodge on a small peninsula nearby, accompanied by an armed park ranger. Other activities include a boat trip to other parts of the lake in two outboard-powered dinghies, and a day visit to a fisheries station at the lake's main outflow.

## Equipment

The only access to this area seems to be by helicopter, and we travelled in a large ex-military machine with a five-bladed rotor, and wheels rather than skids. It is the only helicopter in which I have travelled that taxied on take off like a fixed-winged aeroplane. The fuselage was cylindrical and contained a large, long-distance fuel tank. Noise levels were painfully high, especially after several hours in the air, and we had no earmuffs.

Heavy rain is commonplace in this area, and clients were advised to bring a full set of heavy-duty rubberized waterproof gear including hat, coat, long johns and boots. Pre-trip information material indicates that Gore-Tex® clothing is generally ineffective under these weather conditions, and non-breathable waterproof gear is preferable. The tour operator can provide locally purchased rubber boots on request, to save space and weight in passengers' baggage. Interestingly, both the park rangers at the lake, and one of the guides from the tour company, complained that they did not have sufficient funds to purchase proper wet-weather gear of their own and that they suffered accordingly. The guide, in particularly, was very insistent in asking for my waterproof parka, especially after I had given my waterproof longjohns to one of the rangers. I did, in fact, give it to her, although it seems quite possible that she was simply planning to sell it.

## Accommodation

Accommodation at the lake is in a basic but functional wooden guest lodge built next to the ranger station and housing. It was apparently built and operated by a private individual under concession by the park service. Various hints were made, but never fully explained, as to why such a concession should have been granted. The lodge consisted of a two-storey wooden building about the size of a rather small house, with a kitchen and trestle-table dining room, and remaining rooms equipped as dormitories. There were two outdoor composting toilets in a separate building, and a row of cold-water basins, also outdoors, for washing. There was a small sauna in a separate building nearby, and one could swim in the lake. We brought food and cooks with us in the helicopter from Yelizovo. One of the cooks, apparently a relative of the tour operators, worked particularly hard and fed us well. In Yelizovo itself we stayed for 1 night before the visit to Lake Kurilskoye, and a couple of nights afterwards, in the tour owners' own house, which is operated as a guesthouse or bed-and-breakfast establishment, with a large communal dining room and shared use of bedrooms.

## Statistics

The trip takes 6 days in total, plus the time taken to reach Yelizovo via Vladivostok and Petropavlovsk. Of this we spent 4 days at Lake Kurilskoye itself. The total cost from Yelizovo is US$1600–3600 per person, depending on group size, or about

US$265–600 per person per day. Maximum group size is ten clients. There were four guides at the lake, each with different functions: a logistics guide from the tour company, who was essentially there as a translator; two park rangers, who acted as our principal guides whilst we were there; and the Swiss-Canadian bear guide, who was there to provide interpretation of their behaviour, if we had in fact seen any bears for longer than a brief and distant glimpse.

## Access

Access is by air to Vladivostok and hence Petropavlovsk, and by road to Yelizovo. From Yelizovo to Lake Kurilskoye, access is by helicopter as outlined above. The helicopter lands at the helipad directly by the lodge. At the lake, access is on foot to the bear-watching pavilion, or by boat around the lake. The lake is apparently part of a national park, and we used parks boats and were guided by parks rangers. No doubt there are significant fees for this, but exactly how they are paid and who receives them were never made clear. It seems likely that the private concessionaire who operates the lodge acts as an intermediary and broker in return for additional fees, but I was not able to establish this since everyone denied any knowledge of the details. In any event, all such arrangements are included in the overall price of the tour package.

## Community

Community issues are extremely complicated in this case, because there appears to be a well-organized salmon and bear poaching operation that is armed, wealthy, well-connected and powerful. According to Russell and Enns (2002), these poaching gangs may historically have had connections within the parks service itself. Suggestions were made to us during our visit that this might still be the case, but of course there is no way for a non-Russian-speaking individual, visiting on a holiday for a few days, to distinguish fact from innuendo in regard to issues such as this. Whilst we were there, the parks rangers showed us a makeshift camp on the far side of the lake that they said was a salmon poachers' camp. Apparently, poachers work in secret, netting gravid female salmon and stripping out their roe, which is what fetches the top price. Then a helicopter arrives, flying low to the ground to escape detection, and picks up the roe for immediate sale and distribution. According to the park rangers, even though they can hear the helicopter when it gets close to the lake, by the time they can get across the lake in their dinghy, the helicopter is already gone. Besides, the poachers are more numerous, more heavily armed and less scrupulous than the rangers.

Apparently, salmon are the primary target for the poaching organizations, but they do also kill brown bear. On the black market, the most valuable part of the bear is its gall bladder, and Russell and Enns (2002) give a description of bear poachers catching bears in snares and leaving them in the snare overnight so that their fear and fury enlarges the gall bladder to its maximum weight before they kill the bear. According to the park rangers, poachers do also kill brown bear around Lake Kurilskoye, and for this reason the bears are both wary and potentially dangerous. There seemed to be some differences in opinion between the local Russian park rangers and the Swiss-Canadian guide as to how to best behave towards bears. Since in practice the only bears we saw at close range were two small cubs that immediately ran away, the issue proved academic.

To what degree bear-watching tours may assist the park rangers in combating or at least publicizing poaching is not clear. Even such details as exactly who owns the lodge and where the money goes were never made clear. Whether the park as a whole, or these rangers in particular, earns any of their income from tourism is also uncertain. The two tour companies involved in running this tour both employ local staff, as guides, cooks, etc. Explore Kamchatka also employs two staff at the owners' house.

## Experience

In any wildlife-watching tour the critical issue is to see the wildlife. The Lake Kurilskoye site is known for the opportunity to see Russian brown bears both at short range and in significant numbers. According to the Swiss-Canadian guide, there were indeed good bear sightings later in the same season. When I was there, however, we saw no bears at all from the bear-viewing pavilion; one or two bears crossing open grassland at the limit of our binoculars; and two small bear cubs near a fisheries station.

The timing of this trip was dictated by two of the clients who had apparently specified dates to fit with other commitments, and the tour operator had built the trip around those dates, taking a gamble that the bears would be there. For the clients concerned and the tour operators, this was an informed gamble. For the remaining clients who had been led to believe that the tour dates were within the peak bear-viewing period, however, the outcome was clearly disappointing.

Despite the lack of bears, the trip still had its adventurous components: a long, low-altitude helicopter flight over open rolling hills, apparently quite deserted; the short hike along the foreshore through carpets of flowers; and the boat trip around the lake, including the bird nesting island. None of these, however, were really worth the very considerable cost of getting to Kurilskoye Lake. Information on the poaching problem was also of interest and concern, but essentially unverifiable, and detracting rather than contributing to the tourist experience.

## Environment

There are two principal environmental management issues associated with this tour. The major impact is from the use of a large helicopter. At the Lake Kurilskoye Lodge the toilets are long-drop, and greywater from the kitchen and sinks drains to the ground. Facilities, environmental management and environmental impacts are all limited. The impacts of poaching are orders of magnitude more significant than the impacts of the lodge. Whether tourism helps to counter poaching at all is unknown, but this currently seems unlikely since it is such small scale. Indeed, it is entirely possible that tourism simply represents a small add-on income and a way to legitimize the construction of a private cabin inside the national park, funded from undefined income streams.

## Safety

On a trip such as this, risks are difficult to judge accurately. The ex-military helicopter in which we flew to Lake Kurilskoye seemed rather old and battered, and it is a bit disconcerting to sit right next to an enormous fuel tank, but in reality it was probably no more risky than any other helicopter, and the exact location of the fuel tank probably makes no difference to safety. The pilot certainly seemed competent, skimming his giant machine closely over ridgelines and hilltops, and landing gently on the helipad next to the lodge.

Outside the lodge we were always accompanied by armed rangers, though whether they were more concerned about bears or poachers was never clear. On the lake we did have lifejackets, though we were far from shore and the water was probably too cold to swim any distance. We had two boats, so if one outboard had failed we could possibly have towed one behind the other, and if one sank the other could possibly have carried the entire group, though not in rough water. Fortunately, none of these problems occurred. Indeed, the only significant logistical difficulty occurred when I was trying to leave Russia, and was held for several hours between check-in and passport control because of some supposed irregularity in my visa.

## Marketing

Marketing for this particular tour operator seems to be rather low-key and principally word-of-mouth. The owner does carry out marketing tours in the USA in the off season. In 2005, the 8th World Wilderness Congress in Alaska had a special programme in Kamchatka, and this tour operator was involved, which is likely to give a significant boost to business.

# 21 Aerial Adventures

Ralf Buckley, Lake George, Australia. RB collection.

Carl Cater, Kooralbyn, Australia. CC collection.

© CAB International 2006. *Adventure Tourism* (R. Buckley)

## Sector Structure

Compared with terrestrial and aquatic adventure tours, coverage of aerial activities in this volume is relatively limited, essentially through lack of experience by the authors in relevant commercial products. There are adventure tour companies offering everything from bungee jumps to space flights, at prices ranging from US$60 to US$20 million. Very broadly, the types of aerial activities offered to tourists may be summarized as follows.

There are numerous bungee-jumping products including bridge, crane, upwards, cable, heli-bungee and bridge swings. These were started by A.J. Hackett at the Kawarau Bridge in New Zealand, but have proliferated and have become a standard component of any destination that claims to cater for adventure tourists.

Also spreading rapidly are 'fly-by-wire' rides, where the client is attached to a long, inclined cable in a modified hang-gliding harness, rather like a glorified flying-fox. Flying-foxes of various design have long been used to cross rivers and gorges in many parts of the world, and indeed still are. They also form a common component of 'ropes' courses used for outdoor education programmes, whether for school camps or corporate team-building exercises. The progression to the far longer and faster, fly-by-wire design is relatively recent, and also seems to have started in New Zealand. Cable arrangements are also apparently now common at forest 'jungle lodges' in various continents. In some of the New Zealand 'fly-by-wire' rides, the client travels in a powered capsule that can be steered to some degree.

Hang-gliding is offered as a commercial tourist activity using tandem harnesses, where the client hangs beside the instructor in a standing, seated or prone harness. Recreational and competitive hang-gliders fly at two main types of sites. At ridge-soaring sites there is continuous lift provided by the wind blowing on to a hill or ridge and being deflected upwards. Take-off and landing at these sites is relatively straightforward. There is generally some lift on the kite's wings even before it becomes airborne, and even at low ground speed.

At thermalling sites, in contrast, lift is provided only by large bubbles of warm air rising from the ground, vertically or drifting slowly with ambient wind. These thermals are the air movement that forms cumulus clouds, but often exist even when there are no clouds to indicate their position. In these conditions the hang-glider has to take off in still air, and glide forward and down, searching for a thermal. If one is found, the pilot turns the kite into a series of slow circles so as to rise with the warm air bubble in the same way as a soaring bird or fixed-wing glider.

Flying in thermals is generally much more difficult than ridge-soaring, for various reasons. In ridge-soaring the zone of lift is generally quite stable and the pilot knows where it is and can easily stay in it. On a smoothly sloping ridge with moderate-strength winds, the strength of lift decreases gradually at the edges of the lift zone so the pilot can hunt for the best area. The air-flow is non-turbulent and the lift is smooth. Turbulence can occur at these sites when the wind is strong, the hill sharply cliffed or irregular, or when thermals are mixed in with a steady wind, as often happens at inland sites on hot days.

In thermalling, in contrast, turbulence is the norm. Especially when the thermals are strong and close to the ground, their edges can be very sharply defined and a pilot can fly from strongly sinking to strongly rising air – or vice versa – in a moment. Indeed, one wing can be in rising air and one in still or sinking air, throwing the kite over and requiring very quick reactions to correct. When the atmosphere becomes strongly unstable because of strong temperature gradients between the ground and the air at cloudbase, thermals can become extremely powerful, gathering speed, size and momentum as they rise, and punching thousands or tens of thousands of metres above cloud base to form giant cumulonimbus clouds. A hang-glider caught in one of these clouds is in extreme danger. Even under gentle thermal conditions, the pilot can generally circle in one thermal for a limited time, and must then leave it to glide through still or sinking air in search of another patch of lift. If none is found, the pilot must land, sometimes in difficult circumstances.

To maximize the chance of encountering a thermal soon after the initial take-off, so as to be able to gain altitude and then search for more, hang-glider pilots prefer high take-off points for thermalling, and these are often cliff-faces where the actual take-off itself involves running as fast as possible off the cliff edge into still air. All of these manoeuvres are substantially more difficult and potentially more dangerous than ridge-soaring. Accordingly, commercial tandem hang-gliding is largely restricted to ridge-soaring sites, especially coastal sites where sea breezes provide reliable steady winds of moderate strength.

In Australia there are tandem hang-gliding operations at places such as Sydney's Stanwell Park and at Lennox Head near Byron Bay in northern New South Wales. In New Zealand there is one based in Queenstown, which uses the road to the Mt Remarkable ski field to provide access to a take-off point. There are similar operations in Hawaii, California, Utah, Colorado, New Mexico, Ecuador, Brazil, Chile, South Africa, India, Indonesia, Denmark and elsewhere. Tandem flights in powered hang-gliders or ultralight aircraft are also offered as a tour product in many places.

During the past 20 years, hang-gliders have been partially replaced by parapentes, two-surfaced directional parachutes that can use ridge lift or thermals to ascend in the same way as hang-gliders. Indeed, at many sites the two use the same take-off points. The parapente is launched before its pilot takes off, so the pilot is standing on the hillside with the sail up above inflated by the wind, but adjusted by the pilot's control lines so as not to attain maximum lift. In order to take off, the pilot adjusts the lines for maximum lift and runs forward downslope, as for a hang-glider take-off.

Note that flying a parapente from a hillside is very different indeed from BASE jumping, where the parachutist runs off a cliff or other elevated point with the parachute still folded in its backpack, and freefalls first before pulling the ripcord to open the parachute. BASE jumping requires a very high level of individual skill in parachuting, and is emphatically not offered as a commercial tandem experience. Parapenting also requires a high level of skill for a tandem instructor, but a tandem passenger can be carried with relatively low risk.

Tandem parachuting from an aeroplane, commonly known and marketed as skydiving, is indeed offered as a commercial adventure activity, possibly one of the highest-adrenalin tour products around. The client is strapped into a second harness underneath the instructor and is carried essentially as inert cargo (the phrase 'dead weight' seems unfortunate in this particular application, even if otherwise appropriate!). The client and instructor jump together, but effectively the instructor pushes the client out of the plane. When the pair land, the client pulls up their feet and the actual running landing is made by the instructor. One case study is described in this chapter, but there are tandem skydiving operations worldwide. For skilled skydivers there are also tour operators who will organize logistics for jumps in remote parts of the globe, even the North Pole (for US$12,900) (North Pole Expeditions, 2005b).

Tandem flights in conventional fixed-wing gliders are not a common tourist product, but are available at some aerodromes, especially in rural areas. A two-seat glider is used with a pilot and a passenger, and the glider is launched by being towed aloft behind a powered aircraft. Once it is released from the tow, it is up to the pilot to take advantage of thermals, ridge lift or any other favourable conditions to remain aloft, or else simply to glide back down in a circle and land back at the airstrip. Some two-seat gliders have dual controls, but there is rarely time for the passenger to try using them, even if the pilot permits it.

Tandem flights in powered light aircraft have been offered as a tourist product almost since the earliest aeroplanes. In some parts of the world there was an era of so-called barnstorming, when a pilot would fly his plane to a rural field or paddock and offer flights to anyone who would pay. These were typically biplanes with low take-off and landing speed, which could fly from a rural road or reasonably level field with little difficulty. Such independence would presumably be frowned upon by aviation authorities in most countries today, not to mention insurance underwriters, so scenic flights are generally offered only from registered airstrips and airfields. A range of different light aircraft are used, from two-seaters to ten-seaters or more, depending on the precise product. There are also variants where ski planes and float planes are used so as to take off and land on snow or water, respectively.

Scenic helicopter flights are also available in many adventure tourism destinations, and indeed also in urban tourist destinations. In a few instances, helicopters are also used to watch wildlife, as well as inanimate scenery, but most animals flee from helicopters so the views are often brief. Examples include polar bear watching by helicopter in Canada's Hudson Bay, described in the wildlife chapter (Chapter 20), and helicopter flights to see sperm whales offshore from Kaikoura in New Zealand (Buckley, 2003a, p. 216). Both of these do seem to have significant impacts on the wildlife concerned. Indeed, impacts on wildlife are also of concern where helicopters are used for other purposes. Concerns have been raised that heliskiing in the Canadian Rockies may be affecting caribou populations (Piore, 2002); and that helicopter sight-seeing flights in Australia's Purnululu National Park may affect native bird species such as bowerbirds (Buckley, 2004b).

Hot-air balloon flights provide a much quieter option, but are only feasible in sites with adequate take-off and landing areas, and relatively calm and non-turbulent wind conditions. Balloon flights are now available at sites ranging from wilderness wildlife reserves in Africa to tourist beach towns in Australia. One case study is described in this chapter.

Tourist flights are by no means restricted to light aircraft. There are aerial sightseeing trips to Antarctica, tandem flights in ex-military jet aircraft, and even – for the extremely well-heeled – opportunities for private citizens to experience space travel. These are reviewed briefly in the next chapter.

## Mission Beach, Australia: Jump the Beach

### Place

Mission Beach is a small residential and tourist township on the coastline south of Cairns in Queensland, Australia. It is surrounded by agricultural landscapes, principally cane and cattle farms. Inland lie the steep forested slopes of the Wet Tropics of Queensland World Heritage Area. Offshore lie the reefs and islands of the Great Barrier Reef, also World Heritage listed. Long treated as a small residential outlier to Cairns, in more recent years Mission Beach has become like Port Douglas to the north, a significant tourism destination in its own right.

## Operator

Jump the Beach is a specialist tandem skydiving company based in Mission Beach. It employs around 20 staff and takes around 3000 clients per year. The operational base for Jump the Beach is a residential house, garage and grounds at Mission Beach. Marketing is mainly in Cairns, largely by handing out leaflets in backpacker haunts. At the operations centre there are ground staff responsible for welcoming clients, distributing and checking liability waivers, and managing bookings, payments, transport arrangements, and sale of videos and souvenirs. The parachutists themselves are responsible only for their equipment and for their individual clients once they reach the airstrip.

## Activity

In tandem skydiving, the client is attached to the guide in a special harness, and the parachute is attached to the guide, who is generally referred to as an instructor. In descent, therefore, the client is suspended face-down immediately below the guide. In leaving the plane, the client and guide have to move together to the open door, and the client has to move out of the door and support their feet on a wing strut. The actual jump, however, is made by the guide who effectively pushes the client in front of them. Likewise, at landing the client draws up their feet so that the pair land only on the guide's feet, with the client hanging in harness from the guide's chest. Throughout the jump, the client does not have to know anything about parachuting and the guide effectively makes the jump with the client as an inert weight slung beneath them. If clients are interested to do so, however, the guide can let them take the controlling lines and steer the parachute for a while during the descent.

All the clients for the day are collected by bus from Cairns in the morning and driven to the operational base at Mission Beach. The base is close to the beach and next door to a beachfront hotel, and whilst waiting for their turn to jump, clients can walk on the beach, swim in the hotel pool, watch skydiving videos, or visit the hotel bar and café. Clients are shuttled to the airstrip in groups of four, and land on the beach directly in front of the operational base. At the end of the day the entire group is driven back to Cairns.

At the airstrip, clients are fitted with harnesses and goggles and given a detailed safety briefing. They are then loaded into the jump plane with their guides, in reverse jump order. Clients can elect to jump from different altitudes at slightly different prices.

## Equipment

All equipment is provided by the operator. Clients are fitted out with tandem harnesses and tight plastic goggles at the airstrip. The goggles are essential because of the high relative wind velocity, even once the parachute has opened. The parachutes are re-packed by the guides at the operational base between each jump. Guides and clients don their harnesses before getting into the jump plane, but the guide does not clip the harnesses together until shortly before the jump. The jump plane has only a pilot's seat, with an empty cargo bay where skydivers sit on the floor, and a large doorless opening immediately behind the starboard wing.

## Accommodation

The tour does not include accommodation. Clients stay either in Cairns or in Mission Beach itself.

## Statistics

Whilst the jump itself lasts only a few minutes, the activity as a whole takes an entire day. Clients are taken to the airstrip in groups of four, with one guide or instructor per client. Groups continue to jump throughout the day, and the guide makes a number of jumps with a different client each time. The cost is AUD225–372 (US$160–260) depending on jump altitude. This includes transport from and to Cairns. Videos of the jump, including sequences shot from the air, cost from AUD100 to 125 (US$70–87).

## Access

Access to the operational base is by road in the tour operator's bus or private car. All permits, insurances, etc. are obtained by the tour operator.

## Experience

Skydiving, even a tandem jump, is an intense adrenalin experience for most clients, particularly first-time clients. There is ample time to contemplate the landscape thousands of metres below as the plane ascends. Edging out on to the wing strut, even knowing that one is harnessed to a highly experienced parachute instructor, is still an intuitively alarming activity.

The jump itself and the ensuing freefall somersaults are moments of confusion, at least for the client. For the instructors, no doubt, they are routine. Once the parachute has opened, the guide may demonstrate manoeuvres such as tight spins, and may offer the client a chance to steer the canopy. There is sufficient altitude to fly well out over the ocean, watching manta rays glide through aquamarine waters, before turning back to land on the beach. It is certainly an intense experience. The rest of the day, of course, goes more slowly as clients wait their turn to jump, or relax and exchange stories afterwards.

## Environment

Skydiving contributes pro rata to atmospheric environmental impacts through its use of aircraft, but this is inseparable from the activity and beyond the control of the skydiving tour operator.

## Safety

Safety is, of course, an extremely critical aspect of all skydiving, commercial tandem jumps included. Jump the Beach advertises that it has an 'A-grade safety record', but no actual details are given. The safety briefings, however, are detailed and understandable.

## Marketing

Jump the Beach advertises via its website (Jump the Beach, 2005), printed leaflets and agent sales in Cairns. Its marketing materials feature the excitement of the jump, the range of jump altitudes available, and combined packages such as skydiving and kayaking or skydiving and whitewater rafting.

# Queenstown, New Zealand: AJ Hackett Bungy

## Place

The Kawarau Bridge, spanning the Kawarau River downstream of Queenstown, New Zealand, is the site of the world's oldest and probably best-known commercial bungee jump. The bridge itself, 43 m above the river, was falling into disrepair in 1988 when AJ Hackett (2005) obtained permission to operate the bungee jump. The river is also used by commercial whitewater raft tours, which run under the bridge. Queenstown is described in more detail by Cater in Chapter 24.

## Operator

AJ Hackett is the world's oldest commercial bungee-jump operator. Its founders, Henry van Asch and AJ Hackett himself, are credited with the invention of the modern bungee cord, a technological improvement on the vines used for 'tower diving' by islanders on Pentecost Island in Vanuatu. The company operates jumps at six sites in New Zealand: Auckland Harbour, Kawarau Bridge, the Lake Wakatipu 'Ledge' bungee, Skippers Canyon, the Shotover River 'Pipeline' bungee and the Nevis Bluff 'Highwire'. The last of these has a 143 m drop, and jumpers can reach a velocity of over 128 km/h (AJ Hackett, 2005). The three Queenstown sites are now wholly owned by Henry van Asch and the remainder by AJ Hackett. The company manufactures its own line of wool and synthetic fleece clothing.

## Activity

Bungee jumping probably needs no description. It is perhaps the archetypal short-duration no-skill thrill. Briefly, it involves jumping voluntarily off a high structure such as a bridge or crane, attached by a long elastic cord known as a bungee. Each jumper is weighed carefully, several times, and the effective length of the bungee cord adjusted accordingly before the jumper is attached, so that they will not hit the ground. For jumps into water, clients generally have the option of choosing a 'head dip' or deeper immersion.

There are various types of harness. The most common is a pair of padded cuffs around the ankles, but full-body harnesses are also available, and some jumpers choose less orthodox rigs such as jumping on a mountain bike or in a kayak. Tandem jumps are also possible.

Once attached and checked, the jumper is hauled up by a crane, or shuffles to the edge of a bridge or platform, and, on the count of five, launches themselves outwards – forwards, backwards, upside down or however they prefer. There is a brief period of free-fall, just long enough for the jumper to experience a major adrenalin surge, and then the bungee cord starts to stretch. If the jumper is attached by the ankles, this tips them head down, causing momentary disorientation.

After the cord stretches to its maximum extent and then springs back, the jumper has a very short stationary moment at the top of the first bounce, just enough to regain orientation. The bungee operator then lowers them to the ground, or to a pick-up boat for over-water jumps.

## Equipment

A bungee-jumping operation needs several critical pieces of equipment. Foremost of these is the bungee cord. According to AJ Hackett (2005) each of their jumpmasters knows how to make these cords themselves. They are made of numerous individual strands of latex, twisted or woven together into a rope a few centimetres thick and roughly half as long as the jump is high.

Equally critical are the attachments, both to the jumper and to the jumping platform. Climbing webbing and carabiners are commonly used. The jump platform must have ample clearance around the vertical fall line, in case the jumper swings or bounces sideways. It is not like a BASE parachute jump where the jumper can continue outwards from a cliff face or building. The upper end of the bungee cord also needs a mechanism to lower the jumper to the ground after they have stopped bouncing. Commonly, the cord is attached to a rope that can be winched up or down. Finally, for overwater jumps, a pick-up boat is also needed.

## Accommodation

Bungee jumps do not take long, even with all the attendant paperwork, watching and waiting, weighing and harnessing, and buying of souvenir videos. Bungee jumps therefore do not include accommodation – with the possible exception of the jump at The Last Resort on the Bhote Khosi in Nepal. For the Kawarau Bridge jump, certainly, clients stay in Queenstown.

## Statistics

Bungee jumping is generally a solo activity, unless clients decide to jump together, or in tandem with one of the company staff. There are thus many staff for each individual jump and client – but, of course, many clients per day. The current price for the Kawarau Bridge jump is NZD140 (US$98), including a souvenir t-shirt. For the Nevis Highwire it is NZD199 (US$140) (AJ Hackett, 2005). The company offers a three-jump combo package with one jump at each of the Kawarau, Nevis and Ledge sites, for NZD299 (US$210). In conjunction with other town operators, it also sells the 'Awesome Foursome' combo package including a jump, a jetboat ride, a helicopter flight and a whitewater rafting run on the Shotover River, for a total price of NZD495 (US$350).

## Access

Access to the Kawarau Bridge site is by road from Queenstown, in private vehicles or the company shuttle bus. The same applies for the other sites, except the Nevis Highwire site, which is on private land and can be accessed only in an AJ Hackett 4WD. The Skippers Canyon road, which also provides access to the Shotover Pipeline Bungee, is off limits to rental cars and most clients would take the company bus. Clients on the Awesome Foursome package arrive by helicopter. Most of the sites are publicly owned, and managed by the New Zealand Department of Conservation (NZDOC). AJ Hackett pays a fee to NZDOC for each jump.

## Community

Bungee jumping is one of the icon activities in the Queenstown adventure tourism portfolio, and contributes pro rata to the tourism economy and society, described in more detail by Cater in Chapter 24.

## Experience

Bungee jumping is certainly a high adrenalin activity. Especially after their first ever jump, it is commonplace for people to babble incomprehensibly for several hours and develop a fixed grin that wraps several times around their head and lasts for days. Unfortunately, it doesn't work quite so well on subsequent jumps. Some students of mine, however, once made a deal with an operator in Cairns to jump as many times as they wanted in 1 day, for a fixed price. They jumped 12 times. When we saw them that evening they couldn't string two coherent words together.

The critical component of the experience, I think, is that you have to make the jump yourself. In tandem parachuting, you are effectively pushed out by the instructor, and besides, the ground seems too far away to be real. In bungee jumping you can see the faces of people looking up, the ripples on the water. Part of the brain – the same part that is preoccupied with trying to look cool and composed in front of the jumpmaster – tells you that kids and grandparents jump safely, so stop being a wuss and get on with it. A much more powerful part, however, is convinced that you are committing suicide. No wonder you develop an unstoppable grin when you are still alive afterwards.

Of course, bungee operators will happily sell you videos, photos and souvenirs to help you remember the event. But it's not something you'll forget.

## Environment

Bungee jumping generally takes place at heavily modified sites where environmental impact is not a very significant issue. Toilets are essential. Local trampling and littering can occur from the concentration of people, but sites generally have hardened visitor areas and ample rubbish bins. Platforms and supporting structure may have a significant visual impact in some areas.

## Safety

AJ Hackett (2005) apparently wrote the New Zealand *Code of Practice* for safety in bungee jumping. Since 1992 the company has also been recognized for its safety practices by Standards New Zealand. These are audited externally by international safety auditors Bureau Veritas. Jumpers must be over 10 years old, and over 13 for the Nevis Highwire. The AJ Hackett (2005) website advertises that the company has had 'no jump-related deaths'. This seems slightly ambiguous but can presumably be taken at face value.

## Marketing

AJ Hackett has a highly sophisticated marketing programme. Its bungee jumps are advertised widely in Queenstown, throughout New Zealand, and in international New Zealand tourism marketing materials. It cross-markets extensively with adventure tour operators in other sectors. It promotes its own line of clothing, AJ Gear. It runs its own café, AJ Café. It sells branded souvenirs, videos, photos and DVDs. It develops new jumps at intervals to expand its market and maintain the interest of its existing clientele. As the company slogan says: 'fear of falling comes through inexperience' (AJ Hackett, 2005).

# Kaikoura, New Zealand: Kaikoura Helicopter

### Place

Kaikoura is a small town on the northeast coast of New Zealand's South Island. Over the past 20 years it has transformed itself from fishing village and farm supply centre, first to a domestic coastal holiday destination and backpacker stopover and subsequently to a well-known whalewatching destination. Its rocky coastline supports a colony of New Zealand fur seal, *Arctocephalus forsteri*, which are highly habituated to human presence, easy to approach, and have been known for several decades as an attraction for domestic tourists. The icon attraction, however, is the opportunity to watch sperm whales surfacing after squid-hunting dives. There are few places worldwide where sperm whales can be seen reliably and close to land, because they hunt in very deep water. There is a deep ocean trench close offshore from Kaikoura and this provides the necessary habitat (Buckley, 2003a, pp. 215–217). There is a local company with a monopoly on boat-based whalewatching, and one company that offer helicopter flights to watch the whales from above.

### Operator

Kaikoura Helicopters Ltd (2005) is a relatively small, local operation based in Kaikoura itself. It has offered whalewatching flights since 1991. Currently it also offers scenic flights to mountain areas inland.

### Activity

The company offers 30, 40 and 50-min flights. The longer flights provide a greater opportunity to search for whales offshore, to wait until they surface and to watch them until they dive again.

## Equipment

The company uses Bell 206 Jetranger and Robinson R44 helicopters equipped for overwater flights.

## Accommodation

This is a part-day tour and does not include accommodation. Various types of tourist accommodation are available in Kaikoura, or tourists may simply stop off briefly whilst driving through.

## Statistics

The Bell 206 helicopter can carry four passengers plus the pilot, and the Robinson R44 carries three passengers plus the pilot. Flights generally do not take off until they have a minimum number of paid-up passengers. The website does not say how many precisely. Current costs (Kaikoura Helicopters Ltd, 2005) are NZD185 (US$130) per person for a 30-min flight, NZD215 (US$150) for 40 min and NZD295 (US$210) for 50 min.

## Access

Access to Kaikoura is by road only. All permits are arranged by the tour operator, and are included in the tour price.

## Community

The tour contributes to the portfolio of nature and adventure tourism products available in Kaikoura, and hence to the local tourism economy, including accommodation, restaurants, cafés and souvenir shops. According to Asia-Pacific Economic Cooperation (APEC) (1997), prior to the establishment of the whale-watching industry in Kaikoura, the town's Maori population suffered high unemployment, lack of education and drug problems. The implication is that the whalewatching operation has overcome or at least reduced these problems, but this may be speculative. Kaikoura is now a routine destination on backpacker and self-drive circuits, and whalewatching, though an icon attraction, is not the sole driver of visitor growth.

## Experience

The flight is relatively straightforward. The whalewatching area is some distance offshore, and the helicopter flies straight to the most likely area. If whales are not sighted immediately, it flies up and down searching. If whales surface, it hovers over them until they dive again or the flight time is up.

For the tourist, it is certainly an experience to see the blunt-headed sperm whales, very different from the grey or humpback whales seen in most whale-watching tours. The aerial view also provides a much clearer sight than typical sightings from on-shore lookouts, though much further away than a close encounter by boat.

The helicopter hovers quite low, however, and one cannot help wondering what impact the disturbance has on the whales.

## Environment

The helicopters hover over surfacing sperm whales at a relatively low altitude. The whales do remain on the surface for 10 min or so at a time whilst under helicopter surveillance, but since this is the minimum time required for them to replenish their oxygen supplies after a deep dive, this behaviour may not be a matter of choice or indifference (Buckley, 2003a, p. 216). Indeed, anecdotal evidence suggests that when helicopters are present, the whales do not remain on surface longer than the minimum time required by physiological necessity, and dive more steeply and more rapidly than is otherwise the case. The company website does not mention environmental issues at all.

## Safety

According to the company website (Kaikoura Helicopters Ltd, 2005), the helicopters carry floats, life rafts and life vests, and all the pilots have completed a course in Helicopter Underwater Evacuation Techniques, repeated every 2 years.

## Marketing

The product is not marketed very heavily. In Kaikoura it seems to be promoted principally through the Whalewatch Kaikoura retail shopfront, presumably on a commission basis. The website uses the phrase 'world of whales', which helps tourists to locate it. The company is also listed in a group marketing website for tourist flight operators in New Zealand. The Kaikoura Helicopters Ltd (2005) website itself emphasizes that this is, apparently, the only place worldwide where sperm whales can be seen year-round. It suggests that the helicopter provides an advantage over a boat tour for the hurried, aged, disabled, children or those prone to seasickness. It also emphasizes the 'bird's-eye' view, with the slogan 'see the whole whale'.

# Gold Coast, Australia: Balloon Down Under

## Place

The Gold Coast is Australia's archetypal 3S/4S beach tourism town. Conveniently located halfway up Australia's eastern coastline, it has a subtropical climate and easy international access. It is very much a mass tourism destination, with the majority of development concentrated in a high-rise strip along the beachfront. Besides the beach itself, the principal attractions are nightclubs, retail stores, theme parks, and golf courses and marinas for the well-off. Whilst the economy does include a variety of manufacturing enterprises and other light industries, together with services, information technology and education, it is driven by real estate development and tourism. It is a major retirement area, with a high proportion of older citizens and a large retirement industry.

Essentially, the Gold Coast is Australia's Miami or Waikiki, though probably cleaner, cheaper and more friendly than either. This is a city where a casino, a convention centre or a car race is hailed as a major civic achievement; where the Council has been under investigation for corruption; and where a property developer has far higher social status than a professor. It has golden sands and golden sun, blue skies and blue seas; except when it rains and the innumerable canal estates disgorge their disgusting contents into the ocean. Coincidentally but unfortunately, it also happens to lie in one of Australia's most diverse biological regions, where temperate and tropical ecosystems overlap. As the suburbs continue to expand and fill in, the urban footprint impinges increasingly on the World Heritage national parks to the south and west of the city, and the Ramsar-listed wetlands to the north.

Despite these relatively unfavourable circumstances, the Gold Coast tourism industry is keen to promote the area as an adventure destination, perhaps in competition with Cairns, which occupies a similar coastal position in Australia's tropical northeast. With this aim in mind, the Gold Coast City Council has recently established an adventure tourism task force. Its aim seems to be to persuade backpackers to stop off for a few days, instead of skipping straight from Byron Bay to Brisbane and heading immediately north to Fraser Island and Cairns.

Adventure tourism options on the Gold Coast, however, are currently rather limited. The city is known for its theme parks, with names such as 'Dream World', 'Movie World' and 'Sea World', and some of these have fairground-style thrill rides. The Gold Coast is a well-known surfing destination, hosting several international competitions each year. Over the last few years, a number of surf schools have been established. Most of their clients are backpackers and other visitors who buy a 1-day 'learn-to-surf' package, essentially as a tour rather than training. These packages commonly feature a guarantee that if any client fails to stand on the board by the end of the day, they can come back for free the next day. The instructors interpret standing rather liberally, however, and since most clients want the day's experience rather than a lasting skill, they are unlikely to complain.

Apart from surf schools, the principal adventure tour activity on the Gold Coast is probably hot-air ballooning, described in this case study. There are also regular multi-sport competitions, but these are surf-lifesaving ironman and ironwoman competitions, not adventure events. There is a major nature resort in the forest hinterland that offers commercial abseiling, but this is not within, or run from the Gold Coast itself. There is an equestrian facility within the Gold Coast, a number of recreational trails open to horse riding and a number of farmstays in the surrounding regions that offer horse riding options, but none of these is comparable to the horse-riding tours and ranches described in Chapter 17. There is an extensive network of hiking trails in the World Heritage forests and many international tourists take advantage of these individually. Commercial multi-day hiking tours have been proposed by the management agency, but are not currently on offer as commercial tour products. Currently, therefore, hot-air ballooning may reasonably be described as the principal adventure tourism activity on the Gold Coast.

## Operator

There are two companies offering commercial balloon flights on the Gold Coast, and they seem to share information and airspace quite amicably. The company described here, Balloon Down Under (2005), is a family company that has been operating on the Gold Coast for 17 years, and has received a number of tourism awards. It specializes entirely in balloon flights.

## Activity

The group assembles well before dawn and is driven to the launch site in a company 4WD vehicle, towing a trailer with the balloon and basket. Wind velocities at various altitudes, obtained previously from the local meteorological service, are re-checked by releasing one or two helium-filled balloons and tracking their progress. The intended flight path and landing area are checked on a local large-scale topographic map. Coffee and tea are provided to the clients whilst company staff unpack and inflate the balloon and attach the basket. Once airborne, the balloon drifts over the city and surrounding rural areas at altitudes of up to 1000 m or so, providing excellent views for the passengers. A balloon has no steering mechanism, and the pilot maintains course by adjusting altitude so as to take advantage of slightly different wind directions at different heights. After about an hour's flight, the balloon lands in a large open paddock, and the passengers assist in deflating the balloon, packing it up, and loading it and the basket back on the trailer. Finally, the group drives to a local resort for a champagne breakfast and a short ceremony recalling the traditions of hot-air ballooning.

## Equipment

Balloon Down Under operates two different balloons for its main commercial flights, able to carry 8 or 16 passengers, respectively. Each balloon carries advertising for an unrelated local company, providing additional income for the ballooning operator. This advertisement, essentially the company name writ large, also provides an easy way to identify the balloon whilst in flight, which is useful for the ground crews that track each balloon to the landing site. All the balloons in use in Australia are apparently made by a single company based in Sydney.

The basket is a padded rectangular box with a wooden floor, woven cane walls and interior partitions, and an open top. The partitions separate the pilot and gas bottles from the passengers, and help to keep the passengers in stable positions. A stainless steel frame above the basket holds three gas burners, of which only two are generally used, typically one at a time. There are two large gas bottles for each of these burners. An additional bottle is attached temporarily whilst first inflating the balloon on the ground, and then removed before take-off. The balloon has a small vertical vent on one side, controlled by the pilot, which allows him to rotate it around its vertical axis. There is no mechanism to steer it relative to the ground, except by changing altitude as outlined above.

## Accommodation

This is a single-day tour and does not include accommodation. A variety of tourist accommodation is available on the Gold Coast and Balloon Down Under can pick up clients from the hotel if required.

## Statistics

Every balloon flight has a pilot on board and a ground crew of at least one, travelling by vehicle along approximately the same route. The number of passengers depends on the size of the balloon and the basket. For the flight in which I took part, there were six passengers on the day, but the basket has a capacity of eight, corresponding to a client-to-pilot ratio of 8:1 or an overall client-to-staff ratio of 4:1. The actual flight takes about an hour and the entire tour, including breakfast, takes about 4 h. The cost is AUD285 per person, around US$215.

## Access

Balloons are a type of aircraft, and the airspace they use overlaps with that available to light aircraft of various sizes. Balloon flights are therefore regulated by aviation safety authorities in broadly the same way as other aircraft, but with special dispensations. In Australia the relevant authority is the Civil Aviation Safety Authority, CASA. Pilots must be trained and certified, with a minimum of 15 h flight experience before their first solo flight. For balloon flights over the Gold Coast, Balloon Down Under is not required to file flight plans, but the balloon must maintain phone or radio contact with the ground vehicle, which acts as the designated Search and Rescue (SAR) vehicle should any incident occur. Access to take-off and landing areas must be arranged with the relevant landowners, though in the early hours of the morning this may not be a critical issue. All such arrangements are made directly by the operating company and all associated costs are included in the tour price.

## Community

As outlined earlier, tourism is a significant contributor to the Gold Coast economy, and balloon tours provide something very different from the standard fare of beaches, nightclubs and theme parks. Even though ballooning is a relatively small subsector, therefore, it contributes visibly to the Gold Coast tourism portfolio.

## Experience

On the flight on which I took part, the other passengers were tourists visiting the Gold Coast from England and New Zealand, and they all seemed well satisfied with the experience. To see one's own hometown from relatively low altitude, with plenty of time to look around and identify landmarks, is an enlightening experience in itself. Perhaps the most interesting aspect from my own perspective, however, was to watch how expertly the pilot adjusted altitude with minimum fuel use and no overshoot; and how accurately he could anticipate the balloon trajectory, given that altitude manoeuvres had to be made many minutes in advance, in order to steer the balloon to the selected safe landing spot. Whilst the short-term hand–eye coordination required to turn burners on and off is clearly far less than that required to fly a hang-glider, a helicopter or a light plane, for example, the far slower response time for a balloon means that pilots must have a highly developed sense of the balloon's momentum and cooling rate, the extra lift imparted by any given blast from the gas burners, and the directional changes caused by moving into different wind layers. From a passenger's perspective, the air feels completely still when the balloon is drifting horizontally, but one can feel a small relative wind when it crosses vertically into a different airflow.

In the flight I experienced, the balloon remained aloft for an hour, and then landed very gently in a large grassy paddock a small distance outside the suburbs. The hot air is released through a large vent at the top of the balloon, which collapses sideways. Once it has deflated partially, the passengers can climb out and assist the staff in completing the deflation, packing the balloon into its bag, and lifting the balloon and basket on to the trailer. The group then drives back to the original assembly point for breakfast.

## Environment

Environmental impacts are negligible. The principal impact is consumption of propane fuel for the gas burners. This consumption, however, is presumably far below the fuel requirements for a corresponding flight in a light plane.

## Safety

Commercial ballooning in Australia has a very good safety record, but safety precautions remain critical. The balloon is laid out and inflated by the pilot and ground support crew, with no involvement from the clients, to ensure that all lines and cables are properly attached and none is tangled. The passengers are also kept well away from the balloon during the initial inflation, which involves firing the propane burners horizontally into the half-inflated envelope. The basket is secured to the support vehicle with heavy-duty webbing during the final inflation, and whilst the passengers climb aboard. The webbing is untied only when the balloon is ready to take off. Passengers receive a safety briefing aboard the basket, and again before landing. Passengers who are short of hair, or 'follicle challenged' as the pilot puts it, whether through age or design, are given baseball caps to protect their scalps from the heat of the burners just above their heads. Passengers are reminded not to drop anything outside the basket, because of the danger to people below; and to keep their knees bent and their hands inside the basket on landing, because of potential danger to themselves in the event of a heavy landing.

## Marketing

Balloon Down Under maintains its own website, which is easily found by any search for balloon tours on the Gold Coast. Of course, the competing operator's website also shows up. Since ballooning, or adventure tourism more generally, is not what the Gold Coast is known for, however, most tourists probably do not discover the ballooning option until they have already arrived. To reach this market, Balloon Down Under distributes brochures in tourist hotels and similar venues. The two Balloon Down Under balloons can routinely be seen floating over the Gold Coast in the early morning, so the marketing strategy must be successful.

# 22 Other Sectors and Issues

Zorbing, New Zealand. Photo Carl Cater.

Snowmobile, Svalbard. Photo Carl Cater.

# Introduction

The main focus of this volume has been on outdoor recreation activities that have been packaged as commercial tourism products and marketed with an adventure label. These activity-based products arguably constitute the core of the commercial adventure tourism industry.

As noted at the outset, however, there are some activity sectors where no case studies have been presented, for various reasons. Some of the main examples are considered briefly below.

In addition, there are aspects of tourism that do not conform well with the activity-based paradigm presented here, but that may still be treated as adventure tourism since either the tourists themselves, or tourism marketing materials, see it as such. Some examples are also considered briefly in this chapter.

Finally, all human activities that may be labelled as adventure tourism, under any definition, lie within a broader context of human social behaviour patterns. Such broader links, patterns and trends are significant for the future of adventure tourism both as a commercial industry and as a social phenomenon, and are hence equally relevant to adventure tourism research. Selected examples are therefore also considered below.

# Activity Subsectors

### Criteria for inclusion

The selection of individual adventure tourism activities for detailed case-study consideration in this volume was influenced by a number of factors. The principal criterion was simply that the activity concerned is indeed offered worldwide in the form of commercial adventure tourism products. Thus, for example, this excludes activities where the only commercial products are courses of instruction.

The second major criterion was reasonable familiarity by the author, or contributing authors, with commercial tour products in the activity sector concerned. As noted earlier, for many tours this requires a degree of skill at the activity concerned, and we only have such skills for a subset of activity sectors.

The third general criterion is that the activity is sufficiently widespread and large-scale to form a significant component of the tourism industry, but not so large-scale that it is typically treated as an entire sector of the tourism industry. At the lower end of the economic scale, there are many outdoor recreation and adventure tourism activities that as yet form only a very small component of the commercial adventure tourism industry. Some of these were listed in Table 3.2 in Chapter 3. At the upper end, the principal examples of very large-scale adventure sectors are those such as marina-based boating and resort-based skiing, which are very tightly associated with coastal and mountain resorts and residential developments.

### Resort-based sailing and skiing

Many coastal resorts, on large lakes as well as oceans, incorporate boat marinas that serve as a base for private and commercial yachts and fishing vessels. Whilst multi-day yacht tours and sailing charters may indeed be considered as part of the adventure tourism industry (Chapter 8), in financial terms the coastal resorts and marinas are more accurately classified as part of the property development sector. For the entrepreneurs, investors, regulators and operational managers of such enterprises, issues such as land-use zoning, residential land sales, amenity migrants, strata titling, time-share arrangements and mass marketing of vacation packages are of far greater significance than potential opportunities for adventure tours; and there is a self-contained research literature that examines such resorts specifically (see, for example, Devaux, 1997).

Similar considerations apply for mountain resorts. Such resorts may have been established for many different reasons. In tropical areas, for example, some were set up in colonial times as an escape from the summer heat on lowland plantations. In temperate regions many mountain resorts started as ski fields, often using antecedent infrastructure from former mining and farming communities. Irrespective of their origins, however, most mountain resorts now feature a range of both summer and winter activities, and their development and finance is heavily linked to retail precincts and to residential land sales. Increasingly complex arrangements for part-ownership of property, and cross-marketing between tourists and amenity migrants and between outdoor activities and other goods and services, have become standard in this sector. In addition, whilst backcountry skiing on either telemark or randonnée equipment may be marketed as adventure tourism, resort skiing is more commonly marketed as an outdoor sport, though such a distinction may be far from clear (Hudson, 2002). In any event, in tourism terms resort skiing is so tightly tied into mountain resorts, and the latter are so large and complex a sector on their own, that downhill resort skiing cannot really be compared directly with the other types of adventure tourism considered in this volume.

## Surf cf. sailboard tours

The case study chapters describe tour products that provide a specific activity. Tour products that simply provide a travel and accommodation package to an existing generalized tourist destination are not included, even if that destination is well-known for a particular outdoor recreation activity, unless the package also includes components such as guides, equipment or specialized local transport that are related specifically to that activity.

Such distinctions are not always clear-cut. For example, surfers, sailboarders and kiteboarders all expect to bring their own boards with them when they travel. Commercial surfing tours in Indo-Pacific nations, however, include either live-aboard charter vessels or local boat transfers to particular surf breaks, local knowledge of those breaks and in some cases exclusive access rights to use them. Most sailboarding or kiteboarding packages to Mediterranean or Caribbean destinations, in contrast, simply take the person to the place and leave them to play on their own. Surf tours have therefore been included in this volume whilst sailboard tours have not, even though the author has far more years' experience in sailboarding than in surfing.

Note that this distinction can only be drawn when the structures of tour products throughout the entire activity sector are considered. It does not necessarily apply when comparing individual products. For example, in the surfing sector there are tour packages that take surfers to well-known coastal resort towns in Australia, Indonesia, South Africa or the USA and then leave them to find their own way. Indeed, even for the case studies considered here, some have a local surf break that can be reached by paddling directly from the beach. In each of these case studies, however, the destination is generally known principally to surfers; the accommodation is used almost entirely by surfers and sometimes their partners; and the tour package includes on-demand availability of local boats to shuttle surfers to and from other nearby surf breaks, with local expertise to identify which are likely to have best conditions on any given day. These tour products thus include more than simply generalized travel and accommodation.

On the other hand, some of the kiteboarding tour packages currently on offer do apparently include instruction; and no doubt there are particular sites, and indeed particular hotels, which are heavily patronized by kiteboarders. Perhaps, as in other forms of adventure tourism, there may be particular hotels and kiteboarding schools that are owned by amenity migrants, people who moved to the area for its recreational opportunities and then set up so-called second-tier tourism businesses to support their own lifestyles. I did not have sufficient information on such factors to include kiteboarding case studies in the current volume, but no doubt this omission will be remedied in a later edition.

Of course, kiteboarding is not the only example. In addition to sailboarding, hang-gliding, parapenting and skydiving, a second edition might consider chapters on ballooning, blackwater rafting and caving; and perhaps also on activities such as bungee jumping, cable flights and even zorbing.

## Millionaire thrills

All of the activities mentioned above fall within the same broad price spectrum and product structure, and appeal to similar markets, as those activities that are included in the case study chapters. Equally interesting, perhaps, is to consider types of tourism that may still be treated as adventure, but that are structured rather differently and appeal to different market sectors.

At the most exclusive and expensive end of the scale, there are commercial adventure opportunities that are so high-priced and in consequence so low-volume that they can perhaps barely be treated as tourism at all. The archetypal example is the opportunity for suitably well-heeled private citizens to travel into space, purely for their own amusement.

To date only one private citizen has visited an orbiting space station, as part of an 8-day programme that cost US$20 million. During 2005, however, a joint venture between a commercial airline and a specialist small-scale aircraft construction company announced that they will offer brief commercial trips to an altitude of 100 km at a cost of around US$200,000 per person per flight (Virgin Galactic, 2005).

In the same general league, though one step down in cost and exclusivity, are the opportunities offered to fly in various ex-military combat aircraft, principally from the former USSR, and commonly at a price of around US$3500–4500 per person for an hour's flight in Australia or America, or US$16,500 for three flights over 6 days in Moscow.

## Overlanders and backpacker buses

At the other end of the scale in terms of cost and exclusivity are commercial tours designed principally for backpackers, notably the so-called overlander bus safaris and other backpacker bus trips. There seem to be two main models.

In the overlander model, particularly common in Africa, participants purchase a place on a specially outfitted bus that follows a flexible but reasonably well-defined itinerary across a number of countries. These trips have fixed prices and predefined starting and finishing dates, and the same group of participants travels in the same bus for the entire journey. In many cases the tour includes opportunities for participants to take part in additional optional adventure tourism activities such as wildlife watching or whitewater rafting: i.e. the bus visits the relevant sites, allows time in the itinerary for such activities and may well have prior arrangements with a particular local tour operator. The activities themselves are optional for the overland participants and the prices are not included in the overlander tour price itself, though the marketing materials and pre-trip information may show options and costs.

The overlander buses are commonly set up for camping, and the tour price is essentially the price of the bus journey. Food and drink are generally purchased as a group rather than individually, using a kitty system. This so-called 'local component' may also include entry fees for national parks. It is a compulsory cost for all participants. Typically, the tour price is payable in advance but the kitty is payable in cash to the tour leader at the first point of embarkation. Presumably, this system has evolved for tax and currency transfer reasons. International transfers of sufficient funds to feed a busload of people for several weeks or months involves conversion costs, currency hedging and international exchange control regulations. In addition, receipts will rarely be available for food bought at local African markets, so if catering costs are included in the trip package price, the tour operator may have a large component of taxable income for which no corresponding deductions can be demonstrated.

There are many different tour operators offering overland trips, most of them taking 2 weeks to 3 months or more. Some of these companies print glossy brochures that are distributed through travel agents, whereas others advertise in backpacker magazines and outlets. The former are presumably more reliable and more expensive. Well-known examples include Guerba (2005), Kumuka (2005) and Budget Expeditions (2005).

In countries such as Australia, New Zealand and Fiji, backpacker buses operate according to a somewhat different model. A company trading as 'OZ Experience' (2005), 'Kiwi Experience' (2005) or 'Feejee Experience' (2005) runs large green buses along fixed itineraries, visiting places with backpacker accommodation and/or activities. Clients purchase tickets that give them the right to get on and off the bus at any of its routine destination stops, as many times as they want during a fixed period. The price of the ticket depends on the geographical area covered and the period it remains valid. The ticket's price includes only the transport component. Costs are around US$60 per day.

For the better-known overlander operators such as Guerba (2005), prices are around US$70–US$80 per person per day for trips of up to 2 months' duration or longer. Kumuka's prices are around US$70–80 per person per day for 30–45 day African trips, and Think! Adventure (2005) charges around US$101 per day for a 42-day trip in Kyrgyzstan. Budget Expeditions (2005), whose slogan is 'Price Does Matter' charges around US$50 per person per day for a 6-week South American overland bus trip, including a mixture of camping (70%) and hostels (30%).

These rates, however, are not directly comparable to the rates for the case studies outlined in the earlier chapters, because they cover different components of an overall adventure holiday. The costs quoted in the case studies include the activity itself, plus accommodation, meals and local transport where these are part of the overall package. For single-day activities, the prices quoted refer only to the 1-day activity package excluding accommodation.

In the case of the overlander and backpacker bus trips, however, the prices quoted are principally for long-distance transport. Arguably, the overlander tours are somewhat comparable to the activity-based tour products described in the case studies, since: (i) they do include accommodation in the form of camping and (ii) for most participants, travel on the overland bus itself is an adventurous activity, with optional add-ons as a bonus for the better-funded participants.

The backpacker buses in Australia, New Zealand and Fiji, however, travel mostly on main roads where local buses and long-distance coach transport are also available. They do take some rural roads to particular farmstays and similar sites, but the main reason people purchase these tickets is probably for the convenience of getting on and off the bus at short notice, and perhaps also for the easy opportunities to meet other backpackers and share plans for ancillary activities.

## Social Context for Adventure Tourism

### Behavioural linkages

Like any other aspect of human behaviour, adventure tourism is strongly influenced by other components of human social structures and behaviour, and may influence such other components in return. Such links can exist, for example, with amenity migration and other types of longer-term population mobility (Johnson *et al.*, 2003; Hall, 2005; Moss, 2006); entertainment, fashion and clothing (Buckley, 2003b; Cater, 2005); and materials technology and equipment manufacturing.

In addition, there are links within the tourism industry itself, as towns or regions promote themselves as adventure tourism destinations, either in their general marketing materials or by sponsoring adventure events and competitions of various kinds. Detailed examination of these linkages is beyond the scope of this volume, but since they may well become increasingly important in future they deserve at least some mention.

### Amenity migration

The link between adventure tourism and amenity migration is conceptually straightforward but largely unstudied. Opportunities for outdoor recreation provide one of the major attractions for amenity migrants in many areas. Many such migrants bring their livelihoods with them. For example, they may own a manu-facturing or service corporation that they can relocate in its entirety. They may work for such a corporation and move with it. They may work as consultants or in the finance and information industries, and be able to continue their existing profession through telephone, Internet and courier connections. They may have adequate income from investment, trust or retirement funds.

At least some amenity migrants, however, establish new businesses catering to tourists and to other amenity migrants. These include equipment stores, restaurants and cafés, and a variety of professional services that may not previously have been available; but they can also include commercial adventure tourism businesses.

Adventure tourism and amenity migration may thus grow hand in hand. This link has been considered elsewhere (Johnson, 2004; Buckley *et al.*, 2006), but does not yet seem to have been studied quantitatively.

## Fashion and status

Links between adventure tourism, recreation and clothing sales are equally straightforward but equally little studied (Buckley, 2003a; Cater, 2005). At the simplest level, outdoor recreation requires functional outdoor clothing: but this is not the only link, or even the main market.

Outdoor recreation at an advanced level, especially in remote areas, can confer social status as well as immediate enjoyment (see Chapter 2), and this applies to commercial adventure tours as well as private trips. To claim that status, however, particularly beyond the participant's immediate peer group, requires some kind of label that is both recognizable and acceptable to the target audience. Outdoor clothing or other accessories for the activity concerned, branded by a well-esteemed manufacturer, commonly provide one of the easiest options, since they are relatively cheap to change when the whims of fashion so dictate. A 4WD vehicle, or in some areas a mountain bike, may also be an option, albeit a much more expensive one.

There are several more subtle secondary considerations. First, the branded item must serve a functional purpose in its non-adventure status-advertising use, otherwise the latter intention becomes too evident and hence self-defeating. And not only must the item be functional in a strictly technical sense; its capabilities as an adventure item must be not too disproportionate to its role in general use. For example, wearing a Gore-Tex® parka in town, instead of a city raincoat, might be appropriate, but wearing a survival suit would not.

Secondly, self-labelling in this way can only contribute to social status in places with an appropriate subculture, where expertise in the particular activity concerned is of social value. A Gore-Tex® parka may look good in Bozeman, but probably not in downtown Washington, DC. A heliski suit may confer status if worn at a ski resort where there are routine heliski operations nearby, as long as the wearer also skis well; but not otherwise.

Thirdly, the item must be used, but not worn out. Ideally, perhaps it should look as if it is regularly replaced by sponsors, but since there are now so many fake sponsor labels, this effect may be difficult to achieve.

Fourthly, there may be fine distinctions in brand and design. Examples in the surf clothing industry are summarized by Buckley (2002a, 2003b), but the situation is similar for many other items. In much of Australia, for example, Toyota® station-wagons and so-called troopcarriers are so widespread and commonplace, amongst urban as well as rural or residents, that they confer no particular cachet. To suggest adventure, they need a roof rack with extra spare tyres, an elephant jack on an external bracket, a winch, wide tyres and some well-ingrained mud. A dust snorkel or bullbar means little, since they are fitted as standard to most vehicles.

There is strong brand sensitivity for 4WD vehicles. If you show up in a Landrover®, a Ford® or a Jeep®, other 4WD vehicle owners will immediately make inferences about your character, depending on what particular brand they prefer themselves. Such influences would be even more extreme if you were to arrive in a Range-Rover®, a Mercedes® or a Hummer®.

Of course, such distinctions are highly place-sensitive. Opinions on different

4WD vehicles are likely to be very different for residents of Texas or Oregon in the USA, residents of the Northern Territory in Australia, or residents of the North-West Frontier Territory in Kenya.

Similar place distinctions apply for clothing. Compare, for example, a well-worn, soft and shapeless thigh-length waistless Gore-Tex® parka made to be worn with waterproof trousers for backcountry tramping in the rain, with a brand-new, heavily shaped and waisted hip-length Gore-Tex® parka made to be worn with bib-and-brace trousers for cross-country skiing and snowshoeing. The former would receive preferred recognition in, say, Te Anau in New Zealand, the latter in, say, Banff in Canada.

Links between adventure and fashion extend far beyond clothing. As noted by Cater (Chapter 24) on Queenstown, New Zealand, they can even include issues such as which nightclubs are fashionable to visit. Clearly, this could well merit further research, but I shall leave that to a younger generation.

Queenstown is also particularly interesting through its highly successful use of adventure tourism to market the destination as a whole. As outlined in Chapter 23, this practice is becoming more and more widespread. Also of particular interest is the deliberate promotion of participatory adventure events as a marketing tool. This is considered later in this chapter.

## Equipment and manufacturers

Most adventure tourism activities are heavily dependent on specialized equipment that is made using technologically advanced materials and manufacturing processes. Even for the more popular adventure activities with a relatively large number of devotees worldwide, designs and models evolve quickly, production volumes are low and prices are high. There are also high price premiums for particular brand names. For items that also have high-volume urban or mass markets, such as small backpacks, running shoes and board shorts, the best-known brands can cost an order of magnitude more than no-brand analogues, even if the items are effectively identical.

Items manufactured from fabrics and plastics, in particular, are often produced in developing nations under contract to the major brands. It is therefore relatively straightforward for new companies to copy the designs and even to contract the same factories.

In China, for example, it is now possible to buy a wide range of locally branded outdoor equipment and clothing. These items are labelled in English with European or American-sounding brand names, but in fact seem to be sold only in China, at a fraction of the prices that internationally branded equivalents would cost. Since China is not a signatory to the Berne Convention, which governs international copyright and patent law, the better-known manufacturers would have little redress. In any event, the similarities between these Chinese items and their international equivalents are probably no greater than those between corresponding models produced by two different competing international brands.

In addition to new low-cost local brands such as those described above, in some countries it is now possible to buy ostensibly top-brand equipment at heavily discounted prices. Such items may or may not be genuine. In some cases they may simply be copies, with the brand label and logo copied along with the rest of the design. The example of fake Nalgene® water bottles sold in Nepal is mentioned in Chapter 16.

Sometimes these items may indeed be identical to the items bought through authorized dealers, if factories manufacture more items than their contracts stipulate and sell the overrun secretly to another distributor. This is one reason why most internationally known brands restrict distribution to networks of authorized dealers: to provide a guarantee that the items sold are genuine, have passed quality control procedures, are subject to warranties and guarantees, and are covered by the manufacturer's insurance policies. Another reason for such networks, of course, is to keep prices and profits high by preventing end-of-season discounting and similar practices.

In practice, therefore, low-cost local brands and copies will generally only have a market: (i) where the item is cheap and can be tested or inspected adequately on the spot, such as a water bottle or basic backpack; (ii) where the purchaser wants the item for its appearance rather than its function, such as some shoes and outdoor clothing; or (iii) for entry-level items where the user has low expectations and there is little risk involved if the item fails, such as basic tents and sleeping bags.

For enthusiasts in most types of outdoor recreation, however, good equipment is essential for safety, and people are hence prepared to pay a premium in order to be confident of reliability. Importantly, this includes materials as well as manufacturing. One may be able to see easily if a parka or backpack is well-stitched, but not whether it is really made from Gore-Tex® or Cordura®. One can check whether the gate on a carabiner opens smoothly and closes cleanly, but not the composition of the alloy or whether the carabiner can really support the weight claimed. Plastics used for whitewater kayaks may look much the same, but some are cross-linked and others are not. Even something as simple as a water bottle may or may not begin to leak after a period of use.

For commercial adventure tours, the quality of equipment required depends strongly on the market sector at which the tour is pitched. For any trip where participants and their gear will be put severely to the test, top-quality equipment is an essential investment, for insurance as well as practical purposes. For high-volume, low-risk trips where equipment is used repeatedly, the most critical issue is durability. Many companies that offer tours of this type have routine strategies to replace all of their equipment at the end of each season. Often they sell the old gear second-hand: either to former clients; to guides for private use; or in developing nations especially, to lower-priced operators offering the same activity. This last practice may well be a significant source of safety risk for bottom-tier operators in some areas.

For tour operators that offer trips for unskilled clients who do not know how to look after their equipment, it is pointless to provide expensive gear that will only be damaged. There is thus a significant market for entry-level equipment in the commercial adventure tour sector as well as for private recreational use.

All these considerations apply equally to motorized equipment. Different models and designs of helicopter, off-road vehicle or custom-built truck may have very different range, capacity and handling characteristics; different fuel and maintenance requirements; and indeed, very different environmental impacts, especially as regards noise and exhaust emissions.

## Associations and lobbying

Some outdoor and recreational equipment manufacturers and retailers are very large corporations, and use a variety of indirect approaches and alliances to promote sales.

Adventure tour operators may be involved directly and intentionally in such schemes; or sometimes, indirectly and inadvertently.

For example, there are various alliances of manufacturers and outfitters that have formed consortia to contribute to conservation of the natural environment. They may contribute a proportion of revenues to environmental trusts or conservation associations; or they may adopt mutually agreed codes of environmental practice, or even establish their own eco-certification schemes as in the case of IAATO, the International Association of Antarctic Tour Operators. Companies that adopt measures such as these may do so because of the personal convictions of their founders or owners; or perhaps more probably, in order to gain a market advantage with environmentally conscious consumers.

Other manufacturers, however, have taken the opposite tack, though perhaps not explicitly. Some of the main manufacturers of snowmobiles, jetskis, trail bikes, specialized all-terrain and off-road vehicles, and even unspecialized 4WD passenger vehicles seem to have devoted considerable sums and efforts in political lobbying, particularly in North America. These associations have lobbied strongly, and often successfully, against the designation of wilderness or even roadless areas, and in favour of open access to national parks and other public lands. In some cases they have formed political coalitions with groups representing horse riders and livestock packers, even though the detailed issues and impacts may be rather different. The best-known example is perhaps the Blue Ribbon Coalition (2005) in the USA. Interestingly, this particular group is also supported by extractive industries such as mining, oil and gas, and logging (Viles and Delfino, 2000), which also spend very large sums on their own account lobbying against wilderness or protected-area designations. By sponsoring lobbyists for high-impact recreational uses, these industries may gain a broader political support base.

From a social, community and environmental perspective, such coalitions are not necessarily either good or bad. It depends what they do; and, of course, they are not restricted to the outdoor recreation and adventure tourism sector. The British Columbia Helicopter and Snowcat Skiing Association, BCHSSOA (2005), for example, aims to improve the environmental management practices of its members, as well as lobbying for continued access to public lands for commercial purposes. The relative environmental costs and benefits of these two aims, one localized and the other wide-ranging, have been debated extensively (Piore, 2002; Buckley, 2003a). The Access Fund (2005) exists to lobby for access by climbers to climbing sites, especially in national parks and other public lands. It is supported by climbing equipment manufacturers as well as climbing clubs and associations. The Sporting Goods Manufacturers Association, SGMA (2005), is a US-based association that publishes an annual financial report on recreational equipment markets, and represents the manufacturing sector in public fora.

Commonly, only a few of the larger adventure tour operators hold direct memberships in associations and lobby groups such as these. Particularly dedicated or charismatic individuals can have a strong influence on such groups, even if their own companies are relatively small in financial terms. Irrespective of any such direct links, however, almost all adventure tour operators need equipment of various kinds, and access to appropriate sites for the activities concerned, whether publicly or privately owned. In addition, in many nations it seems that politicians pay greater attention to taxable cash flows that can yield government revenue than to social welfare contributions that can reduce government expenditure. The commercial adventure tourism sector may thus receive more political attention than the non-commercial adventure recreation sector, even if it is much smaller in numbers or effective economic value. Links between adventure tour operators and equipment manufacturers may hence extend to political levels as well as simply purchasing business supplies.

## Safety, Liability and Illness

### Guide training and certification

As noted in the introductory chapters, this volume aims to focus on products rather than people, so guide training and certification issues are not considered in detail. Where the individual tour operators considered in the case studies advertise their guides' qualifications, this is mentioned under the heading of Safety. Such qualifications are generally of particular concern for activities that are perceived as relatively high-risk, and that are long established, so that a certification system has had time to develop.

Currently, in most developed nations at least, adventure tourism companies that offer diving, climbing or mountaineering tours would be expected to have certified guides – either because of statutory, permitting, insurance or client requirements. Activities such as whitewater rafting and kayaking do have guide certification systems, but these are not mandatory and not all guides are necessarily qualified. Activities such as heliskiing do not have their own internal qualification systems, but heliski guides are generally expected to be qualified ski instructors, experienced mountain patrollers, and to have completed avalanche rescue and wilderness first responder courses. Many are also qualified mountain and climbing guides.

For activities such as surfing and seakayaking, horse riding and hiking, there are generally no formal certification systems for adventure tour guides, except for first aid. Most countries do not have certification schemes for wildlife-watching guides, though South Africa is an exception (Field Guide Association of Southern Africa, 2005). Some individual companies have their own internal training and qualification systems. For example, Conservation Corporation Africa (2005) trains and tests its own wildlife rangers and trackers. For some activities, success in professional or amateur competition is used as a form of surrogate certification, e.g. in surfing or horse riding. For all these activities, companies will generally require guides to be familiar with the activity and area concerned.

There can certainly be major differences between tour operators in the precise skills and qualifications they require of their guides. For many activities and tour operations worldwide, guides with formal qualifications may well be the exception rather than the rule. This seems likely to change in future, however, if only because of increasingly stringent requirements for insurance.

### Liability, waivers and insurance

The potential liability of adventure tour operators for any injury to their clients, and the costs of insurance to protect against such a possibility, have become an issue of major concern to operators in all developed nations. These issues apply even if the companies concerned only operate in developing nations where the domestic framework for legal liability is rather limited: tour companies and their agents may still be subject to lawsuits in their countries of origin, even if they try to insulate themselves by operating through separate corporations in each destination country.

For activities that are seen as high-risk by underwriters, insurance premiums have grown so high that in some countries it seems some former tour operators have simply been forced out of business, at least in that particular activity sector. Horseriding tours in Australia provide an example (Ollenburg, 2006). Historically, many farmstays offered low-key trail rides as an integral part of their tourist product, but currently only those operators that specialize in equestrian activities and charge a sufficiently high price to cover the insurance costs can continue to offer horse riding.

Some States in the USA have enacted statutes that specifically limit the liability of commercial providers for any injury sustained by clients during the commercial tourism activity concerned. The best-known of these is probably the Colorado Ski Safety Act, which governs the liability of ski resorts in that State towards their customers. A number of other States have followed suit, with liability-limiting statutes for horse riding as well as skiing. This approach has been taken furthest in New Zealand, where private liability for personal injury of any kind is capped by statute, but where there are publicly funded programmes for medical treatment and accident compensation.

For most activities, operators and countries, the main mechanism to limit potential liability is through waivers, disclaimers and indemnities signed by the client as a condition of taking part in the tour or activity concerned. These documents then become part of the contractual arrangements between the commercial provider and the customer. Some of the legal issues involved were reviewed by McDonald (2003).

Requiring clients to sign a liability waiver can indeed reduce an adventure tour operator's risk of potential legal or financial liability in the event of client injury, but it does not provide complete protection. Many jurisdictions have consumer protection laws that can override such contractual arrangements, even if the contract purports to exclude the operation of the relevant statute.

If a waiver is signed under conditions of duress, or without adequate time for the client to read or understand it, or under circumstances where the client does not have a reasonable option not to purchase the tour product, then the waiver may be invalidated. This might well apply, for example, to waivers that are passed around to the clients for signature when they have already bought the trip and are on a tour-company bus heading for the destination where the activity takes place. These limitations may still apply even if the waiver includes clauses where the client supposedly acknowledges that they had time to read and understand the document, if in fact they did not.

There are many such issues. To mention just one more, some generalized waivers contain clauses that are invalidated by local statutes. Unless the waiver also includes a separability clause specifying that the other clauses remain operative even if one is invalid, it might well prove that the entire waiver could be judged invalid.

These are legal questions and far beyond the scope of this book. The bottom line seems to be that an adventure tour company may still be subject to a lawsuit even if all its clients have signed a liability waiver; but the more watertight the waiver, the more likely the tour operator is to win any such case.

Given the financial and legal importance of these waivers, and the significance of their precise wording, it is perhaps surprising that every waiver seems to be different. One might have thought that some degree of standardization would have occurred. Of course, there are some components that differ between activities, such as a listing of potential hazards; and some that differ between regions, such as local statutes. Even so, there must be many aspects that remain much the same. Perhaps some enterprising legal researcher will address the issue in due course.

## Injuries and illnesses

As noted in the introductory chapters, research into medical aspects of the adventure tourism sector seems to have been more thorough than for most other aspects. The works of Wilks and Page (2003) and Page *et al.* (2005) provide some recent examples. Even so, however, such statistics are quite restricted, because of the difficulty of obtaining primary data. Only in some countries are operators themselves required to file incident reports. In some cases such reports may only be required for certain types of activity – for example, if motor vehicles, boats or aircraft are involved. There do not seem to be any published studies that test how thoroughly operators comply with such reporting obligations. It seems likely that because of its liability-capping laws that reduce the potential consequences, reporting is more complete in New Zealand than in other nations.

The other main route to assemble injury statistics is by collecting data on the medical treatment of injured clients or other personnel. This is possible only if: (i) researchers can gain access to medical records, generally modified so as to preserve confidentiality; (ii) these records include information on the circumstances of injury; and (iii) the patients actually provided the doctors with accurate information on those circumstances.

For example, if patients do not seek treatment at all, or do so only once they have returned home to another town or country, it is unlikely that the medical record will be matched with the incident. If the client's medical or travel insurance policy specifically excludes particular adventure activities, then the patient may not tell the doctor the real cause of injury. As a result, medical records can probably only provide accurate and relatively complete data for serious injuries that need immediate emergency treatment. For the same reasons, attempts to compare accident statistics between activities, or between places or countries for the same activities, must be interpreted in the light of likely reporting.

Perhaps equally interesting, but even harder to quantify, is the incidence of disease contracted during adventure tourism activities. Especially for tours in remote areas or in developing nations, tour clients may be exposed to pathogens and disease vectors that do not occur in their country of origin. They may also eat food, or visit places, that are less hygienic than at home. They may or may not have appropriate immunizations or preventive medicines.

They may get infected whilst on holiday, but they may not develop symptoms or receive treatment until they return home. Diagnosis may be incomplete, and the illness may not be linked to the place or activity where it originated. Even if all this is done, it may not be feasible in practice for researchers to link the medical records to the place or activity. Only for so-called notifiable diseases, where there is a central data coordinating authority in each country concerned, is there likely to be relatively comprehensive information.

Overall, therefore, it is perhaps a near-impossible task to compile statistics of illnesses associated with particular adventure tourism activities. Even if appropriate medical records could always be located, there are difficulties in diagnosis of illness, identification of pathogen and assignment of cause. This is certainly not to discourage such medical research – which is extremely valuable – merely to point out its complexities.

## Adventure Events

Many places use sporting events to promote themselves as tourist destinations. The rights to host the Olympic Games, the Winter Olympics, the Commonwealth Games, and so on are hotly contested, with fierce bidding and lobbying by countries, chambers of commerce and tourism associations. So also are the rights to host events such as the America's Cup, but in this case that right is won through the sporting competition itself.

With the increasing popularity of adventure tourism and recreation, it is not surprising that the number of adventure events has also grown rapidly. The term is applied two rather different types of events.

There are participatory events, generally single-activity, which aim to involve enthusiasts for recreation rather than competition. Some of these have been running at the same site for many years or decades. Often they are billed as festivals. Prizes, if any, are relatively small.

There are also competitive adventure events, either single-activity or multi-sport, where the competition itself is intended to attract sponsors and spectators and to sell television and advertising rights. These may run at different sites each year, and often have significant prizes. Many surfing, snowboarding, kayaking, mountain biking and multi-activity competitions and challenges fit this model.

Adventure events, in either category, may sometimes be packaged as part of a commercial adventure tourism product, either for participants or spectators. The Naadam Festival in Mongolia, mentioned under the Boojum Expeditions case study in Chapter 17, is one example where the tour clients are spectators at the event. The World Powder Eight Championships, run annually by Mike Wiegele Helicopter Skiing as outlined Chapter 12, provides an example where the tour clients are participants in the event.

Adventure events may also be used to market adventure destinations so as to attract tourists outside the period of the event itself, as suggested for Moab, Utah, in Chapter 23. The links between the event itself, its use in marketing and tourist arrivals do not yet seem to have been examined quantitatively in this case.

Some examples of adventure events, of various types, are summarized in Table 22.1. This is an interesting area for further study, a crossover between event tourism and adventure tourism.

Sporting and cultural events are widely used worldwide as a way to attract visitors to tourist destination towns outside the principal holiday season, so as to provide a continuing supply of customers for hotels, restaurants and other components of the hospitality industry. This practice is so widespread that so-called event tourism has become a significant subfield of academic enquiry in tourism. The same applies for conferences and conventions, which in tourism terms are used for the same purpose. From a tourism perspective, spectator sports such as professional surfing or yachting, car-racing, cricket, baseball or the various codes of football can usually generate more bed-nights than participatory competitions. The main exceptions are for national inter-club competitions, e.g. for surf life-saving, which involve a large number of participants.

**Table 22.1.** Selected adventure events.

| Place and country | Event name (website) | Activity | Length, numbers |
|---|---|---|---|
| Various countries | Raid World Series (www.theraid.org) | Multi-sport | 7 days, ~500 |
| South Island, New Zealand | Speight's Coast-to-Coast (www.coasttocoast.co.nz) | Multi-sport | 2 days, ~750 |
| Morocco | Marathon des Sables (www.darbaroud.com) | Endurance running | 6 days, ~800 |
| Costa Rica | Ruta de los Conquistadores (www.adventurerace.com) | Mountain bike | 3 days, ? |
| Moab, UT, USA | 24 Hours of Moab (www.grannygear.com) | Mountain bike | 2 days, 5,500 |
| Fernie, BC, Canada | Trans-Rockies Challenge (www.transrockies.com) | Mountain bike | 7 days, 350 |
| Blue River, Canada | World Powder Eights (www.wiegele.com) | Skiing | 7 days, ~100 |
| Moab, UT, USA | Easter Jeep Safari | 4WD vehicles | 9 days, 40,000 |

There are also a number of long-standing competitive outdoor sporting and recreational events that are run annually at particular places and do, in fact, bring tourists to those destinations, but where that event is not used to market the area as an adventure destination. Examples include fishing competitions in west coast Canada and Alaska, or on the large sand islands of east coast Australia; endurance races such as the Marathon des Sables in Morocco; and multi-sport competitions such as the Hawaii Ironman or the Speight's Coast-to-Coast in New Zealand.

What does not seem to have been noted previously, however, but is reported for Moab, Utah, by Claudia Ollenburg in Chapter 23, is the apparently deliberate sponsorship and promotion of large-scale adventure events that involve thousands of participants and many tens of thousands of spectators and that are used not only to fill beds on the days concerned, but to promote the town as an adventure destination during the rest of the year. Such an approach seems not to have been reported previously and does not, in fact, seem to be commonplace in practice. Clearly, however, it would be straightforward for other areas that market themselves as adventure tourism destinations to mimic this strategy.

# 23 Adventure Destinations

*Contributed by Ralf Buckley, Jerry Johnson and Claudia Ollenburg*

Arches National Park, Moab, USA. Photo Ralf Buckley.

## Introduction

The case studies presented in the preceding chapters are retail adventure tour products. Most of them are marketed worldwide, and many of them are run in relatively remote regions far from major mass tourism routes.

Some of the case studies, however, show the opposite features. They are clustered close to mainstream tourist destinations, and sold to tourists who decided to visit a particular place for their holiday, rather than to take a particular tour. These tourists' choice of destination, however, may well have been influenced by prior knowledge of the tours available once they arrived. It may therefore be worthwhile for tourism providers and tourism promotion agencies to market the destination and the adventure tour opportunities jointly. It is these synergies that have given rise to the concept of adventure tourism destinations.

Adventure destinations may be considered in two main categories on the basis of their history. There are those with a long history of tourism, often tourism for a particular activity, but that have recently expanded the portfolio of activities available and refocused their marketing using an adventure label. And there are those that have a very short history of tourism, and are trying to use an adventure label to gain recognition as a tourism destination.

Perhaps the best-known example of the former is Victoria Falls, on the border of Zambia and Zimbabwe. For over a century, the Falls has had hotels and trails catering to visitors who wanted only to see the scenic splendour of the actual waterfall itself. This volume of travellers supported a tourist infrastructure, providing access as well as accommodation. This allowed the area to evolve into a tourist gateway for wildlife and nature tours, especially in nearby national parks. More recently, a variety of adventure tour products have been developed in the area right around the township, and for younger market sectors the destination is now known more for its adventure opportunities than its scenery or wildlife.

There are several similar examples in the mountains of Europe and North America. Areas that were initially visited only by skiers gradually acquired club huts, ski tows, ski lodges, chairlifts, ski hotels, gondolas and all the trappings of ski resorts. To keep this accommodation and infrastructure operational outside the ski season, a variety of summer sports such as golf were added at some resorts. Many younger skiers and snowboarders, however, are interested only in more adventurous and adrenalized activities, so mountain resorts have an interest in promoting and developing tours that can offer visitors such activities: climbing local cliffs; rafting or kayaking on rivers; sailing, sailboarding or kiteboarding on lakes; hiking, horse riding or mountain biking on mountain trails; tandem skydiving, parapenting or hang-gliding from the slopes; searching for wildflowers or wildlife in nearby national parks; and in some cases, fishing and hunting in public or private estates. Chamonix and Interlaken in the Alps, or Banff, Bozeman and Bend in the Rockies, fit this model well.

Not everywhere advertising itself as an adventure destination, however, has such a long history in tourism. There are now a number of new destinations that historically have had little tourism at all, but that are currently attempting to establish such an industry by marketing an adventure image. Often they start with one particular activity and then graft on others. Some of them started this process decades ago and now have a mature and diverse adventure tourism market; others started much more recently and are as yet relatively unknown.

Nepal, for example, was known first for its mountaineering opportunities; later for trekking; subsequently for whitewater rafting; and more recently, for a wide range of adventure tourism activities. The Thamel area in the capital city of Kathmandu has become the base for marketing many such tours. Namche Bazaar on the route to Everest Base Camp has established something of a reputation for adventure opportunities. And The Last Resort on the Bhote Khosi, David Allardice's current venture, offers a portfolio of adventure tourism activities including bungee jumping as well as rafting, kayaking and trekking.

A much more recent addition to this category of adventure destinations is Pacific Habour on the so-called Coral Coast of Fiji, the southern coastline of Viti Levu. Pacific Habour is a small township with two major hotels and various additional accommodation options, but it is the departure point for Fiji's only whitewater rafting trips, for local lagoon and shark diving ventures, for day trips to an internationally known surf break at Frigates Passage, and for shuttle boats to dive, surf and island resorts, lodges and camps in Bega Lagoon and further offshore at Kadavu Island. It has therefore claimed the title of adventure capital of Fiji. This may or may not be successful: as yet there seems to be no coherent marketing on this theme, and the northern island of Vanua Levu may also lay claim to the same title. The critical issue is simply that Pacific Habour has seen it as worthwhile to describe itself in these terms, which differentiates it from the 3S/4S beach resorts on the main southwestern sector of Fiji's Coral Coast.

A similar example is perhaps provided by the Geraldton region of Western Australia, which for some years (though apparently no longer) advertised itself as the 'Adventure Coast'. The main activities include sailing and sailboarding, surfing, snorkelling and diving, and watching whales, whalesharks and manta rays in particular places and seasons. The tropical city of Cairns, gateway to the Great Barrier Reef and to the World Heritage rainforests of the hinterland, has long been known for its diving and sailing opportunities as well as its coastal resorts with their golf courses and marinas full of game-fishing charter boats. In more recent years it has added a variety of additional adventure options including rafting, parasailing and bungee jumping. It also serves as the hub for skydiving and seakayaking out of Mission Beach a little to the south; for diving and nature tours out of Port Douglas a little to the north; and for wildlife-watching, horse riding, hiking and off-road opportunities in the tablelands to the west.

The differences between Pacific Harbour and Kathmandu, Cairns and Banff illustrate a different possible classification of adventure destinations, at least as useful as one based on development history: some adventure destinations are in the mountains, some on the coast. A few, such as Moab in Utah, USA are in arid areas, though Moab does also have the Colorado River, the Green River and the La Sal Mountains nearby.

Not surprisingly, adventure destinations with different terrain, climate and location tend to offer different types of adventure activities. Diving needs plenty of water and something worth looking at underneath it. Warm coral reefs are by far the favourite, but coldwater kelp forests, sharks and rays, lakebeds and ice floes also offer tourist attractions now that warmer wetsuits and drysuits are routinely available. Rafting needs rivers, but operators at different destinations package trips that range from flatwater float trips to Class III–V whitewater trips in guided rafts. Off-road opportunities and challenges can be created almost anywhere, whether on coastal dunes and near-coastal sand islands, swamps and mud, dense forests or steep mountain slopes, or desert dunes and slickrock.

Advertising varies accordingly. Queenstown in New Zealand claims the title to Adventure Capital of the World (Cater, Chapter 24), but unless they have trademarked the name worldwide, this is presumably open to contest. Various other destinations claim to be the adventure capitals of continents, countries and regions (Table 23.1). Shearwater Adventures (2005) in Victoria Falls claims to be Africa's largest adventure tour company. *Outside* magazine (Brandt, 2005) claims that 'adventure is mainstream'. One might argue some ulterior motive for this particular publication, but the theme is echoed in travel, lifestyle and fashion magazines elsewhere.

Destinations also vary by the demographic niche they seek to exploit. For the most part, adventure tourism obviously targets affluent young risk-takers. However, three trends serve to diversify the adventure tourism market globally toward those enjoying their retirement years. First, enhanced post-retirement health and longevity ensure that more of the aged are capable of outdoor pursuits for a longer period of time. Skiing, scuba diving and parasailing, to name just a few, are increasingly practised by 'mature' participants. Second, in developed economies the record transfer of wealth from the World War II generation to the 'baby boomers' means that the purchase of leisure time is increasingly a lifestyle option for greater numbers of those born during the post-war economic boom. Finally, equipment has become more user-friendly, stylish, warm and functional. Enhanced overall comfort makes outdoor sport possible for those in their later years. Advertising in magazines aimed at the older market reflects the interest in attracting mature wealth to communities

**Table 23.1.** 'Adventure capital' claims.

| Place | Country | Area claimed* |
|---|---|---|
| Queenstown | New Zealand | The World |
| Victoria Falls | Zimbabwe | Africa |
| Livingstone | Zambia | Africa |
| Interlaken | Switzerland | Europe |
| Dominican Republic | Dominican Republic | The Caribbean |
| Cairns | Australia | Australia |
| Lake District | United Kingdom | England |
| Voss | Norway | Norway |
| Perthshire | Scotland | Scotland |
| Ahipara | New Zealand | The North Island |
| Freycinet | Australia | Tasmania |
| Port Stephens | Australia | New South Wales |
| Marquard | South Africa | The Free State |
| Moab | USA | Utah |
| Bryson City, NC | USA | The Smokies |
| Maine | USA | The East |
| Fort William | Scotland | The UK |

* These claims were extracted from the first 200 hits on a Google® web search for 'Adventure Capital' on 24 October 2005. The last three listed claim to be 'Outdoor Adventure Capitals' rather than simply 'Adventure Capitals'. Maine, USA also claims to have trademarked its preferred designation. Livingstone, across the Zambezi River from Victoria Falls, is claimed as the 'new' adventure capital of Africa.

like Bend and Bozeman in the USA, Interlaken in Switzerland and Mt Hotham in Australia.

To illustrate some of these patterns, the remainder of the chapter provides comparative reviews of individual adventure tourism destinations, effectively case studies at the destination scale. The following chapter (Cater, Chapter 24) examines one such destination in much more detail: Queenstown, New Zealand, self-styled Adventure Capital of the World.

The destinations selected for comparison are listed in Table 23.2, with a summary of major features. The principal authors of each destination case study, relevant for descriptions of experiences, are indicated by initials.

## Queenstown (RB)

### Place

Queenstown lies on the western side of Lake Wakatipu in the central southern part of New Zealand's South Island, southwest of Mt Cook and southeast of Mt Aspiring. The surrounding terrain is mountainous, and the principal surrounding land use is sheep farming. The area has a history of former gold mining. Further detail on these aspects, and all the issues summarized below, is given in Chapter 24.

### Operators and activities

As noted earlier, Queenstown markets itself as the adventure capital of the world, and it does indeed offer a broad portfolio of adventure activities, especially if nearby Wanaka is included. In winter the principal activity is downhill skiing and snowboarding at the resorts of Coronet Peak, Mount Remarkable, Cardrona and Treble Cone. There are also several heliski operations based at Queenstown and Wanaka, and a large cross-country ski area across the valley from Cardrona. Some of the

**Table 23.2.** Activities at selected adventure destinations.

| | Climbing | Skiing | Rafting | Jetboat | Hiking | Biking | Horse ride | ORV[4] tour | Heli-rides | Hang-gliding[5] | Balloon | Skydive | Bungee | Diving | Seakayak | Surf/sailboard |
|---|---|---|---|---|---|---|---|---|---|---|---|---|---|---|---|---|
| Queenstown[1] | | * | * | * | * | * | * | | * | * | * | * | * | | | |
| Banff | * | * | * | | * | * | * | * | * | * | * | | | | | |
| Bozeman | * | * | * | | * | * | * | | | * | * | | | | | |
| Interlaken | * | * | * | | * | * | * | | | * | * | * | * | | * | |
| Chamonix | * | * | * | | * | * | | | | * | | | | | | |
| Kathmandu | * | | * | | * | * | * | | | | | | | | | |
| Victoria Falls[2] | | | * | * | | | * | | * | * | | | * | | | |
| Moab | * | * | * | | * | * | * | * | * | | * | * | | | | |
| Cairns[3] | | | * | | | | * | | | | * | * | * | * | | |
| Pacific Harbour | | | * | | | | | | | | | | | * | * | * |

Notes: [1]Including Wanaka and Arrowsmith. [2]Including Livingstone. [3]Including Port Douglas and Mission Beach. [4]Off-road vehicle. [5]Including paragliding.

summer activities, including whitewater rafting on the Shotover River, are also available during winter.

In summer, the area is best known for whitewater rafting, jetboating, bungee jumping and scenic helicopter flights, the so-called Awesome Foursome. Tandem skydiving and hang-gliding, river sledging and other adventure activities are also offered, together with a range of scenic, nature-based and farm tourism opportunities. The major heliski and whitewater rafting operations are described in the relevant case study chapters. Most of these are single-day activities, based out of accommodation in Queenstown or Wanaka. A variety of combination trips are available in summer, and ski packages in winter. Almost all the adventure tourism operations are relatively high-volume.

## Access

Access to Queenstown itself is by road, or by air from Christchurch or directly from Australia. Access from Queenstown to Wanaka is by the so-called Crown Range road, daunting to some international self-drive visitors but driven at speed by ski resort shuttle buses in all weathers. Access to all the other adventure tourism activities is by road. Clients generally have an option to travel from Queenstown in the tour operators' shuttle buses, or in some cases to drive their own vehicles. Bungee jumping and whitewater rafting on the Shotover River are accessed on the so-called Skippers Canyon road, which is off-limits to rental vehicles. For rafting trips on the Kawarau River, the shuttle bus returning from the take-out point does pass the put-in point, so clients arriving in their own vehicles can recover them. For the Shotover River, this is not the case. For most other adventure activities, including heliskiing, access by private vehicle is perfectly feasible. Since the shuttle bus from town is included in the price of the tour for most activities, however, there is little to be gained unless clients do not intend to return to Queenstown.

Most adventure tours in this area take place either on private land owned by sheep farmers or public land managed principally by the New Zealand Department of Conservation. Permission or permits are required in either case, and these are negotiated in advance by the tour operators.

## Community

Queenstown is a heavily tourist-oriented town, and a large proportion of local residents earn at least part of their income either directly or indirectly from tourists. Wanaka is less tourist-dependent, with a more up-market clientele and a significant and growing proportion of amenity migrants. Residents not involved in tourism are mostly involved in farming, and there is some cross-over between the sectors. Some farmers, for example, routinely use helicopters and at least one working sheep station, Walter Peak Station, also runs its own farm tourism operations as well as acting as a staging base for heliskiing.

## Experience

The social side of Queenstown's adventure tourism sector is described in much more detail in Chapter 24, where Cater describes the après-adventure nightclub scene and its links to daytime adventure activities. My own (RB) experiences of Queenstown have been brief and intermittent over a period of 30 years: passing through on occasion on private hiking or kayaking trips; as a tour guide for an American natural history tour company; auditing case studies for this book; or on one occasion taking part in an environmental law conference at the time of the notorious rabbit milkshakes. My impression, certainly, was that it is a strongly tourist-oriented destination, with equal focus on family and backpacker markets.

## Environment

Queenstown itself is a medium-sized town, and its hotels, resorts and other tourism accommodation are subject to normal urban planning and development regulations and are connected to municipal services. The surrounding valleys and uplands are used principally for sheep farming, with consequent modifications to native vegetation and water quality. The large ski resorts have their own waste treatment systems. Adventure tourism makes a pro rata contribution to the environmental impacts of urban accommodation and of local and long-distance transport (Simmons and Becken, 2004).

Localized impacts from particular types of adventure tour activities are summarized in the relevant case studies. Most of these tours use areas that are already heavily modified. The principal exception is heliskiing, which leads to increased helicopter noise in backcountry areas during winter. The potential significance for native birds that may inhabit the small patches of forest in the valleys and gullies remains unstudied.

## Safety

Accident statistics for various adventure activities in New Zealand, as a whole, have been summarized by Page et al. (2003b), but these figures are not broken down by geographic areas. There have been one or two deaths from drowning on commercial whitewater rafting tours out of Queenstown, described in more detail by Cater in Chapter 24. No doubt there are also occasional incidents and injuries from other adventure tourism activities in this area, but detailed statistics are apparently not available.

## Marketing

As noted earlier, Queenstown promotes itself heavily as the adventure capital of the world, and there are strong cross-marketing links: between different activities; between tours, accommodation, retail outlets and entertainment venues; and between airlines, destination and ski resorts.

# Victoria Falls, Zimbabwe (RB)

### Place

Along with Niagara and Iguazu, Victoria Falls is one of the world's most heavily visited scenic waterfalls. The entire Zambezi River, which in this section forms the boundary between Zimbabwe and Zambia, plunges into a narrow slot that crosses its course. This creates an extremely impressive spectacle that is visible principally from the Zimbabwean side and has attracted tourists ever since its first European discovery.

## Operators and activities

Until a few decades ago, the only significant tourist activity was to walk to the various lookouts and gaze at the Falls themselves, which are certainly well worth the visit. During recent decades, however, a wide variety of additional activities has begun to be offered. Best-known of these is the 1-day whitewater rafting trip immediately below the Falls themselves. Other commercial tour activities include: horse riding, single or multi-day; elephant-back rides; canoeing on the calmer portions of the river upstream of the Falls; bungee jumping from the bridge between Zambia and Zimbabwe; scenic helicopter overflights to view the Falls; running the rapids on boogie boards; and surfing a particular standing wave that forms at one of the rapids for a brief period each year. In addition, Victoria Falls acts as a gateway for wildlife-watching tours in nearby national parks, notably Mana Pools and the much larger Hwange National Park further west.

The best-known adventure tour operator at Victoria Falls is Shearwater Adventures, described in more detail in the rafting chapter (Chapter 6). Shearwater started its operations some decades ago by offering whitewater rafting trips downstream of the Falls, and canoe trips upstream. The former is still its principal product, though the latter seem to have been abandoned, as outlined in the Upper Zambezi case study in Chapter 5.

Currently, however, Shearwater offers a range of other adventure activities, either singly or in combination packages. Most of these activities were offered by independent tour companies in the past. It is not clear whether Shearwater has bought these companies, set up in competition with them, arranged to act as their exclusive retail marketing agents under the Shearwater brand name, or simply sells places on commission. Whatever the business structure, however, Shearwater has certainly been able to establish itself as the dominant adventure tourism provider at Victoria Falls, though not the only one. In particular, for some activities there are tour operators based at Livingstone on the Zambian side of the river as well as the Zimbabwean side.

## Accommodation

Victoria Falls offers a wide range of tourist accommodation, from the stately tra-ditional Victoria Falls Hotel built long since for travellers viewing the Falls, to recently built riverside lodges upstream of the Falls, marketed more to modern adventure tourists and backpackers. There are also a number of intermediate hotels and motels that cater to package tours of all types. Many tour company websites and packages seem to recommend these other hotels in preference to the Victoria Falls Hotel itself. This, however, does not necessarily indicate in itself that those other hotels necessarily have better facilities, location, service or even value for money. They may have such advantages; but equally, they may simply give greater discounts or commissions to tour companies.

## Access and community

Victoria Falls has its own airport, and most international tourists arrive by air via Harare or Johannesburg, or a local domestic flight from another southern African tourist destination. Visitors from within Zimbabwe, or to a lesser extent South Africa, may arrive by road. Since tourism at Victoria Falls provides one of the major opportunities in the region for local residents to earn a cash income, many people seem to have moved there from surrounding areas. Some have formal employment, whereas others make a living in the informal sector, e.g. selling carvings or other artefacts by the roadside; selling bottled drinks by the roadside where tourists stop to buy carvings; carrying equipment up from the river after rafting trips, and so on. The social impacts on surrounding communities, or the environmental impacts of increased population in the Victoria Falls region itself, do not seem to have been studied.

### Safety and liability

Domestic liability laws and safety regulations within Zimbabwe itself are probably of little comfort to an international visitor concerned about the risks of adventure tours at Victoria Falls. Most of the major adventure tour operators rely principally on international clients, however, and many of the individual activities are booked through international tour companies and travel agents. A local tour operator will generally need to satisfy international safety standards to be included in prepaid packages, or even to be mentioned by name in international itineraries. These standards would include, for example: adequate third-party insurance; appropriate measures for medical evacuation if required; appropriately qualified and certified guides; and standard safety equipment for the activity concerned. If local operators do not meet the standards to be included or named in international packages, then they have to rely on a walk-up cash clientele, visitors who simply find the operator on the spot during a visit to Victoria Falls, so that no liability is transferred to any other tour operator.

### Marketing and packaging

Victoria Falls is generally seen as the adventure capital of Africa, and Shearwater Adventures markets itself as Africa's largest adventure tour company. Backpackers and other independent travellers, and tourists travelling through Africa on so-called overland buses, do indeed focus on the adventure opportunities around the Falls. A large proportion of visitors to Victoria Falls, however, still visit principally for its scenic splendour, or as one stop in a nature-based or wildlife tour. Some of these travel by bus in packaged tours, others independently by air. These tourists tend to be older than the more adventure-oriented visitors, though there is certainly considerable overlap. Depending on how they arrive, what they do and where they stay, different visitors to Victoria Falls may have quite different experiences and gain quite different impressions. The demographic profile of clients signing up for a 1-day raft trip at the Shearwater headquarters, for example, is typically rather different from the demographic profile of visitors taking afternoon tea on the terraces of Victoria Falls Hotel. Only on the walkways and lookouts at the Falls itself, or perhaps the roadside artefacts markets, do the different groups mix on equal terms.

## Cairns, Queensland, Australia (RB)

### Place

Cairns is the principal gateway town to two World Heritage Areas: the Great Barrier Reef and the tropical rainforest immediately inland. Both the reef and the rainforests stretch for a large distance north to south, and there are many other local access points, but most of these are reached via Cairns. The town has a long commercial history in logging, mining, cane farming and fisheries, with tourism a relatively recent addition.

## Operators and activities

Many visitors, and indeed perhaps the majority of the market, are there for the resorts, restaurants and retail opportunities in a tropical climate and coastal setting. There are also numerous nature-based tourism products, from the 'Skyrail®' gondola through and over the rainforest canopy, to birdwatching boat tours and nocturnal wildlife-watching trips.

In addition, there is a significant adventure tourism market, focusing principally on marine diving, sailing and fishing trips, but also including off-road driving, whitewater rafting, seakayaking, tandem skydiving, bungee jumping and other activities. Some of these products are described in relevant case study chapters. Of course, as at other destinations, the same individual tourists may combine adventure, nature and urban activities in a single trip.

The adventure tourism sector, in particular, seems to be highly competitive, and no single tour operator seems to dominate the entire market. Quicksilver Cruises (2005) and Great Adventures (2005) Reef Cruises, for example, each have a large component of the single-day reef-snorkelling market, though with slightly different products, but there are many other smaller operators that also offer 1-day reef trips. There is a largely separate market for multi-day live-aboard diving tours intended only for qualified and experienced divers. There are a number of dive boats and tour operators, with Taka Dive (2005) and Mike Ball (2005) perhaps best known. There are several whitewater rafting companies, but the lion's share of the market seems to be shared between two operators of approximately equal size, as described in Chapter 6. Similarly, there are many different sailing and fishing operators. Currently there seems to be only one skydiving operation, described in the relevant case study chapter; and only one bungee-jumping operator. Perhaps this plethora of competing operators is possible because the overall size of the Cairns tourist market is growing; perhaps it is an unstable situation due to historical factors, and will not last; or perhaps there are particular factors at this destination, which foster such an oligopoly of operators.

## Accommodation

Cairns has a very wide range of tourist accommodation, from luxury hotels and waterfront resorts to backpacker hostels in the city and specialist ecolodges in the hinterland. There are also a number of resorts on the various offshore islands.

## Access

Cairns has its own international airport, and a number of carriers fly there directly from major Asian cities. For domestic tourists, or those arriving into Australia through other gateways, Cairns is accessible by air, rail or road from Brisbane to the south, and somewhat less readily from Darwin to the west. There are regional road and air links to a range of local tourist areas, island as well mainland.

## Safety

Cairns has generally had a good safety record, except for one or two instances when clients on dive boats have been left behind inadvertently, and disappeared.

## Marketing

Despite the range of adventure tourism activities available out of Cairns, the region does not seem to market itself specifically as an adventure destination. Perhaps it does not want to pigeonhole itself, since currently it attracts a very wide range of tourists with the general theme of 'reef and rainforest'. Current advertising does feature 'outback' and 'adventure' as well as 'reef' and 'rainforest' – but it also features 'golf', 'self-drive' and 'gay and lesbian travel' with equal prominence (Tourism Tropical North Queensland, 2005). The main tourism area of town is effectively in the city centre, with hotels, restaurants, cafés and shops clustered close to the waterfront, and tourists walking from one to another along a grassy esplanade. This walk-in clientele is captured by a large number of small local tour agencies along the esplanade itself, scattered between the cafés. These agencies sell tour places on commission. Often they display coloured-chalk blackboards out the front, advertising supposed bargain sales and specials, which may or may not represent real savings. Most of the hotels in town also advertise the same trips and can make bookings on their guests' behalf.

Cairns is something of a party town and there are cross-marketing links between adventure tour operators and entertainment venues, though not so marked as the links described for Queenstown, New Zealand by Cater (Chapter 24). If we compare Cairns to Queenstown, we should perhaps also draw parallels between Port Douglas, a somewhat smaller and more up-market tourist and amenity migrant town north of Cairns, and Wanaka, its equivalent north of Queenstown.

# Banff, Alberta, Canada (RB)

## Place

Banff is perhaps the largest and best-known of the tourist and amenity migrant towns in the southern part of the Canadian Rockies. It lies within Banff National Park, and the expansion of the town, its suburbs and outliers and its major access highway, create continuing conservation impacts.

## Operators and activities

Banff is surrounded by mountain resorts and ski-fields, and in winter its tourism focus is entirely upon skiing and snowboarding, including downhill resort skiing, backcountry telemark skiing and heliskiing in the mountain ranges to the west. Banff is the headquarters for the large heliski operator Canadian Mountain Holidays, profiled in Chapter 12.

In summer, Banff is the gateway for self-drive or bus-borne sightseeing tourists, and for hikers and backcountry campers in the nearby national parks and public lands. There are many trails open for horse riding and mountain biking, either independently or with commercial tours; and there are commercial whitewater-rafting tours on the Kicking Horse River a little to the west. There are backcountry lodges, climbing sites, hot springs, off-road trails and more.

### Accommodation

Banff and the surrounding area have a wide range of tourist accommodation, including historic edifices such as those at Banff Springs or Lake Louise, originally built by Canadian Pacific Railroads. In more recent years these have caused various environmental controversies as they have sought to expand their capacity and conference facilities, with potential costs to conservation in the national park.

### Community

To visitors, downtown Banff feels very much like a tourist trap, with its high concentration of souvenir shops and upmarket clothing stores. Only a street or two away, however, there are local supermarkets, libraries, eateries and equipment stores, and many residents seem to see tourists more as a hindrance to their own outdoor recreation opportunities than as a source of income. No doubt one has to live there to appreciate the details.

### Access

Most visitors arrive either by road from Vancouver on Canada's west coast, or by air into Calgary at the eastern margin of the mountains. Calgary is accessible by air from Vancouver, Toronto or directly from London. Even though Banff is not far from the border with the USA, direct road connections are relatively poor. There is one connection from the eastern side of Waterton-Glacier International Peace Park, and one on the west. For those travelling north there is the Icefields Parkway, which runs up the Rocky Mountains to Jasper and beyond. Access around the Banff region is almost entirely by road.

### Marketing

Banff markets itself principally as the gateway to the Canadian Rockies rather than as an adventure destination, and its economy is probably driven more by tourism-related residential property development than by tourism itself. It has a relatively small downtown area crammed with souvenir, clothing and outdoor equipment stores, surrounded by residential suburbs that continue to grow wherever planning law allows.

## Moab, Utah, USA (CO)

### Place

Moab is a former mining town in Utah, USA. It is close to the Colorado River, about 250 km upstream of the Grand Canyon. It is the gateway town for nearby Arches and Canyonlands National Parks, and is also famous for its so-called slickrock bike trails. In the 1950s it was known as the uranium capital of the world. Its stark red-rock scenery was also made famous in various 'western'-style movies. As of the 2000 Census, its resident population was a little under 5000, but it also has a large tourist population including over 100,000 mountain bikers each year. Though the town itself is in a hot, arid environment, the La Sal Mountains nearby provide a cooler escape, and Moab is perhaps becoming a minor destination for amenity migrants (Dowling and Newsome, 2005).

## Activities and operators

Moab is well supplied with adventure tour providers and equipment hire companies. There are around seven companies offering guided off-road tours, and six that rent 4WD vehicles. There are a dozen or so whitewater rafting companies; at least three that offer horse-riding tours; three that offer rock climbing; and two that offer guided mountain bike tours, plus several bike rental companies. There are also tour operators offering hiking, canyoning, skydiving and scenic flights either by helicopter or light plane. The National Park Service conducts very high-quality guided walks into isolated parts of Arches National Park.

Moab is perhaps best-known worldwide for its mountain biking opportunities, notably the 15 km Slickrock Bike Trail, which is visited by over 100,000 enthusiasts annually. The name slickrock was bestowed by early settlers who found that their horses' metal-shod hooves would not grip on the steep surfaces. Studded rubber mountain bike tyres, however, grip the sandpaper-like rock surface extremely well, providing sufficient traction for suitably skilled and fearless riders to traverse steep sections at gravity-defying angles.

Perhaps paradoxically, in view of its arid desert appearance, Moab is also within easy access of several well-known rafting rivers. A variety of tour operators provide a range of rafting tours, including tranquil float trips on the Green River, family oriented trips on the intermediate-level rapids of the Colorado River north of town, and more difficult and exciting rapids in Westwater Canyon and Cataract Canyon.

## Accommodation and access

Moab has a wide range of tourist accommodation including: around 23 motels; 13 campgrounds; 21 lodges, hotels and B&Bs; and one youth hostel. Moab is reached by road from Colorado, Arizona or northern Utah, or by air from Salt Lake City. The air link, though supposedly a scheduled service, is in our experience (RB) highly erratic. Lands around Moab are held in various tenures, including Arches and Canyonlands National Parks, Manti-La Sal National Forest and – principally – grazing lands leased from the US Bureau of Land Management, the BLM.

## Community and environment

Moab has undergone major social changes over the last half-century, from mining to ranching, to tourism, to amenity migration. Currently it is still the regional service centre for the ranches, which are largely leasehold BLM lands; but it is also the main gateway to internationally famous Arches and Canyonlands National Parks, and one of the gateways to the Colorado River above Glen Canyon Dam. Tourism is hence a major part of the modern Moab economy, and tourists are viewed ambiguously by local residents as in most tourist towns. Tourism does also produce significant environmental impacts, particularly because of the prevalence of off-road vehicles (ORVs). Those, however, must be compared with the historical impact of mining and grazing. In fact, only one mile from Moab, 11.9 million tons of radioactive waste from uranium mining in the 1950s lies just metres from the banks of the Colorado River.

## Marketing

As the gateway to several famous national parks and rivers, Moab perhaps needs little marketing on its own account. In practice, it seems to have adopted an unusual strategy focusing on 'adventure events'. Most famous of these are the Easter Jeep Safari and the Moab Mountain Bike Race, but there are also rodeos and barrel races, marathons and fat-tyre festivals.

The Easter Jeep Safari is a 4WD trail rally, by no means restricted to Jeep® vehicles. It has been run since 1967 and is currently hosted by the Red Rock Four-Wheelers Inc.®, the local Moab off-road club. The event runs over 9 days, finishing on Easter Sunday, and can involve over 1000 4WD vehicles on 30 trails with around 40,000 participants and spectators. Drivers bring their own vehicles, equipment and food. ATVs and motorbikes are not permitted.

The annual 24 Hours of Moab mountain bike race is a team relay competition running for 24 h over ORV trails, sand and slickrock. There is also an annual skydiving festival, the Moab Boogie, where over 100 parachutists make over 1000 jumps during a 4-day period.

# Bozeman, Montana, USA (JJ)

### Place

Bozeman, Montana is the northern gateway to Yellowstone National Park, one of America's most famous attractions both for tourists and amenity migrants (Johnson *et al.*, 2003; Johnson, 2004). The Yellowstone region as a whole, known as the Greater Yellowstone Ecosystem or GYE, has become a major destination area for amenity migrants within the USA, attracted principally by outdoor recreation opportunities such as hiking and fishing in summer, and skiing and snowmobiling in winter.

### Activities and operators

As an adventure tourism destination, Bozeman in winter offers downhill skiing and snowboarding locally at Bridger Bowl and the nearby resorts of Big Sky and Moonlight Basin. Cross-country skiing, snowshoeing and snowmobiling opportunities are available both within Yellowstone National Park and outside it; and for those suitably skilled, ice climbing opportunities on a number of frozen cliffs and waterfalls, as outlined Chapter 14. In summer, Bozeman plays host to innumerable self-drive tourists heading to Yellowstone National Park, and offers a wide range of hiking, climbing, mountain biking, horse riding and whitewater kayaking opportunities to local residents. Three commercial whitewater concessions operate on the nearby Class IV Gallatin and Yellowstone rivers.

### Accommodation and access

Accommodation is available in a range of hotels, motels, hostels and campgrounds, both in Bozeman itself, local national forest lands and at Yellowstone National Park.

Big Sky and Moonlight Basin ski resorts have their own accommodation, including private residential housing. Access is by air or road. Scheduled flights are available only from within the USA, not directly from nearby Canada.

## Environment and community

There have been a number of significant environmental conflicts during recent years, associated particularly with the increasing use of snowmobiles within Yellowstone National Park itself, and with the rights of surrounding ranchers to kill bison and the recently reintroduced wolves when they leave the park. The dynamics of land use change, as former cattle ranches have been bought and subdivided for rural residential development, and stock and station agents in the towns have supposedly given way to coffee and chardonnay bars, has been the subject of particularly detailed investigation (Johnson *et al.*, 2003). Access to recreational lands is an increasingly contentious issue as private lands change ownership.

## Marketing

Bozeman does not market itself extensively as an adventure tourism destination: indeed, it does not need to market itself at all, since people have to pass through it to get to Yellowstone. Unlike many adventure tourism towns, Bozeman is home to a major state university and an important regional airport. These two attributes act as major attractants for lifestyle migrants seeking a rural lifestyle based, in large part, on outdoor sport and a quality environment. Bozeman is frequently cited as being on many top ten lists of small towns in the USA in which to live.

The Bozeman area is also home to the private Yellowstone Club. This exclusive 13,000 acre resort community has its own self-contained ski resort, golf course and adventure offerings – snowmobile tours, cross-country skiing, wildlife viewing and horse packing.

# Pacific Harbour, Fiji (RB)

## Place

Pacific Harbour is a small town at the eastern end of the so-called Coral Coast region on the south coast of Fiji's main island of Viti Levu. Its mangrove-lined lagoon and river mouth do indeed provide a convenient harbour for a variety of small boats, an opportunity that is lacking along most of the Coral Coast. Equally, however, Pacific Harbour does not have the open sandy beaches and fringing reefs that the Coral Coast resorts can offer.

## Operators and activities

Pacific Harbour is the departure point for the whitewater rafting and inflatable-kayak tours offered by Rivers Fiji on the upper Navua and 'Luva Rivers, described in Chapter 6. It is the pick-up point for the shuttle boat to Lalati and other resorts in Bega Lagoon immediately offshore. This lagoon, and Lalati Resort in particular, is famous for its diving, with the focus on the smaller and rarer species that appeal particularly to internationally experienced divers. There are also dive tours that operate directly from Pacific Harbour, but these focus on feeding sharks. Lalati Resort, and also a surf camp on Yanuca Island, also offer surfing at Frigates Passage, an opening in the western end of the Bega reef. Frigates Passage is known for a relatively consistent and powerful swell, and along with Tavarua in the Mamanuca Islands west of the Viti Levu, and Nagigia off Kadavu Island to the south, is one of Fiji's best-known surfing locations. The break is accessible only by boat, either from the island resort and surf camps as above, or directly from the mainland. Pacific Harbour's one surf shop, and one of the nearby coastal resorts, offer day trips to Frigates Passage.

### Accommodation and access

Pacific Harbour is by no mean large, but it does have a range of adventure tourism opportunities in the immediate vicinity. In addition, it has a new resort hotel that is sufficiently upmarket to be featured in national tourism promotions, and a slightly older hotel nearby that has gained some advertising advantages by playing host to a number of major film productions. Offices and pick-up points for the various adventure tours in the surrounding region are either in the grounds of one or other of these two hotels, or on the short stretch of road between them. This road forms part of Fiji's principal highway, the south coast road linking the capital city of Suva in the east to the international airport and main commercial hub of Nadi in the west.

Fiji currently plays host to around half a million international visitors every year, and most of these tourists stay in the various Coral Coast beach resorts immediately west of Pacific Harbour. The day trips operating from Pacific Harbour are easily accessible from these beach resorts. Currently, Pacific Harbour perhaps acts principally as a departure point for adventure tours purchased by visitors staying at these resorts, either before or after they arrive. It has not yet developed a reputation as an adventure tourism destination in its own right. As the new resort develops an increasing reputation, and a range of adventure activities continues to expand, it may soon pass the threshold to be labelled as a destination in its own right.

### Marketing

Pacific Harbour has recently started to market itself as the adventure capital of Fiji.

# Chamonix, France (JJ)

### Place

Chamonix is the undeniable birthplace of mountaineering. Over 200 years ago, wealthy Britons hired locals to guide them to the tops of the French Alps. The town of Chamonix is the commercial heart of the Chamonix Valley in the far northwest Alps, near the juncture of the borders of France, Switzerland and Italy. The dominant view of the valley is Mt Blanc, 4800 m in elevation, but some of the most spectacular mountain scenery in Europe can be seen in all directions. Tourism, and adventure tourism in particular, is the basis of the regional economy since the first guesthouse was built in 1770. Skiing was introduced to the valley at the end of the 19th century, and in 1924 Chamonix hosted the first Winter Olympic Games.

## Operators

While other communities may market themselves as adventure capitals, Chamonix is the original and still the best. Chamonix has long been known as a downhill ski destination and as a base for climbing in the Alps, but now virtually every high-adrenalin sport imaginable is practised, developed and guided by the highly trained members of the International Federation of Mountain Guides Associations (IFMGA, aka UIAGM). Guides can be hired for paragliding, on and off-piste skiing and snow-boarding, heliski tours, alpinism, rock and ice climbing, via ferrata tours, canyoneering, whitewater kayaking and rafting, to name but a few. Guides are available for almost any language.

## Access

For a rather isolated mountain valley, access is easy thanks to the Mount Blanc Tunnel. Begun in 1957 and completed in 1965, the tunnel is 11.6 km long and 8.6m wide, and provides access to Chamonix from Courmayeur in Italy's Aosta Valley to the south. From the west, access is over the Col des Montets from Geneva and Lyon. Geneva, Switzerland has the closest airport: 1 h by car and 1.5 h by bus. The valley has a free rail service for those holding ski tickets. Expensive but fast transfer is available via Chamonix Mont-Blanc Helicopters.

In 1999 a serious fire broke out in the Mont Blanc Tunnel, killing 41 people and blocking access to the valley for nearly 3 years. Today, after a great deal of retrofitting and safety provisions, the Tunnel is considered safe.

## Community

The Chamonix Valley is approximately 20 km long; there are only about 10,000 permanent residents. In summer, however, there are up to 100,000 visitors per day, and in winter approximately 60,000. Traffic congestion, crowded recreational venues and high prices for lodging, housing and food are the inevitable results. Until the end of the 19th century, the mountain guides were the main economic power in Chamonix. From the beginning of the 20th century, however, with the construction of numerous hotels, the hoteliers have become the foremost economic power in the valley. The views of the mountains are surprisingly well preserved in a town so densely developed. Numerous cable-car 'des glaciers' provide access from town centre to alpine retreats and the well-developed hut system.

## Experience

My own experience in Chamonix is based on winter and summer visits for both skiing and climbing. My impression is that of a well-preserved tourist destination with little sense of community. Older buildings are continuously being restored, and new ones built so as to provide more accommodation. Most accommodation is decidedly upscale, although good value can be found in B&Bs (at around US$30 per night) and in the large campgrounds located in the valley. Prices for apartments more than double during the summer months.

## Environment

With six ski areas within the valley, hundreds of kilometres of hiking trails, massive visitation in summer and dense traffic, the environment of the valley certainly receives heavy use. Yet, when hiking the well-used trails one still gets a sense of relative isolation and quality. Certainly, many of the climbing routes are crowded, but solitude can be found in out of the way places. Ski trails are predictably crowded.

The major impact to the valley is from the numerous trucks that use the tunnel as a shortcut to and from Geneva and Lyon. The noise and accident rate are causes for sustained environmental protests within the valley.

## Safety

The quality of the Chamonix guides has historically been high. The local guild traditionally tried to keep non-residents of the valley from guiding, but today most creditable guide services can do business in Chamonix. The UIAGM has certification agreements with the American Mountain Guides Association as well as other national guiding organizations. Lischke *et al.* (2001) examined the accident rates for the European Alps between 1987 and 1997. They concluded that whilst accident rates had increased significantly over this period, the number of known deaths showed no significant increase.

Given the number of adventure practitioners and clients, and the number of high-risk sports practised in the region, it is not surprising that accidents occur.

## Marketing

The Chamonix Valley is part of a larger region of alpine playgrounds that includes all the mountain sports covered in this book. The valley is a 'must-do' destination for enthusiasts of mountains and mountain sports. Most marketing materials focus on the historical significance of the region to the sport of mountaineering and skiing. Chamonix is one of 12 classic alpine resorts that have joined forces to establish the 'Best of the Alps' branding group. The resorts seek to cooperate on an image based on name recognition, history and quality of the natural environment. Such a strategy is relatively easy to implement, given the highly developed transportation network in Europe.

# 24 World Adventure Capital

*Contributed by Carl Cater*

Kirsten Cater, Bungy Jump, Queenstown NZ. CC collection.

# Introduction

## Place and perception

In an era when the themes of adventure detailed within these pages have become increasingly popular, and adventure society pervades many aspects of our lives, it is worth considering the spatial organization of such activity. In a tourism context, a number of destinations have attempted to build on the popularity of adventure tourism and offer a wide variety of adventure activities in one place. This has led to the emergence of a number of adrenalin 'hotspots' around the world. Travel media frequently publish lists of these destinations. On 14 September 1997, for example, the UK broadsheet *Independent on Sunday* published a list that, among others, included Queenstown (New Zealand), Cairns (Australia), Victoria Falls (Zimbabwe) and Chamonix (France). These areas have been marketed by the media as places where tourists can partake in adventure tourism pursuits in spectacular natural settings. Nature is thus packaged as a spectacular backdrop for these activities.

The marketing of places and activities is an important avenue through which they are endowed with anticipatory meaning. Through this commodification of place, certain destinations emerge as being 'the opening of a space of places at which activities can intelligibly be performed' (Thrift, 1999, p. 311). As a result of these trends some very strong 'place-myths' emerge that become reinforced through touristic practices. Wilson (1992, p. 20) discusses how tourism is projected out into nature and then brought back on itself as part of our imaginations. He shows how the Caribbean holiday is a product as well as place, corresponding to an equation of palm trees, sandy beaches, sunshine and a clear blue sea, irrespective of actual geographical location. This applies equally to adventurous tourism: you *can* bungee jump off a crane in a car park, but people would far rather do so off a bridge across a deep canyon with raging rapids below. This is the image that is circulated most often, and hence it is the one that the tourist seeks to replicate.

These adventurous places are typically perceived as marginal locations, frequently rural, that form an alternative to the highly developed West. The reality is that these are as much part of the global system as the places where the participants originate, in that they are well-served by air links and have the best hotels and nightlife for 'après adventure'. What is important is that these places *look* like they are at the 'edge of the world', and this look adds to that feeling of adventure without compromising the 'safe' regulatory frameworks that holidaymakers have come to expect (Ritzer and Liska, 1997). One of the most successful of these adventure destinations has been that of Queenstown in New Zealand, to the extent that it brands itself the 'adventure capital of the world'. New Zealand benefits in this brand from being geographically on the edge of the world, although it is clearly not in terms of its development. Many of the reasons that Queenstown has been so effective at marketing such a brand are shared by a number of other adventure destinations. This chapter attempts to describe these and provide insights into their management.

## Existing attractions and infrastructure

Clearly, the nature-based orientation of most adventure tourism activities requires a destination that has a bounty of natural environments in which they can be performed. For many contemporary sites of adventurous tourism, their reputation carries 'meanings of excitement, thrill, youthfulness (and) freshness' that are communicated through the meanings invested in nature (Cloke and Perkins, 1998a, p. 190). At first glance it may seem that Queenstown has a perfect natural environment for the practice of such activities, being nestled in a pristine forested valley on the shores of a deep blue lake, surrounded by magnificent towering peaks all around. These physical attributes clearly make the practice of a variety of adventure tourism pursuits possible.

However, in order to understand how the destination has emerged as a premier site of adventure we need to consider a range of organizational developments that have stimulated the foundation of a successful adventure tourism industry. In line with many adventure tourism destinations, Queenstown has a long history of tourism that pre-dates the adventure tourism term. Initially founded on gold mining, the town soon became popular for scenic tourism in the summer months, and, in line with early resort tourism in Europe, tourism to Queenstown was firmly situated within ideas of the therapeutic value of a holiday. Nevertheless, it is interesting to see how even early brochures hint at the wide range of opportunities for engaging with nature available in the region, as one from 1914 states:

> Mankind's holiday tastes are as diverse as his business pursuits, but Nature is a never failing storehouse. And surely in no part of New Zealand, nay, of the world, has there been packed into one corner of the storehouse such a wondrous variety of the chiefest delights of nature as is to be found in the neighbourhood of Queenstown.
>
> (Sinclair, 1914)

The active nature of the destination was supplanted in the post war-period with the emergence of skiing at sites around the town. The development of Coronet Peak in the late 1940s by the Mount Cook Company meant that, for the first time, accommodation in Queenstown was fully utilized during the winter months. Indeed, ski development is important to consider in the majority of so-called adventure destinations. The development of tourism infrastructure, and the need to promote visitation outside the winter months, has in many cases been a cause to promote adventure products. In some cases ski infrastructure may be used, for example chairlifts for hiking and mountain biking in the summer season.

## Iconic activities

A second major factor that may be identified as being important in the development of adventure destinations is the emergence of iconic adventure pursuits. In Queenstown, the 1960s saw a clear change in course for the resort, away from 'purely scenic excursions to more sophisticated and unusual activities with a peculiarly New Zealand flavour' (Lampden, 1968, p. 85). One of the first of these was that of the Shotover Jetboat ride, which commenced operations in 1963, and claimed to offer 'a blend of scenery and excitement' (Pearce and Cant, 1981, p. 10). Interestingly the ride was never envisaged as a long-term venture, originally set up as a fundraising exercise for a Christian youth camp by two Invercargill brothers (Brown, 1997, p. 65). Although the ride was, and still is, largely passive, its place at the softer end of adventure tourism has ensured its long-term popularity, and it has been significant in establishing an adventurous brand for Queenstown. In a similar way to the introduction of jetboats, whitewater rafting in Queenstown was an early adventure activity. In common with rafting worldwide, the availability of cheap ex-military equipment was the catalyst for river exploration. In Queenstown's case it was the arrival of an old US navy life raft acquired in 1972, which was used by locals to navigate several local rivers. This prompted the formation of the first commercial venture, Kon Tiki Rafts, the first rafting company in Australasia.

The one adventure activity that has really captured the imagination of New Zealand and the world, however, is that of bungee jumping. Perhaps it is the fact that it is such an unnatural act that makes it all the more appealing, or the way that it is a display and validation of self. Indeed, it does differ from many other adventure tourism activities in that it requires virtually no skill, beyond a will to leap, although in some senses this may be the ideal commercial situation, with very little left up to the individual. When AJ Hackett and friend Henry van Asch saw the footage of the world's first bungee jump engineered by the Oxford University Dangerous Sports Club from the Clifton suspension bridge in Bristol in 1979, they were taken by the commercial possibilities. After developing the technology involved and a few trial sites, the pair set up the first permanent jump from the Kawarau Bridge on the road into Queenstown in 1988. Instantly popular, the activity had a major impact on the destination as a place of 'crazy' adventurous pursuits as well as boosting numbers of participants in existing adventure activity. Discussions with jetboat operators highlighted that when bungee was introduced, it had the unexpected result of increasing numbers of their participants. This was put down to the effect of being 'the next most crazy activity', whereby those tourists seeing themselves as 'extreme' would pursue the bungee jump, and the larger numbers of people who were less adventurous were happy to take the jetboat. This was seen as the cause of numbers of jetboat tourists increasing from 60,000 people to 95,000 in one year between 1988 and 1989, and an average age increasing from 35 to 42.

## A spectrum of adventure

The majority of adventure tourism destinations invariably have a wide selection of activities available that cements their reputation. Despite the fact that the three activities listed above are clearly the dominant ones in Queenstown, it is part of the very character of the destination that there are a number of smaller scale adventure activities also on offer. These are no less important to the adventurous ethic of the town, since the presence of these pursuits is part of a symbiotic, two-way, catalytic process that operates between them and the larger operations. These include traditional activities such as hiking, climbing and mountain biking and the less so, such as river surfing, canyoning and fly-by-wire (the latter incorporates a two-stroke powered capsule suspended across a canyon that participants can 'fly' between the walls). Not all of these activities are permanent fixtures, and some may only survive for a season, but all of the larger activities were once small operations, and the nature of seeking the latest craze means that the market is always there.

Of course most of the activities we discuss in this example are commercial in nature, and may be termed 'quick-fix' in the adventure tourism spectrum. Queenstown offers a host of independent opportunities for adventure, which are also an important part of this spectrum. Many of these are popular with the adventure tourism company employees, who live and work in the region precisely because they can engage in such activities. However, the commercial pursuits are very much the public image of the destination, and responsible for the adventure capital branding.

## Cooperation and collaboration

Cooperation between different adventure operators is vital for a successful adventure destination. It is suggested that much of this is grassroots based, as many of those involved in managing and operating these activities will have similar interests. These social networks are vital to the development and promotion of existing and new activities. In Queenstown, for example, combination packages have become popular, involving a selection of a number of adventure activities, often completed in the space of a few hours. The pinnacle of these became the 'Awesome Foursome' combination of a helicopter ride, bungee jump, jetboat and rafting, for the adrenalin junkie seeking to cram as many activities into as short a time as possible in a 'cocktail of thrills' (Cloke and Perkins, 1998b, p. 280). Cooperation may also take place between direct competitors. For example, two of the rafting operators got together on realizing it was better to run full boats than half-full ones. As a result, in 1998 Challenge Rafting came to an agreement with Queenstown Rafting whereby the on-river trip was contracted out to the latter, meaning that the Challenge Rafting name is merely a booking route.

# The 'Adventure Capital of the World'

### Origin of the brand

As a result of this range of activity, Queenstown has established a reputation that cements this allegiance with adventure. It is also important to recognize that the town performs *as is expected of it*. Queenstown has clearly established itself as a premier adventure tourism resort, and the phasic nature of this reputation is clear, from the early grassroots development of commercial jetboating and rafting, to the more recent, but still notably home-grown, bungee jumping, all capitalizing on Queenstown's history as a place associated with frontier adventure.

However, to see this reputation as merely self-generating would be wrong, and ignores the importance of the adventure tourism companies' efforts to be recognized as such. Such advertising strategies clearly reinforce the reputation of Queenstown as a place where adventurous activity takes place. One also needs to recognize the manner in which

> such place meanings not only change the ways in which places are represented and experienced, they also influence the ways that those places are managed. Seen in this way, advertising isn't just simply a technique for attracting business; it is a medium through which places and experiences are made in order that particular interests are served and others downplayed.
>
> (Cloke and Perkins, 1998b, p. 271)

The circuit continues, for these interests then translate into particular senses of place, for whilst 'place is a negotiated reality, a social construction by a purposeful set of actors ... the relationship is mutual, for places in turn develop and reinforce the identity of the social group who claims them' (Ley, 1981, p. 215).

These tensions can be observed in the development of the influential 'Adventure Capital of the World' group of the leading Queenstown adventure tourism companies. Nick Flight, the marketing manager of Shotover Jet, gives an insight as to how the phrase was coined:

> Well we actually started that phrase, because we got a little bit worried, Queenstown promotion came up with promotion from other areas like the scenery and the free walks, the wineries, the passive adventure stuff, and we kind of perceived that that wasn't really why people were coming here so we said well, why don't we start up a group called the adventure capital of the world, we've got that, I mean you can go anywhere to a winery, we are famous for the adventure, focus on what we've got. Now we are working with Destination Queenstown and they've really got the adventure side, all the great visuals, and they can go out and show them to the journalists and that. I mean I think people come to New Zealand, especially Queenstown, for an adventure holiday.
>
> (personal communication, 1998)

However, the identity was not without contention, particularly from those tourism operators in Queenstown who felt that being labelled as adventurous would be detrimental to their image. This was of particular tension when the council decided to use the phrase as part of its letterhead slogan (Cooper, Queenstown Lakes District Council Mayor, personal communication, 1999). Irrespective of such conflicts, Queenstown has achieved a world-renowned status as an adrenalin capital, and is understood by many as a *place* for such activity. Thus New Zealand, and Queenstown in particular, have become world-renowned as a site of adventure tourism, and *the* destination for adventurous activity.

In addition, the availability of heavily branded souvenirs has served to strongly reinforce this reputation. It is interesting to see how, for the adventure tourism operators, souvenirs such as t-shirts are positioned just as much as a form of advertising, and therefore product reinforcement, as they are a business venture in themselves. For example, Queenstown Rafting's selection of a fern as their symbol has been reinforced by, and reinforces, the existence of the fern as a New Zealand icon, and has also resulted in a wide range of branded merchandise. Again this is as much for brand recognition as it is to generate profits. Over one-third of respondents who were asked confirmed that they intended to purchase some form of adventure merchandise. The sheer effectiveness of such branding processes in Queenstown is shown by a visitor's categorization of the resort, when asked about their main reason for visiting Queenstown, as based on 'Scenery, Adrenalin, Partying'. Furthermore, it is suggested that even those who do not actively perform the adventure experience do consume the entire concept of Queenstown as a place of adventure, as they still buy into the myth of adventure in both a literal and metaphorical sense. Many of the adventure activities are attractions in their own right, and it is not just the participants who purchase the merchandise discussed here.

## Après adventure

In addition, Queenstown does continue to espouse the ideals of adventure 24 h a day. Nowhere is this as self-evident as in the après-adventure establishments of the bars and nightclubs. Even the names seem to confirm an adventurous ethic, with markers such as 'The Edge', 'The World' and 'Surreal'. Although these are much smaller compared to the establishments that most participants may be used to at home, this is part of their attraction, and their importance in the circuit of adventure cannot be overlooked. By their very nature they become places to which triumphant adventurers retire, in order to celebrate the successful completion of an activity, and in some senses continue the adventure. However, the links run much deeper than this, because there are much more hypostatic links between these establishments and the adventure providers. In several of the nightclubs, television monitors show video segments of the various activities, and often footage of that day's participants, thereby the performance of the activities continues in a reiterative process.

There may be strong advertising, in the manner in which the dance floor of one club is emblazoned with the logo of the Pipeline bungee jump. Another nightclub, 'The World', has a central atrium, down which willing partygoers can perform a mini-bungee jump on a special night once a month, organized by the bungee companies. Many of the clubs have competitions or raffles during the course of an evening in order to win an adventure activity trip. For example, one club would offer a raffle prize of an adventure tourism activity to give away to the clientele each night, provided by the adventure tourism companies free of charge. This makes business sense for the companies, for not only does this provide free advertising, the odds are that the winner would bring along at least one paying customer in the form of a travel companion.

## New Zealand policy dimension

Queenstown's emergence as an adventure destination has also been assisted by a number of peculiar features in New Zealand legislation. Indeed, some industry sources suggest that a major factor in New Zealand's particularly fast uptake of commercial adventure opportunities may be the Accident and Rehabilitation Compensation Act, administered by the Accident Compensation Corporation (ACC). The Act provides complete medical cover for overseas tourists on a no-fault basis during their visit to New Zealand. Interestingly, in 1996, 44.3% of overseas claims to the ACC were for injuries resulting from recreation and sporting activity, of which adventure activities are clearly a major part (Page, 1997, p. 12). The ACC is clearly proactive in the pursuit of minimizing claims to itself, demonstrated by the fact that the development of the New Zealand codes of practice for bungee jumping, which evolved into a concrete legislated Standard (AS/NZS 5848), was sponsored by the ACC (Standards New Zealand, 1992).

Another piece of legislation that has been an important feature in the development of adventure tourism is the Resource Management Act (RMA). The Act's 'overt and emphatic intent is to promote the sustainable management of physical and natural resources' (Kearsley, 1997, p. 56). The Act brings together a range of disparate legislation covering pollution, land-use planning, water and soil management and heritage protection in a consolidated framework. It was an innovative piece of legislation, attempting to enshrine the concept of sustainability and define sustainable management (Cheyne and Ryan, 1996, p. 18).

The Act removed previous approaches to zoning activities, and instead looks at the effects of the activities themselves. Clearly there have been increased costs associated with the Act, which may be divided into compliance costs for meeting new standards and penalties for not meeting them; and transaction costs for consultations, submissions and environmental assessment (Cheyne and Ryan, 1996, p. 26). This has led to some fears that the RMA may have stifled investment in tourism development. However, as Kearsley points out, although 'many potential developers have been required to provide more detailed environmental impact reports than was previously the case, this is clearly in the long term interests of the industry' (Kearsley, 1997, p. 57).

## Adventure playgrounds

Within this framework it becomes apparent that Queenstown undoubtedly has established itself as a significant adventure tourism resort, not only within New Zealand, but also on the global scene. Although only a minority of visitors actually participate in adventure activities in the town, this in no way diminishes the fact that the adventurous ethic is still a dominant one in the place-myth. In addition, one cannot get past the fact that, in terms of visitors per year, over twice the resident population will go whitewater rafting, over five times will do a bungee jump and over ten times will go jetboating whilst in the town. The activities themselves have become more focused on maximizing the adventurous thrills, as shown by the story of rafting and jetboating. Why Queenstown has been so successful at establishing its reputation should be clear from the discussion above, but some distinct factors emerge.

The existence of an already established market and tourism infrastructure cannot be overlooked. The fact that tourists have progressively become more inter-national, and thus are more willing to part with significant amounts of money in order to *experience* Queenstown is paramount. However, this is not to say that the relationship is one-way, with adventure tourism merely creaming off the existing tourism product, as in itself it has the potential to boost tourism, especially in terms of length of stay. As Jim Boult, the managing director of Shotover Jet, states, 'the mountains, the lakes, the hiking, the biking and the adventure tourism is likely to attract overseas visitors for a week or two rather than just the two or three nights common now' (*Otago Daily Times*, 19 July 2000).

The New Zealand, and particularly the 'Southern', ethic has also been instrumental in adventure tourism's growth. Indigenous innovation and a can-do spirit have undoubtedly fostered the rapid introduction of adventure provision. The close networks between the various adventure providers have also meant that new activities are bred in an environment of appropriate knowledge and implementation. Undoubtedly the sector has 'grown up' since its inception, and adventure tourism is a considerably more sophisticated and safer product in 21st century Queenstown. However, it is clear that the value of being the first commercial operator in any new activity cannot be overlooked, as is shown by the continuing dominance of Shotover Jet and AJ Hackett in their respective pursuits.

Attempting to map this space of adventure is an interesting exercise, since it further clarifies the commodified nature of these practices in the resort (Figs 24.1 and 24.2). Although there is an acknowledgment that some travel is part of the feeling of entering 'into' an adventure, clearly tourists do not wish to travel for excessive periods, despite the beautiful scenery. As a result, most of the adventure activities radiate from Queenstown in a radius of no more than a few hours' drive. This hub and spoke effect is characteristic of many adventure destinations where the resort provides the support, booking and infrastructure, whilst the surrounding rural areas provide the playground. This *playground* metaphor seems to confirm the ideals of these spaces and their locales. The author was struck by the poignancy of this phrase when observing

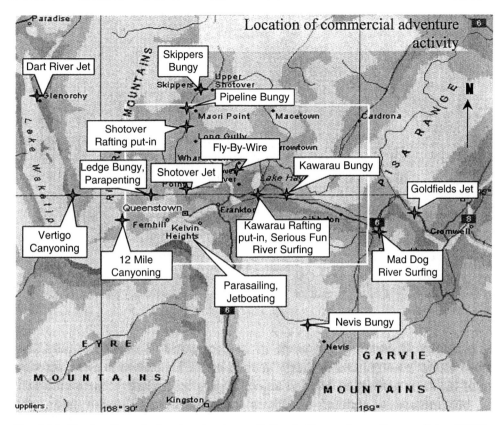

**Fig. 24.1.** The location of adventure tourism activities in Queenstown. Source: Cater (2001).

rafts emerge from the tunnel at the end of the Shotover River as a jetboat performed a 360 degree spin in the melee, or whilst joining a river surfing trip on the Kawarau River, being passed by more rafts whilst a helicopter buzzed low overhead. The cries of delight of playful bodies being thrilled in a distinct spatial environment reminded one powerfully of the sounds of a school playground at lunchtime.

Of course the metaphor has further links if we consider attributes of the *'adventure* playground' of significance in many childhood experiences. These were places of play, enhanced by the environment of swings, death slides, rope bridges and monkey bars. In addition, these places were notionally *safe* places to play, being bounded, and often supervised, and with plenty of woodchips to prevent injury from falls. It should be clear from the discussion that many of these attributes can just as easily be applied to adventure tourism in Queenstown, and indeed this is an attribute further used in the marketing of the destination:

> Welcome to the world's adventure playground for grown-ups. Jetboating, bungee jumping, skiing, white water rafting, parapenting – you can try all of these and more in one place.
>
> (*Holiday Planner*, 1998/99, p. 46)

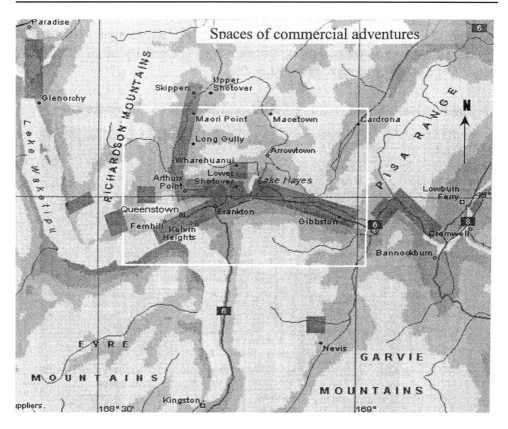

**Fig. 24.2.** The restricted space of Queenstown's adventure playground. Source: Cater (2001).

## Mimicry

However, Queenstown is certainly not alone in its promotion of adventure pursuits. Many long-established tourist resorts have similarly latched on to the growth in these activities, and exhibit some of the same processes detailed above. Examples include those mentioned in the Introduction, but include a number of others such as Bend, Oregon and Interlaken, Switzerland. A number of other destinations have attempted to grow their product offerings through learning from Queenstown experience directly. In New Zealand certainly, it is likely that Queenstown's pre-eminence for adventure tourism has altered the character of many rural locations. Many have, understandably, tried to copy the success of Queenstown by establishing their own adventure activities. This may be direct emulation as in Wanaka, a similar resort the other side of the mountain chain to Queenstown, or the promotion of more indigenous forms, like those based in the caves around Waitomo in North Island. It is undeniable, however, that these developments have had considerable impacts in the place-nature of these settlements. The example has been used elsewhere of Hamner Springs, a thermal resort close to Christchurch. The singular presence of an old bridge and a deeply incised river led to the commercial development of bungee jump, jetboating, rafting and helicopter operations, and the rebranding of the site as 'Thrillseekers Canyon' (Cloke and Perkins, 1998b, p. 282).

Thus the identity and meaning of place is completely altered by the commodification of adventure.

This mimicry has not been limited to New Zealand, as a delegation from Voss, a popular mountain resort in Norway, visited Queenstown for this purpose in 1999. The characteristics of the two destinations are remarkably similar, both sharing a lakeside alpine setting. They have long-established ski industries, a similar population size and a community of outdoor sports enthusiasts. Voss has pursued this niche further in the development of an extreme sports week, which had its sixth year in 2003. Originally a grassroots adventure competition for the large number of outdoor enthusiasts who live or spend a significant amount of time in the Norwegian mountains, the event has become progressively bigger since its early incarnations. Sports showcased in this 'alternative' Olympics included skydiving and paragliding, rafting and kayaking, climbing and downhill mountain biking, and the infamous BASE jumping. In 2001, Nike's All Conditions Gear® brand was brought in to sponsor the event, ensuring global coverage and exposure. In 2003 the event attracted approximately 1000 competitors, 3000 spectators and employed over 300 staff. Such events are increasingly recognized as important in creating a name and place for a destination like Voss.

## Dangerous Places

There is, however, a danger in destinations relying excessively on the adventure tourism product. Despite increasingly active measures to ensure the safety of adventure activities worldwide, accidents in the industry do occur. Some would argue that the very nature of the thrill pursuits is that real physical risk is a vital part of the activity. However, the responsibility of the commercial operator is to minimize the opportunity for loss, to as low a level as possible. For example, McLauchlan (1995) suggests that, since rafting operations began in Queenstown in 1974, approximately one fatality a year has occurred. The highest profile of these were a spate of whitewater rafting deaths in the mid-1990s. Five deaths in an 18-month period sharply focused attention on safety standards in the industry.

The booming adventure industry, and the popularity of rafting, with the relatively low capital costs for entry, meant that by the early 1990s there were over five companies operating on one stretch of river. An article in *Mountain Scene* (Queenstown's free weekly newspaper) in early 1994 highlighted the dangerously narrow safety margins that were becoming the norm in Queenstown rafting operations. Originally accused of scaremongering, the paper was vindicated when, barely 10 days after the report, an Australian tourist drowned when the raft he was in flipped. Later that year a British tourist also drowned when the raft capsized on a trip with Kawarau Rafts. In the following season two further deaths occurred with Danes Rafting, both again drowning in the turbulent currents of the Shotover. In the accident reports for all of these deaths, the overriding factor is clearly human error, with conclusions such as 'negligence', 'trip should not have taken place', 'pressure on guides due to late start' and 'failure to fully explain the trip and what happens when a problem arises' being suggested (Page, 1997, p. 49).

The economic effect of the fatalities was considerable and it is estimated that the rafting market fell dramatically from about 500 a day to less than 50, and led to an estimated drop in tourism expenditure in Queenstown from NZD5 million to NZD2 million (Page, 1997, p. 27). Criminal proceedings were undertaken in respect of the death of the British tourist, Sean Farrell, who died in November 1994. Whilst other companies cancelled trips due to warnings of heavy rain and snow melt, a Kawarau Rafts trip went ahead with two boats. In the event, both the trip leader and the director of the company were collectively charged and convicted with 24 counts of negligently or recklessly operating a vessel to the peril of passengers under section 290 of the Shipping and Seamen Act 1952 (McLauchlan, 1995, p. 74).

In addition to legal proceedings the deaths prompted a comprehensive review of whitewater rafting standards by the Maritime Safety Authority (MSA). Despite the MSA's report, including a rather peculiar method of cost-benefit analysis of 'saving lives' of participants (MSA, 1995), it also highlighted the numerous errors in judgement, and firmly placed the blame at the door of the rafting companies:

> Personnel in the industry are predominantly young men with a desire for excitement and adventure. Many are quite immature and live life 'on the edge'. This severely affects safety judgements and assessment of client capability. There is a significant difference between the guides' perceptions of an exciting trip; the guides' perceptions of client expectations; and the actual clients' concept and expectations of the trip. This leads to guides running trips for their own entertainment without due regard for the need of their clients.
>
> (cited in Morgan, 1998, p. 4)

The effect of an accident in the adventure industry is likely to go beyond the activity concerned, as shown by a drop in participants at Shotover Jet after the rafting deaths. Again the influence of the media circles is highlighted, as tourists assimilating the news of a death on the Shotover would often associate this with the jetboat (Brown, 1997, p. 136). However, Shotover Jet is not unfamiliar with the possibility of fatalities in their activity, as was demonstrated in late 1999 when a Japanese honeymooner was killed after the boat he was travelling in collided with the canyon wall. Although the Marine Safety Authority concluded that mechanical failures caused the crash, the report took pains to point out that the driver had been involved in previous incidents in the gorge. In addition, it was stated that the boat was 'operating closer to the canyon wall than necessary to achieve an appropriate level of thrill for the passengers', and that, had the boat been travelling with a wider clearance than half a metre from the wall, the consequences of the impact may not have been as severe (*Otago Daily Times*, 3 November 2000).

It has been suggested that the principal problem with adventure tourism accidents is the lack of any coherent central framework for their reporting and prevention. As Page (1997, p. 34) emphasizes, there is a considerable lack of data and knowledge about accidents in adventure tourism, and what little there is tends to be 'fragmented, scattered across a range of sources and not available in a manner that permits a systematic assessment of the issue', making comparison with other tourist activities very difficult. Instead, conflicting statistics emerge, such as overseas tourist fatality rates being below 1 per 100,000 in terms of adventure tourism, suggested in *Mountain Scene* (Page, 1997) or the 8 per 100,000 suggested in the *Otago Daily Times* (18 November 1999). 'Despite these reassurances, more accidents occur in the adventure tourism industry than people are led to believe' (Brown, 1997).

What is more difficult to gauge is the number of minor accidents that occur in adventure tourism. Most reporting comes in the form of media interest, particularly the stance that *Mountain Scene* has taken against poor standards in the industry. In 1999 the paper reported on an accident that occurred during a Dart River Jet trip, when a boat was unable to navigate shallow water and flipped over, pinning several people underneath (*Otago Mirror*, 24 February 1999, p. 22). The report into the accident once again highlighted that driver error was the cause of the incident. However, the media is not a reliable source of accident information, as sifting through articles one gets a very blurred picture of the accident rate. To take the example of the month of the Japanese death at Shotover Jet, despite papers confirming that it was Shotover Jet's first fatality, there is no clear picture of other adventure accidents. The *Otago Daily Times* reports that three Queenstown rafting boats flipped on the Kawarau River the previous Friday (*The Press*, 13 November 1999). Meanwhile *The Press* highlights that 'the MSA is still investigating an accident in which a Shotover Jetboat hit a rock and a passenger suffered a fractured wrist' (*The Press*, 13 November 1999). This not only emphasizes the lack of clear data concerning adventure tourism accidents, but also confirms that they are actually relatively common.

So far, however, Queenstown has managed to avoid the sort of mass tragedies that have plagued European adventure tourism destinations in recent years. Four British tourists drowned during a whitewater rafting trip in Austria in June 1999 (*The Times*, 8 June 1999). The high public profile of such a catastrophe was shown when the BBC cancelled the screening of the Meryl Streep film *The River Wild* the following weekend. Barely a month later 21 people were killed whilst canyoning in Interlaken in Switzerland. A torrential flash flood swept down the valley, wiping out almost half of those on the trip. On recovering the bodies, rescue teams noted that many of the participants 'had lost their protective helmets and rubber boots' (*Glasgow Press and Journal*, 31 July 1999). The company running the trip, Adventure World, was severely criticized for ignoring storm warnings on the day of the trip (*The Guardian*, 28 July 1999). The safety procedures of Adventure World were further called into question by the death of an American bungee jumper in May the following year, when the bungee failed to slow his descent and he went head-first into a car park (*The Times*, 15 May 2000).

Clearly then, there is an underlying problem with commercial adventure activities, in that participation does involve the handing over of a significant part of the responsibility to the adventure provider in question. If these providers are not regulated, there is a danger that places of adventure will become synonymous with injury and even fatalities. From a destination marketing perspective it is vital that the best possible frameworks are in place to ensure that the certificates and training are truly up to the required standard for the elimination of foreseeable risk. In addition, it is important that participants have a way of assessing the actual risk that they are placing themselves in, and this calls for greater transparency in the industry. It is notable that the Royal Geographical Society (2000) has recently drawn up a code of conduct for adventure tourism operators. Such codes should contribute to a safer operational standard that is clearly in the interests of all involved.

## Places to Play

The emergence of destinations with a strong reputation for a spectrum of adventure tourism activities practised in a safe regulatory environment has thus created a number of globally recognized adventure playgrounds. Queenstown may position itself as the premier adventure destination, but many of the characteristics of adventure tourism seen here may be observed in a number of other destinations. An accessible natural environment, a history of tourism, and existing facilities and infra-structure, often based on the ski industry, have all promoted an adventurous ethic in these locales. This is often commodified to form what we acknowledge as the adventure tourism industry. However, it is important to stress that it is the social organization of these places that is as powerful in establishing their adventurous credentials as these physical characteristics. A large number of outdoor enthusiasts, cooperative destination marketing and an active après adventure scene are all important in this process. This echoes Lash and Urry's (1994) contention that it is important not to succumb to 'technological determinism', which sees 'travel as derived demand'. Instead *organizational* innovations should be emphasized as key to the success of technological advances and, hence, the social organization of travel as part of a wider 'social organization of the experience of modernity' is paramount. The example of the charitable inception of Shotover Jet, which has been instrumental in Queenstown's adventure branding, is a clear example of the importance of social actors in this process.

Furthermore, it should be clear that not everywhere can be the 'adventure capital of the world'. A consideration of the activities contained within these pages must acknowledge a burgeoning number of practices, and places in which to engage in them. As Sheller and Urry (2004) suggest, 'a global stage is emerging, bringing up the curtain on new places and experiences for play'. The most successful adventure destinations, therefore, will be those that blend adventure activities with a host of more traditional tourism pursuits. As suggested above, the vast majority of 'adventure tourists' are at the softer end, and appreciate a selection of other tourism 'hats' for their holiday experience. It is notable, for example, that Australia's Gold Coast is developing a destination adventure travel network to promote adventure activities, whist capitalizing on the existing tourism infrastructure (Gold Coast Adventure Travel Group, 2005). The popularity of adventure activities as a destination branding tool will therefore continue, although it is suggested that it may become subsumed within a broader tourist desire for experience. Places that provide such playful interaction will ultimately be the most successful.

# 25 Cross-case Analyses

Mt Kenya (see Chapter 16). Photo Ralf Buckley.

Torres del Paine, Patagonia (see Chapter 17). Photo Ride World Wide.

# Introduction

With 15 different activities, and 15 different parameters for each, including the four different measures summarized under the heading of statistics, the case studies in this volume provide a potential opportunity for over 200 different cross-case comparisons. To consider each of these in turn, however, would be rather repetitive. Accordingly, in this chapter I have selected only four such comparisons, and have endeavoured to set them briefly in the context of previous parks, recreation and tourism literature, where available and relevant, to illustrate the relation between commercial adventure tour products and individual outdoor recreation.

The information to make many more such cross-case comparisons is contained in the various case studies presented in this volume. Indeed, as university courses in adventure tourism gradually supersede or supplement those in outdoor recreation and education, this book may perhaps provide the opportunity to use such comparisons as student exercises.

For cross-case analyses to be useful, a reasonably robust and representative set of cases is a basic prerequisite. For many of the adventure tourism activities considered here, however, only a relatively small number of case studies are considered, with no guarantee that these particular products presented are typical for the sector. The features chosen for cross-case analysis in this chapter, therefore, are those that apply (i) across several related activities so as to increase sample size, and (ii) where cases are available from a reasonable selection of the main geographic areas where commercial adventure tours featuring that activity are offered.

There are other possible comparisons that do also satisfy these criteria, but where products offered by different operators are so similar, at least in regard to these specific attributes concerned, that there is essentially an industry standard. This may apply, for example, to safety procedures used by heliski operators as outlined below.

# Safety Procedures for Heliskiing and Heliboarding

Heliskiing and boarding is all in backcountry terrain with no avalanche control, and safety depends on the guides' abilities to select runs that are suitably challenging for their clients but with low risk of avalanche, and the clients' abilities to follow the guides closely down these lines. In some operating areas, the terrain is steep and heavily treed, requiring a significant degree of skill from the clients. Indeed, for some of their operating areas, some companies will only accept clients who have been pre-qualified by first visiting one of the company's less demanding areas.

In the Canadian, New Zealand and Himalayan heliski operations, the helicopter lands at the top of each run, and skis are unloaded from a cargo basket by the guide whilst the clients get out of the machine. For at least some heliski operations in Russia, apparently, clients jump from the hovering helicopter on to the snow at the top of each run, adding a further risk factor.

The principal safety concern for heliski operations worldwide, however, is avalanches. As with any form of backcountry skiing, heliskiing involves a greater avalanche risk than skiing within resort areas where potential avalanche slopes are pre-triggered with explosives. Commercial heliski operations routinely supply all clients with avalanche transceivers, and train and re-train both new and repeat clients in avalanche search techniques. Commonly, one client in each helicopter group, as well as the guide(s), carries a snow shovel, avalanche probe and radio.

Some operators carry safety precautions even further. Himachal Helicopter Skiing (2005) in the Indian Himalayas issues every skier with an avalanche airbag carried in a small backpack. These are designed to help keep the wearer on the surface of an avalanche flow. Each skier and boarder at HHS also carries a small individually coded radio beacon so that they can be located rapidly using a helicopter-based receiver, in addition to ground search.

By far the most important safety factor for all heliskiing and boarding, however, is the skill of the guides in keeping clients away from danger areas. Despite all these precautions, heliskiers are occasionally caught in avalanches or tree wells, and helicopters do occasionally crash. Few of these incidents, fortunately, are fatal, but heliskiers and heliboarders certainly need to remain alert to these risks at all times.

An even greater level of skill is required to maintain safety in new or exploratory heliski operations, where there is no permanent base or associated pool of guide knowledge and where the terrain, snow conditions and weather are less well-known. In the last one or two years, for example, several small operators have begun offering charter heliski tours in Greenland. These are staffed by guides from established heliski operations elsewhere in the world, and rely largely on those operations for their clientele. If these prove commercially successful, they may well lead to the establishment of routine heliski operations in the areas concerned.

The heliski operators audited for this book all follow effectively the same safety procedures and use essentially the same equipment. The main differences in procedures are in client-to-guide ratios, and in whether the guides ski in front of the clients or behind. These factors also depend heavily, however, on terrain and helicopter type. If the most critical safety issue is threading a route through cliffs obscured by dense trees, it is safest for the guide to ski or ride in front so the clients can follow. If the main safety concern is the risk of high-speed falls on steep terrain, as may be the case in some of the Alaskan operations that were not audited here, it may be safer for the guide to ski behind and above, so as to be able to render assistance as quickly as possible. Where it is critical for the guide to evaluate slope stability in avalanche-prone areas, the guide needs to go first. Where there are simultaneous risks from route-finding, slope stability, tree wells and cliffs, the safest options is to have one guide at the front and one at the rear of each group of clients. This procedure is indeed followed by Mike Wiegele Helicopter Skiing. Other operators in the same general area use only one guide, but equip one of the clients to ride at the rear and act as a kind of guide's assistant.

Whilst the various Canadian and New Zealand heliski operators considered have slightly different guiding practices, as outlined above, they all issue standard Ortovox® or similar avalanche transceivers, and teach clients essentially the same searching techniques. There are some differences in the search techniques taught, and in the thoroughness of client training and testing. Mike Wiegele Helicopter Skiing (2005) was particularly thorough. The Canadian operators offer Avalungs® for sale, but do not supply them routinely.

Only Himachal Helicopter Skiing in the Indian Himalayas routinely issues all its heliski clients with avalanche float bags, of their own design. Himachal also supplements the standard transceivers with miniature radio beacons that can be pinpointed from a helicopter overhead, as described in the relevant case study. These innovations were developed by the owner of HHS and may have limited availability at present, but will perhaps be adopted more widely as their reputation spreads, particularly if they prove critical in an avalanche rescue.

## Environmental Management for Rafting and River Journeys

Many commercial whitewater rafting and kayaking tours, particularly the longer ones, travel through national parks and other areas of high conservation value. Typically, there are relatively few convenient campsites, and as a result these are heavily used. The availability and attractiveness of these sites is a significant limiting factor for commercial operations, and the impacts of waste disposal, washing detergents, etc. on water quality are a significant issue for land managers in determining how many commercial permits to issue, and to which operators.

Impacts at campsites and on water quality are highly dependent on specific environmental management practices by the operators, including techniques and equipment for waste disposal, and training and supervision of clients. The Australian, NZ and US trips described in this volume are run under very different conditions from those in Africa, Asia and South America. The former are all in national parks or other publicly owned reserves and are subject to regulation. In addition, most are subject to heavy commercial use and have facilities for treatment of human wastes, accessible from the take-out point. Most of the areas concerned are already reserved for conservation, and the principal human pressures are from the tourism sector itself. The exceptions are the Tully, subject to hydroelectric development, and the Nymboida, which is in a former State Forest subject to past logging.

In general there is a high standard of environmental performance for all the case studies reported here. The main environmental management issues are: disposal of human wastes; cooking and cleaning; litter; and trampling and erosion at campsites. World Expeditions and Expeditions Inc. carry portable toilets for faecal material. World Expeditions, which operates on low-volume oligotrophic rivers in high-rainfall areas, advises clients to urinate away from the water. Expeditions Inc., which operates on a high-volume high-turbidity river in a low-rainfall area, advises clients to urinate directly into the water. On the basis of currently available scientific data, each of these is the lowest-impact option available in the circumstances.

All of these operators use fuel stoves rather than fires for cooking, although some light occasional low-impact fires in areas where this is permitted by land management agencies. None allow soap or detergents to be used for washing directly in rivers, but only some distance back from the riverbank. Most screen or filter used washing-up water and pack out solid residues with other trash. All are scrupulous in checking campsites before departure to ensure all litter is packed out; though as with individual travellers and land-based ecotour operators, some microlitter typically escapes such searches. Similarly, all train their clients in minimal-impact camping techniques to reduce trampling and erosion.

Rafting tours in Chile, China, Nepal, Tibet, Zimbabwe and Uganda, in contrast, operate in areas with substantial local populations and extensive agricultural, pastoral and fisheries industries. Tourism provides an alternative to other commercial activities. The rivers in Chile and China, and perhaps also Uganda, are under immediate threat from hydroelectric power developments.

For Expediciones Chile, human wastes are generally disposed of in a deep-drop toilet at the basecamp. Cooking, cleaning and trash collection are likewise centralized. Earth Science Expeditions and Shangri-La River Expeditions use land-based catholes for human waste disposal in China, even though the rivers concerned are relatively large and already suffer from agricultural and industrial pollution. David

Allardice's company in Nepal used temporary pit toilets at campsites and Ultimate Descents New Zealand uses individual catholes. These are reasonable options in view of river volume, annual floods, surrounding land use and current intensity of tourist use. The pits used by Ultimate Descents in Nepal were dug by clients and were too small and shallow. Since the river beaches are completely remobilized by monsoon floods each year, however, and the rivers already contain human and animal wastes from agricultural settlement, this is principally of aesthetic rather than fundamental ecological concern.

These operators use fires as well as stoves for cooking and heating. As with the US and Australian operations, these operators also take out all trash and use minimal-impact camping techniques. Their owners and principal operators all had extensive previous experience in the developed nations, some over several decades, so their individual skills and knowledge are at least as extensive as those of current US and Australian operators. This does not necessarily apply to other operators in those areas.

Though I did not set out to study environmental education programmes or contributions to conservation, some information on these aspects was also available. NOLS is the only one of the operators listed to incorporate a formal education programme in its curriculum; and indeed, NOLS very definitely considers itself as an outdoor education organization, not an adventure or ecotour operator. All of the other operators were well-informed about environmental management issues, particularly those affecting the areas where they are based, and guides discussed these issues with clients. Some also possessed a degree of knowledge about the geology, flora and fauna of the area. Not surprisingly, this was most evident for guides who had run the same trip in the same place many times over many years. It also varies considerably depending on the interests of individual guides running the same trips for the same company, as in World Expeditions or Expeditions Inc.

Many of the operators audited also contributed to conservation in one way or another, though none made direct financial contributions other than mandatory park entrance and licence fees. Most increase the environmental awareness of their clients, with a corresponding potential influence on their future lifestyles. Most increase their clients' awareness of particular threats to the natural environment in the areas traversed. Expediciones Chile and World Expeditions endeavour to enlist clients' support in current lobbying efforts. Many of the others provide local employment and equity opportunities in a low-impact industry, reducing impacts from other sectors.

Results reported above reflect practices by industry leaders. Overall, commercial raft and kayak adventure tour operators differ enormously in their environmental management practices. Many follow some or all relevant minimal-impact or leave-no-trace guidelines for wilderness travel and camping, but some do not. Performance tends to be better in national parks, in developed countries and for longer multi-day trips.

Environmental management performance also depends on the principal clientele for the particular tour concerned, and on the structure of the rafting industry. Typically this contains three tiers. Retail marketing is carried out by large and often international adventure travel companies, which are big enough to establish well-known brand names and to support marketing campaigns and office staff. Some of these companies also own equipment and run tours directly, but more commonly the logistics are handled by smaller localized specialist companies that own equipment and obtain many of their clients through the larger retail travel companies. This balance differs for some particular destinations, where the on-ground operators are known directly. The ability of small operators to advertise through the World-wide Web has also changed purchasing patterns. Irrespective of these, however, individual trips are actually led by individual guides, who are generally employed on a trip-by-trip or sometimes a season basis by the on-ground logistics operators.

Broadly, it appears that best-practice environmental management is only achieved if all three tiers are involved, i.e. where: the retail operators refer to minimal-impact practices in their marketing materials, generally because they perceive this as an aspect of their market niche; the on-ground operators provide appropriate equipment, typically because this is prescribed by land managers or a local industry agreement; and the guides practise and teach minimal-impact behaviours, generally because of their own personal convictions.

The overall outcome is highly significant to the tourism industry. Best-practice environmental management in the whitewater rafting industry is low cost and easy to implement, but it can increase the allowable maximum volume of commercial tourism by an order of magnitude or more.

## Safety Considerations for Hiking and Wildlife Watching

Watching large wild animals in their own native habitats at close range, as is commonly the aim of wildlife adventure tours, can involve potential dangers from the animals themselves. The same applies for hiking or other human-powered activities in areas inhabited by large and potentially threatening wildlife species, herbivores as well as carnivores. Thus, for example, a person on foot in bear, buffalo or big-cat habitat is potentially at risk, whether or not the main aim of their visit is to look for the animals concerned. The same applies for many other species, in the water as well as on land.

In most areas where large and potentially dangerous wildlife occur, safety procedures and wildlife-watching opportunities for commercial tour clients in private reserves are different from those prescribed for commercial tours operating under permit in public protected areas, which are commonly different again from procedures prescribed for private individual visitors to the same public protected areas. In the private game reserves of eastern and southern Africa, for example, such as those operated by Conservation Corporation Africa, clients watch wildlife from open-topped 4WD safari vehicles at night as well as by day, and often approach individual animals quite closely. In nearby national parks, in contrast, visitors must travel in fully enclosed vehicles where windows and roof hatches can be closed rapidly if required.

The reason for this difference is that the safari vehicles in private game reserves are driven by highly skilled and experienced guides who can interpret the behaviour of individual animals accurately and reliably. Indeed, in many cases they recognize the individual animals concerned, and have learned their temperaments and idiosyncrasies by observing them over several years and discussing them with other guides and trackers. These skills allow the guides to judge how closely a vehicle can approach an animal without disrupting the animal's normal behaviour or risking an attack. Commonly, these animals are habituated to daily visits by safari vehicles and have learned to ignore them, or even to take advantage of them either for shade or stalking cover.

In a similar way, visitors to national parks in eastern and southern Africa are not generally permitted to travel on foot except with a specific permit and purpose. Such permits may be granted to wildlife researchers, for example, who are expected to understand the niceties of animal behaviour and to follow appropriate safety procedures. In the private game reserves, in contrast, commercial tour clients are indeed permitted to walk on foot, accompanied by an armed guide. Again, the difference is due to the guide, who can track, locate and identify animals that would be hidden from unskilled tour clients; interpret the animals' behaviour; advise clients how to respond; and as a last and very rarely used resort, stop a charging animal with a well-aimed close-range rifle shot. Ideally, this should never be necessary. When a safari guide shot a rhinoceros to protect his clients a few years ago, it was debated widely whether the guide could have avoided the situation.

Park rangers who lead tourists to watch mountain gorillas in Uganda are unarmed. Hikers in Denali National Park, Alaska, are allowed to hike and camp in grizzly bear country, but only after they can answer a series of safety questions correctly. Hikers in Glacier National Park, Montana, USA, known for a high frequency of bear attacks, are encouraged to hike only in groups, but are permitted to hike alone as long as they carry a chilli-oil bear-repellent spray. Visitors to Svalbard are permitted to hike outside town only if they carry a high-calibre firearm. In many countries, however, firearms are not permitted in parks, and capsicum sprays are illegal.

There are significant distinctions between animal species with a history of attacking humans as prey, such as crocodile or polar bear; those that could do so but commonly don't, such as other bears and most big cats; herbivores that do quite often attack humans, such as hippopotamus and buffalo; and herbivores that might attack, but generally only if humans approach too closely, such as rhinoceros, moose, elk, deer or antelope.

Similar safety considerations apply in watching marine wildlife. Different species of sharks, for example, can behave very differently if encountered by divers. An experienced dive instructor who is familiar with a local dive site will be able to distinguish an inoffensive species, such as ragged-tooth or grey nurse sharks, from potentially aggressive species, and to tell from an individual shark's behaviour whether it is likely to attack or is merely inquisitive. Similarly, whilst it is considered safe to swim with seals playing in underwater caverns in the Galapagos Islands, it would be considered quite risky to swim with seals in the cold kelp forests of north-west America, where the dominant males might be quite likely to attack.

In all these cases, a detailed behavioural understanding of the particular species or even individual animals concerned is critical to safe interactions at close range, whether deliberate or incidental. The expertise of an experienced tour guide is essential in providing detailed local knowledge; in teaching tour participants how to behave so as to maximize safety; and in managing the behaviour of the group as a whole so as to minimize risks. By taking part in a commercial tour with appropriate equipment, local knowledge and skilled guides, a client can safely take part in a close-range wildlife-watching experience that they would not be able to carry out safely on their own. This, of course, is precisely the role of tour operators in other adventure tourism activities, and justifies the treatment of these particular wildlife-watching tours as a form of adventure tourism.

In each of the wildlife-watching adventure tours described in Chapter 20, clients come within close range of the animals observed and would potentially be at risk were it not for safety measures adopted. In one case, namely the polar bear watching tour run by Natural Habitat Adventures in Canada's Hudson Bay, the bears are considered to offer such a threat that clients and guides are protected by physical barriers such as a lodge or tundra buggy whenever bears are in sight. Since the bears are hungry enough to eat dog food or dishwater, and do test these barriers repeatedly, this precaution does indeed seem to be essential. Individual bears occasionally walk through the streets of Churchill itself, apparently without attacking people, but the risk is still high. There are two occasions on this tour when clients are permitted to travel briefly on foot, but only once the guides have assured themselves that there are no bears in the vicinity: a short walk from the lodge in the mother-and-cubs area, and a short walk from the helicopter to examine abandoned dens.

The Aurora expedition cruise and seakyak trip around Spitzbergen, described in the respective chapters in this book, also include polar bear sightings. Most of these are from the expedition vessel or from kayaks or inflatables, with the bears on land some distance away. The trip does also involve numerous landings and walks across tundra terrain, however, in areas where bears could be present. Each of these walks were accompanied by at least two armed guides. Depending on terrain and visibility, clients were generally kept in a reasonably tight group, with the guides continually moving ahead to check the periphery. On this particular trip we only encountered one bear on foot at close range. The encounter involved a guide rather than clients, and both he and the bear, a young male, backed off startled. Clients were later able to watch the same bear from the safety of the boats.

In watching Russian brown bears in Kamchatka on the tour operated by Explore Kamchatka, clients walked a few hundred metres from the lodge to the bear-viewing tower, accompanied by an unarmed guide and an armed ranger. In practice, no bears were sighted on these occasions. On the one occasion when we did see bears on foot at close range, during a walk at another area some distance from the lodge, there was no such protection, but the bears were cubs and ran away.

It is worth noting that independent visitors hiking in a number of North American national parks may encounter both black and grizzly bear quite commonly. In Yellowstone National Park in 1974, for example, I found a group of tourists standing on the roadside to photograph a large adult male grizzly bear that was trying to lift a log. A rather stressed-looking ranger was trying to persuade the people to get back in their cars, but since he was facing away from them in order to keep the bear in his rifle sights, they paid no attention. I also saw a bikie engaged in a very close-range altercation with a young black bear which was attempting to break into his panniers. The bikie won.

As these anecdotes illustrate, even where park management agencies have regulations and education programmes for appropriate behaviour in the presence of bears, visitors do not necessary follow them. Attacks are rare, and commonly seem to involve solo backcountry hikers who have failed to follow safe protocol for storing food at least 100 m from their tents.

The commercial bear-watching tours described here did not involve backcountry camping, but they do involve bears that are potentially more dangerous than those in most North American national parks, because of the bear species concerned, because the bears are extra hungry or because they are hunted by poachers. Accordingly, the safety measures outlined above are a critical part of the tours concerned, and allow clients to venture into bear territory in ways that they would be foolish to do on their own.

Likewise, tiger-watching in Bardia National Park simply would not be feasible for an independent traveller on foot. One could, perhaps, walk safely through the open forest areas, and no doubt local villagers do so routinely. The areas frequented by tigers, however, seem to be the very dense thickets and tall coarse grasses alongside the swamps and river channels. In these areas it would be difficult for a person on foot to navigate, to see more than a few metres at most, or indeed to make much forward progress. Any encounter with a tiger would be at the tiger's choice, and at very close range. The elephant-back tour overcomes all of these problems, with the elephant providing safe transport through all types of terrain and vegetation and a good view over the tall grass. It is also the elephants, the mahouts and the trackers who find the tigers, predict their movements and position the clients to see them safely. Even so, most sightings are relatively brief.

Lion and leopard sightings in the private conservation reserves of east and southern Africa, in contrast, such as those operated by Conservation Corporation Africa, can be quite extended. Clients commonly get the chance to watch these species by night as well as by day, continuing unconcernedly with their routine daily activities, whether feeding, breeding or simply resting. Some of these encounters are at very close range, with guides and clients sitting motionless in open-topped safari vehicles, and the big cats crunching on their kill only metres away.

During visits to various reserves run by Conservation Corporation Africa, for example, I have found myself parked beneath tree limbs with leopard lying overhead, or face-to-face with a large male lion strolling by within touching distance at night. I have also watched leopards mating, and a lioness suckling very young cubs, close enough that they were well aware of our presence and might have shown us off unceremoniously if they had not had other priorities at the time.

In each of these cases, and many more, there were three critical factors contributing to client safety. First, clients and guides were in a vehicle: an open-topped vehicle, but a vehicle none the less. Indeed, when approaching close to lions or leopards in particular, the tracker who normally sits on a jump seat on the bonnet of each safari vehicle so as to get a clear view of spoor, will move back into the body of the vehicle so as to not expose any recognizable full-body human profile.

Secondly, the particular animals concerned have been habituated to human presence over a number of years, and have come to consider a carefully driven safari vehicle as a neutral object, neither a threat nor an opportunity. Thirdly and most importantly, the Conservation Corporation Africa guides have all undergone training, served an apprenticeship and accrued many years' experience in interpreting animal behaviour, in driving a safari vehicle quietly and slowly, and in keeping clients still and quiet when necessary.

These factors apply equally when watching other potentially dangerous wildlife in these private game reserves. These include buffalo, rhino and elephant; hippopotamus and crocodile; and smaller but potentially aggressive species such as baboons, snakes and perhaps honey badgers. In Lake Manyara National Park, for example, an elephant walked past a CCAfrica safari vehicle in which I was sitting, within touching distance, trunk swinging gently. We sat quietly and it gave us merely a glimpse from an attentive eye, unhurried and unworried.

Things were rather less tranquil when a baboon tried to make off with our food from a national park's picnic ground on the access road, a publicly accessible area where resident baboons have perhaps become used to stealing or begging food. On that occasion, there was a fair amount of mutual snarling, gesticulation and a minor punch-up before the baboon retreated, having first hurled most of our food into the dirt. Such cases, which can occur with many animal species worldwide, illustrate the risk of habituating wildlife to inappropriate behaviour, whether intentionally or inadvertently (Buckley, 2004a; Newsome *et al.*, 2005).

At some of CCAfrica's Northern Circuit lodges in Tanzania, and indeed in many private game reserves and concessions in east and southern Africa, guests also have the opportunity to watch wildlife on foot as part of a guided walk. Such walks are commonly carried out in the heat of the day, typically in late morning or early afternoon, when wildlife are likely to be least active. They focus on tracks, plants and the smaller wildlife species, but must still be alert to potential risks from larger animals. They are accompanied by an armed guide. In most cases the animals encountered are inoffensive, such as dikdik and other small antelope. Occasionally, however, one may encounter a potentially dangerous animal such as solitary male buffalo, calling for a degree of caution in backing away unobtrusively.

Wildlife safety issues can also arise in boat and river trips. There are hippo and crocodile on the Nile and Zambezi, for example; caiman in the Amazon; and estuarine crocodiles in the lower reaches of the Drysdale River in Australia. As with encounters involving purely terrestrial wildlife, in such circumstances a knowledgeable guide is invaluable.

## Marketing and Magazines in Surfing and Snowboarding

There are estimated to be about 10 million surfers worldwide, though not all of these are active (Buckley, 2002a). Most of them are young recreational surfers, and surfing is a very high priority for their disposable income and leisure time. A significant proportion is older, with established careers and families, very short of time but with greater financial resources. Currently, most active surfers are male, but the number of female surfers is increasing, particularly in younger age groups. As with several other adventure sports and outdoor activities such as skiing, snowboarding, sailing and even sunbathing on the beach, there is a strong fashion component to clothing and equipment. In surfing, there are a rather small number of surfwear manufacturers that dominate world markets for surf fashion, including street wear as well as gear to wear in the water.

Each of these major surf-clothing and equipment manufacturers sponsors surf competitions, a team of professional surfers and surf trips to remote locations to produce magazine articles and surfing DVDs (Buckley, 2002a, 2003b).

All this is a marketing exercise, and a very effective one. It only works, however, if: (i) it reaches potential customers; and (ii) it persuades them to buy these manufacturers' products. Such persuasive communication is achieved through high exposure in specialist magazines and dedicated websites, plus less frequent but broader exposure in generic lifestyle magazines and TV adventure shows, i.e. the lifestyle entertainment sector.

Historically, the main lifestyle marketing medium for specialist surf-clothing companies has been specialist surf magazines, and these are still a key component. In recent years, however, both individual corporate websites, and broader mass entertainment, have become critical in expanding sales to customers who are not surfers themselves. Specialist surfing magazines aimed at recreational surfers have existed for decades, but were few in number and low in circulation. In recent years, new magazines have proliferated, and circulation has become much more mainstream, e.g. through city newsagents worldwide as well as through specialist surf shops. The original surfing magazines have also spawned a series of specialist subsector magazines, e.g. for bodyboarders and longboarders. At least one of these is specifically aimed at surf travel, including commercial surf tourism.

There are three main components to these magazines. There is trade information on competitions, competitive rankings, recent sponsorship deals, personality profiles and so on. There are advertisements for surfboards, wetsuits, accessories, clothing, surf tours, videos and so on; and sometimes also for snowboards, skateboards, 4WD vehicles, etc. The main bulk of these magazines, however, consists of heavily illustrated articles, most of them featuring sponsored surfers at locations visited by surf tour operators, photographed by professional surf photographers. Video footage from the same trips is used to make surf videos and DVDs, which are advertised through the same magazines, and sometimes packaged with the magazines for retail sale.

These magazines help to sell surfing equipment and surfing tours, and the equipment advertisements and surf tour stories help to sell the magazine. That works fine, but in financial terms it is only a small part of the picture. The big money is in selling surf-branded clothing and accessories to non-surfers, few of whom are likely to read surfing magazines. To reach these broader markets needs communications channels with a wider reach, which convey four messages: surf clothing is cool; particular brands are coolest; here's what you need; here's how you get it (Buckley, 2003b).

This is very much a fashion message, and indeed, the big surfwear companies see themselves as being in the 'fashion apparel business' (Billabong, 2005). Note that whilst selling surfwear to actual surfers certainly involves an element of fashion, it does also require underlying functionality: boardshorts whose pockets are streamlined for paddling, wetsuits that keep you warm with minimum restriction, reef booties that save you from coral cuts but still let your feet feel the board, bags that let you carry your gear and your board on your bicycle or an airplane. For the urban streetwear market, none of this matters – clothing can be identical to no-name equivalents, and the brand alone makes for many times the mark-up.

On the basis of simple statistics rather than stereotypes, there are still relatively few female surfers. There seems to be no published information on actual numbers. My impression is that the proportion is increasing, but is still well below the proportion of women in other adventure sports such as rock climbing, whitewater kayaking or mountain biking. One of the main reasons why the major surfwear manufacturers have grown so fast over recent years, however, is that they have successfully created a fashion market for surf clothing and accessories as urban streetwear, for both women and men who do not surf and live far from the ocean. Indeed, both the degree of brand consciousness, and the number of items purchased, is probably higher for non-surfers than for actual surfers.

The growth, decline and social implications of such fashions are themselves an interesting topic in human behaviour, but beyond the scope of this contribution. The critical issue for surf tourism is that the major sponsors for the world's top surfers, the world's top-ranked competitions, and the world's most spectacular surfing trips and stories, are clothing manufacturers who make most of their money not from selling functional surfwear to surfers, but by selling surf-branded fashion clothing to non-surfers. The total economic scale of these surf-clothing businesses is around US$6.3 billion per annum (Buckley, 2003b). Indeed the scale and significance of the surf-clothing industry is such that it was recently the subject of a cover article in *The Bulletin* magazine (Gliddon and Syvret, 2002). The release of the mainstream feature movie *Blue Crush* (Universal Studios, 2002), with the lead characters clad ostentatiously in Billabong® clothing, marked another step in surfwear marketing.

In 2002 the website for Voodoo Dolls® (2002), ostensibly a women's surfwear manufacturer, incorporated a range of lifestyle images with little connection to surfing as such, and sold a range of fashion accessories as well as clothing. 'Young, free and single' was the tagline, and the top banner said 'ask your sex question here'. The website sold make-up packs and 'girlie stuff' (their words not mine!), with barely a surfboard in sight. Currently, however, the website (Voodoo Dolls, 2005) is much more conservative, citing the company's associations with fashion designers, and offering snowboard gear as well as bikinis.

The mainstream surfwear companies all have girls' lines, and some have separate websites such as Roxy® and BillabongGirls®. Rip Curl® no longer seems to operate its former site RipCurlGirl®, but now includes women's clothing in the main site. They offer girls' street gear in demure pastels with flowers and butterflies and understated logos, as well as more lurid lines. There's even a second-hand Internet market for Mambo Goddess® clothing. In the early 2000s, the major surfwear manufacturers developed separate product lines for children in various age groups (Buckley, 2003b), though these now seem to receive less emphasis. Even more surprisingly, the surf industry seems to have successfully created surf fashion for male surfers and their street imitators, with rapidly changing style factors such as the precise length and pattern of boardshorts, tabs or cord loops on pockets, ankle strings or zips on cargo pants, and so on. This constant market repositioning has kept surfwear share prices on the rise for many years.

Perhaps equally important is cross-marketing between adventure sports. Companies such as Quicksilver® produce snowboarding clothing as well as surf clothing. And most recently, core snowboard manufacturers such as Burton® have also started to put their brand on running shoes and summer gear, and to use professional surfers to advertise them. Their 2005 product catalogue, self-described as a 'Rider's Journal' (Burton Inc., 2005) features famous surfers David Rastovich, Kalani Robb and Sanoe Lake, co-star of the *Blue Crush* movie. As well as snowboards, boots, bindings, bags and snow clothing, it also features a range of 'clothes you'll live in' (p. 125) and accessories such as the 'WMS hook-up kit', subtitled 'your walk of shame quick fix kit' (p. 129) – a very American phrase and reminiscent of the Voodoo Dolls® website in 2002. Hey, whatever works. With Burton® team riders such as Victoria Jealouse carving under a cornice at Mt Cook (p. 57), Kelly Clark airborne with Mike Wiegele Helicopter Skiing in Canada (p. 47) or JP Solberg in the Montana backcountry (p. 75), Burton® has more than enough credibility in its markets to sell lounge pants (p. 127), purses or anything else.

Surf fashion isn't new: by the 1960s 'surf chic was a cultural phenomenon' as the Quicksilver website says. What is new this decade is the growth in 'adventure' imagery: in lifestyles, clothing and accessories, and entertainment. Adventure is fashionable. Adventure tourism may have grown from outdoor recreation, but both have now become inseparable from the clothing, fashion and entertainment sector. This is not immediately apparent to consumers and tourists; but a glance at corporate financial figures tells the story loud and clear.

# 26 Product Patterns

## Introduction

The case studies presented in this book cover only a small component of the range of adventure tourism products currently available. Even so, however, they indicate an enormous diversity in the design, duration, places, prices, environments and expertise involved. Are there any general patterns that can be identified, either across the entire adventure tourism sector or within individual activity subsectors, with regard to any of the aspects considered in the case studies? In particular, are there any characteristic features of adventure tourism products that distinguish them from the rest of the tourism industry?

The previous chapter contains more detailed cross-case comparisons that examine the similarities and differences in particular aspects of individual tour products offering the same activity. Can we make broader generalizations across different activities? For example, are the differences between individual products within a single activity subsector larger or smaller than the differences between subsectors? That is, does each different adventure activity have its own characteristic product structure for commercial tours, or is the structure of the product independent of the activity it offers? This chapter makes a first attempt at such an analysis.

Such approaches, incidentally, have not previously been possible because there were simply too few published descriptions of individual tour products in the academic literature, and corporate advertising materials, or even editorial write-ups in commercial magazines, do not form a reliable substitute. Such marketing materials can indeed show us how adventure tourism products are sold, but not how they are actually structured.

## Place

Almost anywhere that human beings can go, they can now also go as adventure tourists: peaks, poles and even outer space, though not yet the moon. The deep ocean trenches are still out of reach except for unoccupied remote-control devices, but there are dive tours to open-ocean submarine seamounts, beneath the polar ice and amidst sharks. Commercial surf tours do not yet take surfers to the giant mid-ocean tow-in waves of the Cortez Bank, but this is surely only a matter of time. For several years now, the summit of Mount Everest has been a tourist destination for those with sufficient skill, strength, motivation and money.

As noted previously (Buckley, 2004a), skilled commercial adventure recreation in remote areas (SCARRA) has become the apex of the commercial adventure tourism industry. The base of the industry, in contrast, consists of high-volume low-skill thrill-seeker trips easily accessible from major tourist gateway towns. A few people run rivers in Tibet; innumerable tourists go whitewater rafting near Cairns, Queenstown or Victoria Falls. A few people take specialist dive tours in caves or the Antarctic; but by far the majority of dive tours are in the Caribbean, the Indian Ocean and the Great Barrier Reef. In Europe and North America, many people pay to go horse riding, either for themselves or their children; not many, however, ride across Mongolia. Of course, it costs more to reach remote areas, and it usually takes longer. Adventure tour companies may be able to take you almost anywhere, but in actuality, most of them stay fairly close to town.

For any kind of adventure tourism, the place where it takes place is a critical component of the product. There are particular mountains, particular cliffs and particular climbing routes which are famous for climbers; particular rivers and individual rapids which are famous for whitewater rafters and kayakers; particular waves which are well-known to surfers worldwide; particular destinations where divers would like to dive. Such sites are described and illustrated in the articles and editorials in adventure sports and travel magazines and featured in videos, DVDs and television programmes. For these activities, adventure tour clients commonly have particular destinations in mind, because the places concerned contain a natural challenge. For other adventure tourism activities such as hiking, seakayaking, diving, whalewatching and wildlife watching, particular places are famous for their natural attractions rather than natural challenges. Attractions commonly include general scenery, or individual icon species such as bears or big cats, whalesharks or pygmy seahorses. Once again, commercial tour clients want to go to these particular places, which therefore become differentially valuable as tourist destinations.

## Operator

Not surprisingly, adventure tour companies that offer activities requiring higher levels of skills and that take place in more remote areas tend to be smaller and more specialized than companies offering highly accessible, low-skill, high-volume products. As in many other types of tourism, and indeed other industry sectors, there are many small adventure tour companies and relatively few large ones.

Adventure tour companies that are large in financial terms seem to fall into three major categories. There are some that offer a single activity at high volume, such as Quicksilver's day-trip tours on Australia's Great Barrier Reef. To maintain dominance in their particular market sector and region, such companies may rely on factors such as exclusive access arrangements negotiated with government agencies; high capital investment requirements as a barrier to entry; or particular equipment and technology that are not generally available.

Some companies achieve a high total financial turnover by offering similar products at a range of different sites. At each individual site, numbers are relatively small and prices are high, but the company can continue to grow by adding more sites. Examples include companies such as Conservation Corporation Africa in the wildlife tourism sector and Canadian Mountain Holidays in the heliski sector.

The third category consists of companies that offer a large portfolio of different activities in different areas, essentially acting as a retail packager for numerous small specialist operators. Examples include Abercrombie and Kent or World Expeditions. Perhaps surprisingly, there do not seem to be many examples where specialist adventure tourism companies have been bought out by large generalized tour operators. There is the well-known instance where Mountain Travel-Sobek was purchased by Microsoft some years ago, but this precedent does not seem to have been repeated. Many companies that offer adventure tours, however, also offer nature and ecotours. Indeed, many tours combine nature, eco and adventure components (Buckley, 2000). It is for this reason that some tour operators featured in this book also appear in the companion volume on ecotourism (Buckley, 2003a), though from a different perspective.

## Activity

Some outdoor sports and adventure recreation activities are much more popular with commercial tour operators than others. There seem to be several different reasons for this, which might be considered in three main categories: access, equipment and expertise. In each of these cases, there is a commercial opportunity for tour operators to sell something to customers at a price that is higher than the operator's cost to provide it, but lower than the customer's cost to obtain it independently.

Many adventure tourism destinations are difficult to get to, and especially difficult to get to quickly. By dealing routinely with local air and boat charter operators, for example, and by assembling groups of clients who have had no previous contact with each other, adventure tour operators can take people to places they would otherwise be unable to go. The same applies where access is dependent on developing a long-term relationship with a particular landholder, whether legal or customary; or obtaining a hard-to-get permit, such as those for gorilla-watching tours in Uganda or first descents of whitewater rivers in China.

Equipment is a second significant constraint, because outdoor adventure gear can be quite expensive to purchase, store, maintain and transport. For the more expensive items, it is only worth owning one's own gear if it will receive a lot of use. Very few recreational divers, for example, could afford to run their own compressors: and even if they did, it would be difficult to transport them to new sites. Most divers are thus already tied to commercial dive shops to refill their tanks, and from this it is a short step to equipment rentals, dive tenders, dive resorts and liveaboard dive charter boats. Many recreational divers do indeed have their own equipment, but increasingly, dive shops and tour operators have everything available on the spot, often already included in the tour price.

Similarly, most whitewater kayakers own their own boats, sometimes several, but relatively few whitewater rafters own their rafts. Families who live in an area with plenty of rafting opportunities may well consider it worthwhile to buy their own boat, but most whitewater tour clients are travellers who buy a raft trip as one part of a longer holiday. Even seakayaks, though not nearly as expensive as rafts, are difficult to transport by air because of their length, and whilst excellent collapsible seakayaks are available, these cost at least three times as much as their hardshell equivalents. So once again, in many parts of the world it makes economic sense to buy a seakayak tour rather than buying one's own seakayak. And even if you own and paddle your own seakayak at home, when you want to paddle elsewhere it may be easier to buy a tour.

Similar considerations apply for tours that involve livestock, whether riding or pack animals. If you are a keen rider you may well have your own horse at home, but unless you are a successful and sponsored international competitor, you are unlikely to take your own horse with you on an intercontinental holiday. And if you are planning a camel ride in Australia's Simpson Desert or India's Rajasthan, you are even less likely to bring your own camel.

In addition to access and equipment, commercial adventure tours offer their clients the accumulated skills and expertise of specialist guides. For some types of adventure tours, such as guided ascents of high mountain peaks or guided kayak descents of Class V+ rapids, the guides must generally possess world-class skills in the activity concerned, and the ability to train and lead experienced but less expert clients through relatively difficult routes.

For other adventure tours, such as tandem skydiving or whitewater rafting, the guides need to be skilled but the clients are purely passengers. For others again, such as hiking, seakayaking or looking at large animals, the activity itself is not particularly difficult, but the clients rely on the guides' expertise to find their way around safely; to assess factors such as weather, tides or snowpack; or to understand animals well enough to know where to find them and how they will behave. In any of these categories, the critical issue is that relative to the clients, the guides possess particular skills or knowledge that either gives the group a more interesting experience, keeps them out of danger, or commonly both.

## Equipment

As a general trend, outdoor adventure equipment is becoming more and more technologically sophisticated. Established types of equipment such as skis, kayaks, saddles, climbing ropes and outdoor clothing are constantly being refined, with new designs and materials. Today's whitewater playboats, for example, are stubby flat-bottomed plastic bubbles that look almost like large sit-on-top boogie-boards, a far cry from the long, pointed, round-hulled fibreglass kayaks of a few decades ago, let alone their chine-hulled plywood predecessors or their skin- or canvas-covered forebears. Surfboards have undergone several revolutions in design and construction, with giant wooden single-fin longboards giving way to lightweight multi-fin shortboards of various designs, and most recently to the stepped rails and footstraps on tow-in boards. Sidecut skis made from metal, plastic and carbon fibre with hardshell plastic boots are very different from the long wooden skis and cable bindings from 40 years ago.

Synthetic fleeces, polypropylenes and breathable waterproof fabrics such as Gore-Tex® and Reflex® have revolutionized cold-weather clothing. This applies from the most basic parka, to the technical survival suits used in mountain or polar expeditions, or the drysuits used for ice-diving and cold-water kayaking.

In addition to these design and manufacturing refinements, there are many pieces of outdoor equipment that have only come into existence in recent years or decades. Some of these combine old ideas or components in new ways, such as snowboards, sailboards, kiteboards and hang-gliders. Some have been designed specifically to move a particular activity into more and more difficult realms, such as the many new protection devices used in rock and mixed rock–ice climbing. Some solve old problems with completely new approaches, such as digital dive computers instead of decompression tables and analogue calculators; or hand-held global positioning systems (GPS) instead of compass and altimeter. Many other items of equipment undergo constant small changes and improvements, from engine designs to water filters and headlamps.

Despite this general trend to more high-tech materials, there are some items where traditional materials are still best, or are even experiencing a resurgence. Down sleeping bags are still the warmest, and the best hiking boots still have leather uppers. The lightest sleeping bag liners and thermal underwear are still made of silk, and new manufacturing processes for superfine merino wool are now giving it warmth and wicking capabilities beyond those of its synthetic competitors. Most commercial seakayak tour operators use mass-produced plastic boats, but some aficionados build their own boats using traditional Inuit designs and even materials. This counter-trend, however, is small in comparison.

Though all this new equipment does generally become more affordable as the volume of production increases, little of it could be considered cheap. As noted earlier, this may well be one of the reasons why many people opt to purchase an all-inclusive adventure tour where the operators supply all the equipment, sometimes including specialist clothing, so that participants do not need to purchase their own.

## Accommodation

Accommodation used in adventure tours varies enormously, from tents and tumbledown huts to luxury lodges and live-aboard charter boats. It is difficult to draw any generalizations except for the more obvious ones. For example, tours can only use local accommodation in places where people are living. In remote, seldom-visited areas accessible only on foot, tents are generally the only option; and to build luxury lodges, operators need both security of land tenure and sufficient political stability to be confident of a long-term flow of customers.

Apart from overriding constraints such as these, different tour operators offering similar activities in similar areas may use very different styles of accommodation, with tour prices pitched accordingly at different market segments. At many well-known wildlife-watching areas, for example, visitors can choose to camp in a national park's campground using their own tent, to stay in a low-key local guesthouse or to live in an internationally renowned luxury lodge.

Likewise, one can visit Pond Inlet at the northern tip of Baffin Island in the Canadian Arctic travelling either with tents and seakayaks or in a cruise liner. If one has the time, one can reach almost any of the famous Indonesian surfbreaks using local fishing boats; but surfers with more money and less time will generally opt for a live-aboard surf charter boat. Indeed, if the major surfwear manufacturers Quicksilver® and Billabong® carry through with reported current plans, there may soon be an even more upmarket option, though one that will perhaps be available only to professional surf teams: large float-planes or flying-boats equipped with living quarters and also with jetskis carried in special pods, for tow-in surfing on the world's most remote surfbreaks.

## Statistics

The various product statistics provided for each of the case studies are summarized in Table 26.1. The hundred or so case studies presented here are not a random or rep-

**Table 26.1.** Product statistics for audited case studies.

| Place and country | Operator(s) (abbreviated) | Length of tour (days) | Price/ day (US$) | Client: guide ratio | Typical group size |
|---|---|---|---|---|---|
| *River journeys* | | | | | |
| Qamdo Gorge, China | Shangri La River Expeditions | 28 | 180 | n/a | ** |
| Chuya/Katun, Russia | Team Gorky | 10 | 90 | 3 | *** |
| Various (4), Nepal | Allardice's UD | 2–10 | 50 | 6 | *** |
| Drysdale, Australia | Raleigh, NOLS | ~35 | 140 | 2,7 | ** |
| Jatapu, Brazil | Colares | 10 | ? | 1 | * |
| Yangbi, China | Earth Science Expeditions | 20 | ~170 | n/a | ** |
| *Whitewater kayaking* | | | | | |
| Futaleufu, Chile | Expediciones Chile | 4–14 | 170 | 3 | ** |
| Various, Costa Rica | Endless River | 8 | 170 | 3 | ** |
| Karamea, New Zealand | Ultimate Descents | 3 | 285 | 5 | ** |
| Colorado, USA | Various (3) | 13–16 | ~260 | 4 | *** |
| Franklin, Australia | World Expeditions | 9 | 190 | 4 | * |
| Upper Zambezi, Zimbabwe | Various (2) | 1–2 | 150 | 3 | ** |
| *Whitewater rafting* | | | | | |
| White Nile, Uganda | Adrift | 1 | 95 | 9 | *** |
| Zambezi, Zimbabwe | Shearwater | 1 | 95 | 7 | *** |
| Nymboida, Australia | World Expeditions | 4 | | 4 | * |
| Nymboida, Australia | Others (3) | 1–2 | | 6 | *** |
| Toachi/Blanco, Ecuador | Yacu Amu | 2 | 97 | 6 | ** |
| 'Luva, Fiji | Rivers Fiji | 1 | 110 | >1.5 | ** |
| Tully, Australia | Raging Thunder | 1 | 148 | 7 | *** |
| Tully, Australia | R'n'R | 1 | 131 | 7 | *** |
| Kawarau, New Zealand | Various (3) | 1 | 104 | 7 | *** |
| Shotover, New Zealand | Various (3) | 1 | 111 | 7 | *** |
| Rangitata, New Zealand | Rangitata | 1 | 111 | 7 | *** |
| *Seakayaking* | | | | | |
| Baffin Island, Canada | Blackfeather | 16 | 175 | 2 | * |
| Svalbard, Norway | Aurora/SSV | 11 | 400 | 10 | ** |
| Prince William, Alaska | NOLS | 12 | 240 | 4 | ** |
| Yasawas, Fiji | Southern Sea Ventures | 7 | 205 | 3 | ** |
| Hinchinbrook, Australia | Southern Sea Ventures | 7 | 180 | 5 | ** |
| Abel Tasman, New Zealand | Natural High | 3 | 105 | 8 | ** |
| Abel Tasman, New Zealand | Ocean River | 3 | 95 | 8 | ** |
| Phang Nga, Thailand | John Gray's Sea Canoe | 3 | 70–135 | 5 | ** |
| *Sailing* | | | | | |
| Faeroe Is., Denmark | Private yacht | 7 | | 4 | * |
| Bay of Islands, New Zealand | Various (11) | 1–7 | 50–225 | 4–8 | ** |
| Baja Peninsula, Mexico | NOLS | 21 | 150 | 2.5 | ** |
| *Diving* | | | | | |
| Great Barrier Reef, Australia | Taka Dive | 5 | 250–350 | 6 | *** |
| Kimbe, New Guinea | Walindi | var | ~260 | 4 | ** |
| Mnemba, Zanzibar | CCAfrica | var | 585–730 | 3 | ** |
| Maldives | Delphis Diving | var | 420–560 | 7 | ** |
| Bega, Fiji | Lalati | var | 385 | 1.5 | * |
| Rocktail Bay, South Africa | Wilderness Sararis | var | 300–500 | 10 | ** |
| Great Barrier Reef, Australia | Quicksilver | 1 | 250 | | **** |
| Ningaloo, Australia | Ningaloo Blue, King Dive | 1 | 270 | 20 | ** |

**Table 26.1.** *Continued.*

| Place and country | Operator(s) (abbreviated) | Length of tour (days) | Price/ day (US$) | Client: guide ratio | Typical group size |
|---|---|---|---|---|---|
| *Surfing* | | | | | |
| Dhonveli, Maldives | Dhonveli Beach Resort | 7 | 275–340 | ~10 | ** |
| Savaii, Samoa | Savaii Surfaris | var | 65 | ~10 | ** |
| Upolu, Samoa | Salani Surf Resort | var | 90–130 | ~6 | ** |
| Kadavu, Fiji | Nagigia Surf Resort | var | 100–160 | ~15 | ** |
| Mentawais, Indonesia | Mentawai Sanctuary | 11 | 140–250 | ~6 | ** |
| *Heliski/boarding* | | | | | |
| Manali, India | Himachal Helicopter Skiing | 7 | 1000 | 5 | ** |
| Banff, Canada | Canadian Mountain Holidays | 7 | 1100 | 11 | *** |
| Blue River, Canada | Mike Wiegele Heli Skiing | 7 | 1300 | 4 | *** |
| Wanaka, New Zealand | Harris Mountains Heli-ski | 1 | 600–700 | 4 | ** |
| Christchurch, New Zealand | Methven Heliski | 1 | 700 | 4 | ** |
| *Cross-country skiing* | | | | | |
| North Pole via Norway | Global Expeditions | 11 | 1500 | 5 | ** |
| Snowy Mountains, Australia | Paddy Pallin | 5 | 120 | 5 | ** |
| Yellowstone, USA | Yellowstone Expeditions | 5 | 200 | ? | ** |
| *Ice climbing* | | | | | |
| Banff, Canada | On Top, BAU, Yamnuska | 1–5 | 110–500 | 2–5 | * |
| Ouray, Colorado USA | Various | 1–2 | 135–325 | 1–4 | * |
| North Conway, USA | IMCS, EMS | 1–3 | 115–230 | 1–3 | * |
| Quebec, Canada | EELA, COGEQ | 1–4 | 65–430 | 1–6 | * |
| *Hiking and bushwalking* | | | | | |
| Loja, Ecuador | Surtrek | 4 | 180 | ? | * |
| Annapurna, Nepal | World Expeditions | 11 | 110 | ?5 | ** |
| Purnululu, Australia | Willis's Walkabouts | 7–21 | 110 | 5 | ** |
| Mt Kenya, Kenya | Various | 2–6 | 200–240 | ? | * |
| Routeburn, New Zealand | Ultimate Hikes | 2–3 | 250 | ? | ** |
| Pacific Northwest, USA | Oregon Peak | 3 | 100 | 3 | * |
| *Horse riding* | | | | | |
| Khovsgol, Mongolia | Boojum Expeditions | 19 | 165 | 5 | ** |
| Snowy Mountains, Australia | Reynella Station | 5 | 200 | 8 | ** |
| Torres del Paine, Chile | Ride World Wide | 12 | 270 | ? | ** |
| *Mountain biking* | | | | | |
| North America | Ski areas, various | 1 | 20–33 | n/a | **** |
| Colorado, USA | Hut systems, various | 7 | 28–80 | n/a | ** |
| USA, various states | Multi-day tours, various | 5–9 | 180–360 | ? | ** |
| White Rim Trail, UT, USA | Supported tours, various | 3–4 | 170–205 | 9 | ** |
| Spain, Sri Lanka | Mountain bike resorts (2) | n/a | 75–90 | var | ** |
| *Off-road safaris* | | | | | |
| Taklamakan, China | Various | ~10 | 350 | ~5 | ** |
| Simpson, Australia | Various | 8–20 | 140 | ~5 | ** |
| Chalbi, Kenya | Various | 8–10 | 65–85 | ~5 | ** |
| Namib, Namibia | Various | 11–16 | ? | ? | ** |
| Qinghai, China | Various | 10–12 | 160–275 | ~15 | ** |
| *Wildlife* | | | | | |
| Serengeti, Tanzania | CCAfrica | 5–10 | 450–600 | 2 | ** |
| Bardia, Nepal | Tiger Tops Karnali | var | 75–150 | 2 | ** |
| Mgahinga, Uganda | Various | var | 450 | 2 | ** |

**Table 26.1.** *Continued.*

| Place and country | Operator(s) (abbreviated) | Length of tour (days) | Price/ day (US$) | Client: guide ratio | Typical group size |
|---|---|---|---|---|---|
| Kalahari, Botswana | Jack's Camp | var | 650 | 4 | ** |
| Churchill, Canada | Natural Habitat Adventures | 9 | 700 | 14 | ** |
| Kamchatka, Russia | Explore Kamchatka | 6 | 265–600 | 4 | ** |
| *Aerial adventures* | | | | | |
| Mission Beach, Australia | Jump the Beach | 1 | 160–260 | 1 | ** |
| Queenstown, New Zealand | AJ Hackett Bungy | 1 | 98–140 | 1 | * |
| Kaikoura, New Zealand | Kaikoura Helicopters | 1 | 130–205 | 3 | * |
| Gold Coast, Australia | Balloon Down Under | 1 | 195 | 4 | ** |

Notes: *, 1–5; **, 6–20; ***, 21–50; ****>50.

resentative sample, so statistics for these particular examples cannot necessarily be generalized to the sector as a whole.

Around 65% of the tour products featured typically take groups of 6–20 clients at a time (Table 26.1). Only about 13% take groups with five clients or fewer, and only 22% or so commonly take groups of 21 clients or more. The small-group tours are commonly those that need little equipment, such as hiking; or conversely, have equipment-driven limits to the group size, such as some aerial tours. The large-group tours are either those such as whitewater rafting that can readily replicate smaller units to form a large group; or those such as expedition cruises, where a vessel of adequate size has a large passenger capacity.

For the more difficult, arduous and dangerous trips, such as mountaineering ascents, there may well be one or more guides for each client, as well as a support crew. For easier trips where the main function of the guide is to manage logistics, there may only be one guide per 20 or 30 clients, though such trips may perhaps barely qualify as adventure tourism. For a wide range of activities and trips, the characteristic client-to-guide ratio is between 5:1 and 7:1, either because this represents the capacity of an individual vehicle or boat, or because this is about as many people as a single guide can keep an eye on at any one moment. Interestingly, in countries that have adopted standards for outdoor recreation and outdoor education, similar figures seems to be recommended for the ratio of instructor to clients or students.

For many adventure tours, client-to-guide ratios are constrained by equipment, such as rafts or helicopters. Raft tour operators generally have one guide per raft, so those using small paddle rafts may have only four clients per guide, whereas those with larger rigs will typically have seven or nine (Table 26.1). Taking into account the multiple tour companies audited for some rivers, 60% of the rafting tour products in Table 26.1 operate with a client-to-guide ratio of 7:1.

Kayaking tours have a lower ratio, typically around 4:1, since the clients are paddling independently and are hence harder to watch, instruct and protect. Ratios for seakayak tours range from 2:1 to 10:1, with the highest figure for a boat-supported trip, and the lowest for a self-supported Arctic tour. There is a similar range for dive tours, with ratios between 3:1 and 7:1 for most expert trips. Heliski companies generally operate with four or five clients per guide, except for companies that use clients as 'para-guides' and hence run with double this ratio.

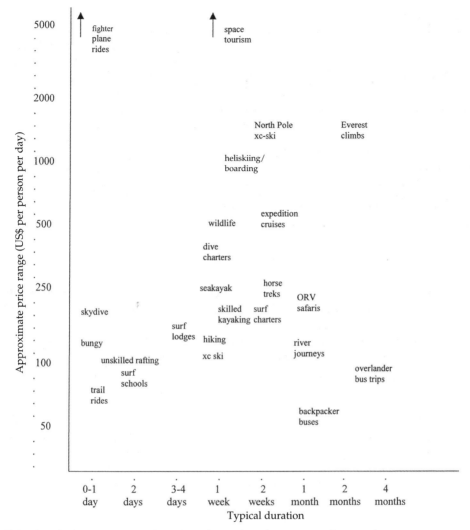

**Fig. 26.1.** Typical prices and durations for major adventure tourism products.

Most cross-country skiing, hiking, horse riding and off-road vehicle tours seem to operate with around five clients per guide.

For many activities, such as diving, whitewater rafting, whalewatching or horse riding, the greatest volume of commercial tour clients purchase single-day trips: but the same tour operators often also offer more specialized multi-day trips to a smaller clientele. Indeed, for some adventure tourism activities such as tandem parachuting or bungee jumping, the activity may last only a few minutes or even seconds, even though the tour experience as a whole may take most of the day.

At the other end of the scale, an attempt to make a guided ascent of a major Himalayan peak such as Mount Everest requires a commitment of many months, as well as many tens of thousands of dollars. There are some activities, such as heliskiing, that are commonly sold as single-day trips in countries such as New Zealand, but as 1-week packages in Canada and elsewhere.

Tour prices depend not only on the length of the trip, but on the level of luxury, the equipment needed, the costs of transport and access, and the number of guides. Anything that involves helicopters, for example, will necessarily be expensive: and tours that use helicopters as an integral part of the activity, such as heliskiing, commonly cost between US$600 and 1300 per person per day. Similarly, if the tour operator has to pay to get specialist equipment to a remote area, such as seakayaks to Baffin Island or whitewater rafts to Tibet, the trip will necessarily be costly.

Prices per person per day, measured in a common currency such as US$ (Table 26.2), vary with the country, the activity and equipment, the cost of access, the level of comfort or luxury, the client-to-guide ratio, and other factors such as length of season, insurance costs, etc. Some broad patterns between activities are shown in Fig. 26.1, which also indicates typical tour lengths for each activity.

## Access

Access to different adventure tours depends on the destination, the type of activity and the price. Not surprisingly, access by air is most popular for the majority of tour companies and their customers, simply because of speed, comfort and convenience. For some areas, however, air access is not feasible: either because of legal constraints, safety considerations or cost. In some areas, for example, the winds are routinely too strong, the altitude too high or the visibility too poor for light aircraft to operate safely; or there may be nowhere for a fixed-wing aircraft to land, and nowhere for a helicopter to refuel. In some cases, there is in fact an actual scheduled air service, but it is so often disrupted by poor weather or politics that it is more reliable to travel by road.

Private or commercial air access is not permitted for national parks in many countries, though there are some notable anomalies such as scenic overflights at Grand Canyon National Park in the USA. Some countries treat aerial access, or even reconnaissance, as military intelligence and ban it accordingly. In the attempted first descent of the Qamdo Gorges in the Tibetan section of the Mekong River, Shangri La Expeditions and its Chinese counterpart organization were refused permission to conduct a reconnaissance flight along the river before starting the descent, even though this would have greatly improved the expedition's safety.

Some adventure tour operations are carried out on private land, and access is available only with permission from the landholder. This applies, for example, to many rock climbing sites, hang-glider take-off and landing points, river access points, off-road driving areas and some private game reserves. In some jurisdictions there is a degree of uncertainty over the precise bundle of rights granted by private land-ownership. For example, on some rivers in Colorado, USA, there have apparently been disputes as to whether landowners on the river banks have the right to prevent rafters running the river itself. Such conflicts may be intensified where there are competing uses, e.g. if the landowners want to use the river for recreational angling, but are disturbed daily by commercial raft trips.

In some parts of the world, permission for access must be sought from traditional or customary owners. This applies, for example, to Aboriginal and First Nations lands in Australia, Canada and the USA. It also applies to surf breaks in many South Pacific nations.

Many commercial adventure tours take place in publicly owned land, such as national parks or state or national forests, and these land management agencies generally operate permit and fee systems for commercial tours, and often also for

**Table 26.2.** Price ranges for various commercial adventure activities.

| Activity | Number of audited tour products in price range (US$) | | | |
|---|---|---|---|---|
| | <100 | 100–200 | 200–500 | >500 |
| River journeys | 3 | 2 | | |
| Whitewater kayaking | | 4 | 2 | |
| Whitewater rafting | 5 | 6 | | |
| Seakayaking | 1 | 4 | 3 | |
| Expedition cruises | | | 3 | 1 |
| Diving | | | 6 | 2 |
| Surfing | 1 | 4 | 1 | |
| Heliski and snowboard | | | | 5 |
| Cross-country skiing | | 2 | | 1 |
| Ice climbing | | (5) | (5) | |
| Hiking and bushwalking | | 4 | 2 | |
| Horse riding | | 2 | 1 | |
| Mountain biking | (4) | (2) | (2) | |
| Off-road safari | 1 | 1 | 1 | |
| Wildlife | | 1 | 2 | 2 |
| Aerial adventures | | 3 | 1 | |

Note: Numbers in brackets are approximate only, because of range in prices for different products offered by single operators and lack of detail for case studies covering several operators.

individual recreational activities. In most cases, an indefinite number of permits may be issued and the system is designed for safety and rescue, to regulate specific and potentially harmful activities, and to offset management costs.

In some cases, however, permit systems on public lands are also used to control the number of people carrying out a particular activity at a particular place and time. Commercial tour operators may have preassigned rights to a particular quota, or they may have to apply for places along with everyone else. For float trips on the Colorado Grand Canyon, for example, there are strictly enforced quotas for group sizes, launch dates and total time on the river; and by far the lion's share of this quota is allocated to commercial tour operators, with private groups stuck on a 15-year waiting list for a launching permit. The quota for gorilla-watching permits at Mgahinga National Park in Uganda is even more strict, but the permits are apparently sold by a more equitable process rather than pre-allocated.

Access and activity permit systems in public land have many variations, some very simple and others quite complex; but in general, commercial tour clients do not need to figure out the details, because the tour operators will do so on their behalf. One interesting aspect, however, is whether the tour operators factor the price of permits into the tour package, or leave their clients to pay permit fees separately. In some cases, particularly in developing countries, national parks and other land management agencies will insist on being paid the permit fees directly, in cash, on the day concerned; perhaps because this is the only way they can be sure of keeping the money on site.

In many cases, often in developed nations, the land management agencies require the tour operators to collect permit fees on their behalf, and pay them over to the authority as part of a routine visitor accounting system. In other cases again, a commercial tour operator may deliberately choose to collect permit fees on behalf of its passengers, for various reasons. One such reason is to guarantee in advance that permits are available. Another is to minimize delays in the payment of fees, e.g. in driving a busload of passengers through a permit booth on a park entrance road.

In general, it appears that the practice of factoring permit fees into tour package prices is common but by no means universal. The general pattern, if there is one, seems to be that tour operators show permit fees separately under two principal sets of circumstances. The first is where they object to the fee: whether in principle, or because of its size, or because they have to collect it on behalf of the land management agency. This may apply, for example, to the AUD4 per person fee for 1-day boat trips on Australia's Great Barrier Reef, or the US$300 per person fee for a week's heliskiing in Himachal Pradesh.

The second case is where tour operators are competing on price and want to advertise the lowest possible rate, so they include only the basic tour product in the advertised package price, and any permit fees and levies as add-on extras. This applies, for example, to many of the day-trip adventure tours out of Cairns, Australia, e.g. to snorkel on the Great Barrier Reef or run the whitewater rapids of the Tully River. As noted earlier, there are also occasions when the systems established by the land management agency force this permit fee to be collected separately. This applies, for example, to whaleshark tours in Western Australia, where tour boats are supposed to sell their clients a special marine-parks permit that is printed as a colourful souvenir-style tag.

## Community

Most adventure tours do not include significant interactions with local communities, except in remote areas where they may be reliant on local residents. Depending on the area and activity, guides and other company staff may be citizens of the county concerned or expatriates. Even if the former, they are not necessarily members of local communities, but may well have come from the country's capital city or other areas where there were opportunities to learn foreign languages.

Many adventure tour operators have indeed made particular efforts to train and hire local residents, sometimes with great success, sometimes less so. There are now local kayakers on the White Nile in Uganda, for example, and local surfers in the Maldives and Mentawais.

Well-intentioned and successful adventure tourism entrepreneurs such as John Gray in Thailand and David Allardice in Nepal, however, found their businesses under attack from within the countries concerned. In Gray's case, copycat companies set up in competition and then used mafia-style methods to attack his local manager. He was able to survive these attacks and continue operating as the premium operator amidst a number of copycats. In Allardice's case, his original local partner staged a hostile takeover of the company using local laws, copying Allardice's company name and logo. Allardice, however, still had the international network, Internet domain and trademark protection, and after a hiatus of several years was able to establish a successful new and upmarket second edition of his original company, with a broader range of products. Such disputes, fortunately, appear to be relatively rare.

In most multi-day adventure tours, the local residents in remote rural areas are very friendly and interested, especially in equipment. The contrasts can certainly be intriguing. Modern-day Inuit living at Pond Inlet in the Canadian Arctic may well wonder why tourists should pay large sums to spend 10 days paddling sea kayaks in the hope of seeing narwhal, whilst they themselves hunt narwhal very successfully using high-calibre rifles from high-powered speedboats. To a local villager living by the Yangbi River in Yunnan, China, in contrast, a bunch of Western kayakers in multi-coloured boats, helmets and drysuits may well look more like aliens than people. Not necessarily, however: a traditional lifestyle does not automatically guarantee unfamiliarity with modern technologies. Tibetan villagers in the Qamdo Gorge, accessible only by several days of hiking along narrow cliffside trails, live in traditional dwellings made of mud and timber and grind their locally grown barley with stone grindstones driven by a wooden paddle wheel. In at least some of these mud houses, however, there are modern DVD players powered by solar cells on the roof.

## Experience

Most adventure clients want fun and thrills. This applies especially for low-skill, short-duration tour products such as bungee jumping, tandem skydiving and many whitewater raft trips. On longer trips, participants may want extended challenges and lifetime experiences; and depending on the precise activity and price, they may be prepared to put in considerable effort and put up with considerable discomfort.

Since different clients on the same tour may often have different expectations, skills and interests, they are likely to experience the same tour in different ways. Someone with extended practice in backcountry hiking trips will see the camping component of a multi-day seakayak, river-rafting or off-road vehicle safari as luxurious in comparison. Someone with experience only in urban apartments and luxurious resorts may find any form of camping to be a considerable challenge.

Similarly, the greater the prior skill of a tour participant in the particular adventure activity concerned, the more likely they are to pay attention to the broader aspects of the tour and terrain, rather than focusing on the immediate activity. And finally, the longer the trip, the smaller the group and the lower the client-to-guide ratio, the greater the opportunities for the participants to learn something new, whether it be improving their outdoor skills or understanding local communities and environmental issues.

## Environment

Adventure tours do not set out to be ecotours, even though there are often many similarities and indeed overlaps. Adventure tours do not necessarily set out to contribute to conservation of the natural environment, to support local communities or even to use the lowest-impact forms of transport and accommodation. In practice, however, most reputable adventure tours do indeed follow recognized good practices in environmental management, and some have become industry leaders.

Environmental management issues for adventure tours may usefully be considered at three different scales. At the most local scale are the various environmental management practices, technologies and training techniques that adventure tour operators may adopt to minimize the local impacts of a tour once it is operational.

At a broader scale is the selection of adventure activity and transport. Motorized vehicles generally make noise, consume fuel and emit exhaust. Horses and other livestock are more likely to cause soil erosion and to introduce weeds and pathogens than hikers without livestock. Some types of motorized equipment, such as snowmobiles, all-terrain quad bikes, jetskis and helicopters are particularly noisy and generally cause unavoidable disturbance to both wildlife and other people.

At the broadest scale, the environmental impacts of tourism, including relatively high-impact adventure tourism, may be compared against the likely impacts of potential alternative land uses, which in some areas might include large-scale industrial logging, agriculture, fisheries, mining or manufacturing. Some adventure tour operators, such as Expediciones Chile on the Futaleufu River in Patagonia, or World Expeditions on the Franklin River in Tasmania, or John Gray's Sea Canoe in Phangna Bay, Thailand, have themselves become strong advocates for conservation. If such efforts are successful, the impacts of their own tour operations will be negligible in comparison.

Most of the focus on environmental management in adventure tourism has been at the smallest scale, with relatively minor modifications to operational practices and equipment. This includes, for example: the design and operation of wilderness lodges so as to conserve energy and water and minimize the impacts of greywater discharge, sewage treatment and waste disposal; minimal-impact travel and camping techniques in backcountry areas and wildlife habitat; the use of four-stroke rather than two-stroke engines in jetskis, snowmobiles, etc., and hush kits in helicopters; and a wide range of minimal-impact practices specific to particular activities. Many of these are outlined in minimal-impact guidelines, such as the *Leave-No-Trace*® or *Green Guide* series (Buckley, 2004e), or may be specified in national park permit conditions. Environmental issues such as these are considered in much more detail in books that focus on ecotourism (Buckley, 2003a, 2004e).

For adventure tourism operators, three very broad patterns may be identified here. First, the environmental impact of any adventure tourism activity depends far more strongly on the type of activity and the place it is carried out than on the operational details of environmental management. Helicopters are always more noisy than balloons, and helicopter noise will almost always create greater impacts on wildlife or people, irrespective of the type of machine or how carefully the pilot flies.

Secondly, adventure tours will only adopt minimal-impact operational practices in general if they have strong direction from the company owners and managers as well as relevant equipment and guide skills. In practice, in developing nations where permit conditions and park management agencies do not define environmental management practices in any detail, companies with expatriate owners who learned these minimal-impact approaches in their home country before setting up adventure tourism businesses overseas are likely to have better environmental management than companies established by local residents, for whom small-scale environmental management issues may seem trivial relative to other social concerns.

And thirdly, whilst environmental guidelines may be followed by leading operators because of concerns to protect their product or concerns expressed by their clients, most tour operators pay little attention to such guidelines unless they are either enshrined in legislation and enforced through on-site policing and prosecution, or are strongly endorsed by other tour operators in the area that are in a position to exert significant peer pressure.

## Safety

If thrills are a core component of adventure, then safety practices are a core component of adventure tours. Serious accidents, and especially fatalities, can cause a dramatic drop-off in the number of clients for the entire activity and country concerned, not merely the particular operator. This applies especially for activities where participants are looking for fun and thrills and have little idea of real risks. For adventure tours carried out at more expert level, clients are more likely to have an informed understanding of risks, whether from falls, hypothermia, drowning or avalanches. New fatalities may encourage them to re-evaluate probabilities, but are less likely to lead to them abandoning the activity.

Actual safety measures are highly specific to the particular activity concerned. There are relatively few factors that can be applied across a wide range of activities. These include, for example, a low client-to-guide ratio; routine maintenance and replacement of all equipment; detailed client briefings before any specific part of the activity; and training of clients in safety procedures and the use of safety equipment at the beginning of any tour.

Such training may include, for example: teaching people how to float through a whitewater rapid (feet first, face up); how to belay someone safely on a climbing rope; or how to search quickly and efficiently for a companion buried under an avalanche. For activities that involve animals, whether riding horses or watching large and potentially dangerous wildlife, additional sets of safety skills are needed to interpret the animals' behaviour and respond accordingly.

Within any given activity sector, there is generally a standard set of safety practices and equipment used by the majority of commercial tour operators, though there are always individual operators who are either more or less careful than their competitors. Nearly all raft tour operators issue their clients with lifejackets, for example, and with helmets in narrow rocky rivers, and wetsuits in cold water. Safety briefings, however, can be extremely sketchy for some operations, and not all companies use safety kayakers, even on fast-flowing, high-volume rivers where they can make the greatest contribution to safety.

Similarly, all heliski operators issue clients with avalanche transceivers, but whilst some companies train and test their clients quite thoroughly in avalanche search techniques, others are rather cursory. Some heliski operators have one guide per group, whilst others have two. For those who have one, some have the guide ski or ride at the front of the group and others at the rear. Most operators have one or two clients in each group, as well as the guide, carrying a safety pack with a radio, snow shovel and avalanche probe. Of the heliski operators in the case studies described here, however, only one fits out every client with a safety pack that includes avalanche float bags.

Safety issues are not restricted to the adventure activity itself. Sometimes getting to and from the site can be the most dangerous component, particularly in some developing countries where road rules are rather rudimentary. The choice of vehicle and the defensive skills of the driver may well make a major contribution to the overall safety of the tour.

## Marketing

As with other specialist types of tourism, the methods used for marketing adventure tours depend strongly on the size of the company. For large-volume operators, it is worth their while to print colour brochures and catalogues and distribute them through tour packages and travel agents, trade shows and specialist slide nights, and their own mail-out lists and retail shopfronts. This applies equally for single-site, single-activity operators such as Quicksilver Cruises; multi-site, single-activity operators such as Conservation Corporation Africa or Canadian Mountain Holidays; or multi-site, multi-activity operators such as Natural Habitat Adventures or World Expeditions. Such broad-scale retail-level marketing approaches are expensive and contribute significantly to the overall price of a trip, but they keep up a continuous flow of new clients, which is essential to maintain a high-volume operation.

For small specialist companies that offer products aimed principally for clients already skilled in the particular activity concerned, it is generally more cost-effective to advertise only in specialist magazines, since these target the potential clientele much more directly. Once readers know the company exists and where it operates, they can find further information from its website and then contact it directly by phone or email, with no need for agents or a retail shopfront.

Not everyone who reads such recreational magazines has the money or inclination to take a commercial adventure tour, but some do; and a majority of people who have the skills for an expert-level adventure tour do also read relevant recreational magazines, at least occasionally. A small advertisement in the back pages of every issue hence provides a good marketing approach.

In addition, many such tour companies sponsor places on occasion for travel journalists, so as to obtain editorial coverage. For relatively upmarket trips that do not demand a high level of skill, such as many of the large-animal wildlife-watching safaris, the most worthwhile coverage may be in general upmarket travel magazines such as *Condé Nast Traveler.* For more skilled and specialist activities such as surfing, it may generally be more valuable to get editorial coverage in specialist surfing magazines. Indeed, for many adventure tourism activities there seem to be strong links between tour operators, magazines and video producers, equipment manufacturers and sponsored professional competitors (Buckley, 2003b).

For a one-off commercial expedition, such as a first ascent, descent or crossing, even a single magazine advertisement may be too expensive, unless the expedition organizers can obtain sponsorship or free editorial coverage. Such trips, arguably the leading fringe of the commercial adventure tourism industry (Buckley, 2004a), rely particularly on word-of-mouth and e-mail contacts directly from the organizers.

For high-volume, single-activity adventure tour operators based in a well-known adventure tourism destination, a different marketing strategy is needed. Examples include, e.g. 1-day dive, snorkel or rafting trips from Cairns, Australia, or 1-day rafting, bungee-jump or combination trips from Queenstown, New Zealand or Victoria Falls, Zimbabwe. For these companies, the bulk of their business comes either from walk-up clients who arrive at the destination with no prior plans or bookings, or from generalized package tours where the activity is either included or an optional add-on expense for which time is allowed in the itinerary.

For these companies, retail packaging and price are critical issues, since they are commonly in direct competition with similar operators at the same destination. Extreme examples occur for trekking and rafting tours in Kathmandu, Nepal, or the sea canoe operators at Phang Nga Bay in Thailand. In those cases, there are so many copycat operators, and so many agents on-selling places in multiple different trips, that a potential client can easily become confused as to exactly what they are buying from whom. Even in Cairns, Australia, there are rows of small travel agents scattered amongst the tourist cafés on the esplanade, all of them selling a multiplicity of tours on commission. Most of the actual tour operators do also have their own, much larger retail shops and offices in Cairns, but clients may not find them unless they already know where to look, and this provides opportunities for touts and commission agents.

One interesting new pattern that seems to have occurred at several of these adventure destinations is that individual tour operators, who formerly offered only a single activity, have subsequently started or bought up operations across a range of different activities so that they can offer a single package product that includes everything a visitor might wish to do. In Queenstown, New Zealand, the individual companies seem to have remained distinct, but have got together to market multi-activity packages, presumably with a cross-commission structure. At Victoria Falls, Zimbabwe, Shearwater Adventures has apparently taken over a range of other activities, though of course it is never reliable to infer company structure from marketing materials, and the Shearwater portfolio may represent branding rather than ownership.

## Signatures

As outlined above, even though adventure tours are different and there are exceptions to all generalizations, some broad general patterns may still be discerned with respect to each of the major characteristics considered. Are these patterns also linked – that is, are there patterns in the patterns?

An analysis of over 170 case studies in ecotourism, for comparison (Buckley, 2003a), suggested that in that sector there are regional signatures, i.e. that different types of ecotourism products, and indeed different combinations of products, are differentially common in different regions of the world. Can we identify comparable signatures in the adventure tourism sector, perhaps characteristic of different activities rather than different geographic regions? Maybe, but only weakly.

Heliski packages offered by the major companies in Canada, for example, and also the only company in the Himalayas, are rather similar in general structure though different in detail. For example, their basic products are all 1-week integrated packages that include well-appointed accommodation and excellent meals, similarly sized helicopters and similar pricing structures. The details of guiding, guarantees and pricing are different, but these differences are minor compared to the similarities. They even have similar incentive programmes to encourage repeat clients. So it might appear that heliskiing has a standard signature.

Heliskiing operators in New Zealand, however, have a very different package structure; and those in Russia, apparently, use very different ex-military helicopters. There is thus nothing sacrosanct about the 1-week package: it is simply a convenient response to market demand and cost control, and perhaps some convergence between competitors. Interestingly, one of the New Zealand operators does also offer a 1-week package, but because of uncertainty over weather conditions, not many clients buy it and so it has never become a standard.

Many multi-day, live-aboard surf and dive charters seem to be 7–10 days in duration, but this probably reflects the length of time that people can take for holidays, balanced against the investment it takes to fly to the region concerned. This is also a convenient period to restock the boat's food and freshwater supplies; but if clients were prepared to pay for longer trips, it would be easy to organize resupplies at sea.

Whilst there are certainly similarities between tour products and operators in some activity sectors, therefore, it is difficult to argue that there are standardized signatures, or even that there are identifiable nodes within the overall continuum of adventure tour products.

Within each activity subsector, there are often similarities between products offered by different operators in regards to some, or indeed several of the features considered for each case study.

My impression, however, is that there is little correlation between the patterns in different parameters. For example, the overview of marketing techniques above identified four major approaches, but these are connected partly with company size, partly with the degree of specialization and partly with the popularity of the destination for adventure tourism more generally. Similarly, there are variations in safety and environmental management practices, but these do not seem to be connected to company size or marketing strategy. Evidence for activity-specific signatures, therefore, seems weak.

## Icon Sites

At a broader scale still, is there anything that characterizes and distinguishes the adventure tourism sector as a whole from other components of the tourism industry? The aspect cited most commonly is risk, or at least thrills, and indeed since these seem to be how adventure tourism is defined, it is not surprising that it should be a characteristic of adventure tourism products. As noted elsewhere, however, one person's panic is another person's ho-hum, so risks are not necessarily a universal defining characteristic, though certainly an important one. Equally, though many adventure tours take place in remote areas, this is not necessarily a universal defining characteristic.

I should like to propose another possible defining characteristic for consideration. It seems to me that in almost all forms of adventure tourism there is a set, or perhaps a series or even a hierarchy, of icon destinations that people want to visit, either for personal challenge or social capital. They are therefore prepared to pay tour operators to take them there safely and look after them once they are there. This applies not only to places like Mt Everest, which is known worldwide as well as to mountaineers, but equally to famous climbing, kayaking, surfing, horse-trekking or even hiking sites.

Such icon destinations are not necessarily obvious or even fixed. There are traditional classic sites such as Mt Everest for mountaineers, the Yosemite Half Dome for rock climbers or the Colorado Grand Canyon for rafters, which are well-known to the general public as well as aficionados of the activity concerned. But beyond these, there are constantly changing lists that are perhaps set as much by fashion as by fact. Rapids such as Throne Room, Terminator and Infierno Canyon on the Rio Futaleufu in Chile are world-famous amongst whitewater kayakers, and rightly so; but there are perhaps equally or even more gnarly rapids in the Qamdo Gorge of the Mekong in Tibet, which hardly anyone has even heard of. The classic big-wave challenges for surfers are on Hawaii's North Shore, but over recent decades and years other waves have become equally famous: at Mavericks off the coast of southern California, Teahupo'o in Tahiti, Shipstern in Tasmania and Cyclops in Western Australia.

Of course, not everyone can tackle the most difficult of climbs, the deepest of dives, the steepest of slopes or the wildest of rapids: indeed, in many cases only a tiny minority of young, athletic, sponsored expert professionals can do so. But the icon sites are there none the less; and within the icon set or series, there are other sites that less skilled exponents may still pit themselves against, especially with an expert guide. Specialist adventure recreation magazines perpetuate the notion of icon destinations by publishing lists: great walks of the world, the ten best paddleable waterfalls, 20 sites to dive before you die, the world's top 100 waves, and so on.

Of course, it is not only adventure tourism that has its icon destinations. Golfers go to St Andrews, horse racing fans to Ascot, car racing fans to Daytona or Indianapolis, marathon runners to Boston, art lovers to the Louvre and Elvis addicts to Graceland. But these are human heritages, not natural challenges or attractions.

My suggestion here is simply that in adventure tourism, the precise place where you go for your preferred activity is a critical component of the commercial product. In this book, I have examined the structure of the products, including place as only one of a dozen or more parameters considered. As noted at the outset, this does not seem to have been done before and I trust it will form a useful basis for future analysis. But to understand the adventure tourism industry more thoroughly, I would submit, it is not enough to examine the activities, we must also catalogue the places where people go. Such a task goes well beyond the 100 case studies I have compiled here and I commend it for future research.

# 27 Conclusions

Baffin Island, Canada (see Chapter 7). Photo Ralf Buckley.

# Trends and Patterns

## Introduction

Looking even more broadly than the comparisons in Chapter 26, can we identify any trends and patterns in the adventure tourism sector as a whole? Such trends are of interest in research, as they may be worth tracking and testing in future. They are also of interest to tour operators and tourism agencies, for commercial reasons. A dozen such trends and patterns are therefore identified below.

## Growth

Over recent decades, the commercial adventure tourism sector has continued to grow from, and within, the overall outdoor recreation industry. Many cash-rich, time-poor people with reasonable general fitness now seem to treat adventure activities more as a purchasable holiday package than as a lifetime personal investment in skills and equipment. This has led to expansion at both the low-skill and high-skill ends of the sector.

## Insurance

In keeping with an overall increase in litigation in North America, and indeed many other countries, there has been growing concern among adventure tourism providers regarding issues of potential liability. This has led to increasingly lengthy and complex pre-trip waivers and disclaimers, as well as much-increased insurance premiums. For some activities in some countries, it has simply driven many former providers out of the market. With reduced competition, remaining operators have increased prices so as to cover increased insurance costs.

## Adventure destinations

Especially in recent years, there has been a marked increase in the number of tourist destinations marketing themselves specifically as adventure destinations. Some of these are long-standing tourist destinations that have simply added new products or changed their marketing strategies. Others are relatively small-scale destinations that are seeking to promote growth in tourism by focusing on a portfolio of adventure products and opportunities. There are enormous differences in the scale of visitation and the scope of activities offered between different destinations that have adopted the adventure label. Some use adventure events as a destination marketing tool. To date, however, there are probably only a few dozen adventure destinations at most, as compared to many thousands of adventure products.

## Copycats and takeovers

There are a number of cases where one individual has invested enormous personal time, effort and resources to establish an adventure tourism product, but has then had to fight over copycat operators or hostile takeovers. Examples include John Gray's Sea Canoe in Thailand, David Allardice's Ultimate Descents in Nepal, and perhaps Chris Spelius' Expediciones Chile on the Futalefu. There are also many examples, of course, where adventure tour companies and products have changed hands, or names, through perfectly fair business dealings, as in the case of Queenstown Rafting and Challenge Rafting in New Zealand.

## Combo products

There seems to be a trend for many individual tour operators to offer a range of different adventure activities at a single destination, often packaged as a discounted bundle of individual tours that is marketed as a 'combo' product. This approach is generally more common for companies that have an on-ground operational base at the destination concerned. In some cases it is simply a syndicated marketing strategy, where the actual on-ground activities are still operated by separate independent companies. In other cases, a single company has either bought up local companies that offer other activities or has purchased equipment, hired staff and acquired permits so as to conduct those activities itself in competition with any other operators. These strategies have parallels in many other industry sectors.

## Retail packaging

There are also many tour operators that offer a portfolio of products at different destinations. Such companies, however, do not necessarily maintain an operational base at each of the destinations concerned. Instead, many of them are larger retail packagers that use their branding and distribution channels to maintain a clientele to whom they can sell a range of local tour products. In addition, there are specialist tour operators that offer similar products or activities at a range of different destinations, from wildlife lodges to whalewatching, surf charters to ski tours. They may actually operate all these products themselves, or they may retail a range of similar products offered by local operators in different places.

## Cross marketing

Currently, there seems to be a strong trend to increased cross-marketing links between adventure tourism products and other products purchased by the same consumers. These links are made through magazines, mailouts, inserts, Internet sites, television, films, fashion, shops and merchandising, mobile phones and music players, and entertainment venues such as nightclubs.

## Amenity migration

In some areas, outdoor recreation opportunities, and to a lesser extent commercial adventure tourism, have triggered amenity migration; and this in turn has led to an increase in adventure tourism as the amenity migrants seek commercial opportunities to maintain their lifestyles.

## Exploratories

A number of top-end adventure tourism companies now offer 'exploratories' as well as routine tours. These are not necessarily first ascents, descents or traverses, but they are generally new itineraries, for that operator at least. Effectively, the term is used both as a marketing device, to advertise adventure, and as a kind of additional legal disclaimer, to warn clients that the trip may not necessarily run smoothly or according to plan.

### Flexible itineraries

Other tour companies also make a virtue of necessity by advertising that their schedules or itineraries are flexible and that this is part of the adventure. This approach is used at both ends of the economic scale, from overland buses to polar expedition cruises.

### Unreliable conditions

Where weather-related aspects of the tour product are concerned, however, many tour companies take the opposite approach: their marketing features ideal conditions, and fails to mention that such conditions may rarely occur. This applies particularly for activities that require prior skill and where the client experience depends very heavily on actual conditions at the time, be it weather, insect pests, snow cover, river flow, swell size or wind direction.

### More luxury

The level of luxury available in adventure tours continues to increase. Backpacker buses are more comfortable. Wildlife heliski and diving lodges have spas and massage therapists. Dive boats, surfboats and heliski operations offer private charters with especially luxurious facilities. Expedition cruise boats have suites with satellite phones, and sometimes even a helicopter. It has almost become a truism that successful adventure tour operators continue to move up-market.

## Research Priorities

### Introduction

Growth and change in the adventure tourism sector itself, it seems, have far out-stripped growth and evolution of adventure tourism research. It has been argued recently that such concerns apply for the entire tourism sector, and that the tourism research literature provides, at best, a very incomplete description and analysis of tourism either as an industry or as a social phenomenon (Ritchie *et al.*, 2005). For adventure tourism in particular, it appears that the relevant theoretical framework is derived almost entirely from the outdoor recreation and education literature, with relatively few analyses of commercial adventure tourism products.

### Case studies and audits

One of the principal aims of this book, of course, is an attempt to remedy this deficiency to some small degree. To describe 100 or so case studies out of the tens of thousands of adventure tourism products that exist worldwide, however, clearly leaves ample opportunity for additional case studies. This applies particularly to those activity subsectors that have not been covered in this volume, but also to those that are. Until we have numerous examples of actual adventure tourism products described and documented by reliable researchers, how can we hope to identify any general patterns, explore any general trends or test any general theories?

To compile such case studies is not a trivial task. Analyses of marketing materials alone are not enough. To determine actual practice and performance requires on-the-spot audits, and these take time, expertise and funding. The first call for future research, therefore, is very simple: more case studies. There is, of course, nothing sacred about the particular style and structure used in this volume. Other researchers will no doubt adopt an emphasis that reflects their own disciplinary backgrounds. Indeed, we see that even within this volume, the various contributing authors have adopted different but equally valid approaches to analyse their own particular activity subsectors.

## Commercial statistics

Adventure tourism is part of the tourism industry, and if we are to build up any general picture of it, surely we need to know basic things such as how many businesses offer what products where, how many people buy them and what they spend. We need to know where those people travel from and to, at what times of year, and for how long. We can ask how often individual people take multiple adventure tours that involve the same activity, and how often they take tours that involve different activities. For the latter, we could examine whether particular combinations of activities are more common than others and if so why, and we can ask whether such patterns differ with the age or relative expertise of the individual concerned. We could examine whether demand is more sensitive to price or political instability, and whether such patterns differ between activities or client age-groups.

Any of this information would be both new and relevant to understanding the real-world tourism industry. Such suggestions are not intended to belittle the psychological research that currently seems to dominate this field, nor the highly valuable body of research from outdoor recreation that focuses on the management of specific visitor activities in public lands. It is simply to suggest that we can hardly claim understanding of an industry if we cannot yet describe the products or identify the buyers and sellers, the product prices and the size of the markets.

## Leadership

Similarities and differences between adventure tourism and non-commercial adventure recreation also present a high priority for future research, because it is these similarities and differences that determine the degree to which results, models and paradigms derived from research in outdoor recreation may be applied to commercial adventure tourism.

One might hypothesize, for instance, that leadership roles are basically similar, but that the relative authority of the leader over the participants may be different between commercial and non-commercial groups. Such patterns are unlikely to be straightforward, however. Certainly, commercial tour clients have paid to be led and looked after, and they may also be significantly older than their guides and hold positions of authority in their own working lives. School-age participants in educational or other non-profit activities, however, may well have rich and litigious parents who may be even more concerned about their children's experience than they would be about their own.

Equally, in a private recreational trip put together by friends, there is commonly a leader who is acknowledged at least informally either because of greater skill or greater familiarity with the particular area visited. The difference in skills between that leader and the other participants in such a private trip is likely to be far less than the difference in skills between a professional guide and paying clients in a commercial adventure tourism trip. Such factors may reduce the relative authority of the leader over the rest of the group.

Overall, therefore, it is not automatically apparent whether leaders in private groups or commercial tours would have greater authority or responsibility. To test these speculations would be relatively straightforward, and perhaps such comparisons could help to inform research into organizational behaviour and leadership more generally. Of course, leadership roles are not the only potential issue for such comparisons.

## Behaviour

It seems likely that there might also be similarities and differences in intra-group dynamics and in social and environmental behaviour. For example, my own anecdotal observations lead me to suspect that commercial adventure tours create greater environmental impact than the more highly skilled and careful private and non-profit groups, but less impact than inexperienced or uncaring groups. Managers of public parks in peri-urban areas may think that commercial tours do less damage than private visitors, because the former at least have a leader, whilst the latter include local vandals. Managers of public parks in remote wilderness areas, in contrast, may have the opposite opinion, because the private visitors are experienced backcountry travellers with good minimal-impact skills, whilst the commercial tour clients are inexperienced and inexpert in comparison. To date, however, such observations are purely anecdotal; there seem to be no controlled or comprehensive comparisons.

## Geography

For some research questions, the distinction between commercial adventure tours and private adventure recreation may be insignificant. For example, there is a geography of icon sites for different adventure tourism activities, and the sites are commonly the same for commercial adventure tours as for individual adventure recreation. Specialist recreational magazines for the activities concerned commonly feature the same sites in their editorial articles about recreational trips as are advertised in the same magazines by commercial tour providers.

The locations of these icon sites, however, do not depend solely on features of the natural terrain. They also depend on access, infrastructure, politics, visas, permits, safety, and so on. Perhaps even more importantly, they depend on the availability of information. In heavily used whitewater rivers such as the Colorado Grand Canyon or the Shotover in New Zealand, every individual feature of every single rapid has a name. For the whitewater rivers that tumble from the Tibetan plateau into China, some sections have not yet even been seen. Icon sites can change as skills and technology evolve. Rock faces once considered unclimbable are now scaled routinely. Potentially lethal and misshapen waves such as Cyclops in Western Australia, as well as potentially lethal and perfectly shaped waves such as

Teahupo'o in Tahiti, are now surfed regularly. The changing geography of different adventure activities, both extreme and routine is, surely, a worthy subject for study.

## Marketing

Aspects of marketing might also merit investigation. As more and more destinations scramble to label themselves as adventure capitals, we might ask why they think this will work and how successful it has been in practice. Can a place, for example, market itself successfully as an adventure tourism destination if it only offers one activity, or must it be known for a portfolio of different products? Are there upper or lower size limits to recognition of an adventure tourism destination? Can a place outgrow an adventure tourism label? May it become perceived as too soft or too mainstream? Can a city successfully add an adventure tourism strand to its marketing if it is already known as a beach resort or other mass tourism destination? Comparative longitudinal studies of appropriately selected tourist destinations could shed light on all of these questions, but do not seem to have been attempted.

## Manufacturing

Most adventure tourism activities need specialized equipment: hiking boots, saddles, kayaks, climbing gear, dive regulators, snowboards, mountain bikes, ORVs and many more. As noted earlier, many major equipment manufacturers have a political as well as a market involvement in the adventure tourism sector.

   To date, however, there seems to have been little published academic research on this aspect of the adventure tourism industry. As a very simple example, how are the many different individual models of snowboards, whitewater kayaks or mountain bikes distributed between different manufacturers? How are prices and sales volumes of these models distributed both between and within manufacturers? How have specific manufacturers changed their products, product mixes and target markets over time? What alliances have manufacturers formed with each other, with tour operators, and with other industry sectors or lobby groups, and why?

## Safety and liability

As noted at the outset of this volume, issues of safety, risk, liability and insurance are currently critical to adventure tourism in most parts of the world, but are largely beyond the scope of the current volume. The case studies presented here include information on practical safety precautions taken, but not on legal issues such as the wording of waivers and disclaimers, the legislative frameworks in the countries concerned, any indemnities required by landowners or land management agencies as part of permit conditions, or any details on insurances held by the tour operators. Such issues, however, are certainly worthy of research by appropriately qualified people. Related areas of research such as accident and disease statistics for different areas and activities are equally significant for health and safety.

## Ecology

A relatively high proportion of commercial adventure tours take place either in remote regions, in protected areas, or both. In the former, social impacts on local communities may be of concern; in the latter, ecological impacts on native species and ecosystems may be even more important. Research on impacts, in particular, falls under the general heading of recreation ecology; and recreation ecology research to date is remarkably sparse in relation to the economic scale of the adventure tourism sector and the ecological significance of the species and environments affected (Newsome *et al.*, 2002, 2005; Buckley, 2004e, 2005a).

## Lifestyles

Beyond the immediate confines of the commercial adventure tourism itself, there are research questions relating to its broader social context, such as those alluded to in Chapter 22. For example, the links between adventure tourism and amenity migration certainly deserve further investigation. The same applies to links between adventure tourism and broader lifestyle aspects; and to the use of adventure events in promoting adventure destinations.

# Policy Issues

## Economics

There are large-scale international attempts at present to use ecotourism as a tool in community development and the alleviation of poverty, especially in developing nations. As noted by Buckley (2003a) ecotourism can, under appropriate circumstances, bring money from rich people in rich countries directly to poor people in poor countries in an extremely focused manner. Given that nature, adventure and sometimes also cultural attractions or activities are often coupled together in the same commercial tour product, these goals also apply for adventure tourism, as illustrated by many of the case studies in this volume.

The same pitfalls, of course, also apply. For example, any community or region that shifts from a subsistence economy to a cash economy based on tourism automatically becomes vulnerable to fluctuations in global tourism markets, which may be more sudden and severe than fluctuations in local weather. Any new economic benefits from tourism are unlikely to be distributed evenly within the recipient community. In countries that are simultaneously pursuing many different avenues for development, there is always the risk that regional opportunities in nature and adventure tourism will be sacrificed to national priorities for commodity production or energy generation, as has happened in China and Chile. And in countries that receive significant sums in multilateral or bilateral development assistance, aid-funded infrastructure and related projects can swamp the local incomes earned from nature and adventure tourism.

## Social

Tourism has the potential to divide and disrupt host communities, and this applies for adventure tourism as for any other subsector. Not surprisingly, people who see themselves making a net gain from tourism are generally in favour of it, whereas those who incur increased costs or disruption are generally opposed to it. This applies, for example, to mountaineering, trekking and rafting in the Andes or Himalayas, just as it does to the 'Indy' car race on the Gold Coast, Australia's archetypal 3S/4S beach resort town. People who earn a living or improve their social tourism status through tourism or associated property development, in either developed or developing nations, commonly form political alliances to promote more tourism. Those who see tourism as interfering with their way of life, corrupting their children, or increasing local infrastructure costs, are likely to want tourism restricted.

Commonly, there is no fixed dividing line between the social effects of packaged commercial adventure tours and those of individual tourists undertaking similar activities. The total number of tourists, the goods and services they want, and the ways they behave are the main factors influencing social impacts. In areas that already have a significant tourism industry, new adventure tours generally make only a small pro rata contribution to social change. In areas where tourism is new and adventure tours are its first manifestation, the ways in which adventure tours companies and their clients interact with local residents become more critical.

New economic and employment opportunities provide benefits for some, but the degree to which these benefits are both realized and distributed depends on the local culture, whether more communal or more entrepreneurial.

Social impacts can also arise from differences in the culture, religion, diet and material wealth between tourists and hosts. Such differentials may operate in either direction. Sailors or surfers resident in developed countries may view sailing or surfing tour clients with disdain, whilst residents of developing nations may view such adventure tour clients with envy. Some adventure tourists live on local foods; others bring their own supplies and indirectly influence local eating habits.

From a policy perspective, any measures taken to promote adventure tourism or the economic opportunities it can create in developing nations also need to consider local social impacts on host communities and ways in which these communities can address and manage such impacts, if indeed they want to. The need to appreciate such issues at a policy level may be particularly acute for adventure tourism, for several reasons. In the more remote parts of some countries, adventure tourists may be the only city people that local rural residents encounter. Even if these tourists are from the same countries, but particularly if they are from overseas, cultural differences can be considerable. Secondly, for adventure tourism activities that do not require significant prior skill, numbers can grow very rapidly once a particular place and activity becomes popular. And thirdly, whilst products that are marketed as ecotours may attract clients who are aware of their own potential social impacts and generally try to act so as to minimize them, this may be less likely for products advertised purely as adventure tours.

## Environment

Adventure tours produce impacts on the natural as well as the human environment; and ecological as well as social impacts should be a significant consideration in any policy measures related to adventure tourism. Whilst some adventure tours take place in ecosystems that are already heavily modified by other human uses, others operate in protected areas and similar sites of high conservation value, where environmental impacts are of particular concern. The best-known example is perhaps the littering of Mt Everest with discarded oxygen bottles and other climbing equipment. This particular impact is principally of aesthetic rather than ecological significance, since the area concerned is well above the altitude for plant and animal communities.

Many types of adventure tourism, however, can indeed have major environmental consequences. Helicopter noise, for example has been implicated in disturbance to caribou in Canada, sperm whales in New Zealand and bowerbirds in Australia. Tourists on adventure or expedition cruises to the Antarctic can disturb nesting penguins, albatrosses and other seabirds if they approach too closely during landings. Even seakayakers can disturb seals. Off-road tours can damage soil, vegetation, ground-nesting birds and burrowing animals.

There may also be significant indirect impacts from adventure tours. For example, trekking in the Himalayas has led to local deforestation as residents cut trees for cooking and heating in guesthouses. Even if tours bring tents and fuel stoves for their clients, porters stay in guesthouses that burn wood. When some guesthouses installed fuel stoves and heaters, porters simply avoided those establishments, because they levy an additional charge for heating and cooking, which wood-fuelled establishments do not (Pobocik and Butalla, 1998).

As national policies and international agencies worldwide seek to promote adventure tourism as a tool in rural development and poverty alleviation, its impacts on ecosystems and biodiversity, as well as local livelihoods, need to be taken into consideration. As concluded by Buckley (2003a), the nature, eco and adventure tourism sector can indeed, with appropriate precautions, generate funds for both communities and conservation, but only if conservation laws and land tenures, and systems to promote social equity are in place before the commercial industry starts to grow.

## Policy implications

From a policy perspective, therefore the lessons from this volume may be summarized as follows:

- Anywhere with appropriate natural features will eventually attract commercial adventure tours, if it has not already done so.
- Tourist destinations that want to increase visitor numbers can do so currently by promoting themselves as adventure destinations, but this has limited scope and will generally lead to growth in relatively unskilled, high-volume adventure tourism.
- Areas that can offer prime conditions for any particular adventure tourism activity need only promote themselves to the major international specialist tour operators for that activity, since these companies already have established clienteles and are constantly searching for new opportunities.
- In order to benefit from growth in adventure tourism, countries and communities must ensure that they have environmental, social and economic frameworks in place before promoting industry growth.
- The most critical environmental regulations are those establishing protected area systems and defining what activities are permitted within them and under what conditions.
- The most critical economic regulations are those relating to fees, charges and taxes, which determine how tourism revenues are allocated.
- The most critical social frameworks are those that determine how a particular society or community wants to allocate economic and employment opportunities associated with adventure tourism, and distribute any risks and gains.

- Growth in adventure tourism is also heavily dependent on laws relating to investment, foreign exchange, company structure, land tenure and legal liability, and on safety, security and political stability in the regions concerned.
- Adventure tourism opportunities can easily be destroyed by the impacts of other economic sectors, whether public or private, commercial or aid-funded, so development plans for any area where adventure tourism is one option must consider it as an integral component, not as an add-on or afterthought.

In commercial terms, adventure tourism is commonly coupled with nature, eco and cultural tourism, so policy and planning for anyone of these must also consider the others, bearing in mind that adventure tourism may often be the fastest-growing.

In conclusion, nature, eco and adventure tourism is a valuable component of the tourism industry and tourism development strategies in both developed and developing nations, but well-designed environmental, economic and social policy frameworks are critical, otherwise tour operators will reap the benefits and host communities will bear the costs.

# Epilogue

The case studies described in this volume have been assembled and audited over a period of decades, and brought up to date as far as possible in 2005. Even so, they represent only a tiny proportion of the global adventure tourism industry: and as the details of each case change month by month, they can only reflect general patterns, not specific statistics. For my colleagues and other readers who will, I hope, use and update this text, a few closing comments may be in order.

Adventure tourism is not going away. It is affected by wars, terrorism, disease outbreaks, fuel prices and climate change like other sectors of the tourism industry. Indeed, it is probably much more sensitive to such issues than urban and resort tourism. But since the market demand for outdoor adventure tourism is driven ultimately by a human social megatrend to increasing urbanization (Buckley, 1998), it seems likely that adventure tourism will keep growing. So it certainly seems to be a worthwhile subject for further study.

We need new researchers to take up these opportunities. Not only to find out how adventure tour operators cross-market with nightclubs (Chapter 24), or how outdoor clothing sales are driven by fashion as much as function (Chapter 22), but to audit commercial adventure tours products now on offer (Chapter 3), and report on how they operate.

Adventure tour products on offer change very quickly indeed. Whilst updating information on these case studies during 2005, we have found that particular products appear and disappear from tour operator websites, change their structure or price markedly, or are bought or sold between different tour operators. The tour operators themselves also change their corporate and physical structures quite frequently, and sometimes even their names. So, the case studies described may well change yet again even between proof and printing of this book, and will certainly change over the next few years. Don't rely on these case studies for logistic or statistical information on individual tour products. Check current websites; check when websites were last updated; and make current enquiries by e-mail and telephone, or whatever means of communication may replace them!

I wrote this book not just because adventure tourism is a large but little-studied sector, but because it is closely linked in commercial terms to the nature and ecotourism sector, as indicated through terms such as ACE and NEAT (see Chapter 1). But ecotourism, and its nature and adventure cousins, have real and lasting global significance only in so far as they affect the natural environment, either directly or through social and economic changes. They may provide a tool for conservation; they may represent a threat; or both at once. Either way, as noted above, they are a manifestation of a human social megatrend, so their role as threat or tool deserves scrutiny. This is the real significance in studying adventure tourism, and I trust this volume may make some small contribution.

# Acknowledgements

As noted at the outset of this volume, I was able to take part in some of the adventure tours described as case studies only through generous sponsorships by the companies concerned. Such sponsorships do not affect the factual information present, but they did make a very considerable difference to the range and scope of adventure tours included. This applies particularly to the horse riding, heliskiing and snowboarding, and expedition cruise chapters. I am equally obliged to the many other tour operators who effectively allowed me to work my passage, whether as a guide, a safety boater, or in some cases simply as a researcher. In addition, companies such as Burton® Snowboards and Perception® Kayaks sponsored equipment. I am particularly grateful to the contributing authors, who covered sectors of the adventure tourism activity where they are far more capable than myself. These are: Claudia Ollenburg on horse riding; Julie Schaefers on mountain biking; Rob Hales on mountaineering; Jerry Johnson and Ian Godwin on ice climbing; and Carl Cater on the World Adventure Capital. I should also like to acknowledge the diligence of Karen Sullivan and Michaela Irvebrant in searching out and checking citations and websites, not to mention typing the text; and to the editors and staff at CABI for their assistance and forbearance.

# References

Abercrombie and Kent (2005) Abercrombie & Kent. Available at: http://www.abercrombiekent.com/

Access Fund (2005) Welcome to the Access Fund. Available at: http://www.accessfund.org/

Adams, W.M. and Infield, M. (2003) Who is on the gorilla's payroll? Claims on tourist revenue from Ugandan National Park. *World Development* 31, 177–190.

Adelman, B.J., Heberlein, T.A. and Bonnicksen, T.M. (1982) Social psychological explanations for the persistence of a conflict between paddling canoeists and motor craft users in the Boundary Waters Canoe Area. *Leisure Sciences* 5, 45–62.

Adrift (2005) Whitewater rafting. Available at: http://www.surfthesource.com/

Adrift Adventures (2005) River trips and learning adventures. Available at: http://www.adrift.com/

Adventure Travel Trade Association (2005) Learn. Partner. Grow. Available at: http://www.adventuretravel.biz/

African Adrenalin (2005) African Adrenalin safaris. Available at: http://www.africanadrenalin.com.za/

Aitkens, M. (1990) Have snowboard will soar. *The Physician and Sports Medicine* 18, 114–120.

AJ Hackett (2005) AJ Hackett Bungy, New Zealand. Available at: http://www.ajhackett.com/

Alaska Backcountry Bike Tours (2005) Alaska mountain biking adventures! Available at: http://www.mountainbikealaska.com/

Allison, W.R. (1996) Snorkeler damage to reef corals in the Maldive Island. *Coral Reefs* 15, 215–218.

Alpine Ascents (2005) Alpine Ascents International. Available at: http://www.alpineascents.com/

Alpine Club of Canada (2005) The Alpine Club of Canada. Available at: http://www.alpineclubofcanada.ca/

Ambunti Lodge (2005) Welcome to the Mystical Sepik. Available at: http://ambuntilodge-sepiktour.com.pg/

American Rivers (2005) American Rivers. Available at: http://www.amrivers.org/

Anderson, K.L. (1999) The construction of gender in an emerging sport. *Journal of Sport and Social Issues* 23, 55–79.

Anderson, S. (2000) Expedition health and safety: a risk assessment. *Journal of the Royal Society of Medicine* 93, 557–562.

Archabald, K. and Naughton-Treves, L. (2001) Tourism revenue sharing around national parks in Western Uganda: early efforts to identify and reward local communities. *Environmental Conservation* 28, 135–149.

Arizona Raft Adventures (2005) Arizona Raft Adventures. Available at: http://www.azraft.com/

Arnould, E. and Price, I. (1993) River magic: extraordinary experience and the extended service encounter. *Journal of Consumer Research* 20, 24–45.

Asia-Pacific Economic Cooperation (APEC) (1997) *Tourism and Environmental Best Practice in APEC Member Economies*. APEC, Singapore.

Atoll Adventures (2005) Atoll Travel. Available at: http://www.atolltravel.com/

Auf und Davon Reisen (2005) Auf und Davon Reisen. Available at: http://www.auf-und-davon-reisen.de/

Aurora Expeditions (2005) Cruising the heart of nature. Available at: http://www.auroraexpeditions.com.au/

Balloon Down Under (2005) Welcome to Balloon Down Under. Available at: http://www.balloondownunder.com/

Bardia Jungle Cottages (2005) Bardia Jungle Cottage, Royal Bardia National Park. Available at: http://www.visitnepal.com/bjc/

Barnes, J.I. and Jager, J.L.V. (1996) Economic and financial incentives for wildlife use on private land in Namibia and the implications for policy. *South African Journal of Wildlife Research* 26, 37–46.

Barnes, J.I., Schier, C. and Van Rooy, G. (1999) Tourists' willingness to pay for wildlife viewing and wildlife conservation in Namibia. *South African Journal of Wildlife Research* 29, 101–111.

Basman, C.M., Manfredo, M.J., Barro, S.C., Vaske, J.J. and Watson, A. (1996) Norm accessibility: an exploratory study of backcountry and frontcountry recreational norms. *Leisure Sciences* 18, 177–191.

Bass, R., Ridgeway, R. and Wells, F. (1987) *Seven Summits*. Warner Books, New York.

Beale, C.M. and Monaghan, P. (2004) Human disturbance: people as predation-free predators? *Journal of Applied Ecology* 41, 335–343.

Beedie, P. (2003) Mountain guiding and adventure tourism: reflections on the choreography of the experience. *Leisure Sciences* 22, 147–167.

Beedie, P. and Hudson, S. (2003) Emergence of mountain-based adventure tourism. *Annals of Tourism Research* 30, 625–643.

Beeh, J. (1999) Going green. Adventure vs ecotourism – can the road less travelled get trampled too often? *The Environmental Magazine* 10, 46–47.

Beeton, S. (2005) The case study in tourism research: a multi-method case study approach. In: Ritchie, B.W., Burns, P. and Palmer, C. (eds) *Tourism Research Methods: Integrating Theory and Practice.* CAB International, Wallingford, UK, pp. 37–48.

Bejder, L., Dawson, S.M. and Harraway, J.A. (1999) Responses by Hector's dolphins to boats and swimmers in Porpoise Bay, New Zealand. *Marine Mammal Science* 15, 738–750.

Bentley, T.A. and Page, S.J. (2001) Scoping the extent of adventure tourism accidents. *Annals of Tourism Research* 28, 705–726.

Bentley, T., Page, S.J. and Laird, I.S. (2000) Safety in New Zealand's adventure tourism industry: the client accident experience of adventure tourism operators. *Journal of Travel Medicine* 7, 239–245.

Bentley, T., Page, S.J. and Laird, I. (2001a) Accidents in the New Zealand adventure tourism industry. *Safety Science* 38, 31–48.

Bentley, T.A., Meyer, D., Page, S.J. and Chalmers, D. (2001b) Recreational tourism injuries among visitors to New Zealand: an exploratory analysis using hospital discharge data. *Tourism Management* 22, 373–381.

Bentley, T., Page, S.J., Meyer, D., Chalmers, D. and Laird, I. (2001c) How safe is adventure tourism in New Zealand: an exploratory analysis. *Applied Ergonomics* 32, 327–338.

Bentley, T., Page, S.J. and Laird, I. (2003) Managing tourist safety: the experience of the adventure tourism industry. In: Wilks, J. and Page, S.J. (eds) *Managing Tourist Health and Safety in the New Millennium.* Pergamon, Oxford, pp. 85–100.

Berno, T., Moore, K., Simmons, D. and Hart, V. (1996) The nature of the adventure tourism experience in Queenstown, New Zealand. *Australian Leisure* 8, 21–25.

Berrow, S.D. (2003) Developing sustainable whalewatching in the Shannon estuary. In: Garrod, B. and Wilson, C. (eds) *Marine Ecotourism: Issues and Experiences.* Channel View, Clevedon, UK, pp. 198–203.

Bicycle Business (2005) Lies, damn lies and statistics. Available at: http://www.bikebiz.co.uk/

Billabong (2005) Billabong. Available at: http://www.billabong.com.au/

Bisht, H. (1994) *Tourism in Garhwal Himalaya: with Special Reference to Mountaineering and Trekking in Uttarkashi and Chamoli Districts.* Indus Publishing Company, New Delhi.

Blackfeather Inc. (2005) Blackfeather: the wilderness adventure company. Available at: http://www.blackfeather.com/

Blahna, D.J., Smith, K.S. and Anderson, J.A. (1995) Backcountry llama packing: visitor perceptions of acceptability and conflict. *Leisure Sciences* 17, 185–204.

Blane, J.M. and Jaakson, R. (1994) The impact of ecotourism boats on the St Lawrence beluga whales. *Environmental Conservation* 21, 267–269.

Blue Ribbon Coalition (2005) Blue Ribbon Coalition. Available at: http://www.sharetrails.org/

Blumenthal, T. (2001) Mountain biking at ski resorts – an overview. International Mountain Bicycling Association Print Center. Available at: http://www.imba.com/

Booth, K.L. and Cullen, R. (2001) Managing recreation and tourism in New Zealand mountains. *Mountain Research and Development* 21, 331–334.

Borrie, W.T. and Harding, J.A. (2002) *Effective Recreation Visitor Communication Strategies: Rock Climbers in the Bitterroot Valley, Montana.* USDA Forest Service, Rocky Mountain Research Station, Ogden, Utah.

Borrie, W. and Roggenbuck, J. (2001) The dynamic, emergent, and multi-phasic nature of onsite wilderness experiences. *Journal of Leisure Research* 33, 202–228.

Botswana Odyssey (2005) Botswana Odyssey. Available at: http://www.botswanaodyssey.com/home/index.htm/

Bourdeau, P., Corneloup, J. and Mao, P. (2002) Adventure sports and tourism in the French mountains: dynamics of change and challenges for sustainable development. *Current Issues in Tourism* 5, 22–32.

Bowker, J.M. (2001) *Outdoor Recreation by Alaskans: Projections for 2000 Through 2020.* USDA Forest Service, Pacific Northwest Research Station, Portland, Oregon.

Bowker, J.M. and English, D.B.K. (2002) *Mountain Biking at Tsali: an Assessment of Users, Preferences, Conflicts, and Management Alternatives.* USDA Forest Service, Southern Research Station, Asheville, North Carolina.

Bowker, J.M., English, D.B.K. and Donovan, J.A. (1996) Toward a value for guided rafting on southern rivers. *Journal of Agricultural and Applied Economics* 28, 423–432.

Brandt, R. (2005) Dropping the ball. *Outside* October, 32.

Bratton, R., Kinnear, G. and Korolux, G. (1979) Why people climb mountains. *International Review of Sport Sociology* 4, 23–36.

Breivik, G. (1996) Personality, sensation seeking and risk taking among Everest climbers. *International Journal of Sport Psychology* 27, 308–320.

British Columbia Helicopter and Snowcat Skiing Association, BCHSSOA (2005) Available at: http://www.bchssoa.com/

British Mountaineering Council (2005) Participation statistics sheet. Available at: http://www.thebmc.co.uk/safety/advice/articles/ParticipationStats03.pdf/

Brookes, A. (2001) Doing the Franklin: wilderness tourism and the construction of nature. *Tourism Recreation Research* 26, 11–18.

Broome, L.S. (2001) Density, home range, seasonal movements and habitat use of the mountain pygmy-possum *Burramys parvus* (Marsupialia: Burramyidae) at Mount Blue Cow, Kosciuszko National Park. *Austral Ecology* 26, 275–292.

Brown, M.N.R. (1997) On the edge: a history of adventure sports and adventure tourism in Queenstown. Unpublished MA thesis, University of Otago, New Zealand.

Buckley, R.C. (1981) Alien plants in central Australia. *Botanical Journal of the Linnaean Society* 82, 369–379.

Buckley, R.C. (1994) Carry on up the Amazon. *The Australian Weekend Review* 9 March, 5–6.

Buckley, R.C. (1995) Ecotourism in China: the Yangbi Expedition. *The Australian Weekend Review*, 17 June.

Buckley, R.C. (1998) Ecotourism megatrends. *Australian International Business Review* 1998, 52–54.

Buckley, R.C. (1999) *Green Guide to White Water.* CRC Tourism and Griffith University, Gold Coast.

Buckley, R.C. (2000) NEAT trends: current issues in nature, eco and adventure tourism. *International Journal of Tourism Research* 2, 437–444.

Buckley, R.C. (2002a) Surf tourism and sustainable development in Indo-Pacific Islands. I. The industry and the islands. *Journal of Sustainable Tourism* 10, 405–424.

Buckley, R.C. (2002b) Surf tourism and sustainable development in Indo-Pacific Islands. II. Recreational capacity management and case study. *Journal of Sustainable Tourism* 10, 425–442.

Buckley, R.C. (2003a) *Case Studies in Ecotourism.* CAB International, Wallingford, UK.

Buckley, R.C. (2003b) Adventure tourism and the clothing, fashion and entertainment industries. *Journal of Ecotourism* 2, 126–134.

Buckley, R.C. (2003c) Pay to play in parks: an Australian policy perspective on visitor fees in public protected areas. *Journal of Sustainable Tourism* 11, 56–73.

Buckley, R.C. (2004a) Skilled commercial adventure: the edge of tourism. In: Singh, T.V. (ed.) *New Horizons in Tourism.* CAB International, Wallingford, UK, pp. 37–48.

Buckley, R.C. (2004b) Impacts of ecotourism on birds. In: Buckley, R. (ed.) *Environmental Impacts of Ecotourism.* CAB International, Wallingford, UK, pp. 187–209.

Buckley, R.C. (2004c) Impacts of ecotourism on terrestrial wildlife. In: Buckley, R. (ed.) *Environmental Impacts of Ecotourism.* CAB International, Wallingford, UK, pp. 211–228.

Buckley, R.C. (2004d) Environmental impacts of motorized off-highway vehicles. In: Buckley, R. (ed.) *Environmental Impacts of Ecotourism*. CAB International, Wallingford, UK, pp. 83–98.

Buckley, R.C. (2004e) *Environmental Impacts of Ecotourism*. CAB International, Wallingford, UK.

Buckley, R.C. (2005a) Recreation ecology research effort: an international comparison. *Tourism Recreation Research* 30, 99–101.

Buckley, R.C. (2005b) In search of the narwhal: ethical dilemmas in ecotourism. *Journal of Ecotourism* 4, 129–134.

Buckley, R.C., Pickering, C. and Warnken, J. (2000) Environmental management for alpine tourism and resorts in Australia. In: Godde, P.M., Price, M.F. and Zimmerman, F.M. (eds) *Tourism and Development in Mountain Regions*. CAB International, Wallingford, UK, pp. 27–46.

Buckley, R.C., Witting, N. and Guest, M. (2003) Visitor fees, tour permits and asset and risk management by Parks Agencies: Australian case study. In: Buckley, R.C., Pickering, D. and Weaver, D.B. (eds) *Nature-Based Tourism, Environment and Land Management*. CAB International, Wallingford, UK, pp. 51–69.

Buckley, R., Sander, N., Ollenburg, C. and Warnken, J. (2006) Green change: inland amenity migration in Australia. In: Moss, L. (ed.) *The Amenity Migrants*. CAB International, Wallingford, UK, pp. 278–294.

Budget Expeditions (2005) *Price Does Matter. Tours for 18–35s*. Think! Adventure, Sydney.

Burton Inc. (2005) *2005 Rider's Journal*. Burton, Burlington, Virginia.

Butynski, T.M. and Kalina, J. (1998) Gorilla tourism: a critical look. In: Milner-Gulland, E.J. and Mace, R. (eds) *Conservation of Biological Resources*. Blackwell, Oxford, pp. 294–313.

Buultjens, J. and Davis, D. (2001) Managing for sustainable commercial whitewater rafting in Northern New South Wales, Australia. *Journal of Tourism Studies* 12, 40–50.

Buykx, C. (2001) *The Responsible Travel Guide Book*. World Expeditions, Sydney. Available at: http://www.worldexpeditions.com.au/index.php?section=about_us&id=322/

Byrd, J.H. and Hamilton, W.F. (1997) Underwater cave diving fatalities in Florida: a review and analysis. *Journal of Forensic Sciences* 42, 807–811.

Camp, R.J. and Knight, R.I. (1998) Rock climbing and cliff bird communities at Joshua Tree National Park, California. *Wildlife Society Bulletin* 26, 892–898.

Canadian Avalanche Association (2005) Canadian Avalanche Association. Available at: http://www.avalanche.ca/

Canadian Mountain Holidays (2005) Canadian Mountain Holidays. Available at: http://www.cmhski.com/

Canadian Tourism Commission (1995) *Adventure Travel in Canada*. Tourism Canada, Ottawa.

Carlson, C. (2001) *A Review of Whalewatching Guidelines and Regulations Around the World*. International Fund for Animal Welfare, Yarmouth Port, Massachusetts.

Carothers, P., Vaske, J.J. and Donnelly, M.P. (2001) Social values versus interpersonal conflict between hikers and mountain bikers. *Leisure Sciences* 23, 47–61.

Cater, C. (2001) Beyond the gaze: the reflexive tourist and the search for embodied experience. Unpublished PhD thesis, University of Bristol, UK.

Cater, C.I. (2006) Playing with risk? Participant perceptions of risk and management complications in adventure tourism. *Tourism Management* 27, 317–325.

Cater, C. and Cater, E. (2000) Marine environments. In: Weaver, D.B. (ed.) *The Encyclopedia of Ecotourism*. CAB International, Wallingford, UK, pp. 265–282.

Cater, C. and Cater, E. (forthcoming) *Marine Ecotourism*. CAB International, Wallingford, UK.

Centre d'Avalanche de La Haute-Gaspésie (2005) Centre d'avalanche de La Haute-Gaspesie. Available at: http://www.centreavalanche.qc.ca/

Cessford, G.R. (1995) Off-road mountain biking: a profile of participants, setting and preferences. Available at: http://www.mountainbike.co.nz/politics/doc/profile/abstract.htm/

Cessford, G.R. (2002) Perception and reality of conflict: walkers and mountain bikes on the Queen Charlotte Track in New Zealand. In: Arnberger, A., Brandenburg, C. and Muhur, A. (eds) *Monitoring and Management of Visitor Flows in Recreational and Protected Areas*. Proceedings of the Conference held at Bodenkultur University Vienna, Austria. Institute for Landscape Architecture and Landscape Management, Bodenkultur University, Vienna, pp. 102–108.

Challenge Rafting (2005) Whitewater rafting Queenstown, New Zealand. Available at: http://www.raft.co.nz/

Chavez, D.J. (1996a) Mountain biking: direct, indirect, and bridge building management. *Journal of Park and Recreation Administration* 14, 21–35.

Chavez, D.J. (1996b) *Mountain Biking: Issues and Actions for USDA Forest Service Managers*. United States Department of Agriculture, Forest Service, California.

Chavez, D.J. (1999) Mountain biking – a rapidly growing sport. In: Cordell, K. (ed.) *Outdoor Recreation in American Life: A National Assessment of Demand and Supply Trends*. Sagamore, Champaign, Illinois, pp. 245–246.

Chavez, D.J., Winter, P.L. and Baas, J.M. (1993) Recreational mountain biking: a management perspective. *Journal of Park and Recreation Administration* 11, 29–36.

Chen, R.J.C., Bloomfield, P. and Fu, J.S. (2003) An evaluation of alternative forecasting methods for recreation visitation. *Journal of Leisure Research* 35, 441–454.

Cheron, E. and Ritchie, B. (1982) Leisure activities and perceived risk. *Journal of Leisure Research* 14, 139–154.

Cheyne, J. and Ryan, C. (1996) The Resource Management Act, a bungy operation and problems of planning. In: Oppermann, M. (ed.) *Proceedings of Pacific Rim Tourism 2000*. Centre for Tourism Studies, Waiariki Polytechnic, pp. 17–28.

Chhetri, P., Arrowsmith, C. and Jackson, M. (2004) Determining hiking experiences in nature-based tourist destinations. *Tourism Management* 25, 31–43.

Chicks with Picks (2005) Women's ice climbing clinics. Available at: http://www.chickswithpicks.net/

China Tours (2005) China Tours … viele Wege ins Reich der Mitte. Available at: http://www.china-tours.de/

Christiansen, D. (1990) Adventure tourism. In: Miles, J.C. and Priest, S. (eds) *Adventure Education*. Venture Publishing, State College, Pennsylvania, pp. 433–441.

Ciclo Montaña (2005) Ciclo Montaña España. Available at: http://www.ciclomontana.com/

Clift, S., Grabowski, P. and Sharpley, R. (1997) British tourists in the Gambia: health precaution and malaria prophylaxis. In: Clift, S. and Grabowski, P. (eds) *Tourism and Health: Risks, Research and Responses*. Pinter, London, pp. 97–116.

Cloke, P. and Perkins, H.C. (1998a) Cracking the canyon with the awesome foursome: representations of adventure tourism in New Zealand. *Environment and Planning D: Society and Space* 16, 185–218.

Cloke, P. and Perkins, H.C. (1998b) "Pushing the limits": place promotion and adventure tourism in the South Island of New Zealand. In: Perkins, H.C. and Cushman, G. (eds) *Time Out; Leisure Recreation and Tourism in New Zealand and Australia*. Longman, Auckland, pp. 271–287.

Cloutier, R. (2003) The business of adventure tourism. In: Hudson, S. (ed.) *Sport and Adventure Tourism*. Haworth Hospitality Press, New York, pp. 241–272.

Coffey, M. (2003) The survivors. *Outside*, September.

Coldfear (2005) Conditions. Available at: http://www.coldfear.com/conditions.htm/

Cole, D.N. (1996) Wilderness recreation in the United States – trends in use, users, and impacts. *International Journal of Wilderness* 2, 14–18.

Cole, D.N. (2004) Impacts of hiking and camping on soils and vegetation: a review. In: Buckley, R.C. (ed.) *Environmental Impacts of Ecotourism*. CAB International, Wallingford, UK, pp. 41–60.

Conservation Corporation Africa (2005) Rewaken your soul. Available at: http://www.ccafrica.com/

Constantine, R. (1999) *Effects of Tourism on Marine Mammals in New Zealand. Science for Conservation: 106*. Department of Conservation, Wellington, New Zealand.

Constantine, R. (2000) Increased avoidance of swimmers by wild bottlenose dolphins (*Tursiop truncatus*) due to longterm exposure to swim-with-dolphin tourism. *Marine Mammal Science* 17, 689–702.

Cooperative des Guides D'Escalade du Quebec (2005) Home page. Available at: http://www.cogeq.com/

Cope, R. (2003) The international diving market. *Travel and Tourism Analyst* 6, 1–39.

Cordell, H.K. and Bergstrom, J.C. (1991) A methodology for assessing national outdoor recreation and supply trends. *Leisure Sciences* 13, 1–20.

Cordell, H.K., Green, G. and Betz, C. (2004) *Trends in Activity Participation Since Fall 1999. Recreation Statistics Update Report 2*. US Department of Agriculture, Southern Research Station, Asheville, North Carolina.

Corkeron, P.J. (1995) Humpback whales (*Megaptera novaeangliae*) in Hervey Bay, Queensland: behavior and responses to whale-watching vessels. *Canadian Journal of Zoology* 73, 1290–1299.

Cosley and Houston Alpine Guides (2005) Mount Kenya. Available at: http://www.cosleyhouston.com/kenya.htm/

Crawford, D.W., Jackson, E.L. and Godbey, G. (1991) Leisure activities and perceived risk. *Journal of Leisure Research* 14, 139–154.

Curtin, S. (2003) Whale-watching in Kaikoura: sustainable destination development? *Journal of Ecotourism* 2, 173–195.

Davidson, L. (2002) The "spirit of the hills": mountaineering in northwest Otago, New Zealand, 1882–1940. *Tourism Geographies* 4, 44–61.

Davis, D.C. and Tisdell, C.A. (1995) Recreational scuba diving and carrying capacity in marine protected areas. *Ocean and Coastal Management* 26, 19–40.

Davis, D.C. and Tisdell, C.A. (1996) Economic management of recreational scuba diving and the environment. *Journal of Environmental Management* 48, 229–248.

Davis, D.C. and Tisdell, C.A. (1998) Tourist levies and willingness to pay for a whale shark experience. *Tourism Economics* 5, 161–174.

Davis, D.C., Banks, S., Birtles, A., Valentine, P. and Cuthill, M. (1997) Whale sharks in Ningaloo Marine Park: managing tourism in an Australian marine protected area. *Tourism Management* 18, 259–271.

Deibert, M., Aronsson, D., Johnson, R.J., Ettlinger, C. and Shealy, J. (1998) Skiing injuries in children, adolescents and adults. *Journal of Bone and Joint Surgery [American Volume]* 80, 25–32.

Delle Fave, A., Bassi, M. and Massimini, F. (2003) Quality of experience and risk perception in high-altitude rock climbing. *Journal of Applied Sport Psychology* 15, 82–98.

Delta Sun Peaks (2005) Delta Hotels. Available at: http://www4.deltahotels.com/hotels/hotels.php?hotelId=38/

Derocher, A.E. and Stirling, I. (1990a) Distribution of polar bears (*Ursus maritimus*) during the ice-free period in western Hudson Bay. *Canadian Journal of Zoology* 68, 1395–1403.

Derocher, A.E. and Stirling, I. (1990b) Observations of aggregating behaviour in adult male polar bears (*Ursus maritimus*). *Canadian Journal of Zoology* 68, 1390–1394.

Derocher, A.E. and Stirling, I. (1995) Temporal variation in reproduction and body mass of polar bears in western Hudson Bay. *Canadian Journal of Zoology* 73, 1657–1665.

Devall, B. and Harry, J. (1981) Who hates whom in the great outdoors: the impact of recreation specialization and technologies of play. *Leisure Sciences* 4, 399–418.

Devaux, G. (1997) The sailing resort concept. *Cahiers Espaces* 1997, 128–138.

Diamantis, D. (ed.) (2004) *Ecotourism: Management and Assessment*. Thomson Learning, London.

Dive Kadavu (2005) Dive Kadavu Fiji. Available at: http://www.divekadavu.com/

Diversion Oz (2005) Diversion Dive Travel. Available at: http://www.diversionoz.com/

Dixon, J.A., Scura, L.F. and Van't Hof, T. (1993) Meeting ecological and economic goals: marine parks in the Caribbean. *Ambio* 22, 117–125.

Donnelly, M.P., Vaske, J.J. and Graefe, A.R. (1986) Degree and range of recreation specialization: toward a typology of boating related activities. *Journal of Leisure Research* 18, 81–95.

Donnelly, M., Vaske, J., Whittaker, D. and Shelby, B. (2000) Toward an understanding of norm prevalence: a comparative analysis of 20 years of research. *Environmental Management* 25, 403–414.

Dowling, R. and Newsome, D. (2005) Geotourism's issues and challenges. In: Dowling, R. and Newsome, D. (eds) *Geotourism*. Elsevier, Oxford, pp. 242–254.

Down Under Dirt (2005) Down under dirt. Available at: http://www.downunderdirt.co.nz/

Dreams Travel (2005) Tibet. Available at: http://www.dreams-travel.com/english/travelguide/tibet/index.asp/

Driver, B.L. and Knopf, R.C. (1976) Personality, outdoor recreation, and expected consequences. *Environment and Behaviour* 9, 169–193.

Duffus, D. (1996) The recreational use of grey whales in southern Clayoquot Sound, Canada. *Applied Geography* 16, 179–190.

Duffus, D.A. and Dearden, P. (1993) Recreational use, valuation, and management of killer whales (*Orcinus orca*) on Canada's Pacific Coast. *Environmental Conservation* 20, 149–156.

Duncans Off-Road (2005) Welcome to Duncans Off Road Driver Training and Tours. Available at: http://www.duncansoffroad.com.au/

Dyck, M.G. and Baydack, R.K. (2004) Vigilance behavior of polar bears (*Ursus maritimus*) in the context of wildlife-viewing activities at Churchill, Manitoba, Canada. *Biological Conservation* 116, 343–350.

Dyers, R. (1997) Adventure travel or ecotourism? *Adventure Travel Business* April, 2.

Eagles, P. and McCool, S. (2002) *Sustainable Tourism in Protected Areas. Guidelines for Planning and Management*. IUCN WCPA Best Practice Series No. 8. IUCN, Gland, Switzerland.

Earth Science Expeditions (2005) Shangri-La River Expeditions. Available at: http://www.shangri-la-river-expeditions.com/

Easson, S. (2006) *Philosophies of Adventure and Extreme Sports. Meaning, Motivation and Sporting Danger.* Routledge, New Zealand (in press).

Eastern and Southern Safaris (2005) Eastern and Southern Safaris. Available at: http://www.essafari.co.ke/

Eastern Mountain Sports (2005) About us. Available at: http://www.ems.com/aboutems/about_ems.jsp/

École d'Escalade L'Ascensation (2005) Roc gyms. Available at: http://www.rocgyms.com/

Ecotour Samoa (2005) Samoa Travel Eco Tourism Holidays. Available at: http://www.ecotoursamoa.com/

Edmonds, C. and Walker, D. (1989) Scuba diving facilities in Australia and New Zealand. Part 1. The human factor. *South Pacific Underwater Medicine Society Journal* 19, 94–104.

EMS Climbing School (2005) Welcome to the EMS Climbing School. Available at: http://www.emsclimb.com/

Endless River Adventures (2005) Endless River Adventures. Available at: http://www.endlessriveradventures.com/

English, D.B.K. and Bowker, J.M. (1996) Economic impacts of guided whitewater rafting: a study of five rivers. *Water Sources Bulletin* 32, 1319–1328.

Evolution 2 (2005) Professionnels de l'aventure. Available at: http://www.evolution2.com/default2.htm/

Ewert, A.W. (1985) Why people climb: the relationship of participant motives and experience level to mountaineering. *Journal of Leisure Research* 17, 241–250.

Ewert, A.W. (1989) *Outdoor Adventure Pursuits: Foundations, Models and Theories.* Publishing Horizons, Scottsdale, Arizona.

Ewert, A.W. (1994) Playing the edge: motivation and risk taking in a high-altitude wildernesslike environment. *Environment and Behaviour* 26, 3–24.

Ewert, A. (2000) Trends in adventure recreation: programs, experiences and issues. *Trends 2000: 5th Outdoor Recreation and Tourism Trends Symposium.* Lansing, Michigan.

Ewert, A.W. and Hollenhorst, S. (1989) Testing the adventure model: empirical support for a model of risk recreation participation. *Journal of Leisure Research* 21, 124–139.

Ewert, A.W. and Hollenhorst, S.J. (1997) Adventure recreation and its implications for wilderness. *International Journal of Wilderness* 3, 21–26.

Ewert, A.W. and Jamieson, L. (2003) Current status and future directions in the adventure tourism industry. In: Wilks, J. and Page, S.J. (eds) *Managing Tourist Health and Safety in the New Millennium.* Pergamon, Oxford, pp. 67–83.

EWP (2005) Mount Kenya introduction and trekking guide. Available at: http://ewpnet.com/mount_kenya_general.htm/

Exmouth Diving Centre (2005) Whale shark adventures. Available at: http://www.exmouthdive.com/english/whalesharks.htm/

Expediciones Chile (2005) Kayak Chile. Available at: http://www.exchile. com/kayakchile.html/

Explore Kamchatka (2005) Explore Kamchatka. Available at: http://www. explorekamchatka.com/

Explorers Club (2005) The Explorers Club. Available at: http://www.explorers.org/

Extreme Green Rafting (2005) Extreme Green Rafting. Available at: http://www.extremegreenrafting.com/

Fahey, B., Wardle, K. and Weir, P. (1999) Environmental effects associated with snow grooming and skiing at Treble Cone Ski Field. *Science for Conservation* 120, 49–62.

Farmer, R.J. (1992) Surfing: motivations, values and culture. *Journal of Sport Behavior* 15, 241–257.

Farris, M.A. (1998) The effects of rock climbing on the vegetation of three Minnesota cliff systems. *Canadian Journal of Botany* 76, 1–10.

Federiuk, C.S., Schlueter, J.L. and Adams, A.L. (2002) Skiing, snowboarding, and sledding injuries in a northwestern state. *Wilderness and Environmental Medicine* 13, 245–249.

Feejee Experience (2005) Feejee Experience. Available at: http://www.feejeeexperience.com/

Feher, P., Meyers, M.C. and Skelly, W.A. (1998) Psychological profile of rock climbers: state and trait attributes. *Journal of Sport Behavior* 21, 167–180.

Fennell, D. (1999) *Ecotourism: An Introduction.* Routledge, London.

Fennell, D. (2001) A content analysis of ecotourism definitions. *Current Issues in Tourism* 4, 403–421.

Fennell, D. and Dowling, R. (2003) *Ecotourism Policy and Planning.* CAB International, Wallingford, UK.

Fennell, D. and Eagles, P.F.J. (1990) Ecotourism in Costa Rica: a conceptual framework. *Journal of Parks and Recreation Research* 8, 23–34.

Festiglas du Québec (2005) Festiglas du Québec. Available at: http://www.festiglace.com/

Field Guide Association of Southern Africa (FGASA) (2005) Field Guide Association of Southern Africa. Available at: http://www.fgasa.org.za/

Firag, I. (2001) An exemplary island destination: tourism industry in the Maldives. In: World Tourism Organisation (ed.) *Island Tourism in Asia and the Pacific.* World Tourism Organisation, Madrid, pp. 92–102.

Fix, P. and Loomis, J.B. (1997) The economic benefits of mountain biking at one of its Meccas: an application of the travel cost method to mountain biking in Moab, Utah. *Journal of Leisure Research* 39, 342–352.

Fluker, M.R. and Turner, L.W. (2000) Needs, motivations, and expectations of a commercial whitewater rafting experience. *Journal of Travel Research* 38, 380–389.

Fowler, G.S. (1999) Behavioral and hormonal responses of Magellanic penguins (*Spheniscus magellanicus*) to tourism and nest site visitation. *Biological Conservation* 90, 143–149.

Fred Hollows Foundation (2005) The Fred Hollows Foundation. Available at: http://www.hollows.org/

Fredman, P. and. Heberlein, T.A. (2003) Changes in skiing and snowmobiling in Swedish mountains. *Annals of Tourism Research* 30, 485–488.

Frost, J. and McCullough, J. (1995) Biking trails: the ins and outs, the ups and downs. *Ski Area Management* 34, 78–91.

Gallatin National Forest Avalanche Center (2000) Gallatin National Forest Avalanche Center. Available at: http://www.mtavalanche.com/

GAP Adventures (2005) GAP Adventures. Available at: http://www.gapadventures.com/

Garrabou, J. (1998) The impact of diving on rocky sublittoral communities: a case study of a bryozoan population. *Conservation Biology* 12, 302–312.

Garrick, J.G. and Kurland, L.T. (1971) The epidemiological significance of unreported ski injuries. *Journal of Safety Research* 3, 182–187.

Garrod, B. and Fennell, D.A. (2004) An analysis of whalewatching codes of conduct. *Annals of Tourism Research* 31, 334–352.

Garrod, B. and Wilson, J.C. (2004) Nature on the edge? Marine ecotourism in peripheral coastal areas. *Journal of Sustainable Tourism* 12 (2), 95–120.

Gartner, W. and Lime, D. (2000) *Trends in Outdoor Recreation, Leisure, and Tourism.* CAB International, Wallingford, UK.

Geva, A. and Goldman, A. (1991) Satisfaction measurement in guided tours. *Annals of Tourism Research* 18, 177–185.

Giard, D. (1997) The situation regarding nature sport tourism in mountain areas. *Cahiers Espaces* 1997, 48–57.

Gibbons, S. and Ruddell, E.J. (1995) The effect of goal orientation and place on select goal interference among winter backcountry users. *Leisure Sciences* 17, 171–183.

Giese, M. (1996) Effects of human activity on Adelie penguins, *Pygoscelis adeliae*, breeding success. *Biological Conservation* 75, 157–164.

Gilbert, D. and Hudson, S. (2000) Tourism demand constraints: a skiing participation. *Annals of Tourism Research* 27, 906–925.

Gjerdalen, G. and Williams, P. (2000) An evaluation of the utility of a whale watching code of conduct. *Tourism Recreation Research* 25, 27–37.

Glacier Raft Company (2005) Middle Fork of the Flathead River. Available at: http://www.glacierraftco.com/riverst.htm/

*Glasgow Press and Journal* (31 July 1999) Swiss guides survivors face charges.

Gliddon, J. and Syvret, P. (2002) Riding high: the surfers who built an $8bn business. *The Bulletin* 13 August, 20–24.

Global Expedition Adventures (2005) Ski to the North Pole. Available at: http://www.north-pole-expeditions.com/ski_to_the_north_pole.htm/

Goeft, U. and Alder, J. (2000) Mountain bike rider preferences and perceptions in the south-west of Western Australia. *CALM Science* 3, 261–275.

Goeft, U. and Alder, J. (2001) Sustainable mountain biking: a case study from the southwest of Western Australia. *Journal of Sustainable Tourism* 9, 193–211.

Gold Coast Adventure Travel Group (2005) Australia's Gold Coast backpackers stuff. Available at: http://www.adventuregc.com/

Golden Bridge (2005) Across the Takla Makan. Available at: http://www. goldenbridge. net/SRT26.htm/

Gordon, J., Leaper, R., Hartley, F.G. and Chappell, O. (1992) *Effects of Whale Watching Vessels on the Surface and Underwater Acoustic Behavior of Sperm Whales off Kaikoura, New Zealand*. Department of Conservation, Wellington, New Zealand.

Gorman, D. (1994) Fitness for diving: a review of the critical issues. *South Pacific Underwater Medicine Society Journal* 24, 2–4.

Goulet, C., Regnier, G., Grimard, G., Valois, P. and Villeneueve, P. (1999) Risk factors associated with alpine skiing injuries in children: a case-control study. *American Journal of Sports Medicine* 27, 644–650.

Gramann, J.H. and Burdge, R.J. (1981) The effect of recreational goal on conflict perception: an evaluation and synthesis of research. *Journal of Leisure Research* 13, 15–27.

Great Adventures (2005) Great Adventures Reef and Green Island Cruises. Available at: http://www.greatadventures.com.au/

Great Outdoor Recreation Pages (2005a) GORP. Available at: http://gorp.away.com/index.html/

Great Outdoor Recreation Pages (2005b) Outdoor activities. Available at: http:// gorp.away.com/gorp/activity/main.htm/

Great White Bear Tours (2005) Great White Bear Tours. Available at: http://www. greatwhitebeartours.com/

Green, D. (2003) Travel patterns of destination mountain bikers. International Mountain Bicycling Association Print Center. Available at: http://www.imba.com/resources/science/travel_patterns.html/

Green, E. and Donnelly, R. (2003) Recreational scuba diving in Caribbean marine protected areas: do the users pay? *Ambio* 32, 140–144.

Grijalva, T.C., Berrens, R.P., Bohara, A.K., Jakus, P.M. and Shaw, W.D. (2002) Valuing the loss of rock climbing access in wilderness areas: a national-level, random-utility model. *Land Economics* 78, 103–120.

Guerba (2005) Adventure and discovery holidays. Available at: http://www.guerba.co.uk/

Gyimothy, S. and Mykletun, R.J. (2004) Play in adventure tourism: the case of Arctic trekking. *Annals of Tourism Research* 51, 855–878.

Ha'atafu Beach Resort (2005) Ha'atafu Beach Resort. Available at: http://www.surfingtonga.com/

Hackett, P.H. and Rennie, D. (1976) The incidence, importance, and prophylaxis of acute mountain sickness. *Lancet* 2, 1149–1154.

Hadley, G.L. and Wilson, K.R. (2004) Patterns of small mammal density and survival following ski-run development. *Journal of Mammalogy* 85, 97–104.

Hagel, B.E., Goulet, C., Platt, R.W. and Pless, B. (2004) Injuries among skiers and snowboarders in Quebec. *Epidemiology* 15, 279–286.

Hall, C.M. (1993) Ecotourism in the Australian and New Zealand sub-Antarctic islands. *Tourism Recreation Research* 18, 13–21.

Hall, C.M. (2005) The future of tourism research. In: Ritchie, B.W., Burns, P. and Palmer, C. (eds) *Tourism Research Methods*. CAB International, Wallingford, UK, pp. 221–230.

Hall, C.M. and McArthur, S. (1991) Commercial whitewater rafting in Australia: motivations and expectations of the participants and the relevance of group size for the rafting experience. *Australian Journal of Leisure and Recreation* 1, 25–31.

Hamilton, A., Cunningham, A., Byarugaba, D. and Kayanja, F. (2000) Conservation in a region of political instability: Bwindi impenetrable forest, Uganda. *Conservation Biology* 14, 1722–1725.

Hammitt, W. and Cole, D. (1998) *Wildland Recreation: Ecology and Management*, 2nd edn. John Wiley, New York.

Hanley, N. (2002) Rationing an open-access resource: mountaineering in Scotland. *Land Use Policy* 19, 167–176.

Hanley, N., Koop, G., Alvarez-Farizo, B., Wright, R.E. and Nevin, C. (2001) Go climb a mountain: an application of recreation demand modelling to rock climbing in Scotland. *Journal of Agricultural Economics* 51, 36–52.

Hanley, N., Shaw, W.S. and Wright, R.E. (2003) *The New Economics of Outdoor Recreation*. Edward Elgar, Cheltenham, UK.

Harriott, V.J., Davis, D. and Banks, S.A. (1997) Recreational diving and its impact in marine protected areas in eastern Australia. *Ambio* 26, 173–179.

Harris, R. and Leiper, N. (eds) (1995) *Sustainable Tourism: An Australian Perspective*. Butterworth, Oxford.

Harris Mountain Heli-ski (2005) Home page. Available at: http://www.heliski.co.nz/

Hawkins, J.P. and Roberts, C.M. (1992) Effects of recreational SCUBA diving on fore-reef slope communities of coral reefs. *Biological Conservation* 62, 171–178.

Hawkins, J.P. and Roberts, C.M. (1993) Effects of recreational scuba diving on coral reefs: trampling on reef flat communities. *Journal of Applied Ecology* 30, 25–30.

Hawkins, J.P. and Roberts, C.M. (1994) The growth of coastal tourism in the Red Sea: present and future effects on coral reefs. *Ambio* 23, 503–507.

Hawkins, J.P. and Roberts, C.M. (1999) Estimating the carrying capacity of coral reefs for recreational scuba diving. *Proceedings of the 8th Coral Reef Symposium* 2, 1923–1926.

Hawkins, J.P., Roberts, C.M., Van't Hof, T., De Meyer, K., Tratalos, J. and Aldam, C. (1999) Effects of recreational scuba diving on Caribbean coral and fish communities. *Conservation Biology* 13, 888–897.

Hawley, E. and Salisbury, R. (2004) *The Himalayan Database: The Expedition Archives of Elizabeth Hawley.* The American Alpine Club, Golden, Colorado.

Heino, R. (2000) What is so punk about snowboarding? *Journal of Sport and Social Issues* 24, 176–191.

Heli Ski Russia (2005) Heliski. Available at: http://www.heliski.ru/en/

Hendee, J.C. and Dawson, C.P. (2002) *Wilderness Management*, 3rd edn. WILD Foundation and Fulcrum Publishing, Colorado.

Hendricks, W.W. (1995) A resurgence in recreation conflict research: introduction to the special issue. *Leisure Sciences* 17, 157–158.

Heywood, J. and Murdock, W. (2002) Social norms in outdoor recreation: searching for the behaviour-conditions link. *Leisure Sciences* 24, 283–296.

High Sky Adventures (2005) High Sky Adventures. Available at: http://www.highskyadventures.com/

Higham, J. and Lusseau, D. (2004) Ecological impacts and management of tourist engagements with cetaceans. In: Buckley, R. (ed.) *Environmental Impacts of Ecotourism*. CAB International, Wallingford, UK, pp. 171–186.

Himachal Helicopter Skiing (2005) Himachal Helicopter Skiing. Available at: http://www.himachal.com/

Hof, J.G. and Kaiser, H.F. (1983) Long term outdoor recreation participation projections for public land management agencies. *Journal of Leisure Research* 15, 1–14.

Hoffmann, H. (2001) Mountain travel helps mountain farmers. *Entwicklung* 35, 26–28.

Hollenhorst, S., Schuett, M.A., Olson, D. and Chavez, D.J. (1995) An examination of the characteristics, preferences, and attitudes of mountain bike users of the national forests. *Journal of Park and Recreation Administration* 13, 41–51.

Holyfield, L. (1999) Manufacturing adventure: the buying and selling of emotions. *Journal of Contemporary Ethnography* 28, 3–32.

Honey Charters (2005) Honey Charters. Available at: http://www.honeycharters.com/

Hopkin, T.E. and Moore, R.L. (1995) The relationship of recreation specialization to setting preferences of mountain bicyclists. *Journal of Leisure Research* 14, 47–62.

Horizons Nouveaux (2005) Horizons Nouveaux Verbier. Available at: http://www.horizonsnouveaux.com/

Hornby, N. and Sheate, W.R. (2001) Sustainable management of recreational off-road vehicles in National Parks in the UK. *Environmental and Waste Management* 4, 95–105.

Howard, J. (1999) How do SCUBA diving operators in Vanuatu attempt to minimize their impact on the environment. *Pacific Tourism Review* 3, 61–69.

Hoyt, E. (2000) *Whale-Watching 2000: Worldwide Tourism Numbers, Expenditures, and Expanding Socioeconomic Benefits.* International Fund for Animal Welfare, Crowborough.

Hudson, S. (2002) *Sport and Adventure Tourism.* Haworth Hospitality Press, New York.

Hultkrantz, L. and Mortazavi, R. (1999) Landowner participation in the regulation of outdoor recreation: problems in snowmobiling regulation. *Tourism Economics* 4, 33–49.

Hyalite Canyon Ice Climbing Guide (2005) Hyalite Canyon Ice Climbing Guide. Available at: http://www.montanaice.com/

Illich, I.P. and. Haslett, J.R. (1994) Responses of assemblages of Orthoptera to management and use of ski slopes on upper subalpine meadows in the Austrian Alps. *Oceologia* 97, 470–474.

Indies Trader (2005) Indies Trader marine adventures. Available at: http://www.indiestrader.com/

Inglis, G.J., Johnson, V.I. and Black, F. (1999) Crowding norms in marine settings: a case study on snorkelling on the Great Barrier Reef. *Environmental Management* 24, 369–381.

International Association of Antarctica Tour Operators, IAATO (2005) International Association of Antarctica Tour Operators. Available at: http://www.iaato.org/

International Mountain Climbing School (2005) International Mountain Climbing School. Available at: http://www.ime-usa.com/imcs/

International Wildlife Adventures (2005) International Wildlife Adventures. Your path to nature travel. Available at: http://wildlifeadventures.com/

Intrepid Expeditions (2005) Welcome to Intrepidtravel.com. Available at: http://www.intrepidtravel.com/

Jack, S.J. and Ronan, K.R. (1998) Sensation seeking among high and low risk sports participants. *Personality and Individual Differences* 25, 1063–1083.

Jackson, E.L. and Wong, R. (1982) Perceived conflict between urban cross-country skiers and snowmobilers in Alberta. *Journal of Leisure Research* 14, 47–62.

Jacob, G.R. and Schreyer, R. (1980) Conflict in outdoor recreation: a theoretical perspective. *Journal of Leisure Research* 12, 368–380.

Jacoby, J. (1990) Mountain bikes: a new dilemma for wildland recreation managers? *Western Wildlands* 16, 25–28.

Jakus, P. and Shaw, W.D. (1996) An empirical analysis of rock climber's response to hazard warnings. *Risk Analysis* 16, 581–585.

Jakus, P. and Shaw, W.D. (1997) Congestion at recreation areas: empirical evidence on perceptions, mitigating behaviour and management preferences. *Journal of Environmental Management* 50, 398–401.

Jameson, S.C., Ammar, M.S.A., Saadalla, E., Mostafa, H.M. and Riegl, B. (1999) A coral damage index and its application to diving sites in the Egyptian Red Sea. *Coral Reefs* 18, 333–339.

Janik, V.M. and Thompson, P.M. (1996) Changes in surfacing patterns of bottlenose dolphins in response to boat traffic. *Marine Mammal Science* 12, 597–602.

Jennings, G. (2003) Marine tourism. In: Hudson, S. (ed.) *Sport and Adventure Tourism*. Haworth Hospitality Press, Binghamton, New York, pp. 125–164.

John Gray's Sea Canoe (2005) Seakayaking in Thailand. Available at: http://www.johngrayseacanoe.com/thailand/index.htm/

Johnson, B. and Edwards, T. (1994) The commodification on mountaineering. *Annals of Tourism Research* 21, 459–478.

Johnson, J. (2004) Impacts of tourism-related in-migration: the Greater Yellowstone region. In: Buckley, R. (ed.) *Environmental Impacts of Ecotourism*. CAB International, Wallingford, UK, pp. 171–186.

Johnson, J., Maxwell, B. and Aspinall, R. (2003) Moving nearer to heaven: growth and change in the Greater Yellowstone region, USA. In: Buckley, R.C., Pickering, C. and Weaver, D.B. (eds) *Nature-Based Tourism, Environment and Land Management*. CAB International, Wallingford, UK, pp.77–88.

Johnson, R.J., Ettlinger, C.F., Shealy, J.F. and Meader, C. (1997) Impact of super sidecut skis on the epidemiology of skiing injuries. *Sportverletz Sportschaden* 11, 150–152.

Josephson, J. (2002) *Waterfall Ice: Climbs in the Canadian Rockies*, 4th edn. Rocky Mountain Books, Calgary, Alberta.

Josephson, J. (2004) *Winter Dance: Select Ice Climbs in Southern Montana & Northern Wyoming*. First Ascent Press, Bozeman, Montana.

Jump the Beach (2005) Jump the Beach. Available at: http://www.jumpthebeach.com.au/

Kaikoura Helicopters Ltd (2005) World of whales. Available at: http://www.kaikourahelicopters.co.nz/

Kane, M.J. and Zink, R. (2004) Package adventure tours: markers in serious leisure careers. *Leisure Studies* 23, 329–345.

Kay, A.M. and Liddle, M.J. (1989) Impact of human trampling in different zones of a coral reef flat. *Environmental Management* 13, 509–520.

Kayak the Nile (2005) Kayak the Nile – cutting edge kayaking. Available at: http://www.kayakthenile.com/

Kayastha, S.L. (1997) Tourism and environment in the Himalayan region. In: Nag, P., Kumra, V.K. and Singh, J. (eds) *Geography and Environment: Volume Two, Regional Issues*. Concept Publishing Company, India.

Kearsley, G. (1997) Tourism planning and policy in New Zealand. In: Hall, C.M., Jenkins, J. and Kearsley, G. (eds) *Tourism Planning and Policy in Australia and New Zealand: Cases, Issues and Practice.* McGraw-Hill, Sydney, pp. 49–60.

Kenya Wildlife Society (2005) Mount Kenya National Park. Available at: http://www.kws.org/mtkenya.htm/

King Dive (2005) Ningaloo Reef Exmouth. Available at: http://www.theguncharters.com/

Kiwi Experience (2005) Kiwi Experience. Available at: http://www.kiwiexperience.com/

Knopf, R.C., Peterson, G.L. and Leatherberry, E.C. (1983) Motives for recreational river floating: relative consistency across settings. *Leisure Sciences* 5, 231–255.

Knopp, D. and Tyger, J. (1973) A study of conflict in recreational land use: snowmobiling vs. ski-touring. *Journal of Leisure Research* 5, 6–17.

Knowles, P. and Allardice, D. (1992) *White Water Nepal.* Menasha Ridge, Birmingham, Alabama and Rivers Publishing, Surrey.

Kovacs, K.M. and Innes, S. (1990) The impact of tourism on harp seals (*Phoca groenlandica*) in the Gulf of St. Lawrence, Canada. *Applied Animal Behaviour Science* 26, 15–26.

Kumuka (2005) Kumuka Worldwide. Available at: http://www.kumuka.com/

Lalati Resort (2005) Lalati. Available at: http://www.lalati-fiji.com/

Lampden, R. (1968) Tourism in the Lake Wakatipu basin. Unpublished MA thesis, University of Otago.

Lamprey, R.H. and Reid, R.S. (2004) Expansion of human settlement in Kenya's Maasai Mara: what future for pastoralism and wildlife? *Journal of Biogeography* 31, 997–1032.

Lapierre, S. and Gagnon, B. (2004) *Quebec guide des cascades de glace et voies mixtes.* La Randonnee Edition, Montreal.

Lash, S. and Urry, J. (1994) *Economies of Signs and Space.* Sage, London.

Lawrence, V. (2004) Untitled. *Prime 15* (1), 30. Mills Media Ltd, Port Moresby.

Levy, A.S., Hawkes, A.P., Hemminger, L.M. and Knights, S. (2002) An analysis of head injuries among skiers and snowboarders. *Journal of Trauma* 53, 695–704.

Lewis, S.P. and Wilcox, R. (2002) *Ice Climbers Guide to Northern New England,* 3rd edn. Huntington Graphics, Burlington, Vermont.

Ley, D. (1981) Behavioural geography and the philosophies of meaning. In: Cox, K.R. and Golledge, R.G. (eds) *Behavioural Problems in Geography Revisited.* Methuen, London, pp. 209–230.

Liddle, M.J. and Kay, A.M. (1987) Resistance, survival and recovery of trampled corals on the Great Barrier Reef. *Biological Conservation* 42, 1–18.

Lindblad Expeditions (2005) Lindblad Expeditions. Available at: http://www. expeditions.com/

Lipscombe, N. (1999) The relevance of the peak experience to continued skydiving participation: a qualitative approach to assessing motivations. *Leisure Studies* 18, 267–288.

Lischke, V., Byhahn, C., Westphal, K. and Kessler, P. (2001) Mountaineering accidents in the European Alps: have the numbers increased in recent years? *Wilderness Environmental Medicine* 12, 74–80.

Livet, R. (1997) From sports diving to underwater tourism. *Cahiers Espaces* 1997, 62–68.

L.L.Bean (2005) L.L.Bean. Available at: http://www.llbean.com/

Loeffler, T.A. (2004) A photo elicitation study of the meanings of outdoor adventure experiences. *Journal of Leisure Research* 36, 536–556.

Lopez, E.M. (1980) The effect of leadership style on satisfaction levels of tour quality. *Journal of Travel Research* 18, 20–23.

Lucas, R.C. (1964) Wilderness perception and use: the example of the Boundary Waters Canoe Area. *Natural Resources Journal* 3, 394–411.

Lunn, N.J. and Stirling, I. (1985) The significance of supplement food to polar bears during the ice-free period of Hudson Bay. *Canadian Journal of Zoology* 63, 2291–2297.

Lynch, T.P., Melling, L., Hamilton, R., MacReady, A. and Feary, S. (2004) Conflict and impacts of divers and anglers in a marine park. *Environmental Management* 33, 196–211.

Mace, B.L., Bell, P.A. and Loomis, R.J. (1999) Aesthetic, affective, and cognitive effects of noise on natural landscape assessment. *Society and Natural Resources* 12, 225–242.

Machold, W., Kwasny, O. and Gabler, P. (2000) Risk of injury through snowboarding. *Journal of Trauma* 48, 1109–1114.

Machold, W., Kwansy, O., Eisenhardt, P., Kolonja, A., Bauer, E., Lehr, S., Mayr, W. and Fuchs, M. (2002) Reduction of severe wrist injuries in snowboarding by an optimized wrist protection device: a prospective randomized trial. *Journal of Trauma* 52, 517–520.

MacLellan, L.R. (1999) An examination of wildlife tourism as a sustainable form of tourism development in North West Scotland. *International Journal of Tourism Research* 5, 375–387.

Macnab, A.J., Smith, T., Gagnon, F.A. and Macnab, M. (2002) Effect of helmet wear on the incidence of head/face and cervical spine injuries in young skiers and snowboarders. *Injury Prevention* 8, 324–327.

Malcolm, M. (2001) Mountaineering fatalities in Mt Cook National Park. *New Zealand Journal of Medicine* 114, 78–80.

Mallett, J. (1998) Plenary address. *Seventh World Congress of Adventure Travel and Ecotourism*. Quito, Ecuador.

Manning, R.E. (1999) *Studies in Outdoor Recreation*, 2nd edn. Oregon University Press, Corvallis, Oregon.

Manning, R.E. (2004) Managing impacts of ecotourism through use rationing and allocation. In: Buckley, R. (ed.) *Environmental Impacts of Ecotourism*. CAB International, Wallingford, UK, pp. 273–286.

Manning, R.E. and. Freimund, W.A. (2004) Use of visual research methods to measure standards of quality for parks and outdoor recreation. *Journal of Leisure Research* 36, 557–579.

Manning, R.E., Johnson, D. and Vandekamp, M. (1996) Norm congruence among tour boat passengers to Glacier Bay National Park. *Leisure Sciences* 18, 125–141.

Manning, R.E., Lawson, S., Newman, P., Laven, D. and Valliere, W. (2002) Methodological issues in measuring crowding-related norms in outdoor recreation. *Leisure Sciences* 24, 339–348.

Manning, R.E., Lawson, S., Newman, P., Budruk, M., Valliere, W., Laven, D. and Bacon, J. (2004) Visitor perceptions of recreation-related resource impacts. In: Buckley, R. (ed.) *Environmental Impacts of Ecotourism*. CAB International, Wallingford, UK, pp. 259–272.

Mansergh, I.M. and Scotts, D.J. (1989) Habitat continuity and social organization of the mountain pygmy-possum restored by tunnel. *Journal of Wildlife Management* 53, 701–707.

Marion, J.L. and Leung, Y. (2004) Environmentally sustainable trail management. In: Buckley, R. (ed.) *Environmental Impacts of Ecotourism*. CAB International, Wallingford, UK, pp. 229–244.

Marion, J.L. and Rogers, C.G. (1994) The applicability of terrestrial visitor impact management strategies to the protection of coral reefs. *Ocean and Coastal Management* 22, 153–163.

Maritime New Zealand (2005) Maritime New Zealand. Available at: http://www.maritimenz.govt.nz/

Maritime Safety Authority (1995) *Review of Commercial Whitewater Rafting Safety Standards; Final Advisory Group Report*. MSA, Wellington, New Zealand.

Marsh, J. (2000) Tourism and national parks in polar regions. In: Butler, R.W. and Boyd, S.W. (eds) *Tourism and National Parks: Issues and Implications*. Wiley, Chichester, UK, pp. 125–136.

Martin, P. and Priest, S. (1986) Understanding the adventure experience. *Journal of Adventure Education* 3, 18–21.

Matsumoto, K., Miyamoto, K., Sumi, H., Sumi, Y. and Shimizu, K. (2002) Upper extremity injuries in snowboarding and skiing: a comparative study. *Clinical Journal of Sport Medicine* 12, 354–359.

McDonald, J. (2003) The financial liability of park managers for visitor injuries. In: Buckley, R.C., Pickering, C. and Weaver, D. (eds) *Nature-Based Tourism, Environment and Land Management*. CAB International, Wallingford, UK, pp. 35–50.

McIntyre, N. (1992) Involvement in risk recreation: a comparison of objective and subjective measures of engagement. *Journal of Leisure Research* 24, 64–71.

McIntyre, N. and Roggenbuck, J.W. (1998) Nature/person transactions during an outdoor adventure experience: a multi-phasic analysis. *Journal of Leisure Research* 30, 401–422.

McLauchlan, M. (1995) White water death: why is the Shotover New Zealand's most lethal river? *North and South* December, 70–81.

McNeilage, A. (1996) Ecotourism and mountain gorillas in the Virunga volcanoes. In: Taylor, V.J. and Dunstone, N. (eds) *The Exploitation of Mammals Populations*. Chapman and Hall, London, pp. 334–344.

Medio, D., Ormond, R.F.G. and Pearson, M. (1997) Effect of briefings on rates of damage to corals by scuba divers. *Biological Conservation* 79, 91–95.

Melanesian Tourist Services (2005) Melanesian Tourist Services. Available at: http://www.meltours.com/

Mentawai Sanctuary (2005) Mentawai Sanctuary. Available at: http://www.mentawai.com/

Methven Heliskiing (2005) Methven Heliskiing. Available at: http://www.heliskiing.co.nz/methven/

Meyer, E. (1993) The impact of summer and winter tourism on the fauna of alpine soils in western Austria. *Revue Suisse de Zoologie* 100, 519–527.

Mike Ball (2005) Mike Ball Dive Expeditions. Available at: http://www.mikeball.com/

Mike Wiegele Helicopter Skiing (2005) Blue River, BC. Available at: http://www.wiegele.com/

Mintel Report (2002) *Sporting Activities in the Great Outdoors in the UK*. Mintel, London.

Mitchell, R.G. (1983) *Mountain Experience: The Psychology and Sociology of Adventure*. University of Chicago Press, Chicago, Illinois.

Montana Alpine Guides (2005) Montana Alpine Guides. Available at: http://www.adventuremontana.com/

Mooney Mountain Guides (2005) Mooney Mountain Guides LLC. Available at: http://www.mooney-mountainguides.com/

More, T.A. and Averill, J.R. (2003) The structure of recreation behavior. *Journal of Leisure Research* 35, 372–395.

Morgan, D.J. (1998) The adventure tourism experience on water: perceptions of risk and competence and the role of the operator. Unpublished MA thesis, Lincoln University, Christchurch, New Zealand.

Mosedale, J. (2002) Mountain biking in the Canadian Rocky Mountains: a situational analysis. Available at: http://www.mtnforum.org/resources/library/mosej02a.htm/

Mosisch, T.D. and Arthington, A.H. (2004) Impacts of recreational power-boating on freshwater ecosystems. In: Buckley, R. (ed.) *Environmental Impacts of Ecotourism*. CAB International, Wallingford, UK, pp. 171–186.

Moss, L. (ed.) (2006) *The Amenity Migrants*. CAB International, Wallingford, UK.

Mountain Equipment Co-op (2005) Mountain Equipment Co-op. Available at: http://www.mec.ca/Main/home.jsp/

Mountain Madness (2004) Mountain Madness. Available at: http://www.mountainmadness.com/

Mountain Travel Sobek (2005) Mountain Travel Sobek: the adventure travel company. Available at: http://www.mtsobek.com/

Mt Kenya Clean Up (2005) The Mt Kenya clean up mission. Available at: http://www.mtkenya.org/mtkenya.htm/

Mt Tremblant Resort (2005) Tremblant. Available at: http://www.tremblant.ca/

Mundet, L. and Ribera, L. (2001) Characteristics of divers at a Spanish resort. *Tourism Management* 22, 501–510.

Musa, G. (2003) Sipadan: an over-exploited scuba-diving paradise? An analysis of tourism impact, diver satisfaction and management priorities. In: Garrod, B. and Wilson, J.C. (eds) *Marine Ecotourism: Issues and Experiences*. Channel View, Clevedon, UK, pp. 122–137.

Musa, G., Hall, C.M. and Higham, J.E.S. (2004) Tourism sustainability and health impacts in high altitude adventure, cultural and ecotourism destinations: a case study of Nepal's Sagarmatha National Park. *Journal of Sustainable Tourism* 12, 306–331.

Mvula, C.D. (2001) Fair trade in tourism to protected areas – a micro case study of wildlife tourism to South Luangwa National Park, Zambia. *International Journal of Tourism Research* 3, 393–405.

Nagigia Surf Resort (2005) Amazing Fiji. Available at: http://www.fijisurf.com/

Nathanson, A., Haynes, P. and Galanis, D. (2002) Surfing injuries. *American Journal of Emergency Medicine* 20, 155–150.

National Association of Underwater Instructors (2005) NAUI Worldwide. Available at: http://www.naui.org/

National Outdoor Leadership School (2005) National Outdoor Leadership School. Available at: http://www.nols.edu/

National Park Service (2005) Denali mountaineering summary reports. US Department of the Interior. Available at: http://www.nps.gov/dena/home/mountaineering/summaryreports.htm/

National Sporting Goods Association (2005) Off-road mountain biking statistics. Mt Prospect, Illinois. Available at: http://www.nsga.org/

Natural Habitat Adventures (2005) The world's greatest nature expeditions. Available at: http://www.nathab.com/

Natural High (2005) Natural High adrenalin dealers. Available at: http://www.naturalhigh.co.nz/

Nature Conservancy (2005) The Nature Conservancy. Available at: http://nature.org/

Needham, M.D. and Rollins, R.B. (2005) Interest group standards for recreation and tourism impacts at ski areas in the summer. *Tourism Management* 26, 1–13.

Needham, M.D., Rollins, R.B. and Wood, C.J.B. (2004) Site-specific encounters, norms and crowding of summer visitors at Alpine ski areas. *International Journal of Tourism Research* 6, 421–437.

Neil, D. (1990) Potential for coral stress due to sediment resuspension and deposition by reef walkers. *Biological Conservation* 52, 221–227.

Nepal Tourist Board (2005) welcomenepal. Available at: http://www.welcomenepal.com/

Nepal, S.K. (2000) Tourism in protected areas: the Nepalese Himalaya. *Annals of Tourism Research* 27, 661–681.

Neumann, P.W. and Merriam, H.G. (1972) Ecological effects of snowmobiles. *Canadian Field Naturalist* 86, 207–212.

Newsome, D., Moore, S.A. and Dowling, R.K. (2001) *Natural Area Tourism: Ecology, Impacts and Management.* Channel View, Clevedon, UK.

Newsome, D., Milewski, A., Philips, N. and Annear, R. (2002) Effects of horseriding on national parks and other natural ecosystems in Australia. *Journal of Ecotourism* 1, 52–74.

Newsome, D., Cole, D.N. and Marion, J.L. (2004a) Environmental impacts associated with recreational horse-riding. In: Buckley, R.C. (ed.) *Environmental Impacts of Ecotourism.* CAB International, Wallingford, UK, pp. 61–82.

Newsome, D., Lewis, A. and Moncrieff, D. (2004b) Impacts and risks associated with developing, but unsupervised, stingray tourism at Hamelin Bay, Western Australia. *International Journal of Tourism Research* 6, 305–323.

Newsome, D., Dowling, R. and Moore, S. (2005) *Wildlife Tourism.* Channel View, Clevedon, UK.

New Zealand Department of Conservation (NZDOC) (2004) *Aoraki/Mount Cook National Park Management Plan.* NZDOC, Christchurch, New Zealand.

Nichols, C., Stone, G., Hutt, A., Brown, J. and Yoshinaga, A. (2001) Observations of interactions between Hector's dolphins (*Cephalorhynchus hectori*), boats and people at Akaroa Harbour, New Zealand. Science for Conservation 178. Department of Conservation, Wellington, New Zealand.

Ningaloo Blue (2005) Ningaloo Blue. Available at: http://www.ningalooblue.com.au/

North Pole Expeditions (2005a) Global Expedition Adventures. Available at: http://www.north-pole-expeditions.com/

North Pole Expeditions (2005b) Skydive the North Pole. Available at: http://www.north-pole-expeditions.com/north_pole_skydiving.htm/

Nowacek, S.M., Wells, R.S. and Solow, A. (2001) Short-term effects of boat traffic on bottlenose dolphins, *Tursiops truncatus*, in Sarasota Bay, Florida. *Marine Mammal Science* 17, 673–688.

Nowacek, S.M., Wells, R.S., Owen, E.C.G., Speakman, T.R., Flamm, R.O. and Nowacek, D.P. (2004) Florida manatees, *Trichechus manatus latirostris*, respond to approaching vessels. *Biological Conservation* 119, 517–523.

Ocean River (2005) Ocean River Sports. Available at: http://www.oceanriver.com/

Ollenburg, C. (2005) Worldwide structure of the equestrian tourism sector. *Journal of Ecotourism* 4, 47–55.

Ollenburg, C. (2006) Farm tourism in Australia. Unpublished PhD thesis, Griffith University, Gold Coast, Australia.

O'Neill, M., MacCarthy, M. and Williams P.A. (2002) Dive tourism: evaluating service quality. *FIU Hospitality Review* 20, 47–65.

Oregon Peak Adventures (2005) Oregon Peak Adventures. Available at: http://www.oregonpeakadventures.com/

*Otago Daily Times* (18 November 1999) Safety an issue for tourism.

*Otago Daily Times* (19 July 2000) Fabulous generator of wealth.

*Otago Daily Times* (3 November 2000) Faults caused crashes.

Ouray Ice Park (2005a) Ouray Ice Park Guiding Application Procedure. Available at: http://www.ourayiceparkguiding.com/

Ouray Ice Park (2005b) Interactive Ice Park Map. Available at: http://www.ourayicepark.com/map.php/

Outback Camel Company (2005) Outback Camel Company. Available at: http://www.cameltreks.com.au/

Outdoor Adventure River Specialists (2005) OARS. Available at: http://www.oars.com/

Outdoor Industry Association (2005) *Outdoor Recreation Participation Study*, 7th edn, for year 2004. Available at: http://www.outdoorindustry.org/pdf/2005ParticipationStudy.pdf

OZ Experience (2005) OZ Experience. Available at: http://www.ozexperience.com/

Paddy Pallin (2005) Jindabyne Adventure Centre. Available at: http://www.mountainadventurecentre.com.au/

Page, S.J. (1997) *The Cost of Adventure Tourism Accidents for the New Zealand Tourism Industry.* Tourism Policy Group, Ministry of Commerce, Wellington, New Zealand.

Page, S.J. and Dowling, R.K. (2002) *Ecotourism.* Pearson Education, Harlow, UK.

Page, S.J., Bentley, T.A. and Laird, I. (2003a) Managing tourist safety: the experience of the adventure tourism industry. In: Wilks, J. and Page, S.J. (eds) *Managing Tourist Health and Safety in the New Millennium.* Pergamon, Oxford, pp. 85–100.

Page, S.J., Bentley, T. and Meyer, D. (2003b) Evaluating the nature, scope and extent of tourist accidents: the New Zealand experience. In: Wilks, J. and Page, S.J. (eds) *Managing Tourist Health and Safety in the New Millennium.* Pergamon, Oxford, pp. 35–52.

Page, S.J., Bentley, T. and Walker, L. (2005) Scoping the nature and extent of adventure tourism operations in Scotland: how safe are they? *Tourism Management* 26, 381–397.

Para, R. (2005) Aconcagua Trek – participation statistics report. Available at: http://www.rudyparra.com/stats.htm/

Park, T., Bowker, J.M. and Leeworthy, V.R. (2002) Valuing snorkeling visits to the Florida Keys with stated and revealed preference models. *Journal of Environmental Management* 65, 301–312.

Parker, J.D. and Avant, B. (2000) In their own words: wilderness values of outfitter/guides. In: McCool, S.F., Cole, D.N., Borrie, W.T. and O'Laughlin, J. (comps) *Wilderness Science in a Time of Change – Volume 3: Wilderness as a Place for Scientific Inquiry. Proceedings RMRS-P-15-VOL-3.* USDA Forest Service, Rocky Mountain Research Station, Ogden, Utah, pp. 196–201.

Parsons, E.C.M., Warburton, C.A., Woods-Ballard, A., Hughes, A. and Johnston, P. (2003) The value of conserving whales: the impacts of whale-watching on the economy of rural west Scotland. *Aquatic Conservation* 13, 397–415.

Pearce, D. and Cant, R. (1981) *The Development and Impact of Tourism in Queenstown. Man and Biosphere Report, 7.* University of Canterbury, Christchurch, New Zealand.

Pearson, C. (2004) *NOLS Cookery,* 5th edn. NOLS, Lander, Wyoming.

Pesant, A.R. (1987) Snowmobiling impact on soil properties and winter cereal crops. *Canadian Field Naturalist* 101, 22–32.

Petreas, C.P. (2003) Scuba diving: an alternative form of coastal tourism for Greece? In: Garrod, B. and Wilson, J.C. (eds) *Marine Ecotourism: Issues and Experiences.* Channel View, Clevedon, UK, pp. 215–232.

Pilkington, R. (2002) Articles and archives: Spring. Available at: http://www.ursusinternational.org/

Piore, A. (2002) Trouble in paradise. *Newsweek* 22–29 July, 42–46.

Planet Kitesurf (2005) Kitesurfing holidays. Available at: http://www.planetkitesurf.com/

PNG Tours (2005) Papua New Guinea trans Niugini tours. Available at: http://www.pngtours.com/

Pobocik, M. and Butalla, C. (1998) Development in Nepal: the Annapurna Conservation Area Project. In: Hall, C.M. and Lew, A.A. (eds) *Sustainable Tourism: a Geographical Perspective.* Longman, Harlow, UK, pp. 159–172.

Pomfret, G. (2005) Mountaineering adventure tourists: a conceptual framework for research. *Tourism Management* 27, 113–123.

Prall, J., Winston, K. and Brennan, R. (1995) Severe snowboarding injuries. *Injury* 26, 539–542.

Primack, R. and Corlett, R. (2004) *Tropical Rain Forests: An Ecological and Biogeographical Comparison.* Blackwell, Oxford.

Prior, M.R., Ormond, R., Hitchen, R. and Wormald, C. (1995) The impacts on natural resources of activity tourism: a case study of diving in Egypt. *International Journal of Environmental Studies* 48, 201–209.

Priskin, J. (2004) Four-wheel drive vehicle impacts in the Central Coast region of Western Australia. In: Buckley, R. (ed.) *Environmental Impacts of Ecotourism.* CAB International, Wallingford, UK, pp. 339–348.

Professional Association of Dive Instructors (2005) PADI – the way the world learns to dive. Available at: http://www.padi.com/

Queenstown Rafting (2005) Queenstown Rafting. Available at: http://www.rafting.co.nz/

Quicksilver Cruises (2005) Quicksilver is the Great Barrier Reef. Available at: http://www.quicksilver-cruises.com/

Quicksilver Dive (2005) Quicksilver Dive. Available at: http://www.quicksilverdive.com.au/

Raft and Rainforest (2005) Dive the Reef. Available at: http://www.divethereef.com/

Raging Thunder (2005) Cairns. Available at: http://www.ragingthunder.com.au/

Rainbow, J., Buckley, R.C., Byrnes, T. and Warnken, J. (2000) *Green Guide to Blue Seas.* CRC Tourism, Griffith University, Gold Coast.

Rainbow, J., Warnken, J. and Buckley, R.C. (2002) *Green Guide to Scuba Diving Tours*. CRC Tourism, Griffith University, Gold Coast.

Raleigh International (2005) About Raleigh International. Available at: http://www.raleigh.org.uk/

Ramthun, R. (1995) Factors in user group conflict between hikers and mountain bikers. *Leisure Sciences* 17, 159–169.

Rangitata Rafts (2005) Rangitata Rafts. Available at: http://www.rafts.co.nz/

Recreational Equipment Inc. (2005) REI. Available at: http://www.rei.com/

Recreational Equipment Inc. Adventures (2005) REI Adventures. Available at: http://www.rei.com/adventures/

Reiter, D.K. and Blahna, D.J. (2002) *Slickrock Trail Mountain Bike Survey: Implications for Resource Managers and Area Communities*. Utah Recreation and Tourism Matters, Institute for Outdoor Recreation and Tourism – Utah State University Extension. No. NR/RF/012.

Requa, R.K., Toney, J.M. and Garrick, J.G. (1977) Parameters on injury reporting in skiing. *Medical Science of Sports Exercise* 9, 185–190.

Rescue 3 Australia (2005) Rescue 3 Australia and Shepherd Consultants. Available at: http://www.adventurepro.com.au/sheperd/

Rescue 3 International (2005) Rescue 3 International. Available at: http://www.rescue3.com/

RideLanka (2005) South Asian off road mountain bike and multi sport adventure vacation tours. Available at: http://www.ridelanka.com/

Ride World Wide (2005) Ride World Wide. Available at: http://www.rideworldwide.co.uk/

Riegl, B. and Velimirov, B. (1991) How many damaged corals in Red Sea reef systems? A quantitative survey. *Hydrobiologia* 216/217, 249–256.

Rios Ecuador (2005) Rios Ecuador – rafting and kayaking adventures. Available at: http://www.riosecuador.com/

Ritchie, B.W., Burns, P. and Palmer, C. (2005) Introduction: reflections on the practice of research. In: Ritchie, B.W., Burns, P. and Palmer, C. (eds) *Tourism Research Methods*. CAB International, Wallingford, pp. 1–8.

Ritzer, G. and Liska, A. (1997) "McDisneyization" and "Post-Tourism": complementary perspectives on contemporary tourism. In: Rojek, C. and Urry, J. (eds) *Touring Cultures: Transformations of Travel and Theory*. Routledge, London, pp. 96–112.

Rivers Fiji (2005) Rivers Fiji. Available at: http://www.riversfiji.com/

Riza, Y. (2000) Maldives marine protected areas. In: WTO (comp.) *Sustainable Development of Ecotourism: A Compilation of Good Practices*. World Tourism Organisation, Madrid, pp. 115–116.

Robinson, J. (2001) Socio-cultural dimensions of sustainable tourism development: achieving the vision. In: WTO *Island Tourism in Asia and the Pacific*. World Tourism Organisation, Madrid, pp. 78–86.

Rodger, K. and Moore, S.A. (2004) Bringing science to wildlife tourism: the influence of managers' and scientists' perceptions. *Journal of Ecotourism* 3, 1–19.

Rogers, C.S. (1983) Sublethal and lethal effects of sediments applied to common reef corals in the field. *Marine Pollution Bulletin* 41, 269–288.

Rogers, C.S. (1990) Responses of coral reefs and reef organisms to sedimentation. *Marine Ecology Progress Series* 62, 185–202.

Roggenbuck, J., Williams, D., Bange, S. and Dean, D. (1991) River float trip encounter norms: questioning the use of the social norms concept. *Journal of Leisure Research* 23, 133–153.

Ronning, R., Gerner, T. and Engebretsen, L. (2000) Risk of injury during alpine and telemark skiing and snowboarding. *American Journal of Sports Medicine* 28, 506–508.

Ronning, R., Ronning, I., Gerner, T. and Engebretsen, L. (2001) The efficacy of wrist protectors in preventing snowboarding injuries. *American Journal of Sports Medicine* 29, 581–585.

Roper ASW (2003) Outdoor recreation in America 2003: recreation's benefits to society challenged by trends. Available at: http://www.funoutdoors.com/files/ROPER%20REPORT%202004_0.pdf/

Rouphael, A.B. and Inglis, G.J. (2001) Increased spatial and temporal variability in coral damage caused by recreation scuba diving. *Ecological Applications* 12, 427–440.

Royal Geographical Society (2000) *Code of Practice for Adventure Tourism Operators*. RGS, London.

Ruddell, E.J. and Gramann, J.H. (1994) Goal orientation, norms, and noise-induced conflict among recreation area users. *Leisure Sciences* 16, 93–104.

Russell, C. and Enns, M. (2002) *Grizzly Heart: Living Without Fear Among the Brown Bears of Kamchatka*. Random House of Canada.

Ryan, C. (1998) Saltwater crocodiles as tourist attractions. *Journal of Sustainable Tourism* 6, 314–327.

Ryan, C. (2003) Risk acceptance in adventure tourism – paradox and content. In: Wilks, J. and Page, S.J. (eds) *Managing Tourist Health and Safety in the New Millennium.* Pergamon, Oxford, pp. 55–66.

Ryan, C. and Harvey, K. (2000) Who likes saltwater crocodiles? Analysing socio-demographics of those viewing tourist wildlife attractions based on saltwater crocodiles. *Journal of Sustainable Tourism* 8, 426–433.

Safari Par Excellence (2005) Safari Par Excellence – Zimbabwe and Zambia. Available at: http://www.safpar.com/

Salani Surf Resort (2005) Salani Surf Resort. Available at: http://www.surfsamoa.com/

Salm, R.V. (1986) Coral reef and tourist carrying capacity: the Indian Ocean experience. *Industry and Environment* 9, 11–13.

Samoana Resort (2005) Samoana Resort. Available at: http://www.samoanaresort.com/

San Juan Hut System (2005) Travel our beautiful backcountry hut-to-hut. Available at: http://www.sanjuanhuts.com/

San Juan Mountain Guides (2003a) Ouray Ice Park history. Available at: http://www.ourayclimbing.com/IceParkHistory.shtml/

San Juan Mountain Guides (2003b) San Juan Mountain Guides LLC. Available at: http://www.ourayclimbing.com/

Savaii Surfaris (2005) Atoll Travel. Available at: http://www.atolltravel.com/Samoa/SamoaSavaii.htm/

Scarpaci, C. and Dayanthi, N. (2003) Compliance with regulations by swim-with-dolphins: operations in Port Phillip Bay, Victoria, Australia. *Environmental Management* 31, 342–347.

Scarpaci, C., Bigger, S.W., Corkeron, P.J. and Nugegoda, D. (2000) Bottlenose dolphins, *Tursiops truncatus*, increase whistling in the presence of "swim-with-dolphin" tour operators. *Journal of Cetacean Research and Management* 2, 183–186.

Schaeffer, T.N., Foster, M.S., Landrau, M.E. and Walder, R.K. (1999) Diver disturbance in kelp forests. *California Fish and Game* 85, 170–176.

Schänzel, H.A. and McIntosh, A.J. (2000) An insight into the personal and emotive context of wildlife viewing at the Penguin Place, Otago Peninsula, New Zealand. *Journal of Sustainable Tourism* 8, 36–52.

Schleyer, M.H. and Tomalin, B.J. (2000) Damage on South African coral reefs and an assessment of their sustainable diving capacity using a fisheries approach. *Bulletin of Marine Science* 67, 1025–1042.

Schmiechen, J. (2004) Crossing borders: future directions for heritage tourism in the Lake Eyre Basin. In: Buckley, R.C. (ed.) *Tourism in Parks: Australian Initiatives.* International Centre for Ecotourism Research, Griffith University, Australia, pp. 99–131.

Schneider, I.E. (2000) Revisiting and revising recreation conflict research. *Journal of Leisure Research* 32, 129–132.

Schoen, R.G. and Stano, M.J. (2002) Year 2000 whitewater injury survey. *Wilderness and Environmental Medicine* 13, 119–124.

Schrader, M.P. and Wann, D.L. (1999) High-risk recreation: the relationship between participant characteristics and degree of involvement. *Journal of Sport Behaviour* 22, 426–441.

Schuett, M.A. (1997) State Park directors' perceptions of mountain biking. *Environmental Management* 21, 239–246.

Schuster, R.M., Thompson, J.G. and Hammitt, W.E. (2001) Rock climbers' attitudes toward management of climbing and the use of bolts. *Environmental Management* 28, 403–412.

Scott, N. and Laws, E. (2004) Whale watching – the roles of small firms in the evolution of a new Australian niche market. In: Thomas, R. (ed.) *Small Firms in Tourism: International Perspectives.* Elsevier Science, Amsterdam.

See Xinjiang (2005) Available at: http://seexj.com.cn/en/tour/tc.html/

Sekhar, N.U. (2003) Local people's attitudes towards conservation and wildlife tourism around Sariska Tiger Reserve, India. *Journal of Environmental Management* 69, 339–347.

Selkirk Tangiers (2005) Selkirk Tangiers Helicopter Skiing. Available at: http://www.selkirk-tangiers.com/

SGMA International (2005) SGMA International. Available at: http://www.sgma.com/

Shackley, M. (1996a) *Wildlife Tourism.* International Thomson Business Press, London.

Shackley, M. (1996b) Community impact of the camel safari industry in Jaisalmar, Rajasthan. *Tourism Management* 17, 213–218.

Shackley, M. (1998) "Stingray City" – managing the impact of underwater tourism in the Cayman Islands. *Journal of Sustainable Tourism* 6, 328–338.

Shangri-La River Expeditions (2005) Shangri-La River Expeditions. Available at: http://www.shangri-la-river-expeditions.com/

Shaolin Viaggi (2005) Shaolin Viaggi. Available at: http:// www.shaolin-viaggi.net/

Sharpe, R. (2005) "Going above and beyond:" the emotional labor of adventure guides. *Journal of Leisure Research* 37, 29–50.

Shaw, W.D. and Jakus, P.M. (1996) Travel cost models of the demand for rock climbing. *Agricultural and Resource Economics Review* 25, 133–142.

Shearwater Adventures (2005) Shearwater Adventures. Available at: http://www.shearwateradventures.com/

Shelby, B. (1980) Contrasting recreational experiences: motors and oars in the Grand Canyon. *Journal of Soil and Water Conservation* 35, 129–131.

Shelby, B. (1981) Encounter norms in backcountry settings: studies of three rivers. *Journal of Leisure Research* 13, 129–138.

Shelby, B., Vaske, J.J. and Donnelly, M.P. (1996) Norms, standards and natural resources. *Leisure Sciences* 18, 103–123.

Sheller, M. and Urry, J. (2004) *Tourism Mobilities: Places to Play, Places in Play*. Routledge, London.

Siderelis, C. and Attarian, A. (2004) Trip response modeling of rock climbers' reactions to proposed regulations. *Journal of Leisure Research* 36, 73–88.

Simmons, D.G. and Becken, S. (2004) The cost of getting there: impacts of travel to ecotourism destinations. In: Buckley, R. (ed.) *Environmental Impacts of Ecotourism*. CAB International, Wallingford, UK, pp. 15–24.

Sinclair, W.R. (1914) *A Guide to Wondrous Wakatipu*. Dunedin Expansion League, New Zealand.

Siyabona Africa (2005) Siyabona Africa. Available at: http://www.siyabona.com/

Slanger, E. and Rudestam, E. (1997) Motivation and disinhibition in high risk sports: sensation seeking and self efficacy. *Journal of Research in Personality* 31, 355–374.

Smith Diving (2005) Smith Diving. Available at: http://www.smithdiving.com/

Sournia, G. (1996) Wildlife tourism in West and Central Africa. *Ecodecision* 20, 52–54.

South Australia (2005) Parks Web: Simpson Desert. Available at: http://www.environment.sa.gov.au/parks/simpson_cp/about.html/

Southern Sea Ventures (2005) Southern Sea Ventures – tropical and polar sea-kayak tours. Available at: http://www.southernseaventures.com/flash.htm/

Splettstoesser, J. (1999) Antarctic tourism: successful management of a vulnerable environment. In: Singh, T.V. and Singh, S. (eds) *Tourism Development in Critical Environments*. Cognizant, New York, pp. 137–148.

Splettstoesser, J., Landau, D. and Headland, R.K. (2004) Tourism in the forbidden landscapes. In: Singh, T.V. (ed.) *New Horizons in Tourism*. CAB International, Wallingford, UK, pp. 27–36.

Sporting Goods Manufacturers Association (2005) Recreation market report, 2005. Available at: http://www.SGMA.com/reports/data/2005/m7-000-05.pdf/

Sproule, K. and Suhandi, A. (1998) Guidelines for community based ecotourism programs. In: Lindberg, K., Epler-Wood, M. and Ingeldrum, D. (eds) *Ecotourism: a Guide for Planners and Managers*. Ecotourism Society, North Bennington, Vermont, pp. 215–235.

Standards New Zealand (1992) *Code of Practice for Bungy Jumping. Australian/New Zealand Standard AS/NZS 5848:1992*. Standards New Zealand, Wellington.

Summer, R.M. (1980) Impact of horse traffic on trails in Rocky Mountain National Park. *Journal of Soil and Water Conservation* 35, 85–87.

Summer, R.M. (1986) Geomorphic impacts of horse traffic on montane landforms. *Journal of Soil and Water Conservation* 41, 126–128.

Sung, H., Morrison, A. and O'Leary, J. (2000) Segmenting the adventure travel market by activities: from the North American industry provider's perspective. *Journal of Travel and Tourism Marketing* 9, 1–20.

Surf The Earth (2005) Happy holidays! Available at: http://surf-the-earth.com/

Surf Travel Company (2005) The Surf Travel Company. Available at: http://www.surftravel.com.au/

Surtrek (2005) Surtrek. Available at: http://www.surtrek.com/

Suzuki, M. and Kawamura, M. (1994) Studies on recreational behaviours in the national park. I. Mountaineering in the National Park "Daisen". *Tottori University Forest, Research Bulletin* 22, 83–114.

Swagman Tours (2005) Swagman Tours. Available at: http://www.swagmantours.com.au/

Swarbrooke, J., Beard, C., Leckie, S. and Pomfret, G. (2003) *Adventure Tourism: the New Frontier.* Butterworth-Heinemann, London.

Symmons, M.C., Hammitt, W.E. and Quisenberry, V.L. (2000) Managing recreational trail environments for mountain bike user preferences. *Environmental Management* 25, 549–564.

Synnott Mountain Guides (2005) Synnott Mountain Guides. Available at: http://www.marksynnott.com/synnottmountainguides/

Tabata, R.S. (1989) The use of nearshore dive sites by recreational dive operations in Hawaii. *Coastal Zone* 89, 2865–2875.

Tabata, R.S. (1992) Scuba diving holidays. In: Tabata, R.S., Weiler, B. and Hall, C.M. (eds) *Special Interest Tourism.* Belhavan Press, London, pp. 171–184.

Taka Dive (2005) Taka Dive. Available at: http://www.takadive.com.au/

Talge, H. (1993) Impact of recreational divers on scleractinian corals at Loo Key, Florida. *Proceedings of the Seventh International Coral Reef Symposium,* University of Guam Marine Laboratory, Mangilao, Guam pp. 1077–1082.

Tarazi, F., Dvorak, M.F.S. and Wing, P.C. (1999) Spinal injuries in skiers and snowboarders. *American Journal of Sports Medicine* 27, 177–180.

Tavarua Island Resort (2005) Tavarua Island Resort, Fiji. Available at: http://www.tavarua.com/

Taylor, D.M., O'Toole, K.S. and Ryan, C.M. (2003) Experienced scuba divers in Australia and the United States suffer considerable injury and morbidity. *Wilderness and Environmental Medicine* 14, 83–88.

Team Gorky (2005) Team Gorky Adventure Travel Company. Available at: http://www.teamgorky.ru/index-e.html/

Tenth Mountain Division Huts (2005) 10th Mountain Division Hut Association. Available at: http://www.huts.org/

Teton Mountain Bike Tours (2005) Teton Mountain Bike Tours. Available at: http://www.tetonmtbike.com/

Thapa, B. and Graefe, A.R. (2003) Level of skill and its relationship to recreation conflict and tolerance among adult skiers and snowboarders. *World Leisure* 45, 13–25.

*The Guardian* (28 July 1998) Criticism grows of disaster gorge trip.

The Helicopter Line (2005) New Zealand Helicopter Scenic Flights. Available at: http://www.helicopter.co.nz/

The International Ecotourism Society (2005) The International Ecotourism Society. Available at: http://www.ecotourism.org/

The Last Resort (2005) The Last Resort. Available at: http://www.thelastresort.com/

*The Press* (13 November 1999) Man dead after jetboat accident on Shotover.

*The Times* (8 June 1999) Four Britons die in raft accident.

*The Times* (15 May 2000) Bungee jumper falls 300 ft to his death.

Think! Adventure (2005) Think! Adventure. Available at: http://www.thinkadventure.com.au/

Thompson, M. and Homewood, K. (2002) Entrepreneurs, elites, and exclusion in Maasailand: trends in wildlife conservation and pastoralist development. *Human Ecology* 30, 107–138.

Thrift, N.J. (1999) Steps to an ecology of place. In: Massey, D., Allen, J. and Sarre, P. (eds) *Human Geography Today.* Polity, Cambridge, pp. 295–322.

Thurston, E. and Reader, R.J. (2001) Impacts of experimentally applied mountain biking and hiking on vegetation and soil of a deciduous forest. *Environmental Management* 27, 397–409.

Tourism Tropical North Queensland (2005) Cairns and Great Barrier Reef region. Available at: http://www.tropicalaustralia.com.au/

Townsend, C. (2003) Marine ecotourism through education: a case study of divers in the British Virgin Islands. In: Garrod, B. and Wilson, J.C. (eds) *Marine Ecotourism: Issues and Experiences.* Channel View, Clevedon, UK, pp. 138–154.

Trans-Niugini Tours (2005) General information. Available at: http://www.pngtours.com/info.html/

Tratalos, J.A. and Austin, T.J. (2001) Impacts of recreational SCUBA diving on coral communities of the Caribbean island of Grand Cayman. *Biological Conservation* 102, 67–75.

Travel China Guide (2005) Travel China Guide. Available at: http://www.travelchinaguide.com/

Travel Industry Association of America (2005) Adventure Travel Report. Available at: http://www.tia.org/

Trevett, A.J., Forbes, R., Rae, C.K., Sheehan, C., Ross, J., Watt, S.J. and Stephenson, R. (2001) Diving accidents in sports divers in Orkney waters. *Scottish Medical Journal* 46, 176–177.

Twardock, P. and Monz, C. (2000) Recreational kayak visitor use, distribution, and financial value of beaches in Western Prince William Sound, Alaska, between 1987 and 1998. *USDA Forest Service Proceedings* 4, 175–180.

Uganda Wildlife Authority (2005) Uganda Wildlife Authority. Available at: http://www.uwa.or.ug/

Ultimate Descents Nepal (2005) Ultimate Descents: Nepal's Rivers. Available at: http://www.ultimatedescents.com/nepal_rivers.htm

Ultimate Descents New Zealand Whitewater Rafting (2005) Welcome to Ultimate Descents New Zealand Whitewater Rafting. Available at: http://www.rivers.co.nz/

Ultimate Hikes (2005) Routeburn track. Available at: http://www.ultimatehikes.co.nz/

Uncharted Africa Safaris (2005) Uncharted Africa Safaris. Available at: http://www.unchartedafrica.com/

Universal Studios (2002) *Blue Crush*. Available at: http://www.bluecrush.com/

US Bureau of Reclamation (1995) Operation of Glen Canyon Dam: final environmental impact statement. USBR, Salt Lake City, Utah. Available at: http://www.usbr.gov/uc/envdocs/eis/gc/gcdOpsFEIS.html/

USDA Forest Service (2005) USDA Forest Service. Available at: http://www.fs.fed.us/

US National Park Service (2005) National Park Service. Available at: http://www.nps.gov/cany/home.htm/

Vail, D. and Heldt, T. (2004) Governing snowmobilers in multiple-use landscapes: Swedish and Maine (USA) cases. *Ecological Economics* 48, 469–483.

Valdez Ice (2005) Valdez Ice. Available at: http://www.geocities.com/guide99686/

Valdez Ice Climbing Festival (2005) Valdez Ice Climbing Festival. Available at: http://www.alaskagold.com/ice/

Vaske, J. and Donnelly, M. (2002) Generalizing the encounter-norm-crowding relationship. *Leisure Sciences* 24, 255–270.

Vaske, J., Graefe, A., Shelby, B. and Heberlein, T. (1986) Backcountry encounter norms: theory, method, and empirical evidence. *Journal of Leisure Research* 18, 137–153.

Vaske, J., Carothers, P., Donnelly, M.P. and Baird, B. (2000) Recreation conflict among skiers and snowboarders. *Leisure Sciences* 22, 297–313.

Vaske, J., Dyar, R. and Timmons, N. (2004) Skill level and recreation conflict among skiers and snowboarders. *Leisure Studies* 26, 215–225.

Victory Adventure Expeditions (2005) Victory Expeditions. Available at: http://www.victory-cruises.com/

Viles, A. and Delfino, K. (2000) The Blue Ribbon Coalition: protector of recreation or industry? US Public Interest Research Group. Available at: http://www.georgiapirg.org/blueribbon/orv.pdf/

Virgin Galactic (2005) Virgin Galactic. Available at: http://www.virgingalactic.com/en/

Vitterso, J., Chipeniuk, R., Skar, M. and Vistad, O.I. (2004) Recreational conflict is affective: the case of cross-country skiers and snowmobiles. *Leisure Studies* 26, 227–243.

Voodoo Dolls (2002) Voodoo Dolls. Viewed at: http://www.voodoodolls.com.au/

Voodoo Dolls (2005) Voodoo Dolls. Viewed at: http://www.voodoodolls.com.au/

Walindi Plantation Resort (2005) World famous SCUBA diving in a lush tropical setting. Available at: http://www.walindi.com/

Walpole, M.J. and Goodwin, H.J. (2001) Local attitudes towards conservation and tourism around Komodo National Park. *Environmental Conservation* 28, 160–166.

Walters, R.D.M. and Samways, M.J. (2001) Sustainable dive ecotourism on a South African coral reef. *Biodiversity and Conservation* 10, 2167–2179.

Warnken, J. and Buckley, R.C. (1997) Major 1987–93 tourism proposals in Australia. *Annals of Tourism Research* 24, 974–1019.

Warnken, J. and Byrnes, T. (2004) Impacts of tourboats in marine environments. In: Buckley, R.C. (ed.) *Environmental Impacts of Ecotourism*. CAB International, Wallingford, UK, pp. 99–124.

Waterways Surf Adventures (2005) Offering global surf relief to local surf anxiety. Available at: http://www.waterwaystravel.com/Index.html/

Watkins, W.A. (1986) Whale reactions to human activities in Cape Cod waters. *Marine Mammal Science* 2, 251–262.

Watson, A. and Moss R. (2004) Impacts of ski-development on ptarmigan (*Lagopus mutus*) at Cairn Gorm, Scotland. *Biological Conservation* 116, 267–275.

Watson, A., Cole, D. and Roggenbuck, J.W. (1995) Trends in wilderness recreation use characteristics. In: Thompson, J.L., Lime, D.W., Gartner, B. and Sames, W.M. (eds) *Proceedings of the Fourth*

*International Outdoor Recreation and Tourism Trends Symposium and the 1995 National Resources Planning Conference.* University of Minnesota, Minnesota, pp. 68–71.

Watson, A.E. (1995) An analysis of recent progress in recreation conflict research and perceptions of future challenges and opportunities. *Leisure Sciences* 17, 235–238.

Watson, A.E., Williams, D.R. and Daigle, J.J. (1991) Sources of conflict between hikers and mountain bike riders in the Rattlesnake NRA. *Journal of Park and Recreation Administration* 9, 59–71.

Watson, A.E., Niccolucci, M.J. and Williams, D.R. (1994) The nature of conflict between hikers and recreational stock users in the John Muir Wilderness. *Journal of Leisure Research* 26, 372–385.

Wearing, S.L. (2001) *Volunteer Tourism: Seeking Experiences that Make a Difference.* CAB International, Wallingford, UK.

Weaver, D. (1998) *Ecotourism in the Less Developed World.* CAB International, Wallingford, UK.

Weaver, D.B. (2001) *The Encyclopedia of Ecotourism.* CAB International, Wallingford, UK.

Weaver, T. and Dale, D. (1978) Trampling effects of hikers, motorcycles and horses in meadows and forests. *Journal of Applied Ecology* 15, 451–457.

Wellman, J.D., Roggenbuck, J.W. and Smith, A.C. (1982) Recreation specialization and norms of depreciative behaviour among canoeists. *Journal of Leisure Research* 14, 323–340.

Western Australia Department of Conservation and Land Management (2005) WACALM. Available at: http://calm.wa.gov.au/tourism/whalesharks_swimming. html/

Whinam, J., Cannell, E.J., Kirkpatrick, J.B. and Comfort, M. (1994) Studies on the potential impact of recreational horseriding on some alpine environments of the Central Plateau, Tasmania. *Journal of Environmental Management* 40, 103–117.

Whitney and Smith Expeditions (2005) Legendary Whitney and Smith Expeditions. Available at: http://www.legendaryex.com/

Wielgus, J., Chadwick-Furman, N.E., Zeitouni, N. and Shechter, M. (2003) Effects of coral reef attribute damage on recreational welfare. *Marine Resource Economics* 18, 225–237.

Wild Frontiers (2005) Mount Kenya climbs. Available at: http://www.wildfrontiers. com/ky/wfkyb/

Wild Rivers Expeditions (2005) Utah whitewater rafting on the San Juan River. Available at: http://www.riversandruins.com/

Wilderness Safaris (2005) Wilderness Safaris. Available at: http://www.wilderness-safaris.com/

Wildlife Africa (2005) African holiday destinations and safari tours. Available at: http://wildlifeafrica.com.za/

Wilkie, D.S. and Carpenter, J.F. (1999a) The potential role of safari hunting as a source of revenue for protected areas in the Congo Basin. *Oryx* 33, 339–345.

Wilkie, D.S. and Carpenter, J.F. (1999b) Can nature tourism help finance protected areas in the Congo Basin? *Oryx* 33, 332–338.

Wilks, J. (1992) Introductory scuba diving on the Great Barrier Reef. *Australian Parks and Recreation* 28, 18–23.

Wilks, J. (1993) Scuba safety in Queensland. *South Pacific Underwater Medicine Society Journal* 23, 139–141.

Wilks, J. (1999) Scuba diving safety on Australia's Great Barrier Reef. *Travel Medicine International* 17, 17–21.

Wilks, J. and Davis, R.J. (2000) Risk management for scuba diving operators in Australia's Great Barrier Reef. *Tourism Management* 21, 591–599.

Wilks, J. and Page, S.J. (2003) *Managing Tourist Health and Safety in the New Millennium.* Pergamon, Oxford.

Williams, I.D. and Polunin, N. (2000) Differences between protected and unprotected reefs of the western Caribbean in attributes preferred by dive tourists. *Environmental Conservation* 27, 382–391.

Williams, P., Dossa, K. and Fulton, A. (1994) Tension on the slopes: managing conflict between skiers and snowboarders. *Journal of Applied Recreation Research* 19, 191–213.

Williamson, J.E. (1999) *Accidents in North American Mountaineering.* American Alpine Club, Boulder, Colorado.

Willis's Walkabouts (2005) Willis's Walkabouts Bushwalking Holidays. Available at: http://www.bushwalkingholidays.com.au/

Wilson, A. (1992) *The Culture of Nature.* Blackwell, Oxford.

Wilson, C. and Tisdell, C.A. (2001) Sea turtles as a non-consumptive tourism resource especially in Australia. *Tourism Management* 22, 279–288.

Woodland, D.J. and Hooper, N.A. (1977) The effect of human trampling on coral reefs. *Biological Conservation* 11, 1–4.

Woods-Ballard, A., Parsons, E.C.M., Hughes, A., Velander, K.A., Ladle, R.J. and Warburton, C.A. (2003) The sustainability of whale-watching in Scotland. *Journal of Sustainable Tourism* 11, 40–55.

World Expeditions (2005a) World Expeditions. Available at: http://www.worldexpeditions.com.au/

World Expeditions (2005b) Lobuche East & Island Peak Trip Notes. Available at: http://www.worldexpeditions.com.au/

World Expeditionary Association (2005) WEXAS: the Travellers Club. Available at: http://www.wexas.com/login.php/

World Surfaris (2005) World Surfaris. Available at: http://www.worldsurfaris.com/

Worldwide Fund for Nature (2005) WWF for a living planet. Available at: http://www.panda.org/

Wyder, T. (1987) 175 years of mountaineering in Switzerland. The Finsteraarhorn. *Magglingen* 44, 2–4.

Yacu Amu (2005) Whitewater rafting and kayaking in Ecuador. Available at: http://www.yacuamu.com/

Yak and Yeti (2005) Yak and Yeti. Available at: http://www.yakandyeti.com/

Yamakawa, H., Murase, S., Sakai, H., Iwama, T., Katada, M., Niikawa, S., Sumi, Y., Mishimura, Y. and Sakai, N. (2001) Spinal injuries in snowboarders: risk of jumping as an integral part of snowboarding. *Journal of Trauma* 50, 1101–1105.

Yellowstone Expeditions (2005) Yellowstone National Park. Available at: http:/www.yellowstoneexpeditions.com/

Zakai, D. and Chadwick-Furman, N.E. (2002) Impacts of intensive recreational diving on reef corals at Eilat, northern Red Sea. *Biological Conservation* 105, 179–187.

Zurick, D.N. (1992) Adventure travel and sustainable tourism in the peripheral economy of Nepal. *Annals of the Association of American Geographers* 82, 608–628.

# Index